LAST
MYSTERIES
OF THE
WORLD

LAST
MYSTERIES
OF THE
WORLD

Reader's Digest • Hong Kong • Sydney • Auckland • Montreal

Contributing writers

Jean Balthazar, Jean Batellier, Jean Bossy, Fabienne Bouloc, Olivier Brusset,
Gabriel Camps, Pierre Cornillot, Anne Deburge, Alain Demurger, Michel Dessaint,
Claire Dupré, Jérôme Grondeux, Rémi Kauffer, Azar Khalatbari, Pierre Lagrange,
Valérie Landon, Philippe Lécrivain, Didier le Fur, Jean Lopez, François Luis-Blanc,
Philippe Madelin, Betty Mamane, Florence Méa Batellier, Daniel Nony,
Laure Panerai, Denise Péricard-Méa, Xavier Péron, Fabienne de Pierrebourg,
David Pouilloux, Jean-Philippe Rémy, Agnès Rotschi, Albert de Surgy, Anne Taverne,
Robert Vivian, Olivier Voizeux

English edition
Translators: Petra Noyes and John K. Noyes
Editor: Alfred LeMaitre

The publishers would like to thank the following for their contributions to this book:
Ethné Clarke, Dr Peter Göbel, Dagmar Ortolf, Sabina Piatzer, Birgit Scheel,
Square Edge Design, Christine Unrath, Anne Wevell

First published in Australia in 2000 by
Reader's Digest (Australia) Pty Limited
26-32 Waterloo Street
Surry Hills, NSW 2010

National Library of Australia Cataloguing-in-Publication data
Last mysteries of the world.

English ed.
Includes index.
ISBN 1 876689 42 0.

1. Curiosities and wonders. 2. Antiquities.
3. Civilization, Ancient – Miscellanea. 4. Science –
Miscellanea. 5. Earth – Miscellanea. I. Noyes, Petra.
II. Noyes, John K. III. LeMaitre, Alfred. IV. Reader's
Digest (Australia).

001.94

Printed in Hong Kong

INTRODUCTION

You are about to set off on a journey that will take your mind to faraway places and tell you things about yourself that perhaps you never imagined. It is a journey into the many mysteries and unexplained phenomena that surround us. These range from the world of the insects beneath our feet to the infinite reaches of the universe, and from the dawn of humankind to our own technologically advanced age. We will also look deeply into our myths and legends – collective fantasies that play a role in the life of every individual.

During the journey, you will learn about the ways in which scientists and researchers in a wide range of fields are finding answers to many of these mysteries. You will find out the story behind some of these important discoveries, but also about the doubts, questions and unresolved issues that remain. For every problem that is solved, there is another one already emerging, waiting for an answer.

We begin by delving into the riddles of the past. Where do humans come from? We will look at some of the earth's vanished civilisations and show how their legacy is, in many cases, still with us. The ancient world also gave birth to a rich body of myths and legends. What is the meaning of the great myths and do they still have a role in modern life?

From the distant past, we move into the here and now, turning the spotlight on the darker side of humankind. We will look at the activities of criminals and the detectives trying to track them down, and we will probe the twilight world of organised crime and fringe religious cults. How do international crime syndicates succeed again and again to launder the millions they earn from their shady dealings?

In part three, we will turn to the workings of the body and mind, and to phenomena that seemingly defy rational explanation. These topics, such as how the brain works and the mysteries of ecstatic religious experience, challenge the imaginations and expertise of doctors and psychologists. Is it possible to return from the brink of death? Why do we have dreams? Where do prophets, shamans and faith healers get their powers?

The last part of our journey brings us to the work of natural scientists. How can we explain the behaviour patterns that we observe in animals and even in plants? Are they learned or are they inherited? What secrets does our planet conceal? And do we share this universe with other forms of life?

Many of these question have no final answer – yet. Perhaps there are also certain things that can never be known to our restless minds. And so the search for answers goes on.

MYSTERIES OF THE PAST

MYSTERIES OF OUR TIME

AT THE LIMITS OF SCIENCE AND LOGIC

UNLOCKING NATURE'S SECRETS

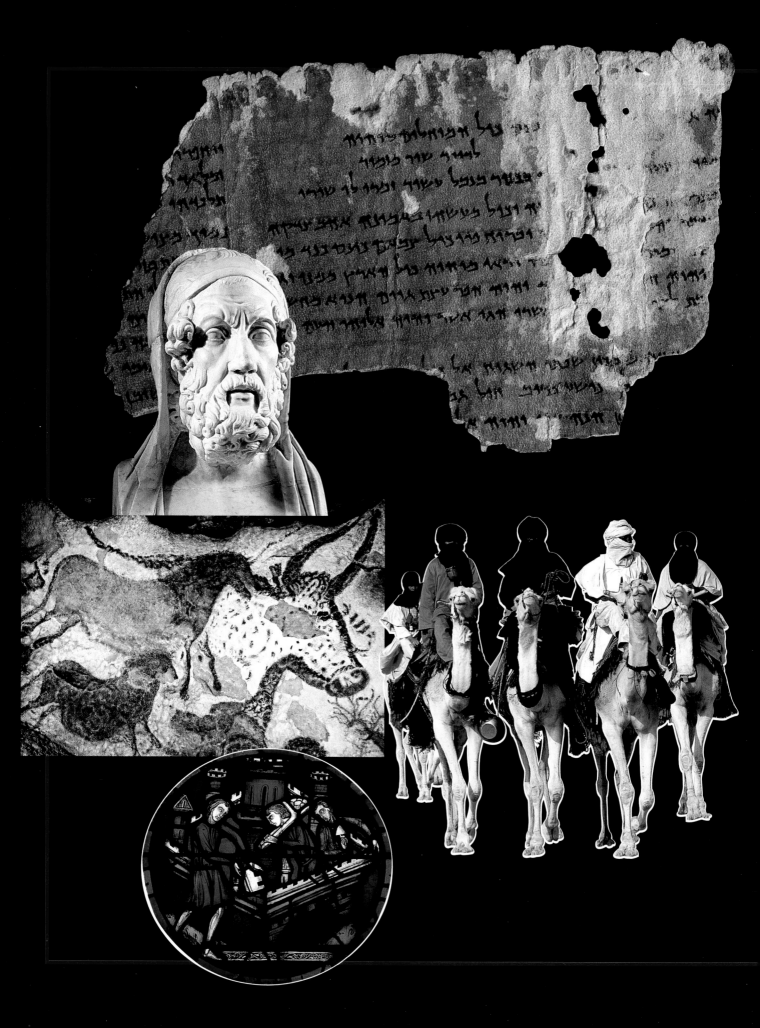

MYSTERIES OF THE PAST

As we enter a new millennium, the future of mankind looks uncertain. Yet while we wonder what the future may hold, there are still many questions to be answered about our past. It is often said that people who know little about their origins know little about themselves. Learning about the past is the best way to understand the present and the future – but only if we succeed in interpreting its mysteries. The following section takes us back through the years to ancient cultures, extraordinary historical figures at the centre of legends, mythical places and legendary events. The spotlight falls mainly on the Middle East and Mediterranean regions, considered by scholars and archaeologists to be the places where human society first evolved. But the story begins on the African continent, where scientists are tracing the beginnings of modern humankind. The first steps that can be recognised belong to Lucy and Abel, who were probably the predecessors of modern humans.

LUCY AND HER BROTHERS

Africa is the birthplace of the human race. Many millions of years ago, the distant ancestors of modern humans climbed down from the trees and began to explore the grassy plains around them. Fossil remains uncovered by palaeoanthropologists have enriched our understanding of these early people, but many unanswered questions remain.

The Afar Basin of northern Ethiopia is one of the most inhospitable areas in the world. But, together with a number of other regions in Africa, it has provided the material for scientists to write one of the first pages in the chronicle of human prehistory. In 1974, a skeleton was found in the bone-dry Afar Basin. Dubbed 'Lucy' by the team of excavators, she was estimated to be over 3 million years old. Others of the same species (*Australopithecus afarensis*) have since been discovered, while remains unearthed at other African sites have added further to our understanding of the development of the ancestors of modern humans. Among these are some of the oldest finds to date, including *Ardipithecus afarensis* (about 4.4 million years old), as well as the oldest examples of modern hominids – the closest ancestors of modern human beings. Most palaeoanthropologists now agree that Africa is the birthplace of humankind, but they are baffled by the lack of evidence of early hominids outside of Africa.

The home of the ancestors

Why have major fossil finds been restricted to certain regions of the African continent? Were the evolutionary conditions there so different from the rest of Africa? In 1984, Yves Coppens, professor at the Collège de France in Paris and joint discoverer of Lucy, put forward one scenario which met with widespread, if not undivided, support in the world of science – at least until quite recently.

About eight million years ago, movements in the earth's crust created the Great Rift Valley, which runs through Africa from the Red Sea to Zimbabwe. This deep fault line separates East Africa from Central and West Africa. The eastern portion of the continent developed from an open savannah to an arid steppe, while the western part is still marked by humid conditions. The movements of the

earth's crust created two regions with vastly different environmental conditions, to which the various inhabitants had to adapt.

While Central and West Africa are still home to anthropoids such as chimpanzees and gorillas, the inhabitants of the eastern regions gradually evolved to the point where they began to walk upright. In the wide, sparsely forested savannah, this gave them a clear advantage over other creatures. The

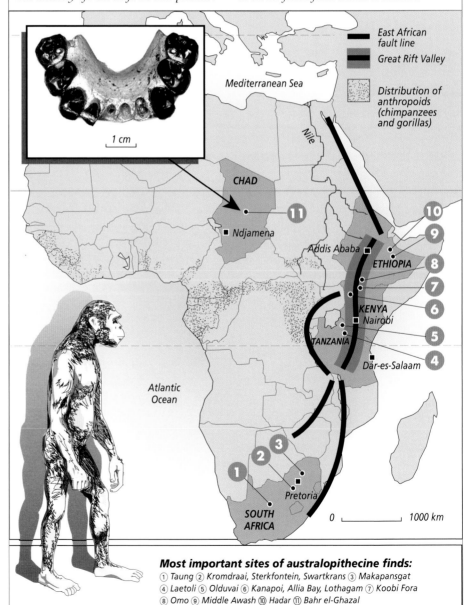

Uneven distribution

The jaw of Abel, an australopithecene, casts new light on the roots of mankind. He was found 2,500 km west of the Great Rift Valley. The discovery of Abel confirms that primitive man was much more widespread in Africa than was previously assumed and that early hominids were not restricted to East Africa, as earlier fossils finds seemed to indicate.

1 cm

East African fault line

Great Rift Valley

Distribution of anthropoids (chimpanzees and gorillas)

Mediterranean Sea

Nile

CHAD

■ Ndjamena

⑪

⑩

⑨

Addis Ababa

ETHIOPIA

⑧

⑦

⑥

KENYA

□ Nairobi

TANZANIA

⑤

④

■ Dar-es-Salaam

Atlantic Ocean

② ③

①

Pretoria ■

SOUTH AFRICA

0 —————— 1000 km

Most important sites of australopithecine finds:
① *Taung* ② *Kromdraai, Sterkfontein, Swartkrans* ③ *Makapansgat*
④ *Laetoli* ⑤ *Olduvai* ⑥ *Kanapoi, Allia Bay, Lothagam* ⑦ *Koobi Fora*
⑧ *Omo* ⑨ *Middle Awash* ⑩ *Hadar* ⑪ *Bahr el-Ghazal*

Is Lucy, shown here reconstructed, our direct ancestor, or does she belong to an extinct side branch of primitive humans?

emergence of bipedalism – walking on two feet – marks the beginning of the evolution of the human race. It was only much later that our predecessors began to explore other regions. First, they moved along the Rift Valley towards the south; in time, they went on to populate the entire African continent, and, eventually, the whole world.

Confusion in prehistory

In recent years, successive discoveries of the fossil remains of prehistoric humans have led to new theories concerning mankind's family tree. In September 1994, a team led by the American scientist Tom White found hominid fossils thought to be 4.4 million years old in the Awash Basin of Ethiopia. White classified these as a new variety called *Ardipithecus ramidus*, which means 'original ground ape'. On closer examination, the finds proved to be very different from the most recent examples of *Australopithecus afarensis*. It appears that *Ardipithecus ramidus* did in fact live in the forest, but already walked upright. However, it is uncertain whether this species is a link between the ape and *Australopithecus afarensis*, or represents a side branch that died out along the way.

A few months later, a considerable number of hominid fossils, between 3.9 and 4.2 million years old, were found by palaeo-anthropologist Meave Leakey near Lake Turkana in northern Kenya. A well-preserved shin fragment proves that this type of proto-human, called *Australopithecus anamensis*, already walked upright, while other bone

finds displayed more primitive features than Lucy. One of those finds, for example, was a lower jaw, where the chin receded strongly and the rows of teeth ran roughly parallel to one another. On this point, scientists are largely in agreement that *Australopithecus anamensis* is the direct predecessor of *Australopithecus afarensis*.

News from the west

In 1995, the French palaeoanthropologist Michel Brunet travelled to Chad and found a lower jawbone in the desert region of Bahr el-Ghazal at Koro Toro. It belonged to an extremely old example of a protohuman, whom Bruno nicknamed 'Abel' in memory of his colleague, Abel Brillanceau, who had died during excavations in Cameroon in 1989.

After a closer examination of Abel's seven remaining teeth, scientists were able to provide a better picture of him. Abel had a sturdy build, with a low forehead and a receding chin;

Hominid fossils, such as these toe-bones and canine tooth provide clues as to how our predecessors might have climbed trees or what they could have eaten.

he probably walked on two legs. Although the 3–3.5-million-year-old lower jaw strongly resembles that of *Australopithecus afarensis*, there are important differences. The molars have only a thin layer of enamel, implying that Abel's diet probably consisted of soft foods such as fruits, buds and young leaves. But the most interesting thing was that Abel was discovered some 2,500 km to the west of the Great Rift Valley, far from the region which until then had been regarded as mankind's official place of origin.

Various theories

How can this great distance be explained? Researchers disagree on this point. Some now reject the theory that the existence of the Great Rift Valley is responsible for the separate development of humans and apes. Michel Brunet believes that the australopithecines spread over the entire African continent long before Abel lived. According to his theory, these protohumans emerged from the forests to the west of the Great Rift Valley, then rapidly fanned out to populate the entire African continent, and so formed the beginnings of Africa's various tribal groups. However, Yves Coppens steadfastly holds the view that East Africa is the Garden of Eden – the birthplace of humanity. In the time between the formation of the Rift Valley, 8 million years ago, and the appearance of Abel, some 3.5 million years ago, other species would certainly have had enough time to emerge and to leave their place of origin in order to explore new and unknown territories.

A family tree emerges

The first australopithecine finds were made in South Africa in 1924, when the skull of a child was discovered in a cave in the vicinity of Taung. Further excavations showed that this protohuman was an example of the so-called *Australopithecus africanus*, who lived on the savannah between 2 and 3 million years ago. Later, the same region was inhabited by

13

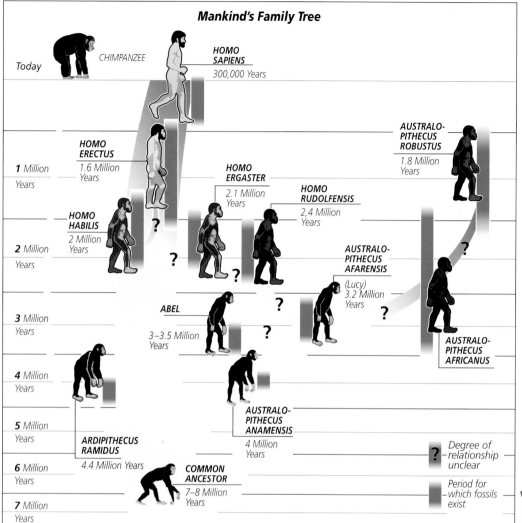

Mankind's Family Tree

Today — CHIMPANZEE

HOMO SAPIENS
300,000 Years

AUSTRALO-PITHECUS ROBUSTUS
1.8 Million Years

HOMO ERECTUS
1.6 Million Years

1 Million Years

HOMO ERGASTER
2.1 Million Years

HOMO RUDOLFENSIS
2,4 Million Years

HOMO HABILIS
2 Million Years

?

2 Million Years

?

?

?

AUSTRALO-PITHECUS AFARENSIS
(Lucy)
3.2 Million Years

?

ABEL
3–3.5 Million Years

?

3 Million Years

?

AUSTRALO-PITHECUS AFRICANUS

4 Million Years

5 Million Years

AUSTRALO-PITHECUS ANAMENSIS
4 Million Years

? Degree of relationship unclear

ARDIPITHECUS RAMIDUS
4.4 Million Years

6 Million Years

COMMON ANCESTOR
7–8 Million Years

Period for which fossils exist

7 Million Years

Creativity versus struggle

The evolution of *Homo sapien sapiens*, or anatomically modern man, can be traced back some 35,000–40,000 years. During this period, humans rapidly developed the use of tools, began to hunt large animals using the bow and arrow, crossed oceans and learned to organize themselves into new and more flexible social groupings. The phenomenon of art made its appearance. Around 9,000 years ago, our ancestors began to settle down, cultivate crops and domesticate cattle and other animals. The earliest cities and written languages – marking the beginning of recorded history – appeared a mere 5,500 years ago.

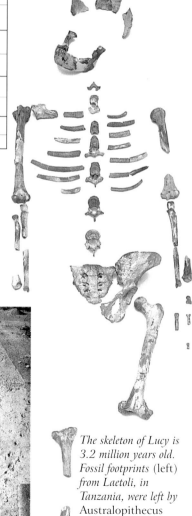

The skeleton of Lucy is 3.2 million years old. Fossil footprints (left) from Laetoli, in Tanzania, were left by Australopithecus afarensis.

another hominid, *Australopithecus robustus*. It had an enormous capacity for chewing, and huge molars were found in its jaw. For this reason, *Australopithecus robustus* is considered to be a specialised herbivore.

The spotlight then shifted to Olduvai Gorge in Tanzania, and the discovery by the renowned anthropologist Louis Leakey of the remains of the oldest of the homo species, *Homo habilis*, dating to between 1.5 and 2.5 million years ago. Its more rounded skull reached an average volume of 630 cm³, with an individual variation of 509–752 cm³. It stood firmly on two legs at a height of up to 1.45 m, weighed around 40 kg and could fashion simple cutting tools such as rough stone knives. These sharp-edged splinters were formed by well-aimed blows on a piece of boulder using a stone as a hammer.

Today we are also familiar with *Homo rudolfensis* and *Homo ergaster*, but science cannot be certain which of these gave rise to a later species, *Homo erectus*, better known

There is general agreement that the birthplace of humanity lies in Africa. But there are still many questions about our direct ancestors, as well as extinct branches of our family tree.

as prehistoric man. The latter had a significantly larger brain, with the oldest measurable skulls attaining a brain volume of 800–1,000 cm³, and the youngest as much as 1.250–1.300 cm³. *Homo erectus* could use fire, and developed symmetrically shaped tools (hammers and axes) as well as other tools of wood and bone.

In 1998, scientists found a complete skull and skeleton of *Australopithecus africanus* – the oldest intact find of its kind ever made – at Sterkfontein, near Johannesburg. The discovery promises to add a new chapter to the story of how our ancestors evolved and spread over the earth.

PILTDOWN

Piltdown Man is one of the most famous frauds in the history of archaeology. The sensational discovery, in a quarry in southern England, of this 'fossil hominid', which supposedly proved that man and ape shared a common ancestor, was in the end revealed to be nothing but a clever counterfeit.

Experts examine the finds: among them are Charles Dawson (third from right, standing) and Arthur Smith-Woodward, of the British Museum (second from right, standing).

On December 18, 1912, headlines in British newspapers trumpeted the names of Arthur Smith-Woodward, a palaeontologist at the British Museum, and Charles Dawson, a prominent amateur archaeologist. At a press conference, the two men announced that they had found the remains of a prehistoric human, about 500,000 years old, next to the fossil remains of extinct animals and some stone tools, in a gravel pit not far from Piltdown Common in the county of Sussex, in southern England. More importantly, Piltdown Man, whom they named *Eoanthropus Dawsoni*, or 'Dawson's early man', was something quite special: it was the long-sought missing link – the common ancestor of both man and ape!

What exactly did these remains consist of? There were small fragments from the top of a human-like skull and a strongly discoloured jawbone. The latter was obviously from an ape, but it had one remarkable characteristic: the molars were worn in a way that could only be compared to the grinding of a human jaw. However, the critical portion of the joint that would confirm that the skull and jaw belonged together was missing. Thus, in order to complete the head, researchers had to imagine how the missing pieces might fit together. Consequently, they had either to make the jaw more human or the skull more primitive.

Free of doubt?

Faced with the need for this type of reconstruction, many expressed doubts that the remains were genuine. But the critical voices were silenced by new findings. Over the following three years, Dawson found more teeth, bones and tools. In 1915, he announced the discovery of teeth and skull fragments of a second human at Piltdown, on a site 3 km from the original findings.

The new finds seemed to banish all doubts about whether or not Piltdown Man was a genuine fossil hominid. However, discoveries made elsewhere by anthropologists quickly cast a shadow over *Eoanthropus Dawsoni*. The remains of fossil hominids found in Europe and Asia, and especially in Africa, had many things in common, but none of these looked at all like their British contemporary.

Who was responsible?

For a long time, the British Museum refused access to the Piltdown fossils for the purposes of comparison. However, its attitude had changed by 1949, and the remains were subjected to a fluorine test, X-ray analysis and isotope markings. The tests showed that the bones were not those of a fossil hominid at all. The skull fragments were those of a modern man – admittedly a few hundred years old – while the jaw belonged to an orang-utan. It had simply been coloured and the teeth filed down.

But who cooked up the swindle? Suspicion fell on the excavators, particularly Dawson. As an amateur archaeologist, he had access to fossils, and the discovery of Piltdown Man had the potential to make him a noted scientist. Nevertheless, nothing was ever proven against him, and the motives of the others involved remain unclear.

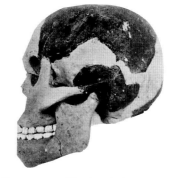

The skull reconstructed by Smith-Woodward (above left) resembled an ape, while another effort (above right) suggested an early human.

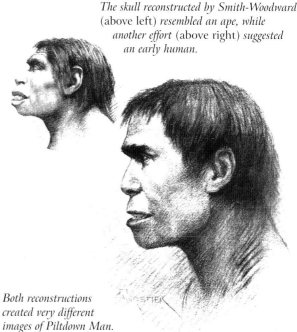

Both reconstructions created very different images of Piltdown Man.

THE NEANDERTHALS AND THEIR SUCCESSORS

For many thousands of years, the Neanderthals – a species of early human named after a valley near Düsseldorf, Germany, where their tools were first discovered in 1856 – ranged over Europe and the Middle East. For reasons that are only beginning to be understood, these people lost the struggle for survival, and passed into extinction more than 30,000 years ago.

Who were the Neanderthals? For much of the 20th century, scientists viewed this early type of human with some disdain. Marcellin Boule, of the Natural History Museum in Paris, once described the Neanderthals as 'huge and ungainly, with a heavy and powerful body, a head, whose robust skull – and jawbones – manifest the prevalence of purely animalistic, instinctive functions over mental processes'.

The development of the Neanderthals (*Homo sapiens neanderthalensis*) and their predecessors can be traced in Europe for around 400,000 years. Certain specialised skull characteristics – bony bulges above the eye sockets, a prominent nose, flat cheekbones, receding chin, as well as large, paddle-like incisors – and a robust bone structure made this early human clearly recognisable. Scientists have disagreed on the question of whether or

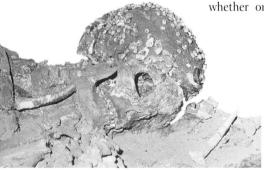

Above: *Analysis of Cro-Magnon remains indicates that these people coexisted with the Neanderthals for several thousand years.*

Right: *Neanderthal stone spearheads and scrapers would be surpassed in quality by the tools of modern man,* Homo sapiens sapiens.

not the Neanderthals could speak, but life in a group undoubtedly required some form of communication between the members. The Neanderthals knew how to use fire, how to make advanced tools from rocks and bones and how to hunt down large herbivores. Neanderthal burials show considerable care for the dignity of the deceased.

Mysterious deaths

Around 35,000–30,000 years ago, all traces of the Neanderthals vanish. At this time, another human type, called *Homo sapiens sapiens*, began to spread over Europe, possibly from a point of origin in the Middle East. The oldest finds of the first anatomically modern man came in 1868 along the rocky banks of the Vézère River in central France. Here, a cave yielded the grave of three men, one woman and one child. These people were named Cro-Magnon, after the site of the finds.

Both types of human seem to have coexisted for approximately 10,000 years in what is now Israel, for example, and for at least 5,000 years in France. Some scientists now ask whether the modern competitor, the Cro-Magnons, perhaps contributed to the elimination of their heavier and more

The Neanderthals lived in a complex social grouping made up of small bands. Hunting was done in groups, with the prey roasted over a fire.

clumsy rivals, the Neanderthals. This concept of genocide seems unlikely, however, judging by the long period of coexistence, and to this day, no trace of massacres has been found. Another theory suggests that certain illnesses passed on by *Homo sapiens sapiens* decimated the Neanderthals, who did not have the necessary resistance. This is also unlikely, as Neanderthal populations were widely scattered and consisted of groups of hunters and gatherers, with each group probably comprising no more than 30 people. The risk of infection was therefore minimal.

Technical superiority

Many researchers are of the opinion that the technological superiority of anatomically modern humans was responsible for the decline of the Neanderthals. The latter already used projectiles, such as spears, and made use of new materials, such as bones or reindeer antlers. But modern humans had perfected the art of sharpening flint to produce tools. Thanks to these technical achievements, *Homo sapiens sapiens* achieved spectacular successes in hunting, even when a new ice age began around 32,000 BC, and it became more and more difficult to find food. Competition for available hunting grounds and the need to share territory could easily have decimated the Neanderthals. After all, we know today that a rise of just 1–2 % in the death rate can wipe out a whole population within a millennium.

SECRETS OF THE CAVE PAINTERS

The works of prehistoric cave painters provide a window into a vanished world, a time when bison and mammoths roamed the plains of Europe. The discovery of spectacular underground art galleries has stunned the world. First there was Lascaux, with its 17,000-year-old cave paintings. Then came the finds at Cosquer, estimated to be about 28,000 years old. But the sensational discovery of the Chauvet Cave in southern France in 1994 has shed new light on the very beginnings of human artistic genius.

The three cave explorers could hardly believe their eyes: after making their way down a long, narrow path, they entered an enormous gallery some dozens of metres underground. On one wall, they saw three lines drawn in ochre, and a small red mammoth. With care, Jean-Marie Chauvet, Eliette Brunel-Deschamps and Christian Hillaire walked to the end of the chamber. There, they found themselves surrounded by bison, rhinoceros, mammoths, horses, bears, wild cats and deer, all of which seemed to run across the walls of the cave.

The discovery of this staggering Stone Age art gallery took place in December 1994 in southeastern France, more precisely in the valley of the Ardèche, a tributary of the Rhône River. The Chauvet Cave, named after Jean-Marie Chauvet, constitutes one of the most extraordinary archaeological finds of modern times. This is partly due to the works of art it contains, but the cave has also opened completely new perspectives for the study of the beginnings of art. These remarkable finds have led to new discussions of old questions: who were the first artists? When and why did they start painting?

An exact copy

For a long time, the Lascaux caves, located in the Dordogne region of central France, were the most famous prehistoric site. This was due to the age of the paintings found there – about 17,000 years old – and because of their exceptional artistic quality.

The discovery, in 1940, of the Lascaux caves brought a great influx of visitors to the site, and aroused fears that the paintings might be damaged by increased humidity,

into a crevice, the muscle of a bison runs along a rocky edge, and the neck of a bull follows the outlines of a ledge. The artists of Lascaux used the rough texture of the rock to give a three-dimensional quality to their creations. By candlelight, the bulls come to life and fill the cave with their presence.

The tools of the artists

Reconstructing Lascaux also involved an attempt to understand the mysterious, nameless prehistoric artists. How did they paint? Where did they get their colours from? And how did they apply them?

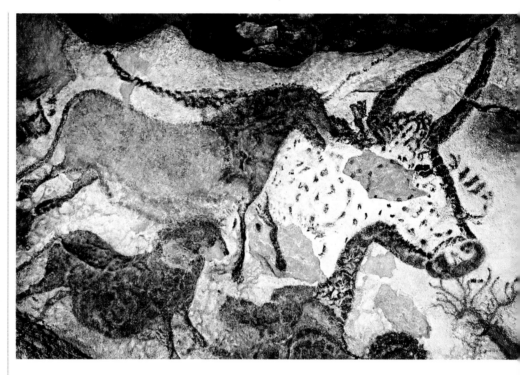

Did the art of our ancestors have a special meaning? Is this ox from Lascaux a work of pure art, or is it a magical means of subduing the spirit of the animal for hunting?

careless contact and even vandalism. The caves were closed to the public in 1963, but, in order to permit people to view the paintings, researchers commissioned Lascaux II, an exact copy of the cave, with its numerous treasures. Opened in 1983, Lascaux II attracts more than 2,000 visitors daily, some of whom travel halfway across Europe to view the replica paintings.

The first sight of the rock paintings is unforgettable. Each animal seems to emerge from the rock face. The spine of a horse melts

To be able to reconstruct the movements of our ancestors, it was necessary for painters and archaeologists to work side by side. Just as the prehistoric artists must have done, the scientists scoured the land for sienna earth, manganese, iron oxide, carbon, haematite and clay – the very same minerals that were ground up by the cave-dwellers to produce pigments. Meticulously imitating their methods, as far as these could be deduced from experiments, modern artists then proceeded to apply the colours with their thumbs, brushes and pieces of fur, or else in powder form by means of blowpipes made from reeds or the bones of birds. Just as the original artists had done, the modern artists worked in the flickering light of fires.

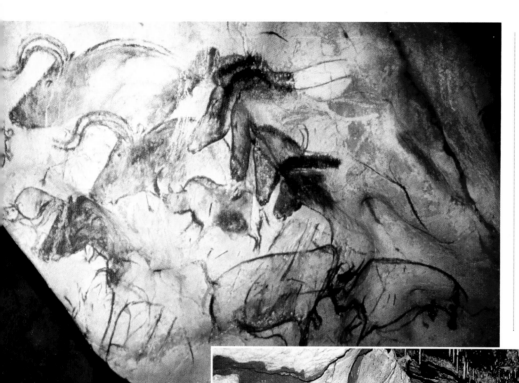

jellyfish, the great deer and all the other animals that can be found in the grotto are – just like the ghostly handprints framed in blown red ochre – early masterpieces of art.

The birth of art

The real sensation came in 1995, when the exact dating of the Chauvet Cave forced experts to revise radically their long-established conceptions of the beginnings of painting. On the basis of the Chauvet finds, we can now say with certainty that prehistoric artists began to scale the heights of artistic achievement at least 33,000 years ago – very much earlier than was previously assumed.

In view of this discovery, some experts have excitedly compared the expressive power and vision of the cave painters to the likes of the Dutch painter Vincent van Gogh. The difference is, however, that the paintings of Chauvet – or at least some of them – are among the oldest in the world, and were probably painted for very different reasons. The latest research has shown that some paintings were completed by later Stone Age artists, sometimes after an interval of as much as several thousand years.

The old idea that mankind needed many millennia to produce works of art is now obsolete. Even those scientists who had previously believed in the slow and gradual development of artistic quality, as shown in cave paintings, had to acknowledge that the paintings from Chauvet are among the most carefully executed of their kind ever discovered. The naturalistic representation of animals, the accurate painting, along with the intentional smudging of contours, the use of perspective – all this was evidence of exceptional skill. So advanced were the Stone Age painters that they could not only endow their creatures with a sense of size, but could also convey the impression of movement.

Unfortunately, the origin of the art of these unknown people remains hidden. Did the paintings have a connection to magic or religious ceremonies? Perhaps the answer lies waiting to be discovered in another of these subterranean museums.

Above: *In the Chauvet Cave, 300 magnificent paintings and etched drawings greet the visitor.*

Right: *Henri Cosquer, the discoverer of the cave that bears his name, wonders if this handprint might not be the signature of a prehistoric artist.*

Radiocarbon dating

By carefully analysing the charcoal that our ancestors used for drawing and etching, it is possible to determine the age of cave paintings to within a few hundred years.

Charcoal contains the radioactive isotope of carbon, $14C$, which decays after the death of the organism. Because its half-life and its relationship to normal carbon ($12C$) are known, it is possible for scientists to determine the relative time of death of the tree that originally provided the carbon. Radiocarbon dating, also known as carbon-14 dating, is applicable within a time period of some 50,000 years.

Paintings under the sea

In 1985, half a century after the discovery of Lascaux, the professional diver Henri Cosquer came across another treasure trove of prehistoric art. Between Cassis and Marseille in the south of France, at a depth of 35 m below sea level, Cosquer found a cave that created a sensation among prehistorians. The oldest known works of art representing people and animals are 35,000 years old, but they cannot compare to the magnificent wall paintings which adorn Cosquer's cave.

The carbon-14 dating method tells us that the oldest part of the cave is more than 28,000 years old. Like Lascaux and the other examples of cave paintings, Cosquer's cave shows the great hunting scenes of the ice age. The small horses, the three penguins, the

THE GLOZEL CONTROVERSY

Over half a century ago, a hoard of ancient objects unearthed at Glozel in the French region of Allier set off a furious argument among archaeologists. Were the objects found by Émile Fradin the remains of some long-forgotten advanced culture or merely a collection of not-so-clever fakes?

One of the famous clay tablets from Glozel.

On March 1, 1924, a young French farm worker named Émile Fradin was ploughing his field when, suddenly, the soil caved in under his team. In the hole that opened up, Fradin found some old clay pots, which he promptly smashed in the hope that they contained treasure. But not a single coin was found. Fradin carried on searching and dug out several other vessels, as well as flat stones, bones, stone tools and clay tablets inscribed with mysterious characters. Shortly afterwards, the farmer showed his finds to a teacher with an interest in archaeology.

The news of the discovery spread rapidly, and soon Antonin Morlet, an amateur archaeologist, announced that this was a prehistoric site, and the objects were at least 12,000–15,000 years old. This assessment, however, was contradicted strongly by professional archaeologists, who believed the finds were not genuine. Morlet saw only professional jealousy and a distortion of the facts. A series of court cases followed, with each side issuing pamphlets and official statements. France became divided into two camps: the one considered the finds genuine testimony to a prehistoric culture, while the other dismissed them as counterfeits.

The clay tablets

The Glozel controversy has far-reaching consequences for our understanding of human history. If the objects found by Émile Fradin were very old, it would mean that the characters inscribed on the clay tablets were written in Europe and not in the Middle East. Several years before, the script system of the Sumerians – assumed to be the earliest written language – had been discovered at sites in the Middle East estimated to be about 5,000 years old. But neither side in the controversy was willing to compromise. As a result, the matter remained unresolved until the 1970s, when new research methods could provide much more precise dating. For example, the carbon-14 method can help determine the age of the organic matter, while thermo-luminescence tells us about when the clay that was used to make a pot was fired. But even modern dating methods have not solved the mystery that surrounds the Glozel finds. Studies show that the clay tablets are barely 2,000 years old and date from Gallo-Roman times, while some of the bones are as old as 15,000 years. But this is not all.

The stones and bones are inscribed with characters that obviously date from the Stone Age.

These inconsistencies seem to support the counterfeit theory: the combination of various objects clearly shows that Glozel is not a genuine prehistoric site. These sceptics suspect instead that someone has collected objects of different origin, some admittedly very old, and marked them with characters. This theory, however, does not in the least deter those who believe in the authenticity of Glozel. In their opinion, modern methods have proven the finds to be ancient. During the 1980s, France's Ministry of Education and Cultural Affairs commissioned new excavation work at the site. But as long as no new finds are recorded, the quarrel is unlikely to be resolved.

Below: *The peaceful valley where the Glozel finds were made.*
Inset right: *Together with his grandfather, Émile Fradin (right) examines one of the artefacts.*

THE MYTH OF THE FLOOD

Stories of an all-engulfing flood are told in many parts of the world. Behind the legends of arks and heroes, though, is there perhaps the record of a real catastrophe, which has been deeply ingrained into the memory of widely scattered cultures?

In the West, the best-known tale of the great flood is found in the Old Testament of the Bible. The story of Noah and the ark, as told in the Bible, was compiled from two texts written sometime between the 8th and 6th centuries BC in the kingdoms of Israel and Judea. The oldest reports on the flood, however, originally came from Mesopotamia (modern-day Iraq). A Sumerian version of the story from the 3rd century BC reports on it in

Above: *On the eleventh tablet of the* Epic of Gilgamesh, *Utnapishtim tells Gilgamesh how to survive the floods.*

This mosaic in St Mark's Basilica, Venice, shows people drowning in the rising waters.

the same way as the famous *Epic of Gilgamesh* from Babylon, which was written about 2,000 years before the birth of Christ. In this account, the Babylonian Utnapishtim describes to the hero Gilgamesh how he escapes a flood sent by the gods which had destroyed everything.

But over and above that, there are many other written records of the legend of the flood. In the holy scriptures of the Mayan

Indians of Central America, a god-fearing man named Tapi assumes the role of Noah; in the Persian text collection known as the *Vendidad*, a protagonist named Yima appears in the middle of a description of a flood; in an Indian tale, the hero is named Manu; in ancient Greek legend, he is known as Deukalion. Legends of the flood are also known from Chinese

mythology, in the South Seas and Australia, among the Inca of Peru and among Native North Americans. Strangely, these stories appear very seldom in African mythology.

Chaos and a new beginning

The myth of the flood always embodies both destruction and rebirth. The destruction of sinful mankind by God's will does mean the return into chaos, but this ending of the world is never final and irrevocable. For out of the floods emerge symbols of the old act of creation: a virgin earth, cleansed of all its sins by the purifying force of the water. And on it, a new mankind will emerge from the few chosen survivors.

In each of the reports, the hero is warned about the impending threat beforehand. Noah and Yima learn about it from God the creator himself, the other protagonists from one of their gods. Thus, the Babylonian god Ea tells the secret to Utnapishtim to ensure that not all of his people will be destroyed. In Greek mythology, Prometheus forewarns his son Deukalion of Zeus's plan. Manu, however, receives his warning from God in the shape of a fish.

In nearly all flood areas, instructions come from the gods to build a boat: Noah builds the ark; Deukalion and his wife Pyrrha a floating chest; and in the legends of Native North Americans, a raft of tree trunks is built for the rescue. One exception is the Persian text: here, the chosen ones retreat into an

enclosed area safe from the flood waters. Most of the heroes flee in boats with their families and a selection of plants and animals; Noah takes one pair from each animal species into his ark.

And then the great flood arrives. In the *Epic of Gilgamesh*, it is caused by a torrent which pours down for seven days; in the Bible, it rains for forty days and nights, until the ocean reaches the tips of the mountains. In the *Vendidad*, the flood is caused by rain and the melting of snow after a severe winter. The boats float on the raging meltwaters and finally end up on a mountain. In the Indian text, the divine fish pulls the boat to the mountain peaks of the Himalayas, and ties it to a tree.

After the flood waters have receded, the survivors are asked to multiply themselves and to help bring forth a new civilisation. Deukalion and Pyrrha throw stones behind

The flood in the Bible

Then God said to Noah: 'I intend to destroy mankind, ... for all men have lived corrupt lives on earth ... Make yourself an ark with ribs of cypress .... And you shall go into the ark, you and your sons, your wife and your son's wives with you. And you shall bring living creatures of every kind into the ark to keep them alive with you, two of each kind, a male and a female ....' The flood continued upon the earth for forty days, and the waters swelled, ... until they covered all the high mountains ... God wiped out every living thing that existed on earth ... and only Noah and his company in the ark survived. (Genesis 6–7)

Above: *In Indian legend, a fish sent by the gods rescues Manu from the flood by towing his boat to the mountains of the Himalayas, which the flood waters could not reach.*

Left: *In this medieval manuscript, Noah's ark floats on an ocean that has covered even the highest peaks.*

themselves, which then come alive. After a sacrifice to the gods, Manu, who is the only survivor, is given a companion. In the Old Testament, God makes a covenant with Noah, his family and the animals for them to populate the earth again.

Science's view

The legends of the flood obviously agree on many points. But does this mean that a great catastrophe gave rise to all these tales? The flood seems to have been experienced in similar ways by peoples living far apart. Did these stories become engraved into the collective memory of mankind? Numerous theories support this thesis.

As all accounts talk about strong and long-lasting rainfall, several scientists deduce that there must have been a major climatic change during the early Stone Age. But, according to them, rainfall alone would never have been enough to create such massive world-destroying floods – even rains as heavy as those mentioned in the Bible. Thus, proponents of the climate-change theory speculate that towards the end of the last ice age – i.e., between 8,000 and 14,000 years ago – rising temperatures caused the rapid melting of the massive ice sheets which had accumulated over many thousands of years. The amount of water thus released would have led to a sudden rise in the level of the oceans and caused great destruction.

The French climatologist A. Capart has pursued this theory even further: in his view, which is hotly disputed by specialists in climate change, an immense glacier that once covered the northern part of Scandinavia was responsible for the floods. Capart suggests that a sudden rise in temperature caused the glacier to shatter, causing an ice block of enormous proportions to fall into what is now the Baltic Sea. The resulting gigantic tidal wave would have spread over Eastern Europe to the Mediterranean Sea.

Other researchers view the myth of the flood in quite a different light. According to their view, an economic revolution took place at the end of the ice age. As the land became fruitful again, groups of formerly nomadic hunters and gatherers settled down and became farmers, securing their survival by planting crops. In the biblical flood, Noah represents this settling impulse, building the ark in order to safeguard seeds and animals, and settling at a particular place after the flood waters have receded.

WHO SPEAKS INDO-EUROPEAN?

Most Europeans, and countless other people outside Europe, speak languages descended from Indo-European. While much is known about modern Indo-European languages, little is known of their origins, because the people who spoke this language lived before the birth of writing.

Compared to other continents, modern Europe – which stretches from the Atlantic Ocean to the Ural Mountains, from the Mediterranean Sea to the Black Sea and from the Caucasus Mountains to the Arctic Ocean – displays a relative uniformity of language. Here, most people speak languages derived from Indo-European. But when it comes to communicating with speakers of another language, it is quite a different story: for an English speaker, the Indo-European languages of Croatia, Russia and Armenia are nearly as incomprehensible as Basque or Hungarian, neither of which belong to the Indo-European family. How then, is it possible to refer to a single, uniform Indo-European language area?

Every second person

When the total number of speakers of Indo-European languages is added up, the total makes up almost half of the human race. Among the 200–300 spoken languages in the world today, there are five 'large' or main languages (English, Hindi, Portuguese, Spanish and Russian), as well as a multitude of 'small' ones – where the language area and the number of speakers is much smaller (for example, Icelandic or Sardinian).

From the late 15th century, European voyages of discovery and subsequent colonial expansion contributed to the worldwide spread of some of these languages, notably the Germanic languages – including English and Dutch – and the Romance languages (based on Latin) such as Spanish,

Portuguese and French. The expansion of the Russian empire spread Russian, a Slavic language, over the northern part of Asia.

The script systems

Surprisingly, regions that share a common language do not necessarily share the same script system, or system of writing. This stems mainly from the diversity of religious and sociopolitical traditions that prevails throughout the world. Thus, out of the five script systems most widely used in the world, no less than four are used by the Indo-European languages, namely Latin, Cyrillic, Arabic and the Devanagari script.

The Latin alphabet – the most widely used in the world – was adopted by the Christian church under the Roman empire, and then passed on to areas influenced by the Roman Catholic Church – chiefly Europe and what has become known as the West. The Latin alphabet was also passed on to the Protestants and to the Catholic Slavs of Central and Eastern Europe.

Although it is derived from Greek, the Cyrillic alphabet has come to characterise the Orthodox Christian/Slav area of Eastern Europe; even Rumanian, although it is derived from Latin, was written in Cyrillic characters up to the middle of the 19th century.

Beginning in the 7th century, the spread of Islam through the Middle East, North Africa and southern and central Asia brought the

The seal of King Mursili II (about 1349–1315 BC) bears an inscription in Hittite, an extinct Indo-European language (from Ras Schamra, Syria).

Arabic alphabet into wide use among peoples who spoke languages as diverse as Persian, Kurdish or Afghan, even to the speakers of Indian languages in the Indian subcontinent.

The modern languages of the northern part of India, notably Hindi and Sanskrit, are written in the Devanagari script. There are a number of other, very old script systems that have survived: for example, the Greek alphabet, which served as a model for the Latin, Cyrillic and Armenian scripts.

A tree with many branches

With so many differences, what do the Indo-European languages have in common? As early as the beginning of the 19th century, linguists detected similarities in texts written in Sanskrit and others written in Ancient Greek. Comparative studies have uncovered a number of other phonetic and grammatical similarities between the languages of the European and Asian regions. This produced the theory that there was one original language, from which many independent languages evolved. Just as a tree forms branches, so did Indo-European – previously called Indo-Germanic – develop subfamilies (Romanic, Slavonic, Germanic or Indo-Aryan), which gave rise to other independent languages (such as French, Italian, Spanish and Portuguese, in the Romance subfamily). But what did Indo-European sound like? Who used it, and when did it exist as a uniform original language?

Striking similarities

The similarities between five languages from the Indo-European family are shown below by the words for the numerals 8, 10 and 100 (simplified, Latin phonetic transcription).

Family	Old Irish	Latin	Gothic	Ancient Greek	Sanskrit
eight	okt	okto	ahtau	okto	asta
ten	deik	dekem	taihum	deka	dasa
hundred	ket	kentum	hund	(he) katon	satam

A 'k' in Old Irish, Ancient Greek or Latin changes to an 'h' in Gothic and to an 's' in Sanskrit.

The home of the Indo-Europeans

Much to the dismay of linguists, there are no written records of this shared original language, as it was spoken at a time before the invention of writing. The oldest known texts – Mycenaean, Vedic and Hittite – stem from the 2nd century BC, and therefore from a time in which the individual Indo-European languages were already markedly different from one another. We can probably assume that the basic language was relatively uniform around the 4th century BC, and that it then diversified into various dialects and then to independent languages through the nomadic movements of its speakers.

From the limited Indo-European vocabulary that could be reconstructed by linguists, it is assumed that the original Indo-Europeans pursued a way of life centred around farming and cattle breeding, and lived together in extended families organised along paternal lines. Their language was strongly inflected and their words had many endings, a feature which probably made their words much longer than our words today.

The most difficult question remains that of determining the original home of the Indo-Europeans. Normally, a comparison of the vocabulary of very old languages makes it possible to trace migrations of population and identify an area of origin. But people don't always move in one direction: they mix with other peoples, exchange goods, news and, consequently, also words. The lines between cultures and languages easily blur. For this reason, it is difficult to determine exactly where the first speakers of Indo-European lived. Some researchers consider the prehistoric Kurgan culture, which flourished on the steppes west of the Ural Mountains from the 6th century BC, to be that of the original Indo-European people. But this is just a theory, much like the assumption that the original Indo-Europeans chose to settle in the centre of Europe.

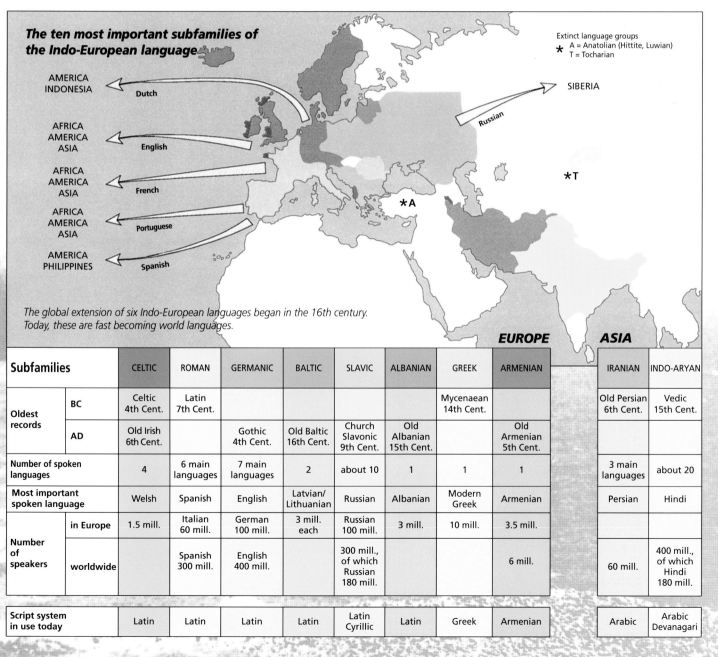

The ten most important subfamilies of the Indo-European language

Extinct language groups
* A = Anatolian (Hittite, Luwian)
T = Tocharian

AMERICA
INDONESIA — Dutch

AFRICA
AMERICA
ASIA — English

AFRICA
AMERICA
ASIA — French

AFRICA
AMERICA
ASIA — Portuguese

AMERICA
PHILIPPINES — Spanish

SIBERIA — Russian

*A

*T

The global extension of six Indo-European languages began in the 16th century. Today, these are fast becoming world languages.

Subfamilies		CELTIC	ROMAN	GERMANIC	BALTIC	SLAVIC	ALBANIAN	GREEK	ARMENIAN		IRANIAN	INDO-ARYAN
Oldest records	BC	Celtic 4th Cent.	Latin 7th Cent.					Mycenaean 14th Cent.			Old Persian 6th Cent.	Vedic 15th Cent.
	AD	Old Irish 6th Cent.		Gothic 4th Cent.	Old Baltic 16th Cent.	Church Slavonic 9th Cent.	Old Albanian 15th Cent.		Old Armenian 5th Cent.			
Number of spoken languages		4	6 main languages	7 main languages	2	about 10	1	1	1		3 main languages	about 20
Most important spoken language		Welsh	Spanish	English	Latvian/ Lithuanian	Russian	Albanian	Modern Greek	Armenian		Persian	Hindi
Number of speakers	in Europe	1.5 mill.	Italian 60 mill.	German 100 mill.	3 mill. each	Russian 100 mill.	3 mill.	10 mill.	3.5 mill.			
	worldwide		Spanish 300 mill.	English 400 mill.		300 mill., of which Russian 180 mill.			6 mill.		60 mill.	400 mill., of which Hindi 180 mill.
Script system in use today		Latin	Latin	Latin	Latin	Latin Cyrillic	Latin	Greek	Armenian		Arabic	Arabic Devanagari

EUROPE   ASIA

THE MUMMY IN THE GLACIER

The discovery of the mummified body of an Iron Age man preserved in a glacier in Austria's Ötztaler Alps stunned the world. After several years of research, though, the Ice Man puzzles scientists. The secret of what drove him to his lonely death in an ice cave over 3,000 metres above sea level remains a tantalising enigma.

The famous mountaineer Reinhold Messner and companion Hans Kammerlander, who happened to be near the site when the dead man was discovered, examine the mummy.

On September 19, 1991, German mountaineers Erika and Helmut Simon made a macabre discovery on the Hauslabjoch in the Ötztaler Alps: sticking out of the ice, a human corpse lay face-down on his stomach, his dried-out upper body covered by a parchment-like skin. The thin ice still held his right leg, which was wrapped in straw and leather strips. The site soon attracted curious people and researchers, who found all kinds of objects scattered around the body. Among these were a copper hatchet and a complete set of hunting equipment. Several days later, the body was officially removed and flown to Innsbruck by helicopter.

The investigation begins

The scientists placed in charge of the investigation all agreed that Ötzi, as the Ice Man was nicknamed, was a sensational find.

They were able to determine the age of the corpse by means of the carbon-14 method, which was carried out at various laboratories in different countries, with each laboratory being given a different sample. Together with the stylistic classification of the objects found around the body, the tests suggested that the man had died around 3300 BC. Apart from the age of the body, scientists wanted to know exactly how it had remained intact in the ice for a period of about 5,000 years. After all, the oldest known corpses previously found in glaciers were only several hundred years old.

The place of discovery

The body had not been found in the middle of a glacier but rather in a rock crevice at the edge of the ice sheet. This was a section where the frozen water was very deep. As this crevice did not have a natural outlet, it had not been affected by movement in the great mass of ice. If the body had been exposed to the forces of a moving glacier, surely no trace of the Ice Man would have been found?

According to the team of scientists and forensic investigators, the Ice Man certainly had the right equipment to survive in the harsh conditions of the Ötztaler Alps. He wore a fur cap, as well as a cape woven from grasses that probably served as a rudimentary raincoat.

The Ice Man had stuffed straw into his shoes, one of which still covers the right foot of the mummy. Above right: the copper hatchet, with a handle made from yew.

Under his cape, he had on a robe made from pieces of fur sewn together. In order to protect his legs from the bitter alpine cold, he wore fur-clad leg-warmers. He also had on a loincloth and shoes made from solid leather which were stuffed with thick grass. The Ice Man carried the equipment necessary for making a fire, as well as a container made from birch bark which was probably used to transport the hot coals which were so laboriously kindled.

The Ice Man's bow and arrow made it possible for him to hunt wild animals, but it is thought that he was not a hunter. By the time of his death, human survival depended less upon hunting than upon farming and raising livestock. Scientists today believe that the Ice Man was probably a shepherd, who may have hunted wild animals but more likely herded his cattle on the high pastures in summer.

Death in the ice

Why did the Ice Man undertake his last, fatal hike into the high mountains? The researchers speculate that he must have either been involved in a serious fight, or perhaps that his home village had been targeted for attack by outsiders. This view is borne out by the fact that he already had several fractured ribs before he set out on his last journey into the mountains. If he really was a shepherd, then he probably knew the highland terrain well enough to hide from his pursuers.

Despite his severe injuries, the Ice Man kept on climbing higher and higher, until he had exhausted his strength. Finally, he reached the bleak, frozen Hauslabjoch area. There he probably encountered a change in weather: perhaps snow began to fall, and the temperature dropped. The Ice Man sought shelter under an overhanging rock, ate some dried meat and desperately tried to keep awake. He knew for certain that he would die if he went to sleep. But he was too exhausted to care any longer; he lay down, fell asleep and never woke up. Several hours later, a thick blanket of snow had covered his cold and lifeless body.

GILGAMESH

The ancient Mesopotamian hero, Gilgamesh, is the earliest symbol in world literature of the search for immortality. But the question remains: did this extraordinary man really live?

Since time immemorial, humans have dreamt of heroes who could grasp the mysteries of the spirit world and the secret of eternal life. Gilgamesh was the first of these – or, at least the first who tried to find answers to these questions.

The *Epic of Gilgamesh* is much older than Homer's *Iliad* or the great Indian epic, the *Mahabharata*. It is undoubtedly the oldest epic text in the world, for we know today that the first version was written down by the Sumerians in the middle of the second millennium BC.

The numerous fragments of the *Epic of Gilgamesh*, of which many versions have appeared, were found in different parts of the Middle East. The most complete part was discovered in Nineveh, site of the famous library of the Assyrian king Assurbanipal. This version of the legend stems from the 7th century AD and was written on 12 clay tablets, three of which have disappeared. Incidentally, this version also contains the story of a great flood, the Babylonian version of the biblical flood.

Half god, half human

The hero of the epic was not just the stuff of legend: relief carvings on Sumerian temples record the heroic deeds of Gilgamesh. He appears to have lived around 2700 BC, and to have reigned as king over the city of Uruk, in southern Mesopotamia. He must have been an important ruler, for he built strong city walls and imposing temples, traces of which can still be seen today. It is not known whether it was these monumental buildings alone that made the king immortal or whether he also performed great deeds. It is known that in Mesopotamian literature, the son of the goddess Ninsum becomes a supernatural being. But despite his godly nature, he comes to accept that he is mortal,

Gilgamesh's superhuman strength enabled him to subdue a lion, as shown in this bas-relief.

and even his character and weaknesses are portrayed as more human than godlike.

Friendship and death

Gilgamesh is the hero of the epic, but he is also a tyrannical ruler whose subjects groan under the cost of his many wars. In order to rid themselves of their king, his people try to get him to fight Enkidu – a creature, half savage and half man, whom the gods of Uruk have created as an equal opponent for Gilgamesh.

A single combat takes place, but it ends in a draw, and the two men become inseparable friends. Their friendship enables them to perform superhuman deeds: together they kill the giant Humbaba, the guardian of the cedar forests of Lebanon, as well as the sky bull, which Gilgamesh has to kill by order of the goddess Ishtar, because he refused her love. This enrages the gods, and they decide to separate the friends by letting Enkidu die of an illness. When Gilgamesh sees the corpse of his friend, he is devastated and goes in search of eternal life.

The search leads him to a land on the other side of the water of death, and to Utnapishtim, a very old wise man and a survivor of the great world-destroying flood, to whom the gods have granted immortality. Utnapishtim's advice to the king is to remain awake for seven days and seven nights in preparation for immortality, but the hero fails this test. Out of pity, Utnapishtim shows him the plant of eternal life, called 'the old man becomes young again'. But this plant is stolen by a snake and so Gilgamesh must remain a mortal. However, he reigns over his people for 126 years.

Eternal questions

The *Epic of Gilgamesh* enjoys widespread, almost universal, interest, in part because it seeks to address mankind's most important questions: the relationship with the gods, the power of friendship, pride and fury, vulnerability, love, death, and even the meaning of life. Because Gilgamesh seeks to answer these eternal questions, he has the chance to become immortal.

The ruins of Uruk reflect the ambitions of its rulers.

THE PYRAMID OF CHEOPS: WHAT MYSTERIES DOES IT CONCEAL?

Even today, almost five thousand years after its completion, the Pyramid of Cheops in Egypt is a technical masterpiece. But its builders left no plans that might explain how it came to be built. It is still not completely clear why the pyramid was erected. With so few answers available, it seems that the Great Pyramid will be surrounded by mystery for ever.

A Hungarian periodical published this fanciful view of the construction of the pyramids.

It was intended to be recognised from a great distance, and the closer you come, the more you are drawn into its spell. The Great Pyramid was probably built around 2580 BC on the instructions of Pharaoh Cheops, on the Giza plateau southwest of modern Cairo, capital of Egypt. It is the largest of a trio of pyramids at the Giza site. But to this day, even with the most modern scientific methods, experts have not been able to solve all the mysteries of this impressive building.

An enormous building site

Everything about the pyramid is on a vast scale. Built on a square ground plan with a side length of 230 m, and an original height of almost 147 m (138 m today), it covers an area of over 5 ha and has a volume of around 2,600,000 m³. The number of stones used is enormous, and each one weighs several tons.

Due to the lack of suitable tools – the artisans only had tools made from copper, which is not hard enough to work stone – the Egyptians selected blocks which did not require very much carving. It is possible that a cleverly devised transport and lifting system was used between the quarries and the building site; however, this hypothesis cannot be proven. The descriptions provided by two Greek historians – Herodotus in 440 BC and Diodorus in 50 BC – probably adapted early accounts of the actual system that was used. Herodotus based his ideas on the assumption that the Egyptians had constructed wooden machines to assemble the blocks in sections – from the base of the pyramid to its top. Diodorus thought it more likely that the Egyptians had built earth ramps to haul the stones into place.

Searching for the answer

During the Middle Ages, people believed that the builders of the pyramids were able to float or use flying carpets. In modern times, archaeologists have come to rely on written texts, which are considerably more reliable. Researchers first thought along the lines of Herodotus's argument and came to the supposition that the pyramid must have been constructed with the aid of mechanical devices – rollers and winches – which were moved with human force or levers.

It was not until the remains of ramps were unearthed and descriptions of them found on grave inscriptions, that Diodorus's ideas were confirmed. Since then, many scholars have assumed that the Egyptians built ramps parallel to the flanks of the pyramid; other scientists are of the opinion that the ramps were positioned at right angles to the side of

Heavenward

The earliest form of pyramid was the step pyramid of Pharaoh Zoser, built by the architect Imhotep around 2600 BC at Saqqara, Egypt. The shape of the stone monument resembles a staircase, and was intended to enable the king to ascend to heaven. In the following 100 years or so, the genuine pyramid form was developed: the relatively smooth sides now sloped gradually to the ground, possibly imitating the rays of the sun.

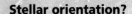

the pyramid, getting smaller as they got closer to the top. Both theories agree that the ramps were covered with a layer of damp clay to allow the stone blocks to slide easily. Massive columns of workers, many of them slaves, pulled sledges full of stone blocks up the ramps.

Facts and fantasy

Even as we come closer to understanding the remarkable methods by which the pyramids were built, we are still far from knowing why the Egyptians mobilised this prodigious effort and expenditure of energy.

Historians and archaeologists agree on one point, however: the pyramids were built as monumental burial chambers for the kings of the 3rd to the 13th dynasties (about 2670–1650 BC). Also, each pyramid always seems to form part of an extended complex of funeral architecture.

At Giza, however, this hypothesis does not work. Herodotus and Diodorus both identified Cheops as being the ruler who commissioned the building, but neither writer said that the pharaoh was buried in the pyramid. The stone coffin found inside was empty. Over the centuries, this has given rise to many different, even fantastic, hypotheses. One biblically inspired interpretation saw the Great Pyramid as a gigantic grain silo. Since the 19th century, the followers of a

pseudo-science known as pyramidology have searched feverishly for an explanation for the dimensions of the pyramid. Some think the geometry of the pyramid reflects the technological know-how that the Egyptians had acquired up to the time of the biblical floods. Others, however, want to see in it a prophetic code for the most important dates in world history.

New perspectives

Those who desperately try to find secrets where there are none can easily find themselves in a position where they miss the real mystery. For a long time, serious Egyptologists have confirmed again and again that the Great Pyramid is really a shrine. Three chambers, which are connected to one another by means of a network of underground passages, have so far been identified. The largest, the King's Chamber, contains the coffin in which the mortal remains of Pharaoh Cheops could have lain. Today the coffin is empty, but it might have been

Above: *The pyramid's entrance, with its lintel, which is oversized compared to the actual opening.*

Stellar orientation?

In recent times, scientific research has shown that the orientation of the three pyramids on the Giza plateau – Cheops, Chefren and Mykerinos – corresponds exactly to the stars in the constellation known as Orion's Belt. In ancient Egypt, Orion's Belt symbolised the god Osiris, the most important of the Egyptian gods.

ransacked by the Muslim leader, Caliph Al-Mamun, who entered the holy chambers in the 9th century. It is true that there are cracks in the ceiling of this room which stem from the time prior to the death of Cheops; surely the pharaoh would not have wanted to be buried in a place that was threatened by collapse? If the corpse did not find its last resting place in this room, the pyramid could have been a giant cenotaph – an empty royal shrine – built for the honour of the departed pharaoh alone.

Even after so many centuries of digging and exploration, the Pyramid of Cheops still harbours plenty of surprises: in recent years, a German engineer, Rudolf Gantenbrink, probed the secrets of some of the narrowest passages – as yet unreachable by human explorers – with the help of a remote-controlled robot camera. Gantenbrink discovered an enormous door at the end of a shaft. But he was never able to find out what lies hidden behind the door.

View through the pyramid

Ⓐ *Royal Chamber*
Ⓑ *Chamber of the Queen*
Ⓒ *Incomplete Chamber*
Ⓓ *Venting Shaft*

① *Entrance to the pyramid*
②③④ *Shafts*
⑤ *Shaft leading downwards*
⑥ *Large gallery*

OF LABYRINTHS AND MAZES

Like the circle, the cross and the spiral, the labyrinth is an ancient symbol common to many cultures. Although it has acquired many meanings over the centuries, the origins of the labyrinth are still shrouded in mystery.

Nowadays we think of a labyrinth as a tangle of constantly crossing paths and blind alleys, a form of entertainment or perhaps a kind of puzzle. In its modern form, the labyrinth has existed for a couple of hundred years. But the original symbol of the labyrinth dates back many thousands of years. Remarkably, the labyrinth crops up all over the world and occupies a place in the religion, philosophy and literature of many different cultures.

The origin of the labyrinth

Where, when and how was this symbol created? Nobody knows exactly. Even the origin and meaning of the word 'labyrinth' have been lost in the mists of history. It has been variously attributed to Greek, Hebrew, Egyptian or Latin roots.

Viking stone bearing a labyrinth motif from the 5th century AD.

As with its name, an aura of mystery surrounds the origins of the labyrinth's form. In Europe, it is closely linked with the island of Crete and the myth of the Minotaur. This creature had the body of a human and the head of a bull, and was born out of a union of Pasiphaë, the wife of Cretan king Minos, with a bull given to the king by the sea god, Poseidon. Faced with this horrible monster, living proof of his wife's adultery, Minos commissioned the exiled Athenian architect and master builder, Daedalus, to build a huge prison with passages so intricate and intertwined that nobody without a map could find their way out. King Minos then locked the Minotaur into the labyrinth.

Far from the Mediterranean, we learn from the Indian epic, the *Mahabharata*, that the magician Droma was the master of the labyrinth in South Asia. Christian tradition attributed it to King Solomon, who was himself a symbol of intelligence and wisdom. But labyrinths have also been found as far afield as Peru and Colorado.

The oldest examples come from the 3rd century AD, and can be seen in the *tomba del labirinto* (labyrinth tombs) of Luzzani on the island of Sardinia. Ironically, the labyrinth of King Minos appears never to have existed. However, some believe that Minos's palace at Knossos, with its myriad chambers, stairwells and winding passageways, could possibly have been the dwelling place of the mythical Minotaur.

Everything runs towards the centre

In general, the classic labyrinth is a closed space with a circuitous pattern of lines that eventually lead to a central point. The winding line is thought to symbolise the difficulties of life on earth, while the centre symbolises death and resurrection.

Even the Christian church has made use of this ancient symbol. Many medieval cathedrals display labyrinths on their walls or columns, or as tile patterns on the floor. Sometimes, these patterns are octagonal, as at Reims Cathedral in northern France, but most are strictly concentric, as at Chartres Cathedral, located southwest of Paris.

Just like the ancient Greek labyrinth, the medieval cathedral has a single entrance, a symbol of the hope of salvation that lies within. The entrance signifies that a genuine Christian need not fear eternal damnation. The intricacies of the labyrinth represent the trials and tribulations through which the souls of good Christians must pass in this life before they reach their goal: salvation.

The famous labyrinth of Crete is shown on this Roman mosaic pavement: in the centre, the hero Theseus slays the Minotaur. At right, Ariadne waits at the entrance for her lover.

Path of penance

Church labyrinths are always situated in the centre of the nave, near the western portal, a symbolic barrier between the outside world and the House of God. With most labyrinths, the entrance points westward, towards the kingdom of the dead. According to the first book of Moses in the Bible, the Garden of Eden was situated in the east – the direction of the sunrise. In Greek mythology, the gates of Hades – the realm of the dead – are situated towards the West, where the sun sets.

If a believer followed the windings of the labyrinth, he could escape from the darkness of earthly life and move towards the light of God. But it was a long journey! The labyrinth of the Cathedral of Sens, in France, required at least 2,000 steps to walk around its 10-m diameter. When performing certain penances, believers shuffled along the meanders of the labyrinth on their knees in order to empathise with Jesus Christ's walk to Calvary. For this reason, church labyrinths are sometimes called 'the way to Jerusalem'.

The modern labyrinth

From the 16th century, a new type of labyrinth made its appearance. The Minotaur's prison and the penitent's path became a place of diversion and contemplation. The new labyrinth often took the form of three-dimensional mazes constructed out of walls or tree-like shrubs. The intertwined crossing paths of the maze are designed to make the

individual quickly lose his or her sense of direction. This kind of labyrinth does not necessarily have a centre; instead, the goal is to find the right path through the winding passages to the exit.

The first of these new labyrinths were built in the gardens of royal palaces in France and England. One of the most popular is the maze at Hampton Court Palace outside London. Perhaps the most famous maze was built at the Palace of Versailles, near Paris, although it has unfortunately been destroyed. At the many crossings of its paths, the wandering visitor, trying to find his or her way, was given the opportunity to think about his position – just like a fable.

This new type of labyrinth did not bring people face to face with the secrets of life and death, nor did it offer the chance of eternal rebirth. But it offered enlightenment, and the opportunity to learn from the experience in order to find the way out. Even if the seemingly endless meanders and frustrating cul-de-sacs of the maze do not represent the meaning of life, they do reveal something of its complexity.

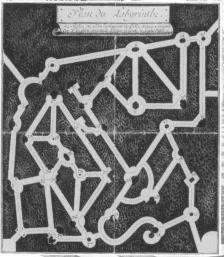

The maze in the gardens of the Palace of Versailles was one of the most modern labyrinths, one which served both as a place of entertainment and of contemplation.

ABYDOS AND THE MYSTERIES OF OSIRIS

The holy city of Abydos in central Egypt was the centre of the cult of Osiris. Here were celebrated the mysteries of this god, whose tragic life became the very embodiment of the cycle of life, death and regeneration for the people of the Nile Valley.

In the world of the Egyptian gods, Osiris is possibly the most complex figure. On one hand, he taught the people basic skills, such as how to work the land; on the other hand, he was a god who would continue to die and be born again. Under the 12th dynasty of the Middle Kingdom (1994 BC–1781 BC), a cult centred on Osiris developed at the city of Abydos, located about 550 km south of modern-day Cairo. Here, an extraordinary ceremony – the mysteries of Osiris – was performed, involving a re-enactment of the burial and resurrection of the god. The city's reputation as a holy place was based on these festivities, and it was one of the most important Egyptian religious centres until the Graeco-Roman era.

Based on findings made by archaeologists, we now know that two types of mysteries were celebrated at Abydos: firstly, there were public theatrical performances, where the various phases of the Osiris myths were retold by actors, priests or courtiers; and then there were the secret rites, which only a few initiates were allowed to witness. We know very little about these secret rites today, but archaeologists have learned much more about the public side of the mysteries. The

A priest of Osiris with a reliquary – in it were supposedly the mortal remains of the god, whom his jealous brother Seth had dismembered.

Pyramid Texts (inscriptions on the walls of the pyramids dating from about 2500 BC) and the writings of the Greek author Plutarch (1st century AD) tell the story of Osiris. According to the Pyramid Texts, Osiris was the son of Nut and Geb – the gods of the heavens and of the earth – and had inherited the throne of Egypt from his father. The god set out to help his subjects. First, he went to the people of the south, who were still quite uncivilised; he taught them the basics of farming and gave them an understanding of the worship of the gods. Matters of state were taken care of by Isis, his sister and wife.

Seth's trap

On Osiris's return from the south, his jealous brother Seth laid a cunning trap for him. During a dinner party, Seth invited his guests, Osiris among them, to lie in a grand coffin, promising that the person who best fitted it would receive it as a gift. But as Osiris lay down, Seth locked the magnificent coffin and threw it into the Nile River. The river carried it to the Mediterranean Sea and the coffin eventually drifted ashore near the

port of Byblos, in what is now Lebanon. There, the body of Osiris fell into the hands of the king of Byblos.

As soon as Isis found out what had happened to Osiris, she hurried to Byblos, convinced the ruler to let her have the coffin containing the mortal remains of her brother and husband, and took the body back to Egypt. But one night, Seth discovered the coffin, took possession of it and hacked the corpse into 14 pieces, which he then distributed throughout the entire country. This was done to prevent Osiris's *ka* – his soul – from living on. (According to ancient Egyptian belief, the soul was bound to the body.) Isis, however,

Above: An illustration of the festive procession with the death boat of Osiris, the symbol of resurrection.

retrieved all of her husband's parts, with the exception of his penis, which she proceeded to have declared holy under the name of Phallus. She collected the other parts of Osiris's body, placed them in a chest and buried it at Abydos.

After his death, the survival of his *ka* enabled Osiris miraculously to conceive a child with Isis. She gave birth to a boy, Horus, who came to be regarded as a protector against evil. The cult of Horus soon

The legend on which the mysteries of Osiris were founded: Isis discovers the dismembered body of her beloved husband, Osiris (detail of a fresco by the Italian artist Pinturicchio, circa 1454–1513).

Osiris's remains – in effect, the planting of the seed in the soil – symbolised the goddess becoming pregnant by Osiris, her brother and husband. The story was a powerful illustration of the importance of water and the force of procreation and renewal.

A royal symbolism

Egyptologists believe that a celebration of renewal was part of the ritual surrounding the accession to the throne. The mysteries marked the death of the old pharaoh and the succession of a new one: 'Horus, the living king, becomes Osiris, the dead king, who again precedes the living king Horus in an eternal cycle.'

During the Old Kingdom (2670–2160 BC), the pharaoh was the incarnation of Osiris. He saw himself as the god's son who would join him after death – becoming a god himself. As his soul survived, the pharaoh was accepted among the gods; from his place in the heavens, he could shower his people with goodness.

In the background on this page is the Djed column, with its four capitals. The column is crowned by a feather cap, the symbol of Osiris (detail from a papyrus of the 21st dynasty. 1075–945 BC).

spread all over Egypt. As soon as he had learned the skills of a warrior, Horus decided to avenge the murder of his father; he fought against Seth and defeated him. Seth tried to deny him the rights of his legitimate inheritance, but the gods would not allow it.

The resurrection of Osiris

The last days of the holidays in Abydos brought the climax of the Osiris mysteries – the erection of the Djed pillar, a column with four capitals that was crowned with feathers and represented an allegory of Osiris. At first, the column lay on the ground, symbolising the dead Osiris. Then a device was operated to lift it, while the people, who were divided into two groups – representing the followers of Osiris and those of Seth – fought a mock battle. The raising of the Djed pillar and the victory of the followers of Osiris symbolised the glorious resurrection of the god.

At this point, a splendidly dressed statue of Osiris was brought in a solemn procession on a galley. This was regarded as the boat of the gods, as it enabled the *ka* to float about

in the cosmos. Aboard the galley, the statue was adorned with a garland of flowers as a symbol of triumph. Afterwards, the statue was returned to the great temple.

These rituals abounded with symbols. Both the Pyramid Texts and Plutarch compare Osiris's death and resurrection with the cycle of planting and harvesting, for the mysteries were celebrated during the season of natural abundance. The ancient Egyptians regarded the semi-annual flooding of the Nile and the lush vegetation produced by the floods as the twofold embodiment of Osiris, and saw the earth as the body of Isis. The onset of drought, when the life-giving waters of the river evaporated, was seen as the trap set by Seth to kill his brother. Seth was helped by the Ethiopian goddess Aso, symbolised by the hot desert winds which blow during the months preceding the Nile floods. Osiris's death corresponded to the lowest water level of the Nile. After the harvest came the time of threshing, which was seen as the dismemberment of Osiris. The cries of Isis, however, let the river rise and burst its banks, while the burial of

Ode to Osiris

'They come, the waters of life, that are in the heavens. They come, the waters of life, that are on earth .... O Osiris! The floods are rising: the abundance is within grasp. The time of flood is imminent, it comes out of the stream which flows from Osiris. May the Gods let you come into life under the name of Orion!'

from the Pyramid Texts

CRETE'S VANISHED CIVILISATION

From the island of Crete came a fabled civilisation that venerated the bull, built stately palaces and traded throughout the Mediterranean world. The disappearance of this advanced culture in the 15th century BC has never been satisfactorily explained.

Up to the beginning of the 20th century, archaeologists did not attach much importance to the island of Crete. However, the ancient Greeks told many tales of this mountainous island in the southern Aegean Sea. For them, Crete was the home of a mighty seafaring people, and was ruled by the legendary king Minos, who was born out of a liaison between Zeus, the father of the gods, and the Phoenician princess Europa. In order to kidnap Europa, Zeus assumed the form of a white bull and carried her away with him to Crete.

According to legend, Minos was a great and just king who ruled a large part of the Aegean islands and the Greek mainland. The legend also tells of the Minotaur – a beast with a human body and the head of a bull – which roamed the coast to keep strangers out. It tells of a labyrinth where Minos locked the monster, and where every nine years seven young men and seven young girls were sacrificed, until the beast was killed by Theseus.

Minos's island

For centuries, these tales were considered highly fanciful, and gave the island of Crete an air of mystery and exoticism. All this changed through the efforts of one man, British archaeologist Arthur Evans. In the early 1900s, based on his excavations of Minos's palace of Knossos, Evans was able to confirm that the legend of King Minos was based upon fact and suggested that Crete had been the seat of an advanced culture more than two thousand years before the birth of Christ. Evans called this civilisation Minoan, in homage to Minos.

According to Evans, the Cretans were the first great maritime power in the world. From Western Europe to Egypt, their culture influenced many others. As a trading and seafaring nation, their power was such that they could exact tribute from the still-barbarian Greeks.

And yet we really have no more detailed information than this. For these people, who were supposed to have played such an important role in history, left almost no written records. The clay tablets found at various excavation sites tell us nothing, for the Minoan script, the so-called Linear A, has not yet been decoded. Therefore, we can only rely on the work of the archaeologists.

This fresco (wall painting), called Ladies in Blue, *once adorned one of the many halls in the Palace of Knossos (around 1600 BC).*

Above: *In the palace of Malia, located on the northeastern coast of Crete, the remains of stone grain silos can still be seen today.*

Right: *A Minoan coffin adorned with geometrical patterns.*

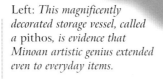

The palace of Knossos

Minoan culture probably appeared around 2500 BC, and reached its peak about 1600 BC. Its political, economic and cultural centre was the city of Knossos on the island's north coast. Here stood the main residence of the Minoan ruler. With a total area of 20,000 m², the vast palace complex was truly imposing. Almost 1,500 rooms were arranged around a central court:

Left: *This magnificently decorated storage vessel, called a pithos, is evidence that Minoan artistic genius extended even to everyday items.*

there were living quarters, audience rooms, baths, storage rooms, galleries and many stairways. The numerous magnificent wall paintings that have been discovered throughout the palace testify that, in artistic terms, the Minoans were far ahead of their neighbours. Knossos, however, was by no means the only important city in the Minoan kingdom. There were also other palace cities on the island, including Phaisto, Malia and Hagia Triada. But this highly developed world inexplicably vanished some 15 centuries before the birth of Christ. Even today, the exact reasons for its demise remain mere hypotheses.

In 1909, a British professor of ancient history, K.T. Frost, published an article in *The Times* newspaper of London, in which he asked whether the Minoan civilisation might be connected in some way to the legend of the lost continent of Atlantis. Frost declared that both Crete and Atlantis had been island kingdoms and important seafaring powers, and both had come to a sudden end.

Was a volcano to blame?

Thirty years later, the general director of archaeological research in Greece, Professor Spyridon Marinatos, brought new insights into the discussion. In the course of his excavations, he had discovered a hollow filled with pumice stone. Based on this find, he suggested that Minoan Crete might have been destroyed by volcanic activity. It was well known that a catastrophic volcanic eruption had wiped out the island of Thera (today's Santorini), some 120 km north of Crete, during the second millennium BC. Marinatos pointed to the devastation caused by the enormous tidal wave produced by the explosion of the volcano Krakatoa in Indonesia in 1883. He suggested that a similar catastrophe could have overtaken Crete. Further excavations on Santorini revealed, amongst other things, a Minoan settlement near the modern town

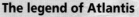

The legend of Atlantis

In *Timaios* and *Kritias*, two dialogues written around 350 BC, Plato speaks of Atlantis: when the gods divided the world amongst themselves, the god of the oceans, Poseidon, was assigned a continent of islands on the other side of the Pillars of Hercules (today's Straits of Gibraltar). There, he fell in love with a mortal who lived on the summit of a hill. With her, he founded the people of Atlantis. To protect them, the god surrounded the island with three rings of land and water. Gradually, Atlantis became wealthy and powerful. Magnificent buildings, temples, gardens, canals and docks were established. The inhabitants, however, became arrogant and tyrannical. Thus, the gods punished Atlantis after an earthquake by letting it sink into the ocean.

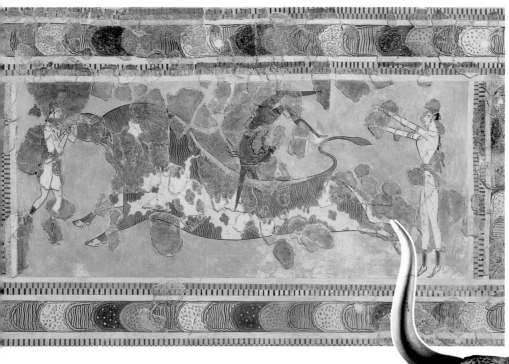

time, however, Minoan culture was at its highest point and would flourish for at least another century. Marinatos's thesis thus became difficult to support.

The Mycenaean invasion

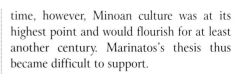

Archaeologists and historians today favour the hypothesis that Crete was gradually conquered by mainland Greeks, especially the Mycenaeans. Rather than rejecting the idea of a catastrophic volcanic eruption, this hypothesis suggests that both natural and human factors contributed to the decline and fall of Minoan civilisation.

From 1450 BC, change was in the air on Crete. Wall paintings feature hitherto unknown motifs and characters. Pottery is decorated with scenes of warfare, but the weapons are different to those originally used on Crete. Weapons, pottery and items of jewellery found in war graves around Knossos are definitely not Minoan in origin. In addition, from 1450 BC Minoan inscriptions are virtually unknown; from that time, all written records appear in Mycenaean Greek, a language known as Linear B.

So there seems to have been an invasion. But why? And when? It is quite possible that Crete had been weakened by an internal crisis or power struggle, which might have led to the concentration of power in the hands of an autocrat, or single ruler; archaeological evidence shows that those Cretan cities already under the rule of the invaders were experiencing a considerable economic upswing. It is likely that the eruption on Thera damaged the island, which had up to that time enjoyed an abundance of fresh water, natural vegetation and pasture. Consequently, it was probably not difficult for the Mycenaeans to land on Crete and to overcome Minoan resistance.

Was Minoan civilisation brought down through invasion, catastrophic floods or a combination of political and natural factors? Only the patient and dedicated work of the archaeologists and scientific researchers can finally reveal the secrets behind the end of Minoan culture.

---

of Akrotiri. Like the Roman city of Pompeii, the Minoan town had been smothered by volcanic ash. For a long time, these findings seemed to support the hypothesis that the Minoan civilisation had fallen victim to a volcanic eruption of unimaginable scale and a subsequent tidal wave. According to Marinatos, this catastrophe took place in 1550 BC. Later work by volcanologists and other experts has placed the date of the eruption much earlier, at 1628 BC. At that

Above: In Minoan culture, the bull was sacred, and numerous representations of bull fights are found on Crete. This fresco from the Palace of Knossos shows the popular sport of bull jumping (around 1500 BC).

Right: A sacrificial vessel, or rhyton, *in the form of a bull.*

The hero Theseus slew the bull-headed Minotaur in the labyrinth.

King Minos and the punishment of Poseidon

King Minos of Crete, the son of Zeus and Europa, was given his throne by the sea god, Poseidon. In order to convince his rivals that the throne was his because of his divine ancestry, Minos maintained that Poseidon would fulfil all his wishes, and prayed to the god to send him a bull so he could perform a sacrifice. When Poseidon made a beautiful bull rise out of the ocean, the king neglected to make the sacrifice. The punishment of the sea god was terrible: Pasiphaë, Minos's wife, fell in love with the animal, and from the union between her and the bull came the Minotaur, which the king locked in the labyrinth. When the Minotaur was slain by Theseus, Minos pursued the labyrinth's builder, Daedalus, to Sicily, only to be murdered in his bath by the daughters of King Cocalos. King Minos then became a judge in the underworld.

VOYAGES TO THE ISLANDS OF OCEANIA

The settlement of Oceania is an epic story of courage and human ingenuity. Several millennia ago, guided only by the stars, the winds and the currents, courageous seafarers set out from South Asia in outrigger canoes to cross the immense Pacific Ocean. Over many thousands of years, this remarkable journey brought settlers to the island chains of Oceania.

Fragments of Lapita ceramics, as found in Melanesia and Western Polynesia.

However small and remote, virtually every island in the Pacific is inhabited. This has puzzled scholars, who have advanced many theories to explain the origins of these peoples, whom we know today as the Polynesians. At various times, they were thought to have originated in Egypt or Scandinavia, or even to be the long-lost 13th tribe of Israel. One fanciful theory even imagined a sunken continent, with the mountain tops forming the island chains. For some time, many people believed that the inhabitants of the islands were descended from Native Americans. Today, though, experts generally agree that the settlement of Oceania started from South Asia.

The first Oceanians

At the peak of the first ice age, sea levels throughout the world were more than 100 m below their present level. At that time, Australia, Tasmania and New Guinea made up a single land mass called Sahul. A narrow strip of water separated Sahul from another continent called Sunda – the continental plate between Sumatra, Timor and the Sulawesi Islands, today occupied by the nation of Indonesia. This boundary between

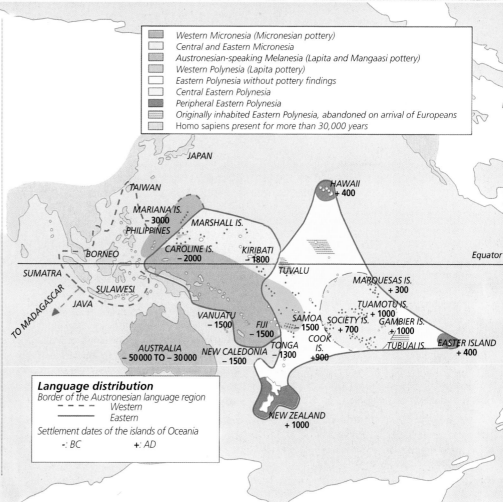

Western Micronesia (Micronesian pottery)
Central and Eastern Micronesia
Austronesian-speaking Melanesia (Lapita and Mangaasi pottery)
Western Polynesia (Lapita pottery)
Eastern Polynesia without pottery findings
Central Eastern Polynesia
Peripheral Eastern Polynesia
Originally inhabited Eastern Polynesia, abandoned on arrival of Europeans
Homo sapiens present for more than 30,000 years

JAPAN
TAIWAN
MARIANA IS. –3000
PHILIPPINES
MARSHALL IS.
BORNEO
CAROLINE IS. –2000
KIRIBATI –1800
SUMATRA
SULAWESI
JAVA
TO MADAGASCAR
TUVALU
HAWAII +400
Equator
MARQUESAS IS. +300
VANUATU –1500
FIJI –1500
SAMOA –1500
SOCIETY IS. +700
TUAMOTUS IS. +1000
GAMBIER IS. +1000
AUSTRALIA –50000 TO –30000
NEW CALEDONIA –1500
TONGA –1300
COOK IS. +900
TUBUAI IS.
EASTER ISLAND +400
NEW ZEALAND +1000

Language distribution
Border of the Austronesian language region
– – – *Western*
——— *Eastern*
Settlement dates of the islands of Oceania
-: BC   +: AD

the two continents corresponded with Wallace's Line – regarded as the boundary between Oriental and Australasian flora and fauna – and was probably easy to cross with primitive boats or rafts.

The very first Oceanians – hunters and gatherers from Sunda – populated Australia and New Guinea. According to experts, they had already settled on the neighbouring islands to the northeast by about 30,000 BC. Around 10,000 BC, the climate got steadily warmer, sea levels rose and many islands were flooded; New Guinea and Tasmania became separated from Australia at this time.

After this first migration, new settlers crossed the ocean from South Asia, bringing with them many cultural innovations. They intermarried with the first immigrants and moved on to discover new territories. People from the Papua language group settled on the islands known today as New Britain, New Ireland and the Solomon Islands. The people who followed them are called Austronesians because their language, which developed 7,000 years ago on the island of Taiwan and along the coast of mainland China, is the likely origin of virtually all the languages of Oceania. Contact and exchange with established populations ensured the spread of the Austronesian language. The new immigrants soon moved on to discover the as yet uninhabited island groups of Melanesia and western Polynesia.

The secret of the Lapita

The people who ventured out into the Pacific Ocean on simple rafts are known as the Lapita. The Lapita produced a characteristic

Did they come from America?

Norwegian anthropologist Thor Heyerdahl won international fame for his attempt to prove the theory that the Polynesians are descended from Native Americans. In 1947, Heyerdahl sailed from South America to the Tuamotu Islands aboard the raft *Kon-Tiki*. Even though a mass of evidence now seems to disprove Heyerdahl's theory, some researchers do not reject his view in principle.

form of pottery, named for the site in New Caledonia where it was found. Fragments of Lapita pottery have been found throughout Melanesia and Polynesia.

Lapita pottery is distinguished by its variety of shapes and its ornamentation, which takes the form of fine lines and dots. Due to its uniformity, we can speak of a single culture, which probably spread over the region through colonisation, but also through intensive exchange and commerce between the inhabitants of the individual islands. Apart from clay articles, the Lapita people also produced other objects, such as shell jewellery worn on the arms and fish hooks cut from pearl oysters.

Migrants ventured into Oceania in graceful, dugout outrigger canoes, like the ones shown in this 19th-century painting.

The sudden disappearance of Lapita pottery around AD 1 is a mystery that still puzzles the experts. While it may indicate that the Lapita were invaded, it is more probable that the production of this pottery simply stopped as tastes changed. Whatever the reason, Austronesian peoples had discovered and populated much of western Polynesia by around 1500 BC. Within one millennium, what was to become Polynesian culture had emerged from the region around the Fiji Islands, Tonga and Samoa.

There were many reasons for the wave of migration from Asia into the Pacific islands, among them the pressure of overpopulation, internal conflict – documented by the construction of fortresses – and the simple desire for new horizons. The migrants set off in large, double-hulled pirogues (canoes made from hollowed-out tree trunks), made with simple stone tools, and able to carry

more than 100 people. They ventured on an uncertain journey westward to Melanesia, to the north into eastern Micronesia – the western part of Micronesia had already been populated in the 16th century BC by seafarers from the Philippines – and, above all, towards eastern Polynesia.

Towards the rising sun

In order to cover such vast distances – no less than 1,800 km separates western Polynesia from the island of Tahiti, and 3,200 km from the Marquesas Islands – extraordinary navigational skills were required. At that time, navigation at sea was a matter of observing the stars, the position of the sun, the direction of the wind and the behaviour of the ocean currents. Certain discoveries probably were made by chance, perhaps when a raft strayed off course and encountered new territory. Most journeys would have been well planned and prepared. The bold seafarers were prudent enough to take everything they would need in order to survive in their new land: tools and equipment, food plants such as taro and yam roots and banana and breadfruit trees, as well as domestic animals such as pigs, chickens, small birds and even rats, which were kept for extra meat supplies.

Around 300 BC, the seafarers reached the Marquesas Islands; soon after, they landed on Tahiti and the Society Islands, the Tubuai and Cook Islands, Hawaii far to the north, and distant Easter Island – all told, around 1,000 new islands were discovered. Apart from New Zealand, where verbal reports told of the arrival of a fleet of pirogues from Hawaiki, the mythical home of all Polynesians, the settlement of Oceania probably took place in successive waves of migration and moved via a network of trading relations between the islands, which were built up and constantly changed over the centuries.

The Asian origins of the peoples of Oceania are now widely accepted, but there are still many gaps in our understanding of the history of human settlement in the Pacific region. Archaeological research is still only in the early stages: the level of research changes constantly, so that dates can only be partially valid.

DID THE TROJAN WAR REALLY TAKE PLACE?

The tragic tale of the Trojan War is one of the world's best-known stories, but is it also part of our history? A century ago, a German businessman named Heinrich Schliemann thought he could prove that the war really happened.

Homer's epic story of the Trojan War, *The Iliad*, is one of the greatest works of world literature. The tragic story of the terrible war between the Greeks and the Trojans is filled with unforgettable events and characters: the beautiful queen Helen, whose love affair with the Trojan prince Paris triggers the 10-year war; the Greek kings Agamemnon and Menelaus, brothers who gather together a great army to win back Helen, Menelaus's wife; the brave but flawed warrior Achilles and his Trojan counterpart, Hector; the Trojan King Priam and his daughter, the seer Cassandra, who foresees the terrible tragedy that will engulf her home city of Troy, but whom nobody believes; and, of course, the wise warrior Odysseus, whose cunning and skill finally tip the balance of the war in favour of the Greeks.

For the people of classical antiquity, there was no question that these people had really lived and that the Trojan War had taken place. Even the Romans attached great importance to their descent from the Trojan warrior Aeneas, who settled in Italy after his flight from the burning Troy. They honoured Aeneas's descendant, Romulus, founder of the city of Rome. But over the centuries, the picture of Troy faded. All that remained was a mystic place, more or less consigned to the realm of fairy tales.

A stubborn archaeologist

However, one man was convinced that Homer's epic was not mere fiction, and that the poet's story contained more than just a grain of truth about the events that took place around 800 BC. Heinrich Schliemann (1822–90) was a businessman from the German state of Mecklenburg. He had already earned a fortune and travelled around the world, when, at the age of 44, he embarked on his childhood dream: to study classical antiquity and to search for the site of the Trojan War.

Unlike many 19th-century archaeologists, he believed that the site of Troy was a hill called Hisarlik, situated near the coast of the Aegean Sea in Asia Minor (modern Turkey). He started digging in 1870, and his efforts were soon rewarded with success. His most sensational find was the so-called Treasure of Priam, a hoard of gold dating from about 2400 BC, but which Schliemann ascribed wrongly to the era of Homer.

The latest discoveries

Today, more mundane items like metal tools, plant seeds or broken pottery represent the real treasure. From these humble objects, archaeologists are now able to draw the most

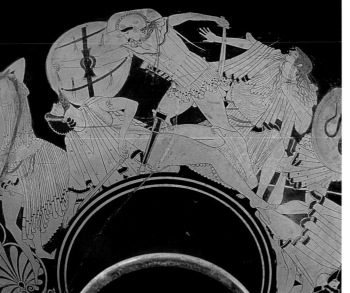

Neoptolemos, the son of Achilles, kills King Priam during the capture of Troy (Attic vase, around 500 BC).

The world owes the story of the Trojan War to the genius of the Greek poet, Homer.

astonishing conclusions, allowing a new and quite different picture of ancient Troy to emerge. A total of 10 settlement densities have been identified by archaeologists at the Hisarlik site. The oldest level, a walled village called Troy I, is dated at 2900–2600 BC. Homer's Troy was hidden in layer VI (1700–1250 BC) and was about 10 times as large as was previously supposed: next to the previously known citadel, with its palaces, there existed a considerably larger sub-city for the common people.

Long before the war, Troy was a rich and powerful city, and therefore was probably often a target for raiders. The head of the excavation team at Troy, Manfred Korfmann of Tübingen University in Germany, believes that instead of a great Trojan War, it is likely that many small and violent clashes for control of the trading centre took place from the Bronze Age onward. The reason for its eventual downfall, around 1250 BC, could even have been an earthquake.

One sensational new find may shed new light on the question: a Bronze Age seal bearing Hittite hieroglyphics – not Greek letters – suggests that the city of Troy might not have been Greek at all, but part of the Hittite culture of central Anatolia. The implication is that, among the many Hittite documents found in Anatolia, there could soon emerge hints regarding the fate of Troy and, perhaps, proof of Homer's Trojan War.

THE MYSTERIOUS QUEEN OF SHEBA

In the Bible, King Solomon answered all the riddles posed by the Queen of Sheba. But who was this mysterious woman from Arabia? And who are the Falasha, who claim to be her descendants?

We don't know what her real name was, nor whether she ever lived at all. But nonetheless, the legendary Queen of Sheba figures in countless tales of the Middle East and Africa. For people today, the figure of the Queen of Sheba still represents all the secrets and allurements of the mysterious East.

The Queen of Sheba is mentioned in the Bible, but not by name. In the Koran (the holy book of Islam), as well as in numerous Arabian and Persian tales, she is called Bilqis. In Ethiopia, she goes by the name of Makeda – Queen of the South – and occupies such a central position in literature and tradition that the emperors of Ethiopia and the downtrodden Falasha (Ethiopian Jews) alike regarded her as their ancestor.

The oldest biblical reference to the Queen of Sheba is found in the first Book of Kings in the Old Testament. According to the story, the queen had heard about the great deeds

In this 16th-century Persian illustration, the Queen of Sheba appears surrounded by angels, with her magnificent caravan and her gift for her host, Solomon.

and wisdom of King Solomon (about 965–926 BC) and gone to Jerusalem to test his knowledge with riddles. The king managed to answer her, but the Bible tells us nothing about the riddles she asked him. In popular belief, however, some of the questions put to Solomon by the Queen of Sheba have been passed down through the ages. The queen's riddles deal mainly with the identification of differences, as well as with sexuality and fertility. For example, the queen showed Solomon two indistinguishable roses, and wanted him to tell her which one was genuine and which one was artificial. The wise ruler then let a swarm of bees show him which was the right flower. In another riddle, the queen asked Solomon to tell her what it was where seven go out, nine come in, two mix the drink, and one drinks. The king answered correctly that this was menstruation (which lasts for seven days),

This fresco by the Renaissance master Piero della Francesca in Arezzo, Italy, is one of countless artistic representations of the visit of the Queen of Sheba to King Solomon.

pregnancy (which lasts for nine months), the mother's breasts and the infant that is nursed, respectively.

The real queen

Where did the queen come from? Today we are almost certain that her kingdom was situated in the southeastern corner of the Arabian Peninsula in what is now Yemen. The desert queen did not undertake the strenuous 2,000-km journey to Jerusalem out of simple curiosity about the wisdom of a foreign ruler. There were much more substantial reasons. The Jewish king's

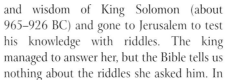

The Queen of Sheba praises King Solomon

'The report which I heard in my own country about you and your wisdom was true, but I did not believe it until I came and saw it for myself .... Blessed be the Lord your God, who has ... set you on the throne of Israel; because he loves Israel for ever, he has made you their king to maintain law and justice.' (1 Kings 10, 6–9)

increasing control of Middle Eastern trade routes endangered Sheba's lucrative trade in myrrh and incense. The Bible indicates that the visit of the Queen of Sheba was successful in this regard, and led to a trade agreement between the two rulers. After the queen had given Solomon '120 hundredweight of gold, an abundance of fragrant oils and many precious stones', and he had fulfilled her every wish, she returned to her kingdom.

The descendants of the queen

While the Old Testament only speaks of the mutual respect and esteem of the two monarchs, the Ethiopian national epic *Kebra nagast* (Glory of the Kings), written in the 14th century, tells of a love affair between Solomon and the Queen of Sheba, or Makeda. Menelik, the son born of this union, is said to have been the first king of Ethiopia. Because of this ancient link to the House of David, Ethiopian emperors – from the Middle Ages until the violent overthrow of the monarchy in 1974 – styled themselves 'Lion of Judah', just as their national emblem, a hexagonal star, was reminiscent of the Jewish Star of David.

But it was not only the rulers of Ethiopia who claimed to have descended from the union of Solomon and Sheba. The Falasha, or Ethiopian Jews, call themselves Bieta Israel (House of Israel) and see themselves as the descendants of the Jewish officials and priests who were ordered by King Solomon to follow his son Menelik to Ethiopia.

The real origins of the Falasha are not entirely clear. They are probably descended from the Jewish traders who came to Ethiopia via the Arabian Peninsula before the Jewish people were sent into exile in Babylon around 600 BC. This may explain why the religious rites of the Falasha differ in part from those practised by Orthodox Jews. For example, the Falasha do not recognise the Talmud or other more recent rabbinical scriptures and their version of the Bible is written in their holy language, Gees, rather than in Hebrew. For this reason, the Falashas' claim to Judaism was a controversial one until the Sephardic Higher Rabbinate recognised them as Jews in 1972. But the world only became aware of the Falasha during the terrible Ethiopian famine of 1985, when Israel airlifted 20,000 Ethiopian Jews out of camps in Ethiopia and the Sudan and brought them 'home' to Israel.

From queen to witch

While the Queen of Sheba has always been held in high esteem in Africa, a quite different picture exists in other traditions and religions. Jewish legends in particular transformed the noble queen of the Old Testament, the equal of the great ruler of Israel, into a seductress, a sorceress and even an evil demon.

Some stories claimed that she had hairy legs, once thought to be a sign of a demonic nature. According to these legends, Solomon ordered a crystal floor to be laid down in his palace so that he would be able to see her legs as she, thinking it was water, lifted her skirt. In these stories, the queen did not come to Jerusalem of her own free will, but was summoned by Solomon to his throne. And it was the sexually promiscuous queen who seduced the king.

But how did the Queen of Sheba's reputation change so dramatically? Possibly, her evolving image reflected the gradual change from matriarchal structures to a

This popular illustration from the 19th century shows the meeting of Solomon and Makeda, an event which the Ethiopians regarded as the founding of their people.

completely patriarchal society, in the course of which women lost more and more power and influence. In Solomon's time, female rulers were not unusual in the Middle East, although this became almost unthinkable in post-biblical times. It was inevitable that a powerful female ruler like the Queen of Sheba would come to be seen as dangerous to the world of men and have to be branded as immoral and evil.

Wise or full of tricks?

According to the Judaeo-Christian tradition, King Solomon and the Queen of Sheba shared mutual respect. She praised his great wisdom, while he fulfilled her every wish. However, in Ethiopian myth, Solomon did not treat the queen quite so well. Driven by sexual desire, he used his fabled wisdom to trick her: Solomon promised not to pester the queen to sleep with him if, in turn, she swore to take none of his possessions. Cunningly, though, he told his servants to bring her heavily salted foods to eat at dinner. During the night, when the thirsty queen drank from the water jug next to her bed, Solomon accused her of theft and thus compelled her to sleep with him.

THE ETRUSCANS: EUROPE'S EARLY TEACHERS

The lost world of the Etruscans – ancient Rome's bitter rivals – is buried deep in Europe's historical memory. The modern world owes much to these sophisticated artists and accomplished builders, even though we know next to nothing about their language.

In the search for their origins, the people of Europe usually consider themselves to have descended from the ancient cultures of the Mediterranean, and therefore to have inherited classical Graeco-Roman culture. Indeed, many of Europe's philosophical, scientific, literary and linguistic roots are originally Greek, succeeded by Roman-Latin, and while Europe's religious heritage basically stems from the Jewish tradition, this was transmitted via the Greeks. Thus, for example, the terms 'Bible', 'gospel', 'Catholic' and 'orthodox' all come from the Greek language. But there are many linguistic, archaeological and mythological features which indicate that other, often immensely old, cultures have made a vital contribution to Europe's cultural heritage – for example, the Ligurians, Etruscans, Germanic 'barbarian' tribes and Basques – not to mention the debt that Europeans owe to the cultures of the Middle East: the Egyptians, Phoenicians and Arabs.

Children of Athens, Rome – and the Etruscans

Modern Europe's most obvious connection to Graeco-Roman culture stems from the fact that the beginnings of Christianity coincided with the flourishing of the Roman empire. But it is easy to forget that Rome, the great unifying power of antiquity, was nothing more than a small market town at a time when more advanced peoples ruled over the western Mediterranean world.

One of these peoples was the Etruscans, whose artistic legacy and achievements as builders still inspire fascination and curiosity. The Etruscans populated the land known as Etruria – the area between the modern cities of Florence, Perugia and Rome. Legend has it that Rome was founded in the year 753 BC – in fact, it was in the 10th century BC – but Rome could only gain supremacy over Italy at the expense of the Etruscans. The Volsinii, who ruled the last of the Etruscan city-states, were finally defeated in 256 BC. Like other Etruscans before them, their subjects were integrated into the Roman world. This process meant that not only were the Etruscans Romanised, but the Romans adopted many innovations and practices originally developed by their neighbours and former enemies. Examples of this included the construction of houses around a central atrium, the construction of aqueducts and sewerage systems, circuses and gladiatorial games, the theatre, the purple-hemmed toga worn by high-ranking officials and the practice of predicting the future by observing the flight of birds and examining the entrails of sacrificial animals. In fact, many of the

The languages of ancient Italy

Celtic
Rhútian
Vinetic
Po
Ligurian
Arno
Illyrian
Picine
Umbrian
Etruscan
Corsican
Tiber
Sabine
Adriatic Sea
Rome
Latin
Oscan
Messapic
Greek
Sicalan
Greek
Tyrrhenian Sea
Elysian
Sicanian
Sicalan
Greek
Punic
(Phoenician)
Carthage
0   100 km

Above: *Some languages of ancient Italy – for example, Etruscan, Sicanian and Rhútian – were not of Indo-European origin.*

The back of this mirror bears images of the heavenly twins – Castor and Pollux, the sons of Jupiter, the father of the gods.

things that we consider typically Roman are actually of Etruscan origin. Therefore, while modern Europeans are certainly the children of Athens and Rome, they can also be regarded in many ways as the descendants of the Etruscans.

Peoples and languages

In their heyday, the Etruscans formed a federation of 12 mighty city-states. Several neighbouring states were also situated on the Apennine Peninsula, and these were also absorbed into the Roman empire. Apart from a few meagre ruins, artefacts and everyday objects found by archaeologists, we know only indirectly about these neighbouring peoples through the works of historians such as Herodotus, who was Greek, and Livy, who was Roman. Their accounts of Roman history also tell us something of the peoples whom the Romans absorbed or crushed in the course of their inexorable expansion.

Even though most of these cultures had already developed their own systems of writing, only fragmentary written records exist, and we have very little information about their languages – as opposed to Latin, the language of the Romans. Today we know that Messapic and Vinetic, like the Celtic and Greek languages, belonged to the Indo-European family of languages, and that many languages were very similar to Latin, for example, Sabine, Picine, Oscan and Umbrian, of which the last is the best known. The links between these various languages can be easily seen through a comparison of words:

Oscan	Umbrian	Latin	English
auti	uti	aut	or
inim	enem	enim	namely

Where did the Etruscans come from?

The origin of the Etruscans is still obscure. Did they come from the Aegean region or from the north, or were they the native inhabitants of Italy? There are solid arguments in favour of each of these theories. But to find the roots of the Etruscans, we must first gain an understanding of their language.

Scholars have gathered some 10,000 written records of the Etruscans: the earliest date from the beginning of the 7th century BC, the last from the early years of the Roman empire. Many of these are grave inscriptions, which, due to their brevity and similarity, are of limited use to linguists. Only three texts longer than a few hundred words have been recorded in ancient chronicles: a property contract from Perugia and two ritual calendars, one of which is inscribed on a linen mummy.

The discovery of these small golden sheets, which date from approximately 600 BC, seemed to promise more detailed information on the vocabulary and grammar of the Etruscan language. Each sheet bears the same text – one in Etruscan, the other in Punic. Much to the disappointment of linguists, however, the constructions used by each language are so different that the structure and meaning of the Punic text sheds no light on the meaning of the Etruscan.

Admittedly, the Etruscan alphabet can be deciphered fairly easily, but the structure, grammar and vocabulary of the language are almost impossible to understand, for it is not Indo-European in origin. At present, linguists can identify only a few elements of declination, conjugation and vocabulary in the Etruscan language, and only about 150 terms have been defined, including the words *apa* (father), *ati* (mother), *clan* (son) and *sech* (daughter).

Unlike Latin, Etruscan is an agglutinative language, which means that the grammatical functions of a word, such as plural or causal, are expressed by means of their own independent endings. You can see from the following examples that Latin and Etruscan share no similarities in vocabulary and structure:

Case	Latin	Etruscan
nominative singular	fili-us	clan
nominative plural	fili-i	clan-ar
dative singular	fili-o	clen-si
dative plural	fili-is	clen-ara-si

However, clear parallels may be found between Etruscan and Rhútian (the language of Rhútia, or modern-day South Tyrol), or Lemnian (spoken on the Greek island of Lemnos). Whether these peoples share a common origin is not yet known.

The heritage of the Etruscans

The Etruscans obviously loved the written word. Etruscan-language readers found among burial objects are of special interest to linguists, by providing information on the letters and sounds of the Etruscan language: for example, there are only four vowels in Etruscan – a, e, i, u. These readers also prove the existence of schools. Thus the greatest legacy of the Etruscans may be their script system, which was adopted by the Latin-speaking Romans. Today, the Latin alphabet is the world's most widely used script system – proof that the teachers of today are in a way the heirs of the ancient Etruscan teachers.

The walls of an Etruscan grave, dating from about 520 BC, on the site of the city of Tarquinia, feature hunting and fishing scenes.

ZARATHUSTRA'S NEW FAITH

More then 2,500 years ago, divine revelation encouraged the Persian prophet Zarathustra to proclaim Ahura Mazda as the only god of a new religion – Zoroastrianism. This ancient religion is still practised today, but the life of its founder remains an enigma.

The period between the 8th and the 5th centuries BC was a time of tremendous religious change. Across the globe, new religious movements sprung up, some of which subsequently grew into the world's major faiths. The Mediterranean region and Asia were particularly fertile ground, giving rise to numerous prophets who bore divine messages: among these were Gautama Siddhartha, the founder of Buddhism; the biblical prophets Ezekiel, Jeremiah and Isaiah, who preached the return of the Messiah; Pompilius, the second King of Rome and creator of the Roman religious system; the Chinese philosopher Confucius, whose teachings have exerted a profound and lasting influence on Chinese culture; his compatriot Laotze, on whose ideas Taoism was founded; and finally Zarathustra, the Persian prophet and founder of Zoroastrianism. Although he ranks as one of the most important religious leaders in history, Zarathustra's name is mainly known to us through the writings of the 19th-century German philosopher Friedrich Nietzsche, and by *Thus Spake Zarathustra*, a musical homage to Nietzsche by composer Richard Strauss.

The life of the prophet

Not much is known about Zarathustra, or Zoroaster, as the prophet is also known. Over the centuries, our lack of knowledge has been strongly

On this bas-relief, dating from around 100 BC, Ahura Mazda is represented as a winged spirit standing on a lion.

coloured by legend, so that today it is difficult to distinguish fiction from truth.

There has been much speculation about the dates when Zarathustra lived, with suggestions ranging widely between 1200 and 600 BC. However, scholars agree that Zarathustra was probably born in Persia (modern Iran) around 630 BC and died in 533 BC. Because of his name, which in the ancient Persian language means 'the one rich

A wall painting dating from around 300 BC in the Syrian town of Dura-Europos bears one of the few portraits of the Persian prophet Zarathustra.

in camels', it is thought that he came from a wealthy family, probably the noble, extended family Spitama of Media, a city in western Iran near the present capital, Teheran. He became a Zaotar (priest), married and had several children. At the age of 30, Zarathustra experienced his first mystical vision and set out to proclaim its teachings. His efforts quickly angered the priests of the Mithraic religion, which was widely practised in Persia (and later in the Roman world). Their opposition probably forced him to flee to Bactria (modern Afghanistan), where he gathered a circle of students and began to spread his teachings.

One god rather than many

Before Zarathustra came on the scene, the Persians shared many religious beliefs and rites with their neighbours in India, for both peoples had common roots. They worshipped many common gods, such as Mithras and Vayu, although over time differences developed over the names and attributes of these gods. However, this pantheon of gods no longer existed for Zarathustra. He broke with tradition, and proclaimed the existence of a single deity, Ahura Mazda. Admittedly, the name already existed in Indo-Iranian mythology, but only as one god among many. According to Zarathustra, Ahura Mazda was the master of wisdom and the creator of the earth, an almighty ruler who created and sustained all life. This new view also incorporated the dual image of a conflict between good and evil: the wise master Ahura Mazda faced his twin brother Angra Mainyu,

For the followers of Zarathustra, the sacred fire is the focus of their beliefs.

which a person lives his life is ultimately his own choice. But after death, people pay the price for their decisions, for the soul has to cross the Bridge of Cinvat, the bridge of separation, after which the good and righteous enter the realm of light and truth, while the wicked and ungodly fall into eternal damnation in the realm of darkness. This concept of individual accountability bears some similarity to Christian belief, but there is a further parallel to the Christian idea of the afterlife: the *Avesta*, the holy scriptures of Zoroastrianism, contain a description of a kind of last judgement, in which a Saoshyaut, or saviour, will sit in judgement. On this day, Ahura Mazda will finally destroy the powers of evil and the world will be made anew. The parallel with Christianity is fascinating, but considerable research remains to be done on the ways in which Christianity, Judaism and Zoroastrianism have influenced one another.

The only record that we have of the Zoroastrian religion is the *Avesta*. The oldest parts of this holy text are the 16 *gathas* (songs or hymns). These were probably written by Zarathustra himself: apart from descriptions of the nature and deeds of Ahura Mazda and injunctions to believers to engage in good, the *gathas* also describe the responsibilities of the individual, such as peaceful coexistence with others, as well as the mandate to abolish animal sacrifice and to strengthen the ancient Persian cult of fire. Surprisingly, certain old gods and religious customs, whose existence the prophet had denied during his lifetime, reappeared in texts written after Zarathustra's death.

The eclipse

The *Avesta* was compiled as a complete text between AD 224 and 642, at a time when Persia formed part of the Sassanid empire. Under the Sassanids, Zarathustra's teachings underwent a revival and even attained the

The Avesta, *written in an ancient Iranian language, contains the holy scriptures of the Zoroastrian religion.*

later also called Ahriman, who had fallen from grace. This evil opponent of the highest god led a host of demons, called the *devas*, and was responsible for all the lies, hatred, strife and darkness in the world.

Freedom of choice

Unlike the adherents of many other world religions, in which destiny is ordained by a deity, Zoroastrians – as the followers of the Zarathustra's teachings are known – enjoy freedom of choice in their deeds and actions. They can choose the good side, that of Ahura Mazda, or the evil side, that of Ahriman and the *devas*. As in Christian belief, the way in

status of state religion, but their appeal was soon eclipsed before the all-conquering tide of Islam, which swept out of the Arabian Peninsula in the mid-7th century. The majority of Zoroastrians migrated to India, where they are known today as Parsee – after Persia, their place of origin. Many followers of Zoroastrianism live in Iran today – in spite of that country's strict Islamic regime – while the Parsee community in India totals almost 100,000 members. Zoroastrians still practise their secret fire ceremonies and lay their dead out in the open air atop the so-called 'towers of silence', where birds of prey gather to feast on the flesh of the departed.

Ahura Mazda the creator

In the *Avesta*, the Zoroastrian god is praised as the creator: 'This is what I ask Thee, tell me truthfully, oh Lord: Who was the creator, the father of the divine laws? Who set the sun and the stars on their course? Through whom does the moon wax and wane? .... Who mounted the earth at the bottom and kept the firmament from falling down? Who created water and plants? Who, oh almighty, is the creator of our senses? .... Which master created light and darkness, sleeping and waking? Who made the morning, midday and evening, to remind anyone with understanding of his duty?'

WHO WERE THE ANCESTORS OF THE TUAREG?

The stark figure of the veiled Tuareg warrior, clad in indigo robes and seated astride a camel, irresistibly evokes images of the vast Sahara. But what are the origins of this mysterious people, who make their homes in one of the world's most hostile landscapes?

The Tuareg call themselves Imuhag, which means 'people of the north', and share a common ancestry with the Berbers, the indigenous people of the northwestern corner of Africa. Today, the Tuareg survive mainly as nomadic herders and shepherds. Although they are quite fair-skinned, the faces of many of them seem to have an unearthly blue tinge – the result of the skin picking up traces of the indigo used to dye their robes.

Of all the Berber groups, the Tuareg are generally viewed as the most intriguing. So great is this popular fascination that they enjoy a special status in scientific literature and have featured in countless novels and films about the Sahara.

One of the reasons for this special aura lies in the mysterious origins of the Tuareg. Because of a lack of hard, scientific evidence, many authors have turned to the realm of conjecture and legend to explain their origins. According to some historians and clergymen, the Tuareg are descended from the crusader knights who came with French king Louis IX (later Saint Louis) to Tunisia in 1270, but were lost in the desert. Others have traced the Tuareg back to the ancient Garamantes people. It has even been suggested that the Tuareg are related to the people of the legendary lost continent of Atlantis, who miraculously survived the destruction of their homeland.

The grave of a princess

Even for the Tuareg themselves, mystery surrounds their ancestry, and so they have developed legends to fill in the gaps. One of these tells of Tin Hinan, a princess who came from southern Morocco on a white camel, and is said to be the founder of the noble tribes of Hoggar, a mountain range in the heart of the Sahara. Even today, Tin Hinan heads the genealogy of Kel Rela, the ruling Tuareg tribe in this region.

According to legend, the grave of Tin Hinan is situated on a hill near Abelessa in southern Algeria. In 1925, a burial structure with 11 chambers was actually found at this spot. In one of these lay the skeleton of a woman, together with hundreds of pearls and semiprecious stones, seven bracelets of silver, eleven of gold and a further eight pieces of jewellery. Other artefacts found in the grave included a Roman oil lamp and, most intriguingly, three gold coins bearing the head of the Roman emperor Constantine the Great, who ruled from AD 306–337 and made Christianity the official religion of Rome. The presence of the coins clearly indicated that the burial must have taken place in the latter part of the Roman empire. Radiocarbon analysis of the leather coffin confirmed this, indicating that it dated from around the year 400 AD.

The traditional dress of the Tuareg consists of loose cotton trousers, cloak, veil and leather sandals.

A chariot drawn by a pair of horses. Rock painting from the Tassili N'Ajjer mountains west of the Fezzan valley.

This important find created a great stir and gave rise to renewed speculation surrounding the origins of the Tuareg. The similarity of the names Tin Hinan and Antinea, the heroine of the popular novel *Atlantide* by French author Pierre Benoit, led many writers to attempt to establish a connection between the real world of the Tuareg and the fictitious ancient world of Atlantis.

The ancient Garamantes

The ancient Greek historian Herodotus, who probably lived around 485 to 425 BC, is considered the 'father of history' due to his detailed accounts of the customs, geography and history of the peoples of the Mediterranean. Herodotus mentioned that among the people living in what is now Libya were the descendants of the legendary people of Atlantis. Herodotus described them as desert dwellers living in the vicinity of the Atlas Mountains, some 20 days' travel westward from the lands of the ancient Garamantes people. The territory of the Garamantes corresponded roughly with the Fezzan valley of west-central Libya on the northern edge of the Sahara. While the inhabitants of Atlantis probably belong to the realm of legend, the ancient Garamantes people certainly existed, for they are mentioned in the accounts of various historians spanning more than 1,000 years.

The settlements built by the Garamantes consisted of houses made of raw bricks or undressed stones. Their most important city,

Garama, lives on today as Djerma. Excavations in the Fezzan area have uncovered imposing stone structures and enormous burial complexes that reveal the range of cultures which influenced the Garamantes.

First among these were the Phoenicians, who set up trading outposts all along the coast of the Mediterranean and developed trading links that extended deep into the Sahara – in ancient times a fertile area teeming with wildlife. From the Phoenicians, the Garamantes adopted elements of writing. From 100 BC onward, the Garamantes enjoyed mostly peaceful relations with the Romans. Ceramic vessels found in Garamantes graves of this period can clearly be attributed to the Romans. There are also written documents describing the relations between the Garamantes and the governors of the Roman province in Africa. According to these records, conflict prevailed between the Garamantes and the Romans following the establishment of Roman rule. Finally, in the 6th century AD, Byzantium – as the eastern Roman empire, with its capital at Constantinople, was known – re-established Roman sovereignty in North Africa and restored friendly relations with the Garamantes. In the year 569, the Garamantes even converted to Christianity.

Chariots in the Sahara

Of all the descriptions of the Garamantes given by Herodotus, perhaps the most vivid is an account of how Garamantes warriors pursued dark-skinned 'Ethiopians' using chariots pulled by teams of four horses. This passage acquired great significance in modern times when researchers and military personnel discovered rock surfaces adorned with hundreds of depictions of chariots drawn by horses or oxen.

Some scientists immediately concluded that these vehicles were the chariots of the Garamantes. Surely such a sophisticated people would have controlled a large territory, or at least an area larger than the Fezzan valley? Some scholars rashly jumped to the conclusion that these people must have been the ancestors of the Tuareg.

Thanks to their camels, the Tuareg can survive in the inhospitable wastes of the Sahara.

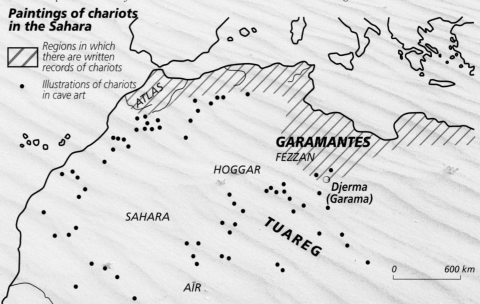

Paintings of chariots in the Sahara

///// Regions in which there are written records of chariots

• Illustrations of chariots in cave art

ATLAS
GARAMANTES
FEZZAN
HOGGAR
Djerma (Garama)
SAHARA
TUAREG
AÏR

0   600 km

Soon enough, new evidence was found to challenge these assumptions. Indeed, with the exception of the Tibesti Mountains of northwestern Chad, illustrations of chariots are found nearly everywhere in the Sahara where rock formations provide a suitable base – from the Atlas Mountains of Morocco to the Aïr Massif of Niger, and from the Fezzan valley to southern Mauritania. Furthermore, apart from the Garamantes, Herodotus mentioned other inhabitants of Libya who made use of chariots.

There was a further misconception about the size of the Garamantes kingdom. The chariots used by these people were drawn by four horses. However, most of the illustrations found in the Sahara depict chariots drawn by two horses. Illustrations of

four-horse chariots have been found only in the Fezzan valley, an indication that the territory controlled by the Garamantes was probably not much larger than this.

The ancient Berbers

Since paintings and etchings of horse-drawn chariots have been found so widely in the Sahara, it is likely that the region's ancient peoples shared many characteristics. It seems that at some point the horse became central to the people of the Sahara. These horse breeders and chariot-builders surfaced in the second half of the 2nd century BC. They replaced an earlier cattle-based culture, in which horses were unknown and oxen were used for farming.

The finest Saharan paintings were made by artists of the cattle culture. These people came from the Mediterranean basin and were lighter-skinned than their predecessors. The horse culture was drawn from the same ethnic group; later, the horsemen would swap their chariots for riding horses, before changing climatic conditions forced them to change to camels.

It is safe to say that the Tuareg do not originate from a single source – whether that might be the inhabitants of Atlantis or the ancient Garamantes. Their predecessors took part in the great wave of migrations that led the ancient Berber from their homeland along the shores of the Mediterranean into the Sahara, where, from the 2nd century BC onward, they made their home.

FABULOUS CREATURES OF MYTH AND LEGEND

The Sphinx and the Minotaur, centaurs and Gorgons, dragons and unicorns – ancient mythology and medieval fables are teeming with strange creatures. Who created the often terrifying and repellent beings that haunt our dreams, and why?

Where does the Sphinx come from? How did the Sirens and centaurs come into being, and how was the Hydra created? How are the Gorgons and the Minotaur related? And why did our distant ancestors invent such bizarre creatures?

The origins of many of these mythological creatures lie with the wealth of stories told by the Sumerians, Babylonians and Egyptians. We owe their survival largely to the Greeks, who included these fabulous tales in the mythological structure of their world and passed them on to Western civilisation. The creatures who feature in these stories all have one thing in common: each is a hybrid, or a creature born out of the union of two different beings. What is unthinkable in nature is made possible through the divine origin of their creators.

The gods' outrageous brood

Greek mythology is full of such hybrids, who were conceived by the various deities or by their descendants. Thus, the old sea god Phorcys and his sister, the sea monster Ceto, produced Echidna, a creature half nymph and half serpent. Echidna herself gave birth to other monsters: the three-headed dog Cerberus, who guarded the gates of the underworld; the Hydra, a nine-headed water snake with the body of a hound, who lived in the swamps of Lerna; the Chimaera, a fire-spitting monster, part lion, part goat and part snake; and the Sphinx, who, unlike the celebrated stone Sphinx of Egypt, was a female creature with the face of a woman, the body of a lion and bird's wings.

Certainly no less horrible were Echidna's three sisters, the Gorgons, the most famous of whom was Medusa. The Gorgons had golden wings and hands of bronze; each had a long red tongue hanging from her mouth

and their canine teeth resembled those of a wild boar. Instead of hair, a repulsive nest of living snakes writhed around their heads and anyone who gazed upon their grotesque faces was instantly turned to stone.

The ancient Greeks regarded the Sirens, maidens with the bodies of birds, whose enticing singing lured seamen to their doom, as the three daughters of the river god Achelous and one of the three Muses. The centaurs, who combined the upper body of a man with a horse's torso and legs, were fathered by Apollo's son, Centauros, with the obliging co-operation of a herd of mares.

Above: *Two deceased souls are drawn on a chariot by winged horses. The most famous winged horse is Pegasus, who emerged from the beheaded Medusa.*

Left: *Hercules killed the Hydra by chopping off its many heads. In order to prevent new ones from growing, he had to seal the wounds with a blazing torch.*

According to myth, human beings have played an important role in the procreation of hybrid creatures. Thus, the famous and feared Minotaur, a human with the head of a bull, was born out of the union of Pasiphaë, the wife of the Cretan king Minos, and a white bull sent by the sea god, Poseidon.

Medieval monsters

The Middle Ages drew on the ancient world's great store of monsters to assemble its own array of fantastic creatures. It is not always entirely clear how these are related to one another, but they also came from the mingling of different species.

The 19th-century painting on the left, by Joseph Anton Koch, illustrates a scene from Dante's Divine Comedy, *in which the hybrid creature symbolises the chaos of hell.*

Right: *The unicorn combines male and female symbols. As an embodiment of both manliness and purity, it integrates almost irreconcilable opposites.*

The unicorn, for example, was first mentioned by the Greek physician Ktesias, who thought the fabulous animal to be indigenous to India. He described its horn as white at the base, red at the tip and black in the middle. Roughly two thousand years ago, the Roman poet Ovid wrote that the unicorn had the body of a horse, the head of a deer, legs of elephants and a tail like a wild boar. Its most familiar shape, though, comes from the Middle Ages, when the unicorn was represented as a small white horse with a little goat's beard and a long white horn.

Just as strange a creature as the unicorn is the dragon, which existed in the mythology of the Sumerians and Babylonians. This creature also combines various elements: even though many dragons were said to live in the water like sea monsters, they still had legs like land creatures and wings like birds. Medieval legends describe a fire-breathing creature that dwelt in caves beneath the earth's surface.

Confusion due to ignorance?

All these mythological monsters can be viewed as a kind of puzzle, with the various pieces taken from real animals. But why did the creators of these beasts draw on existing sources? Is it because our imagination finds it too difficult to work without a firm connection to reality? Perhaps humans prefer to assemble their fantasy images from familiar elements rather than to invent something completely new.

Today, experts on mythology have come up with rational explanations for the ways in which these monsters developed in our ancestors' imaginations. For instance, they speculate that the idea of the centaur may have come from the impression made upon the ancient Greeks by their first sight of nomads on horseback. Thus, it might have seemed to the Greeks that the bodies of the riders merged with those of their mounts to form a single being. The mythological unicorn may originate from Persian bas-reliefs that depicted bulls in profile, with only one horn visible.

At first glance, these theories appear to be plausible enough. But we can hardly expect that the basis of all such fabled creatures lies simply in a matter of wrong interpretations. The hybrid creatures must therefore have a deeper meaning.

The original myths

One way of looking at this would be to view the original myths and their hybrid creatures as having sprung from a prehistorical way of thinking, one which did not yet differentiate between the various components of the natural world, but saw each and every element as part of a whole. According to this view, the boundaries between animals, plants and humans were quite fluid and easy to cross, making hybrids drawn from various forms of life nothing unnatural.

From written records of the origins of peoples and of their gods, we know today that the original myths were built on and developed by later cultures. The key to this process was the rise of a new philosophical

The Germanic dragon

Nordic and Germanic myths feature many terrifying creatures. One of the fiercest is the dragon Fafnir. Breathing poison, this creature guards a ransom extorted from the gods by his father. Fafnir's brother, the blacksmith Regin, wants to take possession of the hoard and talks the young hero Sigurd into killing the dragon with his sword Gram; in the Nibelung saga, the hero becomes Siegfried, with his sword Balmung. By bathing in the dragon's blood, the young hero becomes invincible. According to another legend, Sigurd fries the heart of the dragon and burns his fingers. As he places the heart in his mouth, his tongue touches the blood of the dragon, and he can hear the birds warning him of Regin's deceit.

and scientific way of thinking, which gradually set up barriers between the classes and species. From this time, the hybrid became something objectionable, its mere existence bearing witness to the animal world having entered the human sphere. Crossing this border was now seen to disturb this natural order.

The hero restores order

As the pinnacle of creation, humans felt threatened by such a commingling of the species. In Greek mythology, the law of nature – and of the human world – is restored when a hero and bearer of culture kills the hybrid: for example, when Perseus slays the Medusa, when Hercules cuts off the heads of the Hydra with his sword and when Theseus defeats the Minotaur in the labyrinth. When Oedipus answers one of her riddles, the Sphinx throws herself from a mountain in despair. The Sirens, whose seductive song lure seamen onto the rocks, meet a similar fate. They are overcome by the ingenuity of Odysseus, who puts wax into his oarsmen's ears so they are not able to hear anything, and has himself tied to the mast. With their weapons rendered useless, the Sirens can only watch in frustration as the ship sails away unharmed.

By fighting the monster, the hero banishes all traces of prehistoric chaos. He thus comes to embody the law and becomes the bearer of culture.

The personification of evil

The destruction of the bastard hybrids continued in the Middle Ages, with the best example being the struggle against that monster par excellence, the dragon. In many ancient creation myths, the scaly serpent represented a long-overcome past, and his death symbolised a new beginning out of chaos. In Christian culture, however, the dragon simply represents sin, and is sent by the devil to destroy the souls of human beings. Just as the ancients pitted a hero against the force of evil, Christianity replaced this champion with a saint – usually St George or St Michael.

Top: *This painting of St George slaying the dragon, by the Italian master Raphael, symbolises the victory of good over evil.*

Above: *The hind of Bazalote is an example of a hybrid creature from medieval Spanish art.*

As Christian morality could not allow a demon to have any human features, the Middle Ages confined its demons to animal fables, where they served as allegorical representations of good and evil – much like the centaurs of the classical world. These are portrayed as archers, whose human part points an arrow at their animal part; in this way they show the attempt to keep their animal instincts at bay.

In some mythical creatures, worldly and religious symbols are combined. The unicorn, for example, can only be captured by a virgin. Attracted by her scent, the animal comes up to her and puts its head into the girl's lap; in this way, his horn can be taken off. The sexual symbolism in this is explicit, but over and above this symbolism, Christianity adds another interpretation: the unicorn is a symbol of purity and also stands for Christ becoming human and being born from the virgin body of his mother, Mary.

The significance of the hybrid

According to the modern field of psychoanalysis, hybrids reflect the many-sided nature of human beings. The unicorn, whose name means 'male–female' when translated into Chinese, and which combines female features (a virgin body) with male features (its single horn), bears witness to the two sexes that are latent in each person. Our system of beliefs and norms, however, demands that we confine these thoughts to our subconscious.

The discovery of the hybrid creature, or 'the Other', is part of the process by which humans understand themselves. In a way, it confirms the riddle that the Sphinx posed to Oedipus: 'Which creature has four feet or two or three and is the weaker, the more it has?' 'A human being', answered Oedipus: 'As a child he walks on all fours; when he grows up, on two legs; and when he is old he supports himself on a stick.'

THE SECRET CULT OF THE EARTH GODDESS DEMETER

In a darkened temple, initiates prepare to be admitted to the secret world of the Eleusinian Mysteries. Outside, crowds of pilgrims await the climax of this festival dedicated to the earth goddess, Demeter, the central character of one of the most widespread and popular cults of ancient times. Amid all the hints and speculation, what do we really know of this cult?

A Roman funerary urn bears a carving of one of the mysterious ceremonies in honour of Demeter.

Although it is almost forgotten today, the ancient Greek city of Eleusis was once one of the most important sites of pilgrimage in the classical world. For more than a thousand years – between 700 BC and AD 400 – great crowds of pilgrims came here to worship at the shrine of the earth goddess Demeter. The cult of Demeter attracted men and women, slaves and citizens, high-ranking officials and even the Roman emperors Augustus and Hadrian. Pilgrims came in their thousands to Eleusis to be initiated into the secret rites of the cult. Yet not a single person ever broke the vow of secrecy surrounding the cult of Demeter and described the holy ceremony known as the Eleusinian Mysteries.

A mother's pain

Demeter, whom the Romans called Ceres, was the central figure in the Eleusinian Mysteries. As the earth mother, she was responsible for fertility, agriculture and the flourishing of the crops. Out of a union with her brother Zeus, she had a daughter, Persephone, with whom Hades, the ruler of the underworld, fell in love. Hades was well aware that Demeter would never consent to their marriage and to her separation from her daughter, so he abducted the girl and took her deep underground to his kingdom. Inconsolable at the loss of her daughter, Demeter took on the appearance of an old woman and wandered the earth until she came to Eleusis, where she was kindly welcomed into the royal palace and became a wet nurse to the son of King Celeus. She tried to make the boy immortal by secretly feeding him ambrosia, the food of the gods, and by placing him in the ashes of the fire every night. One night, her activities were discovered by the child's mother, Queen Metanira, who screamed in horror. The furious Demeter revealed her identity as a queen, but was placated by King Celeus's promise to build a temple in her honour at Eleusis. Demeter then taught the king the secret rites – the Eleusinian Mysteries – that were to be practised there.

Demeter continued to mourn for her daughter, and so the earth grew barren because she would

In this bas-relief (from around 500 BC), Demeter and her daughter Persephone welcome the spring, which is symbolised by a flower.

The Eleusinian Mysteries were celebrated in the Telesterion, shown here in model form, a large columned building with roof openings to provide light during the secret ceremonies honouring Demeter.

not allow crops to grow. When it looked as if all mortals would starve, the gods were forced to intervene. Zeus decreed that Persephone would in future spend two thirds of the year with her mother on earth, and one third with Hades in the underworld. Not surprisingly, these periods of time correspond to those of growth and rest in nature and the rhythm of life in general. The daughter of the Earth Mother spends the winter in the dark realm of the dead, but returns to the earth in spring as life emerges once more from the soil.

The initiation into the cult

The *Hymn of Demeter*, which has been attributed to the celebrated Greek poet Homer, tells us the story of Demeter and Persephone and how the shrine at Eleusis came to be founded. But what do we know today about the mysteries of the goddess, which for hundreds of years were concealed by vows of absolute secrecy?

The works of poets and philosophers from Greek and Roman antiquity, as well as the findings of modern archaeologists, can shed light onto the circumstances surrounding the initiation ceremonies and the events of some of the holy days. We know, for example, that the mysteries were part of the state religion of Athens, for Eleusis fell under Athenian rule. But believers came to be admitted into the mysteries not only from Greece, but from the entire Mediterranean region. The festivities took place in September each year and were supervised by a group of priests called the Eumolpides. The mysteries were celebrated in the so-called Telesterion, a large rectangular hall which, unlike most classical temples, was closed to public view. Columns supported the portico,

An offering to Demeter, the Earth Mother.

the Earth Mother and goddess of agriculture and grain, created new life.

and openings in the roof – probably adjustable – allowed light to filter into the darkened interior of the shrine.

By March, the candidates to be initiated into the mysteries – who were known as the Mystics – had taken part in cleansing ceremonies and had performed sacrifices to the gods. In autumn came the great celebration, which lasted for 10 days.

On the first day, the *hiera*, or holy objects, were brought to Athens in a ceremonial procession from Eleusis, a distance of about 20 km. On the second day, the Hierophant, the highest cult official, gathered the initiates together, excluding anyone who did not speak Greek or who had committed a crime. On the third day, the Mystics went to the nearby Bay of Phaleron where they threw themselves into the ocean. The following two days were devoted to preparation, through fasting, cleansing and sacrificial ceremonies, for the great procession held on the sixth day, when the holy cult objects were taken back to Eleusis.

Recent research has attributed the Temple of Ceres at Paestum, on the island of Sicily, to Athena.

On that day, the festive procession of priests, Mystics, choir singers and musicians set out early in the morning along the holy road and did not reach the shrine until dark, guided by the light of many torches. The seventh day was again dedicated to cleansing ceremonies and sacrifices to Demeter and her daughter, who was only referred to as Kore (girl). The real mysteries took place on the last two nights, hidden from public gaze.

Hope for eternal life

Today, we can only speculate as to what happened during those ceremonies held behind the closed doors of the Telesterion. Presumably, a drama brought the story of Demeter and Persephone to life for the Mystics, allowing them to be included in the eternal cycle of birth and death. As with many other initiation ceremonies, the Mystics may have acted out their own symbolic deaths in order to be reborn – analogous to Persephone's return from the underworld. It is thought that the openings in the roof may have been part of the ceremonial transition from the deepest darkness to bright light.

Whatever happened during the mysteries, the connection to the gods at the climax of the celebration gave the Mystics hope for life after death. The mysteries may have served to make the idea of the afterlife seem less forbidding and to ease the fear of death among the initiates.

ORPHEUS, THE SAVIOUR OF THE CLASSICAL WORLD

The story of the beautiful singer who overcame death has fascinated mankind for centuries. As the inspiration of Orphism, which developed from a mystic religion into a philosophical current, spreading from Thrace throughout Greece, Crete, southern Italy and Asia Minor, the legendary Orpheus acquired a lasting if controversial influence.

According to legend, Orpheus was a Thracian singer who sang and played the lyre so beautifully that wild animals would become tame, the trees would bow down and even the rocks would follow him. Orpheus joined the Argonauts in the quest for the Golden Fleece and was often able to make peace among the quarrelsome crew during that adventurous journey. On the return journey to Greece, Orpheus saved his comrades by drowning out the seductive song of the Sirens, which had lured many seafarers to their doom.

When his wife Eurydice died after being bitten by a snake, the despairing Orpheus descended into the realm of the dead, where his singing and playing so moved Hades, the god of the underworld, that he allowed Orpheus to take Eurydice back from the kingdom of the dead. The only condition laid down by Hades was that Orpheus must not look back at his wife until they had reached the surface. When the hero did not heed this warning, he lost Eurydice for ever.

Shortly after his return to Thrace, Orpheus himself met with death when he was torn into pieces by the Maenads, followers of the god Dionysus. There are several possible explanations for their action. Dionysus may have encouraged the Maenads to kill Orpheus because the singer had failed to pay him the appropriate respect. Perhaps each of the Maenads wanted to have him for herself. Orpheus's head was thrown into the river Hebros, from where it floated across the Aegean Sea to the island of Lesvos, where the islanders buried it with the appropriate ceremonies. It is said that, in gratitude, Orpheus endowed the people of Lesvos with great musical talent.

From Orpheus to Orphism

According to legend, Orpheus learned how to defeat death on his journey to the underworld. He then passed his knowledge on to the people by means of initiation rites.

In the 6th century BC, a cult developed in Greece which invoked Orpheus and rejected the entire existing religious and social order. The Orpheans, as the followers of Orpheus were called, differed considerably from those who adhered to the official religion. One difference was the food they ate: the Greek poet Hesiod (700 BC) had declared that the sacrifice and subsequent consumption of meat represented a clear division between ordinary humans and the immortal gods, unifying all people through participation in the sacrificial meal. The Orpheans, on the other hand, refused to eat meat, thereby expressing their opposition to a whole range of religious values. As well as this, they observed their own particular dress codes, such as the wearing of white gowns.

The Orphean religion was based on a revelation which opposed Hesiod's ideas on the origin of the universe. While Hesiod saw the origin of the world in chaos and emptiness, it had, according to Orpheus, emerged from a primal egg – an image that embodied the principle of unity and abundance. For Hesiod, Eros the god of love

This Gallo-Roman mosaic shows how Orpheus enchanted the wild animals and trees when he played the lyre.

An early 18th-century painting by Charles Lamy shows Zeus hurling lightning bolts at the Titans as he banishes them to Tartaros, the dark section of the underworld.

was nothing more than the god of bodily union. The Orpheans attributed a special power to Eros, that of original harmony, or the ability to reconcile differences.

When it came to the history of the gods of Olympus, the Orpheans agreed with Hesiod

The dark realm of the dead

In ancient mythology, Hades was a subterranean place of the gods, and was named after its ruler. After a deceased person was buried as ordained, his soul was conveyed in a rowing boat across the river Styx (or Acheron) to Hades by the ferryman, Charon. In order to secure passage, a dead person would be buried with a coin in their mouth, as Charon had once demanded a fee from one Obolus to ferry him across the river.

on many points, but they differed on the question of human origins. According to Orphean teaching, human beings were created as a result of the crime of the Titans, the sons of the sky and the earth. The Titans had killed and devoured the young god Dionysus. To punish them, Zeus, the ruler of the gods of Mount Olympus, had sent bolts of

Right: Eros, the Greek god of love, invites people to enjoy his pleasures (statuette from 100 BC).

lightning flashing down to destroy the Titans. Out of the ashes of the Titans had emerged the first human beings. As the heirs of the Titans, humans were violent and evil on the one hand, but, on the other, they were also the bearers of the essence of Dionysus.

The goal of the Orpheans lay in freeing the Dionysian soul from the prison of the physical body. This was to be accomplished through cleansing rituals and by attempting to lead an ascetic life.

Orphism, however, was not very popular with ordinary people. As they moved from place to place, the followers of Orpheus were often regarded with a great deal of suspicion. The philosopher Plato contemptuously called them charlatans who promised salvation to the gullible.

The legacy of Orpheus

The teachings of the philosopher and mathematician Pythagoras showed certain parallels to the Orphean religion, but were also widely disregarded. Various writings circulated which offered an introduction to Orphism, but unfortunately these have not survived to the present day.

Gold plaques found in graves in southern Italy and on the island of Crete bear testimony to the Orphean way of life. These were intended to guide the deceased into the afterlife, and they bear inscriptions promising a return to the original state of being. It is possible that the Orpheans believed in reincarnation, and that a level of perfection could be attained by moving from one physical body to the next.

Between 400 and 200 BC, Orphism lost a great deal of influence as a religious movement. A number of Greek philosophers, however, continued to occupy themselves with its teachings. This gave rise to a mystic movement, whose influence can be traced through the classical world and was still influential around 100 BC.

Orphism and Christianity

Because it spread so widely, Orphism may also have exerted some influence on Christianity. The parallels are striking: like Jesus Christ, Orpheus defeated death, conveyed a revelation and founded a doctrine of salvation. Images of Orpheus have been found on mosaic pavements and in buildings, indicating that the master of the house was a cultivated man and a friend of the Muses. The image of Orpheus has also been found on coffins, where he may not always have promised resurrection, but at least pointed to a friendly afterlife. Paintings found in the catacombs – where the early Christians were forced to practise their religion in secret – show Christ symbolised by the figure of Orpheus.

PYTHAGORAS: THOUGHTS AND NUMBERS

He was a philosopher, a teacher, a mathematician, an astrologer, the perfect wise man – for some of his disciples, almost a god. And yet, for a man with so many accomplishments, we know remarkably little about Pythagoras, who led classical Greece to a way of thinking based on rationality rather than religion.

Pythagoras asserted his authority as the master of rational thinking.

The records tell us that Pythagoras was born into a wealthy merchant family, around 570 BC, on the Greek island of Samos. The young Pythagoras learned mathematics and philosophy from Hermondamas, one of the most renowned educators of his time. Hermondamas had taught in the school of philosophers at Athens for 30 years, and his lessons aroused in Pythagoras an admiration for the poet Homer, as well as teaching him the basics of philosophy and mathematics through studies of the writings of the ancient masters.

Upon completing his studies, Pythagoras set out for Egypt, where he lived in a community of priests for about 15 years. During this time, he renounced his Greek name, Mnesarchos, and adopted the holy name of Pythagoras, which is derived from the words *ptah* for God, *ro* for enlightenment and *ra* for sun, and means 'he who knowest God like the sun'. The god-man was born.

A school and its turbulent destiny

Eventually, Pythagoras returned to his home island of Samos and founded a school, which he called the semicircle. But when he failed to attract students in sufficient numbers, he again left the island and travelled to Croton (modern Crotone), in southern Italy, where he settled. At Croton, Pythagoras tried to achieve his moral, religious and political ideals by founding the Pythagorean school.

This time, however, he found success. In time, the thoughts and ideas of Pythagoras came to exert a major influence over all of lower Italy, reaching as far as the flourishing city of Rome. Pythagoras was 70 years old when war broke out between Croton and its neighbour, Sybaris. Even though Croton emerged victorious, the war closed the Pythagorean school. After the war, Croton's rulers decided to distribute the lands of the elite of Sybaris among the ordinary people.

Many of Pythagoras's students came from these aristocratic families, so the philosopher had no choice but to flee, seeking refuge in Metapontum, where he is said to have died around 480 BC. Rumours surrounding his death attributed it to old age, infirmity, a 40-day fast and even to murder. The truth will never be known.

Although the school of Pythagoras had been destroyed, its members went on to form other schools of religious and philosophical thought. For a further 200 years after his death, the ideas of Pythagoras enjoyed wide influence in the Greek world. After that, his teachings seem to have declined in importance, but underwent a revival in the 1st century AD.

Order and discipline

At Croton, Pythagoras's school was ascetic in nature and totally dedicated to the study of philosophy, politics and science. The Pythagoreans subjected their lives to the will of their master. The school was governed by strict rules and entry into this fraternity called for unquestioning observance of the rules and, above all, secrecy. Applicants wishing to be included in the community first went through a three-year probation period, followed by another five years in which they were neither allowed to speak nor to see their master, who kept himself hidden behind a curtain. He demanded that each and every student dedicate a part of his life to public welfare and the rest to the work

Pythagoras and Orphism

For the followers of Orphism, the soul had been locked away in the body as punishment for its transgressions. Only by following an ascetic life could the individual cleanse the soul and free it from the prison of its body. Orphism was a powerful religious current in ancient Greece, exerting a great influence on Pythagoras and his pupils. From Orphism, the Pythagoreans adopted a number of religious concepts. For Pythagoras, the most effective means for cleansing and redeeming the soul was to dedicate one's life to the demands of theoretical studies.

At Croton, Pythagoras founded a school of thinkers with about 600 students.

This detail from The School of Athens, *by the Italian painter Raphael, shows Pythagoras at work in the midst of his students.*

drawn from the ranks of the aristocracy. In his opinion, the perfect state had three foundations: morality, religion and science.

Pythagorean thought

Despite the extremely strict rules of the school, Pythagoras's teachings were a great step forward for his time. To him we owe, for example, the very concept of philosophy. He is also regarded as one of the first thinkers in the search for true wisdom to free himself from an unquestioning belief in the authority of the gods over mortals. Plato and Aristotle both regarded Pythagoras as a great example.

From astronomy to physics and mathematics, all of Pythagoras's works, as well as those of his pupils, were based on the assumption that the nature of matter can be grasped through counting and measurement. They believed that the relationship between all things could be expressed mathematically. Their objective – to unify the basic laws of the universe through pure mathematics, independent of any concrete experience – was revolutionary for the time. This principle was applied in several fields of science, to which the Pythagoreans made major contributions. It can even be said that all of modern rationalism has its roots in the ideas of the Pythagoreans.

While he made a major contribution to science, Pythagoras also was influenced by mystical ideas about the power and influence of certain numbers. These two sides of the man may seem contradictory, but in his teachings there really was no clash between pure mathematics and mystical numerology. In this way, he stands at the very junction of magical and rational thinking.

required by the school. Pythagoras's belief in the religious doctrines of Orphism may explain the discipline enforced in the Pythagorean schools. Rigorous discipline was considered vital for obtaining perfect order and was valued more highly than personal initiative and freedom.

The association of Pythagoreans actually comprised several schools, in which about 600 followers dedicated their lives and

money to the creation of a philosophic-scientific community. The members of the community were recruited mainly from the aristocracy or from the wealthy middle class. The Pythagoreans recognised each other through their dress and by certain signs, particularly the pentagon – symbol of the school. Each person swore an oath to keep their work secret.

The Pythagorean community did not have a direct political programme, but the efforts of Pythagoras led to certain changes in the constitution of Croton. For example, he sought to reform the education of children and to integrate women into society. His most important goal, however, was to change the character of the town from democratic to theocratic – that is, a government centred on religion. He formulated laws for other towns in southern Italy and recruited a 'government of the finest' that was

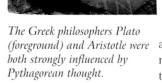

The Greek philosophers Plato (foreground) and Aristotle were both strongly influenced by Pythagorean thought.

Universal genius of antiquity

Most students today are familiar with Pythagoras's theorem – which states that the square of the hypotenuse of a right-angled triangle is equal to the sum of the squares of its two other sides – but Pythagoras is also responsible for multiplication tables and for the discovery of imaginary numbers, values that can be represented neither by a whole number nor by a fraction. In music, the Pythagoreans drew attention to the relationship that exists between the length of a string and the pitch of sound that it produces. Finally, in the realm of astronomy, they were the first to proclaim with certainty that the earth is a sphere.

CYBELE, ISIS AND MITHRAS: NEW GODS FROM THE EAST

For the people of the Roman world, exotic deities imported from the conquered territories of the East offered them the comfort and certainty their own religion could no longer provide. Can we regard Cybele, Isis and Mithras as the forerunners of Christianity?

From around the 3rd century BC, a number of Eastern religions began to spread through the lands ruled by Rome. Some of these involved special initiation ceremonies and gained a wide following among the common people, especially among those who did not have the right to a share in political decisions and who were regarded as minors: the landless classes, the slaves and former slaves – many of whom were women. For all who professed the faith, the new cults enabled them to lead a sheltered life in the community of believers. The faithful were also promised life after death, where they would be united with a charitable god.

The most widespread cults were those of Cybele, Isis and Mithras. They differed from other ancient forms of religion in that their followers could establish a personal relationship with the gods. The cults allowed the believer to share in the divine, and provided hope of salvation.

The jealous goddess of Phrygia

The first Eastern cult to reach Rome was that of the goddess Cybele. It was introduced in the year 204 BC in accordance with the Sibylline Books – a collection of oracles that foretold future events. A statue of Cybele, who was worshipped as the 'Great Mother' of all life on earth, was brought from the small city of Pessinus in Asia Minor (now western Turkey). The statue was made from black meteorite, and its arrival was greeted enthusiastically and with much pomp in Rome. A few years later, the statue of Cybele was erected in one of the shrines on the Palatine Hill – the most important of the seven hills of Rome.

With her lover Attis at her side, the Great Mother Cybele drives her chariot, drawn by a team of lions, in this 4th-century ornamental gold-plated silver plaque.

After the second century BC, calendars bear witness to the Cybele cult's public rites of spring, introduced by the emperor Claudius. The death and resurrection of Attis, the goddess's lover, were commemorated in the second half of March. Cybele was drawn to the beautiful young man, but he succumbed to the charms of a nymph. The jealous goddess responded by making Attis go mad. In his ravings, he castrated himself and then died, only to be resurrected.

The celebrations began with a procession on March 15. This was followed by a week of penance, with general fasting and sexual abstinence. On March 22, the so-called Procession of the Tree took place, in which a spruce or pine tree, symbolising either the genitals of Attis or the tree under which he had castrated himself, was erected on the Palatine Hill and decorated with ribbons, festoons or even blood. Three days later, the tree was placed in a grave in the place of Attis. Before this, loud funeral rites were held, accompanied by frenzied dancing. For some believers, their identification with Attis was so strong that they castrated themselves. After a night of prayer, the celebration of the resurrection of Attis followed on March 25. On this day, which the Romans also regarded as the beginning of spring, the highest dignitaries of the empire – above all, the emperor – paid tribute to Cybele. On March 27, the statue of Cybele was carried from the Palatine to the Almo, a tributary of the Tiber River, where ritual washing was performed.

The return of the goddess to her shrine was celebrated with the Ludi Megalenses, festive circus games which were held around the 4th of April.

Isis, the mourning goddess

In comparison to the cult of Cybele, the cult of Isis and her husband Osiris – or Serapis, as he was called outside Egypt – was looked on less favourably from the beginning. Egyptians residing in

A fresco from Herculaneum (1st century AD) shows a divine service in honour of Isis.

Services were held in the mornings and evenings, during which the statue of Isis was solemnly unveiled and then covered again, to the accompaniment of hymns.

Two great festivities formed the climax of the religious year. On March 5, after a procession to the ocean, where a boat full of sacrificial offerings was commended to the waves, Isis was honoured as the goddess of shipping. In late October, a ceremony lasting several days commemorated the resurrection of Osiris. After three days of loud lamentation for the dead, in which Isis's search for the dismembered corpse of Osiris was re-enacted, the joyful news was proclaimed that the god had been brought back to life. The sufferings of Osiris were also commemorated during the ordination of the priests of Isis. The future official went before the high priest of the cult, who sprinkled him with holy water and strongly urged him to practise

Chastely clad and bearing a container of holy water in one hand, this noble lady is on her way to divine service for Isis following the cleansing rites (marble statue from the Roman era).

the capital first introduced the cult to Rome during the 1st century BC, and Isis soon attained great popularity among the ordinary people of Rome. But when the temple of Isis became a meeting place for prostitutes, the Roman Senate ordered the destruction of cult shrines and their altars. The emperor Augustus also tried to suppress the cult of Isis, albeit for political reasons, since his opponents Mark Antony and Cleopatra had set themselves up as the equals of Isis and Serapis. Following an alleged scandal, emperor Tiberius ordered the statue from Isis's chief shrine to be thrown into the river. It was not until the reign of his successor, Caligula (AD 12–41), that this Egyptian cult was officially permitted to flourish in Rome.

The cult of Isis was based on an Egyptian myth, according to which the god Osiris was murdered and dismembered by his brother,

Seth. But Isis, the wife of Osiris, managed to gather the parts of her husband and awaken him to new life. Osiris then became the ruler of the underworld. Isis's ability to overcome death made her the patron goddess of Egypt, and the veneration of Isis spread rapidly. She became a universal goddess, the 'Mother of All Things' and 'Mistress of the Elements'. Her popularity stemmed from the many responsibilities attributed to her. Initiates and believers knew they would find maternal care and security with Isis.

Wherever Roman culture held sway, there would be a temple to Isis, generally on an enclosed property, where the priests performed cult ceremonies daily.

sexual abstinence for the next 10 days and to consume neither meat nor wine. On a set date, the candidate was taken into the inner sanctum of the temple, where he experienced his symbolic death – a descent into the underworld – in the course of the following night. The next morning, clad in embroidered robes, he would be presented to the other believers as a new priest of Isis.

A god born of stone

The Roman empire accorded more limited acceptance to the cult of Mithras, as opposed to the wide popularity enjoyed by the cults of Isis and Cybele. The reason for this may have been that the cult of Mithras was a purely male religion, whereas the cults of Isis

consecration ceremonies, the cult of Mithras enjoyed increasing popularity. Finally, in the year 307, the emperor Diocletian granted Mithras the status of 'a guardian of the Roman empire'.

Even though the cult of Mithras had hundreds of centres throughout the Roman empire, little is known about its rituals, due to their complexity and the lack of records. We know that it was practised in caves or subterranean chambers (Mithraeum), which held a few dozen devotees at a time.

Originally, Mithras was a god of contracts and of the light of the rising sun, as well as an ally of the beneficial god Ahura Mazda in the fight against evil, but he was also responsible for warfare. Born out of a rock, legend tells how Mithras was first worshipped by

divine services, a type of holy communion was performed, with the consecration of bread, water and wine, and, occasionally, the sacrifice of a bull. The most important festival in the Mithraic calendar took place on December 25, when the god was celebrated as *sol invictus*, or invincible sun.

Parallels to Christianity

Each of the Eastern cults offered believers the possibility of a personal, individual bond with the divine. From these new gods, believers expected to receive health, material happiness and the hope, if not the certainty, of attaining a peaceful afterlife. Apart from these general parallels, there is no connection to Christianity in the Cybele cult – at least, if we disregard the resurrection of Cybele's lover Attis. On the other hand, there is a definite reminder of the Virgin Mary in the grace of Isis, that long-suffering and mighty goddess who confers benefits on all who confess her name. Illustrations of the goddess with her little son Horus may also have served as an inspiration or example for subsequent Christian representations of the Madonna and Child. In its early years, the Isis cult presented Christianity with such a serious competitor that some Fathers of the Church saw themselves forced to denounce it vehemently. There are parallels between the rituals of Mithras and Christianity, including baptism, holy communion, the holiness of Sunday and the acceptance of December 25 – the birthday of Mithras – as the day on which the birth of Christ is celebrated.

The existence of so many parallels between the ancient cults and Christianity may lie in the fact that all these religions endeavoured to provide an answer to the same questions and needs: the common search for the meaning of life and the hope for eternal life.

and Cybele attracted many women and allowed them to participate actively in sacrifices and festivities.

Mithras was originally an Indo-Iranian god, whose worship reached as far as Greece with the expansion of the Persian empire. The cult was brought into the Roman world by merchants, slaves and by legionaries recruited in the East. The worship of Mithras spread, particularly in commercial centres and garrison towns. After the emperor Commodus (AD 161–192) underwent the

Dating from around 300 BC, this Mithraeum – a sacred grotto of Mithras – was discovered under the modern church of San Clemente in Rome. The relief carving in the foreground represents the god slaying the holy bull.

shepherds. He became a creator by killing the sacred bull, from whose body and blood emerged all plants and animals. This scene appears in many sanctuaries of Mithras.

For the followers of Mithras, there were seven degrees of consecration, attained through initiation ceremonies. During the

The end of Mithras and Isis

The decline of the Eastern cults began when the emperor Constantine the Great made Christianity the state religion of Rome. Despite its popularity, the worship of Mithras never became a mass religion, since it was not as well organised as Christianity. By the end of the 4th century, Mithras was almost forgotten, while the cult of Isis lasted only until the 5th century.

HERO OF ALEXANDRIA

The multi-talented Hero of Alexandria was a mechanic, mathematician and scientist whose inventions inspired everyone from the Arabs to Leonardo da Vinci. Nineteenth-century scientists were astonished to find that this mysterious inventor from classical antiquity had even built a working steam engine! Who was this early hero of technology?

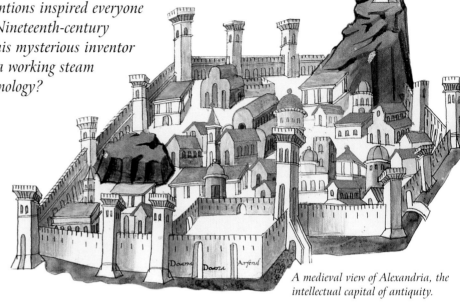

A medieval view of Alexandria, the intellectual capital of antiquity.

He is said to have invented the screw lathe – a machine for cutting screws – as well as the fly press, the fire-extinguisher pump and the water clock. He is also said to have constructed a position sensor that corresponds to our modern odometer. When constructing his painstakingly designed instruments, this craftsman made use of all the mechanical aids at his disposal – for example, pistons and camshafts. Despite these impressive achievements, Hero of Alexandria, one of the most important inventors of classical antiquity, remains virtually unknown today.

For centuries, it was even unclear when he had actually lived. Nowadays, however, historians are almost certain that Hero was active during the 1st century AD. For many years, he was dismissed as little more than a dabbler of humble origins, and it was speculated that he might even have earned his living as a shoemaker. But the discovery, during the 19th century, of one of his manuscripts, the *Metrica*, completely transformed Hero's image. He became recognised as an outstanding mathematician and a physicist of the highest calibre, as competent in the field of hydraulics as he was in astronomy. It is possible that he taught natural science in one of the most significant schools of the classical world, the Museion of Alexandria, in Egypt.

Inspiration for Leonardo da Vinci?

Fortunately for historians, Hero wrote down his work and ideas, and a large part of these writings have survived intact. His seven dissertations, which represent the high point of ancient Greek technology, enjoyed an extraordinary degree of popularity: for example, his dissertation on pneumatics was handed down from one culture to another. In their enthusiasm for a science that was superior to their own, the Byzantines, Aramaeans, Persians and, especially, the Arabs copied his work. Hero's dissertations were read diligently even during the Middle Ages, and some scientists believe that one of them may have provided inspiration for the famed Renaissance painter, inventor and thinker, Leonardo da Vinci.

Counterweights, automata, water pressure: some of the many innovations developed by Hero of Alexandria.

Hero's greatest invention was his famous steam machine, which the Greeks called Aiolipyle. On the basis of the descriptions provided by Hero, the English classicist John Landels reconstructed the device several years ago. The main feature of the Aiolipyle is a rotating water-filled ball fitted with two small pipes facing one another. When the water is heated, steam forms and escapes through the pipes. The resulting forces cause the ball to spin on its axis, attaining a speed of 1,500 r.p.m.

A visionary's toy

By the standards of modern technology, Hero's celebrated steam engine is very inefficient, due to its excessive friction and loss of heat. In order for the machine to give the same performance as the muscle-power of a man, Landels calculated that it would have to burn several hundred kilograms of wood for several hours. It would require the efforts of three or four men to provide the machine with sufficient fuel. Without coal, without cast iron and without such important components as gaskets and valves, the ancient Greeks had no chance of mastering the force of steam. Hero's ball was probably little more than a toy, but the Alexandrian inventor's brilliant gifts deserve our admiration even today.

THE GREAT FIRE OF ROME

Could a ruler, even one as eccentric as the Roman emperor Nero, set fire to his own capital? The disastrous blaze that devastated the city of Rome in 64 BC has never been satisfactorily explained.

The great fire broke out during the night of July 18–19 and raged for several days and nights. By the time its fury was spent, the flames had consumed some 40,000 blocks of rented apartments, 132 villas belonging to the Roman nobility, a part of the emperor's palace and numerous temples and shrines. Although he was not in Rome when the fire broke out, the emperor Nero hastily returned to the city and supervised the erection of emergency shelters for the homeless. He also saw to it that supplies of food were distributed and that wheat was made available at low prices. The citizens of Rome were deeply disturbed by the catastrophe and held ceremonies of penance to appease the anger of the gods.

Since the days of antiquity, an air of mystery has surrounded the exact cause of the fire. It has been suggested that the fire was an accident, the result of inadequate city planning and poor construction methods. No plan had governed the expansion of the city, which sprawled over seven hills, and the great metropolis had become dangerously overpopulated. During the Roman Republic (around 470–427 BC) rampant speculation in real estate, fuelled by high rents, had compounded the problems of overcrowding.

Not surprisingly, fires occurred at regular intervals in Rome. Flames could spread easily between the houses, which were often several storeys high, and were built close together along the narrow lanes and streets. Cooking was done on simple, sometimes open, fireplaces, and families often used pans filled with charcoal for heating, which increased the risk of fire. Many houses adjoined temples, the roofs of which rested on thick wooden beams.

Was Nero the arsonist?

Hanging over all this was the unbalanced personality of the emperor Nero. He has always been labelled as a tyrant and an eccentric, and the long list of his evil deeds – the murders of his mother and wife, for example – certainly give grounds for suspicion. The possibility that Nero himself might have been the one to set fire to Rome occurred to many people at the time. The emperor's passion for the theatre fed rumours that he wanted an opportunity to sing a poem about the burning of Troy. By coincidence, the fire cleared much of the land that Nero needed to build his Golden House, a magnificent and extravagantly furnished palace of which hardly anything remains today – the colonnade was said to have been 1.5 km in length. The emperor, however, ducked the question of his possible guilt, and instead laid the responsibility at the feet of a handy minority, the Christians.

Ideal suspects

It was an easy matter to blame the Christians for the blaze. Small in numbers and poor, they were considered foreigners by the citizens of Rome. Lurid descriptions of their religion, which was banned and practised in secret, circulated through the city. The fire gave Nero the perfect opportunity to begin a systematic persecution of the Christians, in the hope that he could placate the anger of the people and turn opinion in his favour. Countless arrests were made and many Christians met a gruesome death – torn apart by wild beasts in the arenas, nailed to the cross or set alight as living torches to illuminate the emperor's gardens at night.

The question of guilt will never be completely settled. Admittedly, Nero himself lost almost as much in the catastrophic fire as those citizens who lost all their household possessions: his palace was badly damaged, and the Circus Maximus, the symbol of imperial power, was reduced to rubble. After the death of Nero, especially in the second century AD, Roman emperors began to follow a careful and more conscientious system of urban planning in order to minimise the risk of another great fire.

A painting by the late 19th century artist Jan Styka shows Nero, surrounded by his court on a terrace on the Palatine Hill, singing about the burning of Troy, while all around Rome goes up in flames.

THE BASQUES AND THEIR STRANGE LANGUAGE

The Basque people present one of history's more perplexing enigmas: their language bears absolutely no relation to the other languages of Europe. The Basques have lived in their rugged homeland astride the Pyrenees Mountains for thousands of years, but scholars and linguists are only now beginning to unlock the mystery of their origins.

The homeland of the Basque people lies on the shores of the Bay of Biscay, straddling the border between Spain and France. Since 1979, the Spanish portion of this territory, comprising the provinces of Guipuzcóa, Vizcaya and Alava, has enjoyed a special status as an autonomous region.

The Basque population totals only about 2 million, but the Basque people display a lively awareness of their distinctive heritage. This sense of tradition is expressed in dances and games: for example, spectacular sword and stick dances, or the ball game known as *pelota*, which resembles squash. Among the Basques' unique customs is a law of intestate succession, handed down through the ages, which states that the first-born child – whether male or female – will always inherit the parents' land.

But the most remarkable feature of the Basque people is their language, which is called Euskara. Of all the many languages of Europe, the language of the Basques is one of the few that are not derived from the Indo-European language family. More importantly, the Basques are the only people in Europe who define their sense of

Iberian bronze coins: celse (above) was the name of a town; unticesce (left) denoted a people.

national identity solely through language. A Basque calls himself *Euskaldun*, or one who commands Euskara, and he calls his land *Euskadi* or *Euskal-herri*, the land of the Basque language. In other words, being Basque means speaking the Basque language.

Settlers with a long history

In spite of a great deal of research, it has not yet been possible to trace the origins of the Basque people. However, scholars know that Basque settlements go back a very long time in the regions that they occupy today, and

The Basque dialects

Linguistic boundaries of Basque today
Border between Spain and France
Baiona — City name in Basque
(Bayonne) — Name in Spanish or French
BISCAYAN — Basque dialect

that the Basques have had relatively little contact with other population groups. Tests have revealed blood group B as extremely rare among Basque people, while group 0 is disproportionately common, and the occurrence of a negative rhesus factor is the highest in the world. Furthermore, Basque family names have a distinctive sound and are often identical with place names,

Wilhelm von Humboldt, the Prussian statesman and scientist whose writings on the philosophy of language formed the basis of modern linguistics. In 1821, he published a major work on the Basque language.

indicating strong links to dwelling places. Basque culture is also reflected in family names: because the house (*exte*) is the centre of life, it is not surprising that many Basque people are called Etxe-a (the house), Etxe-berri (new house) or Etxe-gorri (red house).

Three-quarters of the Basque linguistic region lies in Spain and one-quarter in France. However, only about half the Spanish Basque population speaks Basque in their daily lives. In France, this figure is even lower, as the Basque language is not taught at school.

There are six main dialects in the spoken language. Because this variety makes communication difficult, a type of artificial uniform Basque – Euskara batua – is promoted by the Academy of the Basque Language as a common written language. It is taught in schools and universities in parts of the Spanish Basque country.

Compared to Indo-European languages, such as English, French, German and Russian, the Basque language has numerous peculiarities. For example, there are only a few abstract terms such as 'animal' or 'weather'. Even the linguistic forms are unusual. An example of this is the so-called ergative construction: while the subject of an intransitive verb – a non-possessive verb – requires the nominative, the subject of a transitive, i.e. possessive, verb calls for the ergative, which is marked by the suffix -k. An example of the nominative would be '*Baigorri mendi artean da*', or 'Baigorri lies in the middle of the mountains'. An example of the ergative construction would be '*Baigorri-k partida irabazi du*', which roughly means 'Baigorri wins the game'.

These and other linguistic peculiarities have always presented a challenge to linguistic research. The most recent theories see Basque as an isolated language with no definite relation to any other language. However, scientists have advanced several hypotheses regarding the origin of the Basque language.

Did Adam and Eve speak Basque?

One outlandish notion was published by a Basque priest during the 18th century. He believed Basque to be the oldest language in the world, and that it had been spoken by Adam and Eve. However, the first real research into the historical roots of Euskara was conducted by the Prussian philologist and educational reformer, Wilhelm von Humboldt (1767–1835).

Historical research is of vital importance in the quest for the origins of the Basque language. The Basques themselves are convinced that the Iberian people, who gave their name to the Iberian Peninsula (containing Spain and Portugal), already lived on the peninsula in the second half of the first millennium BC, and that the Vascones, the forerunners of the modern Basque people, had settled in their present homeland before the Roman conquest of the Iberian Peninsula during the 3rd to the 1st centuries BC. In their minds, this implies a strong mutual influence between the Iberian and Vasconian languages.

Unfortunately, it has not yet been possible to verify this hypothesis. In its written form, Basque has only really been known since 1545, the year in which the first book was printed in Basque. Records of the Iberian language, on the other hand, exist from as early as pre-Roman times, but have not yet been deciphered.

A Caucasian connection?

In antiquity, Caucasian Iberians lived on the shores of the Black Sea in what is today the republic of Georgia, leading some linguists to assume that Basque was related to the Indo-European languages of the Caucasus region. They see the Caucasians and Basques as the heirs of a vast Indo-European linguistic region, people who were subsequently forced into the mountainous areas of old Europe. While individual linguistic features seem to support this hypothesis, most linguists are of the opinion that it is not possible to determine how the Caucasian languages relate to one another, let alone to identify a link with the Basque language.

On one side of this lead sheet, found in 1921, there is an inscription from the 5th century BC in both the Iberian language and Greek-Ionic letters. The Latin transcription at right bears a remote resemblance to Basque.

IUNSTIR SALIRG BASIRTIR SABARI DAR BIRINAR GURS BOISTINGIDSDID SESGERDURAN SESDIRGADEDIN SEAIKALA NALTINGE BIDUDEDIN ILI NIRAENAI BEKOR SEBAGEDIRAN.

In fact, it seems to make more sense to look for linguistic affinities closer to home – for example, around the Straits of Gibraltar. The North African city-state of Carthage established a number of trading ports in what is now Spain: Cartagena, for example, in southeastern Spain, which was founded around 226 BC, was also visited by the Vascones. Some years later, the great Carthaginian commander Hannibal (247–182 BC) led his state's challenge to Roman power. Hannibal put a large army into the field, which included elephants and horsemen from Numidia – ancestors of the Berber people of North Africa.

The Romans allowed Hannibal to land his troops north of Barcelona in 218 BC, thus initiating the conquest of the Iberian Peninsula. About 900 years later, the Arabs occupied Spain; their troops included Berbers under the leadership of Emir Tarik, from whose name Gibraltar is derived. It is certain that the Berbers of North Africa, the Iberians of eastern Spain and the Vascones of the Pyrenees Mountains had considerable contact with each other, suggesting that their languages may be related.

To answer this question, thorough research is underway into the Berber languages, which have only really become known in the 20th century. However, linguists are not yet in a position to make sense of the ancient inscriptions of the Berbers. Success has also been limited in deciphering the language of the Iberians. Thanks to the works of the Spaniard Manuel Gómez Moreno, which were published during the 20th century, it is now possible to read the inscriptions and coins of these people, but they cannot yet be understood.

Because of the complex relationships between the Carthaginians, Greeks, Romans and Iberians, there is still hope that texts with two or more languages might be discovered – much like the Rosetta Stone. This would solve the riddle of the Iberian language and allow scientists to compare it to the language of the Basques.

This Iberian bronze horseman, dating from the 3rd century BC, was found at La Luz in the Spanish province of Murcia.

THE DEAD SEA SCROLLS

The discovery of a collection of 2,000-year-old manuscripts concealed in a network of caves stunned the world. Examination of the Dead Sea Scrolls has offered new insights into Jewish culture, into the character of an emerging Christian faith and into the world of the Essenes, the austere Jewish religious community who hid the fragile manuscripts near their settlement of Qumran.

In 1947, a shepherd stumbled upon a network of dusty caves in a rock face on the north coast of the Dead Sea near the ruins of Qumran in what is now the Israeli-occupied West Bank. Little did he know that, over the next few years, the caves would yield up some of the world's most precious treasures. But these were not jewels or bars of gold. Inside the 11 caves were numerous papyrus rolls – many of them gnawed, frayed or otherwise decayed – wrapped in leather and concealed in clay containers. In 1948, these scrolls were hailed as 'the greatest manuscript discovery of modern times', and were dubbed the Dead Sea Scrolls. But the discovery also raised the possibility that the origins of Christianity might have to be viewed in a new light.

Treasure from the rock

The 700–800 manuscripts date from the period between the 2nd century BC and the 1st century AD. They consist of leather, papyrus or copper; several are largely intact, while only fragments remain of others.

The manuscripts were written in Hebrew, Aramaic and Greek. Roughly a quarter consist of copies of texts from the Old Testament, and their sources are more than 1,000 years older than previously known versions. The others are partly texts from the Old Testament which the modern church does not recognise as authentic, as well as previously unknown non-biblical texts. These non-biblical texts, which were to give rise to the most passionate reactions, display such a consistency of ideas that many scholars believe they can only stem from a mystic religious community not far removed from the beginnings of Christianity.

The community of Qumran

A settlement once stood in the vicinity of the caves of Qumran, the ruins of which show clear traces of an ancient community centre: the site includes a dining room, kitchen, storage rooms, halls, workshops, a burial ground, as well as cisterns and baths, which were supplied with water by means of an aqueduct. A long table, benches and an ink bottle were also discovered – clear indications that scribes and scholars worked at Qumran. However, excavators never found any manuscripts at the site. For this reason,

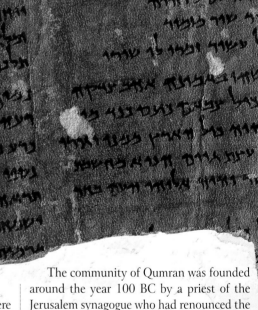

The ruins of the Qumran community, the centre of the Essene sect, still present an impressive sight.

researchers believe that the people of Qumran probably placed the Dead Sea Scrolls in nearby caves when danger threatened their settlement.

The evidence shows that Qumran was a centre for a tiny breakaway Jewish sect called the Essenes; in the 1st century AD, the Roman historian and writer Pliny the Elder (AD 23–79) mentioned the existence of such a community to the north of the Dead Sea. Furthermore, a description of the lifestyle of the Essenes found at the Qumran site corresponds closely to the accounts of two Jewish historians who wrote in Greek: Philon of Alexandria (20 BC–AD 45) and Flavius Josephus (AD 37–100). This thesis has been confirmed through archaeological findings and is generally accepted today.

The community of Qumran was founded around the year 100 BC by a priest of the Jerusalem synagogue who had renounced the official doctrine, and who was called 'Teacher of Justice' by his followers. To find room for their services, it is thought that the Essenes settled in the ruins of an 8th century BC fortress at Qumran.

Admission into the closed community of the Essenes was a rather arduous process. Flavius Josephus tells us that a novice first had to break off contact with his family and spend a year outside the community. This was followed by a two-year novitiate – a kind

of trial period – which entitled the novice to participate in the cleansing rituals of full members and to share in a communal meal that was considered holy. Life in the community was strictly regulated by various rules and ordinances. A violation of the disciplinary code was apparently severely punished and could lead to the exclusion of a member from the community.

Strict regulations

The daily life of an Essene was rigidly organised; there were fixed times for prayers and prescribed tasks for each member. Each member of the congregation had to attend to his duties in the same way. Apart from this, the Essenes dedicated themselves to

Was John the Baptist an Essene? A number of scientists believe that he may have belonged to the community of Qumran.

studying apocalyptic scriptures, and lived in anticipation of the Last Judgement and the advent of the kingdom of God. The liturgy is described in the songs of praise, written in the style of the psalms in the Bible. Even though the Essenes showed great respect for the Law of Moses and their own rules, some of their special festivities differed from those of official Judaism, for example, the festival of the new wine or the oil festival. They also followed a calendar, which originated in the work of the Greek philosopher Pythagoras.

The Essenes left behind a body of writings – some of which are in code – that range from weather predictions to treatises on physiognomy (the art of judging a person's character from their facial features).

The settlement was attacked between 67 and 63 BC, and the Teacher of Justice was banished to Damascus. His adherents followed him there, but he died some time before 63 BC. About 40 years later, the surviving members of the community returned to Qumran to anticipate the return

Above centre: *This fragment of a Hebrew psalter was one of the parchments discovered in the cave of Qumran.*

Above: *The linen-wrapped scrolls were placed in a protective leather pouch.*

of the Teacher of Justice as the Messiah at the end of the world. There they remained until AD 68.

Christianity and the Essenes

According to some scientists, there are indications that the early Christian Church had its roots in the Essene community. During the 18th century, King Frederick the Great of Prussia wrote that 'Jesus was actually an Essene'. In the following century, the French religious historian and writer Ernest Renan believed that 'Christian teaching is a teaching of the Essenes that has found widespread acceptance'.

According to scholars, many beliefs and ideas that were previously considered to be Christian in origin are to be found in the Dead Sea Scrolls. It has also been suggested that John the Baptist was a member of the Qumran community. This hypothesis is based on the fact that John, like the Essenes, expected the end of the world and the Last Judgement, and prepared for it in the desert. In addition, ritual washings played an important role among the Essenes, a fact which could explain the significance of baptism for John. These similarities may be chance; many apocalyptic movements sprang up during the 1st century AD, and seem to have strongly influenced one another. Until new research is made public, we can only speculate.

Cause for scandal?

Rumours surrounded the Dead Sea Scrolls from the beginning. Because many of the manuscripts consisted of fragments, they could not be made public without reconstruction work. Because of the long delay in publication, rumours spread that the scrolls revealed that the origins of Christianity differed from official doctrines. The claim also circulated that the Vatican had tried to suppress this information because it challenged the authority of the Pope. Since 1991, scholars have had free access to photographs of the manuscripts. A growing number of documents are available, and the results of ongoing research are eagerly anticipated.

PEOPLE OF THE TUNDRA, PEOPLE OF THE PUSZTA

The tundra of northern Finland and the broad plains of Hungary's puszta share more than a lack of trees. Both regions are home to peoples speaking languages belonging to the Finno-Ugrian family, the smaller of Europe's two main language families.

The Uralic language family

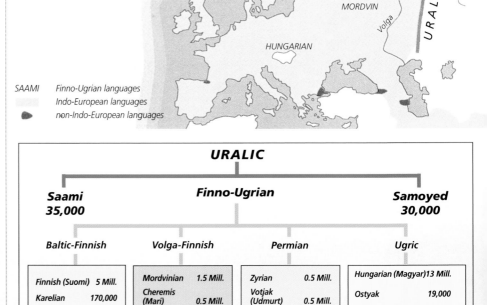

SAAMI — Finno-Ugrian languages
Indo-European languages
non-Indo-European languages

W ith the exception of Basque, some Caucasian languages and Turkish, most modern European languages belong to two families: the large Indo-European and the much smaller Finno-Ugrian, which is part of the Uralic family. In spite of their differences, there are clear similarities between the languages of the Indo-European group, which includes the Germanic, Romance and Slavonic sub-families. But for a person whose mother-tongue is of Indo-European origin, the languages of the Finno-Ugrian group sound very strange indeed.

Finno-Ugrian languages are spoken in the north of Europe, particularly in the tundra – originally a Finnish word for the cold savannah north of the tree line – and in Hungary, in the *puszta*, which means 'wasteland' in Hungarian.

Nomadic origins

In prehistoric times, the Finnish-Ugrian tribes were scattered over the great forests between the Volga River and the Ural Mountains, where they lived as hunters and fishermen. Gradually, they spread northward to the coast of the Arctic Ocean, to the west as far as Norway and to the east as far as the mouth of the Ob River. Only the Magyars – as the Hungarians were called – moved southward. Under their leader Árpád, these nomadic horsemen appeared in the valleys of the Tisza and the Danube rivers in 895. The

URALIC

Saami 35,000	Finno-Ugrian		Samoyed 30,000
Baltic-Finnish	Volga-Finnish	Permian	Ugric

Finnish (Suomi)	5 Mill.
Karelian	170,000
Ingrian	1,100
Livonian	11,000
Weps	16,000
Estonian	1 Mill.

Mordvinian	1.5 Mill.
Cheremis (Mari)	0.5 Mill.

Zyrian	0.5 Mill.
Votjak (Udmurt)	0.5 Mill.

Hungarian (Magyar)	13 Mill.
Ostyak	19,000
Vogul	6,000

The Uralic languages can be classified into the sub-families Saami, Finno-Ugrian and Samoyed. While Finno-Ugrian is spoken by millions of people, the others are spoken by only a few thousand.

Magyars settled in the Danube valley after their defeat in 955 at the hands of German King Otto I at the battle of Lechfeld.

The minor languages of Europe

While the literature of the Indo-European world languages, such as English, French, Italian, Spanish or Russian, is of general interest, and can be learned at schools or in adult education centres in nearly every city, the Finno-Ugrian languages are little spoken outside their home regions. Apart from three national languages – Finnish, Estonian and Hungarian – the Finno-Ugrian family also comprises dialects which are only used by a couple of thousand people. Examples of these are Mansish, Ingrian, Weps and Livonian, all of which are languages spoken by small groups in the former Soviet Union.

The Finno-Ugrian languages, which are native to Scandinavia (Denmark, Norway, Sweden and Finland), the Baltic States (Lithuania, Latvia, Estonia) and Hungary,

This inscription was made by Hungarian messengers in Constantinople, and refers to the activities of ambassadors. The lines are read from left to right; however, deciphering the text is made more difficult by the fact that some letters have been written upside down.

make use of the Latin alphabet. The Volga-Finnish and the Uralic languages of the former USSR, however, are normally written in the Cyrillic script.

Interrelated vocabularies

There are about 20 Finno-Ugrian languages, and they form a scientifically identifiable family. Linguists use the phonetic method – the study of the sounds of speech – to determine their relationship to one another. If two or more languages show a close correspondence in vocabulary, then they are likely to be related. This statement seems quite obvious, and it is the key to the unity of both the Indo-European and Semitic language families. However, there are certain features of Finnish and Hungarian that make the linguist's task more difficult. A comparison of four Finnish and Hungarian words illustrates their close relationship:

	Hungarian	Finnish
hundred	száz	sata
horn	szarv	sarvi
to talk	mond	manaa
winter	tél	talvi

From an early date, Hungarians and Finns were aware of how different their languages were from the Indo-European languages spoken by their neighbours. Not surprisingly, both nations have distinguished themselves in the field of linguistics. In the late 18th century, the Hungarian linguists, Janos Sajnovics and Sámul Gyarmathi, were the first to demonstrate the close relationship between the Finno-Ugrian languages, while the first serious studies of the Indo-European family only appeared in 1816.

In comparison to the Indo-European languages, the Finno-Ugrian idioms have remarkable grammatical structures. One of these is the so-called harmonisation of vowels, in which a word or a term comprising several word units will often repeat the same vowels. Two examples taken from Hungarian show how the vowels in the root are repeated in the suffix:

házanban   in my house
    haz-an-ban   (house-mine-in)
kertemben   in my garden
    kert-em-ben   (garden-mine-in)

In addition, the grammatical forms of these languages are exceedingly complex. Many students despair of ever learning the numerous declensions of Latin or Russian, but these seem like child's play in comparison to Hungarian or Finnish. In Hungarian, the word *fog* (tooth) can be declined in no less than 17 different cases!

Last but not least, the Finno-Ugrian languages are rich in illustrative and expressive words: for example, the Finnish words for 'wind' include *suhina* (the wind which blows), *suhahdus* (the wind that blows fast), *tohina* (the storm wind), *kohina* (the howling wind) and *humina* (the wind that whispers in the branches).

Linguistic borrowings

Naturally, there has always been contact between the Indo-European and Finno-Ugrian peoples, and a number of words have been borrowed from the Finno-Ugrian family: for example, the word 'sabre' is derived from the Hungarian *szablya*, and the word 'couch' from the Hungarian *kocsi*. The word 'ski' probably came to us from the Saami language via the Norwegian, while the word 'sauna' is of Finnish origin, like the sauna bath itself. With the growing political and economic integration of Europe, the continent's languages are destined to grow together even more in future. It seems certain that the modern vocabulary will be further enriched by the contribution of the Finno-Ugrian languages.

While the Hungarian puszta (left) is used largely for cattle herding, the fragile tundra (above), with its magnificent spectrum of colours, remains largely untouched.

THE DISAPPEARANCE OF THE MAYA

The jungles of Central America are slowly revealing clues to explain the disappearance of Classic Maya culture, which reached its high point in the 8th century AD. The sudden decline of this highly advanced civilisation still puzzles scientists. What happened?

Ever since the cities of the Maya were discovered deep in the tropical jungles of Central America in the 19th century, intense speculation has surrounded their culture and its mysterious demise. The Maya left behind the ruins of monumental temples and pyramids, as well as castles and palaces built on hilltops. The dedicated efforts of archaeologists, art historians and linguists have enlarged our understanding of Mayan culture and its development to the point where it is now possible to date the decline of the culture to between AD 790 and 909. This period saw the collapse of what is known as Classic Maya culture, which had developed between approximately AD 300 and 900 in the southern part of the Maya lowlands, an area bounded by the Guatemalan state of Petén, the tiny nation of Belize, part of the Mexican states of Chiapas and Tabasco, and the northwestern portion of Honduras. The reasons for the decline of the Classic Maya are still not known, but new hypotheses continually appear. Was their demise caused by ecological, agricultural or social problems? Did devastating natural catastrophes destroy the magnificent cities, with their ball courts and public baths? Or did the invasion of a foreign power lead to the fall of the Maya?

Above: *The plaza of Tikal, with its pyramids and carved stelae.*

Right: *This stele, dating from 731, was discovered at Copán, in Honduras; it shows the ascension to the throne of a monarch accompanied by strange creatures.*

The period of growth

The history of the Maya can be divided into two great epochs. During the Early Classic period (AD 350–600), Maya civilisation underwent a period of growth, with the city of Tikal as the ruling centre. Then came a period of around 60 years (AD 531–593) during which few monuments were built. This was succeeded by the Late Classic period (AD 600–800), in which the culture flourished once again. The Late Classic period saw the number of Maya settlement centres increase markedly; previously deserted settlements were repopulated, new ones were founded, and existing centres underwent a period of expansion.

Over time, regional differences emerged, and Tikal lost its supreme position. Some researchers believe that political control of the southern lowlands at that time was divided amongst several cities. The most important of these – Tikal, Calakmul, Palenque and Copán – would have controlled a large region and delegated powers to secondary centres, which in turn owed allegiance to the metropolis. But the basis of this power-sharing was weak, for it was largely based on shaky political alliances and family ties. We know that there were numerous conflicts between the cities, and it appears that there were frequent changes of ruler. For this reason, archaeologists have changed their ideas about the ancient Maya, and no longer view them as a largely homogeneous and peaceful people.

Structure of society

The core of each city was the temple precinct, which was generally built on high, pyramidal foundations, together with the neighbouring houses of the elite, with their characteristic corbelled (stepped) arches – for some reason, the Maya never discovered the round arch. The temple precinct formed the centre of administration and worship, with the buildings arranged in the form of an acropolis on a hill or around a central plaza. Surrounding the acropolis were the more humble dwellings of the ordinary people.

The governing elite consisted mainly of warriors, and was supreme in matters both religious and political. The elite controlled a complex, hierarchically structured society which depended on maize production for food. A tribute system ensured that the peasants who lived in the adjoining villages and hamlets supported the non-productive population in the cities, which included specialised artisans and scholars versed in the scriptures, the calendar system and astronomy. The workers were probably slaves, just as they were on the Yucatán Peninsula between 1527 and 1546, during the Spanish conquest.

Reconstructing the decline

One of the most important indications of the decline of Maya culture is the point at which the dates of the calendar, which was based on the so-called long count – beginning on August 11, 3114 BC – ceased to be recorded. Archaeologists can also pinpoint the start of a city's decline by examining the most recent calendar inscriptions to be found on stelae, the carved stone slabs erected in rows in front of Maya temples. Even the fact that monumental buildings were no longer being erected points to the disappearance of the elite. A further indication is the disappearance of the colourful ceramics considered typical of the Classic Maya, and the appearance of a new kind of fine ceramic brought into the interior from the coast of the Gulf of Mexico. Finally, it is clear that the populations of the Maya cities began to shrink, especially in the west and in the Petén.

Communities along the lower reaches of the Rio Usumacinta in the northwest were probably the first to be affected. The once-great cities of Palenque and Piedras Negras, as well as Yaxchilán and Bonampak, fell into ruins between AD 790 and 810. Things moved faster at Altar de Sacrificios, where the construction of monumental buildings and the carving of stelae ended abruptly in AD 779. For some reason, however, the population of Altar de Sacrificios stayed relatively stable until the early part of the 10th century.

The city of Seibal on the Rio de la Pasión, a tributary of the Usumacinta, represents a special case, for here a new ruling dynasty established itself until AD 890. The new rulers appear to have come from the Yucatán Peninsula to the north, or at least from the same group as assumed power in the Yucatán at this time.

The decline of the cities of the Petén took place later on, and there are fewer signs here that external factors played a major role. At Tikal, there was a decline in population and a decrease in building activities

This broken statue from the city of Toniná represents a prisoner.

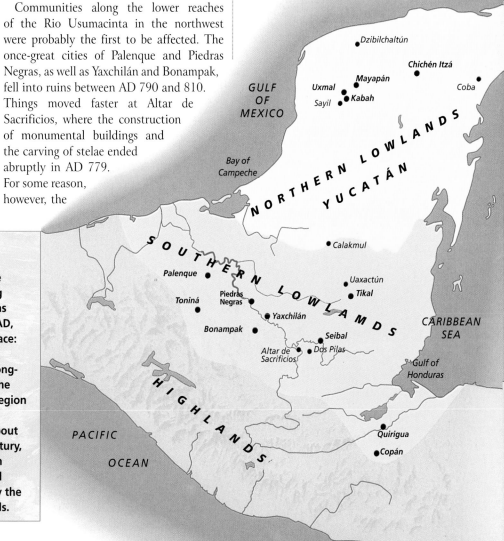

between AD 810 and 830, but only in AD 909 was the city finally abandoned. It was around this time that the last Mayan stele was erected at Toniná; not long afterwards, the sculptures at Toniná were systematically destroyed.

At this time, new centres were developing on the Yucatán Peninsula. According to many specialists in Maya archaeology, these Post-Classic sites were influenced by the arrival of foreign population groups, mainly from the Mexican highlands, such as the Toltec. The immigrants introduced a range of cultural influences into the Yucatán, with sometimes splendid results. This is evident in the north of the region, at Chichén Itzá, a city that attained great significance in the Post-Classic period, and is a popular tourist site today. Among the numerous magnificent buildings at Chichén Itzá is the famous Temple of the Warriors – a spectacular, four-sided temple pyramid.

Possible explanations

Archaeologists long ago abandoned the hypothesis that the destruction of Classic Maya culture was caused by a natural catastrophe, such as an earthquake or a hurricane. Such phenomena normally only occur sporadically and are very localised. However, in recent years evidence has emerged to suggest that a prolonged drought may have played a decisive role. According to a team of American climatologists, the equilibrium of the Maya settlement area could possibly have been upset by changes in climate that took place between 800 and 1000. This assumption was based on the evidence of snail shells found in the sediments of a small reservoir at Chichancanab in the Yucatán Peninsula, which scientists have analysed to determine the presence of the oxygen isotopes O^{18} and O^{16}. Drying causes the lighter isotope O^{16} to evaporate, while the isotope O^{18} is enriched in the shells. According to D. Michelet, a scientist at France's CNRS (National Centre for Scientific Research), 'this discovery is very important, for it allows us to differentiate between the effects of natural catastrophes and those of human land cultivation'. However, M.C. Arnauld, also of the CNRS, notes that, not far from Chichancanab, the cities of the Puuc culture were flourishing at this time, even though they would have been affected first by this ecological crisis. Here, there was no permanent source of available water, and the Puuc lacked the technology to reach the ground water level.

According to others, farming production collapsed in the Maya lowlands, the result of soil leaching caused by many centuries of slash-and-burn agriculture. We have known for several years, however, that the Maya also practised agriculture on elevated or terraced fields, in addition to the cruder slash-and-burn method. These factors are in no way all contradictory, nor do they exclude a further one, in which the decline was triggered by famine. This idea is supported by the examination of bones found at certain sites.

Revolt or invasion?

Many scientists are unconvinced by these hypotheses, and are studying the political, economic and social structures of Mayan culture. We know that the number of cities grew during the Late Classic period, and that regional differences became more marked. This probably weakened the terrritory of the Maya. Competition between the regions seems to have intensified, with conflicts arising more frequently.

The weaknesses of Mayan culture may also have manifested themselves within cities and regions. One school of thought suggests that an increasingly power-hungry elite exacted higher and higher levels of tribute from the peasants, eventually triggering popular uprisings. It is, of course, difficult for archaeologists to find proof of such peasant revolts, but monuments have been found in Toniná and Dos Pilas which had been destroyed on purpose.

However, this violence can just as easily be attributed to invasions by foreign peoples from the Gulf Coast or the Mexican highlands. The newcomers may have settled on the banks of the Usumacinta or in the Yucatán and won control of the river and ocean routes by the end of the Classic period. The presence of foreign peoples is well documented, especially in the western part of the southern lowlands and in the Yucatán, but was this an invasion or a sporadic infiltration over a long period of time?

Waiting for clues

The reasons for the downfall of Classic Maya culture are still not clear. It is possible that a combination of factors contributed to its demise. Ecological problems could easily have led to territorial conflicts; increased social tensions may have occurred at the same time, since the cities had to control larger amounts of territory. In addition, environmental changes and foreign invasion could have exacerbated an already precarious situation, while climate change and invasion would undoubtedly have dealt a body blow to the economic equilibrium of the Maya lowlands. Whatever the exact causes, the work of scholars in the years to come will certainly shed new light on the disappearance of the Maya.

The Temple of the Sun at Palenque dates from the end of the 7th century AD (Late Classic period).

THE THOUSAND-YEAR KINGDOM OF GOD AND THE END OF THE WORLD

During the Middle Ages, great anxiety surrounded the approach of the year 1000. Many people feared that the new millennium would mark the end of the world – just as it had been described in the Book of Revelation in the Bible. How did the people of the time deal with this fear? And what was it about the year 1000 that made them think it would bring the end of humankind?

In the 1890s, a number of historians observed that the approach of the year 1000 in Europe had been accompanied by fears about the end of the world. These fears were fed by the Church, which apparently wanted Christians to believe that they could secure their place in paradise by transferring their property to the clergy. Many Christians did so, thereby securing the church's power base for years to come. It is not difficult to imagine that this caused a sensation, and that the Church angrily denied that anything of the kind ever took place.

Anxiety on all fronts

We know that the level of anxiety among the medieval population rose as the year 1000 drew nearer. Naturally, they looked to their priests and to the Bible for guidance. The Bible gives a detailed description of a number of catastrophes and plagues that would lead to the end of the world. This would fulfil God's will, and the new Jerusalem would descend from heaven. The problem was that the Holy Scriptures did not give an exact date, but some scholars estimated that the period around the new millennium would be the likeliest time. This led to proclamations such as that of a Parisian cleric, who announced around 975: 'the Antichrist will come at the end of the year 1000 and the Last Judgement will follow shortly thereafter'.

According to Revelation 9:7, gold-crowned locusts appeared on the earth, and their appearance was 'like horses equipped for battle'.

Many people believed such statements, in part because a string of natural disasters that took place towards the end of the 10th century led them to fear for the future. In the year 987, parts of western and central Europe were stricken by torrential rains; a severe drought followed in 990; and shortly afterwards storms again devastated these regions. France in particular was badly hit by natural disasters: in 997, a terrible epidemic claimed countless lives, while in Burgundy, a severe famine even produced outbreaks of cannibalism.

Faced with the signs of imminent chaos, it was easy for people to believe in the legends that 'the end of mankind is at hand'. The appearance of a comet in 1014, and a solar eclipse in 1033, were both interpreted as harbingers of further horrors.

The revelations of St John the Divine

All these events were meticulously recorded by the monks, who were the chroniclers of history during the Middle Ages. The various disasters and strange celestial occurrences certainly seemed to confirm the apocalyptic predictions of the Church. Raoul Glaber, a monk from the abbey of Cluny in central France, wrote around 1050: 'After all the signs and wonders which occurred before or after the year 1000 of our Lord, there was no shortage of innovative people who predicted no less important events for the thousandth return of the Passion of the Lord. And

The flagellants

Formed in 1260 in central Italy, the brotherhood of flagellants believed in doing penance by whipping themselves in the mornings and evenings. Flagellation was a response to chiliasm, the widespread belief that the end of the world was coming, as well as a reaction to the teachings of the Italian monk, Joachim of Floris. The flagellants spread over western and central Europe from the late 13th century, with the Netherlands becoming a stronghold of the movement. The flagellants were banned in 1349 by Pope Clement VI, but the movement persisted until the 15th century, at which time interest in flagellation seems to have waned.

indeed, there is no doubt that such signs were manifest .... They fulfilled the prophecy of John, which states that Satan shall be let loose after a thousand years'.

The monk was referring to the Revelation of St John the Divine, the last book of the New Testament. Since the 8th century, its vivid descriptions of heaven, hell and the end of the world had been the subject of much detailed commentary by theologians. But not all these learned clerics interpreted the biblical text in the same way. Raoul Glaber, for example, did not believe in the end of the world, and stated: 'I contradict this opinion in the strongest terms and am supported in this by the Gospel, the Apocalypse and the book of Daniel'. Accompanying the scholarly debate about the significance of the Book of Revelation, however, was a marked increase in activities which supposedly served to purify the souls of believers, including

According to this doctrine, the souls of the just will be resurrected and will rule with the Messiah. Then, Satan will be freed for a short time, and the end of the world will follow.

The Last Judgement

This belief is founded on certain passages in the New Testament, especially in Revelation, which predicts the end of the world. 'After the passing of a thousand years,' the Antichrist – Satan – will be let out of his prison and will lead the people of the world into temptation. Thereafter, the heavens will open and Christ will hold the Last Judgement – over the living and the dead, who will rise from their graves. Finally, a new kingdom of splendour will be established for the chosen ones. The Gospels cite Jesus: 'Heaven and earth will pass away; my words will never pass away' (Mark 13:31).

Above: *Satan returns, but Christ will defeat him. In the background is the New Jerusalem, the Kingdom of Glory, where the chosen ones are admitted.*

The resurrection of the two witnesses: '... there was a violent earthquake, and a tenth of the city fell. Seven thousand people were killed in the earthquake; the rest in terror did homage to the God of heaven' (Revelation 11:13).

penance, excommunication and even the burning of suspected heretics at the stake.

The expectation of a thousand-year reign of Christ on earth before the end of the world is known as chiliasm, and was a widespread belief in the first centuries of Christianity.

The theme of the end of the world, linked to the hope for a better world to come, has its roots in Jewish apocalyptic beliefs about a messianic kingdom. The most extensive description of the Jewish apocalypses is to be found in the Old Testament, in the Book of Daniel (7–12). In highly symbolic language, this account states that the future kingdom of God will be established according to the will of Jehovah. The Messiah, the son of God, will appear and be established in his ministry by God.

Various other passages in the Old Testament present apocalyptic scenarios that are older than those of Daniel. These texts (Isaiah 24–27, Joel 3 and Zechariah 12–14) prophesy the decline of Jerusalem and the intervention of Jehovah, who will lead the battle to a victorious end. But none of these events has been fixed in time.

The apocalypses were written during one of the most tragic periods in the history of the Jewish people, the time of suppression by the Romans, which led to the disastrous

Jewish uprising in AD 66, and finally to the plundering and destruction of the Temple of Jerusalem by the Romans in AD 70. It is a literature of hope for times of crisis, enabling the subjugated Jews to look beyond history to the work of the Lord, who will finally defeat the powers of the evil one.

Opposition to chiliasm

The first centuries of Christianity produced widely differing interpretations of these apocalyptic texts. Papias, the bishop of Hierapolis in Phrygia (ancient Asia Minor) stated in the 2nd century: 'After the resurrection of the dead, 1,000 years will pass and the kingdom of Christ will be manifest here on earth'. St Irenareus, Bishop of Lyon, France, in about 180, expressed a belief that the just would be resurrected after the Anti-christ appeared. A number of heretical beliefs also circulated, some based on interpretations of the apocalyptic texts that predicted 1,000 years of sensual pleasures to would follow the destruction of the world.

At the beginning of the 5th century, chiliasm was dealt a devastating blow by St Augustine (354–430), bishop of Hippo in North Africa, and one of the Fathers of the Church. In *The City of God*, Augustine denounced chiliasm, and interpreted the idea of the thousand-year kingdom of God as an allegory. In his opinion, '1,000' is merely any large number. For him, the thousand-year rule is the period in sacred history between the first and the second appearances of Christ – the time when Satan is temporarily defeated, which each believer begins with his baptism. St. Augustine refers to St. Mark's gospel (13:32), which states: 'But about that day or that hour no one knows, not even the angels in heaven – not even the Son; only the Father.' Finally, in 431, the Council of Ephesus rejected the literal interpretation of the millennium.

Medieval protest movements

Chiliasm prepared the ground for numerous protest movements, since the anticipation of the apocalypse was supposed to be rooted in earthly evils. A number of groups protested against society and against the established church. Of these, the Italian monk Joachim of Floris (around 1130–1202) was the most outspoken. His interpretation of history, known as Joachimism, was very influential during the Middle Ages. From his studies of the Bible, Joachim concluded that the end of the medieval world would come in 1260. His ideas were partly accepted by other movements, notably by the Franciscan spiritualists, who tried to follow the doctrine of poverty formulated by St Francis. This brought them into opposition to the Pope, the head of the established church in Rome.

Around 1420, a new Jerusalem – as an alternative to Rome, with its corruption – was founded at Tabor in Bohemia (now the Czech Republic) by a radical group known as the Taborites. The Taborites were an offshoot of the Hussites, the followers of the Czech religious reformer, Jan Hus (1370–1415).

During the Reformation, another radical group called the Anabaptists broke away from the new Lutheran doctrine to found a new Jerusalem without government or social classes, which they saw as the kingdom of God. Under the guidance of the tailor Jan van Leiden, they occupied the German town of Münster for a long period during 1440.

These and other movements like them were strongly suppressed as false doctrines, but they had one thing in common. Each testified to the deeper fears of the human soul, which only need a small impulse – like the approach of the millennium – to bring them to the surface.

Chiliasm in the name of freedom. The Czech reformer Jan Hus preached a return to the simplicity of the early church in order to fight against the corruption of Rome.

DIVINE JUDGEMENT: CRUEL AND RELENTLESS

In the Middle Ages, when a crowd gathered for a trial, they knew they were in for quite a show. In those days, guilt or innocence could be determined by divine judgement. Not surprisingly, these proceedings struck terror into the hearts of the accused, for the appeal to a supernatural jurisdiction was usually associated with unbearable cruelty.

Even to modern ears, the term 'divine judgement' has an ominous sound to it. Even more disturbing, though, is to associate the idea of a divine entity with the workings of the justice system. But in the Middle Ages, this was very often the case: in legal cases where the question of guilt or innocence could not be determined with certainty – and that was very often the case in judicial proceedings at that time – the authorities would call upon higher powers to decide whether or not the accused was guilty.

With divine judgement, proof of the truth is entrusted to an omnipotent and just God. Today, it is difficult to imagine that such an arbitrary method of investigation, one in which the outcome is largely dependent on chance, was accepted for thousands of years. Divine judgement was well known in ancient Egypt, in Babylon, in biblical times as well as in Ancient Greece, and was practised in Africa, and in large parts of the Western world, right up to modern times.

Contrary to all reason

Divine judgement is based on the idea that God will protect an innocent person, and will enable that person to withstand trial without harm. But divine judgement can take many forms. It can be harmless, or it can be gruesome in the extreme, and can be experienced

actively or passively, as an individual or in a group. An example of the former would be to solve a dispute by means of a legal duel, relying on the assumption that whoever is in the right will receive help from God.

The so-called cross-trial, for example, was relatively harmless for the people involved. Representatives of both parties, or the accused themselves, had to stand in front of a cross with their arms outstretched; the first person who lowered their arms was seen as the guilty one.

Above: *The legal duel was a favourite method to decide the legality of a disagreement between two people; the winner was in the right.*

Left: *In trial by fire, the accused is put to the test by having to grasp a piece of red-hot iron.*

Water or fire

The most common and widely applied form of divine judgement was the trial by water or by fire. Both procedures were exceedingly unpleasant, especially when boiling water or a red-hot iron was used. In trial by water, the so-called kettle trap, the accused had to lower his or her arm into a kettle filled with boiling water and remove a ring or a stone. The scalded arm was then wrapped in cloth. After a fixed period of time, the dressings were taken off, and the judge ruled according to the condition of the burns whether the person concerned was guilty or not. In trial by fire, the suspect had to grasp a red-hot iron rod and walk for several paces, or walk barefoot over red-hot ploughshares.

The origins

The early Christian church was influenced by Roman law and did not acknowledge so-called divine judgement as an option for legal proceedings. But as the Germanic tribes beyond Rome's frontiers were baptised and became Christians, it became clear that divine judgements were permitted as evidence in Germanic law. Since the Christian faith trusted in divine intervention in matters outside the law, it was difficult for church leaders to denounce Germanic divine judgements. As a result, the era of Charlemagne, first of the Holy Roman Emperors, saw an increasing resort to divine judgement as a recognised legal mechanism. Although many people were opposed to the use of divine judgement, clerical circles promoted this development. New forms of divine evidence were introduced, such as the trial of the cross and of communion. Subsequently, divine judgement became a recognised Christian institution.

The critics prevail

As early as the 9th century, the opponents of divine judgement criticised this dubious form of jurisdiction. Towards the end of the 12th century, differing attitudes to divine judgement cut a deep rift through the Western clergy. Finally, in the year 1215, the fourth Lateran Council under Pope Innocent III distanced itself from the concept of divine judgement. From then on, the clergy was prohibited from active involvement in such judgements. A few years later, in 1234, Pope Gregory IX prohibited this practice throughout the realm of the Western church.

In spite of this, civil authorities continued to employ divine judgement as evidence in reaching a verdict. Thus, trial by red-hot iron

A popular image during the Middle Ages was that of a single combat between a murderer and the dog belonging to his victim. The animal usually won.

and boiling water continued to be used in reaching a verdict right up to the modern age, notably during the European witch-hunts of the 16th and 17th centuries.

Divine justice

In Christian belief, divine judgement is based on a simple idea: God expresses himself through the force of the elements, and he will not favour the guilty. The circumstances surrounding divine judgement may seem cruel, and were almost always painful, but we should not forget that the subject's unshakeable belief in God's justice and power meant that he never believed he was doomed from the start – as we might be inclined to believe. A person was innocent if his evidence corresponded to natural experience and did not go against the laws of nature.

Even the apparently cynical premise of trial by water – if a person sank and drowned, then he or she was innocent – was based on a view which was considered just at that time. If we consider the crucial factor for people at that time – their faith and trust in God – then trial by water does not seem so senseless and illogical: the water was baptismal water and was consecrated by God. Since only a pure person could be baptised, the person who was innocent was logically accepted by the water, even though he or she may have drowned in the process. According to this logic, an evil person was sure to be renounced by God; in effect, a guilty person was rejected by the water, and so he or she would float.

Even though the medieval belief in divine judgement had strong links to pre-Christian superstition, it always followed a Christian ritual. Thus, for example, a person who was about to undergo heavy beatings prepared for punishment through fasting. The objects to be used for the trial were usually consecrated during a mass. Finally, the priests prayed to God and asked for his help and guidance during the trial.

Help from a saint?

One renowned case of trial by water concerned a French woman whose husband accused her of a crime, although he could produce no proof of his wife's guilt. A judge duly sentenced her to submit to trial by water, and she was thrown into the Rhône River with a millstone tied around her neck. She instantly sank out of sight, but the woman called upon St Genesius for help, and rose from the bottom of the river. When the crowd saw this, they immediately pulled her from the water. From that time on, she was never

Trial by water was often used in the Middle Ages.

troubled by her husband or the judge. The woman had passed the divine trial: a person could only be considered guilty if he or she did not sink at all but floated from the beginning.

CATHEDRALS AND THEIR BUILDERS

The Gothic cathedrals of Europe are a majestic hymn to the glory of God, and represent the steadfast, unquestioning faith of medieval times. But the most astonishing thing about these mighty edifices is that we know little about the men who built them. For the most part, the master builders, stonemasons, glass-stainers and other artisans have remained anonymous.

Europe is full of fine old buildings. There are palaces and castles, museums and country villas. But perhaps the true glory of European architecture is the medieval Gothic cathedral. These majestic structures soar above the rooftops of cities and towns to proclaim that here stands a house of God. The construction of these massive edifices took many years, and called on the services of many skilled craftsmen. The word 'Gothic' originates with the ancient Germanic tribes, but really signifies a style of architecture featuring tall pointed arches, ribbed vaulting and flying buttresses.

The order to build a cathedral normally came from a clerical landowner, such as a bishop or the abbot of a large monastery. Chartres Cathedral near Paris, considered one of the most beautiful of Europe's cathedrals, owes its modern form to the decision taken by Regnault de Mouçon, Bishop of Chartres, to rebuild the church after a devastating fire in 1194.

The landowner or his representative then selected a master builder, who was essentially the architect. The master builder drafted the plans for the structure and took responsibility for its construction.

The heart of construction activity was the so-called site hut, established solely for the period of construction. The workshops that comprised the site hut were usually situated in the immediate vicinity of the cathedral building site. There, the various artisans and artists lived and worked for many years.

Financing a huge project like a cathedral was always a major problem. The bishop or abbot depended on donations from the faithful, especially the nobility and the guilds – an early type of trade union – but their generosity often left a great deal to be desired. Lack of funding for materials and workers sometimes brought work to a stop for years at a time. Ordinary people were

Above right: *This 15th-century illustration shows a cathedral under construction, which is already being visited by the faithful.*

Above: *The ribbed vaults of the abbey of St Denis enabled the master builder to replace large sections of the load-bearing walls with beautiful stained-glass windows.*

Right: *One of the finest windows in St Denis shows Abbot Suger, who commissioned the abbey. There is no memorial to the master builder.*

usually reluctant to make donations, so money was sometimes obtained by force. A bishop with good connections to the king, though, could be sure of receiving a generous donation from the ruler.

The earliest Gothic cathedrals were built in the 12th century on the Île-de-France – the region around Paris – after the rulers of the Capet dynasty had consolidated France's power, making it one of the wealthiest kingdoms in Europe. Imposing cathedrals, with their prominent spires, were not only centres of the Christian faith, but also demonstrated the political and economic power of the clergy and the nobility.

St Denis: the nucleus

In the suburbs of Paris stands the royal abbey of St Denis, a superb example of Gothic architecture. By the mid-12th century, the old medieval church of St Denis was in need of major repairs. The idea of rebuilding St Denis belonged to Abbot Suger, the head of the abbey, and an adviser to kings Louis VI and Louis VII.

Suger's account of the building of St Denis was written down in two detailed volumes. The combination of architecture, stone-carving, glass-staining, ironwork and painting gave rise to a masterpiece of Gothic architecture. Suger wrote: 'The structure of the building is supported by twelve columns in the middle of the choir, corresponding to the twelve apostles of the New Testament. There are just as many columns in the aisles, standing for the number of the prophets, as described by the apostle, who builds in spirit: "Now therefore ye are no more strangers and foreigners, but fellow citizens with the saints, and of the household of God"'. According to observers at the time, the Gothic building of St Denis represented a promise carved in stone, heralding the glory of future epochs.

In order to give an impression of soaring space, and to allow light – regarded as the outflow of divine grace – to penetrate into the otherwise dark interior of the church, the abbot convinced the builders to construct ribbed vaults. This allowed the construction of tall pointed arches, and also the provision of beautiful stained-glass windows. He also mentions a group of goldsmiths from Lorraine, in eastern France, who were working under his supervision. Suger was conscious of his position as initiator of the rebuilding and did not hesitate to immortalise himself, in the pose of the founder, above the portal under the illustration of the Last Judgement. In addition, he had the following inscription placed in the church: 'It is I, Suger, who caused this building to be enlarged in my time. This happened under my supervision.'

The cathedral of Bourges, begun in 1192, is the only Gothic church building with five portals opening onto five aisles.

In subsequent years, mighty cathedrals were built all over Europe, each greater, more magnificent and more beautiful than the previous one. Some of the most famous are Notre Dame in Paris (1163), Canterbury (1185), Bourges (1192), Chartres (1194), Reims (1211), Amiens (1220), Strasbourg (1220), Burgos (1221), Toledo (1226), Freiburg (around 1235), Wells (1240),

An 11th-century image shows the reconstruction of the temple of Jerusalem. At the top, God commissions Serubabel and the high priest, Joshua. Below them, the work goes on.

Regensburg (circa 1250), Gloucester (1351) and Ulm (1377). Many of these houses of God were never completed, while some of them were rebuilt again and again. Cologne Cathedral took the longest to build: construction work began in 1248, but was only completed in 1880 – 632 years later – and was marked by a dignified ceremony.

The master builder

In his reports, Abbot Suger describes all kinds of technical difficulties and problems encountered during the construction of St Denis. But not once does he give the name of the master builder. And it was this individual, above all, who deserved the honour and the fame of being called the creator of Gothic architecture.

However, the nameless master builder of St Denis is not an isolated example. Little is known about the master builders of any of the early Gothic cathedrals. We know nothing about the life and work of the architects who built Chartres Cathedral – not even their names. What is known is that the master builders generally came from the respected trade of masons. Many of them were German or Italian, or came from parts of France with traditions of building in stone, such as Limousin.

The master builders were continually on the move. When the building of one cathedral was completed, they moved on to the next construction site, where they traded their know-how and experience for cash. Competent builders were rare in the Middle Ages and an experienced individual could therefore earn a lot of money. We know that Bernard de Soissons, who worked on the construction of Reims Cathedral for almost 40 years, was one of the highest taxed people of that town.

With their success, the importance of the master builders grew and so did their self-confidence. From the 14th century, they emerged from anonymity, and immortalised both themselves and their achievements. In a hidden place in the building, they would

Mark of the master

The reputation of the master builder grew tremendously during the 13th century. At Reims, an inscription states that construction of the apse commenced in 1211 under Jean d'Orbais, and continued under Jean Le Loup and Gaucher de Reims, and that the facade as well as the large rose window were the work of Bernard de Soissons. In Notre Dame Cathedral in Paris, the architect of the right transept left this inscription: 'Master Jean de Chelles has commenced this work on the 11th of February 1258'. At Amiens Cathedral, the portraits of the commissioning bishop and the three architects are inlaid in the floor of the church.

inscribe their sign or name, together with an indication of the date when construction had begun or was completed.

Complex tasks

An important feature of the master builder's activity was the supervision of the building work, but he never did any construction work himself. 'It is common', a contemporary source reports, 'for there to be a single master builder who arranges the work through his word alone and never lends a hand. But he receives higher wages than the others. The master builders direct things, they give orders and do not work'. Records left by the master church builder Villard de Honnecourt give a clear picture of the problems an architect had to cope with at that time. Among other things, his sketch books deal

Left: *This 14th-century miniature shows the construction of a basilica over the grave of St Denis, patron saint of France.*

Below: *In the medieval manuscript* Hortus deliciarum, *written at the end of the 12th century, craftsmen of the various guilds are seen building a cathedral.*

with his efforts to improve mechanical procedures, develop new hoisting equipment to save labour and speed up construction, as well as the calculation of construction formulas.

The great masters were conscious of the fact that they had to preserve the skills and secrets of their craft, and not make them accessible to all. The 13th-century *Book of Trades* contains the following instruction: 'The master builders may employ as many craftsmen and workers as they deem necessary, but only on the condition that they do not tell anything about the skills of their trade to anyone'.

The work of the guilds

At any time, several hundred people might be busy at the site hut. They formed a dedicated community, whose thoughts and actions were all focused on one goal: the construction of the Gothic cathedral. To achieve this ambitious goal required many

Above: *When choosing their motifs, the stonemasons enjoyed a great deal of freedom. This capital illustrates the sleep of the Three Wise Men.*

capable people with the most varied professional skills. The labourers occupied the lowest social level. They were often former serfs (slaves) who had fled from their lords, or were the sons of farmers seeking work in the city. They had no rights, and had to perform the most difficult and tiring

Stained-glass windows often depicted motifs from the construction of the church: here, a bricklayer smoothes the plaster with his trowel, while two others bring stones.

tasks: excavating foundations, transporting the earth in sacks and lifting stones.

The guild of stonemasons occupied a totally different position. Stonemasons were considered specialists and were allowed to employ assistants to help them with their difficult work. They received about three times the amount of wages as the labourers and enjoyed certain privileges. Among other things, it was the stonemason's task to select the stones, cut them to the right size and organise their transport to the construction site. Other stonemasons worked directly on site on the shell of the building. With strong, skilled and purposeful blows, they shaped the raw blocks of stone. When it came to ornament, their fantasy knew no limits.

The windows were richly decorated, and sculptures of saints and kings could be found on every niche or ledge.

The sculptors took special care in decorating the portals. In medieval times, the portals were not only the entry to the church, but also symbolised the gateway to the Kingdom of Heaven. Thus, the entrances were splendidly framed with carved figures and ornamentation.

Bricklayers were also organised in a guild. The higher the construction of a cathedral progressed, the more difficult their work became. They worked at dizzying heights on wobbly scaffolding without any safety nets, carefully laying the stone blocks. A moment of carelessness could be fatal. In addition to their wages, bricklayers received a bonus when they laid the keystone, the last stone of the vault. It was a symbol for the durability of the building.

The carpenters played just as important a role as the masons and bricklayers. They were responsible for the construction of the enormous roof truss, the form over which the stone vaulting was laid. Several thousand trees had to be felled for the roof truss. Blacksmiths supplied the saw blades, wall supports, beam ties and nails.

The Gothic cathedrals propelled one trade to unprecedented fame: glass-staining. The stained-glass windows still preserved in some cathedrals are of a rare beauty. These artists developed techniques to produce and colour glass, but their secrets were lost in later years. Unfortunately, even the names of the artists have not survived.

The working day was normally 17 hours, and no work was done on Sundays and religious holidays. Many of the artisans worked their whole life at the same site hut. Each site hut had its own rules, which all members had to observe. For example, no one could work for free, as Renaut de Montauban found when he volunteered to help build Cologne Cathedral, in order to do penance for his sins. Enraged over this unfair competition, the other workers beat him and threw him into the Rhine River.

Mark of quality

In antiquity, stonemasons often signed or marked their work, but this did not become general practice until the end of the 12th century, during the Gothic Age. The signature was a mark of quality, but was also proof for accounting purposes, showing exactly which stones a particular mason had laid. The portal above the cathedral of Autun reads: 'Gilbert has done this work'. On the portal of the church of St Ursin in Bourges is the signature of a man named Giraud; and in the year 1233, a certain Durand carved the following sentence into the keystone of Rouen Cathedral: 'Durand has completed me'.

Signature on the tympanum of Autun Cathedral.

JEWISH MYSTICISM: THE WONDERS OF THE CABBALA

Originating in Palestine, the many-faceted teachings of the Jewish mystics, or Cabbalists, soon found their way to Europe, giving rise to a rich tradition of scholarship and religious and moral thought. In spite of the active hostility of the Christian Church, the followers of the cabbala strove to understand the nature of God, man's place on earth and the principles surrounding creation itself.

Mysticism was widespread among French Jews from the 13th century.

Few people have any idea what lies concealed behind the term 'cabbala'. In English, the word 'cabal' means conspiracy, but is rarely used today. To understand the significance of the cabbala, we must go back into ancient times. The word originates from the Hebrew language, where it means tradition and custom. Since antiquity, it has been used to refer to Jewish mysticism and the esoteric traditions of Judaism. These do not form a uniform system, but consist of an amalgamation of different teachings. Over the centuries, this has resulted in a complex juxtaposition of widely divergent movements, all grouped under the heading of Cabbalism. The Cabbalists wrestle with some of the fundamental questions of Judaism. In what form is God present? What principles form the foundations of creation? Has human suffering any meaning? In the eyes of the Christian Church, and particularly for the popes, Jewish mysticism was long considered to be the work of the devil, and any Christian scholars who made reference to it were condemned and branded as heretics.

The spread of the cabbala

The cabbala had its origins in Palestine and can be traced back to the 2nd century AD. In the following century, the movement spread to Babylon, where there was a lively exchange among its followers. This period produced the *Sefer Jetsira* (Book of Creation), an anonymous theological scripture that explains how the order of the world can be decoded with the help of 32 Paths of Wisdom: the 22 letters of the Hebrew alphabet and the 10 basic numbers, or the Sefirot. The book was very significant, for it opposed the ideas of the Gnostics, a heretical Christian group who maintained that full insight into the ways of God was only given to a few individuals.

From the 8th century onwards, the insights of the Jewish mystics gradually spread to Europe. In southern Germany and in the Rhineland, a movement called

Towards the end of the Middle Ages, cabbalism flourished in the West.

Hasidism (or Chasidism), which grew up between 1150 and 1250, later won acceptance in other parts of Germany, Bohemia and northern France, and flourishes even today. One of its chief representatives was a scholar named Jehuda hä-Chasid (approximately 1146–1217), who came from Regensburg, in southeastern Germany.

Hasidic insights

Jewish scholars had maintained that God is in the highest Heaven, far away from his creatures. By contrast, the German (also known as Ashkenazi) Hasidim – members of the Hasidic movement – saw God's presence in all things. They backed up this belief with the idea that God is a spiritual being who, therefore, cannot be restricted in any way. The presence of the Creator will be revealed by wonders and supernatural phenomena.

Even misfortune and pain have a deeper meaning for the Hasidic movement. One of their basic tenets is that 'reward is measured according to the suffering'. In other words, only those who have passed through numerous difficult tests in the course of their lives will achieve eternal salvation. Those who try to avoid problems will only harm themselves in the end. In their nature, divine

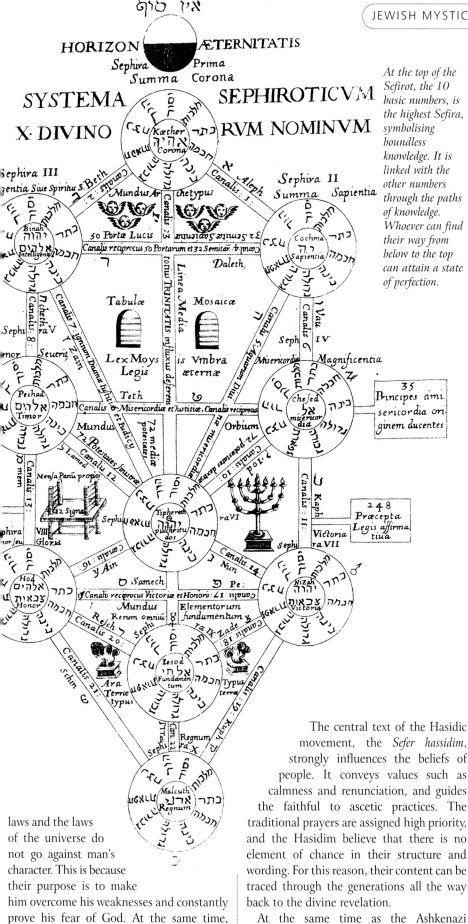

At the top of the Sefirot, the 10 basic numbers, is the highest Sefira, symbolising boundless knowledge. It is linked with the other numbers through the paths of knowledge. Whoever can find their way from below to the top can attain a state of perfection.

especially in Languedoc and Catalonia. Renowned Jewish study centres were established in Béziers, Lunel, Montpellier, Narbonne, Barcelona and Burgos. Prominent Cabbalists, such as Abraham ben Isaac, his son Isaac the Blind and Jacob Nazir wrote the *Sefer ha-Bahir* (Book of Compassion), a challenging book of extracts and short commentaries on various biblical verses. In order to give it more authority, the authors credited the book to previous rabbis rather

This engraving from the late Middle Ages shows Jewish theologists in conversation. The scholars usually maintained a lively exchange of ideas.

The throne of God

Between the 2nd and the 5th centuries, a considerable number of scriptures dealt with the question of how God's glory was revealed, and many Cabbalists were concerned with perhaps the greatest wonder: the physical nature of God and his throne. These writings were a kind of handbook, and described the journey into heaven in great detail. They described God as a being whose bodily dimensions were far beyond the capacity of human imagination. In this way, they did not intend to convey objective facts but to clarify the idea that the size of the Creator may not be captured in words.

The central text of the Hasidic movement, the *Sefer hassidim*, strongly influences the beliefs of people. It conveys values such as calmness and renunciation, and guides the faithful to ascetic practices. The traditional prayers are assigned high priority, and the Hasidim believe that there is no element of chance in their structure and wording. For this reason, their content can be traced through the generations all the way back to the divine revelation.

At the same time as the Ashkenazi theology was flourishing in central Europe, other doctrines appeared in the south,

laws and the laws of the universe do not go against man's character. This is because their purpose is to make him overcome his weaknesses and constantly prove his fear of God. At the same time, Hasidic ethics oppose the pursuit of earthly possessions and carnal desires.

than to themselves. What was new about the *Sefer ha-Bahir* was its central thesis that God's omnipotence was represented by the cosmic forces of the tree of life, from which the souls embark on their journey, and to which each individual then returns.

Discovering God's purpose

The Cabbalists devoted all their efforts to discovering the will and wisdom of God through the interpretation of revelation. They maintained that the hidden meanings of God's commandments will be understood through studying them in great detail. To accomplish this, God gives the devout person three aids: the scriptures, the spoken word and the number. Because the law of Moses – the Torah – was written in Hebrew, the Jewish mystics believed that there was no other language through which people could grasp how the world is ordered.

But the central part of Cabbalistic scholarship involved numbers. The Sefirot (the 10 basic numbers) from the *Sefer Jetsira* achieve divine qualities in the *Bahir*. The principle is simple: one number and one concept correspond to each letter. By combining or changing terms, it is possible to find various hidden meanings in the same biblical verse.

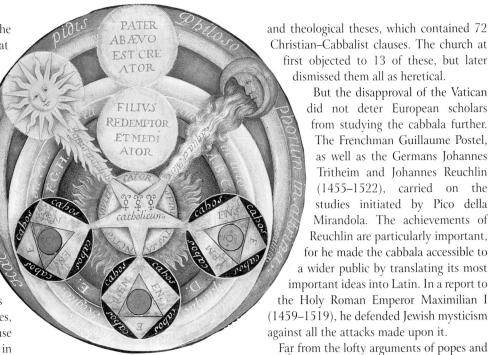

A Christian–Cabbalist adaptation of the order of the Sefirot: it contains the Trinity of God the Father, the Son and the Holy Spirit.

From the 14th century, Cabbalism became increasingly known outside the centres of Judaic scholarship. Many Christian scholars, as well as magicians and astrologers, became interested in the works of the Jewish mystics. Theologians were interested in similarities between Christianity, Judaism and Islam, and, of course, some wanted to convert the Jews to Christianity.

The humanist perspective

The Italian humanist Giovanni Pico della Mirandola (1463–1494) of Florence found that the Jewish esoteric traditions seemed to confirm Christian doctrines of the secret of the Trinity and the creation of the world. After a careful study of the rules of numbers and letters, Pico argued that only through magic and the cabbala could humans be sure of the divinity of the Messiah. He wrote 900 philosophical

and theological theses, which contained 72 Christian–Cabbalist clauses. The church at first objected to 13 of these, but later dismissed them all as heretical.

But the disapproval of the Vatican did not deter European scholars from studying the cabbala further. The Frenchman Guillaume Postel, as well as the Germans Johannes Tritheim and Johannes Reuchlin (1455–1522), carried on the studies initiated by Pico della Mirandola. The achievements of Reuchlin are particularly important, for he made the cabbala accessible to a wider public by translating its most important ideas into Latin. In a report to the Holy Roman Emperor Maximilian I (1459–1519), he defended Jewish mysticism against all the attacks made upon it.

Far from the lofty arguments of popes and scholars, many a humble fortune-teller made use of cabbalistic methods, such as certain correspondences between letters and numbers. If someone needed to know about their fate, for example, the letters of his or her name formed the basis for a prediction.

A resistance movement?

Whether theological or superstitious, all cabbalist movements encountered prejudice, especially from the church. For centuries, many Christian theologians regarded Jewish mysticism as simply a resistance movement. In their opinion, the mystics used magic to protect themselves against attempts to convert them to Christianity. The Vatican considered resistance to be unforgivable. Nevertheless, the cabbala prevailed, and continued to uncover new knowledge.

A religious masterpiece

The *Sefer ha-Zohar* (Book of Splendour) was first attributed to the Rabbi Simeon Ben Jochai, a Talmudic teacher, who is said to have lived in the 2nd century AD, but probably never lived at all. Historians now agree that the author of the Book of Splendour was in fact Rabbi Mose de León, a 13th-century Castilian (Spanish) Cabbalist.

The book contains a variety of texts which analyse sections of the Bible. León intended his writings to bring back onto the right path those Jewish intellectuals who had broken with traditions and discarded the religious orders. He found an unexpectedly large readership and, for many Jews, his work ranks on a par with the Bible and the Talmud.

Pico della Mirandola (left) and Johannes Tritheim (right) were among the first Christian theologians to study the cabbala extensively.

THE VEMGERICHT: ROUGH JUSTICE OR REIGN OF TERROR?

Medieval Europe was an often lawless place, with one law for the rich and another for the poor. One solution was the establishment of courts known as vemgerichts, whose ferocious sentences spread fear and terror. However crude and cruel, this helped to rein in the 'justice' meted out by the nobility, and to redress the lack of rights enjoyed by the common people.

If you are summoned to appear before a court in a democratic country today, you can be fairly sure that the court procedure will be quite clear, but this was not the case during the Middle Ages. In those days, jurisdiction was divided between many individuals, judgement was pronounced according to a variety of laws, and many crimes went unpunished. As a result, many people – especially the nobility – took charge of protecting their own rights, and bloody feuds were the order of the day. In the course of the 13th century, the lack of a strong imperial power in Europe increased the general sense of insecurity in matters of law. It was at that time that a form of jurisdiction developed in Westphalia, western Germany, which was to gain great influence in the following 200 years: the *veme*, meaning either co-operative or punishment. Coupled with the word *gericht*, or law, a new court was born.

A short trial

The origin of the vemgerichts probably lay with local courts administered by noblemen. The 'jurisdiction of blood' – the authority to sit in judgement over life and death – had been granted to these men by the Holy Roman Emperor Charlemagne (747–814). In the 13th century, the courts came under the control of a Master of the Bench, usually a bishop or a prince. He authorised a count (nobleman) to occupy the bench, and to pass judgement with the aid of several lay judges. Normally, there were seven judges, but if a criminal was caught in the act, the presence of three lay judges was sufficient. Lay judges were free men of a good reputation, who had to have been born in Westphalia.

The crimes that were investigated by the vemgerichts included cases of murder and robbery. As well as denying recourse to legal action, the judgement of a vemgericht could only be acquittal or death. The deliberations took place according to rules known only to initiates. The public was excluded, and anybody found eavesdropping was hanged. The execution of a death sentence was carried out on the spot using a rope strung up 'on the next closest tree'.

The secrecy surrounding the proceedings of the vemgerichts gave rise to rumours: the lay judges, it was said, were a secret group of masked henchmen, making their judgements in remote places, mostly under a lime tree, which also served as a handy gallows. It was commonly known that many of the accused underwent torture during the trials.

In spite of all the rumours and horror stories, these courts came to enjoy wide regard and power in the 14th century. People accused of committing crimes were brought from far away to be put on trial before a vemgericht. If an accused person did not appear, he or she became *vervemt*, (outlawed). These outlaws could be executed as soon as a lay judge caught them. Because of their powers, the courts grew too strong, and the number of trials – often for petty offences – increased.

When the vemgericht passed a death sentence, a sword was laid on the judge's table as a symbol of the 'jurisdiction of blood'.

The position of lay judge brought with it material advantages, and many vemgerichts became infiltrated by shady or corrupt characters. By the end of the 15th century, legal agreements between the sovereign princes and the cities caused the *veme* to lose a large portion of their legal functions and their reputations, so that the once infamous courts lost their importance.

Tortures such as the iron maiden (above), where the body of a criminal was pierced upon closure, were unjustly imputed to the vemgerichts.

ALCHEMY IN THE MIDDLE AGES

From early times, men with an interest in the sciences experimented with various substances, and developed laboratory instruments and chemical procedures. These alchemists, or natural philosophers, came to enjoy a high status and were respected at the new universities. Just as important, they also had a reputation as capable craftsmen, whose services were required in mining and the metal industry. Their most important goal, that of turning base metals into gold, was never achieved, but the alchemists tried hard to provide European kings and princes with the money they needed for their incessant wars.

A 15th-century marble floor panel in the cathedral of Siena, Italy, shows Hermes Trismegistus (right). The Egyptians and Greeks worshipped the god of arts and sciences as the founder of alchemy.

Even today, alchemists are represented as sinister, bearded old men who experiment in dark laboratories with formulas from magic books in order to create the philosopher's stone or the elixir of immortality, or to turn base metals into gold. Sometimes the alchemists are portrayed as greedy men producing counterfeit money.

We know now that these images bear little relation to the historical facts, and yet legends persist. Who were these men, who were often suspected of dabbling in black magic? Were they Europe's first serious scientists or simply dangerous charlatans?

The first philosophers of nature

As far back as the first advanced civilisations, priests and scholars began to explore natural phenomena. They invoked a god that the Egyptians called Thoth and the Greeks Hermes Trismegistus. The deity was credited with a series of revelational scriptures that formed the basis for chemical and technical studies, a field that came to be known as natural philosophy.

One of the most fundamental questions asked by ancient researchers concerned the composition of stones and metals: were they living or not? Many natural philosophers thought that substances which were considered dead did, in fact, possess a certain form of life, and that this could be activated with the assistance of magic texts. Most scholars, however, opposed this assumption, and agreed with the Greek philosopher Aristotle (384–322 BC), who maintained that all substances consist of different quantities of the four elements: earth, water, fire and air. These elements emitted vapours – cold, damp, hot or dry – according to the relation of the components. This produced the clouds, rain and snow above the earth, and the minerals beneath its surface. In the case of minerals, vapours first condensed to form mercury or sulphur, which were known as the father and mother, or, together, the *prima materia* of metals.

Around 200 BC, the Greeks produced a variety of formulas for dyeing and counterfeiting minerals and precious stones, and instructions appeared on how to make the necessary equipment. All these investigations formed the basis of alchemy as a related discipline to physics, which in ancient times was considered a branch of philosophy. Not until the 17th century was a distinction made between the terms *chymia* (chemistry) and *alchymia* (alchemy) for the science of natural substances.

From the East to Europe

Between the 9th and 13th centuries, alchemy progressed in the Islamic world. This period saw the development of special ovens, distillation and the discovery of organic substances such as sal ammoniac (ammonium chloride).

The Arabic texts only reached the West after the beginning of the 12th century, but they immediately met with keen interest.

Europe was in the throes of a huge economic upswing, which produced new industries, and gave new impetus to traditional trades such as metalwork. For this reason, any new knowledge was eagerly welcomed.

Within about a hundred years, alchemists were active in many fields, including mining – the exploitation of the silver mines near Freiberg in the German state of Saxony had begun in 1170, for example – and medicine, in which it had long been suspected that substances could be extracted from plants or metals to delay the ageing process. In the 13th century, alchemists began the search for the so-called quintessence, a liquid obtained from repeatedly distilling alcohol, which was supposed to have the effect of an elixir of life. But the alchemists never believed in immortality: the human body was to remain in good condition for the period of time that God gave to the individual.

Theory and practice

Soon the practical, specialised knowledge that the alchemists needed for transmutation granted them a special status in society. Among other things, they used imitation gold to manufacture jewellery and decorative articles such as vases. As a result, people regarded them as craftsmen rather than scientists. Perhaps this

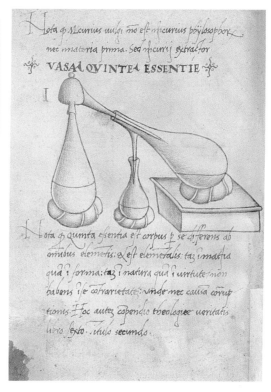

This drawing of a distilling apparatus for the production of quintessence comes from a 15th-century text, which gave an overview of the status of research at that time. By then, however, scientific endeavour had stagnated.

is why it is often said that the Middle Ages actually produced two alchemies – a theoretical and a practical one. Whatever the truth of this statement, the practical handbooks of the time generally included explanations of a general nature, while even

extremely speculative texts refer again and again to laboratory results. By the end of the 14th century, there were scholars researching alchemy all over Europe, and there was a lively exchange of ideas among them. Questions of how to form metals were also discussed at the universities. A document with exam questions dating from around 1230 deals with alchemical matters.

Did the philosopher's stone exist?

The alchemists believed in an ever-repeating cycle of dissolution and unification. As a symbol of this, they used a mythical dragon eating its tail. The dragon signified that a certain number of set procedures had to be used; these included pulverisation, liquefaction and oxidation. The aim was the transmutation and refinement of matter, preferably into precious metals. To achieve this, however, the alchemists needed the philosopher's stone – a substance they never found. It took a long time for the natural philosophers to learn that they would never be successful in the production of silver or gold.

Nevertheless, their experiments had positive side effects. The alchemists greatly improved distillation techniques and produced mineral acids to replace the organic acids, mainly vinegar, that had been used until then. They also discovered phosphorus, black powder (gunpowder) and porcelain. Their research provided an important basis for modern chemistry.

Coded language

The people of medieval Europe believed that God revealed the secrets of creation to the alchemists, and that only a certain group of initiates were allowed access to that knowledge. In order to protect their knowledge from abuse by outsiders, the natural philosophers committed themselves to secrecy; whoever broke their oath had to

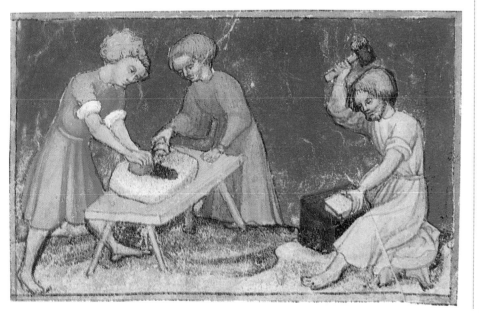

This late 12th-century painting shows alchemists at work. Natural philosophers knew seven metals from antiquity and the Arab world: gold, silver, bronze, copper, zinc, iron and lead.

reckon with a punishment from God. Some feared that competitors could imitate their techniques and contest their monopolies – for example, in the manufacture of drugs and medicines.

To protect themselves, the scientists devised coded names for chemical and physical processes, as well as for the substances and their qualities. They changed the sequences of letters, added characters from foreign languages such as Hebrew or Arabic and even invented new letters. In addition, their writings made use of strange abbreviations and a variety of terms that had several meanings – without specifying the meaning in each case. Some authors left information out or deliberately avoided using a logical textual structure.

Last but not least, the texts of the alchemist authors made use of colourful language and analogies with biological processes. The stages of life – conception, birth, maturity and death – corresponded to alchemistic processes. In principle, they differentiated between male and female

Because of his knowledge of physics, chemistry and mechanics, the Dominican monk Albertus Magnus had the reputation of being a magician. His scientific work enhanced this reputation, which spread through popular books of magic. The fresco shown here is in the monastery of the Dominican order at Treviso, in Italy.

substances. According to their ideas, metals had a body, soul and spirit, and were created from seeds. They were born, grew and could grow sick or healthy; if sick, they needed to be healed according to the diagnosis.

Furthermore, the old natural philosophers adopted numerous images from classical mythology and Christian belief. They called their procedures 'the wedding of sun and moon', and replaced the scientific names of substances with the names of ancient gods and heroes, as the Babylonians had done. If they heated tin and copper together in a crucible, for example, this symbolically unified Jupiter and Venus. Furthermore, they

frequently drew parallels between their own actions and the creative work of God, comparing Christ to the philosopher's stone.

Good and bad instructions

Even if the alchemists sometimes recorded scientifically sound results on paper, the obscure coded language meant that their contemporaries could not easily make use of the research. A series of instructions could only be reconstructed under laboratory conditions. Moreover, the person who had originally carried out the experiments might well have made unreasonable or unfounded statements. Thus, it is not surprising that few people were able to detect a crystal in the blood of a billy goat by following their instructions, or

A page from the Book of Secrets of My Lady Alchemy *by Constantinus (14th century). From top to bottom: four oceans represent the freezing point of mercury. From the union of Adam and Eve came the philosopher's stone, symbolised by the pelican. At the bottom, the earth appears as a triangle; earth, water and the heavens are visibly divided from one another.*

A demonic affair?

It was not until the late Middle Ages that the church criticised alchemy, but it did not oppose the alchemists' scientific pursuits. What the clergy feared most was the appearance of a Satanic cult. A handbook for inquisitors, dating from the 14th century, mentions as one of the 'signs, with which blasphemers can be recognised is the fact that some have dedicated themselves to alchemy .... For many alchemists nearly always ... call upon the demons. As soon as they do not reach their goals, they ask them for help; they implore them, beg, plead and publicly or secretly bring them sacrifices'.

were able to make gold using sweet basil and the blood of a red-haired person.

The alchemists' recipes are hard to follow, in part because they tried to cover their tracks, but also because the records they left behind were full of errors. This is understandable, for we must remember that they were exploring unknown territory!

Modern chemists analyse matter or combine elements before they draw conclusions from their procedures. By contrast, natural philosophers first formulated a hypothesis, which they then tried to prove by experiments. This prejudiced their views, and they tended to interpret individual results incorrectly. If an experiment failed completely, they did not alter the basic theory, but simply reinterpreted their observations to fit in with their expectations.

Author unknown

As was the case with many medieval authors, the Arab and European alchemists either did not sign their work at all or they used the names of authorities from previous centuries. Thus, the translation of a chapter of the *Book of Remedies* written by the Arab author ibn-Sina, better known as Avicenna (around 980–1037), was published around 1200 supposedly as the work of Aristotle. The *Corpus Gabirianum*, an important source for research since antiquity, was erroneously attributed to an Arab doctor, Jabir ibn-Haijan, who lived in the 8th century and was often mistaken for Geber, a 14th-century Christian scholar. Geber's true identity was probably a Franciscan monk named Paul von Tarent.

Problems of attribution arose in particular with collections of texts that were distributed under the names of famous doctors and philosophers. The philosopher and cleric Albertus Magnus (around 1200–1280), his pupil Thomas Aquinas (1225–1274), Roger Bacon (around 1214–1292) and Jean de Roquetaille (14th century), never studied alchemy as intensely as other people claimed. Albertus Magnus only used the new laboratory techniques when he wrote *Meteora* and *De mineralibus*, both published between

In the 14th century, the English writer Geoffrey Chaucer condemned alchemy in The Canterbury Tales, *a collection of stories in verse form. The title page to one of the chapters shows experiments being carried out in a laboratory.*

1250 and 1254. He described, among other things, the production of inexpensive metal alloys. He also furnished information on the gold- and silver-plating of inferior metals, as well as the production of gold and silver lacquers, and gave a detailed description of the element arsenic. Thomas Aquinas – who never compiled a comprehensive study on alchemy – formulated the principle that such techniques would be permitted as long as no forbidden practices, namely magic, were

applied or any fraud intended. This shows that the study of transmutation was still taken seriously.

By the end of the 13th century, the situation was changing. Laymen increasingly tried their hand at experiments, and there are many references to 'peasant alchemy'. Gradually, the entire field of natural philosophy fell into disrepute. For example, famed Renaissance authors such as Dante Alighieri (1265–1321), Francesco Petrarca (1304–1374) and Geoffrey Chaucer (about 1340–1400) mocked the vague language of the alchemists. In their view, the coded language of alchemy was intended to conceal failure and a lack of expert knowledge.

In this respect, they were not altogether wrong. While alchemy had wide practical uses, the theory behind it had not progressed very far. As it became clear that the natural philosophers had reached their limits, their texts grew wilder and more speculative. Since the alchemists could offer nothing new, they searched in literature for proof of their theories; between the 15th and 18th centuries, innumerable commentaries were produced on such works as the Bible, the

The so-called House of Nicolas Flamel in the Rue de Montmorency in Paris. In fact, Flamel's house was torn down in 1852. In memory of this famous citizen, the city named a small street after him. Certain buildings, which the supposed gold-maker had financed, served as meeting places for the alchemists of Paris.

Böttger's white gold

The pharmacist's assistant Johann Friedrich Böttger (1682–1719) was reputed to be an alchemist. In order to obtain gold, the Elector of Saxony, Augustus the Strong (1670–1733), took him into his employ. But, in 1708, instead of converting metal, Böttger achieved something quite wonderful: he invented porcelain. Böttger's discovery gave the Elector, who was a passionate collector, independence from expensive Chinese imports. Soon after, Augustus founded the famous porcelain works at Meissen.

legend of King Arthur, the *Metamorphoses* of the Roman poet Ovid (43 BC–AD 17/18) and the *Roman de la Rose* (Romance of the Rose), the most important French literary work of the 15th century.

In the early modern era, much mystical thought was channelled into alchemy, which was supported by secret societies, such as the Rosicrucians. This amounted to a step

towards a pseudo-doctrine. At the same time, the universities adopted empirical methods, with theories now formulated according to verifiable observations.

Alchemy and counterfeiting

Even if the scientific aspect of alchemy faded into the background, interest in its procedures continued right up to the 18th century. The reason for this was that European kings and princes needed greater and greater sums of money to defend or extend their territories. Since the late Middle Ages, most of these rulers had slipped into chronic debt. First, England and France had fought the Hundred Years' War (1337–1453) to decide who would rule France, while the immensely destructive Thirty Years' War (1618–48), in which most of the leading European states took part, consumed enormous financial resources.

From about 1300, many European rulers ordered experts to come to their courts, and commissioned them to make coins from counterfeit precious metals. In 1329, King Edward III of England (1312–1377), desperate to finance his wars in France, summoned two alchemists to appear at his court – if necessary, by force. There are numerous similar reports of rulers who put pressure on scientists with practical experience to provide them with services which the royal mints could not. The result, however, was that the currencies of the states concerned rapidly lost their value.

The natural philosophers were probably not motivated by dishonesty, unlike a number of their royal customers! Of course, the

The Hôtel d'Escoville in Caen, whose founder, Nicolas de Valois, supposedly belonged to a 16th-century circle of alchemists.

alchemists had their share of swindlers and charlatans, men who devoted their efforts to lining their own pockets.

Taking their cue from their rulers, the middle classes also tried to attain riches through producing counterfeit money. Once again, rumours spread that the philosopher's stone had been found. Later, many newly wealthy people found themselves accused in retrospect of illegal practices, although few of the accusations could be substantiated. Every city was reputed to have alchemists among its wealthy families. Nicolas de Valois of Caen, in Normandy, was believed to be an influential alchemist, supposedly proved by the hieroglyphics which he incorporated into the Hôtel d'Escoville.

The gold-maker of Paris

Another example of wealthy alchemy was Nicolas Flamel (1330–1418), who worked in Paris as a writer and copier. His respected trade, successful property speculations and shrewd marriage to a wealthy widow brought him prosperity. He donated magnificent buildings to the church, which made him popular with the public. There is no evidence that Flamel or any of his circle produced counterfeit precious metals. Around 1600, however, an alchemical treatise called *Le livre Flamel* (The Book of Flamel) was published. This was a French adaptation of a Latin text written in the 14th century – allegedly by Flamel, although the existence of the book was not mentioned at the time. The connection between Flamel and alchemy solidified when a certain Robert Duval pointed out the alchemical symbols on buildings that Flamel had donated. Other authors soon took up the thread – and the myth of the gold-maker of Paris was born.

Protecting the market

It is often said that the church prohibited its monks from dabbling in alchemy during the 13th and 14th centuries. The reality is that the Pope's edicts of the time were directed against magic and counterfeiting rather than alchemy itself, and were aimed at preventing the spread of non-Christian practices and protecting the shaky European money market.

THE CASE AGAINST THE TEMPLARS

Dark tales of immorality and heretical practices surrounded the Order of the Templars in October 1307, when King Philip the Fair ordered the arrest of all the Templars in France. Under torture, many of the Templars confessed to heresy; many of them were burned alive for their crimes. But the scandal surrounding the Templars was also a convenient excuse for the French king to pursue his vendetta against the Pope.

A 13th-century seal of the Order of the Templars shows two knights on one horse. Contemporaries observed cynically that the warrior monks must be very poor if two men had to share a horse.

In 1096, with the launching of the First Crusade, Christian Europe began a 200-year campaign to regain control of the Holy Land, or Palestine, from the Muslims. The struggle gave rise to the so-called military orders, men who combined the vows of a monk with the warlike skills of a knight. These warrior monks swore to protect the Holy Land against the Muslims. The three main orders were: the Knights of St John, also known as the Hospitallers, founded in 1120; the Knights Templar, generally known as the Templars, founded in 1119; and the Teutonic Knights, founded in 1190.

In 1291, the armies of the Mamelukes of Egypt captured the remaining Crusader footholds in the Holy Land, and seized the city of Acre, which had been the Crusader capital for 100 years. The Christian forces went home, and the Templars withdrew to the island of Cyprus.

Crusaders flee the fall of Acre in this illustration from the year 1291.

Blaming the knights

The loss of the Holy Land was a heavy blow for the West, and it was easy to blame the Crusader armies. Some people claimed that the Crusaders had been too lenient. The conduct of the military orders, especially the Templars, was seen as treasonable, as they had left the Holy Land without a fight. The order also attracted criticism for its wealth – especially in France, where it owned large estates – and for its internal power struggles. In 1274, the Council of Lyon had suggested a union of the Templars and Hospitallers, but the church and the nobility had objected.

In late 1306, Jacques de Molay (around 1245–1314), the Master of the Order of Templars, travelled to a meeting with Pope Clement V in the Poitou region of south-western France. The results of this meeting paved the way for tragedy.

Pope Clement told De Molay of the unpleasant rumours about the Templars that had been circulating for some time. At the court of the French king Philip IV, called the Fair (1268–1314), the chief minister Guillaume de Nogaret (around 1260/70–1313) had been collecting vast amounts of evidence against the knights. His files mentioned heresy, immorality and the use of forbidden magical practices. The Pope did not believe the accusations, as the order answered to him alone; at De Molay's request, Clement ordered an investigation.

On August 24, 1307, Clement informed the king of his intentions. In spite of this, Philip the Fair acted swiftly: he ordered all Templars in his kingdom to be arrested on the morning of October 13, and confiscated the entire wealth of the order. What was behind his swift and decisive action?

The monarch said that he wanted to save Christianity from the heretical practices of the Templars, but of course he did not act out of piety. Philip the Fair was a calculating ruler who directed a powerful state. Several years before, he had fought a bitter struggle against Pope Boniface VIII (1235–1303), because the Pope had tried to exempt the clergy from taxes. France emerged stronger from this contest between royal and religious power.

The king's power grows

At the same time, Philip needed money to continue fighting his expensive wars in Flanders and Aquitaine. He also planned to undertake a new crusade to the Holy Land. However, the crusade was merely an excuse for the royal treasury to collect more taxes and for the king to impose his authority on the clergy. By turning against the Templars,

An illustration from Renart le Nouvel *(The New Reynard) mocks the decision to unite the Templars (right) and the Hospitallers (left).*

Philip was able to get his hands on their lands and wealth and to deal a blow against the authority and prestige of the Pope.

Clearly, the action against the Templars had a lot to do with French politics rather than heretical beliefs or the use of magic.

Philip counted on again being able to defeat the weak and sickly Clement V. But even if Clement could not stand up to the will of the French king, he did not blindly follow orders. When he found out about the imprisonment of the Templars, the Pope issued a type of decree known as a papal bull, on November 22, 1307, stating that all Templars – both within and outside France – be put in jail and their possessions handed over to the church. Most European rulers complied with the bull, but it took nine months to carry out the order.

In a second bull, Clement ordered committees in each diocese to try the Templars as individuals. The innocent ones, and those who reconciled with the Church after an admission of guilt, would receive a pension and be allowed to live in a monastery of their choice. Those who failed to confess or returned to

The punishment for convicted heretics was always extreme: a group of Templars is burned at the stake in this contemporary miniature. On the left stands the French king, Philip the Fair.

their old ways, however, 'have to be executed with the greatest strictness'. The Pope reserved for himself the power of passing judgement on prominent Templars who had confessed to heresy.

In addition, Clement appointed papal commissioners to assess the status of the order in each state. A council was covened at Vienne, in southeastern France, to decide whether the entire order should be dissolved.

The arrest: brothers wearing brown rather than white habits were simple monks, not knights.

A cry of protest

In 1311, Rinaldo da Concorrezzo, the archbishop of Ravenna, convened a commission for his diocese in Bologna. Thirteen Templars were tried and acquitted. The interesting thing about this case was the critical manner in which the commission dealt with torture. In 1252, the church had permitted the use of torture in heresy trials. Clement V had specifically requested it this time, as he was dissatisfied with the course of the trial. Rinaldo, however, argued that the court 'must consider those innocent who had been subjected to torture and confessed and who afterwards had withdrawn his statement'. The archbishop was certainly ahead of his time!

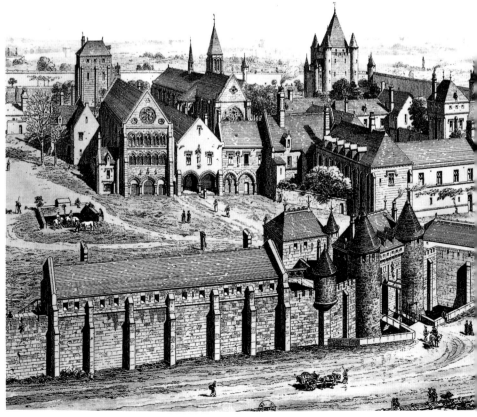

In the meantime, Philip the Fair put his henchmen to work, with the aid of Wilhelm of Paris, the Grand Inquisitor. Interrogation of the Templars began right after their arrest, and the king's agents did not hesitate to use extreme cruelty. In the French capital alone, 134 out of 138 knights of the order admitted guilt under torture. Among other things, they admitted to betraying Jesus, spitting on the cross, worshipping idols and engaging in homosexual acts.

The records speak

Because the records of most of these trials of October 1307 have been preserved, they can tell us things about the proceedings against the Templars. Most of the records document confessions; after a knight confessed, it is almost certain that no proper trial took place. Those who admitted their guilt were almost all French, or came from regions and states allied to France, such as the Duchy of Provence and the Kingdom of Navarre. It is clear that they broke under torture and told the authorities what they wished to hear.

Philip the Fair thought he had won when the papal commission finally assembled in November 1309. In a burst of generosity, he said that any imprisoned knight who wanted to make a statement could come to Paris. But this is where he miscalculated: against all expectations, 600 Templars appeared and reaffirmed the innocence of their order. This brought the whole justice system to a standstill.

But the loyalty of the diocesan commissions lay with the king, not the pope, and this provided Philip with the opportunity for revenge. Fifty-four Templars, who had confessed two years before but now defended their order, were condemned for heresy, and were burned alive. Faced with this terrible punishment, not one of the condemned men withdrew their statements. However, the resistance of the rest crumbled.

This 19th-century engraving shows the Templar district of Paris, circa 1450; by that time, the lands and buildings had passed to the Order of Hospitallers.

Critical voices

Few chroniclers went against the official version of the destruction of the Order of the Templars. Here are two critical voices:

Christian Spinola from Genoa, an informer of the King of Aragon, wrote: 'I believe that the Pope and the King are doing this, because they want to have the Templars' money and also because they want to combine all the orders, Templars, Hospitallers and all others, and make one order ....'

Villiani, a chronicler from Florence, thought that 'many people are saying that they (the Templars) had been killed and destroyed unjustly and for sinful motives, as their possessions were wanted, which the Pope then gave to the Order of Hospitallers ....'

Philip the Fair breathed a sigh of relief, and the papal commission concluded that the knights had been judged fairly. Outside France, only a few Templars were sent to prison; autonomous judges usually let the accused go free. The French members of the order had clearly fallen victim to the greed of a ruthless king.

Clement V gives in

At the end of 1311, the Council of Vienne was supposed to make a unilateral decision on the future of the Templars. However, Philip pressurised the Pope to the point

where, on his own authority, he issued the bull *Vox in excelso*, which dissolved the order but did not pronounce it guilty. With the exception of a special decree pertaining to the Iberian Peninsula, the wealth of the Templars was given to the Hospitallers.

According to historians, it is probable that some of the Knights Templar committed the offences for which they were accused. The majority of the order, however, were certainly not heretics or members of obscure sects. Over the years, they had proved their unshakable Christian faith by fearless actions in defence of the community and by their readiness to give their lives in battle.

The fall of the Grand Master

The Grand Master of the Templars had first admitted to crimes, but later withdrew his confession in front of two messengers of the

From the mid-12th century onwards, the Templars received many gifts from the rulers of the Iberian Peninsula; among them was this castle.

Pope. He finally placed his destiny wholly in the Pope's hands. Philip, however, would not let De Molay make the journey to Clement in order to have his own trial.

It was not until the end of 1313 that the Pope set up a commission of three cardinals authorised to judge De Molay in the pope's name. The commission sentenced De Molay to life imprisonment. After the judgement, De Molay broke a year's silence and spoke in defence of the order. When the king heard of the Templar's defiance, he ignored the papal judgement. On the instructions of Philip, the Grand Master was burned at the stake on March 18, 1314.

WHERE DO THE MASAI COME FROM?

The tall, slender Masai, who roam the grassy plains of southern Kenya and northern Tanzania with their herds of cattle, are for many people the symbol of Africa. With their aristocratic appearance and tradition of independence, the Masai seem to be the epitome of a free people. But despite all the interest from outsiders, it has taken ethnologists many years to understand the Masai. And recent history has not been kind to them.

The stages of life

The social life of the Masai is governed by age: after childhood, there is a time as a warrior, when boys are initiated into manhood and learn the ways of the hunter. Then follows the phase of marriage and starting a family. Finally, people reach the stage in which honorary social positions are taken up. The forms of address used by the Masai reflect this social hierarchy; they do not use terms for family relations but have developed an impersonal terminology relating to a person's age. This makes it nearly impossible to trace the family tree of one individual over the span of several generations.

The Masai people of Kenya and Tanzania certainly rank among the most fascinating peoples on earth. Their unique style of dress and bodily adornment sets them apart from their neighbours. Like the great herds of wildebeest, zebra and antelope that inhabit the grasslands of the Great Rift Valley, it is easy to assume that these people have always lived here.

The homeland of the Masai is located to the east of Lake Victoria, straddling the border between Kenya and Tanzania. With a population of some 600,000 people, the Masai are the epitome of proud and fearless nomads, whose apparently independent and unhurried way of life is in stark contrast to the pressurised lifestyle of our society.

For a long time, there was almost no reliable information about the origins of the Masai. This led to wild speculation, with some ethnologists suggesting that they were the descendants of a scattered legion of the Roman empire. Others regarded them as one of the lost tribes of Israel, immigrants from Egypt or even wanderers from the far-off Tibetan highlands.

Right: *According to custom, young Masai warriors let their hair grow and braid it artistically.*

In the background are the grassy tree-dotted Masai plains, with snowcapped Mount Kilimanjaro towering above the plain. The indigenous people call it the White Mountain.

The creation of a myth

Although the coastal region was well known to Arab traders and seafarers for centuries, European exploration of the interior of East Africa only began in the mid-19th century. English explorers featured prominently, among them Richard Burton and John Speke (who together determined the source of the River Nile), the journalist Henry Morton Stanley (who was actually American), as well as the Scottish missionary and doctor David Livingstone. Despite the activities of these pathfinders, a huge area of land, reaching from Mount Kilimanjaro to what is now the nation of Uganda, remained unexplored. This uncharted region was the territory of the Masai. Because Europeans lacked knowledge about them, myths grew about a secret and unknown, possibly even a violent, people.

A veritable flood of books and newspaper articles turned these rumours into accepted facts. Henry Morton Stanley (1841–1904), who had never had any previous contact with the Masai, declared in a lecture to the Royal Geographical Society in London: 'If there is anyone amongst you who definitely wants to become a martyr, then I can tell him with certainty that for this, he need only go to the country of the Masai, where this will happen faster than at any other of the numerous places I have visited'. A different tone was adopted by Danish writer Karen Blixen (1885–1962), who wrote *Out of Africa* (1938) – later filmed under the same title. Blixen lived on a coffee plantation in Kenya from 1913 to 1931, and wrote: 'The Masai, a people who came from the Sudan in search of pastures for their herds and had walked right to the central highlands of Kenya plundering villages on its way, were wild and courageous in battle'.

In many ways, our knowledge about the Masai remains just as sketchy today. As an illustration, consider the following passage, written in 1987 by a French economist: 'The Masai, supported on his spear, with ear lobes hanging very low under the weight of his earrings, arms adorned with heavy jewellery, beads braided into his hair, where does he come from, where is he going to? From a historical perspective, the cape, sandals and spear are unique in Africa, and are of Roman origin .... The Masai are endlessly proud of the fact that they can live without money and only depend on their herds. They live exclusively from the blood of cows, mixed with their milk and some urine .... The Masai regard us with no interest or with contempt. We have before us the last people of Africa who ostentatiously refuse to become involved with Western civilisation'.

Migration to the south

On the basis of their language, linguists and anthropologists classify the Masai among the Nilotic peoples of the African plateau. The term 'Nilotic' (derived from the Nile River) refers to a group of northern African peoples whose type, language and culture are closely related and possess Hamitic (related to Semitic) elements.

Right: *Much of the Masai territory, as it existed in the 17th century, particularly the region on the north from Lake Baringo to Lake Naivasha, was lost to colonisation. More recently, the boundaries of their homeland, which lies mainly in Tanzania, have shifted eastward.*

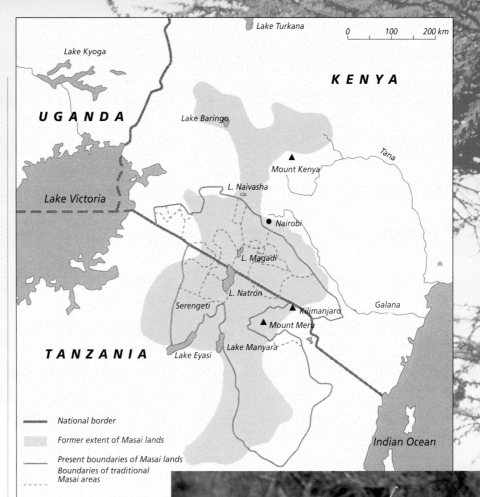

The Masai themselves maintain that they originate from Endigirr ee Kerio, a steep escarpment in the north of Kenya where the Kerio River begins. The river flows eastwards into Lake Turkana (formerly Lake Rudolf). This area is now populated by another group of Nilotic pastoralists, or herders – the Turkana – after whom the lake is now named.

The latest linguistic and archaeological studies support the Masai view. It is now assumed that the Masai gradually moved southwards almost 500 years ago, perhaps in response to a sudden change of climate and the onset of drought conditions over the region. From the beginning of the 17th century, the Masai probably began to settle on the open plains of the Serengeti, to the northeast of Ngorongoro Crater (the caldera of an extinct volcano, and now an important wildlife reserve). At that time, the Masai numbered only about 50,000 people. Gradually, though, they took control of an enormous area along the East African Rift Valley, extending 1,200 km from north to south and 300 km from east to west.

The early inhabitants

The area settled by the Masai was by no means empty. The Serengeti had been populated from the 9th century by nomadic and semi-nomadic people, who pursued a way of life that was similar to that of the Masai. A Chinese chronicler wrote: 'In the interior of Popali (East Africa), the people live on meat .... They bleed their cattle and drink the blood mixed with milk'. In terms of language, it has been proven that the tribes who preceded the Masai into the Rift Valley were also Nilotic. The semi-nomadic groups developed irrigation techniques that made the grasslands fertile, a development that would be of great benefit to the Masai.

Centuries of growth

It is clear that the Masai people did not simply spring up out of nowhere on the border between Kenya and Tanzania. Instead

Right: *Uncircumcised Masai boys are often entrusted with taking care of the herds.*

their culture developed over the course of the centuries in close conjunction with other peoples of the East African Rift Valley. There was little competition between these peoples, but rather a kind of intense co-operation, a process of more or less permanent economic and cultural exchange. Here, three different ways of life converged: the lives of the semi-nomadic cattle breeder, the settled farmer and the hunter-gatherer. It is true that the pastoralists or herders were the dominant group, but the three types could not always be strictly separated. If, for example, cattle were stolen or the herds decimated by an epidemic – as happened towards the end of the 19th century – even the nomadic people had to till the soil and plant crops for a while, or else subsist by hunting. After breeding new stocks of cattle, they could again take up their traditional herding lifestyle. Other

people strived towards the same goal: having built up a herd, they hoped that they would be accepted by the Masai people.

The territory controlled by the Masai shrank drastically during the 20th century, primarily as a result of the British and German colonisation of East Africa (the British took over the German possessions in Tanzania after World War I). Nevertheless, most of them continue to live as nomads today, since cattle breeding still holds the highest social status. However, a large portion of their ancestral grazing land has been converted to growing crops.

PILGRIMAGES AND PEOPLE'S CRUSADES

Time and again, the streets of medieval Europe filled with crowds of the young or the poor, desperate to show their faith in Almighty God. Many chose to demonstrate their piety through pilgrimages to distant shrines. Others joined crusades to free the Holy Land from the Muslims. Tragically, many of these young crusaders never returned.

From the 13th to the 15th centuries, Europe was filled with wandering groups of people. These groups included children, young people and the poor, but also priests, homeless people, criminals and ordinary pilgrims. Huge crowds came together, united by their wish to journey to Jerusalem and other Christian places of pilgrimage. These people's crusades first appeared in the year 1212, when two mass movements emerged, one in a small French village on the Loire River, the other in the Rhineland region of western Germany.

Up to that time, the ideal of a religious life in defence of the faith had been embodied by the knights, who had fought in the Crusades – the series of military campaigns to recapture the Holy Land from Muslim control. But the Crusades were a failure, and ordinary people also wished to contribute towards the defence of Christianity. Unlike the nobility, ordinary folk felt that a true crusade must be a peaceful campaign. The power of God alone was their weapon, they said, and they set out unarmed on the road to the Holy Land.

Many rulers reacted with suspicion when they saw people giving up all their possessions and setting out for distant goals in order to prove their faith. But others reacted more positively towards the enthusiasm of their fellow citizens.

Charismatic shepherd

In June 1212, a 12-year-old shepherd boy named Stephan from the French town of Cloyes-sur-le-Loire met a poor pilgrim who asked him for bread. Stephan believed that he had met Christ himself, and felt driven to do something

for the faith: he decided to lead a crusade. The idea was not unusual; for some years, preachers had appealed for people who were willing to fight against the heathens and heretics. Many people were still inspired by the crusade of Peter the Hermit, also known as Peter of Amiens, a wandering monk whose charismatic preaching had convinced thousands of rural people to follow him to Palestine in 1096.

The young boy travelled to the royal abbey of St Denis outside Paris, where he appeared before the king, Philip II Augustus (1165–1223). The king was not impressed

A statuette of a child pilgrim; with only a few exceptions, children did not take part in crusades or pilgrimages without their parents.

by the boy's plan, but Stephan got a completely different response from the people of Paris and its surrounding districts, who were inspired by his eloquence and his message.

Gradually, masses of people – especially children – gathered in the city, eager to follow Stephan. When the king ordered the crowds to disperse, they only did so under threat of force.

Stephan began to travel around, calling upon his compatriots to gather at Vendôme, near Paris. Officials took advantage of his appeal, and recruited people for the war against the Albigensians (also known as the Cathars), a heretical Christian sect with many followers in the Languedoc region of southern France.

Shepherds often reported heavenly revelations. This may be why the people often chose them to lead their marches of faith (illustration from the late Middle Ages).

Meanwhile, Stephan led about 6,000 children on the long march to Marseilles, where a pair of merchants arranged for the children to board seven ships. Two of the vessels sank before reaching the island of Sardinia. The remaining passengers probably ended up in North Africa and Egypt, sold into slavery by the unscrupulous shipowners.

Departure for the Holy Land

A few months after Stephan's crusade, Nicholas, an 18-year-old boy from Trier in the Rhineland, claimed that an angel had appeared before him and ordered him to go to Jerusalem in the company of like-minded people. When he got to Cologne, the young man convinced many people to join him in his non-violent crusade to liberate the Holy Sepulchre – the tomb in which the body of Jesus Christ was placed after his crucifixion – from Muslim hands. At the beginning of July, a large crowd set out across Alsace towards the Alps.

The weak ones soon died under the strain of the march, but the others could not be deterred. They firmly believed in Nicholas's promise that the waters of the Mediterranean would part to allow them to reach the Holy Land.

When the group reached the Italian port of Genoa on August 25, the expected miracle did not happen, nor could they find any space on a ship for the journey to Palestine. Some individuals turned back, while others boarded ships near Pisa. Not one member of this group was ever heard of again.

A second group of children reached the southern Italian port of Brindisi, and demanded to cross the Mediterranean. The local bishop prevented them from carrying out their plan, so the boys and girls decided to walk to Rome and ask Pope Innocent III (1160/61–1216) to receive their vows of crusade. The Pope barely took notice of this undertaking, let alone announced it publicly. Nevertheless, the sincerity of these young people never wavered.

The Pastorals

When King Louis IX of France (1214–1270) was captured

The deeds of St Michael are recorded in this beautiful medieval manuscript.

by the Muslims while on a crusade in Egypt in 1250, a number of Frenchmen decided to save their king – but without the support of the knights or clergy. 'God has no pleasure in the pride of man,' they cried. In memory of the shepherds and labourers who followed Peter of Amiens, they called themselves the Pastorals.

A former Cistercian monk called the Master of Hungary became the leader of the Pastorals. He justified his position by producing a 'letter from heaven' which he had supposedly received from Mary, the Mother of God. The Master of Hungary dressed in royal robes or in a bishop's cloak; he was frequently seen wearing a papal mitre on his head. His radical ideas swayed large numbers of people, and before long the movement had grown to 100,000. Soon, the Pastorals lost sight of their original goal and became involved in violence against the nobility, clergy and minorities.

The disturbances were subdued by the soldiers of the Queen Mother, Blanca, who ruled the country in the absence of her son Louis. The royal forces defeated the Pastorals at the battle of Villeneuve-sur-Cher. The Master of Hungary died in the battle, and all those taken prisoner were hanged. The Pastorals re-emerged in 1320 around the cities of Toulouse and Carcassone in southwestern France, but this second uprising was also crushed.

The road to Mont-Saint-Michel

In the year 1333, a Benedictine monk from the abbey on the island of Mont-Saint-Michel, just off the coast of Normandy, reported a 'most wondersome thing': 'An enormous crowd of small children, calling themselves shepherd boys, came to this church from many far-off countries, some in groups, the others alone. Many of them saying that they had heard heavenly voices, that spoke to them, saying "Go to Mont-Saint-Michel!" They had followed the charge without hesitating, leaving their herds in the fields and saying farewell to no-one'.

In the years after 1450, the holy island – the most famous shrine of St Michael north of the Alps – drew a vast tide of teenage pilgrims. We know that the archangel Michael had been worshipped for a long time, but why did such huge crowds of adolescents come to worship him at this particular time? Moreover, these young pilgrims flocked to the shrine from the most remote regions of Europe.

According to the chroniclers of the time these pilgrimages were a phenomenon that gripped 'the kingdom of France as well as other kingdoms and countries'. If a source from 1421 can be trusted, then we know that

these journeys of faith developed into a socially accepted custom. The 'kitchen boys', it states, were given money 'in order to go to Mont-Saint-Michel at the time of fasting'.

City chronicles record an enormous influx of pilgrims from all parts of Germany between 1455 and 1457. Other records show that similar movements of people took place from the area around Liège, and from Lorraine, Alsace and Switzerland.

A determined band

Neither heat nor bitter cold could deter the young pilgrims from their goal. For example, on a Tuesday in the carnival week (a festival held annually to mark the beginning of Lent), a group set out from the town of Weissenburg, when 'everything was covered in a blanket of snow and it was bitterly cold'. In the town of Biel, in Switzerland, eight adults agreed to accompany a children's pilgrimage after it became clear that the children were determined to go. In 1441, the inhabitants of the town of Millau said their children had left 'of their own accord' – that is, without their parents' knowledge and, presumably, against their will!

It seems strange to us today that the parents of these children were unable to intervene to stop the pilgrimages. In those days, when someone expressed the need to do penance – by making a pilgrimage, for example – most people took this decision seriously. They were also convinced that God would bestow special grace on innocent children who came to him as petitioners. It is likely that the religious enthusiasm of the adolescents greatly impressed their elders. Last but not least, we must remember that the cult of Michael and the practice of making pilgrimages had great significance in religious practice. Since ancient times, Christians had made pilgrimages to shrines and holy places in order to demonstrate their faith and repentance. This belief in the power of pilgrimage must have influenced the young as much as it did the old.

After about 1450, the wave of children's pilgrimages to Mont-Saint-Michel gradually subsided, but the reasons for this are still unclear. In the end, these mass movements became nothing more than a curious episode in medieval history.

Deep religious commitment

Although we may be doubtful about some individual circumstances, it would be wrong to say that the crusades and pilgrimages of the young and poor cannot be explained. Historians specialising in the medieval period know very well what motivated people to set out on a crusade or pilgrimage.

Above all, people were influenced by the crusading zeal of their rulers to win back control of the Holy Land from the Muslims. The many travelling preachers encouraged pious laymen to become involved in religious acts. Religious and social factors also played a role. The insecurity and poverty endured by the peasants probably made it easy for them to give up their everyday existence and take to the road. For some of the under-privileged, joining a group of crusaders or pilgrims offered a level of personal security which they had never known. And last but not least, many people yearned for more freedom; adolescents in particular were often delighted at the opportunity to free themselves of family ties.

During the Middle Ages, many individuals travelled great distances to visit holy places. As the illustration shows, not everyone had shoes. Even poor people, such as farmworkers, day-labourers and servants, joined in.

JOAN OF ARC: WAS SHE A WITCH OR A SAINT?

She came from humble origins to save France from chaos. But tragedy followed triumph, and Joan of Arc was burned as a heretic, the victim of political rivalries and the scheming of her enemies. In death, she became a legend, and eventually a saint. But who was the Maid of Orléans, whose meteoric rise and fall left such an impact on the history of her native soil?

Joan of Arc played her role in history for a brief period – between February 1429 and May 1431 – but her fame lives on even today. She became a legend in her own lifetime, and her reputation grew after her death at the stake. Few 15th-century figures are as well documented as the Maid of Orléans, but many aspects of her life have remained controversial to the present day.

A divided land

In 1392, France was shaken by the news that King Charles VI of the Valois dynasty had become insane and could no longer govern. The duchies of Armagnac and Burgundy both claimed the regency, and the resulting struggle plunged France into civil war. The Burgundians were allied with the wife of Charles VI, Isabeau of Bavaria, as well as with the English, who also laid claim to the French throne. In 1420, Isabeau pressurised her husband, by now completely deranged, to exclude their son Charles – known as the *dauphin*, or heir – from succession to the throne, and to declare King Henry V of England his successor.

When both Charles VI and Henry V died two years later, France was torn between two rival monarchs – the dauphin Charles VII (1403–1461) – proclaimed by the princes of the country, and Henry VI (1421–1470/71), who was backed by England and Burgundy.

A young woman goes to war

Joan of Arc was the daughter of a prosperous peasant family from the village of Domrémy in Lorraine, and was just 17 years old when she began her mission to save France. From the age of 13, the young girl had heard voices. Eventually, they implored her to come to the aid of Charles VII. She went to the royal captain of the town of Vaucouleurs to ask for an escort. He first rejected her, but her persistent pleas made him allocate some men to protect her. The captain preferred not to go against divine providence – in the Middle Ages, people did not question supernatural phenomena.

On February 22, 1429, Joan departed for Chinon, on the Loire River, site of the desperate dauphin's court. At first, Charles refused to see the peasant girl who claimed to be his saviour. After a few days, he consented to receive her. He then sent the Maid to Poitiers, where a committee of scholars and clergymen examined her for three weeks, and concluded that Charles should trust her.

Joan rapidly gathered wider support during the months that followed. She marched with the troops to the besieged city of Orléans, where she fought in the front line against the English until the siege was lifted. Her fearlessness in battle seemed to be proof of her calling. Over the following months, she led the dauphin's troops to victory in further battles, and ordinary people became convinced of her divine calling.

On July 17, the coronation of Charles VII was celebrated in Reims Cathedral. The Maid of Orléans stood at his side, holding a banner with an image of Jesus Christ. She had reached the climax of her career.

Death in the flames

Perhaps the taste of victory made them complacent, but the French commanders no longer listened to Joan's advice, and the royal forces suffered new defeats. After a battle near the town of Compiègne, she was captured by the Burgundians on May 23, 1430. As was the custom, negotiators tried to determine the amount of money to be paid as a ransom, but King Charles was unwilling to pay. In November, the Burgundians turned the Maid over to the English, who brought her to the town of Rouen, in Normandy, and ordered her to be tried by a French church court that was loyal to them.

On the surface, the trial was a religious matter, but the English were anxious to eliminate such a potent enemy. Presiding over the court was the Bishop of Beauvais, Pierre Cauchon, an adviser to Henry VI. Without any help from lawyers, Joan had to defend herself against allegations that she was an 'idolatress, conjurer of demons, schismatic, apostate and heretic'. Not

When Joan was burned, she wore a cap with these words:'heretic, relapse, apostate, idolatress'.

surprisingly, the judges found her guilty and condemned Joan to be burned at the stake. On May 30, crowds looked on as she was put to death in the marketplace of Rouen.

The Lady of Armoises

Only after her death did France's leaders express remorse for their failure to support the Maid of Orléans. Vast numbers of ordinary people, however, regarded her as a martyr; they said prayers and lit candles for her in the churches. In 1436, another of Joan's prophecies was fulfilled when Charles VII made his triumphant entry into Paris. Many people no longer doubted that the Maid was a saint and must therefore have escaped the flames. In their view, another woman must surely have died at the stake.

A false Joan appeared on May 20, 1436 in the vicinity of Metz, in eastern France.

This 19th-century mural, located in the church of Domrémy, shows the Maid of Orléans being put to death by the English at Rouen.

Inspiration for artists

In his drama *The Maid of Orléans*, German poet Friedrich Schiller allowed the heroine to die honourably on the battlefield. The Irish playwright George Bernard Shaw wrote *Saint Joan* in response to her canonisation, while French playwright Jean Anouilh's *The Lark* re-creates the historical events. In 1928, the Danish filmmaker Carl Theodor Dreyer directed *The Passion of Joan of Arc*, a silent epic that is considered one of the 10 best films of all time.

Towards the end of 1437, she married the Knight of Armoises and lived with him in Lorraine. Two years later, she travelled to Orléans, where she was welcomed with much pomp. Even though she called herself Claude, her two brothers and the noblemen of the area recognised in her the 'Virgin Joan of France' Nevertheless, the supposed saint left the town in a hurry when friends of the real Joan of Arc arrived. Gradually, people began to believe that she was an imposter. In 1440, the true identity of the false Joan was revealed when the Lady of Armoises made a public confession.

In 1439, sightings of Joan were widely reported. For example, a woman wearing men's clothing was arrested and displayed before the people of Paris. When tried, the accused stated that she was married to a knight and had two sons. In Poitou, a 'so-called Joan who calls herself a maiden' lived near Gilles de Rais, a friend of the Lady of Armoises.

Late recognition

Finally, in 1456, Charles VII initiated yet another rehabilitation process when he declared Joan 'free of any disgrace and without a single flaw'. Since then, fact and fiction have become thoroughly mixed. In the 16th and 17th centuries, historians of the city of Orléans acknowledged the heroic deeds of the Maid in various documents, which were widely circulated. The official chroniclers of Charles VII saw Joan as a tool of God, while the English and Burgundians represented her as a helper of the devil. Joan figured in books dealing with virtuous women, but in the first French history of 1570, the historian Girard du Haillan took the view that she had been the mistress of some of her comrades.

In the first part of his historical drama,

Joan could only write her name; shown here is her signature, from a letter to the citizens of Reims.

Henry VI, William Shakespeare made her the mistress of Charles VII. In the 18th century, the Maid's supposed miracles were scornfully denied.

In the 19th century, a new rumour spread that Joan was the child of Queen Isabeau and Louis of Orléans, the brother of the mad king, Charles VI. The girl was hidden in Domrémy to prepare her for her mission.

The people of France consider Joan their national heroine. Following her beatification in 1909, she received a place in the church calendar as a saint – the patron saint of France – on May 16, 1920.

FLEMISH PAINTING: THE MAGIC OF LIGHT AND COLOUR

During the first half of the 15th century, Flanders was the setting for a revolution in the history of painting. It was at this time that Flemish painters attained the highest degree of perfection in the realistic representation of objects. Their work fundamentally changed the aesthetic values of the time. We have learnt much about the special techniques they developed, but certain things will probably never be known.

In the 15th century, the Dukes of Burgundy were among the greatest patrons of art in Europe. The court of Burgundy employed artists from all parts of the lands ruled by the duchy, including Flanders, which had been a part of Burgundy since 1385. There, in the windswept north, a major artistic change took place which left a permanent mark on painting. How did this pioneering style develop?

An acute gaze

Jan van Eyck (around 1390–1441) is rightly considered to be the father of Flemish painting; some critics even refer to the so-called Eyck Miracle. But other artists, such as the Master of Flémalle (alias Robert Campin), Rogier van der Weyden, Dirk Bouts, Hugo van der Goes and Hans Memling, all made important contributions to the new Flemish school of painting. These artists led the way from the stiff, formalised style of the Gothic era to the more naturalistic style of the Renaissance.

Van Eyck's achievement

It was long asserted that Van Eyck invented painting in oils. Art historians no longer consider this to be the case, but, together with his brother Hubert, Van Eyck did contribute decisively to the development of the technique of oil painting. Because he employed assistants, it has not yet been possible to ascertain the nature of his contribution to certain important works.

The centrepiece of the altarpiece in the Cathedral of St Bravo in Ghent is The Adoration of the Lamb *by Jan van Eyck. Angels surround the lamb, symbol of Jesus Christ, which stands on the altar, while the faithful gather around.*

Wealthy patrons made sure that their protégés lived well and could concentrate entirely on their work. After about 1424, van Eyck worked for Duke Philip the Good of Burgundy (1396–1467), who appointed him both court painter and official artist of the city of Bruges, in what is now Belgium.

What made the achievements of the Flemish painters so important? First of all, they observed everything in the most minute detail: the human body, animals, plants and everyday objects. What we see in their pictures appears within our grasp, and the proportions and detail correspond perfectly. Frequently the artist adopted an elevated perspective to give the viewer a bird's-eye view, and make pictorial space seem endless.

The Flemish painters also broke with medieval traditions in their choice of themes. Generally, medieval artists chose to paint religious scenes, and paid little attention to landscape and background. The Flemish artists discovered the beauty of everyday life, placing people into interior spaces such as living rooms and bedrooms. This marked an important development: artists no longer orientated themselves exclusively towards God, but also focused on their earthly lives. For the first time, the sacred and the secular were combined in harmony.

Bathed in rays of light

Never before had there been paintings of comparable brilliance. The Flemish masters used their colours in the most subtle ways to achieve particular lighting effects: for example, to create the natural interaction of light and shadow.

The artists worked on wooden boards, which they sanded down and then coated with a paste of chalk and gelatinous glue. This priming process added considerably to the brilliance of the colours when they were applied. Charcoal, a sharpened goose quill or the ash of burnt bones were used to make preliminary sketches.

The next stage in the process was to apply the paints, or pigments. Because pigments were expensive and difficult to obtain, they were applied layer by layer. Pigments were made from ground-up minerals and organic substances. The blue used for backgrounds, for example, was made from azurite, while pigments used for the glaze were made from lapis lazuli; because the latter did not cover well, it had to be applied in very thick layers. Copper resinate mixed with malachite yielded green tones, while yellow and white came from salts of lead or tin.

The painters (or their assistants) crushed the pigments to powder and mixed them with certain binding agents, according to their qualities. The Van Eycks experimented for many years until they had developed a durable binder which would dry evenly. To achieve this, they mixed oils of flax, hemp and nuts, to which they added resins. But we do not know the exact recipe. We also don't know how they made the clear varnish used to coat completed paintings. All we know is that it contained natural resins.

There are good reasons for our lack of knowledge. At that time, artists passed their knowledge only to their own pupils. If they did not protect their secrets, imitations would have appeared on the market, robbing the leading workshops of their popularity and originality. More importantly, the unique Flemish traditions were lost as the techniques of Italian painting spread through northern Europe after the middle of the 16th century.

Deep devotion

The appeal of the Flemish style, however, cannot be explained simply through the technical skill of the artists. It is clear that deep religious feeling is also involved. For example, the altarpiece of the Cathedral, of St Bravo, Ghent, known as *The Adoration of the Lamb*, completed by the Van Eycks in 1432, has a complex religious programme. The central panel (shown on page 97) shows a sacrificial lamb – symbolising Christ – on

The Mourning of Christ *by Dirk Bouts tenderly expresses the suffering of Jesus and the grief felt over his death.*

an altar, with its blood flowing into a cup. Angels carrying the instruments of Christ's suffering – the cross, the crown of thorns, the spear and the whip – have gathered around the Saviour, while crowds of the faithful – prophets, martyrs, popes, virgins, pilgrims, knights and hermits – flock from the four corners of the earth.

The natural world, as presented in the Ghent altarpiece, is a product of fantasy, and provides a perspective to survey the whole earth: we can see cities, the ocean, mountains, trees and the sky, and are able to grasp the magnitude of creation.

The message of the Flemish painters is that man can feel accepted by God and live in the awareness of his presence. The people in the paintings have understood this revelation, and radiate inner confidence and serenity. But the many paintings that depict Christ's descent from the cross also testify to deep sadness. In a moving work (shown above), Dirk Bouts shows the Virgin Mary, Mary Magdalene and St John sinking to the ground in pain after the death of Jesus: a young man has died and those close to him are in agony. This tender scene evokes boundless sympathy, and yet it also leaves the viewer with the freedom to admire the beauty of the illustration. The true magic of Flemish painting lies in this arousal of both emotion and admiration.

Analysis of a masterpiece

The double portrait known as *The Arnolfini Wedding*, painted by Jan van Eyck in 1434, ranks as one of the most important works in the history of art.

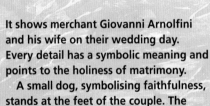

It shows merchant Giovanni Arnolfini and his wife on their wedding day. Every detail has a symbolic meaning and points to the holiness of matrimony.

A small dog, symbolising faithfulness, stands at the feet of the couple. The window opening onto the street symbolises their cosmopolitan attitudes, while the fruit below the window symbolises fertility and the joys of paradise lost. A statuette of St Margaret, patron of expectant mothers, is carved into the backrest of the high armchair. The single burning candle in the six-branched candelabrum can be interpreted as eternal light. On the far wall hangs a convex mirror framed by a ring of ten medallions; the medallions tell the story of Christ's Passion, while the mirror reveals two other people in the room – probably a witness and the painter himself.

QUESTIONS ABOUT COLUMBUS

In 1492, Christopher Columbus's voyage across the Atlantic to the Caribbean forever altered our picture of the world. And yet the fearless seafarer was remarkably vague about himself. There are hundreds of books on Columbus, but even 500 years after the discovery of America, there is no end in sight to the controversy surrounding this enigmatic character.

Christopher Columbus is probably the most famous adventurer of all time – and perhaps the most mysterious. Even to his contemporaries he was a riddle, and was largely responsible for the speculation about his origins. In his autobiographical writings, he always omitted certain aspects of his past. On the other hand, both friends and enemies were only too happy to spread stories and rumours about him. This has made it very difficult for historians to sort out the facts from a mass of hypothesis and speculation. Who was the man who talked Queen Isabella into sending him forth on the great journey?

Off to sea

For a long time, even his exact birthdate was unclear, but it is now generally agreed that Columbus was born near the Italian port of Genoa in 1451, and that he came from a family of weavers. In some documents he appears as Cristófero Colombo, while others use the Spanish form, Cristóbal Colón. Biographers have shown that this is the same person.

Columbus began his adventurous life at the age of 10, when he went to sea. At 15, he is supposed to have served on a privateer (raiding ship) launched by René of Anjou in his fight against King Alfonso V of Aragon and Sicily for the throne of the Kingdom of Naples. The young Columbus was probably involved in the seizure of Spanish ships, which might explain why he later concealed this phase of his youth.

As a young man, Columbus made his way to Portugal. From there, he went to the court of Queen Isabella of Castile and King Ferdinand II of Aragon – their marriage in 1469 had united the two kingdoms – to present his proposal to sail westward. He had contacts with scholars of the time, men who knew that the earth was not a flat disc – as was widely believed during the Middle Ages – and who advised him to travel towards the west.

In August 1492, he was allowed to set sail, and reached the Bahamas, Cuba and Haiti. It was not until his third voyage (1498–1500) that he set foot on the American continent, near the island of Trinidad.

A Genoese-speaking Castilian

But certain things about this remarkable man are unclear. Shortly after Columbus's death, both Spanish and Italian sources claimed him as one of their own citizens. In this context, some researchers mention an interesting point: Columbus almost never spoke or wrote Italian, but chose to use

Christopher Columbus (left) went ashore on the Bahamian island of Guanahani on October 12, 1492. He called it San Salvador.

The Santa Maria, *Columbus's flagship for the first crossing of the Atlantic to the New World.*

Castilian – the dialect of Castile, now accepted as the standard form of European Spanish. In his biography of the explorer, the Spanish historian Salvador de Madariaga claimed that Columbus's family was Jewish, and had fled Spain towards the end of the 14th century because of the persecution of their religion. Within their family they had continued speaking their mother tongue. One question was left unanswered: Why would Columbus return to the country of his supposed forebears just at the time when the Inquisition against the Jews was being ruthlessly implemented? In 1492, the year of Columbus's historic voyage, the Spanish authorities crowned almost a century of persecution by expelling the Jews.

MAPMAKING: KNOWLEDGE AND POWER

The 15th and 16th centuries were a time when increasing geographical knowledge altered Europe's vision of the world. It was a time when mariners set sail on journeys of exploration, making use of advances in ship design, navigation and, above all, mapmaking.

Following the end of Muslim occupation under the Moors during the 13th century, the kingdom of Portugal began a period of expansion. European trade with the East was slackening, mainly because the hostile Ottoman Turks occupied the eastern Mediterranean. It thus became increasingly difficult for Europeans to obtain such highly prized luxury items as sugar, spices and silks. Governments also had an immense hunger for gold, which is why many European rulers devoted all their energies to finding the sea route to Guinea, a gold-rich region of West Africa, and on to India, the gateway to the spice trade. Luck and determination enabled the Portuguese to become the first to obtain reliable knowledge of winds, ocean currents and the southern stars. It was this small but stable country that provided the impulse for the age of exploration, a period of European expansion which would transform the world.

seafarers in order to pass on the new nautical and geographical knowledge. It was here, too, that a new type of ship was developed – the caravel. Smaller, faster and more manoeuvrable than conventional vessels, the caravel would be used for all the major voyages of discovery. At the port of Lagos, to the east of Sagres, Henry established an office for the study of maps.

The new era of exploration was also the beginning of colonisation and the slave trade: along with annual expeditions, Henry supported military campaigns in Morocco and the exploration of West Africa.

Meanwhile. Spain grabbed the Canary Islands off the African coast and established a trading post in Morocco. The Spanish island of Majorca in the Mediterranean became an important centre for sailing and cartography.

Above: *Prince Henry the Navigator promoted Portugal's overseas explorations.*

Right: *Juan de la Cosa, Columbus's companion on two voyages, produced this, the oldest map of the Americas.*

The competition between Spain and Portugal grew more intense during the Castilian War of Succession (1474–1479), but the Treaty of Alcáçovas in 1479 brought peace. Portugal renounced its claim to the throne of Castile, was given the island of Madeira, the Azore Islands, Cape Verde Islands and West Africa south of Morocco's Cape Bojador in exchange. The Canary Islands remained in Spanish hands.

Both states soon recorded new and

Splitting up the world

The influence of kings and princes helped to usher in this new age. The Portuguese prince, Henry the Navigator (1394 – 1460) was a keen supporter of voyages of discovery. Henry invited sailors, astronomers and ship-builders from all corners of the Mediterranean to come to his court. All of them would help him in furthering the systematic exploration of the world. At Sagres, on Portugal's southwestern tip, Prince Henry founded a school for

In 1494, Pope Alexander VI confirmed the rights of Portugal and Spain in the Atlantic. Rivalry between them would not affect the conversion of the native peoples of the Americas.

spectacular successes. Portugal's King John II (1455–1495) was an even more enthusiastic supporter of voyages of exploration than Henry the Navigator. While the Portuguese seafarer Pedro de Covilhão was the first to reach India and discover parts of the East African coast, Christopher Columbus set sail for the Americas under the Spanish flag in 1492. The results of these expeditions once again produced bitter rivalry between Spain and Portugal.

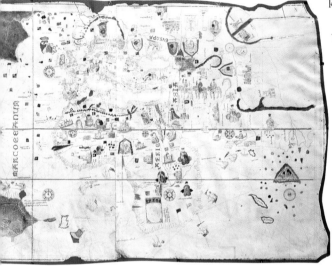

King Ferdinand II of Aragon and Queen Isabella of Castile, who ruled Spain following the union of the crowns in 1469, asked Pope Alexander VI – who happened to be Spanish – to resolve the conflict. The Pope, who was especially keen on Christianising the newly discovered peoples of the New World, produced five bulls (papal decrees) on the subject. In 1494, the adversaries signed the Treaty of Tordesillas, which set out a north-south demarcation line running 370 miles (595 kilometres) west of Cape Verde, on Africa's western tip. West of this line lay the sphere of influence of Spain, and to the east was that of Portugal – with the exception of the Canaries. The line agreed to in the treaty was some distance west of the original papal line, enabling Portugal to hold onto Brazil, which was discovered in 1500.

The exploration of previously unknown regions decisively changed the picture of the world, and the science of cartography flourished for the first time since antiquity. Because maps frequently contained state secrets, rulers kept them under lock and key. Only scraps remain of the resources that were available to discoverers such as Columbus, Bartholomeu Dias (around 1450–1500) and Vasco da Gama (1468/69–1524).

Few people were permitted to know when an expedition of discovery was due to depart. From the end of the 15th century, foreign spies lurked around Portuguese harbours hoping to glean new information, since the other European countries also wanted to secure overseas possessions for themselves. Rival states were prepared to pay large sums for maps and the power and knowledge they contained.

However, their activities were generally in vain. In 1501, for example, the Venetian Pietro Pasqualigo wrote a letter to the civic authorities in Venice complaining that he could not obtain in Portugal a map showing the route to India. It was claimed that King Emmanuel I of Portugal (1469–1521) had ordered the death sentence for any person placing such documents 'at the disposal of strangers'. We know of a later order of secrecy issued by the same king to protect Portugal's pepper monopoly. In November 1504, Emmanuel I prohibited cartographers from illustrating the African coast south of the islands of São Tomé and Príncipe off the coast of Guinea. He also ordered that new geographical illustrations be presented to the royal map office for censorship.

The Cantino map

Nevertheless, the Portuguese *padrão real*, the continuously updated cartographic standard, became known to interests outside Portugal. In 1502, an illegal copy of the map of the world was printed in a large format. The Duke of Ferrara ordered his representative in Lisbon, Albertino Cantino, to obtain the map for commercial purposes. The latter bribed a diplomatic representative of King Emmanuel and smuggled the so-called Cantino map to Italy.

Secrets were hard to keep at that time, for Portuguese cartographers often sold their services to foreigners. Besides, cartographers easily changed from one prince to the next, and it was common practice in all states to recruit these foreign specialists. Bartolomeu Velho, for example, author of a famous world map dating from 1560, worked at the French court before he lost his life under mysterious circumstances.

Many seafaring states resented Spanish and Portuguese control of the seas. They indignantly protested that the Treaty of Tordesillas rested on the assumption that the Iberian states had an inviolable claim to the oceans. They disputed the legal basis of the agreement, claiming that the oceans should be accessible to all. In the end, the Iberians were unable to hold on to their monopoly over the new territories. Finally, the British, Dutch and French broke their monopoly.

Extract from the Cantino map, a pirated copy of the Portuguese standard map of the world.

A star to steer by

The so-called portulan maps that were produced from the 13th century onwards answered the practical needs of a ship's crew. These maps gave detailed illustrations of coastal areas and harbours, and also contained lists of the specialities of certain regions. When compiling this material, cartographers chiefly applied information that they obtained from sailors; they also made use of navigational instruments and made calculations themselves. All of this information was then drawn onto parchment, with a grid added to indicate wind direction.

ASTROLOGERS AND FORTUNE-TELLERS

Some thought they were prophets, others thought them swindlers. Whatever the truth of their predictions, there were plenty of people prepared to believe in them. Astrologers and fortune-tellers became valued royal advisers, and even influenced the course of history. Despite their prominence, mystery still surrounds figures such as Nostradamus.

There is a saying that to rule means to act with foresight. But how is a person to make sense of the future? And who knows what natural forces will upset our plans? During the Middle Ages, princes and kings often turned to the advice of astrologers or fortune-tellers to help them make political decisions. The astrologers, who were often skilled in medicine, pharmacy, physics and alchemy, used prophecies to help the ruler form an opinion.

In the 16th century, the occult sciences were at their peak in Europe. At that time, almost everyone believed in astrology. The church, on the other hand, believed that Christians should trust in God rather than resort to what it considered non-Christian practices. However, many bishops and senior church officials employed astrologers, and often rewarded them generously. Thus, Giovanni de Medici (1475–1521), who later became Pope Leo X, awarded a bishop's diocese to his employee Luca Gaurico, after the latter had predicted that De Medici would be elected Pope.

A gullible queen

One of the most ardent followers of occultism was Catherine de Medici (1519–1589), who reigned over France for three years following the death of her husband King Henry II in 1560. Despite a reputation for political intrigue, she had a tendency to trust every charlatan and con man who happened to come along. One of these was an astrologer by the name of Cosimo

Above inset: *After his medical studies, Michel de Notre-Dame began to call himself Nostradamus.*

Left: *The French royal court at Blois, outside Paris, where Nostradamus was employed after 1555.*

Ruggieri, a power-hungry individual with a shady past. Like Catherine, Ruggieri came from Florence, and soon found favour with the queen. Ruggieri drew up horoscopes for the court, and became known for his talismans and wax figures, which, he claimed, could induce love or lead to death, as required. In 1574, he was imprisoned on charges of conspiring against the young King Charles IX. We shall never be sure of his exact intentions.

Nostradamus: physician and astrologer

The most famous astrologer of this epoch – and one who still fascinates many people today – is without doubt Michel de Notre-Dame (1503–1566), who is widely known under his Latin name of Nostradamus. The descendant of a Jewish family who had converted to the Catholic faith, the young Nostradamus completed his studies at Avignon and Montpellier, where he became a physician. He helped to combat an epidemic in the Languedoc region of southwestern France and was subsequently awarded the titles of doctor and professor. Later, he developed a new concept of hygiene, which enabled him to fight an outbreak of the plague in Aix-en-Provence and Lyon.

Gradually, Nostradamus's interests shifted towards the writing and publishing of selected recipes; he produced a work covering the various ways of using make-up and fragrances, as well as recipes for jams. In the 1550s, Nostradamus turned increasingly towards the occult sciences, and published an almanac containing weather forecasts, horoscopes, remedies and advice on nutrition. It was in this venture that he achieved lasting fame.

The scholar soon came to enjoy a reputation for prophesying the future, and, in 1555, he published the first three of his ten *Centuries*, which contained descriptions of mystical visions. When completed, the *Centuries* contained more than 900 predictions, arranged in sections of 100 verses each. The book met with immediate interest among the French royal family, and King Henry II invited Nostradamus to come to the court, where he was hailed as a visionary. Soon, Catherine de Medici commissioned him to draft horoscopes for her family. The astrologer prophesied that Charles IX, whom he also served as personal physician, would have a long life. However, the monarch died at the age of 24. Nostradamus also prophesied that the Valois family would amass great riches, but this was never fulfilled either.

With a certain amount of good faith, it is possible to find a prediction of the death of Henry II, during a tournament in 1559, in Nostradamus's *Centuries*. Here is the verse:

The young lion will overcome the older one.
In single combat in an arena.
In a golden cage, he shall put out his eyes.
Two wounds in one, and he shall die a horrible death.

The original prophecy is even more obscure than the translation, for this highly educated man used French, Spanish, Latin and Hebrew terms. His writings also made use of his extensive knowledge of Christian and Jewish mysticism, as well as natural philosophy.

What was the reason for the success of the *Centuries*, both in Nostradamus's lifetime and after? We should not forget the turbulent times in which he lived. Two of Catherine de Medici's sons were crowned kings as children: Francis II died one year after his coronation, and thereafter the 10-year-old Charles IX succeeded him on the throne. The frequent changes of ruler, coupled with rivalry between political factions, created an atmosphere of great insecurity in France. This was also the period when the country was torn apart by bitter religious wars between Catholics and Huguenots (French Protestants).

But apart from the wars and politics of the day, it is well known that a heavily symbolic text can be interpreted in many different ways. This may be a reason why the writings of Nostradamus, which were placed on the Vatican's index of prohibited books in 1781, continued to be a source of controversy. Even today, many people are convinced that the scholar had prophetic qualities and correctly foretold many historical events, including the Great Fire of London (1666), the French Revolution (1789) and World War II (1939–1945). His followers maintain that he expressed himself in a deliberately muddled manner, since he feared the attention of the Inquisition – the church courts that worked to suppress heresy – and did not want the public to have ready access to his discoveries.

According to Nostradamus, the end of the world for mankind is definitely not close at hand. He calculated that doomsday will take place in the year 3797.

The alchemist and astrologer John Dee (above) knew how to manipulate Queen Elizabeth I of England (right).

An intelligent swindler

France was not the only state where astrologers influenced royalty. In 16th-century England, an astrologer named John Dee (1527–1608) wielded considerable political influence for almost 44 years as part of the circle of advisers surrounding Queen Elizabeth I (1533–1603). Dee was very well read, had travelled the world as a seafarer and had acquired esoteric knowledge as an alchemist and magician. He is supposed to have been the inspiration for the character of Prospero in Shakespeare's drama *The Tempest*.

When Elizabeth was still just a child, Dee had apparently prophesied that she would be monarch one day. Later on, he gave Elizabeth support when important decisions had to be made, and was frequently able to manipulate her in a very subtle way. He announced the death of Mary Stuart (1542–1587), better known to us today as Mary, Queen of Scots, as a means of encouraging Elizabeth to execute her rival. For his advice, Dee won truly royal rewards, and soon amassed immense wealth. Finally, he became too powerful, and his opponents accused him of fraud. He died penniless and forgotten.

Apocalyptic visions

The prophecies of Nostradamus consist of 900 enigmatic four-line verses. Over the centuries, they have been translated into many languages, and subjected to different interpretations. Literally hundreds of books have been written about Nostradamus. For the most part, his texts contain dark and pessimistic visions of natural catastrophes, murders, revolutions and wars. However, scholars point out that Nostradamus drew on a Christian tradition beginning with the Apocalypse of John, the last book of the New Testament – also known as Revelation – which prepared believers for the horrific events that would precede the return of Christ.

An edition of the Centuries *from the year 1589. These mysterious volumes continue to fascinate many people.*

KING SEBASTIAN OF PORTUGAL AND HIS DOUBLES

Deluded by dreams of knightly glory, he led his army and much of Portugal's nobility to disaster in Morocco. And yet, many Portuguese refused to believe that the young King Sebastian had perished under the pitiless Moroccan sun. While Portugal endured decades of Spanish rule, numerous false Sebastians made their appearance.

As recently as the 19th century, the people of Portugal still mourned the death of King Sebastian I, who fell in battle in 1578 at the age of 24. His memory was kept alive in novels, poems, songs and legends. The cult that surrounded the fallen monarch expressed the hope that, one day, he would return as a hero and lead his country to new glory.

During his lifetime, however, Sebastian was not particularly liked by his subjects. Why then did he become a national myth?

Portrait of Sebastian I (1565)

Shattering defeat

Sebastian was born in January 1554, only a few days after the death of his 16-year-old father, the youngest of King John III's ten children. Since all his uncles had died young, the succession to the throne fell to the young Sebastian. He was brought up by the Jesuits, the austere religious order founded in 1534 by Ignatius Loyola to defend the Catholic faith, and his youth was dominated by asceticism and military drill.

In 1571, the Christian states of Europe, led by Spain's King Philip II, won an important naval victory over the Ottoman Turks at the Battle of Lepanto. The battle inspired the deeply religious King Sebastian, who was also fond of tales of knighthood. These stories of quests and knightly honour were very popular in 16th-century Europe. Like many of the heroes of the novels, the king dreamt of leading a crusade. He got his chance in 1574, when he led his troops on an unsuccessful campaign in Morocco.

Four years later, Sebastian set sail for Morocco once again, this time at the head of a force of 20,000 men, including all the adult noblemen of Portugal. On August 4, his troops suffered a crushing defeat in the battle of Ksar-el-Kebir. The Moroccan armies captured about 10,000 Portuguese soldiers; only a couple of hundred horsemen escaped. The fate of the king was unknown.

Sebastian's uncle Henry took charge of the government. But in 1580 he too died, and King Philip II (1527–1598) then occupied Portugal, which became a province of Spain.

Will he return?

Even though it was assumed that Sebastian had died in the battle, rumours soon spread that he was still alive. The rumours were greeted with excitement, for his return would have brought an end to Spanish rule. In 1584, a man appeared who claimed to be the king. He declared that he had done six years of penance to redeem the shame of defeat. After being identified as the son of a potter, he was sentenced to forced labour.

The next false Sebastian was a hermit from Ericeira, who gathered an 800-man 'army', around him. Philip II's investigators questioned the hermit, but when the latter had two of the commissioners murdered by his followers, justice was swift and ruthless: the rabble-rouser and 200 of his followers were themselves executed.

In 1598, another swindler appeared, this time in Venice. His claim was weak, however, mainly because he could not speak Portuguese. The Spanish ambassador had him arrested, and it was soon established that the imposter came from Calabria, in southern Italy. He too was put to death.

In later years, people claiming to be Sebastian popped up again and again. Even after Portugal regained its independence in 1640, the cult of the lost king did not come to an end. Although he had brought Portugal to the brink of ruin, the young monarch lived on in the consciousness of the people. Sebastian embodied the glory of a bygone era when his country had ruled the oceans of the world and stood up to the might of Spain.

A contemporary view of the battle of Ksar-el-Kebir, in which the Portuguese armies suffered devastating losses.

WHO WAS WILLIAM SHAKESPEARE?

Shakespeare's plays are among the finest literary achievements of all time. Audiences around the world are still fascinated by these timeless tales of love, revenge, war and madness. But is it possible that other authors wrote the plays?

During William Shakespeare's lifetime (1564–1616), nobody dreamed of suggesting that the Bard of Stratford-upon-Avon did not himself write the plays that his theatre company performed to such acclaim. But from the 18th century onwards, doubts arose about the authenticity of his writings. The controversy lasted for years: in 1903, the American novelist Henry James (1843–1916) remarked 'I am convinced to the point of obsession that the Godly William is the biggest and most successful swindler who has ever played games with the world's patience'. Other respected writers, politicians and scientists shared this scepticism.

The Anti-Stratfordians

If we disregard a few, very obscure early statements, a certain William Henry Smith was the first person to attempt to prove that the tragedies, including *Hamlet*, were in fact the work of the philosopher and politician Francis Bacon (1561–1626). Smith provided support for his startling theory by drawing statistical parallels between the works of both authors. Many people supported Smith; a certain Mrs Henry Pott claimed to have discovered no less than 4,400 similarities between the works of Bacon and the plays of Shakespeare. However, most of these similarities consisted of mundane expressions like 'good morning', 'I assure you' and 'amen' – commonplace phrases that were probably used frequently by every writer of the period.

Were the great English plays of the 16th and early 17th centuries the work of William Shakespeare (above)? Some claimed that Francis Bacon (left) was the actual author, while others believed it was Christopher Marlowe (right).

The Anti-Stratfordians – the term for the opponents of the otherwise highly respected man of the theatre, in reference to his birthplace – formed a sizeable group, and over the years, almost 60 'genuine' Shakespeares have been proposed. As well as Francis Bacon, another noble candidate suggested as a plausible author for the plays was Edward de Vere, Earl of Oxford. The most prominent advocate of this thesis was

the founder of psychoanalysis, Sigmund Freud (1856–1939), who interpreted some of Shakespeare's dramas psychonanalytically and changed their dates in such a way that they corresponded to events in the Earl of Oxford's life.

A much more plausible candidate was Christopher Marlowe (1564–1593), since he had been the most famous British playwright before Shakespeare, and his dramas, among them *Edward II* and *The Jew of Malta*, had been well received by his contemporaries. Marlowe had died in a tavern brawl the night before he was to be arrested on charges of atheism. These unusual circumstances led Canadian journalist Calvin Hoffmann to suspect that Marlowe's death had in fact been staged. This allowed the playwright to escape execution and go into exile; he kept on writing – but under the name of Shakespeare – and secretly sent his plays home for performance.

Most of the Anti-Stratfordians saw Shakespeare's function primarily as providing an alias for others: either colleagues from the theatre who were persecuted because of their political convictions, or noblemen who did not wish to be associated with common actors.

Sketchy evidence

Shakespeare's critics also maintained that only a well-travelled and highly educated aristocrat could have produced works of such overwhelming genius. They ignored evidence of the dramatist's outstanding education and took advantage of the lack of documents, engaging in wild speculation.

Very few documents have been preserved that might allow us to reconstruct the dates of Shakespeare's life: a birth register in the church of Stratford mentions a baptism on April 26, 1564; there are documents for the purchase of houses and pieces of land, some notes on legal disputes, as well as a three-page will signed by Shakespeare himself. Strangely, his will contains no mention of his 38 dramas. While this may seem unusual, there were no copyright laws in force at the time. Even though common law did protect intellectual property, Shakespeare may have wanted to keep quiet about his achievements.

First publications

The controversy over authorship should come as no surprise, since none of Shakespeare's original manuscripts has survived. Furthermore, his 16th-century contemporaries held a very different view of the dramatic art than do critics today. In those days, the drama was considered an inferior form of literature to the lyric and epic forms. No dramatic artist would have presumed to present such texts before an

Title page of the Folio edition of 1623, in which some of Shakespeare's dramas were first published. At that time, plays were rarely published, since they were considered inferior literary works.

educated and prosperous readership under his own name. This also applies to the Stratfordian, even though he soon enjoyed high esteem in London. His contemporary, Francis Meres, wrote of the impact of Shakespeare on the theatre of his time: 'If the muses used the English language, they would use the polished style of the amiable Shakespeare'.

London publishers showed an early interest in his dramas, and printed versions of some of the plays, although these are based on incomplete or incorrect documents. The carefully compiled, so-called Folio version was only published posthumously in 1623. It contained a total of 36 works, of which 18 – *Julius Caesar* and *Macbeth* among them – appeared in print for the first time. The publication was sponsored by John Heminges and Henry Condells, two actors who had worked with Shakespeare. In the dedication and the foreword of the collection, they lamented that the author was not able to supervise the printing – further compelling evidence concerning the origin of the texts!

Adaptations of well-known tales

Last but not least, the sources used by Shakespeare gave rise to speculation that he had merely copied the work of others. But nearly all the dramatists of the time preferred to use the same prototypes. For example, the tragedy *Romeo and Juliet* is based on a 15th-century drama by Masuccio de Salerno, which was brought to England by the poet Arthur Brooke. He published a 3,000-verse poem on the unhappy couple of Verona.

Nor did Shakespeare invent the legend of Hamlet. This was a traditional Scandinavian narrative, recorded by the Danish historian Saxo Grammaticus in the 12th century. Gradually, these narratives were worked into a series of literary texts, which Shakespeare probably knew well. A tragedy of later origin, entitled *Gorboduc*, which provided the prototype for *King Lear*, dates from 1562.

Does this mean that Shakespeare was not original? Not at all. Like other writers, he borrowed plots and general themes – love, death, intrigue, greed and madness – but his achievement lay in the development of complex characters and the presentation of universal conflicts. This is why audiences are still spellbound by the power of his dramas.

London, here I come

In 1588, Shakespeare left his family in Stratford-upon-Avon for the lure of London. As a gifted actor, the author of popular dramas and a partner in the acting company, The Lord Chamberlain's Men, he soon won success in the English capital. After the death of Queen Elizabeth I (1533–1603), King James I (1566–1625) took over the patronage of the troupe, which changed its name to The King's Men. The company owned the Globe Theatre on the south bank of the Thames River – now rebuilt exactly as it was – but after a fire destroyed the building, performances moved to the covered Blackfriars Theatre. The actors also performed at court and toured the provinces.

In public theatres like the circular Old Swan in London, plays were performed under the open sky.

THE ORDER OF THE ROSY CROSS

There must be few influential societies that started out as an elaborate prank. Few Europeans suspected this was the case when the manifestoes of the Order of the Rosicrucians were published during the 17th century. But the appeal of the Rosy Cross was so great that the brotherhood spread from Germany throughout Europe and is still alive today.

Christian Rosenkreuz is said to have founded the brotherhood which bears his name.

The story of the Rosicrucians began in the German city of Kassel in the year 1614, with the publication of an anonymous document entitled the *Fama fraternitatis* (Testimony of the Brotherhood). This was followed a year later by a second document, the *Confessio fraternitatis* (Confessions of the Brotherhood), and, in 1616, by a third, *The chymical wedding of Christianus Rosenkreuz*. These three documents set forth the history, statutes and programme of a previously unknown brotherhood, known as 'the laudable order of the Rosicrucians'. In a time of great political and religious turmoil, these documents praised the significance of spirituality, which could save man from the errors of his earthly ways. The texts reached an unexpectedly large readership and were published in several countries. The whole of Europe became enthusiastic about the figure at the centre of the new teachings, a figure steeped in legend: Christian Rosenkreuz.

The legend of C.R.

The *Fama fraternitatis* states that Christian Rosenkreuz – at first known only by the initials C.R. – was born in 1378 on the banks of the Rhine River, the son of a poor but noble family. At the age of four he was given into the care of an abbey, where he learnt Greek, Latin, Hebrew and magic. At the age of 16, he was entrusted to a brother who took him on a pilgrimage to the Holy Land. But his companion died in Cyprus, and

Rosenkreuz continued his journey alone, until illness forced him to remain for a time in Arabia. There he was healed by wise men, received extensive instruction in ancient wisdom, and was introduced to the secret sciences. He was then entrusted with the mission of conveying this knowledge to the Christian world in Western Europe and of establishing a secret community, which 'possesses enough of gold and precious stones, and shall educate the monarchs'.

With God's help, faith and science are combined in wisdom, symbolised here as a winged being.

Rosenkreuz returned to Europe and spent five years in Spain. There, he attracted three companions who swore allegiance to him and, under his guidance, wrote the basic documents of the brotherhood. At a secret location, the four men founded the 'New Temple of the Holy Spirit', in which they healed the sick and comforted the forlorn. Rosenkreuz gradually built up the brotherhood which bore his name and conducted missionary work. Once a year, the brotherhood met in the Temple of the Holy Spirit.

In order to keep the number of its members constant, each Rosicrucian was supposed to nominate one successor prior to his death, if possible. The founder himself is said to have died in 1484, at the age of 106. His grave was discovered in 1604, 120 years after his death – just as he himself had predicted.

The far-fetched story of C.R. sounds as if it was intended to symbolise other, deeper things. Fortunately, the records give us an insight into the ideas of the brotherhood.

The *Fama fraternitatis* consists of three sections. The first one deals critically and, in part, satirically with the social and spiritual conditions of the time. It provides numerous suggestions to solve all problems in the areas of religion, art and science. The document claims that redemption can only occur through a religion of the heart and mystical enthusiasm. The second part of the *Fama fraternitatis* opposes alchemy, that 'atheistic and accursed' business that strives to make gold out of base metals. The third section contains the life of C.R.

The mystery of the creation of the world is discussed in the *Confessio fraternitatis*. In this document, the Pope is called a serpent and an Antichrist. We also learn that the brotherhood uses a secret code, attributes great importance to astrology and rejects the Ptolemaic picture of the world – which places the earth in the centre of the solar system. It is at this point that the complete name of Christian Rosenkreuz is revealed.

French philosopher René Descartes dedicated his work to the Rosicrucians.

The last text, *The chymical wedding*, was published in Kassel and the French city of Strasbourg. In sentences filled with symbolism, it tells of a decisive episode in the life of Christian Rosenkreuz – an experience of enlightenment lasting seven days, which took place when he was 81 years old. During this episode, the hermit went through a succession of revelations and tests which formed the foundation of his spiritual experiences.

Early best sellers

At any other time, these three books would probably have been regarded as little more than interesting, if unusual, reading. But this was not the case. In a Europe torn apart by religious wars between Catholics and Protestants, the contents of the Rosicrucian manifestoes fell on fruitful ground. The manifestoes circulated rapidly, and the ideas of the brotherhood were soon widely known.

There were several reasons for this great success. Many people were attracted to the personality of Christian Rosenkreuz and to the independence of his thought. Also, progressive-minded Europeans embraced the goals and statements of the brotherhood. For when it came to accepting new members, the Rosicrucians did not discriminate on the basis of race, sex or social status. Instead, they felt that intelligent people throughout the world should come together to improve the fate of mankind and to gain knowledge of God and nature.

These aims of the order corresponded to the social, spiritual and intellectual goals of Europe's new literary and scientific elite. As a result, many of the most important intellects of the time asked to be accepted into the brotherhood. The best-known followers – or at least sympathisers – of the Rosicrucians were the English mathematician, physicist and astronomer Sir Isaac Newton (1643–1727), the French

The Dutch philosopher Spinoza is also said to have belonged to the brotherhood.

natural scientist and philosopher René Descartes (1596–1650) as well as the Dutch philosopher Benedict (Baruch) Spinoza (1632–1677).

Surprising exposure

After the documents became known and the brotherhood had been established, the Rosicrucians became an important topic of debate, inspiring a veritable avalanche of publications. By 1717, no less than 1,000 commentaries, theses, notes and pamphlets – by more than 400 authors – had been published.

Among the multitude of documents, just one supplied the key to the formation of the Rosicrucians. In a document published in 1617, the publisher of the third manifesto revealed his identity to be Johann Valentin

This 18th-century etching shows the most important symbols of the rosy cross: the heart and cross flanked by the flower from the fertile plains of Sharon and the lily of the valley; the swan and the Phoenix; the star with the symbols of the metals in its points; the vessel containing heavenly dew; and the all-knowing eye of God.

Andreae (1586–1654) a Protestant priest from Württemberg in southern Germany. Andreae was born into the family of a well-known pastor, and became one of the most highly educated men of his time. Having won mastery of ancient and modern languages, geography, history, genealogy, mathematics and theology, Andreae was an extremely cultured man. He claimed that he had written *The chymical wedding of Christianus Rosenkreuz*. Indeed, everything indicated that the first two texts had in fact come from his pen. It appeared that they had been written by Andreae, with the aid of two friends, Christoph Besold and Arndt Gerhardt. In such violent times, the authors probably wished to be anonymous for their safety.

In the 17th century, Johann Valentin Andreae laid the foundation for the Rosicrucians.

Under the sign of the cross and roses

The cross and the rose are symbols with double meanings. The cross, on the one hand, symbolises Christ's Passion and invokes death. The rose, however, symbolises beauty and life, but also represents the transience of all earthly things, while the cross symbolises life eternal. In this sense, the Rosy Cross – which combines both symbols – can be regarded as a symbol of the union of life on earth and life eternal.

Andreae, who was deeply impressed by the teachings of Martin Luther – leader of the Protestant Reformation – also designed the Rosy Cross, the symbol of the Rosicrucians. Based on Luther's coat of arms, it consisted of the X-shaped cross of St Andrew, framed by four roses.

Just a prank

But Andreae did not simply present himself to the public as an author. In a book entitled *Menippus*, he also divulged that *The chymical wedding of Christianus Rosenkreuz* had been nothing more than a *ludibrium*, a Latin word for a prank, with which he had wished to provide an entertaining and exciting impetus for social reform. In other words, the invention of the Rosy Cross had, in fact, only been a kind of intellectual joke.

But the actual impact of his books was quite different from what he had intended. It seemed that this impetuous young man had unintentionally brought a powerful spiritual movement into being, one which rapidly developed a life of its own and could no longer be stopped by him. While the first brotherhoods formed during the 17th century were mostly loose associations without firm rules and regulations, the communities that evolved from them were much better organised. By the 18th century, increasing numbers of groups were formed which constituted themselves under the symbol of the Rosy Cross.

The best-known Society of Rosicrucians remains to this day the Brotherhood of the Order of the Golden and Rosicrucians, founded in 1710 by Samuel Richter of Silesia (now part of Poland). This secret society had a hierarchically structured social order and was governed by a board. Before being admitted as members, candidates had to subject themselves to certain specified rites of admission. The members of this order wore certain items of jewellery and revealed their identities to each other through words, signs and handshakes. Soon, the rituals of the Rosicrucians came to resemble another secretive fraternal order – the Freemasons, which grew out of the activities and rituals of

medieval stonemasons. Other well-known societies associated with the ideals of the Rosy Cross were the Illuminati of Avignon in the south of France, which was formed in 1716, and the Illuminati of Bavaria, in southern Germany, founded two years later.

Modern groupings

Towards the end of the 19th century, the Rosicrucian movement underwent a revival. In 1888, the French lawyer and poet Stanislas de Guaïta (1861–1897), an ardent follower of occultism, founded a Rosicrucian brotherhood in France together with the novelist Joséphin Péladan (1859–1918). Soon after, however, Péladan left the brotherhood complaining that its outlook was too anti-Catholic for his taste. He founded a new organisation, also under the name of the Rosicrucians, that was to be dedicated to brotherly love, intellectual activity and the arts. Péladan opened a Rosicrucian salon in an art gallery in Paris, and this developed into a popular and influential meeting place, particularly for people associated with the arts.

Rosicrucian orders were also founded in the 20th century; for example, the esoteric society AMORC (Ancient Mystical Order of the Rosy Cross) was established in 1915 in California. Today, this society has branches in more than 50 countries.

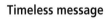

In the late 1800s, lawyer Stanislas de Guaïta founded a Rosicrucian brotherhood.

Timeless message

Even now, more than three centuries after the first manifesto of the Rosicrucians appeared, the teachings of the movement are still surprisingly vibrant. This is particularly astonishing if we consider that this was not the intention of its founder. But even if the *Fama fraternitas*, the *Confessio fraternitas* and *The chymical wedding of Christianus Rosenkreuz* were intended as an intellectual joke, they also convey the restless and curious spirit of their time. The Rosicrucians' message of brotherly love, of striving for knowledge and cooperation between people, is timeless and, even today, appeals to countless individuals.

THE BROTHERHOOD OF THE FREEMASONS

Kings and governments have often tried to ban the free-thinking brotherhoods of the Freemasons. But this secretive organisation, dedicated to improving society and promoting tolerance, has always fascinated ordinary people. The secret rites and traditions of the Masons recall the activities of the master builders of the Middle Ages, but their origins lie far back in the mists of antiquity.

Freemasonry exists throughout the world, but not many people understand its nature or its fascinating origins. The term 'Freemasonry' describes a network of free-thinking male societies which embrace brotherhood, friendship and tolerance. The goal of these communities is to improve society, so that humankind can become a single people composed of true brothers. Each Freemason, usually known as a Mason, must first set himself these goals and must prove his love of man through charity and unselfish endeavour.

The rituals followed by the Masonic brotherhood, and which the members are supposed to keep secret, seem at first to contradict the goals of Freemasonry. Some of the rites appear macabre, but they are actually highly symbolic. An individual who is accepted into the community of the Freemasons must symbolically die and lie in a coffin before being deemed worthy of membership. This procedure is intended to make it clear to the candidate that he has left his old life behind and has now become a different person.

Symbols play a major role in the rituals of the Freemasons. The main symbols are an apron and a trowel, as well as a protractor and compass – all of them tools that are used by stone-masons. All these symbols point to the origins of the brotherhood. As a matter of fact, for a long time the emphasis of the societies really was on masonry

(building in stone), until gradually they turned towards other, humanist goals. Still, the followers of the movement regard the activities of modern Freemasonry – which are called speculative – as a kind of spiritual construction work, where symbolic and class traditions are complemented by ethical and religious ideals.

The sacred art of the masons

The link between architecture and religion dates back to the dawn of urban life. In ancient times, most constructions completed by master builders were intended to honour the gods. The first religious communities dedicated to architecture were found in the area that today is Syria, and later in the Roman empire. In 960 BC, Hiram, the ruler of the Phoenician port of Tyre in the Mediterranean – who was later known as the father of the Freemasons – sent experienced workers to King Solomon, who ruled Israel and Judea, to assist him in the construction of the Temple and palace in Jerusalem.

Some 200 years later, around 710 BC, the second king of the early Roman era, Numa Pompilius, who was allegedly a student of the Greek philosopher Pythagoras (around 580–500 BC), was supposed to have brought the various architectural bodies of the day together

A stained-glass window from the Cathedral of Bourges in France shows medieval masons at work.

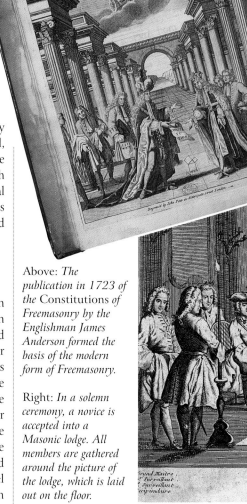

Above: *The publication in 1723 of the* Constitutions *of Freemasonry by the Englishman James Anderson formed the basis of the modern form of Freemasonry.*

Right: *In a solemn ceremony, a novice is accepted into a Masonic lodge. All members are gathered around the picture of the lodge, which is laid out on the floor.*

into so-called colleges. As members, these colleges accepted all master builders who specialised in the construction of religious buildings, as well as civil and military structures, such as dockyards and aqueducts. In the communities of the Roman world, religious and professional matters were very closely linked, and the relationship grew to such an extent that the master builders developed special cults of class based on the pursuit of their trade.

As the Roman world expanded, so did these professional associations, until the year 313, when emperor Constantine declared Christianity the new state religion. As the

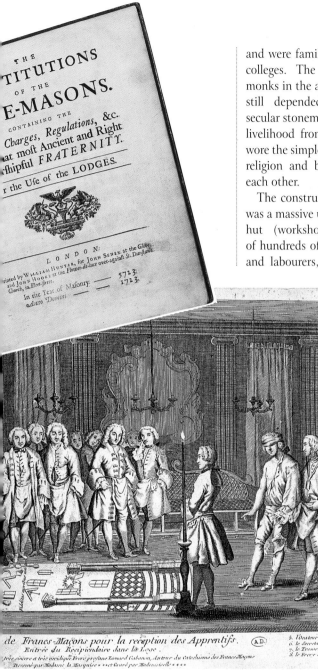

and were familiar with the traditions of the colleges. The master builders instructed monks in the art of building. But the monks still depended on the support of the secular stonemasons who, in turn, drew their livelihood from the monasteries and often wore the simple habit of a monk. Once again, religion and building were closely tied to each other.

The construction of a medieval cathedral was a massive undertaking, and a typical site hut (workshop complex) might consist of hundreds of craftsmen – not just masons and labourers, but also sculptors, painters and glass-stainers – all under a master builder. Brotherhoods gradually emerged from the groups of master builders, whose members used signs and gestures to protect their professional secrets from outsiders. These masonic groups soon came to enjoy certain privileges, which freed them from many of the restrictions of the guild system. For this reason, they came to be known as free craftsmen or, more specifically, free masons.

But when practising their profession, the craftsmen were not free. The church exerted its influence in the construction of all religious buildings – from the initial planning stage all the way through to the actual placing of the stones. The masons had to adhere to all the prescribed deadlines, sizes and specifications regarding the proportions of the building, and every little detail of ornament had to be arranged according to specific mystical numerical relationships and special geometric rules. These rules had deeper symbolic meanings that were known only to initiates.

For this reason, the medieval freemasons felt that their work consisted of more than just placing stone upon stone. They also regarded themselves as workers on the construction site of the universe, where each individual had to play his own part in contributing to the perfection of the whole. This construction exceeded all human dimensions, and they saw their labours as never-ending – with no beginning or end – but proceeding according to a single plan and leading to an illustrious work, the ideal and perfect House of God. Here lies the origin of the tradition of dedicating the work to the glory of the 'Great Builder of all worlds'.

Around the middle of the 17th century, a change took place within the freemasons. The brotherhoods began to accept influential

members of the colleges did not want to oppose the emperor, they let themselves be baptised, but retained their old customs.

The site huts of the cathedrals

The Christianised master builders left few constructions dating from before the 7th century. But as Europe emerged from the Dark Ages following the fall of the Western Roman empire, it became clear that a new religious architecture was triumphantly taking shape. The clergy was intent on building churches, and they appealed to those craftsmen who still knew the old trades

The lodges

The term 'lodge' designates both a physical place where Freemasons gather and the association itself. The term originally described the site hut of the medieval builders and stonemasons, which served as both workshop and meeting place. Each lodge is chartered by a grand lodge.

In this sketch by the Flemish master Jan van Eyck, St Barbara is kept prisoner in the tower of a Gothic church, to which the site hut is directly connected.

patron members, whose lives had nothing to do with the building trade, but whose interests were of a purely speculative nature – that is, their goal was knowledge and enlightenment, for this was also a great time of scientific discovery. The number of these individuals gradually increased until they finally exceeded the numbers of working masons. Traditional freemasonry was in decline, because Europe's long and savage religious wars had virtually put an end to church-building activities. However, the institution did not disappear, for the ideals of the master builders were now replaced by the new humanist ideals of the Renaissance, enriched with influences from alchemy and the world of medieval knighthood.

It was in England especially that the modern form of Freemasonry, generally referred to as speculative freemasonry, was established and organised. On June 24, 1717

The influential French diplomat Charles Maurice de Talleyrand (1754–1838) was a Mason, as was George Washington and Wolfgang Amadeus Mozart.

The symbols of Freemasonry, including dividers and a temple, are depicted on this 18th-century Grand Master's apron.

– St John the Baptist's Day – four London lodges joined together and founded a unified organisation under the designation Grand Lodge of London. They selected a single Grand Master to whom all other members answered. These newly formed lodges were no longer orientated along the lines of ranks. Their goal was exclusively to serve and to develop spiritual values. The actual trade of the medieval stonemasons held only a symbolic character for them.

In 1723, Masonic practices were formally codified with the appearance of the *Constitutions*, published by James Anderson, an English clergyman. Based on traditional concepts, the code stated the duties of a Mason, including the recognition of the 'great master builder of all worlds'. The rules still apply in principle today.

After the publication of the *Constitutions*, the brotherhood entered a period of popularity and was regarded as a very prestigious body. The honourable, intellectually demanding character of Freemasonry made it very attractive to men of various social classes. Members of the upper classes in particular considered it socially desirable to be a member of the brotherhood.

Freemasonry and revolution

Within a couple of years British speculative freemasonry spread to many countries, and its ideas were well received even in France – the two countries were often at war during the 18th century. The first French lodge based on the British model is said to have been established in Dunkirk as early as the 1720s, and in 1736 the first French Grand Lodge was founded. It was not long before Freemasonry penetrated the nobility, the

army, parliament, the clergy, the middle class, writers and artistic circles, as well as the legal profession. Before the French Revolution in 1789, no less than 154 lodges were active in Paris and 322 in the provinces.

But the French Revolution was destined to set Freemasonry back, for many of its members ended their lives on the guillotine. It is doubtful that the Masons influenced the revolution, as has been suggested, for in principle Freemasonry does not follow any political or social goals, but regards itself as a means for the spreading and realisation of liberal thought. In some countries, however, support for Masonic ideals was frowned upon by the authorities, who feared the influence that the doctrine of free thought would have on their citizens. For decades, Catholics were prohibited from belonging to Masonic lodges. However, the ban was lifted in 1983.

In North America, the first Masonic lodges were established in Philadelphia in 1730, and in Boston in 1733. Freemasonry also spread into the German-speaking countries. In 1735, the first lodge was established in Hamburg, and others soon followed in the rest of Germany. In Austria, Freemasonry was established in 1742 and in Switzerland in 1736, with the first lodge being founded in Geneva.

Nowadays, there are two groups of advanced Freemasonry: under the York rite, a Mason can advance through 12 degrees; the Scottish rite consists of 30 degrees. Of the almost five million Masons in the world today, more than three million live in the United States, where the brotherhood has spawned such offshoots as the Shriners.

From apprentice to master

Among the master builders of the Middle Ages, there was a strict hierarchy, which ran from the apprentice to the journeyman to the master. The speculative freemasons retained this classification in their so-called degrees: Freemasons also start out as apprentices and then rise by degrees to the status of journeyman and master. The leader of a lodge is elected by all lodge members and bears the title Lodge Master or Master of the Chair.

THE REMARKABLE CAREER OF COUNT CAGLIOSTRO

He arrived from the East, and boasted of his knowledge as an alchemist, clairvoyant and healer. Within a few months, Count Cagliostro was the toast of France, celebrated as much for his medical skills as for his ability to see into the future. It was many years before his rich and powerful clients realised what a clever scoundrel he really was. But this Italian did in fact possess many talents. And he made some influential friends ....

With his stocky figure and full cheeks, the appearance of the master contradicted his claim that he led a simple life.

At the end of 1779, a remarkable man arrived in the city of Strasbourg in eastern France. He announced that he was an Italian nobleman, Alessandro, Count of Cagliostro, and claimed to have recently returned from Russia, where he had allegedly treated the son of Empress Catherine II. The citizens of Strasbourg were awed to have

Perhaps the mysterious stranger was just lucky, but his talents achieved immediate success in healing the illnesses and complaints of a number of famous people. First, he

helped the childless wife of a banker to fall pregnant at last, then he cured the chronic asthma of the politically influential cardinal and Prince-Bishop of Strasbourg, Louis René Édouard de Rohan (1734–1803). As a result of his achievements in Strasbourg, Cagliostro's reputation soon reached the royal court at Versailles.

A 300-year-old wonder

According to the descriptions of witnesses of the time, Cagliostro was quite short and rather fat, even though he pretended never to eat anything. He dressed simply, but his manners were not exactly modest. He loudly proclaimed his talents, which, according to his boasts, were not just limited to medicine.

He boasted how his knowledge of alchemy enabled him to produce gold and jewels, and how, as a magician, he had found the secret of eternal youth. Many people were quite ready to believe him when he claimed

such a famous doctor in their city. And the Count's methods certainly suggested the skills of a physician: he prescribed laxative herbal teas, turpentine pills, elixirs and Egyptian wines. Not only that, but the master also held spiritualist sessions, where he practised the laying-on of hands and led prayers to God and the angels.

Above: French society ladies question Cagliostro about how to win the royal lottery. He often boasted that he knew the correct answers.

Right: In order to find out about events in the future, Cagliostro put children or young women into a hypnotic trance.

that, by performing a ritual known only to himself, he had attained the remarkable age of 300 years. This truly multi-talented individual also claimed to be a clairvoyant;

he declared that he had predicted the winning numbers of a lottery in London several times. In Strasbourg, he hypnotised children or young women, whom he called doves. By making use of these talents he had learned, among other things, the date of the death of the Empress Maria Theresa of Austria (1717–1780) and the birthdate of the heir to the French throne.

Jeanne de Valois hatched the necklace affair.

Cagliostro's name was widely known within a few months of his arrival in France. The fees he charged for his various services earned him a lot of money. After short stays in the cities of Lyon and Bordeaux, he settled in Paris in 1785. Cagliostro enjoyed financial support from Cardinal de Rohan, who was grateful for having his respiratory problems cured. All the great men of the time – noblemen, politicians, intellectuals – as well as large numbers of society women, wanted to see the divinely gifted Italian.

Cagliostro's recipe for eternal youth

For all those who dreamed of eternal youth, the Count recommended the following treatment:

The treatment should begin on a full moon in May and last for 40 days. For the first 16 days, the patient must live on light soups and biscuits. On the 17th day, he would be bled and be administered 11 white drops. A further blood-letting was due on day 32. Then, the patient was to be administered a universal medicine, in order to induce a deep sleep. Soon, hair on the body and head would grow back, as would the teeth. After a series of aromatic baths and the administration of various beauty drops, the patient could return home completely restored. This process had to be repeated every 50 years.

A disastrous miscalculation

Cagliostro knew how to make himself look and sound impressive. He frequently used Arabic words without bothering to translate them, and – like a king – always spoke of himself in the third person as 'we'. But anyone who makes himself into a cult figure inevitably arouses strong emotions. In Paris, Cagliostro gathered a crowd of admirers around him, but also provoked criticism, envy and aversion.

The Italian's enemies were delighted during the winter of 1785–1786, when the so-called necklace affair became public. Together with Cagliostro and other accomplices, the Countess Jeanne de Valois had spread a rumour that Queen Marie-Antoinette (1755–1793), wife of King Louis XVI, whom she detested, had had an affair with Cardinal de Rohan in order to obtain a diamond necklace. When the plot was exposed and those involved put on trial, only the cardinal was acquitted; the Countess de Valois was sent to prison. But what was really thrilling about the trial was that, finally, the general public learned the true identity of Cagliostro.

Alias Guiseppe Balsamo

After Cagliostro's arrival, rumours about his origin spread wildly. Some said he was the son of a Jew from Portugal, who had made a fortune in Brazil. Others regarded him as the descendant of a Neapolitan wig-maker; still others told the story of how he had been educated by a priest in the passages of an Egyptian pyramid. And yet others saw in him an illegitimate descendant of King Louis XV (1710–1774). Cagliostro himself insisted he did not come from any time or place at all.

In the wake of the necklace affair, the police investigation yielded the following: the 300-year-old count was actually Giuseppe Balsamo, and had been born on June 8, 1743, the son of a tradesman in Palermo, on the island of Sicily. He had been sent to a Franciscan monastery for his education, but the monks had expelled him for bad behaviour.

Lorenza Feliciani was the count's partner in crime.

As a young man, Balsamo had forged copies of famous works of art and sold them in several Italian towns. After he was exposed as a crook, he had to continually change his residence and his identity. In 1768, he had married Lorenza Feliciani in Rome. This beautiful, intelligent and ambitious woman took the name of Serafina, and became his accomplice. The couple travelled throughout Europe, never staying in one city for very long; wherever they went, they were the subject of investigations on charges of theft, fraud, charlatanism and even espionage.

How could this Sicilian con man turn himself so easily into the admired Count Cagliostro? His obvious talents as a healer and clairvoyant do not explain everything. It is possible that Balsamo had help from the Freemasons. We know that he had often been received by small circles of Masonic initiates, and that he belonged to lodges in many countries. In Lyon and later in Paris, Balsamo founded the 'Adoption Mother-Lodges of the High Egyptian Freemasons', whose rituals he probably invented himself. It is possible that Balsamo's goal was to unite all European Masonic groups under his own leadership, but this is only speculation.

In trouble again

Cagliostro's trial in connection with the necklace affair ended with his release and deportation from France. He moved to Rome, where he was again arrested, and hauled up before the Inquisition – a religious court dedicated to stamping out heresy – on charges of witchcraft, heresy and Freemasonry. Although he was sentenced to death, he was later pardoned and sentenced to life imprisonment. Balsamo spent his last years in the prison of St Leo near the Italian capital. When he died in 1795, there was speculation that he had been strangled. There were also rumours that he had fled to Russia or America, or had simply become insane. No corpse was found when his grave was opened, so we will probably never know what really happened to this remarkably gifted man.

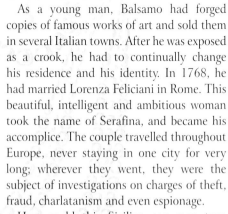

THE JESUITS: RESPECTED AND HATED

Created to defend the papacy and to convert unbelievers in many lands to Christianity, the Society of Jesus – better known as the Jesuits – found themselves embroiled in political skulduggery almost from the beginning of their existence. Most people have an ambivalent picture of the Society of Jesus, one characterised by admiration as well as disapproval. Its great achievements in education and missionary work sit uneasily next to its reputation for manipulation and conspiracy.

A 19th-century cartoon satirises the Jesuits' drive for world dominance. The order engaged in missionary work in many countries.

Few organisations have aroused as much admiration and hatred as the Society of Jesus, better known as the Jesuits. To understand why, we must go back to the early days of this, the youngest of the great Catholic orders. The Society of Jesus was founded during the 16th century, when a young soldier named Ignatius Loyola (1491–1556), from a Basque noble family, was serving in Spain against the French. Ignatius was noted for his intelligence, fiery temperament and immense fighting spirit. In 1521, his leg was severely injured by a cannon shot during the siege of Pamplona. While he was recovering from his wounds, the young nobleman read a life of Christ that was to change not only his life, but Christianity itself.

After he had regained his health, Ignatius Loyola decided to make a pilgrimage to Jerusalem and Rome. On the way, he spent a couple of months in Manresa, a town near Montserrat, a major pilgrimage site in the Spanish province of Catalonia. While he was staying at Manresa, Ignatius reflected on his relationship to Christ and the Church and came to the conviction that it was his calling to consecrate his life to the honour of God. He underwent a mystical experience, which became the basis of a method of spirituality that he compiled in a book entitled *Spiritual Exercises*.

After making the pilgrimage, Loyola went on to study Latin and philosophy at the universities of Barcelona, Alcala and Salamanca. He began his theological studies in Paris in 1528, in order to equip himself with the spiritual knowledge on which he could base his service to God.

In 1534, Loyola and a group of fellow students swore an oath of chastity and poverty at Montmartre, near Paris, also swearing to undertake the journey to Palestine where they would convert the unbelievers to Christianity. Three years later, the four students were ordained as priests.

Because of the conflict between Christian Europe and the Ottoman Turks, it was not possible to conduct missionary work in the Holy Land, so Ignatius started thinking about founding a new order. He went to Rome, where he had an audience with Pope Paul III, and explained his intention to found a kind of reserve unit for God, which he called the Society of Jesus – in Latin, *Societas*

Ignatius Loyola submits his plans for founding the Society of Jesus to Pope Paul III.

Jesu, abbreviated as SJ. The most important tasks of this new society were to be instruction in the faith and pastoral care. In 1540, the Society of Jesus was recognised by the Pope, and in 1558 their goal was clearly defined in the *Constitutions* as 'the defence and diffusion of the faith'.

Missionary work

In the decades following its foundation, the Society of Jesus focused its activities on missionary work among non-Christian peoples in Asia and the Americas. In North America, Jesuit missionaries suffered horrific tortures at the hands of the fearsome Iroquois Indians, and several priests were martyred. But in the 17th century the order was also regarded as the vanguard of the Counter-Reformation, in which the Catholic Church reacted to the rise and spread of Protestantism in Europe. Not only did the order spread around the world, but it actively tried to change the world.

One of the original members was St Francis Xavier (1506–1552), who studied with Loyola in Paris and helped to draw up the rules for the society. Xavier travelled to Asia, where he set up missions in Goa, Travancore, Malacca, the Molucca Islands

and Ceylon (now Sri Lanka). In 1549, he went to Japan, learned the Japanese language and spent two years setting up missions in the country. Xavier died soon after arriving in China to carry out missionary work, and was buried in Goa, in India, where his body still rests. Because of his missionary work,

Wide-reaching influence

A number of expressions stemming from the word 'Jesuit' or compounded from this word illustrate the influence the order has had in many spheres. There is, for example, the Jesuit style of Baroque architecture which was used to build many churches in South America after the missionary period. The Jesuit theatre or Jesuit drama is a kind of didactic theatre, which was staged by the pupils of the Jesuit schools. These plays mainly concerned the legendary deeds of saints, and were staged with a musical backing and lavish scenery. And last but not least, a devious or cunning person's behaviour is called Jesuitical when it is motivated by the motto: 'the end justifies the means'. In their missionary work, the Jesuits were often accused of behaving this way.

A 17th-century Japanese artist captured this image of the activities of the black-robed Jesuit missionaries, whom the Japanese people called the 'barbarians of the south'.

Xavier is considered the patron saint of the Orient; he was canonised as a saint in 1662.

Following in St Francis Xavier's footsteps was the Italian Jesuit Matteo Ricci (1552–1610, who is considered the founder of Christianity in China. Ricci was skilled in science, mathematics, geography and many other fields, and sought to demonstrate to the Chinese elite that European learning was as sophisticated as their own. Ricci's methods aroused controversy, but he is today considered one of the most remarkable men of the 17th century.

Priests without habits

The Jesuit order has several characteristics that distinguish it clearly from older orders. Members of the Society of Jesus do not wear a specific habit, or robe, neither are they obliged to speak a communal prayer – although they must conduct regular spiritual exercises. In addition, the Jesuits do not live in isolation behind the walls of a monastery, but in so-called colleges.

Although the structure of their daily lives appears less rigid, the Society of Jesus is tightly organised. At the top, the superior general of the order resides in Rome, and he is elected for life by a special committee known as the general congregation. Jesuits enter the order as novices, and go on to become scholastics and coadjutors, and can finally reach the highest level, the professed, after a training period of up to 17 years. As well as their oaths of chastity, poverty and obedience – as is customary in other orders – the ordained members of the Society of Jesus make another promise: they commit themselves to strict obedience to the Pope.

Today, alongside missionary work and pastoral care, the Jesuits mainly concentrate on education. Jesuit schools enjoy a high reputation for rigorous intellectual training, and serve as a training ground for new

members of the spiritual elite. Jesuits have distinguished themselves in many fields: some of the members of the order who have won renown include the poet Gerard Manley Hopkins (1844–1889), the social scientist Oswald von Nell-Breuning (1890–1991) and the palaeontologist Marie-Joseph Pierre Teilhard de Chardin (1881–1955).

Difficult subjects

As the confessors and advisers of kings, princes and noble families, the Jesuits were able to exert a strong political influence in Europe and elsewhere. Their influence also aroused hostility, and the order was frequently accused of a hunger for power and a taste for political intrigue. In England, a Jesuit-led effort to re-establish Catholic supremacy almost toppled Queen Elizabeth I (1558–1603). Rulers were not always happy with the way members of the order conducted missionary work in the colonies, and their opposition to the new science-based ideas of the Enlightenment and to liberal political reforms were generally condemned. Some rulers even accused the Jesuits of having masterminded conspiracies aimed at preventing social change.

In this attack on the Jesuits' resistance to new ideas, fathers with clawed feet try to extinguish the light of the great scholars of the past, while others are busy burning books and manuscripts.

Even within the church, the Jesuits had plenty of enemies. Catholic laymen, bishops and some popes were of the opinion that they were much too preoccupied with secular – that is, financial – business, and were stirring up hatred among the people. Thus,

Citizens of Paris are enthralled by the decree of August 1762, which banned the Society of Jesus.

time and again, there were calls for the Jesuits to be reformed. Finally, in 1773, Pope Clement XIV went much further: 'driven by the duty to restore harmony in the church', he dissolved the Society of Jesus. The ban was not widely enforced, however, and 41 years later, the society was authorised once again by Pope Pius VII.

Confrontation in France

In France, the members of the Society of Jesus were in a particularly difficult position. Even before the papal edict, the order had been banned there and the intellectuals of the country heaped scorn on it.

The confrontations between the Jesuits and the French began very early on. Ignatius Loyola was often referred to as 'the black pope', and was accused of a thirst for conquest and of plagiarism, since it was claimed that he had not written the *Spiritual Exercises* himself. Protestant pamphlets slamming Jesuits as sorcerers and makers of poisons found an appreciative audience: 'As creatures of the devil, spat out from hell, in order to poison the youth ... they should be chased away, or better still, true sorcerers that they are, burnt, since what they teach their cursed colleagues is the art of making poison and all occult sciences'.

What the French found suspicious was the strict obedience of the Jesuits towards the Pope. In their opinion, this attitude was unacceptable, since it was a threat to the authority of the French king. There was also opposition to the free classes for children that were given by the Jesuits; it was thought that these were a tool to sow the seeds of their evil ideas in the heads of the young.

It was also very popular to accuse the Jesuits of conspiracy. In the early 17th century, they were accused of supplying weapons to the foes of King Henry IV; there were also dark rumour that the order had masterminded a Catholic plot to overthrow England's King James I.

The Jesuits were attacked with particular force by the Jansenists, a religious movement based on the teachings of Cornelis Jansen (1585–1638), Bishop of Ypres, in northern France. Jansen believed that the human will was completely enslaved and caught in the desires of the flesh, and could only be set free through grace. Jansen preached a God-fearing piety and an absolute morality, which stood in contrast to the flexibility of the Jesuits, who tried to take local conditions into account. The Jansenist movement won many followers in France, Belgium and the Netherlands. Among its followers was the French mathematician and philosopher Blaise Pascal (1623–1662), whose *Provincial Letters* attacked the moral teachings of the Jesuits as too liberal.

A question of rites

The order suffered another major defeat in the so-called quarrel of rites. The Jesuits believed that missionaries had to adapt their teachings to the morality and customs of native peoples, such as ancestor worship. In East Asia, however, the papal cardinals took the opposite view, prohibiting native customs. Finally, in 1742, the Jesuits were forced to change their attitudes and to use their missionary work to try to force native peoples to give up their customs.

In the mid-18th century, the order was forced to take responsibility for heavy debts incurred by a member involved in trade in the West Indies. The case gave the French authorities an opportunity to ban the order; on August 6, 1762, the Jesuits were driven from France 'for good and for all'. However, they returned in 1814 after the papal ban on their activities was lifted.

The honourable fathers

Black-cloaked men
whence come ye all?
We come from the depths,
half fox, half wolf.
We are the sons of Loyola.
Perhaps you know, why they drive us forth.
But we shall return;
remember to hold thy tongue, and that thy children learn our lessons.
For it is we who spank the pretty little ones
time and again.
From within a certain palace
we conduct our offensive,
bound to take all Paris.
And then we shall spank the pretty little ones once again.

(Pierre-Jean de Béranger, 1834)

Liberal authors such as Frenchman Pierre-Jean de Béranger satirised and caricatured the Jesuits.

THE BEAST OF GÉVAUDAN

Many cultures tell stories of brutal part-human, part-animal creatures that prey on the young and the weak. For the most part, these stories belong to the realm of mythology, but one of these mysterious creatures seems to have come to life in a corner of central France during the 18th century. Even after its three-year reign of terror was over, the beast of Gévaudan defied all attempts at rational explanation.

France's Auvergne region straddles the Massif Central, a rugged granite plateau containing a number of extinct volcanoes. In the southeastern corner of this remote and thinly populated area lies the historic region of Gévaudan, near the mountainous terrain of the Margeride. In the summer of 1764, a local peasant woman was grazing her cows when she suddenly came face to face with what she claimed was an enormous monster. The beast tried to kill the woman, but she escaped unharmed when her herd of cows gathered protectively around her.

Others were not so lucky, and many people who encountered this horrific creature were badly hurt or killed. The monster seemed to prefer easy prey when it hunted, and its victims were mostly women and children. In the three years that the monster was active in the Gévaudan area, it killed more than 100 people and injured around 30.

Fruitless pursuit

The savage attacks struck terror into the inhabitants of the area, who were mainly poor peasants and shepherds. They banded together to try to kill the monster, but without success. Every time they managed to get close, the beast escaped; witnesses claimed the creature could leap up to nine metres. On the few occasions that the beast was cornered, the guns of the pursuers misfired or jammed. When the news reached Versailles, King Louis XV sent soldiers to help in the hunt, and the combined force of royal troops and local hunters eventually numbered some 20,000 men. But not even the soldiers could get near the beast. They managed to kill quite a few wild animals, but the beast was not one of them. Even Antoine de Beauterne, the king's chief hunter, had to admit defeat, and eventually gave up the search.

Three years went by. In the end, it was a local man who defeated the beast. In June 1767, hunter Jean Chastel set out calmly and fearlessly, armed only with a rifle and a prayer book, and made his way up the slopes of Mount Mouchet, where the monster had often been sighted. As soon as the monster appeared, so the story goes, Chastel first finished reading the page he had started in his prayer book, then levelled his weapon and fired the fatal shot.

With the monster safely dead, the relief of the people of Gévaudan, and indeed of all France, knew no limits. The carcass was embalmed and taken from town to town where people could inspect it for a small fee. The king, too, wanted to see the legendary beast of Gévaudan and ordered it to be brought to his palace at Versailles, outside Paris. Jean Chastel personally brought his trophy to the court, but the long journey took its toll. The remains of the animal had

The beast of Gévaudan mainly attacked women and children.

obviously not been preserved carefully enough, so that when the box containing the animal was opened at Versailles the king found only a stinking, rotten carcass. The king ordered the remains of the beast to be disposed of, and angrily refused to pay the reward that had been promised to Chastel.

Terrifying appearance

Naturally, the beast of Gévaudan was a particularly popular topic in the press at the time. Newspaper articles and pamphlets containing eyewitness reports of the beast appeared by the thousands. According to

The peaceful mountainous area of the Margeride was the haunt of the beast of Gévaudan.

many of these accounts, and judging from the wounds inflicted on the victims, the beast was quite formidable. It was much larger than a wolf, possessing a girth and weight more like that of a cow. Its giant head had broad, pointed, reddish-tinted jaws. A throat nearly half a metre in diameter gaped wide when it opened its terrible mouth and showed its giant teeth. The beast's ears appeared rather small, and its short fur was light grey and white at the chest, with black markings along the spine. Its tail was as long as that of a wolf or a horse. Large, clawed feet enabled the beast to grab its prey and hold fast.

The beast was able to move fast, and was sometimes seen in several different places on the same day. Some witnesses told of how it stalked its prey, creeping along slowly with its belly to the ground. Once it had chosen its next victim, whether it was animal or human, the beast jumped on it from behind like a cat. It quickly ripped out the throat of its victim, and then devoured the heart and lungs. The great strength of the beast was truly frightening; one shepherd maintained that it was capable of standing on its hind legs and lifting a sheep off the ground. Dogs, it was said, fled from the beast, and only a bull would offer any resistance at all.

The fear spread by the beast of Gévaudan paralysed the entire region, and was all the more intense since no-one could explain the real nature of the horrific creature. But there was one thing the eyewitnesses all agreed on: it could not have been a wolf, for these predators were common in Gévaudan.

Some people have speculated that the beast could have been a giant hyena, or perhaps even an ape, a bear or a cross between a lion and a tiger. Still others would

A 16th-century illustration of a werewolf.

The werewolf

A werewolf (from the Old German word *wer*, or man) is the name given to a person who changes into a wolf at night and sets out to create mayhem. According to legend, such people drink a herbal potion during the period of the full moon and murmur a few imploring verses. They then grow a wolf's head and become covered with wolf's fur, and are overcome by an irresistible urge to kill. As the entire horrific episode is over by the next morning, it is seldom known exactly who lurks within the body of a werewolf.

not discount the possibility that it could be the work of the devil – the spawn of hell.

A werewolf?

For some, the fact that the beast was capable of standing on its hind legs – meaning it could almost walk upright – was food for thought. They feared that the beast that was holding the country to ransom might be a werewolf. Many held similar opinions, believing that the work of spirits lay at the root of the strange happenings. Their belief seemed to be confirmed when it was revealed that even the cows avoided the place where the beast had been killed.

Even today, the real nature of the beast of Gévaudan is far from clear. Was it, in fact, just a very large and savage wolf, or was a particularly brutal criminal behind the beast's three-year killing spree? Some people think that at least some of the numerous murders can be attributed to human hands, perhaps to someone clad in a wolf's skin who knew the area well.

HOW DID NAPOLEON DIE?

Even though the post-mortem showed stomach cancer, rumours spread that the exiled French emperor had not died of natural causes. The controversy still goes on, though in a different form.

Following his defeat at the battle of Waterloo in 1815, French emperor Napoleon Bonaparte (born 1769) was sent into exile on the tiny island of St Helena in the South Atlantic. Napoleon spent five years on the British-ruled island before he died on May 5, 1821. During his exile, the former emperor's health declined steadily.

Since September 1819, Bonaparte had been under the care of Dr Antommarchi – a fellow Corsican. The doctor had performed a post-mortem, observed by five British doctors. He confirmed that the emperor had died of stomach cancer. But many people did not believe the official post-mortem, and, until just a few years ago, the rumour prevailed that the emperor had been poisoned with arsenic.

Unexplained inconsistencies

Bonaparte was first treated on St Helena by an Irishman named Dr O'Meara. In a report written at the end of 1817, he stated that the patient's gums were full of holes, and that he suffered from insomnia, swollen legs, attacks of migraine and hot flushes. In O'Meara's view, Napoleon suffered from a mild case of scurvy caused by a poorly balanced diet.

However, a modern French scientist, René Maury, saw in this description all the symptoms of arsenic poisoning, which was still unknown at the beginning of the 19th century. Specialists in forensic medicine dismissed Maury's hypothesis as nonsense, and referred to the watertight post-mortem report.

Maury put forward a second argument, though, which pointed out that when the body of the dead ruler was returned to France in 1840, the corpse inside the coffin had not decomposed. According to Maury, Bonaparte's body had been preserved by the arsenic that was used to kill him! The problem with this theory was that the damp climatic conditions on St Helena could also have slowed down the process of decay. Also, the emperor's coffin was placed in a nest of three progressively larger coffins, which formed an air-tight barrier.

A more valid question was the identity of the murderer or murderers. Possible suspects included an agent of the Bourbons, the French royal family, who were restored to the throne in 1814 and owed their position to Napoleon's defeat. Another hypothesis pointed to a group of British doctors who would certainly have been in a position to get rid of the emperor. Maury, however, claimed to have discovered the real suspect in the Count de Montholon, who was responsible for the household of the exiled emperor. One of his tasks was to order wine from South Africa; De Montholon could quite easily have put poison into the wine. According to the emperor's will, the count stood to receive a large sum of money, so this could have been a motive for him to kill Napoleon.

In the early 1960s, tests were carried out in Canada on samples of Napoleon's hair. The results shot down the arsenic theory. A second round of testing in 1994 revealed traces of arsenic, but in small quantities. The poison could have come from food or the water on St Helena.

Today, historians are concerned with how to evaluate the cause of death. Apart from cancer, Antommarchi also diagnosed an enlargement and inflammation of the liver, as well as signs of tuberculosis in the lungs. Some French authors asserted that the conditions on the island were unhealthy, and even that the British had tried to hasten the emperor's death by sending him to this damp and inhospitable island. The British, on the other hand, stated that the report of Napoleon's personal physician had been manipulated at a later stage. They pointed to the fact that cancer of the stomach was common in Napoleon's family, and that his death could not be linked to the unhygienic conditions on the island.

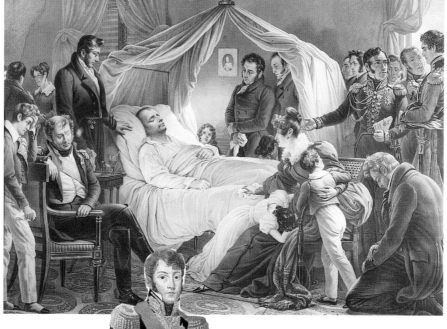

Above: *On May 5, 1821, Napoleon died on the island of St Helena in the Atlantic Ocean. Among others, the Count de Montholon (left) was suspected of having murdered the emperor.*

THE SOCIETY OF THE CARBONARI

The humble German charcoal burner of the Middle Ages came to symbolise much greater things during the 19th century. The secret society of the Carbonari, based around the medieval rituals of the charcoal burners, played an important role in the national unification of Italy.

I f you were taking a history quiz at school, one of the trickiest questions might be the following: is there a connection between the traditions of 18th-century charcoal burners in the forests of Germany and the desperate struggle waged by Italian freedom fighters to forge a single Italian nation on the Apennine Peninsula from the beginning of the 19th century? Their common name – Carbonari – is the clue, for the word means 'charcoal burner'. In 19th-century liberal and nationalist politics, the making of charcoal came to symbolise the purification and spreading of ideas of liberty, morality and progress.

The organisation of a secret society

Originally, the Carbonari were the members of a guild – a kind of trade union or craftsmen's association – which probably came into being in the Middle Ages around the same time as Freemasonry. While the rituals of the Freemasons were based on the trade of stonemasonry, the customs of the Carbonari – which included not only charcoal burners, but also forest workers, carpenters and cabinet-makers – were based on trades associated with woodwork and the forest. Senior officers would be addressed by the names of trees – for example, 'Brother Oak' or 'Brother Elm'; their conference table was called the chopping block, and their chairs were bundles of brushwood. Similar to the Freemasons, the members wore red leather aprons, and, during their regular meetings, they surrounded themselves with objects to which they attributed a certain symbolic meaning: axes, saws, pieces of wood in various lengths and wreaths made from oak leaves.

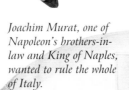

Joachim Murat, one of Napoleon's brothers-in-law and King of Naples, wanted to rule the whole of Italy.

Freedom fighters in Italy

The reason why this male society, based on a venerable trade, changed to a secret society with strong political tendencies has never been completely explained. But we do know that the change took place between 1807 and 1812 in southern Italy, when a certain Marghella, who was the Minister of Police in the Kingdom of Naples and Sicily, became a sponsor of the Carbonari. At that time, the kingdom was ruled by the dashing Joachim Murat (1767–1815), one of Napoleon's leading generals as well as the French emperor's brother-in-law. Marghella had set himself the goal of unifying Italy under a constitutional monarchy, and of toppling foreign-imposed rulers like Murat. He won the Carbonari over to his plans, and it was probably this that changed it into a society with a rigid military organisation, whose members were armed, and which exerted a strong political influence over the years. Many historians are convinced that the Carbonari were involved in nearly all the unsuccessful rebellions that gripped the Kingdom of Naples and Sicily up to 1835. The early liberation movements were finally subdued around 1850, but the dream of Italian unification survived. These ideas spread throughout the entire peninsula, and were eventually put into action by men such as Camillo Cavour, the prime minister of the northern state of Piedmont, and the famed guerrilla leader Guiseppe Garibaldi.

Republicans in France

Even in France, where it was known as the Charbonnerie, the Carbonari developed into a political association. While the members supported the establishment of a constitutional monarchy in Italy, they lobbied for the return of the republic in France, especially after 1820, when the Bourbon kings grew ever more anti-liberal. The French branch of the Carbonari may have played a major part in the revolutions of

Guiseppe Garibaldi, who fought with his red-shirted volunteer soldiers for Italian unity, was venerated like a saint by his people.

1830 and 1848, but this is uncertain. It is known, though, that they gave assistance to Napoleon III – the nephew of Napoleon Bonaparte – enabling him to win power. In Italy around 1870, just as an Italian nation was born, the Carbonari disappeared from the political scene, while the same happened to the Charbonnerie.

MYSTERIES OF OUR TIME

We don't have to go far back into history to track down unsolved mysteries. Every day, our newspapers and television programmes are filled with stories of well-known personalities who die under mysterious circumstances; serious crimes that have never been solved; or secret powers attempting to undermine society. Faced with the ever-increasing menace of organised crime, for example, we need to find out the identities of the masterminds behind these organisations. How do underworld kingpins manage to escape the law time and again? And who are their assistants? Another area for concern lies on the fringes of religious belief, in the profusion of cults and bizarre religious groups. What makes people surrender their free will and give themselves into the hands of cults? It is clear that the influence of some of these religious movements extends very far indeed. Do any of them pose a danger to ordinary people? While we may never know the full story behind some of these individuals and secret societies, we are beginning to put together parts of the puzzle.

UNSOLVED DEATHS

For no apparent reason, former French government minister Joseph Fontanet was gunned down on his doorstep. In the United States, the body of the notoriously corrupt union leader Jimmy Hoffa has never been found. In the United Kingdom, investigators have concluded that publishing magnate Robert Maxwell probably committed suicide. The common thread that connects these cases is that police and investigating authorities still have no clue as to who was responsible.

Joseph Fontanet's last words were, 'They fired at me from a car!' On the night of February 1, 1980, just as he was about to step out of his own vehicle, a bullet struck him down in front of his house in central Paris. Fontanet was a politician who had served as a minister in the governments of three French presidents: Charles de Gaulle, Georges Pompidou and Valéry Giscard d'Estaing. The fatal shot came from a so-called 11.43, a gun widely used by gangs. Police focused their investigation on one group in particular, and were tipped off that some of the gang members had taken aim at passers-by on

Joseph Fontanet held ministerial office in France up to 1976.

the day before Fontanet's murder. However, ballistics evidence cleared the gangsters.

The next lead came on February 2, when Fontanet was scheduled to attend a meeting to discuss a building project in Annecy, a city in the lower Alps. The project aimed to establish a conference centre, a luxury hotel and, in particular, a new casino complex to attract wealthy visitors from neighbouring Switzerland. Participating in the project was a group of companies that operated casinos in Europe and Lebanon. However, this group was in competition with another company operating a casino on the Côte d'Azur, in the south of France, which was frequented by guests with Swiss bank accounts. Speculation grew that Fontanet's death might have been a contract killing arranged by the rival

casino group. When the police looked at this possibility, they found a dead end.

The last lead was a long shot: it was possible that the assassination was a mistake. Early in 1984, followers of Iranian leader Ayatollah Khomeini shot dead the exiled Iranian general Oveissi, who was widely held responsible for the death of thousands of people under the reign of the deposed Shah of Iran. Oveissi, who narrowly escaped the assassination attempt, lived very close to Fontanet. Is it possible that the gunmen made a mistake and shot the wrong person four years earlier?

Ruthless and corrupt

On the morning of July 30, 1975, Jimmy Hoffa said goodbye to his wife for the last time. The ex-chairman of the International Brotherhood of Teamsters – the powerful US transport workers' union – was going out for lunch with 'a couple of guys' in a Detroit suburb. He never returned.

Hoffa had made plenty of enemies during his career. The 62-year-old union leader, first elected in 1957, was notorious for criminal dealings. He was suspected of swindling the Teamsters out of about US$2 million, and of securing his position through Mafia contacts. He became one of the most notorious public figures in the United States.

Robert F. Kennedy (1925–1968), younger brother of President John F. Kennedy, called the Teamsters 'a conspiracy of evil'. In his

capacity as Attorney General – the top law enforcement official in the United States – Kennedy initiated large-scale legal action against Hoffa in the early 1960s. The accused tried to manipulate the court proceedings by bribing the jury, but this only landed him with another law-suit. On March 7, 1967, Hoffa was sentenced to 13 years in prison.

President Richard Nixon pardoned Hoffa in 1971, but only on condition that he did not accept any union office until 1980. As soon as he was released from prison, Hoffa began to campaign against the ban, and attempted to oust Frank Fitzsimmons, his successor as union head. At the time of his disappearance, Hoffa was deeply involved in new intrigues to recapture his control of the Teamsters.

Hoffa's shady past meant that there were lots of

Former Teamster leader Jimmy Hoffa and his wife at a function in 1973.

theories on the reason for his disappearance. One said that he was murdered by opponents within the union. Another theory pointed to the Mafia, claiming that the gangsters wanted to suppress details of their links to transport companies. And finally, Hoffa might have staged his own disappearance. When the police found his car, there were no indications of violence or a struggle. But if Hoffa had not been murdered, where did he go? The answer has never been found.

The strange death of Captain Bob

'No evidence supports the hypothesis of sudden death due to a heart attack. There are also no indications that he could have accidentally fallen overboard. There is just as little evidence for murder ... Robert Maxwell took his own life.' Thus reads the final report compiled by experts for the British insurance companies that were to have paid out £20 million (approximately US$34 million) in case of death – suicide excluded.

Search parties found Maxwell's body on November 5, 1991 off the coast of Tenerife, in the Canary Islands. Detectives concluded that he must have fallen overboard from his yacht, *Lady Ghislaine*, the previous night. But not all the evidence pointed to suicide. This self-made man had attracted the hatred of many, although at that time he was also facing financial ruin.

Maxwell was born Ludvik Hoch, the eldest son of Jewish parents, on June 10, 1923. He spent his childhood and early youth in the Czechoslovakian village of Solotino near the Rumanian border. While most members of his family died in the Nazi Holocaust, the young Ludvik managed to make his way across the Balkans and France, eventually reaching Great Britain, where he joined the army in October 1940. For his bravery during the invasion of Normandy in 1944, he was awarded the Military Cross.

At the end of the war, he changed his name. In March 1945, Ian Robert Maxwell married Elizabeth Meynard, the daughter of a silk producer from the city of Lyon, in France. He also began his inexorable rise in the business world: within 10 years, Maxwell was the owner of Pergamon Press, an important international scientific publisher. He then moved into newspapers, acquiring Britain's Mirror Group, publisher of the mass-circulation *Daily Mirror*. Maxwell also

Robert Maxwell (above left) lived in Britain, but his funeral (left) was held in Jerusalem.

acquired other publications, including the *Jerusalem Post* and the New York *Daily News*. His publishing empire expanded further when he bought the established Macmillan book publishing group, and Maxwell made plans to venture into electronic media. But the new acquisitions overloaded his finances. He found himself faced with immense debts, while the price of his company's shares plummeted. Hounded by the banks and his creditors, Maxwell retreated to his yacht in search of some peace and quiet.

Enormous stress, a weight problem and a lung illness all placed Maxwell at risk of a heart attack. But if that was what took place, he would have collapsed on the deck rather than fall over the railing into the sea. Because there was no wind that night, the probability of an accident is extremely small.

Suicide and murder remain possibilities. A British pathologist found injuries on the body that were consistent with a leap from a

Rape of an empire

In order to finance his numerous acquisitions and keep his creditors at bay, Maxwell stole nearly £900 million (about US$1.5 billion), mainly from the pension funds of the Mirror Group. His theft was only revealed after his death, whereupon the British government paid out compensation to the pensioners. Maxwell had appointed his sons, Ian and Kevin, as silent partners, and after his death they were accused of having stolen the funds. Together with two other business partners, the Maxwell brothers are held responsible for the theft of a total of £22 million (about US$37 million).

great height, suggesting that Maxwell had killed himself. However, murder cannot be excluded, for Maxwell was said to have worked for Mossad, the Israeli secret service. At the same time, the FBI was interested in him because of his business ties with the former Soviet Union and its satellite states. There were rumours that Maxwell had close ties to the KGB, the Soviet secret service. While it seems that many people had an interest in getting rid of Robert Maxwell, it is unlikely that the full story will ever be told.

CRIMINALS ROAM FREE

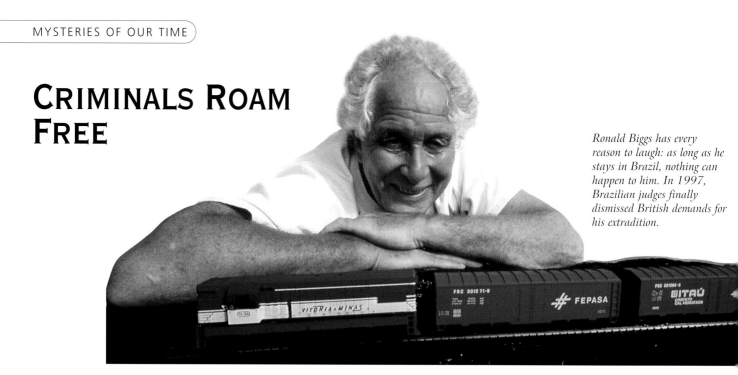

Ronald Biggs has every reason to laugh: as long as he stays in Brazil, nothing can happen to him. In 1997, Brazilian judges finally dismissed British demands for his extradition.

The daring robbery of the Glasgow–London mail train in 1963 counts among the most celebrated crimes of the 20th century. The British police succeeded in tracking down the gang of robbers, but their leader, Ronald Biggs, escaped from prison after only a year. Now a resident of sunny Brazil, he will probably never be put behind bars again. Another case that cannot be closed is that of the 'mad killers of Brabant', who terrorised Belgium in the early 1980s. These pitiless killers left no clues to their identity.

On the night of August 9, 1963, the mail train from Glasgow was moving through London's outer suburbs. Aboard the train, driver Jack Mills was looking forward to reaching his destination, Euston Station. Strangely, the signal on the bridge at Sears Crossing indicated red, so Mills brought the train to a stop, and fireman David Whitby got out to find the reason for the delay. At the next telephone post, the line was dead. On his return to the train, a pair of armed men knocked him down. It was the prelude to the greatest robbery in British history.

A group of 15 gangsters had planned the heist with military precision. They unhitched the locomotive and the first two coaches, and forced Mills to drive the short train well over a kilometre away. The postal clerks in the mail-sorting coach were put out of action and 120 mailbags were loaded into trucks waiting under a bridge. The thieves netted £2.6 million in used banknotes – equivalent to US$37.5 million today. Little of this was ever recovered.

At first, the police found only a few clues. Nevertheless, over the next five years they arrested one train robber after another. Only Ronald Biggs, supposedly the head of the gang, managed to escape from prison, in 1965. He found refuge in Brazil. After his whereabouts became known, British police repeatedly demanded the extradition of the fugitive, but he claimed the right of custody for his child, whose mother was Brazilian. In November 1997, the Supreme Court of Justice in Brasilia, Brazil's capital, ruled that Biggs's offence

Philippe de Staercke (left) admitted his role in three supermarket robberies; below is the site of the 1985 Alost massacre.

Biggs's merry dance

In 1964, when he was sentenced to 30 years' imprisonment, detectives thought they were finished with Ronnie Biggs. But after escaping from prison, the criminal underwent plastic surgery in Paris, adopted a new identity and fled to Australia, where he began a new life with his wife and three children. It was not until 1969 that Scotland Yard again picked up his trail. Biggs then left his family and went on the run. After hiding out in Venezuela and Panama, he finally reached Brazil in 1970. Apparently, this is where he will remain.

was committed too long ago to be punishable under Brazilian law. The fugitive Briton will probably enjoy a happy retirement in his host country, and often appears in interviews and in advertising spots. In the late 1970s, Biggs even made a record with British punk rockers, The Sex Pistols.

Furious murder

The Great Train Robbery appeared almost harmless compared to the brutal wave of terror that swept over Belgium in the early 1980s. Between 1982 and 1985, a series of attacks took place on supermarkets in the Walloon (French-speaking) region of Belgium. The perpetrators soon became known as the 'mad killers of Brabant'. They used modern weapons and equipment, and their attacks were planned in great detail. But they seemed to consider their loot less important than the murder of innocent people. Blind with rage, the robbers shot cashiers and customers, even children.

Their last attack was on the Delhaize supermarket in the town of Alost on November 9, 1985, when the criminals shot and killed eight people. The dead included a woman and her daughter who were shot while they sat in their car. The takings from the robbery were ridiculously small, but the shootings brought the death toll to 28 – all victims of arbitrary violence.

The Belgian police never managed to arrest the killers. However, the case took a dramatic twist when a certain Philippe de Staercke, who was serving a 20-year sentence in a Brussels prison, announced that, in 1985, he had led the gunmen in three of the supermarket attacks. Six-teen people were killed in these assaults. When he was questioned about the motive for the crimes, De Staercke said he and the others had acted 'out of ideological reasons'. In a bizarre twist, he alleged that the orders for the attacks had come from Belgian politicians and top police commanders. De Staercke refused to divulge any names, and so these grisly crimes remain unsolved.

WHEN THE CRIMINAL JUSTICE SYSTEM FAILS

Some criminal cases make history because questions remain unanswered. Perhaps there is just not enough evidence to arrive at a firm conclusion, but a great injustice is done when suspects are wrongly imprisoned, or when the real culprits are not brought to justice. Here are some examples from the files of the French judicial system.

When his trial began in November 1954, Gaston Dominici appeared very calm and composed.

In August 1952, French police examine the site in the Alps where the bodies of the three British campers were found; on the left is their car.

Despite the efforts of detectives and prosecutors, some murder cases just seem to slip through the cracks. Sometimes there is not enough evidence, a lack of witnesses or else no body. The legal system is often not up to the challenge of difficult cases, and sensational reporting in the media promotes gossip and far-fetched hypotheses. In 1994–1995, the public was riveted by the trial of American football star O.J. Simpson, who was suspected of the murder of his wife and a companion. In spite of Simpson's suspicious behaviour and strong motive, as well as solid forensic evidence, prosecutors were unable to secure a conviction, while the intense media coverage contributed to a climate of hysteria. The cases described here are not as well known as the Simpson trial, but in each one the authorities are still far from the truth of what actually happened.

The Dominici case

On August 5, 1952, the bodies of three campers were found along France's National Road 16. They were the British nutritionist Sir Jack Drummond, his wife Lady Ann and their 12-year-old daughter, Elizabeth.

Just 150 m away was the farm Grand-Terre, the home of the Dominici family. Suspicion immediately fell on the family, and detectives homed in on the head of the household, Gaston Dominici, a father of nine children who could neither read nor write. Dominici was an alcoholic and was known to have a quick temper. After some of his sons testified against him, he confessed to the three murders in November 1953.

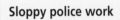

But only Clovis, the eldest son, stuck by his accusations. When his brothers withdrew their testimony, the evidence against their father became contradictory. Because of the discrepancies in the evidence, rumour and opinion ran wild. People anxiously awaited the outcome of the court proceedings, which were held in the town of Digne, in the foothills of the French Alps.

When the trial began, hordes of journalists thronged the narrow courtroom. From the testimony, it soon became obvious that the investigating officers had not prepared their case well, and the atmosphere in court grew heated and emotional.

For example, on the day of the killings eyewitnesses reported seeing a pair of trousers hanging on the line to dry at Grand-Terre. Had someone been trying to remove bloodstains? The police did not follow up this lead and did not present the trousers as evidence. Any observer who thought twice about the trial must have suspected that the identity of the killer would never be known, particularly since the family kept silent throughout the entire proceedings. Nevertheless, the court imposed the death sentence on Gaston Dominici.

After the verdict was handed down, many French people, including several prominent figures, expressed their sympathy with this simple man. For example, the author Jean Giono wrote, 'I do not say he is innocent. I only say his guilt has not been proven'.

Naturally, the British public also paid attention to the case, and were quick to voice their outrage over the bumbling and inept police investigation. One British journalist wrote that it was 'a clumsy crime, a clumsy investigation, clumsy court proceedings and a clumsy sentence'.

The case is still a strange one. It is possible that there was more than one killer, but this is contradicted by Gaston Dominici's confession. He may have wanted to protect one or more of his sons or grandsons, but no-one will ever know for sure.

Because of all the doubts surrounding the case, French President René Coty commuted Dominici's sentence to life imprisonment in January 1957. In 1960, Coty's successor, Charles de Gaulle (1890–1970), ordered Gaston Dominici to be released from prison. In a television interview aired a few weeks earlier, Dominici had told of his extreme despair.

Marie Besnard presented a dignified image during her trial.

Serial murderess?

In February 1952, a few months before the terrible events at Grand-Terre, the city of Poitiers in western France was convulsed by news of murder. Suspicion fell on a woman named Marie Besnard, the so-called widow of Loudon, who was accused of having murdered her husband, Léon. Subsequently, she was accused of a further 12 murders, including those of her father, her mother and her first husband, who had been dead for 22 years. Traces of arsenic were found in all the corpses, but there was no evidence that Besnard had administered the poison. Nevertheless, the courts sentenced her to many years in prison. Upon obtaining remission for good behaviour, she made the following statement: 'You have possibly believed that I was guilty or still believe it. I am not angry at you for that, for so many bad things have been said about me ... But suppose for one minute, just one minute, I were innocent ... for I am. Then you will understand what hardship I had to go through'. Were these the words of a liar or an innocent woman?

Sloppy police work

In October 1984, the police fished the body of four-year-old Grégory Villemin out of the Vologne River in the Vosges, a mountainous

Right: *Grégory Villemin in happier days. The boy's body was retrieved from the Vologne River near the stretch shown below.*

region in eastern France. The next day, the boy's parents received a letter from the 'crow' – a person who for many years had terrorised them with anonymous letters and telephone calls. This time, the crow admitted to having committed the murder.

On the basis of handwriting samples, the police suspected Bernard Laroche, a cousin of Grégory's father, Jean-Marie. His sister-in-law, Muriel, confirmed that she had seen the child being abducted, but she retracted her statement the day after Laroche's arrest. Two months later, Laroche was released due to a lack of evidence.

At this point, the media began a hate campaign against the mother, Christine Villemin. Jean-Marie Villemin became so bitter that he went mad and killed Laroche with a sporting gun in March 1985. Four months after her husband was imprisoned, Christine Villemin was herself placed in police custody for her son's murder.

Her lawyer soon found that the police had been sloppy and had not taken the necessary steps to investigate whether the murderer had drowned Grégory in a bathtub and only

then thrown the corpse into the river. And the letter from the 'crow' had been almost destroyed through fingerprint testing.

When Christine tried to commit suicide, she and Jean-Marie were released from prison. Their terrible ordeal continued, however, as the trials went on for years. Not until June 1992 did Christine actually stand trial. The verdict stated that 'it is impossible to ascertain who has murdered the child', and this was confirmed by a court of appeal in 1993. In December 1993, Jean-Marie was sentenced to four years in prison, but as he had been in detention for that long while awaiting trial, he was able to return to his family a few days later. The Villemins then left their home town, never to be seen again.

An innocent man

Most people at the time were utterly convinced that Guillaume Seznec had, in 1924, killed his friend Pierre Quemeneur, a member of the French National Assembly (parliament) from Brittany. In their opinion, the carpenter deserved his sentence of 20 years' hard labour in Cayenne, the infamous penal colony in France's South American colony, French Guiana.

Twenty years seemed excessively severe, especially when Quemeneur's body had not been found. Witnesses later admitted that they had been pressurised by police officers into giving false evidence. It seems that nobody pointed out the obvious holes in the evidence, possibly because people in high places wanted to see Seznec convicted.

Seznec and Quemeneur had been involved in illegal and highly lucrative business deals, including trafficking in American cars and counterfeit dollar notes. They had also illegally supplied alcohol to contacts in the United States. (Prohibition was in force at that time in the US, and the sale of alcohol was illegal.) Strangely, the public prosecutor ignored these activities. He may not have been aware of them, but he also may have tried to hide the involvement of civil servants, who were anxious not to be linked to Seznec and Quemeneur.

When he returned from the penal colony of Cayenne, in South America, Guillaume Seznec was a broken man.

In 1946, President Charles de Gaulle pardoned Seznec, who returned home the following year. For his family at least, his rehabilitation brought some comfort. As for Quemeneur, he was reportedly seen alive after his last meeting with Seznec. He may have fled to the US, or perhaps his enemies took revenge on him for his shady deals.

FORGED MASTERPIECES

The international art market is awash with forged works of art, some of which are so convincing that even the experts can be deceived. In days gone by, it was virtually impossible to tell the difference between a fake and a genuine work of art, and forgers made millions by hoodwinking the art world. Fortunately, we know a lot more today about how forgers work, and the sudden appearance of a previously unknown masterpiece now raises suspicions. In addition, an array of high-tech tools enables scholars to analyse even the most minute components of paint.

From the great Flemish painters and the Venetian and Florentine artists of the Renaissance to the artists of our day, art has long been the object of forgery. Sometimes, multiple copies may circulate at the same time! In 1989, the heirs of the French painter Maurice Utrillo (1883–1955) sued an art dealer in Bourg-en-Bresse, in central France. They were suspicious of a work, supposedly by Utrillo, that the dealer was selling for 1.8 million francs (about US$360,000). Experts examined the painting closely and concluded that it was indeed a fake.

Top: *The* Supper at Emmaus, *one of the most famous Vermeer copies by Hans van Meegeren (shown at his trial, above), is stored today in a museum in Rotterdam.*

The police quickly located the person behind the fraud. He was a Frenchman living in the United States, whose nephew in France served as his accomplice. After a search of the man's apartment in the town of Blois, the state prosecutor confiscated a number of paintings allegedly by Utrillo, as well as copies of paintings by Marc Chagall (1887–1985), Jean Cocteau (1889–1963) and Raoul Dufy (1877–1953).

Expert evaluations were carried out, but, as expected, not one authentic painting was found, although, as often happens in art forgery, the forgers produced documents proving the authenticity of the paintings.

The paintings confiscated by the French authorities in Blois were only a small blow against the often spectacular world of art forgery. For a long time, a lively trade in forged masterpieces has flourished within the multimillion-dollar art market, and this increased dramatically during the 20th century. The problem now extends beyond paintings and drawings to areas such as sculpture, ceramics and textiles. Oriental art and objects from Pre-Columbian America are also often forged.

A question of attribution

It is an open secret that museums store and even exhibit fake works of art. When we admire a landscape or portrait by a particular artist, we may actually be standing in front of a copy by someone familiar with the style of that artist. In France, disagreement still rages over whether works by the Dutch abstract painter Piet Mondrian (1872–1944) in the famous Pompidou Centre modern art gallery in Paris are indeed the artist's original works. Confusion also comes from the fact that many of the old masters, such as Rembrandt, employed assistants to carry out some of the work. In some cases, paintings formerly attributed to a master are now thought to be the work of an assistant or the painter's workshop.

Many of these controversies are extremely difficult to resolve. In the opinion of a leading French auctioneer, 'Any buyer runs the risk of acquiring a fake. There is a large number of works, particularly those of old masters, whose authorship has not been established. No expert is in a position to come to an indisputable conclusion'.

Collectors who have invested large sums of money in controversial art objects can take some comfort from this, since they can still claim to own a genuine Picasso, even if certain experts contest their claim.

Forgery is not a recent phenomenon. In order to satisfy the demands of enthusiastic collectors, the Romans manufactured copies of sculptures and coins. Later, this practice extended to paintings, particularly during the Renaissance. At that time, however, the copyists were not trying to trick people. They wanted to re-create the genius of great works of art, and even improve on it, for the sake of their fellow human beings.

In the course of time, the profit motive took over, and talented imitators began to sell their paintings as masterpieces. In other cases, artists whose talents were not good enough to develop their own style may have turned to painting fakes in order to achieve public recognition. But there is no doubt that good forgers certainly have talent. They have to be able to use a brush correctly and give the impression of age, by creating hairline cracks, for example.

The Dutch master

A Dutchman named Hans van Meegeren (1889–1947) is probably the 20th century's most famous counterfeiter of paintings. As an art student, he learned, among other things, to mix perfect paints, and he applied his know-how towards the production of remarkably faithful copies. Between 1935 and 1943, he painted 13 paintings in the style of the great Dutch masters, including Frans Hals (about 1581–1666), Gerard Terborch (1617–1681) and Jan Vermeer (1632–1675). Art experts believed Van Meegeren's work to be genuine, and the appearance of 'new' works by famous artists created a sensation. A religious painting in the style of Vermeer, entitled *Supper at Emmaus*, was celebrated as 'the artistic discovery of the century'. Van Meegeren sold eight of his forgeries, mainly to museums and members of Germany's Nazi government, for the equivalent of US$2,289,000, of which he kept more than half.

The extent of Van Meegeren's fraud was exposed after the end of World War II. When the Dutch police confiscated the vast art collection looted by German air force chief Hermann Goering (1893–1946), they found

For years, experts dated this ivory statue of St Katherine, in a museum in Paris, to the 14th century. In fact, it is a 19th-century copy.

a hitherto unknown Vermeer, entitled *Christ and the Adultress*. At first, the authenticity of the painting was not in doubt; investigators merely wished to find out who had acquired the work, and so they established business links with Germany. At the end of May 1945, the trail led officials to Van Meegeren. In spite of accusations of collaboration with the German occupying forces, he remained stubbornly silent.

Two months later, Van Meegeren spilled the beans. 'You are a bunch of idiots,' he screamed at the investigators, 'I haven't sold any of our country's art treasures. I painted them myself.' He admitted to six forgeries, but at first no-one believed him. Finally, Van Meegeren was asked to complete another painting 'in the style of Vermeer'. He did as he was asked, putting his abilities to the test under the eyes of the police. In 1947, a court sentenced the master forger to a year in prison, and he died shortly after his release.

Thirty Van Goghs

In the mid-1920s, art experts pronounced over 30 works by the Dutch painter Vincent van Gogh (1853–1890) as originals. The paintings came from a Berlin dancer and art dealer, who claimed to have obtained them from a Russian travelling from Switzerland to Egypt. When exhibited next to original works by Van Gogh in the German capital in 1928, most visitors thought that the new paintings looked like forgeries. This time, the spectators were right. Since that time, the custodians of Van Gogh's works have reacted with scepticism to any new painting that unexpectedly appears on the market.

Proving a forgery

The eye of the art expert cannot always tell the difference between a forgery and an original work of art. For this reason, experts today make use of the skills of photographers, chemists, radiologists and even atomic physicists when examining a painting or sculpture. There are a number of methods used to analyse pigments: sometimes, when examined under the microscope, samples the size of a pinhead are enough to reveal a forgery. Similarly, X-ray photographs of the layers under the surface of a painting give valuable information about when the work was produced. In extremely difficult cases, art experts may make use of a proton

One of the procedures that are used to identify a forgery is X-ray analysis. The technique is used to uncover layers beneath the surface of the paint.

and ion accelerator to determine the components of paints in extremely fine detail, and to identify particular components that may only be present in tiny amounts.

ECHOES FROM BEYOND THE GRAVE: CAN SCIENCE HELP THE DEAD TO SPEAK TO US?

Of course, the dead cannot really speak to us. However, modern science is providing us with the next best thing. An American research group specialising in the exact investigation of the bones of corpses has developed techniques to enable scientists to examine even long-buried human remains and determine the cause of death – effectively allowing the dead to 'speak'. We can now understand more clearly how a murder was committed or how terrified civilians came to be massacred by brutal Serb or Hutu militias.

By using modern technology, James Starrs is able to analyse the bones of a dead person and determine how that person died.

If the circumstances of a person's death are not straightforward, medical authorities will perform an autopsy, or post-mortem examination, in order to determine the cause of death. The autopsy will tell them exactly how the victim died – from which disease, or whether an accident or murder was involved. In medical and criminal investigations, a post-mortem is now a routine procedure, and is usually carried out quite soon after death, as decomposition of the body quickly destroys important clues.

In recent years, the spectrum of such investigations has increased, particularly after new methods were developed during the 1980s by a research team led by an American professor, James Starrs. The new techniques mean that the bones of a corpse can be analysed as much as 20, 50, 100 or even 200 years after death. Scientists use high-technology apparatus and techniques, and rely on the latest scientific research, especially in the fields of forensic medicine, chemistry and biogenetics. This range of information enables them, for example, to detect even a tiny trace of poison, from the smallest samples, and to determine what is called the genetic 'fingerprint' of a deceased person. In this way, Starrs and his team can take bones that have been in the ground for many years and accurately determine the cause of death.

Scientific detective work

The work of James Starrs and his team has implications for many medical and legal professionals. By examining the bones of deceased soldiers, historians can possibly gain insight into the way a particular battle was fought. More urgently, the new techniques offer UN investigators the chance to shed light on the ghastly massacres of Tutsis in Rwanda in 1994 and the so-called ethnic cleansing operations carried out in Bosnia and other parts of the former Yugoslavia during the mid-1990s, during which so many innocent civilians were killed. In the United States, Starrs's expertise is sought after by city and state criminal investigation units hoping to close many of the unsolved murder cases on their files. Michael Barden, a director of the New York State Police, comments that 'these methods enable an active criminal investigation even after many years have passed.'

The material studied by Starrs, and by many other scientists who are active in this field, is found in cemeteries and mass graves. There are some critics who think that corpses should not be exhumed for analysis. They feel that the dead should not be disturbed to satisfy the curiosity of scientists. Most people, however, support the researchers' activities, regarding them as a way of getting at the truth. For this reason, Starrs and his colleagues are often given permission to exhume and analyse human skeletons.

We should not expect miracles to come from Starrs's work. While the new scientific methods do indeed permit the dead to 'speak', not every remnant of bone reveals its secrets. There are some mysterious deaths that will remain unsolved.

WHO WAS BEHIND THE ATTACK ON THE POPE?

The attempt to kill Pope John Paul II sent shock waves around the world. But the trial of the attackers never really revealed where the order to kill the pontiff came from. It seems that those who were really responsible will probably never be brought to justice.

In the late afternoon of May 13, 1981, Pope John Paul II was standing in an open-topped vehicle greeting the thousands of the faithful who had crowded into St Peter's Square in Rome for a general audience with the head of the Catholic Church. Suddenly the pontiff collapsed and sank into the arms of his companions. The Holy Father had been shot.

The Pope was severely wounded in the attack. The bullets hit his intestines and damaged his nervous system, missing the aorta by only a few millimetres.

The Italian authorities immediately began to investigate the attack, while stunned people around the globe asked themselves who could be capable of such an act. It seemed that only a madman would try to kill a man of peace like the Pope. Various theories suggested that the attack was part of a large-scale conspiracy involving the Red Brigades – an Italian urban terrorist group – religious fanatics or even a Satanist sect. But all of these proved to be dead ends. On the basis of important pieces of circumstantial evidence, we know that the attack was planned in Bulgaria, which was at that time still a Communist-ruled satellite of the Soviet Union.

Links to the KGB

Evidence gathered by the Italian police showed that the Bulgarian secret service had planned and executed the operation. Apparently, the Bulgarians thought that the attack would impress the Soviet leadership in Moscow. For support, they turned to contacts in the Turkish underworld, which was to supply suitable people to carry out the 'mission'.

The two men chosen to carry out the attack were Ali Agca and Oral Celik. They made their way to Rome and waited for the Pope. It was Agca who actually fired at the Pope; Celik was supposed to toss a hand grenade, but lost his nerve when he found himself surrounded by the dense crowd.

The police arrested Agca on the day of the attack. Despite the sensational reports in the media, he was clearly not a madman, nor was he a religious extremist. Little was known about him and Celik; Agca claimed to be a member of the Grey Wolves, a right-wing Turkish terrorist group, and claimed that the attack on the Pope had been masterminded by the KGB, the feared Soviet secret service. Intelligence agencies in the West found this story hard to believe, but rumours about the KGB's role persisted. The Pope had supported Solidarity, the trade union movement that had emerged in his native Poland in the late 1970s. The Pope's moral support took on great importance for the Polish people during the struggle against Communist rule. But for the Soviet Union, anxious to maintain its influence in Poland, the Pope's stance was a dangerous challenge.

Gradually, the police investigation ground to a halt. Three Bulgarians and five Turks, thought to be the brains of the operation, were freed in 1986 on lack of evidence.

The victim forgives

On December 23, 1983, John Paul II visited Ali Agca in prison, and held a 20-minute conversation with him in private during which the Holy Father forgave his attacker. Afterwards, the gunman – who is serving a life sentence – said in an interview: 'The Pope knows everything'. It seems in any case that the Holy Father does not want to find out the truth about the attack. He believes that his life was saved by the Virgin of Fátima.

Ali Agca was in good spirits during his trial in Rome.

Photos taken seconds before the assassination attempt were used as evidence at the trial.

THE OPUS DEI

In the past, many people called it the Holy Mafia, and considered it as some kind of Catholic conspiracy to rule the world. The Opus Dei is one of the Catholic Church's so-called secular institutes, an organisation dedicated to good works and service. For some time, it has enjoyed the blessing of the Pope, who has even presided over the beatification of its Spanish founder.

One of the most influential organisations within the Roman Catholic Church during the modern era has been the Opus Dei, a group of lay people who devote themselves to the pursuit of sainthood through service to the community. The name of the organisation comes from the Latin for 'work of God', and the Opus Dei was founded in Spain in 1928 under the name Community of Priests of the Holy Cross and Opus Dei.

The founder of the Opus Dei was a young priest named Josemaría Escrivá de Balaguer, who was particularly enthusiastic about the idea of sainthood. He was convinced that not only priests and members of religious orders could strive to achieve sainthood – as was traditionally the case – but that lay people, or ordinary Christians, could be filled with this compelling desire in the pursuit of their everyday duties, whether in their family, at work or in society at large.

The members of the Opus Dei are, for the most part, Catholic lay people. Since 1930 there has also been a branch for women. Members come from virtually all countries and levels of society, although academics and members of the upper classes are heavily represented. The process of initiation begins with a trial period, followed by a so-called oblation phase, which lasts for five years. After completing the oblation phase, each member takes lifelong vows.

In accordance with the teachings of their founder, the members of the Opus Dei, most of whom are married, strive to lead a lifestyle that is permeated by the Christian faith.

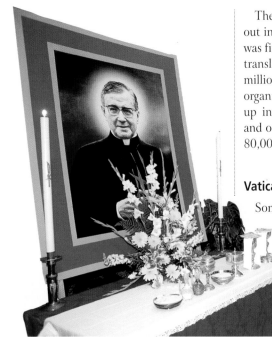

The Spanish priest, Josemaría Escrivá de Balaguer (1902–1975), founded the Opus Dei.

They must observe the regulations laid down by the Church, which include daily prayers as well as frequent attendance at divine services and regular confession. Members attempt to attain personal holiness through ascetic exercises, and the Opus Dei offers its members spiritual support in matters of self-discipline.

The teachings of Josemaría Escrivá are laid out in his book *El Camino* (The Path), which was first published in 1934. It has since been translated into 35 languages, and several million copies have been sold. Soon after the organisation was founded, branches sprung up in Spain, Portugal, Great Britain, Italy and other countries. Today, it has more than 80,000 members, including 2,000 priests.

Vatican connections

Some members of the Opus Dei occupy key posts in the administration of the Vatican City, seat of the Pope. The organisation also controls numerous student residences, schools and universities, such as the one at Pamplona, in northeastern Spain, which was founded in 1952 and has an international reputation.

In 1950, Opus Dei was recognised by the Vatican, when Pope Pius XII granted the organisation the status of a secular institute. In recent years, the community found a strong supporter in John Paul II, who granted it the new status of a personal prelacy in 1982, making the Opus Dei into a kind of

Thousands of people gathered on St Peter's Square in Rome on May 17, 1992 to witness the beatification of Josemaría Escrivá.

'super diocese', answerable only to the Holy Father himself. In part, the reasons for the organisation's privileged status lay in its conservative social policies, which matched John Paul II's own conservative stance on many issues. But many observers believe that the Polish-born pontiff also wanted to pay tribute to the support of the Opus Dei during the rise of the independent Polish trade union movement, Solidarity, which was led by Lech Walesa, who eventually became president of a democratic Poland.

Officials of the Opus Dei gather in front of St Peter's Basilica for the beatification ceremony.

The commandments of the founder

Josemaría Escrivá, the Spanish-born founder of Opus Dei, drew up 999 maxims for members of the organisation to follow. Here are a few samples:

❏ Do not postpone your work to the morrow.

❏ Lose control? You? .... Do you wish to be one amongst the crowd? You who were born to rule! There is no room for half-heartedness among us.

❏ It is my wish that you are happy on earth. This you will only be when you have freed yourself from the fear of suffering.

❏ You yourself are your greatest enemy.

❏ A thread, then another, and another, twisted together form a strong rope, capable of carrying enormous loads. With the power of your combined will, you and your brothers can fulfil the will of God.

❏ You feel within you a great faith .... The one who has given you this faith will also give you the ability to act.

❏ If obedience does not bring you peace, the reason is that you are arrogant.

❏ To be a good example is to sow a good seed.

Critical voices

The Opus Dei's special status has led to criticism within the Church, especially from Jesuits, and from lay people outside the organisation. Many think that the community enjoys too much independence and power. Others accuse it of having supported military dictatorships in Latin America and take offence at its sympathetic stance towards the extreme right wing in Spain. It is well known that Spanish dictator General Francisco Franco (1892–1975) appointed several ministers from the ranks of the Opus Dei during the 1960s. However,

many historians argue that the involvement of the Opus Dei played a positive role in the modernisation of Spain. They maintain that few organisations in Spain were free from complicity in the dictatorship of Franco. Moreover, the Opus Dei does not prescribe any views for members, but allows them to exercise their own free will in political matters. Thus, the organisation itself is not responsible for the political views of members. This extends to the world of business. Critical voices have also attacked the

Since 1994, the Spanish bishop Javier Echeverría has been the leader of the 80,000 members of the Opus Dei.

organisation's financial record, accusing it of involvement in a number of scandals.

From time to time, specific accusations have been levelled against the Opus Dei, mainly in cases of members who have been pressurised to stay in the organisation even though they wished to resign. In some cases, parents of initiates have complained about the strict ascetic exercises and the forced alienation of children from their families. Such statements sound like the accusations made against cults, and this negative aspect is intensified by the general air of mystery that surrounds the Opus Dei.

Beatification

In spite of all the criticism, the Opus Dei has developed into an important constituent of the Roman Catholic Church. Through the backing of the Holy Father, it enjoys special protection, and is no longer referred to as the Holy or Catholic Mafia.

In 1992, the Opus Dei received an even higher blessing: after a preparatory period of over 10 years, the organisation's founder was beatified on May 17 of that year: 300,000 people assembled in St Peter's Square in Rome to witness this momentous event. In his eulogy, Pope John Paul II said: 'Josemaría Escrivá was an exemplary priest who succeeded in opening new apostolic horizons for missionary and evangelical work.'

SECRET WEAPONS FOR THE WARS OF THE FUTURE

Rumours constantly surface about new and more terrible weapons of war, while speculation abounds about how the wars of the future will be fought. If warfare became industrialised in the 20th century, then it looks as if the 21st century will be the age of high-technology war. All over the world, scientists are working hard to refine the ways we use to kill each other. But whether future wars are fought with lasers, chemicals or microwave radiation, one thing is certain: war is not going to go away.

The history of warfare took a new and horrifying turn during World War I, when chemical weapons first made their appearance on the battlefield. On April 22, 1915, during the Second Battle of Ypres, German troops released chlorine gas along a 6-km stretch of the front line. About 5,000 Allied soldiers died and another 10,000 were injured – many of them permanently.

During World War II, the Nazis also planned to deploy chemical weapons against their opponents, but fortunately such attacks never materialised. However, a chemical developed in the Third Reich – and one of the most poisonous pesticides known – is still on the market in France, where it is sold under the name of Bladan. When Iran and Iraq fought a long border war during the 1980s, they frequently used this substance. In the mid-1980s, Iraqi president Saddam Hussein even directed chemical weapons against his country's Kurdish minority.

The harmful effects of chemical weapons became evident during the Vietnam War. During that conflict, US forces sprayed tons of the defoliant Agent Orange on the forests of the Asian country in order to eliminate hiding places for Communist guerrillas. In the process, they destroyed more than 1.4 million ha of trees, causing a massive eco-logical disaster. Exposure to the highly toxic herbicide caused large numbers of deformities in babies and doubled the number of stillbirths.

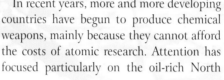

In recent years, more and more developing countries have begun to produce chemical weapons, mainly because they cannot afford the costs of atomic research. Attention has focused particularly on the oil-rich North African state of Libya. In the late 1980s, the world reacted with dismay when it became known that the Libyan government, with the assistance of a German company, was building a poison gas factory at Rabta. A fire destroyed the plant in 1990, but, two years later, according to information gathered by the Central Intelligence Agency (CIA), the government of Libyan leader Moamar al Qaddafi had begun the construction of huge underground facilities near the capital city, Tripoli, allegedly intended for the production of chemical weapons.

Left: *A test dummy sprayed with paralysing foam from the apparatus shown below. Humans would generally survive such an attack, but they would be immobilised.*

Only protective suits and gas masks shield against attacks using atomic, biological and chemical weapons. Decontamination showers are essential before the overalls can be removed.

In 1996, two German businessmen were jailed in their home country for supplying Libya with the necessary material, including several computer-controlled mixing devices, to produce poison gas. For a long time, the North African regime has been suspected of supplying international terrorist groups with highly dangerous substances such as mustard gas and sarin.

It is now relatively easy for radical groups to acquire chemical weapons, a fact that was grimly underlined by the sarin gas attack on the Tokyo undergound railway carried out by Japan's Aum Shinri-Kyo cult in March 1995. The terrorists probably obtained the sarin gas from sources in Russia. This gruesome act of violence took the lives of 12 people, and injured about 5,000 others.

Chemical weapons kill, maim and cause genetic defects, as well as contaminating the environment. Because of the threat these weapons pose, many nations have decided to outlaw them. In April 1997, an international convention came into force, which led to the establishment by the United Nations of the Organisation for the Prohibition of Chemical Weapons (OPCW). The OPCW's mission is to monitor and enforce the terms of the convention. Based in The Hague, capital of the Netherlands, it has more than 200 inspectors who – on a two-thirds majority vote of the members – can conduct surprise investigations of any industrial plant or military facility. The inspection procedures are a step in the right direction, but chemical weapons remain a danger as long as countries such as Iraq and Libya continue to produce them in substantial quantities.

Western defence experts today speak of the 'non-lethal' or even 'humane' weapon systems that will shape the warfare of the 21st century. What exactly does this mean? And is there really anything like a 'soft killer technology', or are these euphemisms simply designed to confuse the general public?

The fact is that, for a long time, military research has been heading in this direction. The US government, in particular, spends billions of dollars on the development of new defence technologies in facilities such as Los Alamos, Edgewood and Picatinny. Here, tests are run under the strictest secrecy.

In spite of this, a few facts have leaked out, and the public has learned about apparently harmless weapons designed to render a person helpless, and others that damage military equipment or make it inoperative. For example, one idea is to counter infantry attacks through the use of sedatives or tranquillisers. It is usually too risky to lace an opponent's food with these drugs, but sedatives can be sprayed from cruise missiles or aircraft. Of course, large quantities are needed, since winds can easily carry such gases away from their target. During the US deployment in Somalia in 1995, troops are said to have tested the effects of such sedatives, but word has it that a particularly brutal act of revenge on the part of Somali rebels forced them to drop the idea of using sedatives again.

Plastic bullets and glue pistols

Technology has been developed that allows soldiers to use soft-impact weapons, such as so-called 'plastic bullets', instead of deadly live ammunition. Supporters of soft-impact weapons claim that their use can prevent deaths, particularly in situations involving civilians. However, they neglect to mention that deaths have resulted from the injuries caused by plastic bullets. Evidence from Northern Ireland, where British troops have used plastic bullets since the 1970s, has shown that the impact of these projectiles leads to severe internal injuries. Apparently less dangerous are special guns which fire nets to entrap enemy soldiers. If resistance is anticipated, the nets can be prepared with glue, irritant gas or pepper spray.

More outlandish is a 'glue pistol', which fires synthetic adhesive foam. The resinous mass dries extremely quickly on contact with air, and forms a kind of straitjacket. The victim can only be freed with someone else's help, but this is by no means a gentle method: the foam can only be removed with a solvent which is very harmful to the skin. Anyone hit in the face would suffocate. The glue pistol is really only suitable for close combat, because it is very difficult to aim with any accuracy, and so is unlikely to come into wide use. Some people argue that such a weapon could be useful to police forces in the future as an alternative to firearms, since it reduces the danger of injury. However, this appears highly improbable at present.

Experiments with laser weapons, on the other hand, are in full swing. Since the 1970s, the United States has developed a number of military applications for lasers, including laser guns and grenades, as well as the so-called infantry laser. These use high-energy, bundled light rays to temporarily blind enemy soldiers from a long distance; at short distances, the lasers can completely destroy their vision. At the same time they interfere with electronic and optical devices. In late 1997, the US Defence Department successfully aimed a laser at an obsolete satellite orbiting the earth. The experiment provided data on the extreme vulnerability of

Problems with lasers

The use of laser technology is not as simple as it sounds. It has proved very difficult to use satellites to position equipment in space that can destroy the steering controls of enemy aircraft. On the one hand, such equipment weighs several thousand tons. On the other hand, to operate it at a height of 1,000 km would require about 60,000 tons of fuel, which would have to be stored on board the satellites. The cost of launching this equipment into space would be prohibitive.

Should laser beams be fired from earth, satellite dishes would have to intercept the laser at a distance of 36,000 km from earth and divert it onto the target. To do this with any degree of precision would be extremely complicated. The strength of the laser beam would also diminish as it passed through the earth's atmosphere.

American communications, reconnaissance and navigational technologies. According to certain sources, Russia, China, Great Britain, France and Israel all have similar equipment at their disposal.

Critics oppose the use of lasers and lobby for a ban on their use, saying that they are not a means of 'revolutionising warfare', but a 'diabolical mistake'. The International Red Cross has argued that the loss of sight is one of the most serious combat injuries, since it is incurable.

The use of psychological weapons is just as controversial. Powerful loudspeakers, for example, can create sound waves capable of penetrating armoured vehicles and rendering the occupants powerless. The sound creates a state of disorientation, then nausea and uncontrollable bowel movements; finally, loss of co-ordination and feelings of madness occur. Intense ultrasonic radiation can have similar effects, leading to deafness or death.

Acid, Teflon and microwaves

Sabotage is another fertile area of military research. Acids for melting metal sound like something out of a comic book or science

fiction film, but reality long ago overtook such fantasies. It is already possible for low-flying fighter-bombers to distribute metal-eating microbes over enemy armoured formations. Diesel engines can be destroyed in seconds by so-called combustion inhibitors incorporating an acetylene concentrate of 3%, normally used in industry for cutting and welding metal.

Other products make the rubber of truck tyres brittle. If this method does not bring enemy transport to a standstill, then Teflon 'confetti' can be sprayed on the streets. This substance acts like soft soap, making it difficult for infantrymen to walk, causing vehicles and trains to skid and preventing aeroplanes from taking off. However, Teflon can only be removed with difficulty, and it also destroys plant life. Strong glues have apparently been invented which can bring tanks and aeroplanes to a standstill.

Research in the area of advanced electonics focuses on projects such as high-performance microwaves. These weapons can knock out battlefield radar and radio systems, cause disturbances in the circuits of power stations and cripple data-processing systems in the same way that computer viruses behave in the modern office. However, the intensive electromagnetic radiation that is released is dangerous to human health, and contributes to bone damage, blood clots and cancer.

There are rumours that US and British researchers have developed high-frequency weapons to disrupt vital computer networks. The prospect is particularly frightening, considering modern society's near-complete dependence on computers. These weapons could also be used to jam electronic systems on aeroplanes, leading to mid-air explosions and disastrous crashes.

Is a 'clean war' possible?

While scientists and military strategists are looking to virtually 'bloodless conflict resolution', many peace researchers and humanitarian organisations paint a bleak picture of warfare in the 21st century. They believe that the 'humane' defence systems developed in recent years are not only harmful, but would also be used to supplement traditional methods of warfare rather than replace them. Rumours abound that some nations are experimenting with new weapons of mass destruction that allow

An artist's impression of the super-secret Aurora. *So far, the US Defence Department has not released any details about the project. Insiders claim that development of* Aurora *could be too expensive, causing tests to be stopped.*

The F-117 Stealth fighter, built by Lockheed Martin, is almost invisible to radar.

Speculation about *Aurora* initially arose following the 1985 Pentagon budget. No details about the aircraft were given, but production was due to start in 1987. In February 1988, the *New York Times* cited unofficial sources within the Defence Department that said the US Air Force was developing a Stealth aircraft that could attain a speed of Mach 6 – six times the speed of sound.

In August 1989, Chris Gibson, an engineer working on an oil platform in the North Atlantic, observed an unusual formation in the sky. It consisted of a tanker aircraft, two fighter-bombers and a fourth machine that looked from below like an isosceles triangle. Gibson was familiar with almost every type

In June 1991, residents of several towns in southern California reported that they had heard pulsating aircraft engines and supersonic booms; the latter had even showed up on seismographic instruments. In Texas, a photographer captured a weird vapour trail on the horizon in May 1992: along a narrow line, small smoke rings were lined up at regular intervals. A few days later, air traffic controllers from Britain's Royal Air Force observed the same trail over Machrihanish air base in Scotland. Experts believe that this indicates a so-called pulsating detonation drive, probably using a methane oxidator mixture as fuel. This technology provides an especially favourable weight-to-thrust ratio. If *Aurora* is the successor to Blackbird, will we ever get to see this high-speed marvel?

an attacker to eliminate an opponent from a distance while remaining unharmed. If such weapons are really being developed, then the concept of a 'clean war' becomes virtually meaningless.

A French comic-book hero melts iron with a mushroom extract. Today, bacteria and other substances can be used to destroy metals.

Towards Mach 6

The field of aircraft design and construction has been marked by more or less continuous innovation. In the 1991 Persian Gulf War, for example, F-117 Stealth bombers were first used extensively in combat. These high-performance aircraft are made from new materials that absorb radar signals, while the angular design means that the aircraft barely shows up on enemy radar screens.

Senior military planners and aerospace companies have many projects of this kind on the drawing boards. Since the mid-1980s, for example, rumours have circulated about a mysterious American aircraft called *Aurora*. Drawings and chronologies of *Aurora*, with detailed listings as to where and when it had allegedly been sighted or at least heard, are widely available on the Internet. However, the US government has remained resolutely silent on the subject.

of aircraft design, yet he had never seen this particular one. Could this have been *Aurora*? There has always been evidence of tests with supersonic aircraft, but never any clear proof.

Nevertheless, a number of facts point to the existence of such a machine. Much to the world's surprise, the Pentagon withdrew the SR-71 Blackbird spy plane from service in 1990. At that time the sleek Blackbird was the world's fastest aeroplane, and could reach a speed of Mach 3. Spokesmen for the Pentagon explained the cost of the aircraft was too high, and that satellites could now do the job. Few observers were convinced. Satellites are vulnerable targets; if they are hit, they cannot easily be replaced. Without reconnaissance aircraft, the US would be at a disadvantage, and it would certainly never voluntarily put itself in this position. So it must have found a better machine for the job than the sleek Blackbird.

Model aircraft

For some time now, the Israeli Defence Force has used remote-controlled model aircraft to monitor its territory, particularly in disputed areas such as the Golan Heights and South Lebanon. Some of these machines do indeed look like oversized toys, but they are, in fact, important reconnaissance devices. The small aircraft are equipped with robust cameras, which are partly used to take photographs in border areas and in other trouble spots. In American weapon laboratories, micro-planes are being developed under the names Black Widow and Microbat. These can be used for reconnaissance, but also for the transport and delivery of conventional and biological weapons.

THE SHADOWY WORLD OF INDUSTRIAL ESPIONAGE

Following the collapse of the Communist bloc and the end of the Cold War, intelligence agencies received a new mission. Old political and military rivals such as the United States and Russia are now competitors in a global marketplace, and employ secret agents to gather data about new technology, corporate mergers and the activities of leading corporations. Even supposedly friendly nations spy on one another, with sometimes embarrassing results. An almost impenetrable web of lies and rumours surrounds the mysterious world of the industrial spy.

In 1995, when representatives of the American government and the European Union sat down to discuss world trade issues, the European delegates were surprised to see how well informed the Americans seemed to be about the European positions. The reason for this emerged the following year: the US government had ordered agents of the CIA (Central Intelligence Agency) – the best-known of America's many secret intelligence agencies – to gain access to the European Union's computer systems. The CIA had obtained exact information about the tactics that the Europeans would pursue in the coming negotiations.

In 1996, France was rocked by the news that MI6 (the British counter-intelligence service) had stolen new and highly classified technology – a satellite system for tracking atomic submarines – from the French naval base at Brest. In 1998, it was revealed that for many years a Chinese-American scientist working at the Los Alamos weapons research laboratory in New Mexico had been passing the secrets of America's missile development programme to China, allegedly permitting that country to produce highly sophisticated ballistic missile technology of its own.

But military and state secrets have always been fair game for secret agents. Far more worrying – and more widespread – are the activities of industrial spies. According to the Swedish secret police, the Säkerhetspolisen, more than half of the 30 employees at the Russian embassy in Stockholm, capital of Sweden, are engaged in industrial espionage. At one time, the KGB – the Soviet secret service – ran 600 decoy or 'front' companies

in Sweden, with most of them still in existence.

The list of cases goes on. Industrial spying is now the order of the day, and it seems that every country or corporation spies on someone else. It seems ridiculous for one state to be outraged by the covert activities of another, when virtually all major industrial nations carry on some form of intelligence-gathering. Industrial espionage flourishes today because the stakes are so high. Any firm that wants to survive in the global marketplace has to obtain solid information about the activities of the competition, be it in advanced electronics, computers, atomic energy, aeronautics, pharmacology or genetic engineering. Indeed, governments often lend their support to industrial espionage.

A billion-dollar business

There are no accurate figures available that would indicate by how much individual national economies benefit from the theft of industrial know-how. But there are plenty of conjectures about the damage suffered by the victims. In a hearing held by the US Senate commission on industrial espionage in February 1996, Louis J. Freeh, director of the FBI, would not give firm figures, but claimed that American companies were losing billions of dollars as a result of such crimes. In 1996, the automobile industry was gripped by allegations that the former Vice-President for

Computers (above) and microphones in cigarette boxes are important devices used by agents.

Purchasing at General Motors (GM), Ignacio Lopez, had taken boxes filled with secret company documents with him when he resigned from GM and joined the German car firm Volkswagen. The case led to a long and very costly lawsuit, with Volkswagen forced to pay out a substantial settlement to its powerful American rival.

Representatives of Japanese business inspect a factory in the Netherlands. Photography is usually permitted during such visits.

But the battlelines in this new Cold War do not run along the former East–West divide. Even friendly nations like the United States and the members of the European Union let their intelligence agencies loose on one another. Despite the close relationship between Israel and the United States, a joint CIA–FBI report lists Israel as one of 23 countries engaged in industrial, economic and trade espionage. The report also names US allies such as France and Japan, as well as such long-standing rivals or adversaries as Russia, China and Cuba.

But what do they stand to gain from the risky business of espionage? Many Western industrial nations believe they will gain an advantage over their rivals if they secretly obtain innovative ideas, if they examine the conditions of contracts before negotiations begin and if they are informed about imminent corporate mergers.

Other nations, particularly Russia and former Eastern Bloc states, are desperate to gain access to more advanced Western technologies. They hope that undercover activities will save them the effort required for research in the high-technology sectors. However, Poland, the Czech Republic and

Business people have always tried to get information about what their competitors are planning. For example, during the so-called 'soft drink wars' in the United States in the 1980s, Coca-Cola always wanted to know what its rival Pepsi was planning, and vice versa. In the car industry, manufacturers would try to find out what colour ranges were being planned by their competitors. But the 1990s saw a increase in systematic spying activities on the part of foreign companies and research institutes. Some insiders believe that there are 500,000 men and women worldwide engaged in espionage to obtain future-orientated knowledge.

The second Cold War

The growth in industrial espionage stems primarily from the end of the Cold War. As the military rivalry between East and West faded, the collapse of Communism high-lighted economic antagonisms. Intelligence agencies no longer had to spy on their political enemies, but they still had to justify their huge budgets, expanded capacity and expensive surveillance equipment. In the US, the CIA shifted its focus from the spread of Communism to the narcotics trade, fighting terrorism, economic information and the spread of sensitive technology. In other countries, intelligence agencies were placed at the service of powerful, often state-owned, corporations. In effect, the world embarked on a 'second Cold War'.

BUSINTEL: a flourishing new business

More and more American companies are wary of using information that they have obtained through covert or secret means. For one, they fear that spies have their own loyalties, supplying some companies with better material than others. But they also doubt the competence of these agents when it comes to evaluating data that relates to competitiveness and future economic trends. For this reason, corporate chiefs are increasingly working with private companies run by top-rate professionals – often former employees of secret intelligence services – who specialise in industrial affairs. The new business is referred to as BUSINTEL – Business Intelligence. According to one survey, the yearly turnover of this fast-growing industry is as much as US$3.3 billion.

Hungary are avoiding banned research fields in order not to jeopardise their acceptance into the European Union.

US government regulations limit the transfer of technology to certain states, making it difficult for these countries to gain

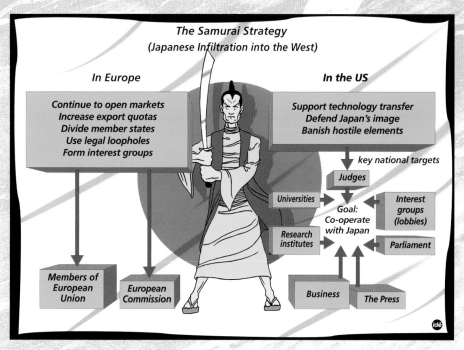

The Samurai Strategy
(Japanese Infiltration into the West)

In Europe

Continue to open markets
Increase export quotas
Divide member states
Use legal loopholes
Form interest groups

In the US

Support technology transfer
Defend Japan's image
Banish hostile elements

key national targets

Judges
Universities
Interest groups (lobbies)
Goal: Co-operate with Japan
Research institutes
Parliament
Business
The Press

Members of European Union
European Commission

A French cartoon depicts the so-called Japanese threat, an illusion based on Japan's reputation for penetrating foreign markets. France itself operates an aggressive programme of industrial espionage.

access to the latest innovations. So they try to obtain it illegally, through espionage. The regulations are aimed at so-called borderline countries such as Iran, Iraq, India, Pakistan, Libya and Syria, whose goals are considered by experts still to be primarily military, and which are seeking to obtain weapons of mass destruction.

According to information supplied by the German secret service, Iranian agents are attempting to obtain technical know-how on so-called ABC weapons (atomic, biological and chemical) and the technologies associated with them. They are also interested in obtaining dual-use weapons – products that

now relatively simple to intercept satellite transmissions, log into data banks or use ultra-modern listening devices to monitor telephone and fax lines.

Many cases of so-called economic warfare reach the public eye, but these are probably only the tip of the iceberg. Even in the most highly publicised crimes, many of the details remain hidden. It comes as no surprise that governments and intelligence agencies are generally reluctant to reveal exactly how they obtained certain items of information. Even teams of experienced journalists are often unable to uncover all the facts of these complex affairs.

America and France have a long history of mutual economic warfare. In recent years, the government-owned French airline Air France taped the conversations of passengers travelling in the first-class section, some of whom were employees of American airlines. The French government apologised for this event, but turned the tables in 1995 when five CIA officers were expelled from France for having mounted an operation aimed at gaining information about France's telecommunications industry.

Japan has only a small foreign intelligence agency, but important business information is collected by the powerful Ministry of Economic Affairs together with private industry. Companies acquire data through their branches throughout the world, and carefully evaluate sources. In 1994, German intelligence agencies acknowledged Japan's great skill in obtaining legal information, especially information pertaining to global patents, economic analyses and studies on future trends. German authorities claim that 'thousands of scientists, translators and experts in the field of technology' are permanently evaluating specialist publications. Japan also makes use of military intelligence and its highly advanced telecommunications infrastructure to conduct spying operations against the former Soviet Union and the United States.

The City of London, one of world's financial hubs, attracts thousands of industrial spies.

have both a civilian and military application: for example, in the fields of engineering and instrument technology. Following the end of the Persian Gulf War in 1991, the UN undertook the difficult task of tracking down and destroying Iraq's weapons of mass destruction, many of which were developed through the purchase of supposedly harmless civilian technology.

A shadowy world

In today's information age, secret agents no longer require the elaborate cloak-and-dagger strategies of the past. Instead of having to shuffle through filing cabinets at night, it is

In the autumn of 1993, two giant German electronics and engineering firms, Siemens and AEG, together bid for a tender in South Korea to develop high-speed trains for the 420-km route from Seoul to Pusan. The British–French consortium of GEC Alsthom was granted the tender, although the German bid was the lower one. Siemens suspected that its communications had been tapped by the rival group, but nothing could be proved. In 1994, information supplied by US secret intelligence agencies enabled the American aerospace firms Boeing Aerospace, McDonnell Douglas and Raytheon to win two multibillion-dollar contracts from Saudi Arabia and Brazil after US President Bill Clinton complained to those governments that rival French companies had paid bribes to win the contracts.

No way back?

In some countries, the theft of industrial or trade secrets is severely punished. In 1996, the US Congress passed a law on industrial espionage, which provides for up to 15 years in prison and fines of up to US$500,000 for individuals or US$10 million for corporations, depending on the severity of the crime. A number of other countries, such as France, have introduced similar legislation.

The illegal gathering of trade secrets will only end when the nations of the world agree that industrial espionage must be banned. In 1997, a committee of the German Bundestag (parliament) took pioneering steps in this direction when it proposed an outright ban on industrial espionage, at least among Western industrial nations. It would be a real step in the right direction if individual states were to announce that they intended to follow Germany's lead. So far, the prospects for this happening are not good.

ATTACK ON THE STATE: THE CRIMES OF P2

The exposure of the secretive P2 lodge revealed a complex web of financial and political corruption that reached into the very highest offices of the Italian government, and even into the Vatican itself. Through money laundering, widespread corruption and support for right-wing extremists, the brotherhood attempted to infiltrate the Italian state and establish a new authoritarian order.

For a long time, Licio Gelli, Grand Master of the P2 lodge was one of Italy's most influential criminals.

In the 1970s and early 1980s, a dangerous brotherhood attempted to topple Italy's democracy. The name of this organisation – a kind of Masonic lodge – was *Propaganda Due*, but it became known to the world as P2. Many questions about its criminal activities remain unanswered today. But there is no doubt that P2 was involved in some of the worst crimes and most notorious financial scandals in Italy's recent history.

Picking up the trail

In March 1981, tax investigators from Italy's Ministry of Finance raided the luxurious villa of businessman Licio Gelli at Arezzo in Tuscany. The officials suspected him of shady dealings, but were surprised to find a list with 962 names of the members of a previously unknown organisation called P2. It turned out that Gelli was the Grand Master of the lodge. The members of P2 included government ministers, more than 40 representatives of political parties, as well as military officers, bankers, industrialists and journalists. The fact that Gelli also

Roberto Calvi, head of the Banco Ambrosiano, was involved in shady financial deals. His death remains unsolved.

had several confidential state documents caused an uproar; he had received these from the heads of the Italian secret service and the Italian armed forces, both of whom were members of the lodge. In May, as the P2 scandal widened, the government of Prime Minister Arnoldo Forlani was forced to resign. In 1982, the lodge was banned.

During the investigation into the activities of P2, Italian police and magistrates were confronted with an extremely complex web of intrigue. They found that the organisation was involved in a range of criminal activities.

In August 1980, 83 people died when a bomb destroyed Bologna's main railway station. A right-wing terrorist organisation claimed responsibility, but the order came from P2.

P2 had links to industry, banks, the Mafia, the CIA, right-wing terrorist groups – and even the Vatican.

For a long time, the investigators had been watching Roberto Calvi, one of Italy's most successful businessmen, suspecting him of illegally exporting funds to accounts in Switzerland. Calvi had made Milan's Banco

Ambrosiano into Italy's largest private bank, and had founded a number of subsidiaries, as well as buying stakes in various corporations. Documents found in Calvi's possession proved that he was responsible for financing P2, and that he did in fact have access to Swiss bank accounts. It seemed that the investigators had the evidence needed to prosecute him. Calvi was sentenced to four years' imprisonment, but was immediately freed when he appealed against the sentence. On June 12, 1982, his family reported him missing, and, six days later, he was found hanging from Blackfriars Bridge in London.

The British police initially assumed that Calvi had committed suicide, particularly

At his trial in 1986, banker Michele Sindona gave evidence on the links between P2, the Mafia and the Vatican. He died of poisoning soon afterwards.

since it was known that his financial empire – with debts estimated at US$1.4 billion – was beginning to crumble. But a number of facts challenged the suicide theory. If he had really wanted to kill himself, it would have been simpler for him to use pills. Calvi was also afraid of heights and presumably would not have climbed under the bridge on his own. There were clear indications that he had been murdered.

The Banco Ambrosiano had borrowed money all over the world, lending it to companies in South and Central America

which were involved in money laundering – buying legitimate businesses or assets with money from criminal activities – for the Mafia-controlled drug trade. These firms were owned by a holding company that turned out to be controlled by the Vatican. At some stage, the amounts transferred by Calvi started disappearing. Insiders claim that they were diverted to Italian political parties, to P2 and even to the Polish trade union, Solidarity – the reform movement that was dear to Pope John Paul II. If Calvi's finances were to be salvaged, the companies in Latin America would have to repay huge amounts of money. The Vatican saw no reason why it should try to force these companies to do so.

Reasons for suspicion

There are various reasons that suggest P2 had a role in Calvi's death. For a long time, Calvi had worked with Michele Sindona, a P2 lodge brother and Sicilian banker who laundered large sums of money for the Mafia and advised the Vatican in financial matters. Sindona had gained access to the Vatican

At a press conference to launch one of his books, Licio Gelli explains P2's harmless nature.

Bank for Calvi, and, for this favour, he demanded that his protégé support his illegal activities. This situation went on for a long time, and Licio Gelli was happy to go along

with it. Then Sindona went bankrupt. Calvi did not help him and made a bitter enemy. It is possible that Sindona arranged for Calvi to be killed, but the evidence is not conclusive. Other members of P2 are also suspects, since Calvi transferred funds for them to Italian fascist groups overseas, and also dealt in arms. He may have made mistakes or earned the hatred of individuals as powerful as Sindona. Certain aspects of his death point to a ritual murder. For example, his pockets were filled with fragments of broken brick, a symbol of failure among the Freemasons.

The Calvi affair offers a revealing picture of P2's criminal ties. At times, its dealings posed a real threat to the health of Italy's democracy. The goals of the lodge were to defend conservative values more vigorously than Italy's constitution allowed. In plain language, it wanted to infiltrate the state and establish a dictatorship.

To carry out this aim, P2 needed power, which it obtained by recruiting generous donors and individuals in key positions. As Gelli's list of members showed, he had a talent for making important contacts. He also spent large sums on bribes to gain favour with civil servants and business leaders.

The Fascist connection

During the late 1970s, Italy was rocked by the activities of terrorist groups, notably the leftist Red Brigades. P2 leaned the other way, and actively supported right-wing terrorism. On August 2, 1980, right-wingers bombed the main railway station in Bologna, a city in northern Italy, killing 83 people and injuring 200. The attack was intended to spread fear and encourage support for dictatorship.

Who was the man that turned P2 into one of the most dangerous secret organisations in Italy? In his youth, Gelli was friendly with Fascist leader Benito Mussolini (1883–1945), who ruled Italy from 1922 to 1943. Between 1941 and 1945, Gelli worked for US intelligence, but was probably a double agent, feeding information to the Fascists in his home country. After World War II, he helped many German Nazis to escape to South America. In 1947, when the Central Intelligence Agency (CIA) was set up, the Americans continued to use him. Documents uncovered in the 1990s show that, in 1956, the CIA formed a paramilitary group, *Il Gladio* (The Sword), to fight communism in Italy, France and Spain. Gelli was active in the group. Weapons provided to Il Gladio were hidden all over Italy, and later fell into the hands of right-wing terrorists.

These details indicate the extent of Gelli's influence. Before P2 was exposed, Gelli fled to Switzerland, where he was imprisoned. However, he managed to escape. In 1986, he surrendered and was extradited to Italy. After spending just one month in jail, Gelli was released in 1988 on the grounds of a heart ailment. However, in 1994, a court in Rome sentenced him to 17 years' imprisonment.

Tommaso Buscetta, the repentant don.

ORGANISED CRIME: THE ITALIAN OCTOPUS

Books and films have made the Sicilian Mafia a household name. Yet the 'men of respect' of the 'honoured society' preside over one of the most ruthless and murderous criminal organisations in the world. Joined since the 19th century by societies such as the Camorra and the 'Ndrangheta, Italy's organised crime families earn billions through drug trafficking and other nefarious activities.

'I want to warn you, your worship: after this trial you will certainly become famous. But efforts will be made to destroy you, physically and professionally. The same efforts will be made on me. Never forget that you will never be able to pay the account that you have opened with the Mafia. Do you still want to interrogate me?'

It was with these ominous words that Mafia boss Tommaso Buscetta and the Sicilian judge Giovanni Falcone began their historic co-operation in 1984. But Falcone, the senior investigator into the activities of Sicily's infamous 'honoured society' was not intimidated by the threat, for he knew that he was entering a minefield. Soon, further other high-ranking mafiosi came forward to provide him with information.

During a mass trial held in Palermo in 1986–1987, cross-examination of the *pentiti* – the inner circles of organised crime – provided unprecedented insights into the workings of the Mafia. The testimony caused a sensation, especially considering the fact that, until then, some politicians and justice ministers had even denied the existence of the Mafia. The detailed statements enabled Falcone to prosecute 456 members of the *Cosa Nostra* ('Our Cause'), as the Mafia is known in Italian. The Palermo trial led to the acquittal of 114 of the defendants, while a total of 2,655 years in prison were imposed on the rest. Nineteen of these were sentenced to life imprisonment.

Buscetta's prophecy was to be fulfilled in every respect: Judge Falcone became very famous; in March 1991, he was called upon to head the division of criminal law at the Ministry of Justice in Rome. But brutal acts of revenge also followed. Buscetta lost 32 of his relatives and friends through murders ordered by rivals. Falcone narrowly escaped assassination in June 1989, but died three years later in a bomb attack, together with his wife and three bodyguards; the assassins had planted several hundred kilograms of TNT under the pavement.

The men of respect

The Mafia was born out of the grinding poverty of rural Sicily, a large island at the southern tip of Italy. For centuries, Sicily and most of southern Italy were covered by the huge estates, or *latifundia*, of the landed nobility. These wealthy barons ruled this region without any interference by the state. Towards the end of the 18th century, the noble families moved to the cities, leaving the latifundia to the poverty-stricken tenants of the estates, who had to supply them with rent and harvest produce and were allowed to sublet small plots of land. More and more men applied to serve as *gabelotti*, a minor administrative post. If the owners declined to employ these men, they had to reckon with arson and the devastation of their land. So, they gradually gave in to the brutal applicants and made them the 'protectors' of the estates. Eventually, the gabelotti were able to set the rents for the tenants. A regular tribute to the gabelotti granted some security to the peasant farmers who rented the land. They had no choice but to accept this repressive system; if they did otherwise, they would be chased away. The peasants also needed protection from the many gangs of armed bandits that harassed and terrorised the countryside.

Gradually, the rural population accepted this situation. Between 1860 and 1900, the new custodians of the law – they increasingly referred to themselves as *Mafiosi* – acquired control of about 400,000 hectares of land, and granted 'protection for a fee' to peasants who wanted to use the land, water or wells. To strengthen their position, the Mafiosi exerted blackmail-type pressure on town councils, judges and the police. Soon, it was the Mafia and not the weak institutions of the young Italian republic which ruled Sicily, especially in the triangle formed by the cities of Palermo, Trapani and Agrigento. If anyone dared to oppose them, brutal revenge was sure to follow.

The Mafia's counter-violence was based on loyalty within a clan, prohibition of any co-operation with authorities and formulation of its own laws. The most important of these was the rule of silence, or *omerta*. In the years to come, centrally organised societies were formed, whose commissions were headed by provincial chiefs.

What does 'Mafia' stand for?

There has been much speculation about the origins of the word 'Mafia', which was first used officially in 1865. One plausible explanation concerns Italian history. Until 1860, southern Italy was ruled by the French. Foreign rule led many patriotic Italians to proclaim the motto *Morte alla Francia, Italia anela*, or 'death to France, gasps Italy'. The initial letters spell 'Mafia'. In the dialect of Palermo, the word means pride, and a sense of national identity, but also a presumptuous manner. Another source may be the Arabic word *mahyah*, which means bragging or boastful.

The only time Italy successfully asserted itself against the Mafia was under the Fascist regime of Benito Mussolini (1883-1945). Rome conferred special powers on Cesare Mori, the prefect of Palermo, who detained thousands of suspects, carried out public trials and instituted tough bans on illegal activities. The Mafia surrendered, and many fled abroad, especially to the United States. However, many Mafiosi returned from exile with the Allied troops who invaded Sicily in 1943 to liberate the island from Fascist rule.

After World War II, the Italian state was unable to provide help for the poor south of the country; their failure opened the way for

Top: *The death of Judge Giovanni Falcone shocked Italy. General Alberto Dalla Chiesa (above left) was murdered for his anti-Mafia activities. His death was probably ordered by Toto Riina (right, at his trial).*

organised crime to re-establish its influence in the countryside. For a while, the Mafia was content to stick to its old activities, such as blackmail, intimidation and smuggling.

In the 1950s and 1960s, the Cosa Nostra became deeply involved in the drug trade. Initially, their operations were carried out in co-operation with Corsican clans in southern France – the so-called French Connection. During the 1960s, the Mafia split with the Corsicans and began to form alliances with Chinese gangs, and to import narcotics from the Far East. Intelligence gathered by the international police organisation, Interpol, meant that detectives were able to smash these connections in 1971–1972.

Until that time, Sicily had served only as an operational base for the illegal trade in morphine, but the island soon became a hub of the international drug trade: the Sicilian Connection operated for a good 10 years. In the early 1980s, according to estimates of the US drug investigation authorities, 20% of the 60 tons of heroin destined for the world market was packaged on the island.

The drug trade was worth billions, and the Mafia made sure that nothing threatened it. The organisation killed anyone who got in their way – even state officials. The public were terrified by the many 'famous' corpses, among them Palermo's top detective, Boris Guiliano, who was murdered in July 1979.

At the same time, a bitter fight erupted within the Cosa Nostra, for the young Mafiosi wanted to get their share of the drug trade, just as the older generation had done. In Sicily alone, the bloody internal strife led to 200 deaths. The situation in Palermo was so out of control that the government sent General Carlo Alberto Dalla Chiesa of the Carabinieri – Italy's national police force – to restore order. Four months later, he and his wife were shot and killed. The murders were apparently ordered by Salvatore Toto Riina

of the infamous Corleone clan, who had murdered several other public figures. He was imprisoned in 1993.

It was the escalation in the war between the rival Mafia clans that led Tommaso Buscetta, who had been detained in Brazil since 1983, to break the organisation's vow of silence and spill his secrets to Judge Falcone. But the bitter feuds continued in spite of the successful mass trial. In recent years, Sicilian and Neapolitan families have co-operated with the cocaine traders from Colombia. As the profits of the international drug business grow, so the tentacles of the octopus, as the Mafia is also called, reach further than ever.

The other 'honoured societies'

Apart from the Mafia, with its 186 clans, there are other smaller, but still extremely dangerous, criminal societies in southern Italy, notably the Camorra in Campania and the 'Ndrangheta in Calabria.

Unlike the Mafia, the Camorra was never a rural organisation. When it was formed in the 19th century, it spread throughout the underworld of the city of Naples; for over 20 years, it concentrated on cigarette smuggling, extortion and robbery. Recently, clans from the Camorra have come to an agreement with the Mafia and now earn substantial amounts from criminal activity throughout the world.

The origins of the 'Ndrangheta, made up of about 140 families, are shrouded in mystery. We know that the organisation was formed in the 19th century, that it operated in mountainous areas and formed alliances with highway robbers. Many of its members were recruited from the lower classes, and its criminal activities sometimes had a political angle, such as the intimidation of unpopular politicians. The 'Ndrangheta has a different structure to the Mafia, for only one family is responsible for matters of direct control.

Through the revelations of Buscetta and others, we now know a great deal about Italy's underworld. In his book *Inside the Mafia* (1991), Giovanni Falcone also offered many insights into their way of thinking and secret rituals. Nevertheless, it appears virtually impossible for the authorities to destroy criminal societies. A rare bright spot came in May 1996, when police arrested Giovanni Brusca, Falcone's killer.

AMERICA'S BATTLE AGAINST ORGANISED CRIME

With its roots in rural Sicily, the Mafia flourished when it was transplanted to the United States. In the 1920s, the gangsters had it all their own way, and, in 1934, formed a syndicate whose influence snaked into every corner of illegal endeavour. For a long time, the Mafia were the baddest of the bad. But the new kids on the block, the Colombian cocaine gangs, are every bit as ruthless and violent as the Cosa Nostra.

For most people, America in the 1920s recalls images of flappers dancing the Charleston, of Dixieland jazz bands, the era of silent films and drinking 'bathtub gin' during Prohibition. The 'Roaring Twenties' was a time of great social change, and of unprecedented economic prosperity. But it also saw a tremendous increase in organised crime, when bloody strife between rival syndicates caused hundreds of deaths. The turning point came when the Italian Mafia forged a single powerful syndicate.

The Cosa Nostra

Between 1880 and 1914, tens of millions of immigrants entered the United States from Europe. The reasons for this influx included crop failures in southern Italy, devastating poverty in Ireland and pogroms against the Jews in Russia. Many of the new arrivals remained in the cities of the East Coast, and especially in New York, where individual neighbourhoods became home to particular ethnic groups. Unfortunately, this ethnic stamp also included particular forms of criminality.

Some of the Italians had worked for the Sicilian Mafia or the Neapolitan Camorra, and they continued their criminal activities in their new country. They blackmailed fellow immigrants for protection money, took part in illegal gambling and operated houses of prostitution. In Sicily, the Mafia was always referred to as the Black Hand, and initially this name was applied to its American branch.

In order to get a foothold in American society, the Sicilians founded organisations along the lines of the secret societies of their homeland. One of these was the Unione Siciliana, founded in 1908, which soon had branches in many other cities. By 1917, in Chicago alone, there were 38 lodges of the organisation, with around 40,000 members.

The Unione Siciliana soon became a vehicle for illegal dealings. One of the key figures in the organisation was James 'Big Jim' Colosimo, who controlled the earnings from prostitution in Chicago and enjoyed a great deal of political influence. Colosimo helped to rig the results of elections, and bribed politicians and city officials to stay away from his activities. When he was shot dead in 1922, more than 5,000 people attended his funeral, including nine city councillors, three judges, two congressmen and a senator.

Colosimo's alleged murderer, Frank Yale, was a long-time leader of the Unione Siciliana in New York. Always on the lookout for new talent, his eye was caught by a 14-year-old boy from Brooklyn by the name of Alphonse Caponie, whose buddies called him Al Capone for short. He came from a poor Neapolitan family whose members belonged to a brutal street gang. Capone and his associates would demand a cut from the teenagers who operated street-corner fruit and vegetable stalls. If a stallholder refused to pay, the gang would smash their windows or destroy their stall.

When Capone was 17, Yale gave him a job as a barman and bouncer in a saloon. One evening, a patron stabbed young Al in the face during a fight, severely wounding him. The resulting scar gave rise to his enduring nickname, 'Scarface'.

Soon afterwards, Capone met Johnny Torrio, Colosimo's nephew, for whom he felt a profound admiration. The link with Torrio drew Capone into the world of serious crime, and, for the first time, he participated in armed robbery and murder. In 1916, Torrio took over the management of Big Jim's brothels in Chicago. Three years later, he asked Capone to join him, and the two shared the profits following Big Jim's death.

Mightiest in the underworld

On January 16, 1920, an amendment to the US Constitution made the consumption and sale of alcohol illegal in the United States. This ban, which lasted until 1933, was known as Prohibition, and offered rich pickings for gangsters. When Prohibition was enforced, Scarface saw his chance. He opened an 'antique store' in the centre of Chicago that was actually a front for the illegal sale of alcohol. Soon he and Torrio had control of the beer market, while Sicilian and Irish gangs had a monopoly on the sale of spirits, some of which were smuggled across the border from Canada. The Torrio–Capone team also set up illegal bars – so-called speakeasies – and gambling dens. Together with the takings from prostitution, their activities made them extremely wealthy. Both travelled in limousines, threw lavish parties and gave generously to their friends.

Above: *Illegal bars, or 'speakeasies', were lucrative establishments during Prohibition. There were an estimated 23,000 in New York alone. In Chicago, Al Capone (right) controlled most of the alcohol trade.*

The turning point came when Luciano convinced Al Capone and other bosses, including Lucky's influential disciple Frank Costello, to come together. Between 1928 and 1934, a number of meetings took place in which the Italians decided to establish a network across the United States that would monopolise certain businesses. Certain non-Italian partners, such as Meyer Lansky, were to be included.

The nature of the huge proposed syndicate was agreed on at two meetings held in New York and Kansas City in 1934. It was to consist of 24 families of equal status, headed by a council of nine godfathers, to be known as dons, who would settle disputes. Criminologists regard this initiative as the real beginning of organised crime in the United States.

Luciano also provided the impulse for peace agreements between the New York bosses. He suggested that the city be

Like Big Jim Colosimo, Capone and Torrio manipulated city authorities and ensured that their candidates became mayor or chief of police. The police and justice system turned an increasingly blind eye to the gang bosses, particularly since any witnesses were invariably pressurised by the gangsters to commit perjury and retract statements made to the police. For example, when the bosses ordered the killing of their arch-enemy, the Irishman Dion O'Bannion, they provided alibis for everyone on their payroll, and – touchingly – even went to the trouble of attending O'Bannion's funeral.

Over the years, bloody gang wars claimed countless victims. When he was finally arrested in 1925, Torrio passed the gang leadership on to Capone, who proceeded to eliminate any remaining competitors. He soon became the mightiest man in the US underworld. Estimates placed the annual turnover of his empire in the region of more than US$60 million. In 1930, the authorities finally found a way to catch him: Capone was put behind bars for the crime of tax evasion. He served eight years of his eleven-year sentence – part of it in the infamous maximum-security prison on Alcatraz Island in San Francisco Bay – after which he was released due to ill health. Capone died of syphilis in Miami in 1948.

The mother of all syndicates

While Al Capone ran Chicago, the Mob was also flourishing in New York. Here the prostitution business was dominated by Italian gangs, while Irish, German, Russian and Polish groups concentrated on gambling and money lending, also known as 'loan sharking'. Among the big names on the New York crime scene were Salvatore 'Lucky' Luciano, a Sicilian who had immigrated to the United States at the age of ten. Together with the professional killer Benjamin 'Bugsy' Siegel and a Russian named Mei'or Suchowljansky – also known as Meyer Lansky – Luciano also entered the high-stakes trade in alcohol.

In the late 1920s, the struggle for control of the bootleg alcohol market escalated, leading to the so-called Castellammarese War. On the one hand, conflicts arose between rival factions within the Cosa Nostra, while on the other the Mafia battled Irish–Jewish groups. Hundreds of gangsters died in brutal contract killings.

Above: *A scene from a gangster film; Hollywood is fascinated by the Mob. Francesco Castiglia (left), alias Frank Costello, was one of Lucky Luciano's most faithful followers. He belonged to the Genovese family and helped to found the huge Italian syndicate.*

divided among the families, each of which would enjoy equal rights. The year 1931 saw the beginning of rule by the Big Five, which consisted of Luciano's own family, the Genovese, as well as the Bonanno, Lucchese, Gambino and Colombo clans.

When Prohibition ended two years later, the families expanded their involvement in prostitution, gambling and casinos. They also entered the heroin trade. In this venture, they enlisted the help of Corsican clans – the so-called French Connection – operating in southern Italy. The Corsicans helped the Cosa Nostra to refine the heroin from Turkish poppy cultures, and send it by ship to the US. The French Connection was interrupted by World War II, but was extended during the 1950s and 1960s. In the postwar period, the Corsicans established connections in Indochina, then a French colony, which became a key source of heroin.

The Cosa Nostra forced the Corsicans out of the heroin trade, and began to operate in co-operation with Asian, primarily Chinese,

Scores of followers attended the elaborate funeral of the gangster boss Lucky Luciano.

Lucky's rise

Before he was finally sentenced by an American court to 35 years in prison on charges of procurement, Lucky Luciano earned a fortune through his control of prostitution and alcohol smuggling, and, later, through trafficking in heroin. In 1943, the powerful godfather used his contacts within the Sicilian Mafia to assist Allied forces in the liberation of Sicily from Fascist rule. In 1946, he was deported to the Italian mainland, and settled in his home town of Naples. In spite of strict surveillance by the Carabinieri, the FBI and Interpol, he soon resumed his underworld activities, primarily in the drug trade. His luck ran out on January 27, 1962, when he died of heart failure while out driving.

organisations. In 1971–1972, investigators broke up the French Connection entirely. Rumours spread that New York's Big Five had provided the police with information that led to the arrest and conviction of their former partners. Only those involved knew for certain if this was the case.

Involuntary surrender of power

After the breakup of the French Connection, the New York Cosa Nostra turned its attention to Sicily, where it made use of family connections to establish a new heroin monopoly: the Sicilian Connection. They received their deliveries from the so-called Golden Crescent – the countries of Iran, Afghanistan and Pakistan.

By the early 1980s, however, change was in the air, as younger Mafiosi in cities like Los Angeles, Miami and Houston forced their way into the drug market. The new generation was no longer content to watch the older gangsters on the East Coast, whom they referred to with a mixture of disdain and envy as the Pizza Connection, cream off millions of dollars in proceeds from the narcotics trade.

It was at this time, too, that the US government intensified its campaign of criminal prosecutions. In 1984, President Ronald Reagan appointed a commission to combat organised crime, which concentrated on the Cosa Nostra in New York. For almost two years, city police and the FBI amassed evidence on Mafia activities. The material was so comprehensive that it enabled federal prosecutors to indict 19 members of the Big Five, including three dons. The testimony of

30 state witnesses was of vital importance in these trials. In January 1987, the court imposed long prison sentences – in some cases up to 100 years – on 18 of the accused.

Similar investigations in Boston, Denver, and St Louis netted many other gangsters. American investigators were able to pass on information to their Italian colleagues, and the Sicilian Mafia suffered a severe blow.

Unfortunately, these successes did not lead to a decline in organised crime. In certain

The wheel of fortune

Mei'or Suchowljansky, alias Meyer Lansky (1902–1983), was born the son of Russian Jews in Grodno, and became the financial wizard in the American underworld. In contrast to other bosses, he kept out of prostitution and the heroin trade in the years following Prohibition. Instead, Lansky became a multi-millionaire through the illegal gambling business. He built up a vast casino empire that employed hundreds of professional criminals. In the 1950s he made massive investments in Cuban hotels and casinos, and helped his fellow bosses by laundering money earned in drug and weapons dealing. When Fidel Castro came to power in Cuba in 1959, he put an end to Lansky's empire. The Cosa Nostra lost a fortune as a result of the Cuban revolution, but Lansky kept his wealth and went on to decentralise the Mafia's finances.

Right: Aged 48, Lucky Luciano arrives in Italy a year after the end of World War II. Even in exile, he maintained his connections to the American Cosa Nostra.

In recent years, Colombian growers have turned to the cultivation of poppies for heroin production. Police often spray herbicides on the crops, causing protests among farmers.

A state within the state

The career of the Colombians took a new turn when they began to move into the trafficking of cocaine, a drug derived from the leaves of the coca plant. The cocaine trade, centred on the city of Medellín, took shape when some of the most brutal bosses of the underground – Pablo Escobar, Jorge Luís Ochoa, Gonzalo Rodríguez Gacha and Carlos Léhder – made a pact. Escobar, born in 1949, soon took leadership of the cartel, which then acquired huge expanses of farmland, not only in Colombia, but in Bolivia and Peru, where the bulk of South American coca is grown. Raw cocaine is delivered to laboratories in Colombia in the form of a paste, which is then refined by chemists and smuggled into the United States and Western Europe.

areas of the US, other organisations stepped forward to replace the Cosa Nostra. For example, the Chinese triad 14K took over the heroin trade in New York, while Korean and Vietnamese secret organisations made their entry into the American underworld. But the most potent of the new arrivals were the Colombians.

Andean gold

From the late 1960s, drug use mushroomed in the United States. The hippie movement and the counterculture of the late 1960s made the use of marijuana – a derivative of the hemp plant – much more acceptable, and demand for the illegal weed grew rapidly. One source of marijuana was the South American nation of Colombia. In the early 1970s, a group of Colombian drug dealers arranged for marijuana to be cultivated along the coast of the Caribbean Sea, from where it could be easily exported to the US. By the late 1970s, the Colombians controlled 70–80% of American marijuana deals. By then, receipts from the export of drugs totalled between an estimated US$1.5 and US$2 billion, far exceeding the export of coffee, previously the most important legal sector of the economy in the poor Andean state. Soon officials, companies and farmers were co-operating with the new drug barons. For example, banks would launder money for the drug dealers, enabling them to convert illegal earnings in US dollars into legitimate Colombian pesos.

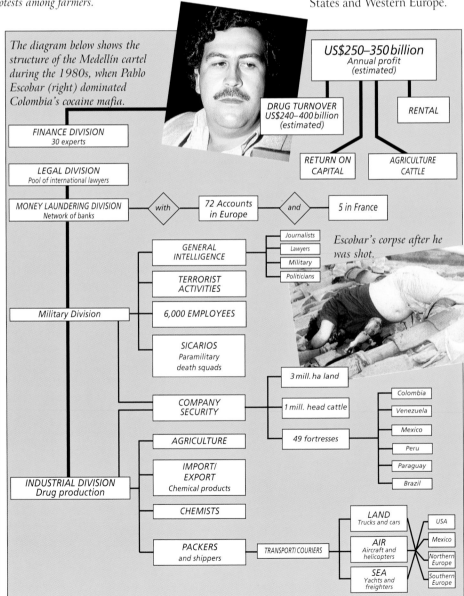

The diagram below shows the structure of the Medellín cartel during the 1980s, when Pablo Escobar (right) dominated Colombia's cocaine mafia.

Escobar's corpse after he was shot.

US$250–350 billion
Annual profit (estimated)

DRUG TURNOVER
US$240–400 billion
(estimated)

RENTAL

RETURN ON CAPITAL

AGRICULTURE CATTLE

FINANCE DIVISION
30 experts

LEGAL DIVISION
Pool of international lawyers

MONEY LAUNDERING DIVISION
Network of banks

with — 72 Accounts in Europe — and — 5 in France

GENERAL INTELLIGENCE
— Journalists
— Lawyers
— Military
— Politicians

TERRORIST ACTIVITIES

Military Division

6,000 EMPLOYEES

SICARIOS
Paramilitary death squads

COMPANY SECURITY
— 3 mill. ha land
— 1 mill. head cattle
— 49 fortresses

Colombia
Venezuela
Mexico
Peru
Paraguay
Brazil

AGRICULTURE

INDUSTRIAL DIVISION
Drug production

IMPORT/EXPORT
Chemical products

CHEMISTS

PACKERS
and shippers

TRANSPORT/COURIERS

LAND
Trucks and cars

AIR
Aircraft and helicopters

SEA
Yachts and freighters

USA
Mexico
Northern Europe
Southern Europe

The cocaine bosses took advantage of falling coffee prices, which meant more and more farmers came to depend on growing coca. The collapse in coffee prices came about in 1989, when the US abandoned a coffee-pricing agreement initiated by them in 1940. Intended to bring economic stability to South America, the pricing agreement had fixed export quotas, ensuring that Colombia became the second-largest coffee exporter in the world. When the agreement expired in 1989, prices for the aromatic beans hit rock-bottom, and thousands of poor farmers were forced to turn to the much more lucrative cultivation of drugs.

At the height of its power, the cocaine cartel employed more than 100,000 people, and earned between US$240 and US$400 billion each year. Its influence was massive: money from the drug trade was used to pay off politicians, judges and police officers. The cartel exerted control over virtually all of Colombia's mass media, as well as its cultural and sporting establishments. Death squads with 15,000 armed members cold-bloodedly murdered anyone who stood in the cartel's way: newspaper editors, critical journalists, politicians, judges and policemen. A state had emerged within the state.

Andean farmers are still strongly dependent on coca cultivation. Only a few of them, as shown here, are willing to fight the drug cartels.

sports facilities, Escobar and his men became hugely popular. For example, he financed a construction programme, 'Medellín without slums', building houses for the homeless, recreational facilities and a zoo. In 1982, his activities won him a seat in parliament. However, he was stripped of his seat a few months later following conflicts with the minister of justice, Rodrigo Lara Bonilla. Escobar's hitmen took revenge and shot Bonilla in 1984.

The assassination of Bonilla convinced the government in Bogotá to sign an extradition agreement with the US. The agreement was unique in the history of international law: no other state had ever agreed to voluntarily bypass its own judiciary and hand over its criminals to another state for trial.

Escobar and his accomplices – who became known as the Extraditables – were not frightened. In 1984, they offered to pay back Colombia's foreign debt – at that time, some US$12.5 billion – if the country's president, Belisario Betancur, ordered a halt to the extradition proceedings. The Colombian government refused – regretfully, according to many insiders. When Luís Carlos Galán, presidential candidate of the Liberal Party and a supporter of tough measures against the cocaine barons, was murdered in front of cameras in August 1989, the government pursued extradition with a vengeance.

A fake imprisonment

After discussions with mediator Father Rafael Garcia Herreros, Pablo Escobar announced on April 18, 1991 that he intended to release two prominent hostages – the wife and sister of senator Alberto Villamizar – and surrender to the

Father Rafael G. Herreros

Colombian judiciary. Four weeks later, the gangster kept his promise and gave himself up to the general state prosecutor, signing a series of admissions of guilt. But Escobar's confession was carefully designed to avoid the thing he feared most – extradition to the United States. Although guarded by armed soldiers, the prison where he was held was furnished according to his designs, and he was able to conduct his business deals without difficulty, a fact that aroused indignation and anger throughout the world. His escape in the summer of 1992 showed that he had retained excellent contacts with the outside world.

continued to direct his empire. A year later, Escobar escaped, but on December 2, 1993 an elite police unit cornered him in a house in Medellín. The king of the cartel died in a hail of automatic weapons fire.

Indecisive action

While the Medellín cartel was busy with its war against the state, competitors in the city of Cali took over the leading position in the cocaine market in the early 1990s. Although investigators imprisoned both Cali bosses in 1995, and an anti-Mafia law of December 1996 paved the way for the confiscation of the drug lords' property and assets, corrupt politicians still aided the criminals.

The cocaine trade will continue to flourish as long as America's demand for the drug remains high. As with the Cosa Nostra, America's struggle against organised crime seems never-ending.

The rise and fall of Escobar

For many of Colombia's poor people, Pablo Escobar became a kind of folk hero, the son of a poor farmer who had risen to become one of the richest men on earth. Through gifts and donations, and the construction of

The Medellín cartel then declared war on the state, and a terrible civil war ensued. In June 1991, Escobar surrendered to the authorities on condition that he be granted privileged status. He chose his own prison, a luxurious hilltop location, from where he

THE RUSSIAN MAFIA: THE DEADLIEST SYNDICATE OF ALL

Instead of heralding democracy and a better life for all, the fall of Communism has allowed criminal gangs to flourish in the former Soviet Union. Instead of fighting the underworld, it seems that many high-ranking officials maintain close connections to the Mafia. The weakness of central authority has allowed the gangs to plunder the assets of the state and legitimate businesses. And the Organisazija has now moved into lucrative ventures in Western Europe and North America.

On March 1, 1995, at around 10:30 pm, Vladislav Listjev, the general director of a leading Russian independent television station, entered his Moscow apartment block. In the stairwell, he came face to face with an armed man. Listjev tried to flee, but it was too late. Two bullets struck him down.

The station suspended all programming on the following day, and broadcast only this statement: 'May our silence be a warning to those in government and to society: a country where criminal societies rule boundlessly has no future'.

Listjev's killing dramatically highlighted the prominence of organised crime in Russia. Among other things, he had tried to keep his station free of advertising companies that wanted him to include as much advertising as possible. A number of these companies were clearly in the hands of the Russian Mafia, and earned spectacular returns. For example, Vyacheslav Ivankov, one of the most infamous of Moscow's Mafia bosses, raked in as much as US$250,000 each month from television advertising. There were signs of his involvement in Listjev's murder. Fearing reprisals, detectives and journalists with more information kept quiet – an extreme example of the climate of fear created by organised crime in Russia.

Anarchy instead of democracy

Despite official denials, there was always crime in the former Soviet Union. Numerous criminal societies were established in the late 1980s, in the wake of the liberalisation of the Soviet system introduced by Mikhail Gorbachev. Following the collapse of the Soviet empire in 1991, many more such groups emerged in the

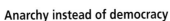

Television journalist Vladislav Listjev opposed the attempts of the Mafia to undermine his TV station. He paid for this stance with his life.

Russian Federation and the various successor states of the Soviet Union. The chaos around the fall of the Iron Curtain and the end of the Soviet Union created the right conditions for criminals of all kinds.

The Russian government made a big mistake when it chose to ignore the fact that criminals had moved into the new private economic sector, making illegal activities acceptable business practices. According to a recent official estimate, the *Organisazija* – as the Mafia is called in Russian – owns about 40,000 private and public companies. These include banks, commercial firms, distribution agencies and real estate agencies. It also controls smuggling, is increasing its influence in the media, operates prostitution rings and earns incredible sums from sales of weapons and drugs. Some insiders maintain that the Mafia uses up to 50% of its income for bribing officials. Last, but not least, the underworld obtains part of its income through extortion; legitimate companies frequently have to turn over between 10 and 20% of their profits to the gangsters. The effect is that prices spiral ever higher and the already impoverished Russian population lurches closer to destitution.

Instead of fighting against the Mafia, it is obvious that greedy politicians and poorly paid officials find it easier to co-operate with them. Fuelled by lavish bribes, corruption has become a fact of life in Russia. Where democracy should flourish, the country seems on the brink of lawlessness.

Just like the Italian clans, these criminal societies use secret codes, carry out initiation ceremonies for new members and submit themselves to a dubious code of honour. But the term 'Russian Mafia' is also slightly misleading, for the gangs are by no means a homogeneous unit. Georgians and Azeris from the Caucasus region are also active in the underworld. However, Ukrainian and Czech gangs have not as yet followed the Russians into the realms of serious crime.

Expansion of crime

Of all the criminal groups in the former Communist-ruled Eastern Bloc, those of the former Soviet Union are expanding the fastest. The first of these gangs made their appearance in Western Europe during the 1970s. At that time, they were involved mainly in counterfeiting, slot machines and the smuggling of gold and icons (painted religious images). Their illegal activities were centred on the divided city of Berlin, which at that time lay deep inside Communist-ruled East Germany.

After the collapse of Communism, the Russian Mafia formed close ties with other criminal syndicates. Their first meetings with the Sicilian Mafia, the Camorra and the 'Ndrangheta took place in March and June 1991 in Warsaw, capital of Poland. The syndicates found that they had much in common, and the links between them developed rapidly. This is hardly surprising, since each side had much to offer the other. They agreed on a worldwide network for dealing in drugs and radioactive materials. According to Britain's National Criminal Intelligence Service, about 60% of the heroin smuggled into the European Union is routed via the Balkans and the former Eastern Bloc states. Even more alarming has been the increase in illegal shipments of radioactive materials from the East. If any of these fell into the hands of terrorists, the results could be terrifying.

International connections

The rapid rise of the Russian Mafia took Western authorities by surprise. Police chiefs found it hard to believe that organised crime had changed so quickly. Until the early 1990s, extortion, hostage-taking, bombing of banks and contract killings were never seen in a global context.

While the Eastern European underground was establishing contacts with its cousins in Western Europe, a new chapter unfolded in America. Russian crime boss Vyacheslav Ivankov crossed the Atlantic to establish bases in the US, where many Russians had emigrated. Using a false name, he and his closest associates travelled to New York. In a short time, they got rid of all rival groups. This war turned Ivankov's gang into by far the most powerful arm of the Russian Mafia in the United States. It is rumoured that the group maintains close contact with New York's Cosa Nostra.

Ivankov, called the 'Red Godfather' by the FBI, soon had bases in Miami, Boston, Denver and Los Angeles. His gang specialises in insurance and credit card fraud, extortion and the sale of black-market fuel – cheating authorities out of millions of dollars in sales tax each year. The FBI arrested Ivankov in 1995, but his gang continued to operate.

A web of international connections means that the Russian Mafia can easily transfer illegal income from one country to another. Another popular way of laundering money is for the criminals to set up commercial companies and sell products to each other at inflated prices. And this system works the other way, too: they sell goods bought with dirty money, such as precious stones and works of art, to their own companies abroad at prices far below market value. The goods then yield high profits when resold.

A photographer snapped this picture near the Kremlin in Moscow: note the New York licence plate of this luxury vehicle.

The international network of the Russian Mafia is virtually impenetrable. According to some estimates, they currently have an annual turnover of about US$100 billion and number well over 1.8 million members.

The army's shady deals

After the collapse of the Berlin Wall in 1989, Soviet leader Mikhail Gorbachev allowed Soviet troops stationed in Germany to enter into commerce. In preparation for the reunification of Germany, new laws came into effect on July 1, 1990, allowing the men of the Red Army to purchase duty-free merchandise. While ordinary soldiers could improve their meagre pay by selling medals and cigarettes outside their barracks, the officers soon made contact with the Mafia. Both sides earned healthy profits through the sale of military equipment, most of which found its way into the wars in the former Yugoslavia.

Russian investigative journalist Dimitri Cholodov conducted extensive research into corruption on Soviet military bases. He was supposed to present his results in October 1994 during a hearing in the Duma – Russia's parliament. Shortly before he was due to appear, Cholodov was killed by a bomb.

Shocked citizens of Moscow read about the assassination of the journalist Dimitri Cholodov. He intended to reveal how the Soviet armed forces had collaborated with the Mafia.

THE YAKUZA: JAPAN'S TATTOOED PROTECTORS

In the 17th century, when Japan was wracked by wars between rival warlords, the Yakuza protected the people from attacks by wandering bands of fierce samurai warriors. Inevitably, the Yakuza began to exploit the population. Today, they are active in all profitable areas of crime, but these tattooed gangsters are also branching out into many legitimate sectors of the economy.

The Yakuza are increasingly active on the Japanese stock market.

During the 17th century, Japan went through a period of great change. After a long era of civil war, peace returned to the islands, and the *shoguns*, or military dictators, began the process of restructuring the state. As a result, the elite samurai warriors lost their influence and their fortunes. Many of them became criminals, raiding villages and cities for food and money.

In order to protect themselves, the people then looked towards the non-criminal samurai – traders, craftsmen and labourers. Among them were many sharp minds and potentially strong leaders. These men began to form local defence committees, and these bodies soon earned the respect of the people; they became the 'Robin Hoods' of Japan, and built up an organisation marked by strong hierarchy and many rituals.

The tables turn

It was not long, however, before they began to prey on the people. They extorted money and opened gambling dens where a popular card game, *hanafuda*, was played. The worst hand consisted of an eight (*ya*), a nine (*ku*) and a three (*za*). The losers were referred to as *yakuza*, but in time the meaning of the word changed. It came to be used for the players themselves, or any type of criminal.

From the early 18th century, the defence committees formed increasingly close links with corrupt bureaucrats; the latter made themselves dependent on the owners of gambling dens, who provided them with labourers. A reliable labour supply was vital for the shoguns, who desperately needed workers to carry out their monumental construction projects.

Despite their criminal activities, the Yakuza have always seen themselves as the guardians of Japan's enduring values, such as loyalty to the emperor. In the 20th century, they began to move into the world of right-wing politics. When US troops occupied Japan after World War II, the American military government took strict measures against the society. But this changed when members of the Yakuza started to express anti-Communist views. The Yakuza did not remain outlawed for long; by the end of the 1940s, the American authorities had turned to the Yakuza as allies in the struggle to halt the spread of socialist ideas and trade unions. In the years to come, funds from the Yakuza flowed into the coffers of conservative political parties. According to police information, it is no longer possible to separate Japan's right wing from the Yakuza.

Many Yakuza have mutilated fingers (top) and extensive tattoos (above).

The Yakuza are organised into families, which of course are not based on actual kinship. The *oyabun* has the final authority, and he takes on the role of father and ruler. From his 'sons', the *kobun*, he demands unconditional loyalty. In order to become full members, they must pass through a difficult initiation phase, at the end of which they have to take a blood oath at a Shinto shrine. Among their secret signs are the ritual greeting, '*jingi*', and the tattooing of the entire body. If a kobun makes a mistake, he cuts off the tip of his little finger and sends it to his oyabun as a sign of penance.

Half-hearted reaction

Officials estimate that there are roughly 900,000 Yakuza in Japan today. The most influential syndicates are the Sumiyoshi-Rengo and the Inagawa-Kai in Tokyo, and the Amaguchi-Gumi in Kobe and Osaka. The illegal traffic in amphetamines provides about half of their illegal income, but the Yakuza do not neglect any area of crime: gambling, illegal bookmaking, extortion, prostitution and trafficking in arms all earn millions for the families. In recent years, they have been involved in property transactions and the stock market.

On March 1, 1992, Japan passed an anti-gang law. The new legislation officially made the Yakuza a criminal society, but certain loopholes mean that investigators may only confiscate the proceeds of drug deals. It is difficult to track down the transactions that the families make between their many front companies. Because the Yakuza now engage in so many legal businesses, more drastic measures are needed to break their power.

The origins of China's secret societies lie as far back as 200 BC. Over the centuries, secret societies flourished in opposition to the Confucian upper class, which prohibited any form of opposition to imperial rule. In those days, the societies attempted to stand up for the rights of the dissatisfied and oppressed lower classes. In the 17th century, when the ruling Ming dynasty was overthrown by the Manchu, whose origins lay in Central Asia, many secret societies directed their efforts towards the expulsion of the 'barbarian' Manchu.

Out of this liberation struggle emerged the Society of the Three in One, also called the triadic league or Triad. The emblem of the league was an isosceles triangle – in which each side is of equal length – whose three sides symbolised the basic forces in Chinese cosmology: heaven, earth and man.

During the 19th century, the huge and increasingly fragmented Chinese empire gave rise to two systems of secret societies: in the north was the White Lotus, while the south was home to the various branches of the Triad. Their resistance was not directed solely against the Manchu rulers, but also against the encroachment of European colonial powers. The 19th century saw the establishment of more and more foreign-administered enclaves, with China forced again and again to accept treaties that favoured foreign powers. Not only did the 'long noses' destroy existing economic structures, but they also introduced the trade in opium, which was first imported from India by the British. Although the imperial government prohibited the import of opium, the trade opened up lucrative commercial prospects for foreign companies. The main result was that countless millions of Chinese, mainly in the new cities that sprang up around the foreign enclaves, became helpless drug addicts.

CHINA'S TRIADS

Secret societies have a long and even honourable history in China, where they were forced to operate in secret to counter the cruelties of imperial rule. China's Triads were born out of the struggle against the detested Manchu regime, but somehow these crusaders for justice embraced the dark forces and turned to crime. Today, the Triads are among the most feared criminal societies in the world, with activities ranging from the heroin trade to the smuggling of illegal immigrants.

The movie Year of the Dragon, *by director Michael Cimino, dramatised the rise of the Triads.*

When the last Manchu emperor abdicated in 1911, the Triads lost their most important political goal: the re-establishment of Ming rule. Over the next three decades, as rival warlords divided up the country, the societies degenerated more and more into criminal gangs. Initially, they made money through piracy, extortion, gambling and kidnapping, but they soon entered the opium trade. The British colony of Hong Kong became a centre for many such gangs. After the Communists assumed power in China in 1949, the colony became the main base for the powerful Triads Sun Yee On, Wo Sing So and 14K. By the early 1990s, these groups totalled over 75,000 members.

Enter the dragon

Because of the impenetrable structure of the Triads, it is difficult to gather information about their activities. The Triads are known to have operated in the United Kingdom and the Netherlands since the 1970s, where they specialise in loan-sharking, prostitution and extortion. According to senior officials of the Metropolitan Police, nearly every Chinese restaurant in London has to pay a percentage of its takings to the Eastern Mafia. The Triads are also active in drug trafficking, exporting heroin from the Golden Triangle – a region covering the remote interior of Burma, Laos and northern Thailand. In the US, the Drug Enforcement Administration (DEA) maintains that the 14K Triad is the biggest supplier of heroin in New York.

There is another cruel business that earns millions for the Hong Kong syndicates: the trade in human beings. Thousands of illegal immigrants are smuggled into Europe and North America each year. In most cases, the immigrants are desperate people searching for a better life, and they generally have to pay the Triads a fee of around US$35,000. Few of the applicants have the money, so they are frequently forced to work for the gangsters in restaurants and gambling dens until they can pay their debts. Women must earn the money through prostitution.

For many years, the metropolis of Hong Kong has been the main base for the Triads.

THE DIRTY BUSINESS OF MONEY LAUNDERING

Awash with cash from peddling narcotics and guns, international crime syndicates dump billions in illegal earnings into the legitimate financial system. Even with tighter laws and more vigilant police investigations, this dirty money continues to pollute the world economy.

For some time, a Dutchman would appear each week at a German bank on the lower Rhine and convert cash from various currencies into Dutch guilders and US dollars. Invariably, the amounts ran into six figures. When Belgian police picked him up in October 1996 after he tried to exchange £240,000 at a bank in Belgium, police in the German state of North Rhine-Westphalia launched an investigation, which revealed that the Dutchman earned his living by laundering money for drug traffickers from the United Kingdom, Scandinavia, Germany and Australia. Altogether, it is thought that he channelled about US$66 million through the German financial system.

acquired'. In plain language, this means channelling money into normal circulation in order to unlawfully conceal its illegal source – be it drug trafficking, arms dealing, blackmail or other criminal activities. Money laundering enables criminals to destroy the evidence of their criminal activity.

Because laundered money is often hard to trace, it is difficult to determine exactly how much is at stake in these transactions, and the estimates differ enormously. According to an International Monetary Fund (IMF) estimate in 1996, more than US$500 billion is laundered annually throughout the world. Money laundering takes place around the world, from the nations of Western Europe

areas of activity. Investigators face an uphill task in determining the source of a particular sum of money. But years of experience have enabled them to distinguish three distinct phases of money laundering:

❑ **Placement**: The most obvious way of introducing illegal earnings into the legal financial economy is to deposit cash at a bank. Syndicates usually use front men for this purpose. In the early 1980s, for example, a German grocer deposited cash amounting to 14 million Deutschmarks (US$8 million) in his bank account over a short period of time. The money had been entrusted to him by drug couriers from all over Europe.

The risk of getting caught is considerable. Because criminals amass huge quantities of cash – from street sales of drugs, for example – they face the problem of depositing large

No-one knows how much of the skyline of downtown Miami was financed by South American drug bosses.

Although the sums of money involved are huge, not many people know exactly what is involved in money laundering. In 1984, an American commission looking into organised crime provided a comprehensive definition. It described money laundering as 'a process whereby the existence, the illegal source, or the illegal use of funds is disguised, in order that these funds appear to have been legally

and North America to newly democratised Eastern Europe and the developing nations of South America, Asia and Africa.

Three phases

The nature of financial transactions makes it easy for organised crime bosses to distribute their profits into a variety of businesses and

amounts of banknotes. Anyone appearing at the teller of a bank with shopping bags full of banknotes is viewed with suspicion by bank officials. A grocer who suddenly has millions to deposit should be a dead giveaway.

The solution is for the criminals to get other people to deposit money for them. Often, restaurant owners are forced to open bank accounts into which dirty money can be paid. An established business is unlikely to attract attention, even if the amounts deposited are as much as tens of thousands of dollars.

But criminals are tending increasingly to mix dirty money with legal profits. For this purpose, they set up 'front companies', including import–export firms, video rental outlets and sex shops. Such companies use decoy sales in order to move illegally earned profits through their cash registers. The owners can then deposit them in various accounts without concern, and even pay taxes to create the illusion of legitimacy.

This technique was used by a Turkish money-laundering gang which operated in many European states. Members of the gang delivered worthless goods, such as rotting food, to a German businessman in Munich. When he took delivery, he issued a receipt for more than half a million Deutschmarks, and usually destroyed the goods. His only objective was to get his dirty money out of Germany. By the time police cracked the scam, he had transferred about 350 million Deutschmarks to accounts in 15 countries.

Who is involved?

Gangsters alone cannot launder their ill-gotten gains. Three groups help the gangsters to integrate illegal profits into the conventional financial world. The first group is the members of the crime syndicates themselves. The second includes volunteers who are otherwise employed in legal professions, such as money couriers or corrupt legal and financial experts who offer their services to criminal organisations. The third group consists of people or institutions that may

A small currency exchange bureau in Cali, one of the centres of the Colombian drug business. Transactions worth billions are concluded in such establishments.

unwittingly support illegal transactions, such as bank employees, trustees, real-estate agents or investment companies.

worthless, loss-making state corporations on extremely generous terms and asked few questions about the accounts of these firms. The new owners could easily declare that the proceeds from drug trafficking, arms dealing and protection rackets were actually legally earned income.

❏ **Layering**: During the second phase in the money laundering process, the money has to circulate. Usually, it moves from one international financial centre to another. Here, an

funds at short notice. The most important offshore havens are Hong Kong, the Cayman Islands, the Bahamas, Panama, the Netherlands Antilles and Bahrain. Apart from Hong Kong, the economies of the tax havens are not highly developed, so they compete fiercely for the illegal capital that serves to increase their national income.

Drug-exporting countries also depend on the flow of illegal money. It is estimated that US$11 billion is channelled from the US to South America by front men working for drug bosses. Of this amount, more than US$1 billion originates in New York City. The money is transferred by telegraph from

After the opening of the Berlin Wall in 1989, international criminals descended on the former East Germany. More than a third of the investments made there after 1989 came from illegally earned millions. It seems that the German government unwittingly participated in money laundering when it set up a trust to dispose of East Germany's state-owned enterprises. The trust sold almost

important role is played by offshore tax havens – countries where there is either low taxation or none at all – which allow the formation of anonymous companies. These conditions make it easy for criminal groups to form front companies. Typically, they grant lawyers power of attorney to conclude transactions, open accounts at local banks and position themselves to invest transferred

small currency exchange bureaus or via established financial services companies. Because these kind of transactions are so easy to carry out, the US government passed legislation in mid-1997 that required the reporting of all money transfers in excess of US$750. Previously, the limit had been US$10,000. But even before the legal framework was tightened, officials from the

Drug Enforcement Agency (DEA), together with US Customs and the French police, exposed the involvement of Rapid-O-Giros, a chain of French currency exchange bureaus, in illegal transactions amounting to millions of dollars. It turned out that the company had links to the Cali drug syndicate.

Successful investigations like this are forcing the criminal organisations to think up new tricks. In 1997, the *New York Times*

smuggling. Gangsters also fit out chemical and pharmaceutical companies for the secret production of drugs and form tourism companies to enable them to sell drugs more easily. Many run their own gambling casinos where money can be laundered effortlessly.

On the surface, it might appear that the industrial nations actually profit from money laundering, since it introduces vast sums into their economies. However, criminologists are

disturbed by the way criminals continue to introduce billions of dollars into many sectors of the economy, because this brings them social legitimacy. For example, South American cocaine gangs have invested in American television stations and newspapers and pumped money into the construction of office towers in centres of the drug trade such as Miami, Florida. On the Costa Del Sol, Spain's popular Mediterranean holiday region, cocaine syndicates now own hotel and restaurant chains, as well as apartment buildings and night clubs.

According to an Italian financial journal, the Mafia owns more than half of the retail businesses, a third of all agriculture, 20% of the credit and financial institutions, 20% of transport companies, as well as 10% of the industrial and service sector in the province of Naples. But the Cosa Nostra is by no means confined to southern Italy. The men of respect own banks, insurance agencies and leasing companies throughout the country, and have also moved into the acquisition of high-value government bonds and letters of credit, which puts the gangsters in a position to affect the national budget deficit. This is a worrying development, for it gives organised crime control over the state.

A branch of the Rapid-O-Giros currency exchange chain in Miami. Investigations showed that the firm was laundering money for the Colombian Mafia.

reported that the drug syndicates were increasingly buying consumer goods such as alcohol, electronics and automobiles in the United States, which they then sold in Latin America at prices far below their actual value. Although the money launderers lose about 20–30% of their expenses through such transactions, the money still remains undetected by the authorities. Even this loss is worthwhile, given the massive profit margins of the cocaine trade.

Experts fear that layering is on the increase through the growth of cash-free transactions, such as those using credit cards, telebanking, teleshopping and so-called cyberbanking – capital transfers made via the Internet.

❏ **Integration**: In the last phase of the process, the newly laundered money flows back to where it came from, and the gangsters can now invest it legally. Often this is done by buying shares on the financial markets or purchasing goods – particularly those that will improve the infrastructure of their syndicates. Laundered money is used to purchase real estate, expand front companies and acquire ships and aircraft to facilitate

The world's offshore tax havens

It is becoming increasingly difficult to distinguish between money laundered by criminals and legitimate funds moved around the world by multinational corporations in order to reduce their tax burden. Large corporations increasingly transfer profits offshore, to underdeveloped countries or to European nations with favourable investment conditions, such as Luxembourg or Switzerland, and form front companies or foundations through which they can channel and invest their funds.

International investigators cannot stop the flood of cocaine shipments – shown here disguised as cheese – and block illegal profits.

There is also a real danger that laundered money might, in the long run, drive out clean money – that Mafia-run enterprises might eliminate competition. Enterprises that are fed by laundered money have no need to worry about making a legitimate profit, and can afford to drive prices down, thereby putting legal businesses out of business. Economic power also determines political influence. The Russian Mafia has close ties to members of the government in Moscow, while the Colombian drug bosses keep their government in check with lavish campaign donations and bribes.

Inadequate laws

Western nations have generally been slow to introduce laws to fight money laundering. Among the first was Italy in 1982, followed by the United States (1986), the United Kingdom (1986–1987), France (1987), Spain (1988), Canada (1989), Switzerland (1990) and Germany (1993). But such laws are often not enough to halt the problem. In 1994, German investigators confiscated 10 million Deutschmarks (US$5.5 million) in suspicious funds, but this represents at most only 0.02% of the total sum laundered by German banks and financial institutions.

Legislation runs into difficulties when it comes to confiscating private property, since this requires considerable legal justification. Prosecutors must be able to demonstrate not only 'sufficient' but 'compelling' cause to believe the accused's guilt. This is difficult to prove, since the origin of banknotes is not written on them.

The weakest link in the chain is the banking system. Some time after Germany passed laws to control money laundering, the journalist Jörg Heimbrecht tested the willingness of banks to report suspicious customers to the authorities. Together with some colleagues, Heimbrecht set up a front company and employed a professional money launderer to 'wash' and invest some 400 million Deutschmarks (US$222 million) – a sum that had supposedly originated from criminal activities – in German, Austrian and Swiss banks. The result was that Heimbrecht received letters of acceptance from a dozen banks. A number of financial institutions did refuse to accept the dirty money, but they neglected to inform either the police or state prosecutors.

Reform of the financial system is clearly needed, for Germany still has the reputation among gangsters as a haven for 'bleaching' black-market money. To get around problems when large amounts of cash are deposited at banks, criminals are starting to invest in property and life insurance.

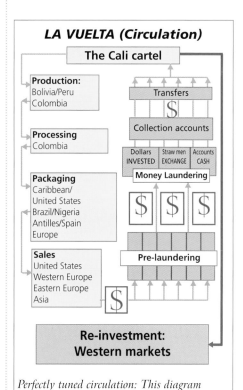

Perfectly tuned circulation: This diagram shows how the Cali cocaine cartel organises its businesses and launders money.

The Basle Statement

There have been several important international initiatives aimed at curbing the spread of money laundering. One of the most important was the Basle Statement of 1988, which aimed to deny money launderers the use of the banking system. According to the Basle Statement, banks should step up efforts to know the true identity of their customers, and to verify the *bona fides* of new customers; they should ensure that their business is carried on in conformity with high ethical standards, laws and regulations; and they should co-operate with law enforcement agencies, especially when there are reasonable grounds for suspicion of money laundering.

Co-operation is needed

Even countries that have worked hard at perfecting their investigation procedures find themselves confronting serious problems, since money laundering often crosses borders with lightning speed. This does not only apply to bank transfers. In 1997, employees of the US Department of Justice admitted that US Customs agents neglected to check many of the trucks leaving the United States for Mexico, since they had their hands full checking vehicles waiting to cross into the United States. Huge quantities of cash could be taken out of the US along this route.

Furthermore, money laundering cannot be detected as long as the offshore tax havens tolerate the influx of illegal funds. For years, the US government has pressurised offshore centres to stop criminal transactions. But most have shown little willingness to co-operate; it is apparently more important to them to secure their positions with short-term profits.

Experts stress that the fight against money laundering requires co-operation between governments, investigating authorities and banks. Many also recommend the formation of a global financial community that would only admit nations with efficient detection measures. Restrictions would be placed on transactions with non-member states. Until more people wake up to the problem, such suggestions will remain wishful thinking.

CULTS: A TICKET TO HEAVEN?

Ever since the late 1960s, and the rise of the hippie culture, the promise of enlightenment and spiritual wellbeing has lured many people into religious cults. While some of these are genuine religious movements, there is concern about the activities of others. Pseudo-religions enjoy great popularity, and have even become big business. Nevertheless, accusations of fraud and dangerous brainwashing surround these movements.

Above: *Maharishi Mahesh Yogi, founder of TM and formerly the guru of the Beatles. Communal meals (below left) are a feature of many cults.*

When we recall the 1960s, many people remember student protests in North America and Europe. That turbulent decade saw many adolescents rebel against what they saw as the materialistic values of their parents' generation. They demanded greater freedom and the right to share in political decision-making. They dressed outrageously, and experimented with drugs such as marijuana and LSD. In attempting to find an alternative to the capitalist way of life, which was perceived as soulless and cruel, many young people were drawn to the teachings of Eastern gurus.

The religious cults of the late 1960s appear relatively harmless to us today. However, times have changed, and some of these movements now seem less benign. Several of the movements that purport to offer salvation and enlightenment have expanded steadily during the past three decades, and many new organisations have made their appearance. Some of these are considered dangerous: by joining, members become isolated from the outside world and from their families, and they grow psychologically dependent on the cult, which often exploits these vulnerable young people.

Indian wisdom

Transcendental meditation (TM) first hit the headlines in the mid-1960s when pop stars such as the Beatles and actress Mia Farrow became involved with the movement. Interest in its philosophy quickly spread through the West. The founder, Maharishi Mahesh Yogi (born 1918), defined TM as a non-religious way of relaxing, one that allows practitioners to be much more creative and to find pathways to inspiration. It is even said that TM can bestow a kind of paranormal capability – for example, levitating off the ground while in the lotus position.

In the final analysis, TM bears many of the hallmarks of a religion. But more than that, the movement professes a kind of universal political status. In 1976, for example, it proclaimed the 'World Government of the Age of Illumination', which was aimed at promoting world peace and a perfect society. The centre of the movement is in Switzerland, and it is estimated to have 2 million followers worldwide.

Above: *Hare Krishna followers from Moscow gather in Calcutta, India. Since the collapse of Communism, many cults have won supporters in Eastern Europe.*

Probably even more people belong to the controversial Bhagwan movement, which was started in 1974 by Rajneesh Chandra Mohan (1931–1990), a former professor of philosophy. The master formed a commune, or *ashram*, at Pune (or Poona) in India, adopted the name Bhagwan (the Sublime One) and began to spread his philosophy, which was shaped by a combination of Hindu theology and Western psychotherapy. Believers could transcend this world, the guru said, by a combination of spirituality and uninhibited sex. Many non-conformists from Europe and the US – often quite wealthy people – were profoundly touched by the Bhagwan's message. His followers called themselves the Sannyasins, although they were often called the Rajneesh. They tried to get away from the alienation and stress of Western society by living according to the motto 'totally relaxed in the here and now'.

The dream turns sour

Pursued by opponents and Indian tax authorities, Mohan moved to the US state of Oregon in 1981, where he began building Rajneeshpuram, the 'city of the new people' – known to sceptics as Rancho Rajneesh. Tensions arose within the community, partly because the master made his supporters work hard for him. They had to establish restaurants and discos in order to increase the wealth of the cult. Finally, Bhagwan came into conflict with the state authorities in Oregon. He was eventually arrested and deported. Back in Pune, he founded the 'World Academy of Creative Sciences'. After his death, news surfaced of the Bhagwan's great personal wealth and his sexual exploitation of female cult members. Still, the ashram remained extraordinarily popular. The enterprising Sannyasins have established businesses in many countries, offering courses in massage, yoga, Tantra and meditation techniques.

In contrast to the worldly Sannyasins, the followers of the Hare Krishna movement earn money mainly through the sale of religious literature and devotional objects and through asking for donations on the street. Members are easily recognisable by their shorn heads with a single ponytail, and by their long flowing orange robes. Hare Krishnas are often seen dancing outdoors,

and are alleged to chant the mantra 'Hare Krishna, Krishna, Krishna' 1,728 times each day. By repetition, members believe they can attain ecstasy, establish contact with the divine and bring 'never-ending happiness' in the world. The followers commit themselves to 'four regulating principles': no meat, drugs, gambling or extra-marital sex.

The Hare Krishna movement is based on the ancient Indian religious scriptures, the *Vedas* and the *Bhagavad-Gita*. The group was founded by Abhay Charan Bhaktivedanta

In August 1992, the Reverend Sun Myung Moon blessed 20,000 newly married couples in a stadium in Seoul, South Korea.

Swami Prabhupada (1896–1977), a Bengali who had worked for a chemical company before moving to the United States, where he formed the International Society for Krishna Consciousness (ISKCON).

The Hare Krishnas are characterised by a rigid hierarchical structure. Cult-watchers criticise Charan for having created a type of spiritualised caste structure similar to the caste system which governs Indian society. There are many levels among the Hare Krishnas, with the lowest composed of those who do the hardest jobs.

When the guru died, a management team of 11 people took control of the running of ISKCON, but the movement soon became linked to illegal activities. The 1990s saw the

introduction of reforms intended to give the Hare Krishnas a more positive image.

The Moonies

Another highly controversial cult is the Unification Church, whose members are known as Moonies. Generally, the Moonies keep a very low public profile, but their influence should not be underestimated.

The Unification Church was founded by the Korean pastor Sun Myung Moon (born 1920). At the age of 16, Moon is said to have experienced a vision on Easter Sunday: his biography relates that 'on a ... mountain, deep in prayer, Jesus appeared to him and the young man was given the mission of creating heaven on earth'.

During the Korean War (1950–1953), Moon moved from Pyongyang, now the capital of North Korea, to the port city of Pusan, in South Korea. In 1954, he formed the 'Society of the Holy Spirit for the Unification of World Christianity'. Four years later, he left his country to work as a missionary. He first moved his operations to Japan and the US, and later expanded into Latin America and Western Europe. In 1973, the master took up residence in America. The Unification Church claims to have a total of 2 million members; however, experts estimate the number of Moonies at no more than 200,000 people.

Moon's book, *Divine Principles*, presents him as Jesus Christ returned, on a quest to redeem mankind. According to Moon, Jesus did not fulfil God's plan for human salvation; as the second Adam, Jesus should have

A Scientology centre in France includes an advertisement for L. Ron Hubbard's book, Dianetics, *the 'bible' of this controversial religious movement.*

People who have broken away from the church have provided information on how the Moonies convert new recruits. After being approached by a church member, novices are invited to participate in a retreat

A special vocabulary

The teachings of Scientology make use of certain terms, including:
❏ Auditing: testing a member in order to establish personal weaknesses. Critics link this to brainwashing.
❏ E-meter: an auditing device, which detects skin resistance and determines whether the person being interrogated is in a state of excitement or calmness.
❏ OT: the desired state of being, in which a person can influence matter, energy, time and space.

united with a true Eve and formed a perfect family. Therefore, mankind had no choice but to wait 2,000 years for redemption from the fall from grace.

Moon and his fourth wife Han Hak-Ja have dedicated themselves to this task. Together, 'without sin', they have conceived 13 children and are therefore father and mother of the 'first heavenly family on earth'. When their son Heung-Jin died in 1984, Moon declared him to be governor of heaven – with Jesus, who had admitted his 'failure', as his representative.

The Unification Church seeks to recruit young and unmarried people. After a trial period, Moon often suggests a marriage partner – with an emphasis on linking people from different nations. At huge ceremonies, Moon blesses the newlyweds. On August 25, 1992, for example, he welcomed 20,000 couples into the Moonie community during a mass wedding held in Seoul, capital of South Korea; a further 10,000 couples were connected via satellite.

in the country. They are never left alone, and are subjected to constant yet subtle pressure to submit to the organisation – a process that amounts to brainwashing. Once they are in, new members must subordinate themselves unconditionally. They break off ties with their family and frequently transfer all their possessions to the organisation.

Over the years, Moon has built up an economic empire, with interests in drugs, fisheries, shipping and newspapers. Moon's fortune is estimated in the millions, but the value of his business empire declined greatly in the late 1990s.

Scientology

The Church of Scientology was founded in the United States by controversial science-fiction writer L. Ron Hubbard (1911–1986). Hubbard developed a philosophy called 'dianetics', which makes use of supposedly scientific methods to help members learn to cope with sickness and crisis.

Opinion has long been divided as to whether the Church of Scientology is simply a community with a common philosophy of life or a shadowy organisation that engages in mind control. In the past, the organisation was repeatedly in the public eye when it was accused of intimidating new members. In 1996, a German court ruled that it was not a religious denomination as laid down in Germany's constitution; in June 1997, both federal and state authorities in Germany ordered that the activities of the organisation be monitored.

The decision caused a storm of protest in America, where this 'church' is recognised as a religious group, and enjoys a high-profile following in Hollywood. But Germany is apparently not the only country to clamp down on the organisation, which, according to its own publicity, comprises about 8 million members. In France, Greece and Italy, Scientologists have been convicted of crimes, including repeated cases of fraud.

What makes this group so controversial? Their main goal is to gain 'spiritual health', a process elaborated by L. Ron Hubbard in his book, *Dianetics*. Scientology prescribes a long path to 'perfection'. Members must attend numerous expensive courses, the results of which can change a person very deeply. Once in the hands of the organisation, it is extremely difficult to withdraw, for the Scientologists have developed an advanced feedback and surveillance system. Many experts believe that the church is actually a corporation, and that it is attempting to infiltrate the economy in order to gain access to power and establish a totalitarian system.

WAITING FOR THE APOCALYPSE

Members of apocalyptic cults believe that Judgment Day is near. Their leaders convince them that they must defend themselves against a hostile world. In all too many cases, cult members have proved that they are prepared to voluntarily give their lives to defend the group.

Some of the saddest stories about cults concern the many people who drop out of their everyday lives and submit themselves unconditionally to self-appointed masters. In recent years, the activities of a number of radical apocalyptic sects have hit the headlines. The members of these groups believe they are beset by demonic forces and that the end of the world is imminent. They are prepared to sacrifice everything – including their lives – to put their fears to rest. Many of these fanatics think they are surrounded by enemies, and their actions follow the logic of warfare. Such groups have stockpiled arsenals of weapons, and even committed murder.

False avenger

On November 20, 1978, tragedy overtook the members of the People's Temple, an American cult led by the charismatic James Warren 'Jim' Jones. On that day, 913 members of the People's Temple, including Jones, took their lives at their commune in the South American country of Guyana. Apparently the majority quite willingly drank a deadly cocktail of fruit juice laced with cyanide that had been prepared on Jones's orders. Only a few had to be forced to drink the poisoned brew.

The event horrified the world, but details soon came to light of a nightmare world of coercion, manipulation and violence. Jones had founded the cult during the late 1950s in Indianapolis, in the American Midwest. In his sermons, the preacher spoke of social justice, presenting himself as a ray of hope in a world damned to destruction. He soon

In 1978, 913 members of the People's Temple killed themselves on the orders of their leader.

attracted a large following, and the group expanded further after 1965, when Jones moved his operations to California. The People's Temple grew to several thousand members, who were recruited mainly among African-Americans, socially disadvantaged women and children and the mentally ill.

Reverend Jones's social commitment found increasing favour among leftist-liberal groups in California. In 1976, he was named chairman of the San Francisco housing office. By that time, however, rumours were spreading of how he exploited the poor by forcing them, for example, to pass their welfare cheques on to him. There were claims that many members had been beaten and sexually assaulted, and there was talk of several mysterious deaths. Press reports implied that these may have been members who had gone astray.

To escape the tide of rumour, Jones transferred the People's Temple to Guyana in 1977. He had purchased land there, and now established the community

at Jonestown. Rumours circulated that Jones maintained an elite armed unit of about 20 people who were the only ones permitted to leave the cult compound. On November 18, 1978, US congressman Leo Ryan, together with Richard Dwyer, an employee of the US embassy in Guyana, and several journalists, flew into Jonestown with the intention of carrying out a more detailed investigation of

The fiery end of the Waco siege, in April 1993; 85 people died, along with guru David Koresh (left).

Above: *The Order of the Solar Temple conducted their rituals in the 'sanctuary'. The group was led by Luc Jouret (right).*

the accusations against the community in exile. However, most of the visitors were cut down by gunfire before they could leave the landing strip. Survivors of the airstrip attack reported how Jones's gunmen had approached them mechanically, without a trace of emotion.

Soon after the killings, Jones delivered a sermon in which he convinced his followers to commit suicide. It is still a mystery why so many people allowed themselves to be sent to their deaths.

Fiery tragedy at Waco

Fifteen years later, a similar tragedy erupted on a ranch outside Waco, Texas. The ranch was home to the Branch Davidians, a tiny group that had broken away from the mainstream Seventh Day Adventists. The Branch Davidians were led by a former rock musician named Vernon Howell. In 1990, Howell changed his name to David Koresh. His first name referred to the biblical King David, while Koresh is the Hebrew form of Cyrus, the ancient Persian ruler who freed the Jews from Babylon.

The head of the Branch Davidians saw himself as the lamb of God, the new Messiah. His group believed him when he claimed to be able to hasten the Apocalypse, but only after he had established a kingdom

in which his many wives would give him numerous children. These descendants would later be the rulers of a better world.

People who had left the cult accused Koresh of acting like a slave-driver, forcing his followers into a life of strict asceticism. It was also said that he had raped teenage girls and had abused children. As with many Christian fundamentalists, the cult expected serious battles on the Day of Judgment. The righteous would go to heaven, and the rest of humanity would suffer a painful death. To prepare for the Apocalypse, the Branch Davidians built up a large stockpile of arms on their ranch.

When authorities heard about the cult's arsenal, the US Attorney General Janet Reno ordered the ranch to be raided. On February 28, 1993, agents of the Bureau of Alcohol, Tobacco and Firearms (ATF) descended on the ranch, only to be forced back by fierce gunfire from cult members. The compound was quickly surrounded by hundreds of

police, FBI and ATF agents. The tense standoff lasted until April 19, when the FBI attacked the ranch with armoured vehicles and tear gas. The wooden buildings quickly caught fire, and 86 people died in the blaze. However, there is evidence that most of these people had committed suicide on Koresh's orders, including Koresh himself.

But the madness continued. On the second anniversary of the raid on the Waco compound, a bomb exploded in front of the federal office building in Oklahoma City, Oklahoma. The massive explosion virtually demolished the building, and killed 167 people, including several children. It was the worst act of terror in the history of the US. The bomber was former soldier and Gulf War veteran Timothy McVeigh, 28, who wanted revenge for the government's actions at Waco. In 1997, a federal court in Denver, Colorado, sentenced McVeigh to death.

Suicide or murder?

On January 8, 1998 Spanish police arrived in time to prevent the suicide of 32 members of the Order of the Solar Temple on the island of Tenerife in the Canary Islands. The group had prophesied that the end of the world would take place on this day, and wanted to end their lives by poisoning themselves on the slopes of Mt Teide. However, this was just one episode in the strange story of this esoteric 'order'. For several years, members had made headlines through successful collective suicides.

The beginnings of the Order of the Solar Temple go back to 1976, when Joseph di Mambro, a Frenchman who had been convicted of fraud, moved to Geneva, Switzerland, to avoid French tax laws. For years, Di Mambro had pretended to be a psychologist, and taught a technique called 'self-contemplation'. This was a lucrative business, so he decided to continue with it in Switzerland, and he founded the Golden Way Foundation.

In 1981, a Belgian doctor named Luc Jouret joined the Golden Way Foundation. Soon afterward, Jouret met Julien Origas, the ageing Grand Master of an occult temple order, and convinced him to name Jouret as his successor. Di Mambro and Jouret then affiliated their two organisations to form the Order of the Solar Temple. The group expanded its activities in Switzerland, and established branches in Canada and France. Di Mambro was apparently responsible for financial matters, while Jouret assumed the function of chief office bearer, converting the group into a kind of secret lodge. Gradually, Jouret came to be seen as a guru.

The members of the Order of the Solar Temple claimed to have special access to divinity. Their ideology combined various

On October 6, 1994, 24 charred bodies were found in this chalet in a Swiss village.

doctrines and contained elements of Roman Catholicism, Eastern mysticism and a UFO mythology. They believed that the 'Lords of the Universe' dwelt on the star Sirius, and that the end of the world would see all faithful members of the order taken there.

Jouret's powers of persuasion attracted many members to the order. He gave esoteric lectures on topics like 'the creation of a new man' and campaigned for organic agriculture and ecology. He also offered management courses, enabling him to recruit wealthy professionals.

The members also gathered stocks of weapons to defend themselves during the coming Apocalypse. For this reason, police in Canada began to monitor the activities of the Canadian members. The order was finally prosecuted in 1993, but the accused received only probationary sentences.

The horror began in the following year. On October 5 and 6, 1994, fire destroyed two houses belonging to Di Mambro and Jouret in the mountains to the north of Montreal, Canada. When police entered the burned-out houses, they found the bodies of the two leaders and three other people. At the same time, fires broke out in two Swiss villages in

which 50 people lost their lives. Investigators later found that electric heaters had caused the fires.

There are several indications that many of the victims had not died willingly. Some of them had plastic bags over their heads, and hypodermic needles were found lying nearby. But since the corpses were badly burned, it was not possible for investigators to come to a conclusion about the exact cause of death.

The members of the San Diego-based Heaven's Gate cult accepted the word of their leader, 65-year-old Marshall Herff Applewhite, when they lay down on their beds to die. In March 1997, San Diego sheriff's deputies removed the bodies of 39 members of the cult from the mansion where they had worked as website developers. The cult's beliefs centred on the need to prepare for the arrival of extraterrestrial beings who would take the cult members to other worlds. In 1997, the appearance of the Hale-Bopp comet seemed to signal that the moment of deliverance was at hand, and the cult members drank a deadly mix of alcohol and painkillers and lay down to await their departure for the stars.

Right: *Emergency personnel tend to the injured following the nerve gas attack on the Tokyo underground system. The man allegedly responsible for ordering the attack, was the near-blind guru Shoko Asahara (below, holding microphone), who preached messages of peace to his followers.*

Chronology of madness

❏ **November 1978:** 913 members of the People's Temple commit collective suicide in Guyana, South America.
❏ **April 1993:** 86 people die when US federal agents storm the Branch Davidian compound in Waco, Texas, following a seven-week siege.
❏ **1994–1997:** 74 members of the Order of the Solar Temple die in various suicide pacts.
❏ **March 1995:** A sarin gas attack on the Tokyo underground by the Aum cult leaves 12 dead and 5,000 injured.
❏ **March 1997:** Mass suicide of 39 members of the Heaven's Gate cult.

Japan's killer cult

Unusually, the Japanese cult Aum Shinri-Kyo (Highest Truth) did not direct their madness against themselves, but against their fellow citizens. On March 20, 1995, members of the group released the lethal nerve gas sarin into the Tokyo underground railway, causing 12 deaths; 5,000 others were injured.

Soon afterwards, Japanese police arrested cult leader Shoko Asahara, together with around 1,000 of his followers. They were accused of producing chemical weapons, illegal drugs and other weapons, partly with Russian support. They were also charged with abduction and murder.

THE FOLLOWERS OF SATAN

The celebration of the black mass and the worship of Lucifer are a source of fascination for those individuals prepared to ridicule Christian values, perform animal sacrifices and abandon themselves to sexual excesses. The exploration of humankind's dark side occasionally strays into acts of violence, and yet not all Satanists are prepared to go to such lengths. Certain people dabble in the black arts because it is fashionable, while others commit crimes under the influence of unhinged cult leaders.

Shortly after midnight on August 9, 1969, three women and one man crept up to a remote villa on Cielo Drive in Bel Air, Los Angeles. In the house was Sharon Tate, the pregnant wife of film director Roman Polanski, and six friends. The horror that then took place is almost impossible to comprehend. The intruders forced their way into the house, assaulted Tate and her guests and stabbed them hundreds of times. Before they left the house, they used the blood of the victims to write the word 'pig' on the front door of the house. When the killers were tried, it was revealed that they did not even know whom they had killed: the attack was completely random.

The brutal slayings still stand as one of the most brutal crimes of the 20th century. The murderers were followers of Charles Manson, a dangerous criminal, who had gathered a cult-like group of about 40 people around him. The Family, as he called them, regarded him as a prophet and obeyed him blindly. He manipulated them with drugs, and many of the female members were his sexual slaves.

At the time of the killings, Manson was under the influence of a Satanic group. He presented himself as both a second Messiah and the Devil. He announced the imminent end of the world, after which the Family would be 'empowered' – whatever that meant. Before their empowerment, though, his followers would have to commit a series of ritual crimes, although Manson himself did not participate in all of them. He later confessed to committing 35 murders, but the number was probably higher. Manson's most highly publicised crime took place on August 11, 1969, when he and six Family members stabbed Leno and Rosemary La Bianca to death. The blood orgy at the Cielo Drive house two days previously had aroused his displeasure, and he wanted to show the right

way to carry out a killing. Even this brutal deed was an act of blind carnage; Manson and his associates had never previously set eyes on the victims.

Soon after the Tate–La Bianca killings, police arrested Susan Atkins, a member of the Family, on charges of prostitution. While in jail awaiting trial, she made the mistake of telling another inmate of her complicity in

Right: *Devil worship during a black mass. Has the notorious Reverend Mackenzie (below) carried out similar rituals on the Orkney Islands? Despite loud accusations, no proof could be found that he had pursued Satanist practices.*

the murders at the Tate house. The inmate passed the information on to prison guards. On December 1, the Manson Family was rounded up by the police.

In one of the most spectacular proceedings in American judicial history, Manson and seven others were tried for the killings. In most cases, the death sentence was imposed, although the sentences were later commuted

Below: *The Satanist and mass murderer Charles Manson went astray at an early age. It is likely that he will remain in prison for the rest of his life.*

to life in prison when California abolished the death penalty. In 1999, Manson was denied parole for the ninth time.

Manson was the unwanted child of a teenage prostitute. His unhappy childhood – marked by a long succession of foster homes, frequent beatings and sexual abuse – may have turned him into a killer. He probably suffered from delusions, which culminated in his embrace of Satanism.

The Manson case is an extreme example of the excesses to which Satanism can lead. A tiny minority of the worshippers of Lucifer stray into such excesses. It is important to be able to distinguish the majority of harmless dabblers from the minority of dangerous and disturbed individuals like Charles Manson.

All Satanists worship the Devil as a deity, effectively reversing conventional Christian values. It is their desire that the power of the evil one – known as Satan, Lucifer or Beelzebub – takes control of the world.

Satanist rituals revolve around the so-called black mass, a parody of the traditional Christian ritual. At an altar with an upside-down cross – symbolising the failure of Christianity and the coming victory of Beelzebub – the followers of Satan desecrate the Eucharist and utter curses against Jesus Christ and the mother of God. During the black mass, many Satanists torture animals, mostly cats, and then drink their blood.

According to some reports, there are 20 occasions for such 'celebrations' throughout the year; many are celebrated at the same time as Christian festivals. But Satanic rituals are not celebrated openly; only rarely can proof be found of their existence. For example, a certain Reverend Mackenzie was accused of having performed such acts during rituals held on Scotland's remote Orkney Islands, although nothing could ever be proved against him.

Shock tactics

Religious scholars have divided Satanists into three groups, even though the differences between them can be unclear: adolescent rebellion, organised groups and secret lodges.

In recent years, researchers have noted a growing interest among teenagers in the occult and in Satanic practices. Most of these people are merely experimenting, and are not genuinely looking for a substitute religion. They enjoy shocking their elders by wearing black clothing, painting their faces white, looking as gloomy as possible and listening to music which mocks Christian tradition.

This interest is reflected in the imagery of heavy metal bands, and in the subculture known as Black Metal, which includes bands such as Black Sabbath, Venom, Slayer, Sodom and Merciful Fate. Posters claim that musicians will perform blasphemous acts on stage, while the lyrics of one song say: 'I am a damned Antichrist, only believe in evil, spit on the church ...' For most teenagers, this is just a passing thrill, but for a few individuals, it can encourage aggressive behaviour.

But of course heavy metal music is not the only thing that contributes to a negative view of the world. An individual with a weak sense of perspective could be persuaded to give up traditional norms of behaviour. Press reports certainly indicate that more and more teenagers are becoming involved in forms of devil worship, which can include criminal acts such as the vandalisation of cemeteries and the desecration of graves and corpses.

Some youths have demonstrated such practices for journalists. However, organised Satanic groups do not divulge information. Their rituals take place behind closed doors. They have very hierarchical structures, and newcomers must show absolute obedience. Their rituals are alleged to include drug abuse and unusual sexual practices, together with sadism and other perversions.

Legitimising violence

Satanic lodges have existed for a long time, and include the Ordo Templi Orientis (OTO), founded as a secret society by the Viennese manufacturer Carl Kellner and the German theosophist Franz Hartmann in 1900. The OTO gave rise to similar organisations around the world, and became more widely known through the activities of Aleister Crowley (1875–1947), who founded a branch in Los Angeles in 1905, then later moved to the Abbey of Thelema in Cefalù on the island of Sicily and became its Grand Master. Crowley masterminded a new cult and formulated its article of faith: '"Do as you wish": this is to be the entire law'. This legitimised the transgression of all Christian moral laws. Crowley openly approved of violence, the violation of women and human sacrifice, especially of male children.

In 1966, the Church of Satan was founded in San Francisco. Among its members was Susan Atkins, who was later to become involved with Charles Manson. The founder, Anton Szandor LaVey, produced a so-called *Satanic Bible*, in which he wrote: 'Satan symbolises pleasure and satisfaction rather than abstinence .... Satan symbolises revenge rather than love .... Blessed be the strong, for they shall rule the earth. Cursed be the weak, for they shall suffer. The hatred of all weakness purifies thought ....' Although LaVey's name has been connected with acts of violence, the Church of Satan continues to be one of the world's largest Satanic sects.

NEW RELIGIOUS BELIEFS FROM ASIA

A growing number of spiritual movements have emerged from Asia, encouraging a widespread revival of traditional religious values. Japanese groups have given the ancient religions of their land a more practical focus, while Indian scholars have reformed Hinduism by adopting certain Christian ideas. Although they share common roots, these movements of spiritual renewal should not be confused with mind-controlling cults.

Several new religions appeared in Asia during the 19th and 20th centuries, particularly in India and Japan. Some of them led to revivals of popular religion. But the new beliefs also responded to people's changing spiritual needs when faced with rapid industrialisation, urbanisation and the import of unfamiliar Western customs. In recent decades, these religions have begun to exert increasing influence in the West.

Secular orientation

Some 20% of Japan's more than 125 million people belong to one of Asia's nearly 400 new religions. These include Rissho Kosei-kai and Soka Gakkai. The new religions can be divided into three groups: older movements that were set up during the 19th century; faiths that originated around the turn of the century; and those that emerged after the turmoil of World War II.

A leader of the lay religious movement, Soka Gakkai.

The new religions have many things in common. For example, they all have a charismatic founder, often a woman, who has carried out a divine injunction or conveyed a set of teachings from another world. The centre of the community is often a magnificent shrine, which serves as both the religion's chief place of pilgrimage and its business headquarters.

Elements of Buddhism, Shintoism and shamanism, as well as Christianity and other religions, all find expression in the new religions. The old beliefs and rituals form the foundations, but the new movements in Japan also have a strongly secular understanding of salvation. They believe that popular medicine, simple meditation exercises and neighbourly love contribute to the attainment of peace, happiness and enlightenment. The human need for personal spiritual care is met by house circles and group discussions. This is one important factor that ensures relatively easy access to religion. Many groups do not even require that new members give up membership of their old religion.

Most of the new religions display an admirable degree of social commitment. For example, Rissho Kosei-kai (Society for the Establishment of Law and Community) boasts a membership of some 6.5 million, and runs aid programmes in Africa, takes part in disaster relief, supports the work begun by Mother Teresa, and finances ecological projects.

Of all Japan's new movements, it is only Soka Gakkai, founded in 1930, that has received negative publicity. The movement is also strongly involved in humanitarian causes, but its ideological position has attracted criticism. Soka Gakkai is the only lay religious movement in Japan that also acts as a political party. It is represented in Japan's Diet, or parliament, as Komeito (Party for Cleanliness). The founders of Soka Gakkai, former teachers Tsunesaburo Makiguchi and Josei Toda, have stated that they have not created a new religion. But their teachings closely parallel those of Buddhism; for example, one of Soka Gakkai's rituals involves the recitation of the lotus mantra.

The organisation is structured on military lines, and new recruits undergo an aggressive conversion procedure that is intended to eradicate 'false modes of thought'. They have to distance themselves from their previous religious rituals and are only permitted to worship the cult object known as Gohonzon. This is a mandala designed by the Buddhist

This university complex belongs to Soka Gakkai.

reformer Nichiren (1222–1283). If members disobey the rules of correct worship, they can be punished severely.

In spite of its rigidity, Soka Gakkai has become immensely popular. It has roughly 8 million members in Japan, with another 1.2 million worldwide – the product of extensive missionary work. According to its own statistics, the group has a number of centres in Europe. It owns a financial empire and a huge public relations division. It also publishes its own daily newspaper with a circulation of over 4 million.

Unlike the other new Japanese religions, which are extremely tolerant, Soka Gakkai rejects the claims of its competitors. It claims

This Indian school is run by the Sahaja Yoga cult.

that Christianity has not achieved any social progress and cannot make people happy. It awaits a 'third civilisation', in which the contradictions between idealism and materialism, socialism and capitalism, shall finally be overcome.

True and false gurus

In India, the imposition of British imperial rule during the 19th century led to a revival of the spiritual heritage of Indian culture, but also to an increased study of Christianity. This interaction of religious beliefs produced reformed Hinduism, which was influenced by Christianity. In contrast to mainstream Hinduism, with its many deities, reformed Hinduism is monotheistic – it recognises only one god – and also emphasises the ethical responsibility of humans. In the 20th century, these aspects made its doctrines very appealing to Westerners.

During the 19th century, the leading lights of the movement were Ram Mohan Roy (1772–1833), Dayananda Sarasvati (1824–1883), Sri Ramakrishna (1834–1886) and Swami Vivekananda (1863–1902). These spiritual individuals also directed efforts towards long-overdue social reforms, such as

the elimination of India's rigid caste system.

India's contribution to the new religion expanded during the 20th century. For example, the father of integral yoga, Sri Aurobindo Gosh (1872–1950) became highly respected. As a student at Cambridge University in England, he studied the history of Western ideas, associating the impressive achievements he saw in England with the Hindu traditions of his native land. When he returned to India, he taught at an ashram at Pondicherry, in southern India, and spread the message that human consciousness could be developed, leading to a general spiritualisation of the human race. Aurobindo's influence is often compared to that of Mohandas Karamchand, better known as Mahatma Gandhi (1869–1948), who led India's struggle for home rule from Britain. Gandhi himself created the

Eastern movements in the West

❑ Ananda Marga: about 2.5 million members.
❑ Bhagwan movement: an estimated membership of several million worldwide; extensive business interests worldwide.
❑ International Society for Krishna Consciousness (ISKON), also known as Hare Krishna: an estimated membership of around 750,000 sympathisers in Europe, more than 300 centres worldwide.
❑ Soka Gakkai: around 8 million members in Japan, 1.2 million in the rest of the world.

These adherents of TM are jumping in the lotus position, a technique often called 'yogic flying'.

For several years, Bhagwan Shree Rajneesh (shown at the wheel of one of his fleet of luxury cars) lived in the US state of Oregon.

Sarvodaya Samaj (Society for the Good of All), which propagated a philosophy of general philanthropy and avoiding harm.

In spite of this rich contribution to human spiritual growth, a number of new Indian religions have come to be regarded as cults with questionable practices. Many of these have found disciples among disillusioned and confused people in North America and Western Europe. A number of groups cut themselves off from society and even resort to brainwashing. Groups that have attracted controversy include the Bhagwan movement, Transcendental Meditation (TM) and the Hare Krishnas (*see* pages 160–162).

Ananda Marga, established in 1955 by Prabhat Ranjan Sarkar (1921–1990), is actually considered to be harmful. Reinhart Hummel, a German theologian, describes the group as an 'explosive mixture of combat unit and monastic community'. Ananda Marga demands an absolute abandonment of the self, including suicide. According to experts, the group propagates extreme right-wing ideas, and is responsible for attacks on members of the Indian government.

Obviously, we must distinguish between the genuine religions and groups seeking to exploit gullible believers. Many of the new religions have adapted religious tradition to the here and now and encourage people to consider spiritual questions, while others are dangerous and misleading. A number of progressive Western theologians believe that the spread of the serious-minded movements will allow religious pluralism to flourish, forcing Christianity to become more open.

HOPE FOR A NEW GOLDEN AGE

The New Age movement promises humanity a future of peace and harmony with nature. All that is required is a little self-knowledge and an expanded consciousness. Sceptics mock the self-importance of the New Agers, who plunder the world's religions for ideas. But the New Age is also big business, and is increasingly accepted by millions of people.

Like so many other trends and fashions, the New Age movement was born in California. Essentially, it is a loose collection of beliefs that purports to offer people the means to answer pressing questions about human existence and our future on earth. The movement first emerged during the 1970s, and now has millions of followers all over the world, including such prominent personalities as American actress Shirley McLaine. Some people even say the heir to the British throne – Prince Charles – has sympathies with the new doctrine.

New Age beliefs have found a ready audience among people who are disoriented or confused by contemporary society. The failure of ideologies, particularly Communism, the lack of tolerance on the part of Christian churches and the general decline in moral values have all encouraged the spread of alienation. As a result, many people choose to set out on a personal quest for alternative paths to salvation. New Age beliefs offer the possibility of self-knowledge and the attainment of harmony with society and nature.

The New Age movement claims that the Age of Aquarius will bring perfect happiness to humanity. This depiction of the sign of Aquarius is a miniature from a 15th-century French book of hours.

The sign of Aquarius

New Age ideas overlap to some extent with other movements such as astrology and the occult, but the movement is just as willing to draw on the insights of modern science. Its adherents also borrow at will from all religions and often jumble statements and traditions in a highly

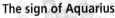

The Hollywood actress Shirley McLaine is a devout follower of the new doctrine.

arbitrary manner. They strive to fuse the knowledge of a variety of cultures and eras. At New Age gatherings, it is possible to see a nuclear physicist squatting placidly beside a Native American healer.

To the followers of the New Age, it is a matter of principle to try to change people and their world. The chief goal is stated as the 'spiritualisation of all humanity' leading to peace on earth. In order for the individual to be able to grasp these changes, he or she must expand their consciousness.

In New Age philosophy, the present is a phase of the final battle between light and darkness – although this is not combined with any apocalyptic vision. According to this view, problems such as the destruction of the environment, nuclear accidents or other catastrophes serve only to purify humanity, which can then look forward to the dawn of the 'Age of Aquarius'. Few people understand the significance of this phrase, although it was first made famous more than 30 years ago in a song from the breakthrough musical *Hair*, a Broadway show later made into a popular film.

The arrival of the Age of Aquarius is signalled by the stars. Certain planetary movements cause the vernal equinox – the position of the sun on March 21 each year – to shift into another sign of the zodiac every 2,140 years. Around the year 0, the earth was moving from the sign of Aries to Pisces. The fish is a symbol for Christ, and with his birth we entered the age of Christianity. The Age of Pisces represents the triumph of rationality, formal religion and organisations such as states and political parties.

The Age of Aquarius will follow the Age of Pisces, and will dissolve formal structures. From now on, people will only support one another in loose networks. The New Age movement, for example, has no particular gurus or leaders. Admittedly, no-one can say exactly when the 'Golden Age' will begin. Many claim that it began in 1961, while others set the date at 2012, 2160 or 2770.

Paths to spirituality

The New Age promises 'immediate contact between the self and the universe, or cosmic energy', but how can an individual experience this promise? The first stage is a new lifestyle. Many followers of the New Age are vegetarians and take ecology very seriously. It is also necessary to free the mind, which can be done using a wide range of techniques. In this respect, the New Age makes use of methods that have long been widespread in circles outside the movement: examples include such respected practices such as homeopathy, various forms of massage, yoga, meditation and Eastern martial arts.

But New Agers go much further, delving into such unusual areas as spiritual healing and gemstone therapy. Spiritualist elements are also important, and these techniques are aimed at awakening the occult powers within the individual. Reincarnation techniques, such as rebirthing, aim at 'going back to the moment of conception, birth and entry into the world'. Alongside techniques such as clairvoyance, Ouija and pendulums, spirit communication is practised using so-called channelling, which is defined as 'the art of making contact with higher forms of consciousness by taking the medial path'.

New religion or hocus-pocus?

Because the doctrines of the New Age combine so many diverse elements, its beliefs cannot be reduced to a core of basic principles. This makes it hard to reach a conclusion about whether the New Age offers hope for the future. But we have to accept that it satisfies certain religious needs. As humanity enters a new millennium, millions feel dissatisfied with society, and fear the future. The optimistic perspectives of the New Age may have a calming effect.

Since this philosophy draws on all religions, it naturally shares some common ground with Christianity – for example, in its attempts to overcome the straightforward instrumental reason of our technological society. Both Christianity and the New Age reject the uncontrolled consumerism of industrial society.

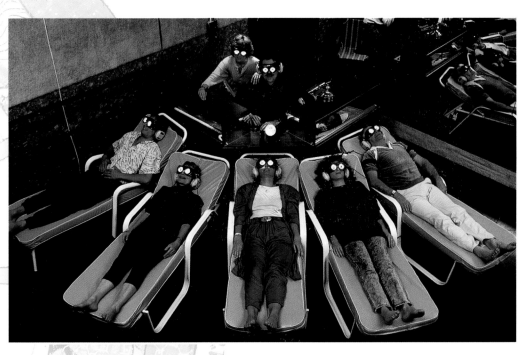

The profits of the New Age contradict its idealism. Book publishers have flooded the market with works on self-help and self-realisation, and the bestseller lists reflect the popularity of such manuals. New Age centres offer a range of seminars and treatments, from Bach flower therapy to channelling.

Critics of the New Age speak of a 'huge business in souls'. But their strongest accusation is that the movement is a kind of 'spiritual supermarket' where anyone can take what suits them. They also point to the fact that the New Age has rehabilitated many ideas that science and Christianity had rejected as superstition in the 19th century,

At a New Age centre, believers settle down for a session in 'mental energy synchronisation'.

such as astrology, magic and shamanism. According to German theologian Reinhart Hummel, the New Age offers believers 'ideological titbits from all possible cultures'.

The articles of faith of the New Age

1. All is one.
2. We have several bodies.
3. The body does not lie.
4. Before me I am myself, after me I am myself.
5. Life after death has been explored.
6. Science speaks for us.
7. There is no such thing as chance.
8. We must work on ourselves.
9. We can communicate with angels.
10. It is true if I believe in it.
11. The earth is a living being and its name is Gaia.

From *France of the mutants: A journey to the centre of the New Age*, by Jean-Luc Porquet (1994).

The alternative scene earns its keep with New Age commerce.

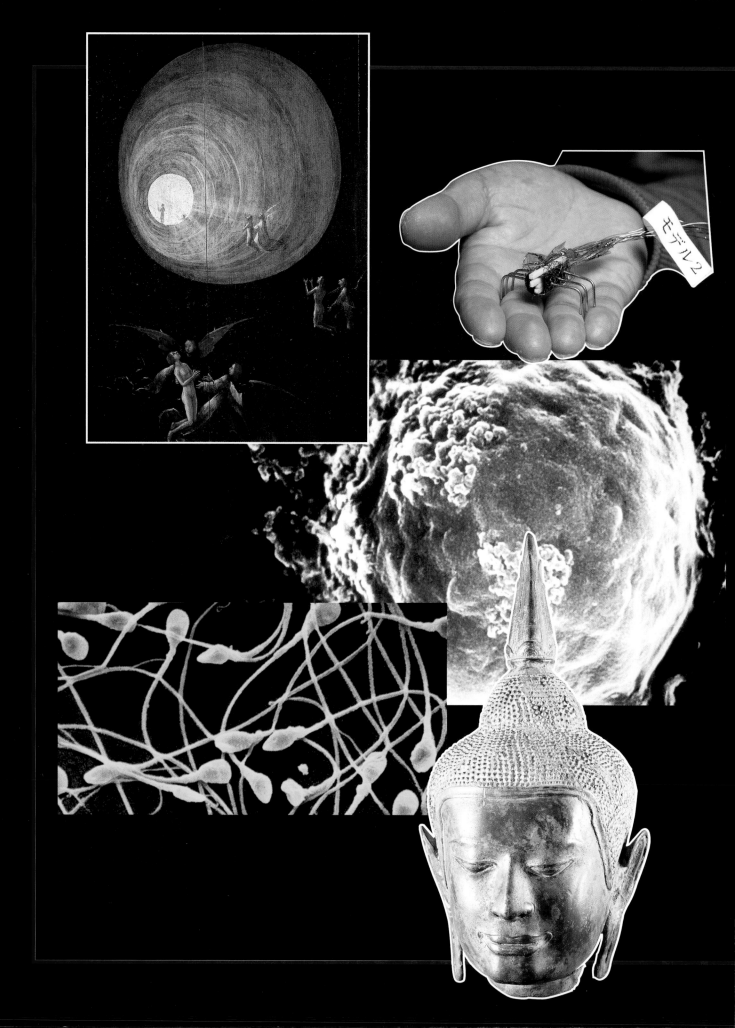

AT THE LIMITS OF SCIENCE AND LOGIC

Within just a few decades, medical research has made enormous progress. Our knowledge about the human body is constantly increasing. For example, new technology enables scientists to understand how the body heals itself and to unlock the secrets of that incredible super-computer, the human brain. A century ago, few people would have thought it possible that diseased organs could be replaced or that infertile couples could have children. And yet our knowledge has limits: the killer virus that causes AIDS rages unchecked; remarkably, we still do not understand the processes at work in acupuncture or homeopathy; and phenomena such as stigmatisation, trances or near death experiences remain inexplicable. Perhaps there are some questions that just cannot be answered.

PSYCHOSOMATICS: ALL IN THE MIND?

Systematic research into psychosomatic medicine only began early in the 20th century, but today this fascinating field enjoys wide acceptance among health professionals. It is difficult to define a psychosomatic illness, but we now recognise the ways in which psychological and emotional states can influence the working of the body.

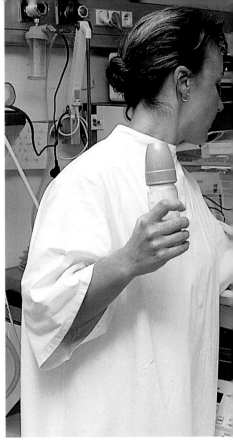

Modern medicine classifies patients into two types. On the one hand, there are people with so-called functional illnesses, where symptoms such as lack of appetite, vomiting, diarrhoea, cramps, muscle aches or an excessively strong heartbeat (tachycardia) cannot be attributed to a particular organic cause. On the other hand, there are those who are organically ill and suffer from so-called somatic afflictions, such as tumours, diabetes, cancer or diseases of the heart or circulatory system, which are caused by pathological processes in one or several of the body's vital organs.

For decades, doctors considered functional illnesses to be psychosomatic – that is, made worse by emotional or psychological factors, such as stress. But today, patients can consult a specialist in psychosomatic medicine, a relatively new field in which medical doctors pursue an integrated, or holistic, approach to healing the body's illnesses.

The psychosomatic method

The basis of psychosomatics lies in the union of body and soul. The term is derived from the Greek words *psukhê* (psyche or soul) and *soma* (body), and designates that branch of the human sciences which deals with the relations between mental and physical processes in physically ill people.

First and foremost, psychosomatics is based on a holistic perspective, in which the physician considers the overall picture of a patient and not just his or her specific complaint. In spite of – or perhaps even because of – the high level of specialisation in modern medicine, there is rarely enough time for a doctor to consider a patient's complete physical and psychological state. If she or he consults a doctor with a physical ailment, specialists will examine different

organs, and try to explain the symptoms in terms of the pathological processes at work in them.

A specialist in psychosomatics is a medical doctor who may also have training in psychoanalysis. He or she attempts to detect processes active in the patient's subconscious mind and to assess their effect on the underlying causes of the disease. While this might diminish the role of the family doctor, this new approach to healing aims to help the patient by uncovering the underlying reasons for his or her illness.

Automatic fear

Sigmund Freud developed the theory that a person can experience continuous agitation as a result of an overstimulation which he or she cannot control. This condition can be compared to the loneliness which a newborn baby experiences as a result of the physiological changes that occur after birth.

Patients who suffer from severe psychosomatic disturbances often show similar behaviour. If they lack a sufficiently protective environment, their mental faculties cannot develop to the point where they will shield the individuals against the many hard knocks that life has in store.

The theories of Sigmund Freud form the basis of psychosomatic medicine.

The subconscious mind plays a role in all illnesses, and the way it manifests itself leads to both physical and psychic disturbances. When a flu epidemic strikes, for example, the virus never affects everyone. Each individual reacts differently to a specific virus, and this reaction is governed by his or her level of resistance, or immunity. Resistance to the virus, in turn, can vary depending on the psychic state of the patient.

Starting early

The development of an individual's psychic state starts early. In order to understand this, let us look at a premature baby. Depending on how early he or she arrives, certain physiological functions, such as breathing, the heart and circulatory system, and the balance of the biological metabolism, must be maintained if the child is to remain alive. A premature baby can only be taken out of the incubator once bodily functions, such as breathing, have stabilised and developed to the extent that the child can function on its own. After that, parental care replaces the electronic monitors and guides the child until he or she becomes capable of leading an independent life.

Our early sensory experiences, whether it is seeing a parent or tasting a new food, are received through our five senses, often in connection with physical contact with our

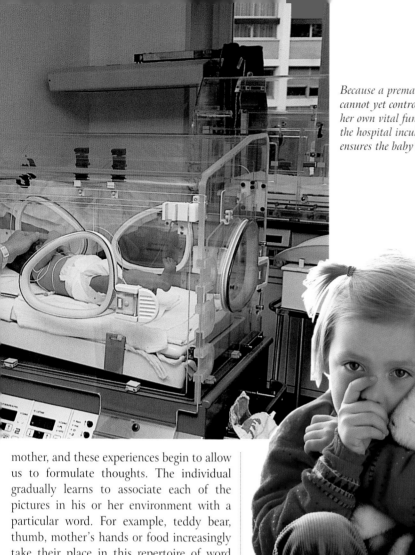

Because a premature baby cannot yet control his or her own vital functions, the hospital incubator ensures the baby's survival.

The result is a very personal symbolic activity, whereby a teddy bear, for example, can come to symbolise a big, likeable boy and protector in the eyes of a girl. Sigmund Freud (1856–1939), the founder of psychoanalysis, used the term 'early consciousness' to describe this unity of representation and emotional attachment. If early consciousness functions well, then mental development will become rich in images, words, pictures and dreams. In other words, associative images will flow effortlessly between the past, present and future, between different symbolic levels, and between feelings that relate to our inner selves and those pertaining to our relationships with others. These processes correspond to a normal mental development, and they equip us with coping mechanisms for dealing with the traumatic events that we will encounter in the course of our lives. If this mental development is disturbed, however, then the individual may become ill-equipped to cope with the unpleasant experiences that are bound to come.

mother, and these experiences begin to allow us to formulate thoughts. The individual gradually learns to associate each of the pictures in his or her environment with a particular word. For example, teddy bear, thumb, mother's hands or food increasingly take their place in this repertoire of word representations. These take on symbolic meanings and enter a circle of images: words and memories that form the foundation of mental development.

Emotional destitution

In 1963, French doctor Pierre Marty and his colleagues at Paris's Institute for Psychosomatic Medicine described

Her thumb and her teddy bear provide this little girl with comfort. They form part of her developing world of images.

The American School

During the 1930s, the American psychoanalysts Alexander and Dunbar developed Freud's work to present a complete psychosomatic theory.

Alexander formulated the concept of organ neurosis, now considered a vital part of psychosomatics. The term refers to the occurrence of certain organic disorders as a result of permanent psychological stress affecting a particular part of the body. For example, a person for whom food is very important might suffer an affliction of the stomach. In the same way Alexander described physical symptoms that are coupled to emotions:

the connection between anger and high blood pressure, for example, or between excitement and respiratory difficulties.

Dunbar was also interested in the possible psychological causes of organic disorders. She examined people diagnosed with personality disorders in order to identify risk factors in the susceptibility to illness. She found that these individuals were indeed more sensitive to external stress. In addition, Dunbar was the first to describe the typical mental picture of sufferers of psychosomatic illness, thereby opening the way for modern research. Dunbar insisted that an emotional experience was at the root of the physical conflict, keeping it alive in the subconscious mind.

Many people believe that it is healthier to release anger and avoid dangerous emotional stress.

A mental struggle

Psychological trauma can strike at any time. When the unexpected happens, a normal, well-adjusted person can react in several ways. First, there is the need to deal with a situation mentally, such as happens through the normal process of grieving. Following the loss of a loved one, there is a time of suffering, when the subconscious mind starts 'sifting' through the qualities and imperfections of the deceased. In a way, the deceased is kept alive in the memory of those left behind, and the accompanying enrichment of their imagination helps them to hold onto that person.

Another possible reaction to the loss of a loved one is more active: sports, painting or fishing, for example, are all activities that allow certain forms of stress to be overcome. In contrast, if you just sit around or drift unhappily through the day, it could have an adverse effect on your health.

Fishing is both challenging and relaxing – an ideal recipe for coping with stress.

a certain mode of existence which they saw in a large number of patients who were afflicted with physical illnesses. Marty and his team called it *pensée opératoire* – literally, operative thinking – or the automatistic-mechanistic condition.

Invalids with this condition have a typical way of talking about their lives and their afflictions. Normally, when speaking about his or her own life, and especially about a serious illness or a traumatic memory, a person will usually try to awaken emotions, pictorial associations and possibly even similar memories for the listener. This allows two people to communicate; in this way, they are able to share a common imaginary world.

People suffering from so-called operative thinking display another pattern of behaviour. Their choice of words and tone of voice is impersonal, formulaic and verges on the mechanical. They are unable to express their feelings, and their fantasy world seems poorly developed – which also expresses itself in dull or banal dreams. If they are asked to describe their illness, they reel off a report with no time frame, presenting it in an unemotional and almost apathetic manner, without any feelings, complaints or fear.

The Parisian doctor Pierre Marty founded the Institute for Psychosomatic Medicine.

In the course of his research, Pierre Marty also identified a phenomenon that he spoke of as essential or unfocused depression. Normally, people suffering from great mental anguish will usually say that this condition set in gradually after a traumatic personal experience, such as loss of a loved one, grief, separation or failure. Their anguish, known as reactive depression, represents an answer to a deep psychic shock. Since they have been deprived of a loved one or a positive self-image, these people react by going into mental suffering. This suffering is accompanied by a weakening of the body's ability to overcome illness. Other symptoms of reactive depression are fatigue, sleep disturbances or loss of appetite. Feelings of guilt may also come to the surface. When a loved one dies, a person will sometimes reproach him- or herself for having treated the deceased badly. Normally, these feelings subside with the passage of time.

A different picture

People suffering from essential or unfocused depression present a totally different picture. In such cases, physical symptoms take the place of complaints directed at specific causes; instead of feelings of self-accusation and guilt, the body bears the brunt of an oppressive, indiscriminate feeling of failure and inadequacy. Apart from some initial anxiety attacks, the individual hardly notices his or her own psychological symptoms. Sufferers are neither interested in themselves nor in the people around them, and generally it is a progressive fatigue or other physical problem that causes them to seek medical advice. Depression sets in unconsciously, and it is often only at a late stage that family and friends will notice that something has changed. Nevertheless, the afflicted person's vitality has been severely upset, and no simple cause can be found to explain the change.

A fatal claim

The third key word in this field is the ego-ideal. This is a force that strongly affects an individual's character and behaviour and is connected to the

Many people suffer from essential depression, a condition that takes away their enthusiasm for life.

excessive demands which the patient places on him- or herself. Such a person often acts according to the 'all or nothing' principle, and experiences any external problem or affliction as a serious blow to his or her narcissistic self-image. If stricken by a serious illness, the patient has the ability to deny the seriousness of the situation and asks not to be pitied. He or she pretends to be healthy and remains strangely calm, while friends and relatives are filled with anxiety as a result of the illness and their concern for their loved one. In reality, such a patient has composed an ideal image of him- or herself: an extremely limiting, even paralysing ego-ideal, which may salvage his or her pride, but can lead to death.

Restriction and trauma

According to the experts on psychosomatics, some patients generally lack a mental mechanism that Freud called para-stimulus, which act as a counterbalance to reality. The reasons for this can lie in a traumatic childhood experience. If a person has suffered the loss of a parent or sibling or become separated from parents in early childhood, this can affect later development. Similarly, if a mother gets depressed shortly after the birth of a child, or if the family is just too big, then this may hold back individual development and lead to a state of psychological instability. Such people are characterised by a limited imagination and reduced pictorial associations. They can be unstable, and the smallest setback can completely upset them.

The second factor that can harm mental development is mental disorientation. This occurs when a person is overburdened, either physically – such as when a virus strikes – or psychologically – if severe losses occur in quick succession. Illnesses such as cancer are thought to develop more frequently in such cases.

The third danger to mental development is suppressing normal mental activity – when a person tries to hold back sexual or aggressive instinctive desires, whose satisfaction would violate deeply rooted ideals or moral values. Some people try to avoid these kinds of thoughts, since they may be linked to painful childhood experiences (for example, the memory of a rape) and would only re-open the old wounds. Thus they gradually ban from their thoughts every image, every association which could have any connection to those hated events. This can result in a severe stunting of normal emotional development.

Psychosomatic treatment

When a patient goes to see a specialist in psychosomatics, he or she usually does so on the advice of their family doctor. The first thing the specialist tries to find out is the position that the illness occupies in the patient's mental balance. A severe flu when the atmosphere in the office becomes unbearable; stomach pains that confine a child to bed the day before school starts: these combinations could explain the onset of illness. In such cases, it is best to treat the illness as real until the mind can take over and solve the conflict in the right way. So the specialist in psychosomatic medicine tries to ensure that both the body and the mind are cared for.

The so-called clinical interview plays an important role in psychosomatic treatment. The clinical interview is a useful way to obtain information about the patient's qualities, conflicts and personal situation. Questionnaires are frequently used to obtain objective measurements of certain aspects of a person's personality.

Once the initial symptoms have been dealt with, the patient can be helped by psychotherapy in the form of weekly therapy sessions. The therapist offers support and listens carefully in order to uncover the source of conflicts and understand the patient's behaviour and thoughts. By encouraging the patient to speak openly about his or her feelings and ideas and by showing interest in his or her dreams, the individual is encouraged to understand their own thought processes by following the explanations given by the therapist. The therapist seeks to improve the patient's mental balance, thereby protecting him or her from future physical afflictions.

Keep calm

Every person has his or her own way of staying calm. These are behaviour patterns which are used in everyday life, often unconsciously, in order to reduce agitation. They can take the form of the need to smoke during work, to walk up and down while speaking or to scribble on a piece of paper during a meeting.

Such practices become obsessive when they are the only way in which a person can find calmness or release excess emotional pressure. When this happens, the situation could become pathological.

High-performance athletes have many methods for attaining calmness.

By keeping his mind and body continuously occupied, rower Gérard d'Aboville refused to allow himself to feel fear or anxiety. This enabled him to conquer the cold and stormy Atlantic Ocean.

The French long-distance rower Gérard d'Aboville, for example, single-handedly crossed the Atlantic Ocean, rowing 7,000 strokes per day over a distance of 10,000 km. This corresponds to 16 strokes per minute, a level that suggests that he was able to make his physical activities virtually automatic. This kept his body and mind continuously busy and reduced the likelihood that he would feel anxious or fearful, in spite of loneliness and mortal danger.

AIDS

Ever since it emerged in the late 1970s, AIDS has presented a profound challenge to medical science. So far, researchers have not been able to discover a cure for the deadly virus, which uses the body's immune system in order to multiply. The rapid spread of AIDS among the nations of Africa and Asia has transformed it from an epidemic into a global pandemic. But new research gives reason to hope that doctors will soon be able to control the infection.

More than two decades have passed since doctors and the public first learned of acquired immune deficiency syndrome (AIDS). This syndrome – the medical term for an illness characterised by a typical complex of symptoms and ailments – was first recognised among homosexual men in the United States in 1978. However, its distant origins are thought to lie in Africa.

In April 1981, the renowned Centers for Disease Control (CDC) in Atlanta noted an unusual increase in the use of the medication Pentadimin, which is used to treat certain forms of inflammation of the lung, in New York State. This revealed the existence of a breeding ground for so-called opportunistic lung afflictions resulting from *Pneumocystis carinii*, a single-celled organism, presumably of the type Sporozoa. Although the pathogen is harmless to healthy individuals, it poses a critical danger for those with a weakened immune system.

In June of 1981, in the American research journal *Morbidity and Mortality Weekly Report*, the CDC reported five more cases of the same illness in Los Angeles. A month later, it reported another 26 cases, establishing for the first time a connection between the lung ailment, a form of skin cancer (Kaposi's sarcoma) and the symptoms of immune deficiency. It was not long before the alarm bells began to ring.

Doctors were already quite familiar with clinical pictures of patients with weakened resistance. Children were sometimes born

The two groups were the French team led by Luc Montagnier (left), and the American team under Robert Gallo (below).

A bitter dispute arose between two scientific teams over which one actually discovered the HI-virus responsible for AIDS. The dispute held back the pace of new research.

with inadequately developed immune systems, and this was also a symptom accompanying various forms of bone marrow cancer. Furthermore, since the late 1950s, medical science has developed a number of therapeutic techniques that can almost completely neutralise the immune system. These include chemotherapy – widely used in the treatment of cancer – cortisone treatment and the use of immune suppressants (drugs that suppress the body's natural defences). In an organ transplant, such as a heart transplant, the body's immune system needs to be artificially weakened so that the body

will not reject the transplanted organ. This is also the case with patients suffering from leukaemia: their treatment is supplemented or concluded with a bone marrow transplant. This procedure is critical to establish a new immune cell system in the place of the old, afflicted one.

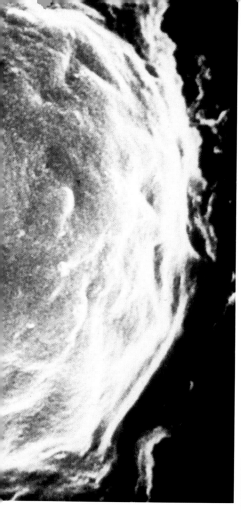

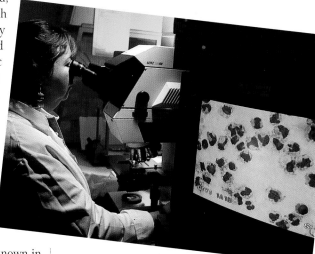

Advanced technology is employed to investigate the AIDS virus. Shown here is an image of a cell seen through an electron microscope.

are the result of bacterial, viral, fungal or monocellular causes. A direct connection has been established between the affliction resulting from the pathogen and the illness. Even in the case of congenital immune deficiency or a deficiency induced by drugs with varying degrees of toxicity, it was possible to identify the causes. But the appearance of AIDS demonstrated that infectious disease could once again become a serious threat.

Research into the causes of AIDS became a rapidly expanding scientific field, in which researchers came up with increasingly detailed results. Many hypotheses have been advanced, and a number of new therapeutic approaches have been tested. Today, we know that AIDS is the final stage in a chronically progressive viral infection, in which the immune system of the victim becomes increasingly weaker. As a result, germs that the body would normally be able to fight can now lead to serious illness and finally death. The cause of the illness is the Human Immune Deficiency Virus (Type 1), or HIV-1, which is known in at least nine variants.

This pathogen can only survive in fluids, and is transmitted through contact with body fluids. High concentrations of the virus

A very sensitive virus

For such a deadly killer, the AIDS virus is surprisingly sensitive. It is sensitive to 70% alcohol or bleach and has little resistance to a number of antiseptics. The virus reproduces in a host organism, which it has entered via the bodily fluids – primarily blood or semen. Initially, homosexual men carried the virus because many practised unprotected sex. Nowadays, it is known that any unprotected sexual activity – whether homosexual or heterosexual – drastically increases the risk of infection.

The Pasteur Institute in Paris is one of the many research centres where scientists are engaged in intensive study of cellular processes.

What was new was not the appearance of an immune deficiency syndrome, but the fact that this ailment had begun to afflict adults, primarily male homosexuals, who had no history of immune system disorders and were not undergoing any therapy that might suppress the functioning of the immune system. Apart from this, the illness appeared to be extremely infectious and to be passed on through sexual intercourse. The virus clearly presented a serious epidemiological threat – perhaps the most serious such threat in modern times.

Isolating a virus

Over centuries, although primarily during the 20th century, medical science has identified many illnesses and discovered their causes. We now know that the great scourges of the past – bubonic plague, cholera, tuberculosis, syphilis and malaria –

A changing clinical picture

HIV infection and its accompanying symptoms have particular characteristics:
❏ The pathogen forms genetic mutations, which alter certain of its qualities and make specific treatment difficult.
❏ The latency period between infection and the presence of detectable antibodies in the blood differs in length.
❏ The latency period between infection and the appearance of the full clinical picture of an AIDS sufferer varies, and can be extended using new therapeutic approaches.
❏ The symptomatic picture can vary widely from patient to patient.

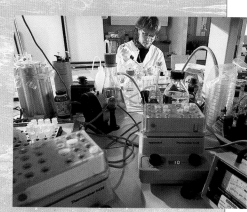

Genetic mutations of HIV-1 are studied in molecular retro-virology laboratories.

AIDS in Africa

There are two related branches of the HI-virus in Africa. HIV-1, the actual pathogen of the acquired immune deficiency syndrome, is prevalent in the so-called AIDS belt. This includes a number of states south of the Sahara, among them tourist destinations such as Kenya and Tanzania. Only about 2% of the world's population live in this zone, but it is home to 50% of all infected persons. Further south, South Africa has recorded one of the world's highest rates of infection.

According to research, there are two reasons for the high degree of infection. First, people engage in high-risk sexual practices, such as frequent changes of partner and sex with prostitutes. Second, there is poor sex education and sexual hygiene.

The second branch of the virus, HIV-2, probably emerged in West Africa. It has not infected as many people as HIV-1, and the clinical picture appears to be less serious.

are found in blood, sperm and vaginal secretions. The host cells of HIV are the so-called T4-helpers, a type of white blood cell and a component of our immune system that is destroyed by the infection.

After a period of between 4 and 26 weeks, it is generally possible to determine by a blood test whether a person is infected or not. This period varies greatly from one individual to another. The period of latency, in which an infected person remains symptom-free, can last up to 11 years.

Is it a pandemic?

As a result of these findings, public health authorities in both rich and poor nations must assume that there are many more HIV-positive people than reported cases of illness. There are many other factors that further emphasise the formidable nature of this illness, among them the proven transmission of the virus from infected mothers to their infants (in 25% of the cases, the child is HIV-positive and is sure to contract AIDS in the coming years), the confirmed danger of infection between heterosexual partners

engaging in unprotected sex and the risk of drug addicts contracting the virus through sharing infected needles.

On top of this, there is the tragic scandal surrounding contaminated blood, which infected thousands of patients in Canada, France, Germany and other countries during

Tragically, the safety of donor blood came into question as a result of the AIDS pandemic.

the 1980s. In the early stages of the AIDS crisis, those responsible for the safety of the blood supply were slow to take the measures necessary to detect the presence of the virus in donated blood. As a result, contaminated blood and clotting products were supplied to haemophiliacs and patients needing large quantities of blood as a result of surgery. Thousands of people contracted the virus, many of whom subsequently died.

Of the approximately 23 million infected people throughout the world, about 90% live in the developing nations, and two-thirds of them are Africans living south of the Sahara. Each year, about $18 billion is spent in the fight against AIDS, but the United Nations has estimated that more than 90% of this money goes to

industrialised nations. Currently, the world spends around $2.6 billion on programmes for AIDS education and prevention, but only 14% of this is spent in the developing world.

Alongside Africa, parts of the Caribbean and some Asian countries have a high rate of infection – AIDS has spread rapidly in India, for example. However, between 1990 and 1994, intensive campaigns against AIDS resulted in the annual number of new HIV infections in Thailand being reduced by half. This shows that education can have a real effect on the transmission of the virus.

Fighting back

The development of therapies against AIDS is based on attempts to slow down the multiplication of the HI-virus in its host cells. In the course of this process, the pathogen transfers its genetic code to the genetic make-up of the cells it attacks. An enzyme known as reverse transcriptase acts as

High-risk practices such as sharing or using unsterilised needles dramatically increase the risks of contracting the HI-virus.

The pathogen that caused bubonic plague, the scourge of the Middle Ages, remained unknown to medical science for centuries.

a kind of writing instrument, making it easier to turn the single-strand RNA (ribonucleic acid) of the so-called retrovirus into the double-strand DNA (deoxyribonucleic acid). This can be inserted into the host's genetic make-up where it can be reproduced as a so-called provirus, which will continue to reproduce and multiply until the infected cell dies. Before the virus can be released, large protein molecules are formed, which another enzyme known as protease cuts to shape. The resulting molecules can serve as protein supports for the virus.

The first strategy tried by researchers was to inhibit the functional mechanism of reverse transcriptase by causing it to produce a false copy of the virus's genetic make-up. Since this genetic structure consists of building blocks known as nucleotides, drugs with similar elements (nucleotide analogues) have been developed, which, once they have been incorporated, prevent the development of a viable virus.

The first medication of this kind was Azidothymanide, known as AZT, which was approved for use in the late 1980s in the United States, and shortly afterwards in the rest of the world. But not long afterwards, it was discovered that the HI-virus had learned

to trick this substance and had developed resistance to it. Scientists were forced to produce other substances capable of acting as transcriptase inhibitors.

Strength in unity

There is another category of substances which attacks the second viral enzyme and are thus known as protease inhibitors. They ensure that the protein necessary for the maturation of the pathogen is not produced. There are, however, two problems here: on one hand, protease inhibitors interfere with the medication needed by the patient to treat opportunistic infections, and, on the other hand, they reach the central nervous system and can even attack the brain.

The real breakthrough in AIDS therapy finally came in the mid-1990s when both nucleotide analogues and protease inhibitors began to be administered

All over the world, educational campaigns, such as this one in Thailand, are driving home the message of AIDS awareness.

in combination – the so-called 'cocktail' approach. Tests carried out with a threefold combination of two nucleotide analogues and one protease inhibitor succeeded in suppressing the virus in the majority of infected people so that it remained below the threshold of detection. Unfortunately, here too the pathogen has proven remarkably resistant, demonstrating its ability to adapt rapidly to new drugs. It is also unlikely that this costly form of therapy can be effective in the poor countries of Africa or Asia.

For this reason, cheaper drugs or mass immunisation are essential. But all efforts to bring this about have been unsuccessful. A

Staying safe

❑ Engage in sexual activity only with adequate protection against infection, and avoid high-risk sexual practices.
❑ Use protective gloves in emergencies.
❑ Employ correct personal and public hygiene.
❑ Reduce the chances of transmission through donated blood by using your own blood for transfusions.
❑ Maintain strict control over the production of vaccines from debilitated virus material.
❑ Support a high level of medical care for HIV-positive individuals.

large-scale study of immunisation has been conducted in the US using a genetically engineered vaccine. Another new approach has been to vaccinate individuals with pure DNA: nucleic acid, which only carries part of the genetic make-up of the virus, is injected into a muscle. Once in the body, it strengthens the immune system. However, the mechanisms involved are not yet fully understood. Researchers in Germany and the US have also succeeded in producing a genetically altered virus which, in laboratory tests, has attacked the host cells of the HI-virus. It remains to be seen how the immune system of a living organism will react to the altered virus.

With the growing body of knowledge about the HI-virus, there may be a chance of a cure in the near future. For now, new drugs and therapeutic techniques are ensuring that HIV-positive patients enjoy a better life and a longer period of survival.

How Dangerous is Cholesterol?

Heart disease is the greatest killer in industrial nations. The onset of heart disease and other illnesses of the circulatory system is greatly influenced by the level of cholesterol in the body. Excessive levels of blood cholesterol slowly build up on artery walls, gradually strangling the circulation. But research has shown that it is not only the level of cholesterol that is important. Individual factors also play an important role.

In recent years, people around the world have become aware of the health hazards associated with high levels of cholesterol. These include the increased risks of heart attacks and strokes. For many people, this has been the signal to cut down on fats and to eat a more balanced diet – particularly in industrialised nations, where the intake of dietary fat is typically high. But cholesterol has also been widely misunderstood, and in the process has acquired a bad reputation.

Cholesterol is a fat-like, waxy material that is a component of all cells. It belongs to the family of fats, also called lipids. Despite its reputation, cholesterol is indispensable to both humans and animals. It is an important component, for example, of cell membranes; it plays a part in the production of steroid hormones, such as stress and sex hormones; and it is also required for the synthesis of vitamin D and the production of bile acids.

A small part of the body's cholesterol comes from animal produce – egg yolks, butter and meats. Such foods should make up only about 15% of a balanced diet. The bulk of the body's cholesterol is produced by the body itself, in organs such as the liver, intestines and adrenal glands.

'Good' and 'bad' cholesterol

Cholesterol is not soluble in the blood, and so it requires some kind of 'taxi' to transport it throughout the body. This role is played by the so-called lipoproteins, molecules with a water-resistant core and a shell formed of water-soluble proteins. The lipoproteins may be subdivided into four main groups.

The first group are the chylomicrons. With their help, cholesterol is taken from the cells of the intestines via the lymph into the blood, and then via the blood vessels to the liver and to other organs (heart, kidney, lungs, muscles), where it serves as fuel. The second group is known as the VLDL (Very

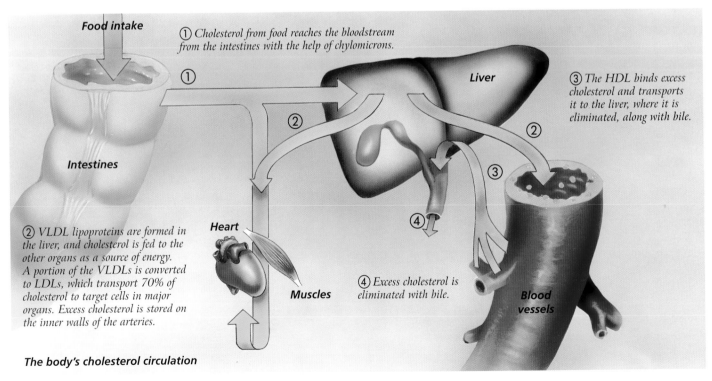

① *Cholesterol from food reaches the bloodstream from the intestines with the help of chylomicrons.*

③ *The HDL binds excess cholesterol and transports it to the liver, where it is eliminated, along with bile.*

② *VLDL lipoproteins are formed in the liver, and cholesterol is fed to the other organs as a source of energy. A portion of the VLDLs is converted to LDLs, which transport 70% of cholesterol to target cells in major organs. Excess cholesterol is stored on the inner walls of the arteries.*

④ *Excess cholesterol is eliminated with bile.*

The body's cholesterol circulation

Cholesterol passes into the bloodstream during the digestive process.

Cholesterol is deposited on the walls of the arteries in the form of crystals, shown here (dyed) under a microscope.

Low Density Lipoprotein); VLDL is formed in the liver, from where it is passed into the bloodstream.

In the blood, a third carrier takes over. Characterised by its low density, this lipoprotein is known as LDL (Low Density Lipoprotein). The LDL can be bound to specific receptors or receptor molecules of the body cells, where it releases the required cholesterol inside the organism. These processes ensure that no less than 70% of cholesterol reaches target cells in the major organs. If the tissues already have sufficient amounts of cholesterol, the LDL stores it on the artery walls. Because of its detrimental effects, this form of cholesterol is called 'bad' cholesterol.

The fourth carrier, HDL (High Density Lipoprotein), circulates in the bloodstream. It scoops up the excess cholesterol from the cells and from the walls of the blood vessels and transports it to the liver, where it will be broken down. HDL actually serves to break down cholesterol and prevent its deposit on the artery walls. For this reason, it is widely referred to as 'good' cholesterol.

LDL and HDL play an important role in regulating the human body's cholesterol metabolism; they either contribute to or counteract the increasing fat deposits on the walls of the arteries. The medical term for this gradual build-up of fat in the arteries is arteriosclerosis. When a doctor tests a patient's cholesterol level, it is not sufficient to determine the overall cholesterol level. The ratio of LDL to HDL also has to be determined if the doctor is to make a prognosis regarding a patient's possible risk of heart disease.

Assessing the risk

Since the early 1990s, there has been considerable progress in the development of tests to measure blood-cholesterol levels. Studies show that, for most people, an overall cholesterol level of 5.5 mmol/litre or less carries with it a low risk of cardiovascular disease. A level of 5.5–6.5 mmol/litre carries an increased risk, and a level of 6.5 or more represents a high risk. The most common problems are illustrated in the following three situations:

❏ First: The overall cholesterol level is normal, but there is a lower HDL level and an increased LDL level. This is a danger sign, and points to an increased risk of heart disease.

❏ Second: Levels of both overall cholesterol and HDL are high. The ratio between the two determines the risk: individuals should seek advice from their doctor.

❏ Third: Apart from increased levels of overall cholesterol (both HDL and LDL), there is also an increase in other lipid forms, such as triglycerides. In this case, the increased risk of heart disease stems from the increased level of all fats.

Arteries and ageing

The progressive accumulation of fats on artery walls, or arteriosclerosis, is a natural symptom which accompanies the ageing process in humans. There is a constant flow of cholesterol within the arteries: LDLs transport cholesterol and deposit it on the surface, where it is absorbed by HDLs and transported back to the liver for digestion. If this equilibrium is disturbed in favour of the LDLs, this can lead to dangerously high levels of cholesterol being deposited on the walls of the blood vessels.

After the second decade of life, cholesterol begins to be deposited on the inner walls of the arteries in the form of small yellowish spots. In time, these so-called lipid stripes

Products derived from animals, such as butter, paté and sausages, are all rich in saturated fats, and likely to raise blood cholesterol levels.

An illness of the rich?

People in developing countries are unlikely to have high cholesterol levels, as their diet, mainly grains, is relatively low in fats.

The incidence of heart disease among North Americans, Europeans, wealthy Javanese and Chinese is higher than among the peoples of less developed regions. The decisive factor seems to be diet. As people grow more prosperous, they tend to eat greater amounts of fatty foods.

gradually merge and form a smooth surface. Over the years, these deposits are absorbed into the walls of the blood vessels; they take on a whitish tinge, with irregular contours, and are known as plaque. As fatty substances such as LDL continue to be deposited, the plaque increases in thickness and hardness. The contours of the deposits become more and more fissured, until they form a kind of bud which gradually restricts the inner diameter of the artery.

In people around 60, the deposits start to harden, until the entire artery wall looks like an eggshell. By this time, the arteries have become stiff and narrow and can no longer transport sufficient quantities of blood. At this point, serious problems can occur.

Fatal consequences

Depending on the strength of the arteries and of the organ which has to be supplied, the various stages of arteriosclerosis have different effects. Once the arterial cross-section has been restricted by about 75%, the reduced blood supply and resultant lack of oxygen to the affected organ produces clinical signs of illness in that organ. The heart is especially vulnerable: a severely restricted flow of blood can lead to angina pectoris (chest pains, usually accompanied by shortness of breath), or even a heart attack. Researchers have determined that the frequency of these ailments go hand in hand with a surplus of LDL in the blood. The statistical risk of a heart attack virtually doubles in people with a cholesterol level of 6.5 mmol/litre or more, as compared to the risks for those with levels of 5.5 mmol/litre or less. Arteriosclerosis can develop in different parts of the body – for example, in the lower limbs or in the brain. In such cases, failing circulation may reveal itself in the form of short motor and sensory lapses, or as a life-threatening stroke.

But the risks are definitely not the same for all people. Some individuals have a genetic predisposition to arteriosclerosis. However, probably the best defence is to manage your cholesterol by eating a balanced diet with a relatively small percentage of animal fats. Even though only a small percentage of blood cholesterol is absorbed from food, a cholesterol-conscious diet has proven effective in reducing the incidence of heart disease.

LIKE CURES LIKE: IS THERE A SCIENTIFIC BASIS FOR HOMEOPATHY?

The basis of homeopathy rests on the amazing principle that tiny quantities of plant, animal or mineral substances – diluted many thousands of times in water and alcohol – can cure the body's ailments. Supporters claim that it is an effective alternative treatment that works with the individual's special make-up to restore the body's balance.

In recent years, there has been a strong worldwide trend towards alternative forms of medicine. Many patients now seek out alternative treatment, especially if they suffer from psychosomatic illnesses, chronic ailments or allergies, for despite medicine's achievements in the development of exact analytic and diagnostic procedures, it is in these areas that science often encounters its limits. Among the bewildering range of alternative therapies, one of the most popular is homeopathy.

Homeopathy has been practised for about 200 years, and has numbered many illustrious people among its proponents, for example, the Dutch painter Vincent van Gogh, who was treated by a French homeopath named Dr Paul Gachet; the British royal family, who even financed a noted homeopathic clinic in London; and the world-famous violinist Yehudi Menuhin. There are also many opponents of homeopathy, who see it as nothing but an illusion. 'Homeopathy,' declared former French cabinet minister Bernard Kouchner – himself a medical doctor – 'is a luxury for those who are not too sick.' But most people know little about the principles and practices of homeopathy. Is it just a fashion made popular by our longing for gentle remedies, or is it a serious therapeutic method?

The basic principle of homeopathy can be explained using the following example. First, a drop of coffee is placed in a bottle with one

The Greek physician Hippocrates realised that 'the same things that have given rise to suffering can also heal it'.

Samuel Hahnemann (1755–1843) is regarded as the founder of homeopathy. His pioneering observations were recorded in The Doctrine of Pure Medication.

litre of water and shaken thoroughly. Then a drop of this solution is placed on a sugar cube and eaten. Although coffee itself is a stimulant, this homeopathic preparation has a calming effect.

The production of homeopathic medicine is naturally much more complex and subject to extremely stringent controls, and the above example may raise more questions than it answers. Among these questions are: why does the end product have the opposite effect to the original substance? How much coffee remains on the sugar cube? Does every drop in the bottle contain coffee? Does this substance have the same effect on all people?

Reverse effect

As early as the 5th century BC, the Greek physician Hippocrates made the following observation about illness: 'They are sometimes passed on by our fellow human beings; and the same things that have given rise to suffering can also heal it'.

The first exact description of this so-called reverse effect of substances was given by the German doctor Samuel Hahnemann (1755–1843), who is regarded as the founder of modern homeopathy. After qualifying as a doctor in 1799, Hahnemann supplemented his income by working as a translator. While he was translating an English pharmaceutical

Three examples of plants from which medications are obtained: henbane (Hyoscyamus niger, right) has an antispasmodic effect in the stomach and intestinal tract; Cinchona bark (Cinchona pubescens, below) relieves nervous exhaustion and general physical weakness as a result of loss of fluids; and deadly nightshade (Atropa belladonna, large picture) is administered in some cases of oversensitivity to light and noise. These plants are used in conventional medicine as well as in homeopathy.

A different perspective

A homeopath will look at a person's tendency to pathological reactions (diathesis), their sensibility type and their constitution. Sensibility type comprises morphological features such as body size, typical qualities such as aggressiveness and various physical characteristics such as sweating or dryness of the tongue. Constitution embraces the morphological, psychic and physiological qualities of a person. For example, the 'carbohydrate type' includes short-limbed individuals, while the 'phosphorus type' covers those with long limbs.

textbook, his attention was drawn to a passage describing the quinaquina tree (*Cinchona officinalis*), which is indigenous to the Andes region and provided a common remedy for malaria at the time – it is the source of the antimalarial drug quinine. Hahnemann read that the bark of this tree had an antipyretic (fever-reducing) effect due to 'its stimulating effect on the stomach', so he decided to try this out on himself. After drinking a few cups of tea prepared from the bark of the tree, he experienced a strong fever, accompanied by trembling and sweating. These symptoms were very similar to those of malaria, which the quinaquina bark was supposed to relieve.

Quite astonished, Hahnemann carried out experiments with other plants, such as deadly nightshade (*Atropa belladonna*) and henbane (*Hyoscyamus niger*). Each time, he thought he observed in himself the same symptoms that the plant was supposed to suppress. He began an exact description and systematic classification of the symptoms induced in healthy individuals by different plants, minerals and animal substances. Hahnemann's observations are collected in his book, *The Doctrine of Pure Medication*.

Shaking all over

The production of homeopathic medications is subject to strict control. Here a technician checks the base substance.

The base solutions for homeopathic medications come from various plant, animal, mineral or metallic substances. These are then classified according to their degree of dilution as D-potency (dilution 1:9), C-potency (dilution 1:99) or Q-potency (dilution 1:50,000). If, for example, one drop of the base solution is mixed with 99 drops of water and alcohol, the preparation is said to be a mixture of C-potency. At each stage, exact instructions govern how much the mixture is to be shaken. This procedure is known as potentiation. At the end of the shaking, the resultant solution is poured onto small pills of pure lactose (a sugar derived from milk), and the fluid saturates the globules. Finally, they are dried and bottled. A person taking a homeopathic medication simply swallows the dry globules.

The foundation of homeopathy was thus laid, and it found expression in the Latin phrase *Similia similibus curentur* (Let likes be cured by likes), or the so-called simile principle. The word 'homeopathy' comes from the Greek *homoio pathis*, or 'similar suffering'.

Hahnemann proceeded to administer the substances he was testing not only to healthy individuals, but to those suffering from illnesses with the same symptoms. If, for example, a person was stung by a bee, the injection of venom would be followed immediately by pain. The skin would begin to redden and swell, indicating the area of the inflammation. Hahnemann's idea was to make use of the honeybee's venom in order to alleviate inflammations of quite different origin.

He soon achieved spectacular results with this method. However, he soon noticed that his results were related to the dosage, with high dosages often making the symptoms worse. For this reason he began diluting the substances with a mixture of alcohol and water until not a single molecule of the active ingredient was detectable in the final product. This formed the second principle behind homeopathy: the concept of potentiation.

Homeopathic medicine makes use of a system to indicate how much a substance has been diluted. A dilution of 1:9 is known as D-potency; 1:99 is known as C-potency; and 1:50,000 is Q-potency. If a homeopathic medication is labelled C200, then the active ingredient has been diluted with water and alcohol 200 times in a relation of 1:99. During this process, it is essential that the mixture be shaken in the prescribed manner.

French researcher Jacques Benveniste has conducted experiments that supposedly prove the efficacy of homeopathy.

In Hahnemann's view, medications prepared in this manner become more potent, or more effective, the more they are diluted. He referred to the process as potentiation.

Since highly diluted substances no longer contain a trace of the original substance, most scientists believe that such substances cannot have healing effects. Homeopaths counter this belief with the explanation known as the imprint theory or the 'memory of water'. The question has caused heated debate among researchers in recent years. In 1988, Jacques Benveniste, who at the time was chief researcher at France's Institute for Health and Medical Research (INSERM), published a study attempting to demonstrate that, even after various stages of dilution and shaking, water retains a clear imprint of the substances that have been diluted in it. In effect, the water 'remembers' information about the substance, even if it no longer contains a single molecule of it.

Opponents of homeopathy are convinced that the small sugar pills soaked in the diluted mixtures cannot possibly contain any significant active ingredients, and that after maximum dilution all homeopathic medicines are identical. In their opinion, the effectiveness of these products rests entirely on the placebo effect. Supporters of a second hypothesis believe that modern analytic techniques are not sensitive enough to detect the difference between untreated water and so-called dynamically rendered water that is marked by the molecules of the medication. In support of their thesis, students of Hahnemann point to the results of various laboratory experiments that indicate that electromagnetic or physical-chemical changes have taken place.

The placebo effect

But doctors and researchers are not only divided on the question as to how homeopathy works. Another controversial area is the successful cures that are cited by its proponents. In order to find out whether a medication has a specific effect, doctors rely on the so-called double-blind experiment, the only testing method that enjoys wide acceptance in the scientific world. In a typical clinical test, researchers try to get rid of any possible human influences: the test group is randomly divided into two, and neither the doctors nor the patients know which of the two groups is going to receive the substance under test, and which will receive a false medication or placebo (usually a harmless sugar pill). The unusual and puzzling thing about the double-blind experiment, however, is that up to 40% of patients who take the placebo experience healing effects. This is explained as psychic in origin, and is known as the placebo effect.

The double-blind procedure is not easy to apply to homeopathy. Unlike conventional medicine, homeopathic medications are not prescribed according to a specific and exact definition of the illness, but are determined by an assessment of an individual's life force, which the treatment seeks to restore to balance. If the life force is disturbed, this weakens the body's defence system, allowing disease-causing germs to enter the organism. For this reason, each patient receives a

medication that is tailor-made for his or her requirements. In conventional medicine, however, the clinical testing of drugs aims to measure the effect of a single preparation on as many individuals as possible. The different approach taken by homeopathy makes it difficult for practitioners to show convincingly that homeopathic preparations are equally effective.

In spite of this difficulty, there have been more than 100 studies testing the efficacy of homeopathic medications. But the results of these studies have been contradictory. When a Dutch research group examined the methodology of all these studies, they concluded that only 23 of them yielded any significant results. In 15 studies, the homeopathic drug was clearly superior to the placebo, a result that surprised even the scientists. Of course, in order to be widely accepted, these results would have to be successfully repeated by an independent team of researchers.

Can substances remember?

On June 30, 1988 the respected Paris-based daily newspaper *Le Monde* reported on 'The Memory of Matter'. This article followed the publication of a study in the influential British scientific journal *Nature* that described the effect of strongly diluted antibodies on human blood cells. The study had been conducted by a team led by Jacques Benveniste.

The results of research studies are normally carefully scrutinised before they appear in scientific journals. In this case, the chief editor of *Nature* took the unusual step of questioning the value of the results in a later issue of the journal. In July 1989, the study was repeated, but the results could not be duplicated.

Don't touch!

It is very important not to touch homeopathic medications with your fingers, as this could neutralise them. The globules are placed directly under the tongue, which has a strong supply of blood. The substance can then rapidly enter the bloodstream.

Body, soul and spirit

Clinical studies conducted in recent years show that homeopathy can be very successful in the treatment of certain conditions, including migraine headaches, hives, allergic congestion and various forms of rheumatism. Significantly, many of these conditions are caused by psychic factors rather than physical ones.

Doctors warn against using homeopathy as the sole therapy in cases of diabetes, cancer or dangerous infectious diseases, because of the danger that precise diagnoses and effective cures will be delayed until it is potentially too late for the patient. We still do not know if the healing effects of homeopathic medication are due to the placebo effect or not. Perhaps, in the final analysis, what really matters is the fact that the individual feels restored to health.

Homeopathic medications are most commonly administered in the form of tiny globules. The lid of this container has three small holes to allow convenient dosing while preventing finger contact with the pills.

How much is there?

The Avogadro constant N has a value of 6.0221×10^{23} and expresses the number of molecules that exist in one mole of any substance (a mole is the number of molecules in 12.011 g of carbon). If the initial concentration of the base solution of a homeopathic medication is known, it is possible to calculate the degree of dilution after which it is technically not present.

FIGHTING PAIN WITH ACUPUNCTURE

Of all the methods for treating pain, only acupuncture – used in China for thousands of years – seems to offer consistent success. Although its efficacy is beyond question, it is difficult to explain. Doctors and scientists are still trying to understand the principles at work when needles inserted into the skin at specific points miraculously banish all feelings of pain.

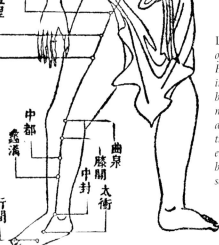

For a long time, the local elimination of pain seemed to be the best method of treating it. In the Mediterranean region, for example, the traditional remedy for pain lay in cauterising the wound – that is, searing or burning the affected tissue. A quite different approach to controlling pain was developed in China many thousands of years ago. Known as acupuncture, this technique now enjoys increasing acceptance around the world. In acupuncture, very thin needles of gold, silver or surgical steel are inserted into the patient's skin at specific points. Unlike other methods of treating pain, acupuncture does not simply concentrate on a local area, but also makes use of points in other areas of the body.

A healing technique

Acupuncture has been practised in China for about 3,500 years. The first medical textbook in which it is mentioned dates from about 400 BC. The technique first came to Europe in the 16th century. Its name comes from the Latin words *acus* (needle) and *punctum* (to prick) and was coined by the Dutch doctor Willem ten Rhyn who learned the technique during a visit to Japan in the 17th century. Because of its Chinese origins, acupuncture was misunderstood and rejected in Europe for many years. It was only really accepted in the 20th century.

Traditional Chinese medicine rests upon a series of concepts which are not only medical in nature, but include ideas concerning all aspects of life, including social structure. The body is viewed as an integral part of nature, in which there is normally a balance between

two opposing and complementary forces known as the Yin and the Yang. The Yin represents the feminine force, and the Yang the masculine. Yin is passive and calm, standing for darkness, cold, damp and expansion. Yang is aggressive and stimulating, and it stands for light, warmth, dryness and contraction.

If there is an imbalance between these two forces, it can lead to illness and other ailments. Too much Yin causes dull aches and pains, shivering, retention of fluid in the tissues, excretions and tiredness. If the Yang is dominant, this can lead to inflammation, headaches sudden pains, cramps, and high blood pressure. In acupuncture, both the diagnosis and the therapy aim to find and to alleviate the imbalance between the two forces.

Points and meridians

Treatment involves inserting needles at specific points on the patient's body. These points are located along invisible lines called meridians, flows of energy that cover the body like a grid and along which flow the forces of Yin and Yang.

Above left: *An 18th-century illustration of a Chinese doctor and his patient.*

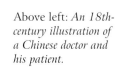

Above right: *The Taiji, or highest principle, embodies the unity of Yin and Yang. In Chinese medicine, Yin and Yang represent opposing forces – the masculine and the feminine – which complement one another and are in balance in the healthy body.*

Left: *The 14 points of the liver meridian. Beginning behind the inner cuticle of the big toe, the liver meridian runs up along the leg, across the stomach and ends below the nipple between the sixth and seventh rib.*

The position in which the needle is inserted and the way it is manipulated have an effect on the flow of energy along the meridian.

Each of these meridians has a privileged functional relationship to a specific bodily region: there are meridians for the solid or hollow organs such as the liver, gall bladder, heart or small intestine; for the sense organs, such as the tongue, eyes or mouth; or for the tissues, such as the skin or a muscle. The network of meridians is also inter-connected, which means that one point can be used instead of another, as long as the practitioner adheres strictly to the rules.

Doctors have not yet been able to demonstrate experimentally the existence of the network of meridians – neither structurally nor functionally. In other words, the relative position of the meridians does not correspond to the functional anatomy of the human body. But the structure of the central nervous system is well known and may partially explain the privileged paths that connect a series of major points with the internal organs or other body regions or sensory zones.

Points for soothing

In the West, acupuncture is used above all to soothe painful afflictions such as arthritis, back pain or rheumatism. It may appear remarkable that the simple act of inserting needles into the skin of a sick person can make their pain go away, but this is exactly what happens.

Acupuncture also provides a useful adjunct to conventional methods of dealing with pain. In conventional medicine, there are three approaches to pain: the first, antalgia, attempts to combat a given pain; the second, analgesia, is used to prevent pain from arising; and the third, anaesthesia, attempts to suppress any sensitivity, not just the pain. The analgesic effects of acupuncture are not very strong, but they are sufficiently effective so that the amounts of anaesthetic that are administered in minor operations can be

reduced. But this method is only suitable in relatively stable personalities – people who are strong in both physical and mental terms. In exceptional cases, where no anaesthetic is administered to a patient, they are often given an injection just before the operation. The injection contains medication to prevent the development of undesirable side effects. As far as analgesia is concerned, acupuncture seems to function as a kind of hyperanalgesic – in other words, it raises the threshold of pain, leading to a higher level of tolerance on the part of the patient.

Acupuncture and the nervous system

From the perspective of today's scientific knowledge, it is very difficult to understand how acupuncture works. The selection of therapeutic points is based on a traditional standard of practice that was developed over centuries. It is known that specific points are

Above: *Acupuncture is widely accepted today.*

Right: *The head of this 15th-century bronze figure is marked with meridians and points.*

associated with certain effects and that their stimulation – whether by manual or electrical means – encourages the release of chemical substances such as endorphins and serotonin, which in turn have an effect on the individual's perceptions of pain. Other points have a purely nervous effect: they interfere with the conducting capacity of the nerve channels before pain even registers in the brain. It has also been established that

certain points have an effect on very specific zones and that stimulation of a group of points can have a diffuse effect on pain, helping to make it manageable.

Today, it is thought that acupuncture acts on various levels of the nervous system in accordance with the chosen points as well as the patient's nervous disposition, and in relationship to the network of the meridians.

The first controlling instance for pain signals is found in the bone marrow. On the level of the so-called reticular formation, a kind of switching station in the brain, the transmission of the painful signal is inhibited by nervous mechanisms and by the release of chemical transmitters. In the thalamus, a region at the base of the brain, there are both neurochemical and nervous mechanisms, while it is in the cerebral cortex that pain is finally registered consciously.

Since pain is seldom the result of a single factor, all of these functional levels and quantities have to be taken into account. According to the nature of the pain, specific points may be chosen to combat fear in certain patients, whereas other individuals will require localised or regional treatment. In certain cases, acupuncture will even focus on distant points – for example, in patients who suffer phantom pains in a limb that has been amputated.

Knowledge and its limits

There is no doubt that acupuncture can combat and prevent pain in humans and animals. But to use it effectively still requires a complete analysis of the existing or expected pain, a thorough knowledge of the nervous system and a good command of the traditional rules for correct selection of the therapeutic points.

Acupuncture has led a secret, marginal existence in the West for more than 200 years. Today it is an accepted treatment, in spite of its radically different conception of the body's circulatory and nervous systems. Despite our lack of knowledge, it is certain that advances in the field of neurophysiology will gradually remove the ignorance that surrounds this effective painkiller.

THE AGONY OF MIGRAINE HEADACHES

The pain of migraine headaches affects millions of people. Migraines are difficult to treat, and scientists do not yet fully understand the processes that trigger an attack. However, new research into the brain is starting to shed some light on this painful subject.

Anyone who has suffered a migraine headache knows the pain and suffering that is involved. In most cases, migraines reveal themselves as a severe headache that is accompanied by a number of other symptoms. What makes matters worse is the fact that, unlike an ordinary headache, a migraine is difficult to treat with drugs, making the ordeal that much worse for the sufferer. Migraines were described by the Greek physician Hippocrates as early as the 4th century BC, but scientists are still baffled by the causes of this ailment. In many countries, severe migraine attacks account for a substantial percentage of all visits to doctors. With so many people affected, the cost of treating migraines presents a genuine public health problem.

An aura of pain

In 90% of all affected people, migraines appear at an early age, particularly in the years between puberty and the age of 30. Women are affected almost twice as much as men. In people over the age of 60, migraines seem to be an exception. Family forms have been reported, but there is no evidence that the condition is passed on from one generation to another. Of course, not every headache is a migraine headache, and it was not until 1988 that the specialists of the International Headache Society (IHS) were able to agree on a general classification of the affliction.

Today, doctors recognise two main types of migraine. The most prevalent form is the common migraine, which can arrive with almost no warning. The first sign is a painful pulsation about the same frequency as your heartbeat. The pulsation begins on one side of the head, but can then spread over the entire region.

The second form of migraine is much less common. It is preceded by several hours of warning signs, including nausea, irritability, weariness, feeling sleepy and depression – although in some cases there can also be the opposite, a kind of elation. The victim might also suffer from disturbed vision, in which he or she sees bright spots or jagged lines, or experiences flickering vision. This stage marks the beginning of the crisis, and is known as the aura, but it fades when the headache appears.

Whichever the type of migraine, there may be other symptoms involved. These include digestive complaints, a pronounced feeling of physical weakness, sensitivity to noise and light, impaired concentration and pale skin. In spite of the pain that accompanies a migraine, doctors regard them as relatively harmless. Depending on the frequency and severity, a migraine is unpleasant, but it is certainly not serious or life-threatening. Nevertheless, proper diagnosis requires an in-depth medical examination. This is done in order to exclude other possible causes of the attacks.

Like a bolt of lightning

In spite of numerous studies in the fields of neurology, vascular medicine and bio-chemistry, scientists have not yet been able to determine the cause of migraines. A major obstacle to research is the fact that people feel and describe the effects of the attacks in different ways. Because the severity of a migraine is so much a matter of individual opinion, it makes it difficult for researchers to evaluate scientific tests such as animal experiments. Accordingly, researchers have focused their attention on the factors that

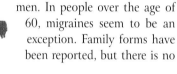

The agony of migraines inspired this cartoon by the French cartoonist Honoré Daumier (1808–1879).

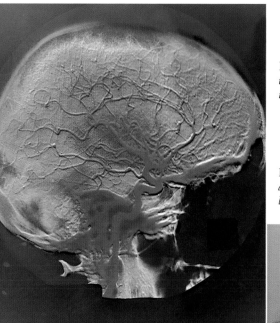

Left: *This image of the blood vessels in the head shows a strong vascular dilation in the minor arteries during a migraine.*

Below: *A migraine sufferer typically attempts to alleviate the pain through light massage pressure on the temples.*

of a number of highly effective drugs for the treatment of migraines. These medications block the serotonin receptors, in order to prevent dilation of the blood vessels that supply the brain.

The pain spreads

The third hypothesis is the so-called neuro-vascular hypothesis, and is based on the fact that the attacks, which are first and foremost a vascular phenomenon, are preceded by a number of symptoms that indicate a malfunction in the nervous system.

According to this hypothesis, the intense pain of a migraine comes from a stimulatory phenomenon in certain nerve cells, which spreads from the back of the head towards the front and is accompanied by a dilation of the blood vessels. The vessels are surrounded by a network of nerve fibres which release a large amount of neurotransmitters, including serotonin. It is conceivable that the nerve endings are activated and stimulated in the course of an attack.

Furthermore, a new suspect has recently appeared in the form of Drillings nerve, or trigeminus, an important nerve in the head. Drillings nerve is also connected to the blood vessels and plays a part in the dilation or constriction of the arteries and the transmission of sensations of pain to the brain. The left and right sides of the head are each supplied by one of its neural strands, which could explain the fact that migraines often cause pain in only one side of the head.

might trigger migraine attacks. The factors so far identified include alcohol, stress, certain foods such as chocolate or eggs, fatigue and sometimes heat, cold or wind. In 50% of women, the attacks are more frequent during menstruation, while in 10% they are more likely to occur during ovulation.

How does a migraine attack come about? In theory, every individual has a threshold of resistance to this form of headache, relative to the particular causes and to that person's disposition. When this threshold sinks, the crisis can occur with greater frequency, while a preventive treatment raises the threshold and can reduce the frequency of attacks. Migraines can therefore be regarded as a pathological reaction to certain stimuli, in which a brain that is susceptible to migraines demonstrates anomalies in the activation of pain and in vascular, or blood vessel, tension.

The vascular angle

Clinical observations have yielded three closely related hypotheses on the origins of migraines. The first concerns the blood vessels, and it has recently been confirmed through the use of modern techniques for measuring the flow of blood through the blood vessels of the brain. There is no proof as yet, but this might be the reason that migraine headaches are often described as pulsating. According to the hypothesis, there is an initial phase in which the blood vessels constrict. This begins at the back of the head, and is followed by the progressive dilation of the vessels of the entire head at a rate of

about 2 mm per minute. The spreading is accompanied by metabolic disorders whose advance corresponds to the spread of the headache. According to Pramod Saxenas, a pharmacologist at the Erasmus University in Rotterdam, the Netherlands, a migraine headache appears when the capillaries – the tiny connections between the veins and arteries – suddenly open, allowing arterial blood to flow into the veins. Experiments carried out on animals show that migraine remedies can partially block the advancing pain by closing the capillaries.

The role of serotonin

A second hypothesis was developed about 20 years ago with the discovery of serotonin, and produced a new biochemical theory concerning the vascular system. Serotonin is a chemical transmitter of the central nervous system. It plays an important role in the awareness of pain and affects, among other things, the blood vessels that supply the brain. It is thought that serotonin is released during the phase of arterial dilation, leading to headaches.

This theory places joint responsibility on the white blood cells (granulocytes), the blood platelets (blood cells that transport serotonin) and the nerve fibres that produce serotonin, and it has led to the development

---

Is it a migraine?

These are the accepted criteria for the diagnosis of a migraine:
❑ At least five attacks which meet the following criteria:
❑ A duration of about 4–72 hours;
❑ At least two of the following three features: a hammering and pulsating sensation, headache on one side of the head, medium to strong level of pain;
❑ Pain intensified through normal physical activity, such as climbing the stairs;
❑ At least one accompanying symptom, such as nausea and/or vomiting, sensitivity to light or noise.

DECLINING SPERM COUNTS: PANIC IN THE GENE POOL

Scientific research shows that male sperm production in industrial nations has diminished considerably over the past 50 years. Do men no longer have what it takes? There is a heated discussion about the role of stress and environmental toxins in this phenomenon. However, if we don't find out the cause of declining male fertility, the future of the human species could be severely affected.

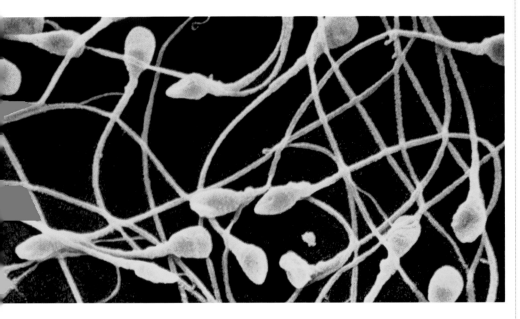

In 1992, the Danish scientist Niels E. Skakkebaek of Copenhagen University clinic published the results of some startling research. Skakkebaek and his colleagues had conducted the research over the preceding 50 years, and had analysed and evaluated 61 studies from 20 countries. They found that the overall sperm count had decreased by nearly half – from 113 to 66 million per millilitre of seminal fluid – and the average ejaculation volume of a man has fallen from 3.4 to 2.7 ml. A study by French scientists, based on sperm donations given by men in France between 1972 and 1993, yielded a similar result. Here too, the concentration of sperm has decreased continuously by about 2% per year.

If we take this research seriously, then the implications for the coming years are quite disturbing. While women produce just one ovum per month, men are continuously producing sperm cells. Their large number

Studies of industrial nations over the past 20–50 years have shown that sperm counts have apparently dropped by some 30–50%.

ensures a high probability of fertilisation, for most sperm cells die before they reach the female ovum after intercourse.

If a man has less than 20 million sperm cells per millilitre, then his chances of becoming a father are dramatically reduced. Fortunately, this is not yet the situation in the industrial nations, where the male sterility rate currently hovers around 8–11% of the population. But the trend is alarming, and scientists are conducting more research into the causes.

Will the earth be female?

The fall in sperm counts around the world needs considerable research. Some scientists believe that the stress of the modern work environment has a strong retarding effect on the production of sperm cells. But scientific opinion increasingly focuses on so-called environmental toxins as the main culprits. Among other things, it has been established that farm labourers working on the banana plantations and cotton fields of Central America who had been exposed to pesticides had a highly diminished level of fertility.

Subsequent studies show that the a similar phenomenon has occurred among the wild mammals of the Great Lakes region of the United States, an area which is heavily polluted by industrial effluents. In the southern state of Florida, where huge quantities of the insecticide Dicofol – which contains large amounts of the poison DDT – were fed into the waters of Lake Apopka in 1981, the fertility of male alligators was greatly affected.

All these cases concerned chemicals whose effects are similar to those of oestrogen, the female sex hormone. So far, it has been possible to identify 50 such substances, which are produced primarily through the industrial manufacture of chemicals, and occur as additional or auxiliary substances – also called plasticisers – in many synthetic materials, such as laundry powder. Research is currently being conducted to find out whether the continuous contact with these pseudo-oestrogens is responsible for the reduction in human sperm production.

Left: *Chemical contamination by the insecticide Dicofol has harmed the reproductive capacity of alligators in Lake Apopka, Florida. Do such toxins pose a threat to human fertility?*

SOUND WITHOUT LIMITS

Low-flying jet planes, rush-hour traffic, rock concerts, construction work – modern life is a noisy business, and our ears are constantly bombarded with sounds, some too low or too high for us to hear. But whether audible or not, sound has a strong influence on our bodies.

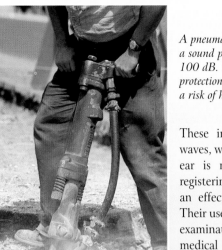

A pneumatic drill produces a sound pressure of over 100 dB. Unless hearing protection is worn, there is a risk of hearing damage.

Whether a jet engine starts up nearby or we listen to music at full volume on a personal stereo, it is not the origin of the sound waves but the pressure they create which has a decisive impact on our health. Sound is harmful when the volume exceeds a level of 120 dB (decibels). The longer the sound wave persists and the stronger it is, the greater the danger of permanent loss of hearing. If a sound wave exceeds 140 dB, the delicate membrane covering the eardrum could tear and the nerve fibres in the inner ear lose their function or die off completely. If this happens, the result will be permanent deafness, for damage to the hearing cells is irreparable.

Fatal repercussions

Above a certain level, noise is not only hazardous to the ear, but is potentially fatal as well. The reason for this is that sound is carried by vibrations which change the pressure of the medium that carries it – be it air, water, metal or living cells. If the sound wave is very strong, it can cause the entire organism to vibrate. The vibration exerts a mechanical pressure on the blood vessels that is strong enough to make them tear. This leads to internal bleeding. The pressure exerted by a modern artillery piece fired within a couple of metres is estimated at 200 dB, and is sufficient to severely injure or even kill a person nearby.

Silence full of noise

From an early age, the human ear is able to pick up sound waves in a frequency range of between 20 and 20,000 Hz (Hertz). Consequently, it can neither hear the very deep frequencies below 20 Hz nor the very high ones above 20 kHz (ultrasound). But what we experience as silence is actually filled with a clamour of inaudible sound waves. Cats and dogs, for example, can register certain ultrasounds, and elephants can communicate by means of infrasonic waves (soundlike waves of less than 16 Hz, or below audible range). Modern technology also makes use of numerous high and low frequency instruments, such as sonar devices – used at sea for navigation and echo location of underwater objects.

These inaudible sound waves, which the human ear is not capable of registering, seem to have an effect on the body. Their use in sonographic examinations and other medical operations is the proof. Low-intensity ultrasound is used to provide a mother-to-be with an image of the foetus developing in her womb. High-intensity ultrasonic waves with a frequency of 0.5–5 MHz (megahertz) are also used to destroy kidney stones, urinary calculus or bladder stones. This procedure, called lithotripsy, involves the focusing of impacting waves on the stone. Surrounding tissue is unharmed, and the ultrasonic waves will not enter the organism unless a certain contact gel is used.

Infrasonic waves pass through the skin and cause the organs to vibrate slowly. This can affect the functioning of the nervous system and impair the blood supply. For this reason, proximity to large, slow-running engines, turbines or muted compressors can lead to nausea and other symptoms of seasickness in some individuals.

During takeoff, the supersonic Concorde emits an ear-splitting noise level of about 140 dB, which can destroy our hearing cells.

HYPNOSIS: A QUESTION OF BELIEF?

Hypnosis has come a long way from the days of Dr Mesmer and 'animal magnetism'. Nowadays, therapists use hypnosis to fight pain, nicotine addiction and the psychological scars of trauma. And yet even its successes have not banished all the doubts that surround this technique.

Hypnosis is one of the oldest methods of physical therapy, and yet it still attracts controversy. Many people worry that if they undergo hypnosis, they will be vulnerable, and be asked to do things that they would not consider doing in a normal state of consciousness. Their fears are made worse by television shows in which people under hypnosis bark like dogs or try to swim across the carpet on the command of the hypnotist.

Hypnosis involves the inducement of a trance, which is a condition between waking and sleeping. A person who is in a trance is unaware of environmental stimuli, but is still open to the suggestions of the hypnotherapist.

For centuries, hypnotists have induced a state of trance by using the eye fixation method, in which the patient stares at a certain point or object – for example, a watch or necklace swinging back and forth. Focusing attention is the first step towards trance, which is then intensified through monotonous words spoken in a uniform, low voice by the therapist. Once a change in the state of consciousness has been attained, the therapist can begin to make suggestions. Generally, a patient is told to imagine a situation intensively. For example, patients suffering from fears or lack of self-confidence could imagine an everyday scene in which they feel courageous, strong or vigorously self-assertive, or chronic asthma sufferers could imagine themselves breathing without discomfort.

Early in the 20th century, the Swiss psychiatrist Auguste Forel differentiated between three degrees of hypnosis: the weakest form, the numb sleepy state, is succeeded by a more intense state, where a person is incapable of moving his or her arms and legs and is insensitive to pain.

Anton Mesmer (right) was a hit in Parisian salons (below), and was often assisted by beautiful young men and women, the so-called touch-servants.

The last and deepest stage is characterised by so-called somnambulism, a type of sleep-walking with complete loss of memory. Even though each form of hypnosis has therapeutic value, the person administering the treatment usually prefers the first or the second state of trance, as the patient tends to co-operate. Studies show that no-one has a predisposition to hypnosis, but they stress that a person should show a certain degree of willingness to go along with the procedure.

For a long time, the hypnotic trance was regarded as a state of relaxation. The ancient Sumerians of Mesopotamia developed the ability to place sick people into a type of healing sleep, while the scriptures of the ancient Egyptians contain references to cults in which trance played a role. In the early Middle Ages, Christian monks used hypnotic techniques in order to drive out demons.

Mesmer's magnetism

On the other hand, for German doctor Anton Mesmer (1734–1815), who worked in Vienna and Paris in the late 18th century, the trance's healing power came from what he called 'animal magnetism'. According to Mesmer, the universe rests in a fluid which surrounds and penetrates all physical bodies. Each person acts as a magnet, where the North Pole is the head and the South Pole the feet. Illnesses are the result of a poor distribution of the atmosphere in the body and can be treated through a gentle massage of the poles or along the equator (the lower ribs). Whether or not we believe Mesmer's far-fetched theory, his legacy remains in the form of the common verb 'to mesmerise'.

In a trance, but still awake

A person in a trance might look asleep, but looks can be deceiving. According to scientific studies, hypnosis – a term derived from the Greek for 'sleep of the nerves' – has nothing in common with actual sleep. An electroencephalogram (EEG) readout of a person in a hypnotic trance shows a normal brain wave pattern in which alpha waves prevail, which resembles the waking state of a relaxed person.

Hypnosis entered the modern era in 1843, when the English physician James Braid first coined the term, which was derived from the Greek for 'sleep of the nerves' (Hypnos was the Greek god of sleep). At this point, the new disciplines of psychiatry and psychology began to enter the picture. Researchers in these fields were less interested in the physical principles behind hypnosis than they were in the potential therapeutic effects of the trance.

For many decades, hypnosis was chiefly used by so-called stage magicians, who put on trance displays for public entertainment. Finally, in the 1970s, a new era began with the work of the American psychiatrist Milton Erickson. The classic, authoritarian treatment, in which the hypnotist tells the patient what to do, was replaced with a new type of hypnosis restricting the power of the therapist, who had to exercise restraint in the treatment of the patient.

The power of the hidden ego

Hypnosis is very much a two-way relationship. Under hypnosis, patient and therapist enter into an intimate working relationship. Since the trance is the desired state of consciousness, the first step is to focus the patient's attention. Then, through verbal instructions, the therapist suggests certain images or pictures.

The far-reaching effects of hypnosis make it an ideal form of deep relaxation in psychotherapy, a type of anaesthesia in surgery and a means to help individuals suffering from loss of memory to uncover traumatic events buried in their past. But it is only people who wish to be hypnotised who can be treated in this way. Any actions which go against a person's moral values or personal dignity cannot generally be induced under hypnosis.

Above: *In sessions held at Paris's Salpêtrière hospital in 1873 and 1884, the French neurologist J.M. Charcot demonstrated that certain nervous disorders can be cured through hypnosis.*

Right: *Today, hypnosis is often used to treat patients suffering from stress symptoms or certain fears.*

In France, the pioneering work of Jean Martin Charcot (1825–1893) did much to restore the reputation of hypnosis. Charcot, a neurologist at Paris's famous Salpêtrière hospital, used the technique to heal patients diagnosed with hysteria. Even Sigmund Freud employed hypnosis for some time after he witnessed Charcot's public displays in the Salpêtrière. However, Freud found that its results were arbitrary and could not be repeated, so he began to explore psychoanalysis rather than hypnosis.

When a person enters a trance, breathing slows, heart rate and blood pressure decrease, the production of stress hormones drops, while the number of lymphocytes, which are important for the immune system, increases. Brain wave patterns measured by means of an electroencephalogram (EEG) show that a person under hypnosis is not asleep but is in a relaxed state of wakefulness. Part of his or her consciousness is directed inwards, while another part continues to register events in the surrounding environment.

New applications

It is still unclear exactly which processes are triggered through concentration on the subconscious. But data collected over the past 20 years proves that hypnotherapy has a healing effect in certain conditions. In Sweden, dental operations are now performed under hypnosis as a matter of routine. Patients who suffer from a fear of going to the dentist or who cannot tolerate anaesthetics are treated while they are in a trance. In other instances, problems such as impotence, nicotine addiction and allergic reactions have been successfully treated through the use of hypnotherapy.

Hypnosis is also helpful when traumatic events have are be uncovered. Trance can unblock emotions which protect the memories of victims of war, torture or accidents. Nevertheless, hypnosis as a form of therapy today remains a controversial issue, since scientific methods cannot prove how it works. This is why some researchers only regard it as a kind of role play, in which the patient tries to please the therapist.

THE UNIVERSE OF THE BRAIN

It contains a thousand million nerve cells and yet weighs just 1.5 kg. Regardless of whether we are lifting our little finger, thinking back on times of happiness or solving an equation, the human brain controls and directs all our physical and mental processes. But scientists are only beginning to understand how the brain works.

Left: Paul Broca (1824–1880) was the first to recognise that mental capacity is linked to specific areas of the brain. He made this discovery after examining the brain of a mental patient nicknamed Tan-Tan. In 1960, Tan-Tan's brain was found in storage (below left).

In the asylum of Bicêtre, in Paris, a patient named Leborgne was known as Tan-Tan, since these two syllables were all he could say. And yet, Tan-Tan understood exactly what was said to him. He played chess, read the newspaper and behaved in a perfectly normal manner. Leborgne died in 1861, at which time French doctor Paul Broca conducted an autopsy. Broca wanted to find out whether Tan-Tan really was insane. The examination showed a noticeable injury to the left side of the brain at the level of the third frontal convolution. Broca concluded that the injured region of the brain must be the part that controlled spoken language.

Subsequent experiments have confirmed Broca's hypothesis. The region in question is the motor area for speech and is known today as the Broca area – after its discoverer. The procedure developed by Broca also led to a new method of research into the anatomy of the brain – tissue damage to specific areas could be made visible by

French neurologist Guillaume Duchenne (below, standing) explored the interaction between the two hemispheres of the brain. He used electro-physiological techniques to measure the activity of nerves and muscles, demonstrated here with his patient Kevin (below right).

marking it, and brain functions whose impairment resulted from this damage could be attributed to these areas.

The man with the separated brain

Another case that was of decisive importance in understanding human thought processes was that of an epileptic named Kevin. In the 1860s, doctors severed his *Corpus callosum*, the slab of nerve fibres that connects the two halves, or hemispheres, of the brain. But instead of a cure, new complications arose. Kevin could only laugh when he was instructed to do so by a person speaking in

the two halves of our brain interact to perform their tasks.

In the crossfire

Every muscle in one half of our body is controlled by nerve cells in the opposite hemisphere of the brain. For example, if you move your right toe, the command comes from cells in the left hemisphere. Advanced intellectual functions also correspond to areas specific to one half of the brain. The reason for this is that each hemisphere is responsible for specific tasks. The analysis of shapes in space, recognition of faces, the memory of sounds and music awareness are all assigned to the right hemisphere, while the left is responsible for tasks such as smiling, calculating and logical problem-solving. This half of the brain also governs the learning of language, as well as written and spoken language.

Although each half of the brain has its specific functions, both hemispheres work in co-ordination to control the tiniest nuances of our behaviour. The necessary connection is made through the *Corpus callosum*, the slab of nerves described above. When Kevin used his eyes to look at the face of a woman sitting on his right side, he couldn't recognise her. The explanation for this is that the left half of his brain, which receives visual information, could not decipher the information from the eyes, since it could not communicate with the right half of the brain, which is responsible for recognising faces.

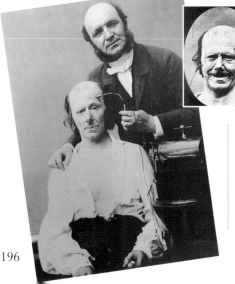

his right ear. In his left ear, which was functionally intact, he was incapable of understanding the message. Furthermore, he no longer recognised familiar faces when they appeared in his right field of vision. These unfortunate impairments provided scientists with important clues about how

If one half of the brain is injured, the opposite side can replace it to a certain extent, particularly in young people. In such cases, cerebral areas which do not have a specific function – and research indicates that there are a large number of such areas – are activated by nerve cells. It seems that these non-functional areas serve as reserve tissue.

The brain in action

Despite a growing body of knowledge, we still do not understand the way our brain assigns different tasks to its two halves. Until now, research has focused on linking specific areas of the brain to certain functions. But the usefulness of Broca's method has now reached its limits, and it has been replaced by the study of the living brain.

This change has been made possible by a range of new imaging technology developed since the 1970s, including computerised axial tomography (CAT), nuclear spin tomography (NST) and positron emission tomo-graphy (PET). These techniques enable scientists to obtain exact images of active organs. For example, the PET technique involves the injection of harmless radioactive glucose into the bloodstream. Brain areas where the glucose is absorbed in greater quantities signal an increased activity, which shows up on a monitor.

Thanks to technology, doctors are now able to examine impaired brain functions in living patients. For example, a woman who had vision only in one eye – although both eyes were healthy – was diagnosed with a localised affliction of the right half of the brain; in another case, it was also possible to identify the damaged brain area of a man who could no longer recognise the members of his family.

Finally, new technology allows scientists to identify the brain's main sensory regions, the control areas of our movements and other regions that area responsible for vision and speech. Research suggests that each activity corresponds not just to one zone, but to a

series of specialised zones, which come into play when these activities are performed.

It has been possible to identify 20 distinct vision zones that independently analyse the form, colour and dimensions of an object and construct a coherent image of it. If only one of the decoding elements malfunctions, then our perception of an object can be faulty. This problem is particularly evident in people who can speak and write but cannot read, or who recognise objects but not their meaning, or who have lost the ability – either through a tumour or a head injury – to comprehend the significance of words.

No two brains are alike

The discoveries of recent years have provided researchers with many of the pieces that will enable them to solve the puzzle of how the brain functions. As our knowledge grows, the mapping of the brain is becoming more and more detailed. We now know that many thousands of neurons and a large number of synapses are involved in each of our activities. The fact remains, though, that each person's brain is unique. Alongside the differences between individuals, there are also differences of age and sex. In some word comprehension tests, for example, women make use of both halves of the brain more often than men, who tend to rely on the left half. Nevertheless, the more we discover about the brain, the more we come to appreciate the miracle of human thought.

The zones and areas of the brain

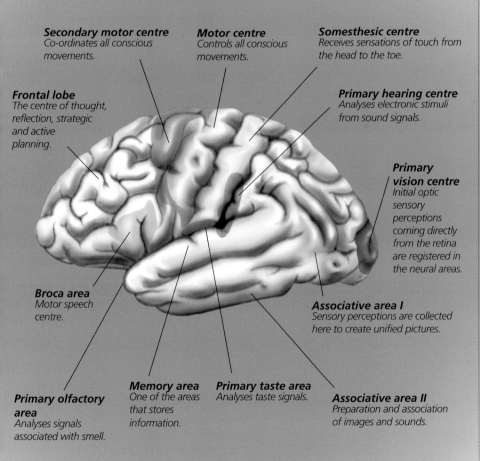

Secondary motor centre
Co-ordinates all conscious movements.

Motor centre
Controls all conscious movements.

Somesthesic centre
Receives sensations of touch from the head to the toe.

Frontal lobe
The centre of thought, reflection, strategic and active planning.

Primary hearing centre
Analyses electronic stimuli from sound signals.

Primary vision centre
Initial optic sensory perceptions coming directly from the retina are registered in the neural areas.

Broca area
Motor speech centre.

Associative area I
Sensory perceptions are collected here to create unified pictures.

Primary olfactory area
Analyses signals associated with smell.

Memory area
One of the areas that stores information.

Primary taste area
Analyses taste signals.

Associative area II
Preparation and association of images and sounds.

WHAT IS INTELLIGENCE?

Why are some people more intelligent than others? What makes men like Nobel prizewinner Albert Einstein or child prodigies like Wolfgang Amadeus Mozart so outstanding? The answers to these age-old questions are helping scientists to learn more about intelligence – and to understand why some people have more than others.

If you've always thought of highly gifted children as little geniuses, maybe you should think again. Psychologists use the term 'precocious', which simply means that these children possess abilities that do not correspond with those of their age group. These boys and girls not only fascinate their families and friends but are a vital link in helping scientists understand the elusive phenomenon of intelligence.

From Mozart to Nadia Comaneci

From an early age, gifted children are capable of exceptional achievements. They learn quickly and efficiently, think as adults do, juggle formulae from mathematics or physics and often learn to read by themselves or learn their way round a computer keyboard by the time they are old enough to go to school. Such children often stand out from others in the areas of science, literature, music, painting and sports.

In music, for example, many a famous virtuoso was a brilliant performer as a child. Wolfgang Amadeus Mozart (1756–1791) learned to play the harpsichord at the age of four, composed his first sonata at the age of six and wrote his first opera, *Bastien and Bastienne*, at the age of 12. The brilliant Italian painter, Primo Conti, was born around 1900, and painted his first self-portrait at the age of 11. At the 1976 Olympic Games in Montreal, Canada, the 14-year-old Rumanian gymnast Nadia Comaneci was the first to achieve two perfect 10s – the dream score.

No anatomical differences

While they are in every way normal children, there are specific features of the brains of gifted children that give them the abilities to excel at mathematics, drawing or sports. It is likely that the difference is not one of anatomy, but rather in their ability to process information. Scientists have not yet been able to pinpoint these individual abilities in the microstructures of the brain, since not enough is known about the brain's complex network of nerve cells, or neurons. At present, it is not possible to make any link between anatomy and a high level of intelligence.

Another difficulty confronting researchers is the lack of a general definition of intelligence. We know that everybody has

Below: *The life of a precocious child is never easy. Mozart's father travelled with him throughout Europe, presenting him to princes and kings.*

Above: *Nadia Comaneci became the star of the Montreal Olympic Games in 1976. As in other Eastern European countries, Rumanian children with a talent for sport received support from an early age.*

Above left: *Christian Heinecken, an 18th century child prodigy and historian, died in 1725 at the age of only four and a half years. His knowledge of sacred and secular history, geography, anatomy and law, and his perfect command of Latin and French, astonished all who met him.*

intelligence, and the concept is used to combine a number of brain functions. Among them are the ability to understand ideas and turn them into action, the capacity for abstraction, for adapting ideas and concepts to new conditions, creativity and the capacity for memory and recall. One important aspect of intelligence, social intelligence, is the ability to understand one's fellow human beings, and to promote

Two men whose early years gave no reason to suspect intellectual brilliance. Louis Pasteur (below) was a weak student and yet became France's greatest scientist. Albert Einstein (below right) showed no special distinction at school. Yet in later life, his research and theories caused a revolution in science and philosophy.

human understanding. Another aspect is common sense, a capacity that we use to assess a situation quickly and to take the appropriate action. Thus, because there are many forms of intelligence, scientists and psychologists avoid formulating an exact definition of the concept, arguing that such an attempt will always be incomplete. Still, they agree that there are certain criteria that researchers can use to determine levels of intelligence.

What is a genius?

The best evidence that there are varying levels of intelligence may be seen in the question of genius. The modern world has seen great strides in many fields of science, with top physicists or natural scientists attracting public attention and acclaim. Perhaps the most renowned 20th-century scientist was the German-born physicist Albert Einstein (1879–1955), whose General Theory of Relativity revolutionised our understanding of the laws of physics and the universe. Many of Einstein's contemporaries were also remarkably knowledgeable, and perhaps just as creative, inventive and intelligent, but Einstein stood out from the crowd because of his genius. His work, his results and his ideas decisively changed our picture of the world and our philosophy.

A 'retarded' genius

Leslie Lemke is spastic. He can hardly speak and is considered mentally retarded. To make matters even worse, he was blinded just a few months after his birth.

These impediments, however, have not prevented Leslie from becoming a musical genius. As soon as he sits down at a piano, he has the amazing ability to mesmerise an audience. Whether he is performing hymns, concertos or popular tunes, Leslie plays everything perfectly, even though he has never studied music. He has a wonderfully developed musical 'ear', and only has to hear a piece of music once in order to play it. After that, he can perform it perfectly.

Moderately gifted people are, of course, much more common than the so-called geniuses. According to statistics, about 5% of all six-year-old children are one and a half years ahead of their age group in terms of their mental development. These children are usually termed intellectually precocious. On average, for every 20 children in a school class, there will be one – that is, roughly one or two in each class – whose mental abilities are far ahead of those of his or her fellow students. In spite of this relatively high percentage, teachers often have great difficulty in identifying the highly gifted children in their classes.

A blessing or a curse?

In fact, gifted children may try not to attract attention to themselves. They may feel uneasy about their unusual abilities, and so they tend to be shy and only rarely stand out as the best in the class. Gifted children may not even achieve extraordinary results at school, as they generally try to restrain their mental abilities in order not to be singled out in the class. Sometimes, they become so bored by the class routine that they can no longer concentrate on what the teacher is saying. When this happens, their marks fall rapidly. Since these children can understand mathematical concepts and complex historical events in the blink of an eye, they may spend much of their time daydreaming or fooling around.

A 'gift' for numbers

You don't have to be a genius to possess a particular gift for numbers – or other extraordinary talent. The American twins Charles and George could name the day of the week for any randomly selected calendar date – in addition to coping with several other complex mathematical challenges.

And yet both were classified as 'mentally retarded'. A test carried out in 1964, when the brothers were 24 years old, indicated an IQ between 60 and 70, against the normal average of 100. Their mental development was assessed as being at the same level.

For various reasons, parents and teachers may be slow to recognise gifted children as exceptional, or their development may be otherwise retarded, making them inhibited and insecure in a school setting. But in an environment that allows their abilities to blossom, some of them awaken to a whole new life. Louis Pasteur (1822–1895), the French chemist who invented pasteurisation and discovered vaccines against rabies and anthrax, was undistinguished as a student. But after he set up a laboratory, the quality of his research proved that he possessed an unusually high level of intelligence.

Although gifted children are often very advanced in subjects such as mathematics or chemistry, their motor development can be weak. They may have difficulty with certain sequences of movement – for example, those which affect handwriting, when it seems as if the hand cannot follow a series of subtle and agile thoughts. Another source of difficulty is the fact that their mental development does not match their emotional development and its range of feelings. Although they may be able to compose pieces of music or solve complicated algebraic equations, they still have the emotional needs and vulnerability of a child. As they get older, this gap often increases, and many of these children require a great deal of parental tenderness and ordinary, childlike play in order to be happy and well adjusted.

In the final analysis, it is hard to identify gifted individuals with certainty. For this reason, psychologists and educators rely on a battery of tests designed to determine an individual's so-called intelligence quotient (IQ). These questionnaires are intended to measure mental abilities, but they are very much orientated towards the ability to retain and project information and images, as well as combinatory or mathematical skills and speed. The result of an intelligence test is given on a scale of points.

The testing system is based on the work of the French psychologist Alfred Binet, who introduced the first IQ test in 1905. Binet wanted to develop a series of short tests that would identify children with learning disabilities who required special education.

Reason for caution

Since IQ tests do not take a person's creativity and imagination into account, they do not really provide a full measure of intelligence. Accordingly, the results of the tests should be treated with caution. A low score on an IQ test does not automatically indicate a low level of intelligence, since only partial functions of the brain have been tested. A precocious child tends to be an IQ whiz: while the average value is about 100, gifted people typically exceed 125 points at an early age.

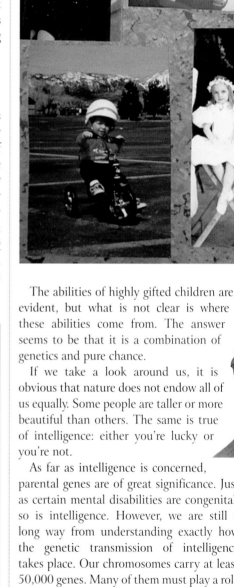

The abilities of highly gifted children are evident, but what is not clear is where these abilities come from. The answer seems to be that it is a combination of genetics and pure chance.

If we take a look around us, it is obvious that nature does not endow all of us equally. Some people are taller or more beautiful than others. The same is true of intelligence: either you're lucky or you're not.

As far as intelligence is concerned, parental genes are of great significance. Just as certain mental disabilities are congenital, so is intelligence. However, we are still a long way from understanding exactly how the genetic transmission of intelligence takes place. Our chromosomes carry at least 50,000 genes. Many of them must play a role in the origin and development of our mental abilities. If you compare intelligence to the design of a machine, you can see that a single defective gear can cause the whole system to break down. And many parts are required for

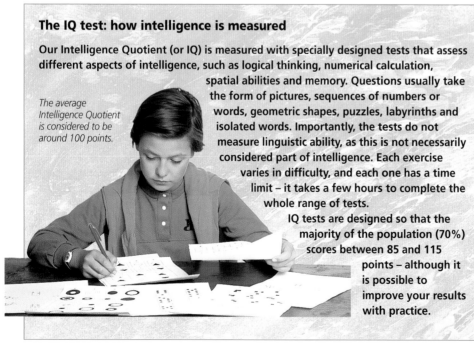

The IQ test: how intelligence is measured

Our Intelligence Quotient (or IQ) is measured with specially designed tests that assess different aspects of intelligence, such as logical thinking, numerical calculation, spatial abilities and memory. Questions usually take the form of pictures, sequences of numbers or words, geometric shapes, puzzles, labyrinths and isolated words. Importantly, the tests do not measure linguistic ability, as this is not necessarily considered part of intelligence. Each exercise varies in difficulty, and each one has a time limit – it takes a few hours to complete the whole range of tests.

The average Intelligence Quotient is considered to be around 100 points.

IQ tests are designed so that the majority of the population (70%) scores between 85 and 115 points – although it is possible to improve your results with practice.

neither Hans Albert nor Edward Einstein, the sons of Albert Einstein, are noted for any special achievements. There is no doubt that the environment in which a child grows up is just as important as genetics for his or her mental development. Education, the family and the social setting all have a lasting influence on an individual's development. If a child's talents and needs are given the necessary attention, then that child has every chance of developing certain abilities.

The search for the elite

Countries like the United Kingdom, Germany and France provide only limited additional support for highly gifted children. Other countries, however, have adopted policies aimed specifically at identifying and promoting precocious children.

In the former Soviet Union, an annual mathematics competition was held in order to identify highly gifted children and enrol them in elite schools. In the US, around one million precocious children enjoy the benefits of specially designed educational programmes. Israel has a systematic selection scheme. Each year, the state conducts a three-month-long campaign to identify precocious children. The Israeli Ministry of Culture devotes 1% of its budget to these highly gifted young people.

Above: *The children of Nobel prize-winners. There is no evidence to link their talents to the genes of their parents.*

Left: *A happy family environment plays a decisive role in the development of a child.*

Chagai Skolminkof, a young Israeli, benefits from his country's support for gifted children. He has distinguished himself through his great abilities in chemistry and physics, and is also studying politics.

it to function correctly. While scientists have made spectacular progress in understanding the complexities of human genetics, there is much research still to be done.

Finding that special father

For several years, a number of sperm banks in the United States have offered women the opportunity to be inseminated with sperm donated by carefully selected men – leaders in business, science and the arts – in the belief that the genes of these members of the elite will be passed on to the next generation. In theory, this is possible, but if we look at the children of Nobel prizewinners, they turn out to be frustratingly normal in most respects. This should come as no surprise, for there is an immense number of possible combinations of the mother's and father's genes. Furthermore, there is a largely random distribution of genes on the grandparents' side, so that a child's genetic make-up tends to be largely a matter of chance. For example,

Helped by a learning programme developed by his parents, Arthur Ramiandrisoa was accepted into university at the age of 12.

If this does not happen, his or her intellect will not be stimulated and any exceptional talents will remain hidden. A gifted child who is born into a family that does not value their child's cultural development, and which does not foster the talents he or she has inherited, will not be able to blossom. However, behavioural scientists still disagree about the relative importance of inherited and acquired abilities.

The elite school

A gifted child's talents confront parents with the problem of finding the right school to allow this talent to develop. In deciding on a suitable school, they must consider their child's special needs, thirst for knowledge, rate of comprehension and natural curiosity. Sometimes, a gifted child is allowed to jump ahead at school, and a small group may be established to stimulate him or her and to encourage the development of his or her abilities. But this also has disadvantages. Any child will face difficulties when the other children are all older and more mature.

Bodybuilding for the brain

Just like the body, the brain needs exercise to keep it in optimum condition. It's vital to keep your brain challenged in order to stimulate and even increase your intelligence, particularly as you grow older. If you're not getting enough stimulation at work, consider learning a foreign language or do the crossword every day. The brain also benefits from a healthy lifestyle – with a low intake of alcohol and no tobacco.

Another possibility is to send the child to an elite school, one that is orientated to the needs of precocious children. There is an ongoing debate between the supporters of such schools and those who believe it is better for children of the same age to learn together in one class, regardless of their different abilities. In many countries, schools for gifted children either do not exist, or exist only in very limited numbers.

Intensive learning

Another alternative for gifted children is the so-called intensive learning group. These are common in Israel, for example, where they offer many extramural activities on a number of levels. Instead of covering the curriculum more quickly, the students can enjoy a more intensive learning experience in subjects they enjoy, such as mathematics, astronomy, physics, chemistry, biology, literature or music. The system is flexible, and caters for talented children who excel in one subject. A large number of children can take part in intensive learning groups, thanks to their versatile structure and the way they promote creativity and motivation – as well as improving academic results.

The final possibility is learning at home. In the mid-1990s, French newspapers profiled Arthur Ramiandrisoa, a French youngster who had never been to school, but had passed all the required examinations as an external candidate. The secret of his success was a tailor-made programme of studies developed by his parents. The result of their efforts was that Arthur entered university at the age of 12! The challenge will be to ensure that Arthur's emotional development keeps pace with his exceptional mental abilities.

Recognising exceptional talent

Liu Ting attends School Number 8 for gifted children in Beijing, China. At the age of 13 she could work out complicated mathematical formulae, and soon surpassed the abilities of her teacher.

A highly gifted child's linguistic abilities usually develop rapidly, and at an early age, with a short transitional phase in baby language.

Before the parents even notice, the child has fallen in love with the world of books and often masters reading skills without adult assistance. Such children come to prefer reading encyclopaedias and dictionaries, which allow them to reach the sources of knowledge. It is often observed that highly gifted children prefer to work alone rather than under supervision.

CAN MACHINES THINK?

Science is a long way from producing a machine as powerful as the human brain. However, the search for artificial intelligence has come a long way since the first robots. New technology enables scientists to produce devices capable of a range of human-like actions, while many scientists now look to the insect world for inspiration for tomorrow's thinking machines.

During the 1960s, popular magazines, science fiction writers and even some scientists predicted that human-like robots would soon come into wide use. In 1961, Unimate, the world's first industrial robot, began operations in an American automobile assembly plant. Its programming allowed Unimate to transport unwieldy metal parts with the same precision as a whole group of human workers. At that time, it was widely believed that thinking machines would soon be able to imitate their human makers. Stanley Kubrick's influential 1969 film *2001: A Space Odyssey* even imagined what would happen when an intelligent computer turned against its human masters. Since the 1960s, a number of inventions have pointed in the direction of thinking machines – for example, the first chess-playing computer (IBM's Deep Blue) and the first computer capable of solving equations or proving mathematical principles. As we move from the Industrial Age to the Information Age, new intelligent machines are going to affect virtually all aspects of our everyday existence.

The idea of a machine that can think, also known as artificial intelligence (AI), grew out of the development of the computer, and in particular the work of the scientists and mathematicians who cracked German military codes during World War II. At first, the idea of artificial intelligence seemed both promising and threatening. Many people felt that such machines could be used to take jobs away from humans. As early as 1950, the American biochemist and renowned science fiction author Isaac Asimov (1920–1992) foresaw the problem in his classic collection of short stories entitled *I, Robot*. Asimov drew up a code of behaviour for the electronic humanoids of the future: 'Law one: a robot shall never harm a human being or expose him to danger through passive hesitation'. In the 1990s, some people in scientific circles even began to speak of a post-human age, a culture of robots which would take over the heritage of humanity.

Artificial workers

Almost four decades after the introduction of Unimate, few people are terrified by the prospect of so-called intelligent machines, but the dreams of scientists have only been partially fulfilled. Computers are an everyday part of our lives, and there are now machines that can warm our food, clean the toilet bowl, make the beds, or call 'Fire!' as soon as their electronic noses detect smoke. But these artificial workers are programmed to execute a specific number of repetitive sequences of movement, or to carry out simple, well-defined tasks. They are useless for anything outside their predetermined functions. At present, scientists admit that the electronic human has not yet been born.

Robots lack intelligence, adaptability and intuition. As a result, they cannot evaluate their experiences, observations and errors and learn new modes of behaviour. While this may seem a major problem, scientists are not discouraged. The pace of innovation in science and information technology makes it likely that more sophisticated robots will be developed in the near future. While first-generation robots could only carry out commands literally and exactly, those of the second generation, which has been in operation since the 1980s, can learn new skills to make the best use of their abilities, or even find their own methods to achieve a certain goal.

Experts needed

One of the driving forces in the efforts to develop artificial intelligence has been the need not only to store information, but to combine it in a meaningful way. Initially, scientists aimed to design machines capable of executing certain specialist tasks. The principle behind these specialised machines was the collection and storage of a considerable amount of knowledge in a specific field, and the development of tools of analytic logic – so-called problem-solving strategies. Faced with a given situation, a computer would analyse the position and recommend the best course of action. Such a machine would be able to modify its data banks as a result of its findings. In other words, the machine would have learnt something from the situation.

Electronic devices that work along these lines are common these days, and are

The robots R2D2 and C3PO, from the Star Wars *film series, are independent, clever, adaptable and sometimes a nuisance – in short, intelligent.*

used, for example, to make medical diagnoses or produce financial projections and analyses. However, even when used to their full potential, the programming, or software, of these machines can overlook certain details that do not fit their code. In a medical setting, this means that they might not recognise certain symptoms – such as a hoarse voice or feverish eyes – that would provide a doctor with clues regarding the nature of the illness. Once the machine's capacity is exceeded, such a system might also shut down, since the world only makes sense to it within the limits of its data.

An artificial nervous system

It is fascinating to wonder whether machines will ever possess real intelligence. In this respect, an important milestone has been the introduction of the so-called third generation of computers. These advanced systems promise a higher level of mental ability for the future. The principle that lies behind third-generation machines is based on the neurons of the human brain. In third-generation systems, electronic components are not arranged in a row, but are linked in a network. Up to 10,000 microprocessors, or chips, are able to function in parallel to one another, performing millions of calculations each second. These machines can exchange information just like the cells in our brains.

The Turing Test

In 1950, British mathematician Alan Turing (1912–1954), one of the founders of information technology, published an article in which he asked 'Can a machine think?' According to Turing, a computer could be said to be thinking if its responses could not be distinguished from a human's. This is the basis of the so-called Turing Test. In 1990, the American Hugh Loebner established the Loebner Prize to implement the Turing Test. During the contest, a human and a computer are placed behind a screen. Jury members can communicate with both. If, in spite of careful questioning, they are not able to tell the computer from the human, then the machine is said to possess intelligence.

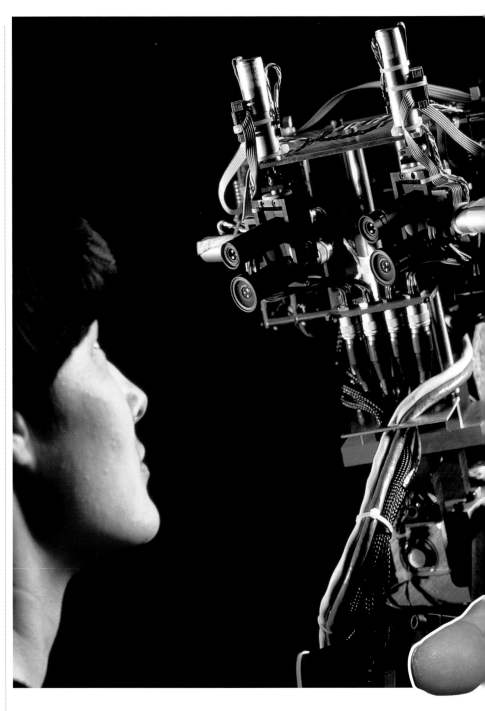

The new technology represented by third-generation computers will give robot systems the scope to complete complex tasks, such as perceiving and evaluating the world around them, that had previously been impossible. For example, it is not enough simply to fit a robot with a camera; like a human, the machine must also possess the means of processing and interpreting the images it receives. Scientists have developed optical recognition systems, derived from the human vision system, enabling some robots to recognise and identify faces.

Above: *Robots have a lot to learn before they become more like humans. This machine, called COG, can recognise faces.*

Collective intelligence

In the 1980s, scientists became interested in the area of communication, or information exchange, which had up till then been neglected, since the necessary technology did not yet exist. The result was a whole new field of research. Now, instead of attempting to develop a single large machine that would imitate all the abilities of the human brain, a number of scientists took a serious look at the collective intelligence of insects. The abilities of a single insect are limited, but in a community they can achieve wonders. The first step has been the development of robot ants, simple machines with a single elementary program. These machines can communicate by means of ultrasound. They can determine the position of other robot ants, register sounds and movement and orientate themselves according to all the information they collect. The robot ants can even walk in single file or find the quickest route out of a room when ordered to leave it immediately. These robots are also unique in their ability to develop new patterns of behaviour for which they were not programmed. This kind of co-ordination, based on creative fantasy, marks a major advance in the field of artificial intelligence.

The fly's eye

Insects provide one of the richest sources of information for the development of robots. By working with flies, scientists have gained a better understanding of the ways in which these creatures see and move. Through studying the 3,000 visual components of an insect's compound eye – with its 24,000 light-sensitive sensory cells linked to more than a million nerve cells –

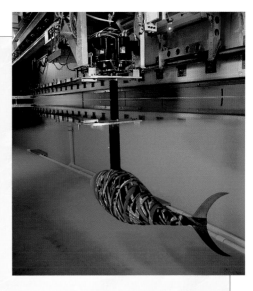

The mechanical tuna

Scientists have been looking carefully at tuna fish in the search for advanced machines. A robot fish named Robotuna has been developed to aid in this research. Tests show that the tuna uses its tail fin to find a way through the turbulence that its body causes when it displaces water. This is more efficient than a ship's propeller, enabling the fish to attain speeds of nearly 50 km/hour.

Robotuna yields a precise analysis of the movements of a tuna fish, one of the fastest fishes. The data is used to design new profiles for ships' hulls.

scientists have been able to construct a robot with similar visual capabilities. Instead of analysing and mapping the environment around it, and then deciding what direction to move in, the model fly detects moving objects and responds accordingly. Insect-like robot devices have potential military uses, as they can provide military vehicles with ultra-fast eyes. In the future, these robots will have to be able to recognise colours and shapes as well as judge distances.

Is mechanical man coming?

In spite of all these advances, there is a long way to go before artificial intelligence will be able to match the mental abilities of humans. Today, there are about 250,000 industrial robots in use around the world, with Japan the leading maker and user of such devices. Most of these are used in assembly lines – chiefly in the car industry – and are used to perform fairly repetitive tasks such as welding, painting and inspection. Other robotic systems are widely used in computer-aided design (CAD). The next development may be machines with human-like features; science fiction is full of fantasies in which humans are modified to resemble machines. Some dream of giving the brain unbelievable powers by

implanting tiny, neuron-sized circuits within the cerebral cortex. Is this just fantasy? Only time will tell.

Fantastic voyage

In the near future, extremely compact mini-robots weighing just a few milligrams may be introduced into the human body to fight tumours and diseases. Scientists are already testing such devices, which are modelled on the creatures of the insect world, who can detect and follow their prey with great precision. These micro-machines would follow the bloodstream and go wherever they were needed. They could attack tumours, administer medications with absolute precision or even provide doctors with an inside view of the body.

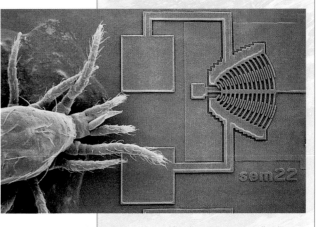

Micro-grips smaller than 0.5 mm – smaller than a mite – could soon be injected into the human body to carry out precision medical procedures.

This machine can imitate the complex motion of an ant. While this is a small step for a robot, it is a giant leap for artificial intelligence.

THE STOREHOUSE OF THE MEMORY

Memory is one of the vital building blocks of intelligence. Without memory there would be no learning, no recall, no communication. Every second of the day, your memory is busy processing images from the world around you and storing them in the appropriate portion of your brain's data banks. The way this process works is still only partially understood.

The capacity to remember is one of the miracles of the mind. We remember all kinds of things – telephone numbers, dates, prices, titles of books. Each person has his or her own capacity for memory, and some people can remember truly stupendous amounts of information: Bhandata Vicitsara,

Chain reaction

If you've ever been bitten by a dog, then even the sight of a small poodle can be enough to make you nervous. Perhaps the smell of a particular perfume reminds you of someone you once knew. In every situation we encounter, our memory tries to determine the best possible reaction by sifting through its libraries in search of past memories. Whether consciously or not, pleasant or unpleasant, this process sets off a chain reaction of embedded memories and associated emotions. In his classic novel *À la recherche du temps perdu* (Remembrance of Things Past), the French writer Marcel Proust (1871–1922) told how the taste of a biscuit was enough to take him back to his grandmother's house. Through this process of associa-tion, he could even feel the same emo-tions he did long ago.

The works of French novelist Marcel Proust delve deeply into his memory.

brains. Hidden there is a complex archiving centre based on the co-ordination of billions of nerve cells. Our memory is so sensitive that sometimes just glancing at a rough outline or hearing a few words is enough to reconstruct an entire picture in our minds.

Save data: yes or no?

Whether it is learning to read, remembering our first love, recognising an aroma or noting a telephone number, not a single moment in

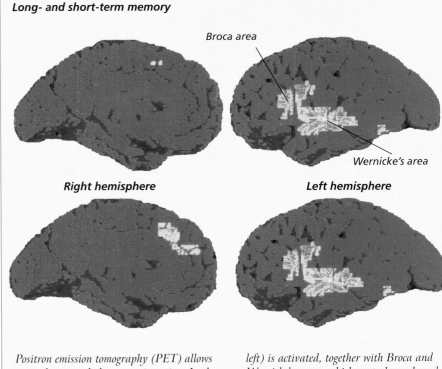

Long- and short-term memory

Broca area

Right hemisphere

Wernicke's area

Left hemisphere

Positron emission tomography (PET) allows us to observe verbal memory in action. In the images shown above, the most active areas of the brain are shown in yellow, orange and red, according to their intensity.

In order for us to repeat a sentence that we have just heard, the short-term memory (top

left) is activated, together with Broca and Wernicke's areas, which control speech and language (top right).

Both hemispheres are active when long-term information is recalled (lower half of diagram), but the activated area of the left hemisphere (above right) is much larger.

from Burma, can recite 16,000 pages of Buddhist scripture by heart; Hideaki Tomoyori, from Japan, can reel off the first 40,000 decimal places of the value of pi (π); and Frenchwoman Dany Sirejean can name the day of the week for any random date of the 20th century.

But in spite of intense investigations into the workings of our memory, scientists are only slowly beginning to understand the functioning of the giant data bank in our

our lives escapes our memory; even dreams can be partially recalled from sleep. From the moment of birth – and even before then – our memory is constantly registering, sorting and ordering the tiniest pieces of information that it considers worth saving. Thanks to this valuable ability, we are able to take note of our experiences and remember them.

Information can be held in the memory, simply forgotten or fade away with time. The key is our consciously increased capacity for retention – in other words, how much attention we devote to it. Without this capacity, the data passing the nerve endings in the brain would simply rush by and be erased within a few tenths of a second. This is fortunate, since forgetting is a very useful tool when it comes to ordering our thoughts and filtering useless information. If our brain cells could retain every scrap of conversation that we hear in the course of the day, we would soon no longer know what was happening in our heads. So our memory is constantly busy selecting and ordering information, a process that depends on how interesting the information is to us at present or will be for the future. A lot depends on the emotions that we associate with the information, as well as the relationship it has to our personality and experiences. Some messages are only stored for about ten seconds – the time needed, for example, to remember a telephone number and dial it – and discarded immediately. We seldom succeed in recalling such fleeting information.

The secret of the super-brains

Along with the constant processing and discarding of information, there are many thousands of pieces of knowledge and memories that we will retain for ever. These pieces of data have been consigned to our long-term memory, a data bank that examines and stores selected information for long-term recording. The long-term memory ensures that these pieces of information will always be there for us.

The long-term memory works by first checking new elements for their significance, then admitting them in proportion to how often they are repeated. This is why so-called swotting, or memorisation – the apparently

endless repetition of whatever has to be learned – is not a torture invented by cruel teachers, but is one of the basic principles of memory retention. In

Left: *The griots are the storytellers, poets and singers of West Africa, who pass on traditional tales from generation to generation. They are the living memory of many African peoples.*

Below: *Reading and more reading, listening and more listening. Repetition is the best recipe for retaining information.*

many cases of extraordinary memory, the secret is simply well-trained abilities. But we do need certain inherited talents if we wish to compete with the likes of Bhandata Vicitsara or Hideaki Tomoyori.

After a period of three years, most people only retain about a tenth of several hundred pieces of stored information. The remainder usually stays in their memory until the end of their lives. But to understand this process better, we need to examine where these messages are placed while they are waiting to be recalled.

The physical layout of the human memory is complicated, since our memory is not localised in one single area of the brain. This can be seen in patients who suffer from memory disturbances but not complete memory loss. Many people forget what they

Memory training

Just like your body, your memory capacity will stay in top form only if you exercise it regularly. The proper development of your mental abilities requires the full use of your intellect. Consider regular study, memorising of information and skills training – even memory games are good practice. The brain uses about 20% of the body's oxygen requirements, so it clearly needs to be in top form. A healthy lifestyle and a balanced diet will go a long way towards keeping the mind young and supple.

did the previous evening or a few hours ago – in extreme cases, even a few minutes ago. This is known as a retention impediment. Other people cannot recall entire periods of their lives. All memory malfunctions indicate that events affecting us activate several areas of the brain.

Data from the senses

The explanation for this lies in the huge variety of messages received by the memory. Every second of the day, we are busy probing our environment through our five senses. From the outer ear to the retina, the tip of the tongue, the mucous membrane inside the nose or the surface of our skin, special sensory cells are constantly sending stimuli via the nerves to the brain. This vast quantity of sensory perceptions is then linked to a large number of previous experiences. The brain has several 'libraries' where impressions from the senses are ordered and stored, and it is these that determine our memories. There is a library for images, for taste impressions, colours, words, music, shapes and smells.

Many of our capacities – such as vision, touch or smell – are processed in specialised regions of the brain. There are also extended areas of the brain known as areas of association, whose task is to evaluate and associate sensory perceptions. Even if we cannot directly remember our first taste of milk or the first time we saw a dog or cat,

How memories are stored

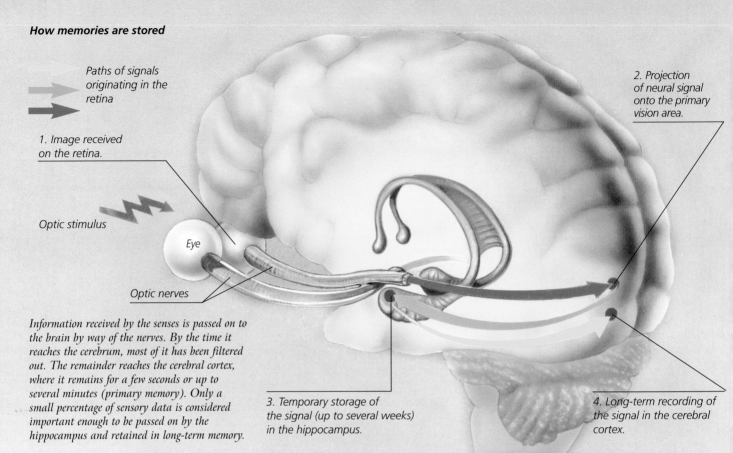

Paths of signals originating in the retina

1. Image received on the retina.

Optic stimulus

Eye

Optic nerves

2. Projection of neural signal onto the primary vision area.

Information received by the senses is passed on to the brain by way of the nerves. By the time it reaches the cerebrum, most of it has been filtered out. The remainder reaches the cerebral cortex, where it remains for a few seconds or up to several minutes (primary memory). Only a small percentage of sensory data is considered important enough to be passed on by the hippocampus and retained in long-term memory.

3. Temporary storage of the signal (up to several weeks) in the hippocampus.

4. Long-term recording of the signal in the cerebral cortex.

new stimulation through similar events is usually enough to refresh our memory. The associative pathways reactivate the formerly activated areas of the brain and enable us to recall the past.

Complicated switching mechanisms

Advances in medical imaging technology have provided a much more detailed picture of how the brain functions. These advances now permit scientists to connect certain areas of the brain to certain memory tasks, an ability that is especially useful for patients suffering from loss of memory, epilepsy or memory impairments.

Research has found that a central role in long-term memory is played by an area called the hippocampus, which is located in the temporal lobe. All new information must pass through the hippocampus, and it retains these impressions for up to several weeks before passing them on to areas in the cortex where they are permanently recorded. In these cortical areas, memories are also connected to specific emotions.

The hippocampus is closely linked to the brain's limbic system, one of the keys to our emotional world. The front temporal lobe contains areas that are responsible for short-term memory. The so-called reticular formation, situated between the brain and the spinal cord, contributes to wakefulness and attention, which are vital for both active and passive learning, as well as the active recall of memories. The cerebellum, situated in the rear cranial cavity, harbours those memories that are necessary for conditioned

The wheels of time

Advancing age definitely affects memory. If you're forgetting things, finding gaps in your memory and noticing your attention span is decreasing, chances are that you're feeling the effects of age. This is part of the human life cycle, and usually begins around the age of 30, when the connections (synapses) between nerve cells begin to weaken. An active 80-year-old has typically lost between 5 and 30% of his or her neurons, and this affects memory. One comfort is that we shouldn't worry about losing our mental abilities, as large parts of our brain are little used.

or acquired reflexes. It also plays a role in maintaining the body's equilibrium.

At present, we possess only fragmentary knowledge about how the mechanisms of memory retention and recall actually work. It is clear that our nerve cells make thousands of connections which are known as synapses. These are specifically re-formed or reactivated when mental processes occur. Together with the arrangement of special groups of nerve cells, the synapses create a neuron network for storing information. But the actual formation of memories is still poorly understood, and remains a subject for future study.

Daily memory training allows a waiter to remember several orders at once.

DO OUR DREAMS MEAN ANYTHING?

Dreams have always fascinated us. After all, we spend more than a quarter of our lives asleep, and a total of several years dreaming! Although we now know much about the processes of dreaming, researchers are still divided as to the meaning and function of dreams.

For thousands of years, people have tried to interpret their dreams. In the Old Testament, the dreams of Jacob, Pharaoh, Joseph and the Three Kings were all seen as prophecies. The Greek philosopher Plato (around 428–348 BC) also regarded dreams as divine signs that pointed to future events. The famed Roman author and orator Cicero (106–43 BC), on the other hand, was far ahead of his time when, in the 1st century BC, he rejected the idea that our dreams might be divine messages. But Cicero's view did not last long, and many centuries passed before dreams were again seen as anything other than messages from above.

It was not until the 17th century that Europeans began to look at dreams as a reflection of the individual's inner life and personality. People began to write down their dreams and search for meaning in them. Some – like Hervey de Saint-Denys, a

Right: *Carl Gustav Jung, one of the pioneers of psychoanalysis, interpreted dreams as an expression of archaic and universal human emotions.*

Below: *For Sigmund Freud, dreams are linked to childhood experiences, and express unfulfilled wishes or desires.*

teacher at the Collège de France in the late 19th century – even believed that they could influence their dreams. Later, philosophers began to look at the interpretation of dreams. For the French philosopher Henri Bergson (1859–1941), for example, dreams were images from the eye; for other thinkers, dreams were mirror images of the soul.

It was not until the early 20th century that the meaning of dreams began to be studied on a systematic basis, chiefly by Sigmund Freud (1856–1939) and Carl Gustav Jung (1875–1961). Freud, who is considered the founder of psychoanalysis, regarded dreams as the expression of certain drives and wishes that are repressed in our waking lives. In his opinion, the images or stories that we experience at night are often chaotic because the subconscious mind makes an effort to negate, displace or distort certain elements so that they are not as easily recognisable and therefore more acceptable. For Jung, who initially worked with Freud, dreams allow access to important archetypes (collective myths) that occur in all civilisations.

The ideas of psychoanalysis have since been supplemented through research in the area of neurophysiology – the study of the workings of the human nervous system. Since the late 1950s, dream research has developed into a discipline which aims to unlock the processes that allow us to dream. Researchers are now able to pinpoint the moment in sleep when dreams begin. Using data derived from electroencephalography (EEG) and several other physiological indicators, researchers have been able to identify three specific kinds of sleep: light sleep, deep sleep and REM sleep. During light and deep sleep, there are low-frequency or slow electronic waves. REM (Rapid Eye Movement) sleep, on the other hand, is characterised by higher-frequency electronic activity in the brain.

The stages of sleep

The first phase of sleep is characterised by a constant slowing of the brain waves. At this stage, the sleeper still responds to sounds and is relatively easy to waken. The body then begins to calm down and slips into the deep sleep phase, in which the eyes do not move, but muscle tone or tension remains as it was. Finally, in REM sleep, the brain becomes reactivated and sends out successions of rapid waves. The eyeballs move under the closed lids – hence the term Rapid Eye Movement – and the general muscle tone falls. Muscle spasms may occur, above all in

---

Furred and feathered dreamers

It may be hard to believe, but animals have dreams too. Humans share with other mammals and birds the capacity for REM sleep – the period when dreaming takes place. Other living creatures, such as fish, amphibians and reptiles, do not display the same type of brain waves as mammals and birds. Scientists accordingly assume that dreaming appeared in the higher vertebrates more than 130 million years ago.

Interestingly, biologists have found that animals whose childhood lasts the longest also have the longest dream phases. Chickens and cows dream for 25 minutes, chimpanzees for 90 minutes, and cats up to 200 minutes. In humans, REM sleep lasts about 100 minutes per night. In birds, dream phases are few and very short, lasting between 5 and 15 seconds.

Up, up and away

Many of us have had dreams in which we fly like a bird or float in space free of the force of gravity. Such dreams usually leave us with a pleasant feeling of lightness when we awaken. For this reason, psychoanalysts interpret them as an expression of the sexual drive. However, neuro-physiologists observe that the muscles are out of action during sleep, and they believe that bodily relaxation helps a person form the content of their dreams. He or she then feels free of bodily constraints and can rise effortlessly into the air.

the fingers and toes. At this point, the sleeper is deep in the dreaming phase and is difficult to waken. This phase is repeated roughly every 100 minutes, and lasts approximately 10–20 minutes.

For an adult, a night's sleep consists of about 75–80% non-REM sleep and 20–25% REM sleep. In a foetus, on the other hand, REM sleep takes place for almost 90% of the night. This has led researchers to conclude that REM sleep phases contribute to the structural maturation of the brain during the first few months of life. The six basic facial expressions characteristic of humans – joy,

fear, surprise, anger, sadness and disgust – are all displayed by young children, but most often during sleep. These expressions are the result of intensive dream experiences; the child's facial expression reflects the stimulus of the dream.

Learning while asleep

Recently, attempts have been made to find out whether there is a connection between REM sleep and learning capacity. French scientist Michel Jouvet, one of the founders of dream research, is convinced that this connection exists. In his view, dreaming is the time when the mind expresses elements of the human collective memory – an idea drawn from the work of Jung – together with the inherent personality traits of the sleeper. This means that ancient patterns of behaviour can be activated according to the genetic make-up of the sleeper, allowing the brain to learn something new each night.

The occurrence of REM sleep in infants and birds and its absence in other highly developed animals seems to support Jouvet's theory. Observations of animals that dream show that the structure of the brain is already well formed at birth. Dreaming thus

Above: *Electrodes on a patient's head measure signals from the brain and display them on a monitor in the form of waves.*

Right: *The smiling face of a five-day-old baby girl during REM sleep. Dreams cause children to display genetically transmitted facial expressions.*

Falling asleep

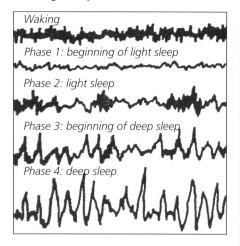

Waking

Phase 1: beginning of light sleep

Phase 2: light sleep

Phase 3: beginning of deep sleep

Phase 4: deep sleep

Above: *Electroencephalograms (EEG) allow us to distinguish various phases of sleep that are repeated in several cycles every night. Each stage is characterised by specific brain wave patterns. In so-called non-REM sleep, (phases 1–4), brain activity steadily diminishes, with brain waves becoming increasingly slower.*

Below: *For about 20 minutes at the end of each sleep cycle, brain waves display a higher frequency, similar to the levels that prevail during waking hours. This is when REM sleep, the period of dreaming, takes place. REM sleep is also called paradox sleep, since the brain is active but the body is completely relaxed.*

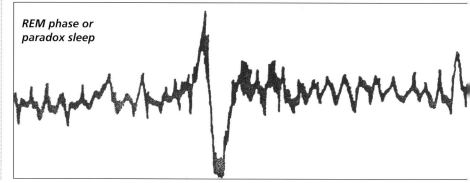

REM phase or paradox sleep

serves to regularly programme the brain's neuronic network. In contrast, the nerve cells of cold-blooded animals, such as fish and reptiles, continue to divide throughout the animal's life, so any regular activation would be pointless.

Nevertheless, specialists generally agree that dreaming is a kind of learning tool; it is the time when the long-term memory stores the information collected in the course of the day. During the day, when we are awake, consciousness hinders the neuronic activity, since extensive areas of the brain are busy processing the flow of data and impressions from our senses.

Dreams of a busy mind

Anyone who learns a lot is bound to dream a lot. An increase in REM sleep is typically observed in students during examination times, when the memory is strongly utilised. Experiments with rats also show that learning is a stimulus to dreaming. If these rodents are made to find their way through a difficult maze, their REM sleep increases by 50–60%. Only after they have learned the route to the exit does the length of the dreaming phase return to normal again.

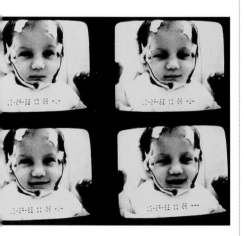

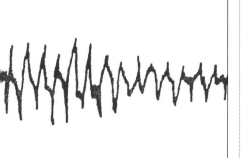

By the light of the moon

Sleepwalking may sound bizarre, but it is a very real phenomenon. People who walk in their sleep may make dangerous journeys up stairways or over rooftops. Next morning, they remember nothing of their moonlight rambles. Statistics show that sleepwalking occurs in 20% of children between the ages of 5 and 12, and that most of them (70%) are boys. EEG analysis of brain waves shows that this phenomenon takes place not during REM or dreaming sleep, but during the phase of deep sleep, when the brain's activity is low. Consciousness is disabled, but the muscles receive co-ordinated commands from the movement centres. Causes of sleepwalking may include genetic predisposition, stress or even the influence of the moon.

Given these results, REM sleep seems essential in establishing acquired knowledge. Scientists have also found that cats and rats will develop learning problems if they are given certain drugs to prevent dreaming. The same is true for humans: if a person is woken as soon as they have begun to dream, then their learning capacity will soon diminish. If dreaming is interrupted for a few days, they will also develop an impediment referred to by researchers as futurograde amnesia. This term means that their ability to think about events in the future is weakened. Such individuals are no longer able to anticipate an expected sequence of events.

Two approaches

There seems to be a link between the findings of the neurophysiologists and the psychoanalytic theory of dreams developed by Freud. While the two disciplines have very different approaches to the phenomenon, they agree that dreams serve to process the many events, emotions and discoveries of our daily lives. Psychoanalysts explain that we recognise in our dreams the unconscious wishes and fears that we repress during the waking hours. For the neuro-physiologists, however, REM sleep enables us to record in our nerve cells the knowledge, information and abilities we have acquired in the course of the day. In spite of their differences, both fields agree that dreams help us to record new situations and ideas, and to process them with help from the emotions. In this way, we learn how to handle similar situations more efficiently in the future. While you may still have a bad dream from time to time, you really needn't worry that this is a sign of things to come.

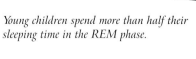

Young children spend more than half their sleeping time in the REM phase.

LIGHT AT THE END OF THE TUNNEL

Is it really possible to cross the threshold of death and yet return to life? Time and again, the survivors of severe accidents have described exactly this scenario. However, doctors and others are sceptical about reports of near death experiences. Could these be the body's way of protecting itself from life-threatening trauma?

Occasionally, people describe experiences that challenge our notions of what is possible. Consider the following: a man is driving along the highway when he suddenly loses control of the vehicle. There is a powerful impact as he ploughs into a tree or other obstacle. The driver is trapped in the twisted wreckage of his car, unable to move. Gravely injured, his life is ebbing away. Suddenly, he feels a force pulling him upwards. While anxious rescuers struggle to free him, he feels himself rising up into the air, leaving behind the battered shell of his body. His role changes: he is no longer involved, he becomes a spectator. Then everything grows dark, and a tunnel opens up to swallow him. There is a long passage, at the end of which he can see an unreal light. He hears sounds and voices that comfort him and make him feel at rest. Then he re-enters the tunnel, returning to the scene of the accident and the sound of human voices – the rescuers. And he begins to feel pain.

Such a description is typical of a Near Death Experience (NDE), a phenomenon that defies explanation. A surprising number of people have undergone such experiences, and have described the journey in detail.

Credible reports?

The question of whether there is life after death has always interested people, but it has recently undergone a revival. In part, this stems from the development of modern medical resuscitation technologies, which enable emergency personnel to save many more lives than was possible in the past.

People who have narrowly escaped death after an accident have described journeys that have taken them into the beyond. After the publication of Dr Raymond Moody's best-selling book *Life After Life* in 1988, such reports became widely known, and NDEs have been the subject of intense debate for about 20 years. Some people dismiss the stories as nothing more than tales of the spirit realm. Others suppose that the survivors are influenced by the tabloid press, and that they tell journalists what they think readers would like to read.

Above: *People who have had a near death experience describe scenes like this, from a painting by Hieronymus Bosch.*

Right: *An engraving by William Blake shows the soul floating above the body.*

Would survivors of NDEs describe such experiences if they had not already heard similar reports in the media? There is a third group, those familiar with the scientific background, who interpret NDEs as simple hallucinations; for them, the main question is what triggers these experiences.

An unreal journey

For the sceptics, people who report a near death experience are certainly sincere, but they have not returned from death. Sceptics see the NDE as simply a mirror of reality, with nothing to do with the afterlife. The question that remains, though, concerns the substance of these cases.

Suppose, for a moment, that the victims had really left their bodies. This would mean that an independent part of their being could detach itself from the physical body. The survivors are convinced that this is what takes place. But there are no rational grounds for believing this to be true.

For many psychologists and physiologists, a near death experience can be compared to conditions of trance and their accompanying hallucinations. Under the impact of an overwhelming physical and mental shock, the brain releases large amounts of chemicals known as endorphins – natural painkillers which bring about feelings of happiness and wellbeing. The effects of the endorphins are similar to those triggered by certain synthetic drugs, and include the feeling of peace described by some survivors of NDEs.

After such a journey into the beyond, some people not only lose their fear of death, but they even regret having returned – not least because it is at this point that the pain begins. But at least they are still alive.

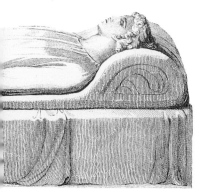

THE HEALING POWERS OF HERBS

Medicinal herbs are increasingly seen as humankind's best bet in the fight against disease and the unceasing quest for good health. Herbs have been used for thousands of years to treat common ailments and ward off illness. Even in this time of genetic engineering and advanced medicine, fully half of all the medications that we use are derived from plants.

People who live in the developed nations of the industrial world often assume that traditional healing methods and the techniques of modern medicine are worlds apart. But if we look closely at the subject, we find that their histories are closely linked. The common thread lies in their use of medicinal plants or herbs. Traditional healers around the world make use of plants to provide remedies for various ailments, while modern synthetic drugs are often derived from plant substances. A very good example is aspirin, a standard medicine that is found in most households, and is used to treat colds, fever and headaches. With its painkilling, anticoagulant and antipyretic (fever-reducing) properties, aspirin has also been found to be beneficial in protecting the body against certain heart diseases. But few people know that it comes from the European meadowsweet (*Filipendula ulmaria*), a plant which is common in central Europe and thrives on river banks and in marshes. The trade name 'aspirin' is derived from *Spiraea ulmaria*, the old scientific designation for the medication.

Morphine and quinine

There are many similar examples: morphine, for example, is known for its painkilling effects and is widely administered as an anaesthetic. The drug is derived from opium, which is extracted from the opium poppy (*Papaver somniferum*). Quinine, used to treat malaria, comes from the quinaquina tree (*Cinchona officinalis*), a species that is indigenous to the Andes Mountains of South America. The heart medication digitalin is prepared primarily from the red foxglove (*Digitalis purpurea*), which grows in upland areas, as well from the sea leek (*Urginea maritima*), which is found in relatively dry regions of the Mediterranean.

But why did people start to use plants for medicinal purposes, and how did they come to discover their special properties?

The first step in the preparation of medicinal plants is to crush them in a mortar.

When we think of how long it takes to discover and test a new drug today, it is fascinating to wonder how our distant ancestors discovered the properties of certain plants. For early humans, the search for food was a process of trial and error. It was largely a matter of personal experience – both good and bad – that helped them to tell the difference between plants that could be eaten safely and those that were poisonous or showed medicinal effects in certain dosages. The knowledge that was gained from these experiences could be passed on from generation to generation.

Human knowledge increased considerably when people began to observe the animal world and to draw certain conclusions: for example, they realised that the plants consumed by fast-running animals such as horses, antelope or bison must have a high concentration of energy. Perhaps they reasoned that these properties could be passed on to the hunters of these animals.

Above: *Acetylsalicylic acid – the scientific name for aspirin – is derived from the European meadowsweet (above) a plant which thrives in wet conditions.*

Right: *Opium is made from the pods of the opium poppy, shown here being harvested in Thailand. The sap of the poppy is rich in alkaloids, such as morphine. It has pain-killing effects, but is also addictive.*

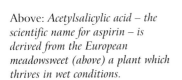

The flying death

For centuries, the hunters of the Venezuelan rain forest have used arrows dipped in curare, a potent poison that paralyses the victim. There are several forms of curare, but it generally contains a cocktail of ingredients drawn from more than 30 plants. Before hunters use it, curare is tested on monkeys. The paralysing effect of curare, which blocks the links or synapses between nerves and muscles, was researched by the French physiologist Claude Bernard (1813–1878). Today, synthetic derivatives of curare are widely administered as muscle relaxants.

A healer from the Mato Grosso region of Brazil prepares medicines using plants.

Many cultures came to associate a so-called magical plant with a certain type of animal, a link that was determined by the plant's effects and its shape, which had to correspond at least partially to that of the animal. The Indians of the Brazilian rain forest, for example, noticed that the bulb of the Piripirioca plant looked like the eye of the tapir (family Tapiridae), a pig-like mammal with a large snout that feeds on fruit, leaves and water plants. The plant had a narcotic effect on the animal, allowing hunters to get closer. Soon, the hunters began to rub the plant on their bodies and arrows, and on the paws of their dogs.

The theory of signatures

It is well known that the peoples of the ancient world made extensive use of the powers of medicinal herbs. Both the Greek philosopher Theophrastus (around 372–286 BC), who wrote about botany, as well as the Roman writer Pliny the Elder (AD 23–79) two centuries later, believed that every drug bears a message – a kind of divine mark. In the 16th century, the Swiss-born doctor and alchemist Paracelsus (1493–1541) published his theory of signatures, which he believed allowed him to read the uses of any plant according to its appearance.

From our point of view, the theory of signatures seems to combine magic and imagination to the extent that it is difficult to separate the two. A basic knowledge of botany tells us that the properties of a plant are arbitrarily accompanied by basic structural characteristics. This is the case with the bloated roots of the figwort (*Ranunculus ficaria*), which leads to excessively enlarged, so-called

hypertrophic veins. The plant contains chemicals called saponins, however, which are effective in the treatment of haemorrhoids. Another example is the common ivy (*Hedera helix*), which winds around the trunks of trees, giving them a slender and venerable appearance. Substances derived from ivy are used in the treatment of obesity and cellulite. Finally, there is mistletoe (*Viscum album*), which is found in compact bundles as a semi-parasite on the branches of trees and therefore looks like a tumour. The plant contains proteins which are used to treat cancer.

There is a persistent but unfounded belief that the cornflower makes blue eyes shine.

The effectiveness of the plant can be connected not only to its form but also to other characteristics such as where it thrives. The bark of the silver willow (*Salix alba*), for example, which especially thrives in marshy wetlands, near streams and on the banks of ponds, contains salicin, an anti-rheumatic substance that is useful in treating the colds and fevers that develop among people living in this kind of environment.

A further indication of a plant's potency is its colour. In China, the active agents in plants are classified according to their colour and warmth. Chinese herbalists attribute their healing effects more to these qualities than to the chemical composition of the plants. An example of this is the liquorice bush (*Glycyrrhiza glabra*), which is widely used in China. Researchers have identified and isolated the molecules that give the plant its yellowish colour, and have proven its anti-inflammatory and antispasmodic effect on the intestines. Nevertheless, the followers of traditional Chinese medicine continue to insist that the effectiveness of the liquorice bush stems from its colour rather than any other factor. They are so convinced of this that they will replace liquorice with turmeric (*Curcuma longa*) if the former is not available in sufficient quantities, even though their only common characteristic is their yellow colour. Interestingly, the same healing effects are reported.

Many of us might be sceptical about such a belief, but it really is no different from the placebo effect – a 'cure' produced by giving a harmless sugar pill to someone who believes they are getting an effective medication. The effectiveness of placebos has been proved time and again. Traditionally, the peoples of

A question of definition

We often use the word 'drug' when we actually mean 'plant drug'. In 1870, a drug was defined as a generic designation for raw materials out of which pharmacists prepare medicines. In practice, a drug is that part of the plant – whether fresh or dry – that contains the active medicinal agents. According to this definition, even such innocuous beverages as camomile or green tea can be said to be prepared from drugs.

Above: *On a street in Rangoon, capital of Burma, a trader offers a wide selection of medicinal plants.*

Right: *Medicinal herbs are consumed in the form of gelatin capsules, tablets and ampoules.*

Above: *The owner of this medicinal plant stall on the island of Mauritius claims that his teas will ease the effects of diabetes, rheumatism, asthma and other ailments.*

Asia believe that yellow symbolises good health, equilibrium and the harmony of the body's organs. If a doctor prescribes a yellow medicine, he shows his patient that he has understood his concerns and meets his expectations. The improvement of health that goes hand in hand with yellow may well be attributed to the placebo effect, but the same may be true of many of the medicines developed by modern medical science.

Reliable medicines

The theory of signatures has drawn attention to certain plants. As a result, a wide range of species has been investigated, leading in many cases to the production of effective medicines. But not every medicinal herb has proven as effective as it was traditionally thought to be. The roots of the yellow gentian (*Gentiana lutea*), for example, have a gall-like bitterness, which is why this plant is widely thought to have a choleric effect, promoting the secretion of bile in the gall bladder. In parts of Africa, it is believed that the phallus-like fruits of the sausage tree (*Kigelia africana*) can confer aphrodisiac or potency-enhancing effects.

In the 20th century, science concentrated on synthetic medicines, but there is now growing interest in natural preparations. Gentle medicines such as teas or royal jelly – the liquid food produced by the worker bees for their queen – enjoy wide popularity, while the health-enhancing properties of ginseng, echinacea and other plants are attracting interest. However, it must be remembered that some plant medicines are very potent, and can be dangerous in high concentrations. Accidents sometimes result from an overdose or an ineffective treatment. Much depends on the conditions under which the plants were produced, harvested and stored, and the concentration of their active substances can vary greatly from case to case.

The major international drug companies have noticed the growing public interest in herbal products. The drug companies make use of the expertise of ethnologists and ethnobotanists, who comb remote areas of Africa, South America or Siberia collecting samples from traditional healers. Botanists test these plants to find out their structure, chemical make-up and properties. Although many years of research lie ahead, there is considerable hope that such plants will one day yield the wonder drugs of the future.

The wisdom of Africa

In many parts of Africa, people attribute all natural phenomena, be they good or bad, to a soul, and seek to gain the favour of the spirits through various magical practices. The use of indigenous plants, among them medicinal plants, is their way of fighting the evil spirits who send illnesses. There is increasing interest in many of the traditional remedies of Africa, but pharmaceutical testing has shown that only a few traditional healing preparations are as effective as synthetically produced medicines.

VOODOO: THE INSIDE STORY

When most of us hear the word 'voodoo', we think only of gruesome rituals, zombies and the living dead. Voodoo is widespread in West Africa and was brought to the Caribbean and South America with the slaves. For the most part, we only hear about its dark side. But in West Africa, voodoo is an accepted part of traditional religious practice, and a way of achieving positive goals.

Many dark tales surround the practice of voodoo, a religious cult involving trance, spirits and ancestor worship that is popular among the peoples of West Africa, the Caribbean and South America. The word may come from the word for 'spirit' in the Fon language of West Africa, or from the word *vodu* (guardian spirit) of the Ewe people of Ghana. But voodoo is overwhelmingly identified with the poor Caribbean nation of Haiti, which shares the island of Hispaniola with the Dominican Republic. In colonial times, Haiti was ruled by France, and French colonists imported thousands of slaves from West Africa to work on the island's vast sugar plantations. The religious beliefs of the slaves were gradually combined with the Roman Catholicism of the French colonists, producing an unusual synthesis in which Christian saints came to be worshipped alongside the ancient gods of Africa.

While consulting an oracle, this Ghanaian voodoo priest paints magical symbols on a table covered with powdered plants.

Voodoo has many names, and its practices vary widely, for the slave trade scattered the peoples of Africa throughout the Americas. In Cuba, a form of voodoo is known as Santeria; in Brazil, Macumba. To understand how voodoo is woven into daily life, let us go back to its roots and put ourselves in the place of Kofi, a young West African.

Kofi is worried because everything in his life is going wrong: he is deeply in debt, his wife has recently fallen ill and he wonders if the path he has chosen is bringing him bad luck. In his search for explanations, he wonders if he has been bewitched, is simply unlucky or is perhaps the object of revenge on the part of visible or invisible spirits. It is possible that he has broken some moral law or neglected to make a ritual sacrifice to honour the spirit of an ancestor.

The paths to the gods

Kofi knows that only a voodoo priest, who commands the gift of prophecy and can invoke the spirits, is in a position to interpret his fate. The priest will ask an oracle for information from various gods and from the spirits of the ancestors, and he will use other magical practices to try to free Kofi from evil influences.

If we assume that Kofi's problems can be solved by voodoo rituals, then there are a number of possibilities. Since he is young, Kofi first needs help in strengthening his

The arrangement of the objects on a voodoo altar signifies which deity is being represented and worshipped.

personality, so he will probably be advised to join a voodoo cult. These are groups of worshippers consisting of several extended families under the guidance of an experienced priest. Prospective members are initiated into the rites that are intended to make them receptive to the spirits. Once the initiation is complete, the spirits will be able to place the individual in a trance or even take control of his or her mind. During voodoo ceremonies, a cult member can achieve a state of ecstasy in which he or she embodies a mythical being that corresponds to a previously unknown aspect of their personality. The ritual ensures the spirit's goodwill towards the community.

It may be that all Kofi needs is support from the outside. Then the priest will probably advise him to arrange for a voodoo fetish, a spirit object that can be conveyed to individuals. His close relatives would also benefit from this. Most of the time, Kofi will have complete control over this holy object, which symbolises a deity. He will not enter into mythical communion with it, nor will it ever possess him. But a sensitive woman from his close circle of associates could become the mystical wife of his protector, for whom she would then serve as a medium, enabling the object to 'speak'.

If Kofi's problems are simply due to a run of bad luck, the priest will generally advise

Above: *Cult members restrain a man possessed by a spirit during a ceremony.*

Haiti's voodoo gods

Voodoo is very much a part of daily life in Haiti. Here, the gods are known as loas and are divided into water, air, fire and earth spirits. Many of these deities bear African names, and some are identified with Roman Catholic saints. Papa Legba, the Lord of the Crossroads, acts as a mediator between the higher powers and the world of humans. Other important loas are Ogun, the god of iron, fire and war; Agwe, the god of the ocean; and Erzulie, the goddess of love and wealth. Baron Samedi is the name given to the Lord of the Dead, who bears similarities to the devil.

him to perform a particular act to please one of the voodoo gods; he may ask for forgiveness, or place himself under the god's protection. If Kofi wishes to ask the god for a favour, he will have to promise this god to perform a sacrifice once the favour has been granted. After that he will no longer be in the god's debt. He may still continue to attend ceremonies dedicated to the god in the hope that his future needs will be more easily satisfied.

A fetish grants protection

If the priest tells Kofi to acquire a voodoo fetish from someone who already possesses one, the young man will have to find this person. Then, in exchange for cash and other goods, he will be told what he must acquire for the ceremony of arrangement, as well as the materials he will need to construct the object with which his voodoo patron god will be identified. The materials range from various plant leaves and stones to pieces of skin

and bones, feathers, hair and teeth. The person who conveys the fetish will guard these ingredients carefully from the eyes and touch of other people by burying it in the ground, hiding it in a pot or wrapping it in cloth or skins. Believers in voodoo assume that the ingredients of a fetish are filled with the powers of the spirit that previously occupied them. The ingredients are supposed to possess an aura that attracts some spirits while repelling others. The ingredients must be arranged carefully; then they can serve as a kind of antenna, that is, they are able to communicate with a supernatural power, as long as this is in harmony with the fetish.

When the person conveying the fetish finally anoints it, he will bring Kofi into contact with the corresponding higher power. At the same time, he will teach him a special magic formula that Kofi can use to call upon the spirit. These formulae are only

effective as a result of these agreements between the conveyor and receiver – the master and disciple. After the holy object has been transferred, a substantial sacrifice is made to thank the higher power for being prepared to serve a new initiate.

Becoming a voodoo priest

Perhaps Kofi is not immediately satisfied with his protecting spirit. If that is the case, he will pay his teacher another visit. The priest may advise Kofi to strengthen the effects of his voodoo fetish by adding one or more extra ingredients. Or he will suggest acquiring additional protectors to fight the evil spirits that must be interfering with the use of the fetish.

If things run smoothly, Kofi's standing in the community will increase. Neighbours and friends will know that he possesses a protecting spirit which is helping him in various ways. It is likely that many people will come to him and ask him to use his magic to assist them.

In trying to satisfy his clients, the young man will study the healing and magical powers of certain plants and herbs. If he acquires several protective spirits, he can offer people solutions for a wide range of problems. If he really wishes to advise his clients to the best of his ability, Kofi will acquire the art of prophecy from an experienced priest and learn how to summon the spirits.

In order to resist evil magicians or at least to be on an equal footing with them, Kofi needs to find a special voodoo protector who

Above: *During her initiation, this Togolese woman has been blindfolded and taken to a holy place in the forest. There, it is revealed to her that voodoo – in this case Hévíéso, the god of lightning – is an inner force and cannot be seen.*

will give him power over the evil spirits that spread misfortune, suffering and death, driving anyone who falls under their spell to insanity. Kofi can use the evil forces to his advantage, or he can resist them; he is now able to act as a magician himself. He can then choose between acting according to the will of a superior being and striving towards good in everything he does, or else helping the dark forces who seek to increase their powers through wilful destruction.

The tale of Kofi shows that the task of the voodoo gods is to help people – no matter what their situation – to lead a better life in accordance with their temperament and

Left: *During a voodoo dance in a village Togo, the participants enter a state of trance.*

The spread of voodoo

Voodoo was born in what are now the nations of Togo and Benin in West Africa, and was brought to the New World by West African slaves. Voodoo is also known in the southern states of the US, particularly Louisiana, where it is known by the French name, *voudou*. The Cuban religion, Santeria, and Macumba, which is practised in Brazil, bear great similarities to voodoo.

ability. Voodoo ceremonies call on the gods to exert a favourable influence on events or to prevent certain things from happening. The gods are simply agents in the range of possibilities that is open to every individual.

A higher being

The deity that presides over the many voodoo gods is Mahou. According to belief, he encourages people to place responsibility for their lives in the hands of the individual gods below him. In this way, the complex religious system of voodoo acknowledges a higher being, while at the same time acknowledging the existence of many other gods of varying degrees of importance.

The world of the voodoo gods helps to recognise and tame the individual's essential powers, which can lead to rage, madness, violence and trickery. Instead of demonising or repressing these qualities, voodoo helps to place them in the service of noble goals.

People are not always ready to receive voodoo spirits and partake in voodoo rituals. This is why voodoo practices are subject to strict control, which is ensured by tradition, the custodians of the culture, the spirits of departed ancestors who have the interests of the faithful in mind and, not least, by the protector spirits, who are concerned for the spiritual wellbeing of the individual. It is only when a voodoo priest dares to confront the temptations of evil forces that he becomes really secure from them. The danger here is that the magic rites of voodoo can be misused, with the priest turning to the manipulation of others through witchcraft.

TRANCES AND VISIONS IN AFRICAN CHRISTIANITY

Trances, visions, speaking in tongues, miraculous healing: all these are features of the independent African Christian churches that emerged during the 20th century. In these denominations, Christian doctrines of salvation taught by the European missionary churches gradually merged with elements of African religion. These African adaptations of Christianity serve the very real need of meeting the spiritual requirements of African people.

Above: *During a service, a 'reporter' notes down the words of one of the faithful, who is describing a vision.*

Right: *Overcome with emotion, a woman falls into a trance.*

Christianity has existed in Africa for many centuries. In Roman times, many of the Church Fathers were active in North Africa, while Egypt's Coptic Church and Ethiopia's Orthodox Church are among the oldest established denominations within Christianity. However, the real spread of Christianity through Africa took place during the colonial period, which began in the 16th century. First came the Portuguese, who brought Roman Catholicism when they established trading posts along the coast. Following the founding of Sierra Leone as a colony for freed slaves in 1808, West Africa received an influx of Anglican, Methodist, Baptist and Presbyterian missionaries. In southern Africa, missionary efforts were led by German Lutherans and a variety of evangelical Protestant groups.

When they arrived in Africa, Christian missionaries encountered a strange world of cults and customs. For the peoples of Africa, the introduction of Western religion and culture was a massive shock to their system of values. Large numbers of Africans converted to the new faith, but many felt the need to adapt Christianity to their own religious and social traditions. This need became acute in the late 19th century as African clergy and lay people realised that positions of power within church structures would be dominated by white priests. Gradually, they freed themselves from the missionary churches and established their own Christian groups headed by indigenous spiritual leaders. Such groups were often inspired by the charismatic faith of African-American churches. In the 20th century, this produced an authentic African Christianity, combining belief in Jesus Christ with ancestor worship, magic, sacrificial rites, fetishism and animism, and a strong emphasis on a sense of community.

Today there are about 60,000 so-called independent African churches of almost all Christian denominations, and they attract people in cities and country alike. Southern Africa has been a particularly fertile area for the growth of such denominations. Perhaps the largest is the Zionist Christian Church of South Africa. Each year at Easter, up to two million church members gather at its shrine at Moria, north of Johannesburg.

Christianity and African tradition

African church congregations tend not to gather for the purpose of quiet worship; instead, they seek to use their own forms of religious expression to establish a more living and immediate contact with Jesus Christ, in order to praise him or beseech him with the full power of their hearts.

Services often involve visions, revelations and trance-like dancing, which sometimes reaches the point of ecstatic possession. A congregation might meet to free its members from evil demons who are preventing their wishes from being fulfilled – be it the wish for children, marriage, or a desperately needed job. Soon, the divine powers invoked by the priest are set in action. The participants begin to cry out and moan, some fall to the floor, others must be restrained. People hum songs and hymns ecstatically. Suddenly a woman stands upright, trembling. As if from the depths of her being, she shouts warnings and advice. Next to her, another member of the congregation takes careful note of what she says.

At another church, several men and women wait their turn at the entrance. They appear uneasy and dissatisfied, and are waiting to ask a priest where their sorrows come from and what prayers or ceremonies they need to perform if they are to receive divine assistance. Examples like these make it clear that Christianity in Africa has a variety of faces, and that it often combines traditional forms of spiritualism with a more conventional Christian message.

Although a charismatic service like the one described above might seem a long way from conventional Christian practice, first impressions are deceiving. The African churches have departed radically from the many gods of traditional animistic religion and have turned unconditionally to Jesus. Their creed is the Bible, and the Holy Scriptures are the source

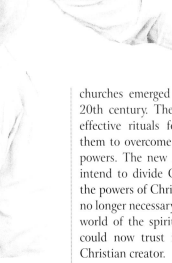

of justification for their religious acts, with which they seek connection to the spiritual spontaneity of the early Christian gospels.

But this transformation has not been easy for the African Christians. In many areas, traditional spiritual leaders, fetish-magicians and so-called witch doctors threatened converts to Christianity with all kinds of occult violence. For this reason there was a constant spiritual battle against the threats of the magicians, a battle in which the words

of the Apostle Paul provided inspiration: 'Put on the whole armour of God that ye may be able to stand against the wiles of the devil' (Ephesians 6:11).

Because European missionary societies were not able to provide their converts with the protection that they required, local

Above: *A Catholic priest carries the host (holy sacrament) in front of the congregation. The host also serves as an instrument for healing the sick.*

churches emerged at the beginning of the 20th century. The local churches provided effective rituals for the faithful, enabling them to overcome their fear of evil magical powers. The new African churches did not intend to divide Christianity, but to reveal the powers of Christ. This meant that it was no longer necessary to turn to the traditional world of the spirits for help, for the pious could now trust in the protection of the Christian creator.

Visions of the Holy Ghost

Many African Christian churches have not hesitated to invoke the Holy Ghost in order to protect individuals from evil. The faithful fall into a trance and receive the prophetic tidings which often warn them of imminent danger. The Holy Ghost is seen as a power that intervenes in earthly affairs, heals illness and grants wealth. It often encourages the congregation to increase its devotion in

prayer or to carry out certain rituals, thereby animating the faithful to develop rich forms of religious tradition.

Occasionally, fortune-tellers are invited to prayer meetings in order to illuminate the workings of the priest during the divine service. They have received their gift of revealing hidden events or future occurrences directly from the Holy Ghost, and they differ from traditional tribal seers in that they base their prophecies on acts of Christian faith alone.

In African Christianity, any faithful person can, in principle, have direct access to the Holy Ghost. Once the spirit is within a person, it reveals itself through fainting, cramp-like states of physical animation and in so-called speaking in tongues – an ecstatic form of speech that requires religious interpretation. It is through this kind of spectacular display, which makes an equally powerful impression on the faithful and on unbelievers, that the Protestant churches of Africa mark the immediate presence of the Holy Ghost.

As in many areas of the world, incidents of miraculous healing in the name of Jesus or God arouse intense interest in the villages

Spiritual renewal through Christianity

The evolution of Christianity has opened new horizons for the peoples of Africa. The great achievement of the independent African churches has been to give a new identity to a foreign religion with its roots in the detested colonial past. The new churches have been able to preserve African culture while at the same time hastening the displacement of outdated religious and social traditions. Unlike the gods of indigenous religions, who are subject to the immutable powers of fate, the Christian doctrine of salvation of the faithful places individual salvation of the soul in the foreground, thus granting the faithful a greater degree of self-determination.

and towns of Africa. Miracles are a visible demonstration of the power of the Christian faith. When a priest heals a sick person by the laying on of hands or frees his or her body from evil spirits through prayer, the person who has been 'healed by a miracle' is called on to make a donation in order to thank God for his help and to compensate the church for its extraordinary act of pastoral care.

In these regions, where almost nothing happens by luck or chance, almost any random event may be counted as a miracle but always requires the consent or action of the spirits. An illness that clears up, a pregnancy without complications, a business that suddenly flourishes, an accident where no-one is killed or the deserved punishment of a blasphemer – these are events that provide the opportunity to wonder at God's powers. The Christian miracle-workers emphasise that they do not make use of black magic, but that God has granted them their spiritual talents. They support their claim with the statement that Christ will help those who believe in him.

Proponents of traditional Christianity accuse the African churches of offering a simplistic picture of the Christian doctrines.

A ritual held by the African Church of the Wisdom of God in Christ takes place in the form of a public exorcism.

Right: *'Satan! Get behind me!' cries a priest, as he tries to drive the evil spirit out of this woman's body.*

Below: *A meeting of an indigenous African Church, held in Benin over Christmas, is the occasion for beachside prayers against witchcraft.*

They believe that God loses his position as an all-powerful being once he intervenes in earthly affairs via holy men equipped with his supernatural powers, which they use to protect people from accidents, lightning, poverty or illness. The counter-argument is that the churches of black Africa have once again proven the resilience and adaptability of Christianity worldwide.

In spite of many variations, the African churches serve the same God, and their activities are based on underlying principles of morality. Individual denominations allow their members to join forces with others to help construct a new society.

THE MAGICAL POWERS OF THE SHAMANS

By invoking spirits through magic, transmutation of souls, ecstatic possession and states of trance, the shaman mediates between the earthly world and that of the spirits. While shamans were often dismissed as primitive magicians in the past, there is increasing interest in the beliefs and practices of shamanism.

A leather headdress with bears' claws, eyes with copper inlay, dogs' teeth, eyebrows and moustache of fur all decorate this carved statue of a shaman from Canada's West Coast.

For many peoples around the world, the natural world is filled with good and evil spirits. In order to influence or control the actions of the spirits, these peoples rely on the actions of a very special individual called a shaman. Also known as a medicine man, the shaman is a kind of priest. In northern Asia, shamanism is a religion – the word 'shaman' comes from the Tungus region of Siberia, and may have its origins in the Sanskrit word *srama*, or 'religious exercise'. In its wider sense, shamanism represents a set of magical-religious beliefs that stem from the depths of our prehistoric past. Shamanic practices are found among the Eskimos (or Inuit) of the Arctic regions, Native American peoples, the Australian Aborigines and numerous other indigenous peoples of Africa, Oceania and South America.

Europeans first encountered shamanism during the eastward expansion of the Russian empire into the wilderness of Siberia. As contact with the east increased, travellers and scientists sent back descriptions of unusual religious practices. In the 17th century, the Russian diplomat Isbrand Ides told of a remarkable experience he had had during a hunting trip in Siberia, near what is now the Mongolian border. One night, he observed his guide performing strange rituals in a log cabin together with a Tungusic shaman. Both men wore arrows in their pierced noses and danced in a circle to the beat of a drum, surrounded by fearsome statues that represented spirits. As they danced, they howled like dogs. According to his tale, ravens and other birds nearby also took part in this strange concert.

Still more amazing was the experience of explorer Johann Georg Gmelin, who set out in 1733 to study the Ural Mountains, Siberia and the Kamchatka Peninsula, under the patronage of the Russian Empress Anna Ivanovna. On his way, he witnessed how a Yakut shaman woman cut open her belly, removed a piece of tissue and proceeded to cook and eat it. Afterwards, she treated the wound with pitch and birch bark, and after only six days it had healed.

Who are the shamans?

Based on accounts such as these, it is clear that a shaman must be an extraordinary person. Generally, they either inherit their status, or else they respond to a call from superhuman beings, either through a dream, a vision or an experience of great suffering, such as a severe illness. After this kind of other-worldly experience, a person destined to become a shaman establishes lasting contact with the spirit kingdom in order to gain extrasensory experience and see the true nature of things. The spirits grant him or her great powers, which are then placed at the disposal of the tribe. Thus the shaman acts as a mediator between the earthly and the supernatural worlds.

In the great Amazon basin of South America, the shaman is initiated by spending long periods alone in the tropical rain forests. In the forest he experiences loss of consciousness and has dreams that bear deep significance. His ordeals give him access to the world beyond. In order to commune with the hunting spirits of the jungle, the lagoons or the Andes Mountains, he improvises the so-called Ikaro song, sometimes distorting his voice while he sings. The Eskimo (or Inuit) shamans of the Arctic attain a state of ecstatic conscious-ness through a coughing breath, interrupted by cries deep in their

The deer antler headdress of a dancing Tungusic shaman permits his soul to travel to the spirit world.

A group of Inuit objects from Alaska: animal masks and a raven rattle serve the shamans as props for ritual ceremonies. The symbolic motif on the shaman's coat represents the seasons and cycles of fertility.

abducted soul back again. The fascinating phenomenon of a journey in search of a soul which took place in the Amazon has been described as follows:

The shaman offers a hallucinogenic drink to those participating in a ritual seance, and they sip it slowly. After that, the magician-priest begins a monotonous song consisting of magical invocations, accompanied by the rhythmic beating of a drum. All the while, the participants shake, grimace and make wild gestures.

The patient has fear written on her face and looks as if she wishes to flee from some terrifying vision. The spirits of the plants have apparently taken hold of her. The possessed person emits short, hoarse cries and turns round and round in a circle. With a blow from his stick – the *chonta* – the shaman stops the woman and she stands as if petrified. Although it makes her burp and sneeze, he forces her to inhale a vegetable decoction through her nose, accompanying every inhalation with a long whistle. The woman contorts strangely, throws her arms in the air and shakes her hands, as if she wants to banish a terrible spirit. Then she falls to the ground in a shamanic trance.

throats. This ability to 'sing' with the throat is shared by the shamans of Tuva, a mountainous territory in Siberia on the border with Mongolia. Siberian shamans complete their initiation rites through a symbolic second birth, by climbing down from a tree head first. The shamans of the Andes must demonstrate their ability to control nature and its powers by surviving a lightning strike.

During his apprenticeship, a shaman must himself by acquiring the tools of his trade such as drums, rattles, reed flutes, animal masks, skins, and twig whips. Shamans use these objects to heighten their ecstatic experience during cult ceremonies, and also to symbolise the ritual acts.

Because shamans are usually regarded as possessing great authority, they live apart from the community. Solitude allows them to embrace the supernatural universe in complete tranquillity.

The social role of the shaman

Thanks to their special relationship to the spirits, shamans are able to heal the sick, influence the success of hunting trips – as well as the weather affecting the harvest – and protect their people from natural disasters. The shaman combines the roles of medicine man, magician, fortune-teller and tribal priest, and it is his responsibility to conduct religious ceremonies, retell the ancient myths, smooth over social conflicts and reassure people who fear supernatural powers.

When a member of the tribe has been possessed by an evil spirit, the shaman enters a state of trance and sets out on a so-called journey to the sky to fetch the

Below: A shamanic healer in Borneo treats a sick girl by laying his hands on her and blowing fragrant sandalwood smoke.

Magician or spirit doctor?

For a long time, the practices of shamanism were dismissed by Western experts as mere primitive rituals. In recent years, however, researchers have identified certain similarities between the mystical experiences of the shaman and certain forms of psychotherapy. Because of its therapeutic potential, researchers are also very interested in trance.

Now the shaman kneels next to his patient and listens to the disjointed words that pass her lips, interspersed with sobs. Then he again invokes the spirits, chews some herbs, takes another sip from the drug mixture and announces to the participants that he is about to set off on a journey to the sky.

has been sent by the wise ones – for example, a serious infection – it exceeds his powers of healing.

In the shamanic trance, a kind of exchange takes place with the spirits – a unification with the cosmos or with divinity. In Brazil's Macumba cult, which is related to voodoo, the person in a trance is ridden by African Orixás gods. On the island of Bali, in Indonesia, *Sanghyang jaran* represents the possession of a person by the horses of God.

The shaman's art of healing and fortune-telling seems to be a 'holy spark' or sixth sense. Their powers enable tribal priests to find out the causes of illness by uncovering hidden conflicts or fears that may disturb spiritual balance and the body's wellbeing.

It is easy to scoff that shamanism is nothing but primitive superstition. But there are many people who believe that it is a form of knowledge about the relationship between humans, nature and the cosmos. This implies that the boundaries of shamanism are much wider than the modern Western world imagines. At present, science has no clear explanations for the phenomenon of shamanism, but we can be sure that this mystical realm will continue to tantalise us with its mysteries.

Above: *The 'Holy Daughters' of the Brazilian Macumba cult enter a state of trance through dances.*

Above right: *A Mayan statuette from Guatemala represents a sacred hallucinogenic mushroom.*

Left: *In a Sanghyang ceremony on the island of Bali, the 'horses of the gods' possess a person.*

From then on, he retreats into himself, as if nodding off to sleep. The air in the room becomes unbearably sticky. The shaman has grown pale and his eyes, when open, have a glassy sheen. His lips move weakly, as if speaking with invisible beings. Then he believes he has found the cause of his patient's problem. When he returns from his journey to the beyond, the shaman brings with him the soul of his patient which had been stolen by the evil spirits, and he gives her therapeutic advice.

The shaman's diagnoses can be harsh, and he might declare that the victim is suffering from an illness, has been disgraced, or has strayed from the path of fate. If the illness

Opening the doors of perception

It is well known that drugs prepared from mushrooms containing psilocybin – so-called magic mushrooms – or other plant substances can alter consciousness. In many cultures, hallucinogenic or mind-altering substances are used by shamans to enter the spirit world. The hallucinogen affects the central nervous system and produces a state resembling psychosis, similar to the symptoms of schizophrenia or epilepsy. In medieval Europe, witches drank potions made of mandrake (*Mandragora officinarum*). In Peru, potent hallucinogenic drugs are prepared from the San Pedro cactus, in Mexico from peyote, and in the Amazon from ayahuasca.

With its human-like form, mandrake root was a much-prized magical herb during the Middle Ages.

POSSESSION

Demonic possession is the almost tangible evidence of one of the oldest of human beliefs – the struggle between good and evil. But expelling demons is not just a medieval ritual: the Catholic Church still sees exorcism as viable, if it believes that evil spirits have taken over a person.

In Christian belief, the ultimate horror is for Satan, the Prince of Darkness, to take possession of an individual's body and soul. However, almost all cultures have similar beliefs concerning the ability of demons to take over a person. In many ways, such beliefs are a way of explaining unusual changes in a person's mental or physical state. In the past, people who suffered from epilepsy, hysteria or schizophrenia, for example, were often thought to be possessed by demons. Such individuals were often gripped by states of wild and uncontrollable excitement, and their disturbed behaviour gave the impression that threatening beings were in control.

The Old and New Testaments both tell of demons who bring disaster, jeopardise a person's health or cause them to commit evil deeds. At the forefront of these dark forces is Satan (from the Hebrew word for 'adversary'), who is regarded as the origin of all evil and the enemy of God. Although the Bible presents him as a part of the original Creation, Satan later came to be represented as a fallen angel. Satan, the most beautiful and intelligent of the angels, was driven by

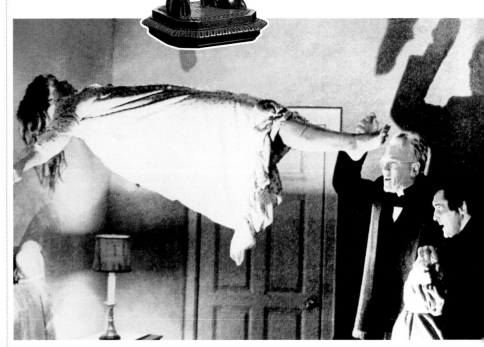

The devil is often portrayed as a well-dressed gentleman ready to offer earthly delights in exchange for possession of an individual's soul. The horns and goat's legs are characteristic features.

Below: *A scene from the 1973 film* The Exorcist. *A demon has given the girl supernatural powers, enabling her to float in the air.*

In order to fight the power of evil, priests have practised the ritual of exorcism for centuries – and the Catholic Church is still convinced of the benefits of this ritual.

God and his dark adversary

The dualism of God and the devil is a fundamental aspect of the Christian faith, and can be traced back to the teachings of the Persian prophet, Zarathustra, who founded the Zoroastrian religion in the 6th century BC. In the collection of holy scriptures called the *Avesta*, Zarathustra described the demonic spirit Ahriman as the enemy of Ahura Mazda, the creator of the world and sole god. This was the first expression of the principle of opposition between good and evil. The idea of a force opposed to God was new, and it posed a great ethical challenge. The idea influenced Judaism during the period when the Jews were held captive by the Babylonians, and was in turn passed on to Christianity.

A thousand million devils

In 1988, Pope John Paul II's former chief exorcist, Monsignore Corrado Balducci, put a number on the extent of Satan's influence. Balducci published figures for the diocese of Rome, and claimed that diocesan records listed an exact total of 1,758,640,176 expulsions of demons. Despite this staggering figure, the Monsignore believed that Satan was involved in only 15 out of every 1,000 cases of possession. He estimated that 40% of all priests doubt the physical existence of the devil.

his pride and arrogance to resist and rebel against God, eventually becoming the ruler of the kingdom of demons.

Close examination of certain passages in the Bible convinced the early fathers of the Christian church that Satan, also known as the devil, exists in physical form and can take control of a person's body and soul. It is said that Jesus Christ healed people possessed by evil spirits through the expulsion of demons.

In recent years, there has been an upsurge in popular interest in the phenomenon of demonic possession and belief in evil. This public fascination began in 1973, when the controversial film *The Exorcist*, by the American director William Friedkin, drew crowds throughout the world. The film's success spawned a sequel, and created a new area of books and films dealing with demonic possession. Interest in possession goes hand

Medieval art usually depicted possessed people as naked and contorted. Here the devil is shown leaving the body of the victim, who is healed by the seal of the bishop.

in hand with the continuing fascination with stories of satanic cults and black masses, which symbolise an obscene inversion of Christian values.

In 1998, a Catholic priest named Gabriele Amorth, who is active under the commission of the Pope as an exorcist in the diocese of Rome, made a shocking announcement. In the Catholic journal *Vita Pastorale*, Amorth claimed that he received requests for help from several thousand supposedly possessed individuals each year, although after careful examination only a fraction of them were treated by expulsion of demons. He also spoke of increasing requests from Germany, Austria and Switzerland.

Evil in the world

In the 18th century, Europe underwent a tremendous growth in scientific and rational thinking – the Age of Enlightenment. The new age led to a great demystification of satanic powers, with many other causes being suggested as responsible for supposed demonic possession. Today, psychiatrists, psychologists and sociologists are influenced by studies of hysteria, neurosis and hypnosis made by French neurologist Jean Martin Charcot (1825–1893), as well as the psychoanalytic theories of Sigmund Freud (1856–1939). Professionals in these fields now regard the devil as a construction of the subconscious mind to give a human form to the evils of the modern world. Faced with the decline in traditional values and the feeling of powerlessness in the face of the tragedies of our time, many people are drawn to religious ideas beyond the bounds of tradition.

This relief from an 8th-century Italian baptismal chapel shows a group exorcism, in which the possessed must touch the bishop's cross.

Many Christian theologians view the devil as purely symbolic. However, the Catholic Church insists on the physical existence of Satan. In the eyes of the Church, certain forms of possession cannot be explained on the basis of medicine or psychiatry, but only as a result of demonic powers.

A priest who specialises in driving out demons is known as an exorcist. Some exorcist priests, who may be holders of a specific office, strictly follow the regulations for the expulsion of demons set out by Pope Paul V in the *Rituale Romanum* of 1614 and revised at the end of the 19th century by Pope Leo XIII. According to this document, the presence of Satan can be recognised by a number of features in the possessed: their smell, an aversion to religious values, sudden fluency in a foreign language and a great strength that is in no way proportional to their physical constitution and age.

In its classic form, an exorcism involves the laying on of hands, prayer, invocation and the presentation of the cross. An exorcist will attempt to expel the evil demon, although he knows that the rituals prescribed in the *Rituale Romanum* can be a shock to a sensitive individual. For this reason, the Catholic Church today requires a doctor to be present during an exorcism.

Most officiating exorcists today seem to want to combine dogma with the findings of medicine and psychology. They aim to establish trust and help people find a new independence. In most cases, exorcist priests support their findings with a psychiatric examination. If there is agreement that an exorcism is needed, the priest will conduct the ritual, beseeching God to free the afflicted person.

Perhaps more moderate forms of exorcism will discourage people from turning to fringe groups and private exorcists. The actions of a number of these self-styled exorcists have contributed to the deaths of supposedly possessed individuals, or so traumatised them that they required psychiatric care.

THE ORACLE SPEAKS

The people of the ancient world placed great importance on prophecies. Whether uttered by a priestess in a subterranean chamber or derived from looking at the entrails of an animal, these prophecies governed many aspects of life. Today, the pseudo-science of astrology has taken their place.

Since ancient times, humans have longed for the ability to look into the future. At one time or another, nearly all cultures and religions have relied on oracles – prophecies of future events delivered by a revered priest or priestess representing a god or goddess. In ancient times, divine prophecies played an important role in evaluating future events.

In the ancient world, there were two types of divination: on the one hand, there was inspirational prophecy, as known in Greece and ancient Israel (Canaan), where humans received the oracle from the gods; on the other hand, there was interpretive prophecy, in which revelations came from reading signs left by the gods. The interpretive type was very common among the Babylonians, the Etruscans and the Romans. Social structure largely determined which type of prophecy was most commonly used. Inspirational prophecy was more common for nomadic peoples whose mythology assigned a special importance to the spoken word, while interpretive prophecy was more suited to the settled cultures whose myths were recorded in writing.

Prophecy through inspiration

The most famous shrines of inspirational prophecy lay in ancient Greece. From the 5th century BC, the oracle of the healing god Asclepius, the son of Apollo, appeared to sleeping pilgrims in his cult temple at Epidaurus. Pilgrims performed cleansing rituals before they went to sleep at night. In the morning, priests interpreted their dreams.

The oracle of Delphi, at the foot of Mount Parnassus, enjoyed the highest reputation, and attracted vast crowds of people between the 7th century BC and the 2nd century AD. Pilgrims came to share in the wisdom of Apollo, who spoke through the priestess Pythia. According to Greek mythology, the oracle stood on the site where Apollo had slain the female snake Python, which guarded a deep fissure in the ground and could foretell the future. The shrine's guardian was named Pythia, after the snake, and all priestesses of the shrine were known as Pythia.

Above: *In the oracle room of Delphi, inspired by the breath of Apollo, Pythia spoke mysterious prophecies to pilgrims who sought advice.*

The Greek biographer and philosopher Plutarch (around AD 46–120) belonged to the select group of priests entrusted with the supervision of the Delphi cult, and he described the rituals that took place. With the support of the temple servants, the priests first assessed whether those seeking advice had fulfilled all their duties, including ritual washings and the appropriate sacrifices. If everything was in order, an animal was slaughtered; by observing its reactions prior to the killing, the priests learned how Pythia was feeling. If the animal remained

Bending over, a Roman haruspex inspects the entrails of a sacrificial bull for divine messages. The liver of a sacrificial animal was considered especially meaningful for predictions of the future.

The early Romans prized the Sibylline Books, a collection of prophecies attributed to the legendary prophetess, the Sybil of Cumae – depicted in this painting by Michelangelo, from the ceiling of the Sistine Chapel in Rome.

Interpretive prophecies

The Romans were very interested in interpretive prophecy, a type of oracle that was based on noting certain signs in nature. These signs allowed a god to be invoked and asked for the gift of special knowledge. This manner of prophecy usually involved examining the entrails of sacrificial animals. Priests would come to conclusions based on the arrangement or appearance of the organs. Interpretive prophecy originated among the Babylonians as early as the 18th century BC, and was taken over by Etruscan priests, who were called haruspices. From the 4th century BC, the practice of interpretive prophecy was adopted by the Romans.

Each of these cultures attributed different meanings to the displays of sacrificial animal entrails. For the Babylonians, the structure of animal organs corresponded to the districts of their city. For the Etruscans, the entrails symbolised the houses of their gods in the skies; the haruspices examined the intestines to turn the decisions of the gods in various directions. In Rome, interpretive prophecy was a civic institution: when the oracle was consulted, the representative of the city informed the Roman Senate of the result, and the Senate decided on measures to be taken.

The Romans also adopted the Etruscan belief in unusual natural occurrences, or miracles. These were thought to express the anger of the gods, who then had to be pacified. For example, lightning came from Jupiter, the highest of the gods, as a sign that the gods were unhappy with humankind.

The will of the gods was also seen in the flight and the call of the birds, which were carefully observed and interpreted. This art of prophecy was called auspices, and was supervised by the augurs, a group of 16 priests. Only they knew the complicated and secret procedures of the auspices. Amazingly, the Romans based many of their political actions on predictions made by the augurs.

Prophecies through oracles have always been criticised. The priests who controlled the oracles attracted criticism for the power they held over pilgrims. Moreover, when archaeologists excavated at Delphi, they did not find the celebrated fissure in the ground.

Because supernatural phenomena tend to elude rational criticism, it is important to consider the psychological factor when it comes to questioning an oracle. It is well known that if humans place their trust in an omen, then its fulfilment becomes much more likely. A good example is our modern-day fondness for astrology, which reconciles knowledge about the stars with supernatural beliefs. Despite its shaky claims to authority, astrology has made triumphant progress since the time of the Renaissance.

calm, the consultation of the oracle was postponed; if the animal twitched, the oracle was consulted right away.

Pythia performed her cleansing rituals and took steam baths before descending into the Adyton, an underground chamber, which was allegedly sited over the natural fissure in the ground. Contemporary accounts say that a supernatural wind blew from the fissure, and this may have been volcanic gases escaping. Pythia would sit on a stone, and, intoxicated by the vapours, fall into a trance and stammer a string of incomprehensible words. It was up to the priests to translate her utterances into enigmatic prophecies, which could then be interpreted.

For the Romans, inspirational prophecy centred on the prophetic books named after a mythical Greek priestess named Sibyl. Given the gift of prophecy by Apollo, Sibyl was thought to have written down many prophecies or oracles, which were expressed as riddles. The name of Sibyl was claimed by many places, but the prophetic books are associated with the Sibyl of Cumae, who offered nine books of prophecy to Tarquinius Superbus, the last of the early kings of Rome. The king bought three books, which were kept in the Temple of Jupiter in Rome, to be consulted in times of crisis.

The Omphalos, a sacred stone that the Greeks proudly called the navel of the world, was located within the famous temple of Apollo at Delphi. These columns surrounded the holy shrine.

THE PROPHETS

An awesome responsibility is borne by those selected to become prophets and proclaim the word of God. In many religions, these charismatic individuals have acted as the interpreters of divine will, mediating between the people and the heavenly powers.

Through his divine inspiration, Buddha stood out in an impure world. His teachings gave rise to a religion which is practised by 333 million people.

As the recipients and proclaimers of the will of the gods, prophets have existed in virtually all cultures. In ancient Greece, for example, the role of prophet was taken by the priestesses of the sites of the oracle. But nowhere did prophets enjoy such an important role as in ancient Israel.

Whether Abraham, Moses, Nathan or Isaiah – the prophets of the Old Testament received divine revelations which they passed on to the people through words and deeds. They demanded justice, criticised the kings, warned the sinful Israelites to turn back, announced imminent divine judgements or inspired hope for the return of the Messiah.

The quality that marked the prophets as different from ordinary people was their outstanding sense of mission. Generally, a prophet received his calling in the form of a vision, or he heard the voice of God inside his head. Often they received the message of the Lord in the solitude of mountains or deserts. God appeared to the prophet Moses in the form of a burning bush, and told Moses to go forth and free the people of Israel from Egyptian slavery and lead them to the Holy Land. Individuals chosen to be prophets had charismatic qualities that enabled them to proclaim the word of God and carry out divine missions.

Fighting for justice

Once they had received divine inspiration, the prophets could often foretell events. But this was only part of their task. Their revelations also exposed hidden truths and communicated them to the people. When events had to be explained, the prophets often resorted to descriptions of the Last Judgement. Their attempts to influence contemporary events often brought them into conflict with political authorities. The prophet Jeremiah, for example, narrowly escaped death when he preached the downfall of Judah, the southern kingdom of the Israelites, which was ruled by King Jehoiakim.

The prophets of the Old Testament were not always successful in awakening a sense of justice among the people. Nevertheless, they set an example through their high ethical conduct, and gave rise to ideals that survive today.

In many ways, these fierce old prophets resemble the prophet Mohammed (AD 570–632), who is regarded as the founder of Islam. From AD 610, Mohammed received a series of divine revelations that told him that he had been chosen as God's messenger to lead the Arabs to a new faith. He preached the message that there is one God – whose name is Allah – warned people against the worship of many gods and advised them to lead an ethical life. Islam recognises other prophets, particularly Abraham, Moses and Jesus Christ, whose life and work can serve as a guide for Muslim believers in matters of correct behaviour.

This image of the prophet Moses was painted in the 14th century by Simone Martini, an Italian artist of the early Renaissance period.

The prophets of the Old Testament

The books of Joshua, Judges, and Kings in the Old Testament contain the statements and actions of the 'earlier' or pre-classical prophets of old Israel, who lived between the 13th and 15th centuries BC. These were written down at a much later period, however. There is also a group of 'later' prophets, who lived from the 8th to the 6th century BC, and are classified as 'greater' or 'lesser', depending on the extent of their written pronouncements. The great prophets are Isaiah, Jeremiah, Ezekiel and Daniel; the 12 lesser prophets are Hosea, Joel, Amos, Obadiah, Jonah, Micah, Nahum, Habakkuk, Zephaniah, Haggai, Zacharias and Malachi.

THE SECRETS OF THE DANCING DERVISHES

The whirling dance of the dervishes symbolises mystic devotion and an ecstatic union with the divine. Although suppressed for many years, the ritual of the sama has survived, and offers a glimpse of the Sufi mystical practices developed in the 13th century by Jalal ad-Din Rumi.

Although they are a celebrated part of Turkish culture, the dancing or whirling dervishes are the modern inheritors of a mystical movement that began in Persia (now Iran). In Turkish, the word 'dervish' means beggar, and comes from a Persian word for 'wandering monk'. The movement grew out of Sufism, a branch of Islam based on direct personal experience of God.

When the Persian poet and mystic Jalal ad-Din Rumi (1207–1273), also known as Maulavi, came to the Turkish city of Konya, then the centre of the empire of the Seljuk Turks, he founded the order of Maulawiyah, which has come to be known as the so-called whirling dervishes – one of many dervish orders inspired by Sufism. Members strived for a mystical union with God through music, dancing and ecstasy, and soon gained popularity. The dervishes wore plain woollen gowns (*suf*), which stood out against the refined, luxurious society of the Seljuk court.

The political attitude of the dervishes had considerable influence under the Ottoman empire. Sometimes the members of the brotherhood supported the policies of the sultan, while at other times they offered fierce resistance. In 1925, Kemal Ataturk (1881–1938), the father of modern Turkey, outlawed the brotherhood of Maulawiyah. Nevertheless, Rumi's death is commemorated each year in December with festivities in which the dervishes perform their mystical whirling dances.

Mysticism of remembrance

The devotion of the dervishes is founded on the idea that there is a spark of divinity within the soul, and that this knowledge must be released for man to achieve perfection. Believers require the guidance of a master familiar with the ritual called *sama*, or 'listening to music', a mystical dance composition.

To the sound of music, the dervishes, clad in black gowns and their distinctive conical felt hats, first quickly walk three rounds. Then they take off their gowns, revealing the white

A 16th-century Turkish miniature shows the various gestures of the dance of the dervishes, which always have a symbolic meaning.

garments underneath. Three dances follow, in which the dervishes extend their arms – the right hand towards the heavens, the left towards the earth. All the time, the dancers whirl around in ever-faster circles. The master joins them in the last round, while turning on the middle line, halving the circle described by the dervishes. The purpose of the dance is to train the spirit to feel the divine. Its hidden pictorial language urges the spirit to discover how the world both conceals and reveals its creator.

The sama consists of three sections. The first signifies the blinding of consciousness. In the second, the music is a means of transforming the senses. The cleansing of the soul takes place in the last section. The sight of the white gown under the black cloak symbolises that the dervish is free of his body, and ready for rebirth.

The whirling of the dervishes symbolises the rotation of the planets. The position of the master indicates that all is an illusion: he stays in the centre, as a symbol for God – the reality which every perfect man resembles. The position of the hands is important: the right hand is the one that receives divine grace, while the left passes it on to the world. They symbolise the passing of wisdom from a master to his disciple, and the point where heaven and earth meet.

In the finale of the sama, *the dervishes receive the highest truth under the guidance of their master, who stands in the centre.*

WONDERS OF INDIA'S SADHUS

Science has yet to explain the extraordinary abilities and feats of the sadhus, the Hindu holy men of India. With their matted hair, they present a startling appearance, but even more startling is their ability to meditate on beds of nails, subject themselves to unusual bodily torments and commit themselves to rigorous ascetic practices.

More than 85% of India's population are classified as Hindu, and Hinduism is considered one of the world's great religions. Unlike Christianity or Islam – the great monotheistic faiths – Hindus worship a multitude of gods, and there is a wide variety of religious practices and observances. One of the most fascinating groups within Hinduism are the *sadhus* (literally, the 'good ones'), extremely devout individuals whose religious conviction causes them to give up their jobs and possessions and live as hermits or wandering ascetics.

The sadhus strive to experience *samadhi*, the point of complete unity with Brahma, who is one of the supreme gods in the Hindu pantheon. In achieving samadhi, a sadhu realises that his soul rests entirely within the creator. Sadhus view any other goal in life as senseless and useless.

These men take vows of poverty and are revered as holy men by their fellow Hindus. Sadhus eat a completely vegetarian diet because of their respect for all living things. They voluntarily give up earthly pleasures to follow the difficult path of asceticism, the object of which is deliverance and eternal bliss. They believe in reincarnation – which is a basic principle of Hinduism – and their goal is to free themselves from the endless circle of rebirth.

Sadhus are usually older Hindu men who have left their jobs and families to pursue an ideal – the renunciation

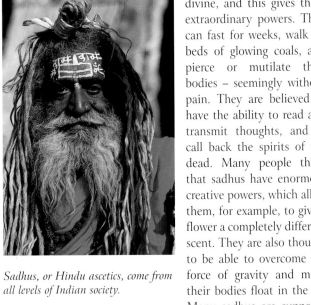

Sadhus, or Hindu ascetics, come from all levels of Indian society.

of worldly things. Many perform strict rites of repentance and live alone, while others undertake communal pilgrimages to Hindu holy sites. Devout Hindus often visit the retreats of holy men as part of the ordinary round of daily worship.

Extraordinary powers

For the sadhus, the entire universe is driven by the urge to unite with the divine, and this gives them extraordinary powers. They can fast for weeks, walk on beds of glowing coals, and pierce or mutilate their bodies – seemingly without pain. They are believed to have the ability to read and transmit thoughts, and to call back the spirits of the dead. Many people think that sadhus have enormous creative powers, which allow them, for example, to give a flower a completely different scent. They are also thought to be able to overcome the force of gravity and make their bodies float in the air. Many sadhus are supposed to be able to duplicate themselves and appear in two places at once.

Researchers in the field of parapsychology have studied the mysterious abilities of these holy men, and have confirmed many of these astonishing observations. Modern science, however, generally rejects any notion that the sadhus possess any special extrasensory abilities, because this goes against our rationalistic mode of thought. For Hindus, though, the abilities of the sadhus are certainly not seen as unusual. Indeed, all the holy scriptures of Hinduism – which include the *Vedas*, the *Upanishads* and the *Bhagavad-Gita* – agree that the human soul, the self (*atman*), is identical with the cosmic principle, the absolute (*brahman*).

Perhaps there is a lesson for the sceptics here, for it seems that the deeper we probe into the enigmas of human life, the closer we come to the mysterious and unacknowledged forces that dwell within us all.

Meditating sadhus are often seen along the banks of the River Ganges.

HOLY PLACES OF THE WORLD

In all the world's great religions, the sublime face of God has made itself visible on earth in the form of certain holy places. Today, large numbers of pilgrims journey to the world's holy sites, where they find comfort, spiritual healing and divine inspiration.

From the earliest times, people believed that the gods dwelt in nature, and revealed themselves at natural features. The first holy places were particular mountains and stones, groves of trees, rivers and lakes, caves and springs. Later on, as human society developed, people began to build temples to honour their gods, often choosing places where events of religious significance had occurred. The faithful came to these holy sites to enjoy communion with the divine, which seemed more present at the holy places than in the world of everyday life.

An apostle's grave

Rome was a metropolis long before it became the headquarters of Christianity. The change occurred in AD 324, when Roman emperor Constantine the Great (AD 280–337) issued the Edict of Milan, which recognised the previously outlawed Christian sect. As a fitting home for the empire's new official religion, Constantine ordered a great basilica to be built on the Vatican Hill, which lies on the west bank of the Tiber River. The new church was built on the spot where it was thought that the Apostle Peter lay buried. In time, Rome became an important place of pilgrimage and later the seat of the Popes, who, according to Catholic doctrine, are the successors to St Peter's Holy See.

Above: Jerusalem, with the Dome of the Rock in the foreground, contains sites holy to Judaism, Islam and Christianity. St Peter's Basilica in Rome (below) is one of the most important Christian places of pilgrimage.

Today, pilgrims come from all over the world to St Peter's Basilica, which was rebuilt with an imposing dome in the 16th century. The church was completed by the renowned Italian Renaissance painter and sculptor Michelangelo (1475–1564), who painted the ceiling of the adjoining Sistine Chapel. Until recently, St Peter's was the largest church in the world, and it is still the architectural and spiritual centre of the walled Vatican City, with its complex of palaces and parks. The Pope continues to celebrate holy mass in the Church of the Holy Sepulchre of the Apostle Peter, and he is present when priests and bishops are ordained. Today, the Vatican is the world's smallest independent state; from here, the Pope presides over almost a thousand million Roman Catholics – by far the largest religious community in the world.

City of three faiths

In the course of nearly 4,000 years of history, Jerusalem has been the holy city for three world religions – Judaism, Christianity and Islam. It has been fought over in many wars, and its political status is still in dispute.

In the 10th century BC, King David brought the Ark of Jehovah to Jerusalem as a sign of the presence of God. Later, King Solomon built his famous temple here, and the city developed into the cultural and religious centre of Judaism. After a long siege, the Romans destroyed Jerusalem in AD 70. The only part of the Temple still standing is the western wall, and it is one of the most important places of pilgrimage and prayer for

The Ark of the Covenant

Before King Solomon built the Temple in Jerusalem, the Israelites' most sacred relic was the holy ark, which was built by the prophet Moses to house the stone tablets on which the Ten Commandments were inscribed. Fashioned from acacia wood, the ark consisted of a box with two carrying poles attached. The ark was regarded as the site of the presence of God, and was taken along whenever the Israelites went to war. Later, the ark was placed in the Temple, but it disappeared for ever in the 6th century BC when the Babylonians raided Jerusalem and burnt down the Temple.

Jews. Known as the Wailing Wall, it is the place where Jews lament the loss of their sanctuary and the scattering of their people.

As the site of the Passion of Jesus Christ, the Old City of Jerusalem contains many sites that are holy to Christians. Emperor Constantine built the magnificent Church of the Holy Sepulchre between AD 326 and 353 on the site where Christ was believed to have been crucified and buried. Jerusalem remained a Christian city for about 300 years, until it was conquered by the Arabs in 637. The Arabs declared it the second holiest site in Islam – the other being Mecca. They built the Dome of the Rock on the site where the prophet Abraham prepared to sacrifice his son Isaac, as described in the Bible, and where the Koran reports that the prophet Mohammed rose to heaven. This splendid mosque, with its landmark golden dome, is the centre of Muslim Jerusalem.

No entry for infidels

The city of Mecca on the Arabian Peninsula is the holy city of Islam. As the birthplace of the prophet Mohammed, it is the chief holy site for the world's Muslims. Its importance is signalled by the fact that, five times daily, no matter where they are in the world, the faithful bow their heads and turn in the direction of Mecca.

According to Islamic law, each believer should make the *haj*, or pilgrimage, to the holiest sites of Islam at least once in their lifetime. Only poverty or a severe illness releases them from this obligation. Each year, about 2 million of the faithful converge on Mecca. Non-Muslims, however, are strictly forbidden from entering the holy city.

The climax of the haj takes place when pilgrims walk seven times around the Kaaba, a cube-shaped structure draped in black in the courtyard of Mecca's Great Mosque. Pilgrims come to touch and kiss the Black Stone, a chunk of a meteorite mounted in the Kaaba's south-eastern corner.

India's holy river

Hinduism is the main religion of India. Over the centuries, it has evolved to the point where it encompasses a range of smaller groups. Each has its own deity and holy sites.

The most popular place of pilgrimage for the Hindus is the holy city of Varanasi (Benares), in northern India, which has an enormous temple district with more than 1,500 shrines. Stone steps lead down to the River Ganges, which, according to Hindu mythology, issues from the foot of the benevolent God Vishnu, and is worshipped as a holy river.

Thousands of faithful Hindus come to Varanasi, one of the seven holy cities of India, to ritually cleanse themselves in the sacred waters of the River Ganges.

Pilgrims journey to Varanasi for ritual cleansing in the waters of the Ganges, to pray on its banks, and to meditate. Many come here to die, in the belief that they will be freed from the cycle of rebirth. Corpses are wrapped in linen and burned along the shore; the ashes are scattered in the river.

There are many holy sites throughout the world. The one thing they have in common is that people come to them to seek traces of the divine, in order to give a higher meaning to their lives. By going to a holy place, the pilgrim gets a glimpse of the world beyond.

The world's holiest places also have a political side, but their very existence makes them tokens of faith. Making a pilgrimage gives people a feeling of belonging to a community. The churches, mosques and temples all testify to the enduring power of the world's great religions.

Pilgrims circle the black-draped Kaaba in Mecca's Great Mosque. Here, the presence of God is revealed to the faithful, for the cube-shaped building is Allah's earthly home.

MIRACLE CURES

From the shrines of ancient Greece and the holy wells of the Celts to the modern shrine of Lourdes, a willingness to believe in miraculous cures is as old as humanity itself. Even with the advances made by modern medicine, there are still people who cling to such beliefs. Today, faith healing still flourishes, particularly in cases of afflictions for which modern medical science has found no effective treatment.

Centuries before the first Christian places of pilgrimage were established, there were religious sites known for their miracle cures. In ancient Greece, pilgrims streamed to the world-famous place of healing at Epidaurus. There they hoped to be healed by the divine powers that resided in the sanctuary of Asclepius, the god of healing and the son of the god Apollo. The shrine of Asclepius flourished as a therapeutic centre in the 4th century BC. Pilgrims were only allowed into the temple after thorough preparation through fasting, prayer, cleansing in the holy spring and the offering of sacrifices. In a hall known as the Abaton, patients lay down on animal skins and waited for the instructions of Asclepius, who was supposed to appear in their dreams. They told the contents of their dreams to the priests, who then decided on the appropriate treatment.

Around 291 BC, the cult of Asclepius was brought to Rome, and the god continued to be worshipped as Aesculapius. His symbol, a rod with a snake wound around it, is the universal symbol of medical doctors. In the 3rd century BC, the cult of the Egyptian god Serapis became popular in the Greek world, and enjoyed a status similar to that of the cult of Asclepius.

From heathen to Christian

The Celtic people of ancient Gaul (modern France), which was a Roman province from the first century BC, worshipped maternal goddesses who presided over springs and fountains thought to possess healing powers.

Such springs were widespread in the British Isles, which were also home to the Celts. Mistletoe (*Viscum album*), a parasitic plant which grows on trees, served the Gauls as a talisman and was used as a medication. From the 2nd century AD, these Celtic practices became increasingly Christianised. Thus, it is possible to trace certain places of pilgrimage, such as the famous French village of Lourdes, where the peasant girl Bernadette Soubirous had a vision of the Virgin Mary in a grotto in 1858, back to ancient Celtic rites held at holy springs.

When they embraced Christianity, the Celts often dedicated their places of worship to the new God. The shrine was not moved, and the only difference was that the healing powers were now attributed to Christian saints. Documents from the early Christian period tell how saints spontaneously healed people suffering from nervous or infectious illnesses by laying their hands on the person or blessing them. Indeed the performance of miracles such as cures was considered an essential condition for becoming a saint. Miraculous cures were reported by people who had spent the night lying in front of the grave of a saint, in order to witness divine revelation in a dream.

Another fertile area of miracles was that of holy relics, which were thought to possess healing powers when a person touched them. When they visited an important shrine, pilgrims often brought back religious artefacts – a piece of a saint's robe, a bone, a stone from a holy grave, even a fragment of the cross on which Jesus was crucified – believing without question that the supernatural powers contained in these relics would continue to benefit them.

A marble frieze from Piraeus, in Greece, shows Asclepius, the god of healing, appearing to a sleeping patient in a dream.

In the late Middle Ages, the king of France was popularly believed to possess the remarkable ability to cure scrofula, a form of tuberculosis which affects the lymphatic glands, producing painful swellings in the neck. This misconception arose after the Capet family, which ruled France from the late 10th century, claimed to be anointed with an oil sent from heaven that granted their dynasty a divine nature. Nevertheless, similar healing powers were ascribed to many

Above: *The French king Henry II (1519–1559) lays his hand on a man afflicted with scrofula. In the 16th century, the motto of the French ruling dynasty was 'The King touches you, God heals you'.*

Right: *Through miraculous cures – such as giving the gift of sight to two blind men – Jesus Christ announced himself as the saviour of mankind.*

Modern medicine in ancient Greece

It may be hard to believe, but some of the miracles performed in ancient times have a scientific basis. There is evidence to indicate that the miracle cures performed in the ancient therapeutic centre of Epidaurus were made possible through the use of psychosomatic and psychotherapeutic methods – techniques used by modern medicine. Reports of cures indicate that the priests of the shrine of Asclepius used fasting and sleep therapy to treat their patients, whose ailments seem to have been mostly psychological or nervous in origin.

European monarchs, and, as late as the 17th century, ceremonies were held in which a sovereign would lay his or her hands on the sick and diseased.

In modern times, many a self-proclaimed healer has used shady practices to make money at the expense of people who believe in miracles. Even in ancient times, the custodians of healing sanctuaries realised that the granting of miracles required an economic system of payments (the sacrifice) and performances (the cure).

A sign of God's rule

Miracles have long played an important role in religious belief, for they provide proof of supernatural powers. Generally, a miracle is defined as an extraordinary event or occurrence that goes against human experience and the laws of nature. In the religious sense, miracles represent a human encounter with the divine, a realm which lies outside everyday experience.

In the Bible, miracles occur when God decides to help or punish his creatures. According to the Old Testament, God provided the prophet Moses with the ability to perform miracles. These included the nine plagues sent to torment the Egyptians and convince them to free the people of Israel from captivity. Moses miraculously parted the waters of the Red Sea to lead his people through the desert to the promised land of Canaan.

In the New Testament, it is taken for granted that Jesus can perform miracles. His ability to awaken the dead, restore eyesight to the blind and make the lame walk are signs of God's mercy, and indicate Jesus's divine mission as the saviour of mankind. By performing miraculous cures, Jesus announces to all

those who are downtrodden or burdened that the Kingdom of God on earth has come, re-establishing the divine order in this world.

Mind over matter

In earlier times, miraculous cures provided people with many different ideas about the cause, diagnosis and treatment of illnesses. Due to the great advances that have been made in medicine, this only plays a small role in modern Christianity. Beginning in the 1970s, however, interest revived in a variety of alternative cures, where philosophies with a religious bent played a central role.

Psychological factors can have a strong influence on mental and physical processes, and play an important part in miracle cures. If, for example, a person recalls the miracles that have taken place at the site he or she is visiting, this gives them the hope of sharing in divine grace. The more than 2 million pilgrims who travel to Lourdes every year do not consider their journey as useless; the Catholic Church has recognised about 60 cures at Lourdes as genuine miracles.

If a person suffers from a condition for which doctors can provide no relief, then the search for divine miracle cures releases them from physical and mental suffering. Perhaps a belief in miracles, which lie beyond rational experience, is an effective way of dealing with pain that defies rationality.

The shrine of Lourdes, renowned for the miraculous cures that have been reported there, attracts millions of pilgrims.

PILGRIMAGES: A QUAINT ANACHRONISM OR TOKEN OF ENDURING FAITH?

The phenomenon of pilgrimages shows no sign of dying out. Indeed, new sites are constantly springing up. While sceptics might argue that these journeys of faith are old-fashioned, making a pilgrimage seems to answer a deep-seated spiritual need in many Christians.

In the Middle Ages, making a pilgrimage to Rome or Jerusalem was considered to be the crowning achievement of a person's life. Today, millions of people – mainly Roman Catholics – travel each year to the leading shrines of the Christian world. Surprisingly, the phenomenon of Christian pilgrimage in the modern age has received little attention from sociologists, psychologists and other researchers who study human behaviour. But while there is little academic information available, the subject attracts a great deal of prejudice. Many people today see pilgrimage as simply a quaint relic of a bygone age, of a time when religion and the church still formed the unquestioned centre of people's lives. They may view the pilgrims as naive victims of charlatans and the flourishing pilgrimage industry.

Such a narrow view oversimplifies the situation, for pilgrimages are still very much part of the life of many Christians. The millions of people who set out on these journeys each year include not only regular church-goers, but also people who might ordinarily seem indifferent to religion – for example, the 7,000 French motorcyclists who ride through Brittany each year on August 15 in order to have their machines blessed by the Virgin Mary.

In fact, almost anybody can turn out to be a pilgrim, and the practice is definitely not limited to the naive, the unsophisticated and the gullible. Many groups of students and schoolchildren travel to the famous shrine of St James at Santiago de Compostela in northern Spain; groups of French students regularly visit the cathedral town of Chartres, outside Paris; and more than 20,000 soldiers visit the famed shrine at Lourdes every year, where they meditate on the meaning of the profession of arms. Clearly, there is more to pilgrimage than an outdated demonstration of blind faith.

Holy sites

There are numerous destinations for pilgrims, with around 6,000 sanctuaries in Europe alone. These are usually places where a person has seen the Virgin Mary, or where the tomb of a saint is allegedly to be found. Some of these holy places have a worldwide reputation, while others are hardly known outside their own country. In Ireland, the tiny village of Knock (An Cnoc), in County Mayo, has grown into one of the world's foremost Marian shrines, complete with a large basilica capable of holding 20,000 pilgrims. The shrine, which draws more than 1 million pilgrims annually, dates from 1879, when a number of villagers first reported seeing a vision of the Virgin Mary, St Joseph and St John the Evangelist. A much more obscure shrine is located in the Rue du Bac in the centre of Paris. Here, the Virgin Mary is said to have appeared before Sister Cathérine Labouré in the chapel of the Convent of the Sisters of Mercy of St Vincent of Paul in November 1830. Today around 1.3 million

Mass pilgrimages to the Black Madonna of Czestochowa are woven into the fabric of Polish life. For centuries, the Black Madonna has been the patroness of Poland.

people make the pilgrimage to this site every year.

Lourdes and Fátima

The Virgin Mary clearly occupies a special place for pilgrims. She is the focus of the two most famous European places of pilgrimage: the village of Lourdes in the south of France and the village of Fátima, located 115 km north of Portugal's capital, Lisbon. In 1858, the Holy Virgin appeared several times before 14-year-old Bernadette Soubirous at a grotto outside Lourdes. Shortly afterwards, the Roman Catholic Church granted permission for a sanctuary to be established at this location, as a destination for pilgrims. The Mother of God was never seen here again, but there have been numerous reports of miracles, usually in the form of inexplicable cures. Gradually, the village at the foot of the Pyrenees Mountains developed into Europe's major place of pilgrimage, and draws some 5.5 million pilgrims annually.

Each year, more than 1 million pilgrims make the journey to Fátima, where, on several occasions in 1917, the Virgin Mary appeared before a group of three children. Pilgrimages began in 1927, and a basilica was consecrated at the site in 1953. Between May and October, processions to the Chapel of Revelation take place on the 12th and 13th of each month.

The tidings of Mary

Sites such as Lourdes, Fátima and Knock are well established, but new apparitions of the Virgin are continually reported in a variety of locations. One of these is the town of San Damiano near Piacenza in northern Italy. There, on a fine autumn day in 1964, a woman named Rosa Quattrini saw the Holy Virgin several times in a fruit-laden pear tree, which promptly covered itself with blossoms. These amazing appearances were repeated until Mama Rosa's death in 1981. Since then, it is said that the Madonna appears every Saturday afternoon. Some pilgrims

The pilgrims who come to Civita-vecchia, in Italy, worship an image of the Madonna of Medjugorje, who cries bloody tears.

claim they can feel the Virgin's presence. Some position micro-phones in the direction they guess she might be found or take photographs in the hope of finding an image of the Madonna on the print. A number of self-appointed prophets claim to receive oral or written messages from the Madonna.

One of the most important new pilgrimage sites has been at Medjugorje, in Bosnia-Herzegovina (until 1991 a province of Yugoslavia). In the early 1980s, the Holy Virgin was seen by a group of six children. She told them to devote their lives to conversion and prayer. Some witnesses report that they still see the Madonna, and 500 miracles are officially claimed to have taken place there. Despite the war that ravaged Bosnia-Herzegovina, a steady flow of pilgrims has continued to flock to Medjugorje.

Miraculous tears

While making a pilgrimage to Medjugorje in 1994, a priest from Civitavecchia, a town near Rome, purchased a picture of the Madonna and gave it to a couple from his congregation, who placed the picture in their garden. To their great shock, on January 2, 1995 the picture began to weep red tears, which turned out to be human blood. After the tears had flowed a dozen times, there occurred a further miracle: the Communist mayor of the town ordered a sanctuary to be built on the site.

The tears of the Madonna of Civitavecchia are by no means unique. Since 1990, about 60 pictures have been reported to church authorities on the grounds that they allegedly weep bloody tears. These reports come from all over Europe and North America. While Pope John Paul II has described such occurrences as signs, there are good reasons to suspect fraud in many reports of miraculous tears of blood. Although there is good reason to be sceptical in many of these cases, hundreds of pilgrims immediately converge whenever drops of blood are reported.

The black Madonnas

Among images of grace, a special place belongs to the so-called black Madonnas, the most famous of which is undoubtedly the Black Madonna of Czestochowa, in Poland.

Tradition has it that the 14th-century icon of the Black Madonna of Czestochowa is the work of the Evangelist Luke.

The image is housed in the Chapel of Mary at the monastery of Jasna Gora in this industrial city in southern Poland. For Poles, the Black Madonna is more than a religious icon, it is the symbol of their country's

Pope John Paul II on pilgrimage

The spirit of pilgrimage is alive and well in Pope John Paul II. Not only has the Holy Father visited numerous countries, he has also made pilgrimages to many of the world's holy sites. In September 1995, 300,000 young people from 35 countries followed his call and gathered in Loreto, an Italian place of pilgrimage south of Ancona. On this occasion, the Pope was connected via conference lines to crowds of pilgrims in churches as far away as Belfast, Paris, Dresden, Santiago de Compostela and Sarajevo, who were able to see him on television screens.

Young people from all over the world gathered in September 1995 in Loreto, Italy.

independence. When the Protestant Swedes threatened to conquer Catholic Poland in 1656, only the fortress of Czestochowa withstood the foreign onslaught. Inspired by this symbol of defiance, the Poles took heart and defeated the enemy, naming the Virgin Mary the Mother of Victory and Queen of the Fatherland. Poles have made the pilgrimage to their Black Madonna ever since. In spite of numerous wars, occupation by the Nazis and decades of Communist rule, nothing has ever stopped the stream of pilgrims to Czestochowa.

The Black Madonna of Altötting, in the southern German state of Bavaria, is much older than Czestochowa's famous icon. Pilgrimages in honour of the soot-blackened Madonna have taken place since 1498, when a small boy drowned in a nearby stream but miraculously revived after his mother placed him on the altar of Mary.

Another area of pilgrimage concerns the tombs of saints. Many places have become sites of pilgrimage because the tomb of a saint is found there, or is thought to lie there.

For example, hundreds of thousands of pilgrims flock to St Peter's Basilica in Rome, which was established on the tomb of St Peter; and around 5 million pilgrims each year visit the last resting place of Saint Anthony in Padua or the tomb of St Francis in Assisi, both in Italy. In France, the burial place of St Martin of Tours on the Loire River is also a popular place of pilgrimage.

The Pilgrims' Way

Probably the most famous of these pilgrimages leads to the town of Santiago de Compostela in northern Spain, where a tomb believed to be that of St James was discovered in the 9th century. Historians have known for a long time that the Apostle never preached in Spain, but this has not affected the popularity of Santiago as a place of pilgrimage.

Since the Middle Ages, the faithful have trodden the so-called Pilgrims' Way to Santiago de Compostela, returning with a scallop shell – the symbol of St James. Many people still make the journey at least partially on foot, or by bicycle. Today, there are four official pilgrimage routes, which cross the rugged Pyrenees Mountains at Roncesvalles and Somport and then merge at the Spanish town of Puente la Reina, forming a single route – the *camino francés*, or 'French road' – leading to the shrine. The beautiful church has been declared a European cultural heritage site, and the route from Puente la Reina to Santiago has

Above: *The Baroque facade of the cathedral of Santiago de Compostela provides the backdrop for a gathering of pilgrims. Behind the facade lies the Pórtico de Gloria, one of the finest works of Romanesque architecture in Europe.*

Below: *Every spring since 1935, thousands of university and high school students have retraced the footsteps of the poet Charles Péguy (1873–1914) from Paris to Chartres.*

been designated a World Heritage Site by UNESCO, the cultural and educational agency of the United Nations.

Big business

The large number of sanctuaries and the millions of pilgrims have inevitably turned pilgrimage into a lively business. Lourdes underwent an economic boom after the initial appearance of the Virgin Mary, and the town has never looked back. Each year, 5 million hotel rooms are booked, huge amounts of money are donated to the shrine and some 800 tons of candles are sold. Many other holy places have also developed a trade in religious paraphernalia, consisting mainly of souvenirs and devotional objects.

What moves the pilgrims?

The sheer number of holy sites, some of which have attracted believers since the Middle Ages, together with the millions of pilgrims, indicate that pilgrimage is still an important force in the modern age. But there is no doubt that the reasons for making a pilgrimage have changed.

During the Middle Ages, pilgrims set out on their difficult journey to obtain eternal salvation for their souls. Today, many people decide to make a pilgrimage for personal reasons, or because they want to ask the Virgin Mary or the saints to cure them of an illness, or at least reduce their suffering. But even if they are not cured, many return from the journey feeling that their condition has improved. They feel that the prayers they spoke in the holy place were not in vain, and that God has heard them. Other pilgrims might have a request to make on behalf of a relative, or they may wish to thank God or Mary or the saints for healing an illness or relieving them of a great spiritual burden.

Apart from the fulfilment of personal wishes, each pilgrimage has another, deeper meaning. The journey is a withdrawal from everyday life in order to experience God and find a new dimension for one's own life. Furthermore, pilgrimages have always offered the opportunity for a special kind of human community. Many pilgrims gain strength from the presence of other people on their journey. These feelings of solidarity give them new hope and perseverance for the rest of their lives.

BACK FROM THE BRINK: A MIRACLE AT LOURDES

Since 1858, doctors have confirmed 3,500 cures at Lourdes. However, the Church has only acknowledged 65 of them as miracles. The most recent miracle cure took place in the mid-1970s, when a young girl from Sicily gallantly fought against a deadly tumour. Her story is an inspiring one, but the reasons behind such cures are the subject of much debate.

When doctors examined her right knee, their diagnosis was devastating. They informed Delizia Cirolli, an 11-year-old Sicilian girl, that she was suffering from bone cancer. It seemed that nothing could halt the disease. Then, in August, 1976, Delizia's mother took her on a pilgrimage to the famed shrine of Lourdes, in southern France. At first, there seemed to be no improvement in the girl's condition. However, a short time later, she regained the ability to walk without pain, and X-rays showed that the cancerous tumour had inexplicably disappeared.

A medical commission immediately began to investigate the girl's case to determine whether she was completely cured. By the end of the year, they issued a report. All the doctors who studied the files on Delizia's illness felt the same: there had never been a spontaneous healing in a malignant tumour of the kind the girl had been suffering from. In July 1980, the doctors' report came to the following conclusion: 'considering the conditions under which it occurred and took place', the cure was 'a phenomenon contradictory to all observations and prognoses based on medical experience, and scientifically inexplicable'.

In the spring of 1982, doctors from Delizia's home diocese of Catania reached the same conclusion. They passed their report on to the medical committee of Lourdes, as well as to other medical bodies connected to the bishops of Lourdes and Tarbes, who also confirmed the findings. The question on everybody's minds was whether this case could be considered a miracle.

Delizia Cirolli as a pilgrim in Lourdes after her cure.

In a situation such as this, the Church authorities have to take a public position. The bishop of Catania had to make an announcement as to whether he attributed the cure to divine intervention or not. In 1989, Monsignore Luigi Bommarto declared that Delizia had indeed been afflicted and that her cure was miraculous.

Debate among doctors

The decision to declare a miracle depends very much on the opinions of doctors. Effectively, it is the doctors who have to decide whether a miracle has occurred in a specific case or not. Of course, individual physicians can have quite different attitudes. Some might deny the extraordinary nature of a supposed cure, claiming, for example, that in pathology there is no such thing as a normal case, and there are thus no 'normal' or 'abnormal' processes. They would argue that numerous aspects of the body's healing processes are still not fully understood, and that it would be reckless to ascribe a cure to divine intervention. Others accept that there may be such a thing as an extraordinary cure. They categorise such cases either as spontaneous healings, for which there is no scientific explanation, but only a religious one, or they take the view that the patient possesses certain spiritual powers: a strong healing faith or a kind of autosuggestion. Whatever their explanation, doctors are put into the difficult position of having to decide whether to place their faith either in the powers of God or of man.

THE MIRACULOUS BLOOD OF ST JANUARIUS

The carefully preserved blood of St Januarius first returned to liquid form 11 years after his martyrdom in AD 304 at the hands of the Romans. Since 1389, the people of the Italian city of Naples have celebrated the annual repetition of this astounding miracle. While sceptics search for a rational explanation, it is still not possible to prove whether this is a natural phenomenon or a miracle.

According to legend, Januarius, Bishop of Benevent, near Pozzuoli in southern Italy, was decapitated in AD 304 during the persecution of Christians by the Roman emperor Diocletian. A local woman collected Januarius's blood in a number of flasks, which she put in a safe place. Eleven years later, when the martyr's body was to be moved to the city of Naples, a few kilometres to the east, the woman decided to hand the flasks over to the bishop. When they were placed next to the head of the saint, the bishop noted with great surprise that the blood in the flasks had turned to a liquid. This remarkable occurrence almost defies belief, for it goes against nature itself. It is easy to understand why at the time it was considered a miracle.

For more than 1,000 years, no-one noticed anything remarkable about the blood. But when a cathedral was built in honour of San Gennaro – as St Januarius is known in Italy – during the 14th century, the blood miracle took place once again. Since that time, it has occurred regularly on holy days associated with the saint, including the Saturday before the first Sunday in May, September 19 and December 16. On these days, the head and blood of the saint are placed on the cathedral altar. Then a priest turns over the flasks containing the saint's blood, so everyone in the congregation can see when the substance it contains has completely liquefied. The believers begin to pray that the miracle will occur, and, soon after, the substance flows down the sides of the flasks.

A picture of blood

There have been other blood miracles, but none as artistic as that which occurred around 1330 in Walldürn, a small German town located southwest of Würzburg. Tradition has it that a young priest knocked over the flask of communion wine while he was celebrating Mass. The consecrated wine – which is seen as the blood of Jesus – spilled over a linen cloth draped over the altar. Miraculously, the liquid formed the image of Christ on the cross, surrounded by 11 smaller images of his divine head wearing the crown of thorns. To commemorate this event, the Church of the Holy Blood was built in Walldürn.

Whenever supposed miracles occur, there are always two sides. The believers explain the event by way of the divine nature of the object, in this case the martyr's blood, and they need no further explanation. Sceptics, however, doubt the divine nature of events and seek a more down-to-earth explanation.

Clever manipulation?

Cynics suspect that the miracle of the blood is carefully manipulated. They point to other cases in southern Italy, where the preserved blood of saints supposedly behaves in a similar manner. There are even cases where the blood will liquefy more or less on demand. In their opinion, the miracle is staged by mixing water and insoluble chalk or a chemical in the flask, or perhaps someone switches the ampoule of dried blood for another which is filled with liquid. Some suggest that there are red wax particles in the vessels, which gradually melt in the warmth of the many candles.

Most sceptics, however, do not wish to accuse anyone of fraud, and they take the view that the faithful crowd is actually experiencing a collective hallucination.

Several times each year, the head and blood relics of St Januarius are carried in a popular procession through the streets of Naples.

WONDROUS VISIONS OF THE VIRGIN MARY

Sometimes she appears on a mountain, or suspended above a bush, her presence heralded by an unusual wind. Appearances of the Virgin Mary have become more frequent over the centuries, but the Catholic Church views such events with caution. Sceptics see them as a kind of hallucination, but progressive theologians urge a broad-minded approach.

Since the early days of Christianity, there have been many reports of appearances of the Virgin Mary, mother of Jesus Christ. Amazingly, these reports generally describe the Holy Virgin as a physical being. While there were only 300 such apparitions recorded during the first 1,700 years since the time of Christ, the number rose sharply during the mid-19th century. In the 20th century, there were 445 cases reported. Researchers have put forward two theories for this tremendous increase: on the one hand, the 19th century saw the church authorities undertake a systematic examination of appearances of Mary, while on the other hand, Pope Pius IX proclaimed the dogma of immaculate conception in 1854. This stated that Mary had remained without sin and in a state of grace from the beginning of her life. The Catholic Church itself acknowledges a direct connection between the proclamation of this dogma and the increase in the appearances of the Virgin, although it now takes a cautious approach to the phenomenon.

Parallels and symbols

Although the individual circumstances differ, descriptions of the appearances of Mary have a number of features in common. For example, the Holy Virgin frequently appears in the open air, usually in a rural setting, sometimes in a cave, and generally slightly above the observers' heads – on a cloud, mountain top, tree or bush.

Those who have experienced such visions report that Mary's approach is announced by certain natural phenomena – a sudden breeze or stormy wind, a bolt of lightning or a gentle glow of light. The light phenomena

that occurred at Fátima in Portugal in 1917 were particularly spectacular. During the event, 70,000 witnesses and countless others within a radius of 50 km reported that the sun rotated three times around itself.

In most cases, witnesses describe Mary as a beautiful young woman. She almost always wears a long garment, sometimes also a cloak of white or blue, which is why she is sometimes referred to as the Madonna of the cloak. Mary often carries other symbolic objects, such as a crown, cross, sword or a flaming heart, which she holds in her hands.

Another remarkable aspect of these apparitions is that the Madonna resembles a living being rather than a statue. She moves

Above left: *On November 27, 1830, the Madonna appeared to the nun Cathérine Labouré in the chapel of a convent in Paris.*

Above: *Bernadette Soubirous saw the Mother of God on several occasions in the grotto of Massabielle near the village of Lourdes.*

and speaks to those around her, and often beseeches them. For example, she has often told people to pray for the preservation of peace. In other cases, she has requested that a chapel or other sanctuary be built, a memorial in stone that will allow believers to retain their experience in a tangible way.

The appearance of the figure, as well as the message she bears, make it immediately clear to most witnesses that they are not dealing with a real historical figure, a flesh-and-blood person, but rather a supernatural being.

On May 13, 1917, the Virgin appeared to three shepherd children in Fátima. She admonished them to recite the rosary daily and pray for peace on earth, and promised that they would go to heaven.

In the first centuries of Christianity, most witnesses were men. However, since the 18th century, an increasing number of women and – in the past 120 years – children have reported appearances of Mary. All these visionaries share a deep sense of religious faith. They have often come from simple peasant families, and often have difficulty making those around them believe what they have experienced. This might help to explain the refutations that occur – sometimes, as in the case of Fátima, many years later.

Psychologists, theologians and others are particularly interested in experiences of children who have reported seeing the Virgin Mary. Since their life experience is much more limited and their minds more open than adults, they are more likely to give an unbiased account of the event. In contrast, adults are much more likely to embellish a vision with their personal religious ideas – perhaps without even realising what they are doing.

Various stances

Even sceptical individuals have to admit that there are many mysteries in heaven and on earth, but they resolutely seek out rational explanations for them. In their view, appearances of the Virgin are in fact images projected by the unconscious mind. Those who report an apparition are actually projecting an intense inner desire onto an external image, perhaps due to their overwhelming or heightened religious emotions. Many scientists believe that a person's expectations can create an object in this way. For this reason, the appearance of the Virgin often resembles traditional models, such as are found in religious paintings.

Although it hailed such apparitions in the past, the modern Catholic Church treats the many reports of appearances of Mary with a great deal of reservation. Before the Church will recognise a vision as genuine, a number of points must be clarified. The Church investigates the trustworthiness of the person in question, as well as asking if the appearance contradicts church dogma and if the message will have a positive effect.

Among the best-known examples that have fulfilled these strict criteria are the appearances of Mary at Lourdes in southern France in 1858 and at Fátima in Portugal in 1917. While the Madonna appeared several times to 14-year-old Bernadette Soubirous at Lourdes, three children were involved in the six visions at Fátima: 10-year-old Lúcia dos Santos, her 9-year-old cousin Francisco Marto and his 7-year-old sister Jacinta.

Popular pressure

But even if the Church does not recognise the visions as genuine, the places where they have occurred often become places of pilgrimage anyway. This is the case with San Damiano in Italy and Zeitoun in Egypt. Despite their lack of formal approval from the church, such sites prove extremely attractive in popular experiences of faith.

A number of progressive-minded Catholic theologians consider it wrong for the Church to apply such strict criteria to appearances of the Virgin. They feel that the decisive point is not the genuineness of the appearance, but the fact that the vision represents an authentic experience of faith that allows the witness to encounter God as an immediate and tangible presence. For the average believer, these events often act as a catalyst, allowing them to experience the works of God in the world. In this way, the witness plays a vital role in mediating between divine and human reality.

The ascension of Mary

About a century after the publication of the dogma of the immaculate conception, another important article of faith concerning the Mother of God was accepted by the Catholic Church. On All Saints' Day (November 1), 1950, Pope Pius XII announced as 'the truth revealed by God', that Mary had been accepted body and soul into heaven. This dogma was intended to document the unique status of Mary as the Mother of the Son of God. It acknowledges an ancient tradition that was already popular among Christians in the 6th century, according to which Mary, like Jesus Christ, rose to heaven at the end of her earthly life. Catholics celebrate the ascension of Mary each year on August 15.

THE MYSTERY OF STIGMATISATION

In one of the most bizarre phenomena ever recorded, hundreds of devout Christians have reported that the wounds suffered by Christ have spontaneously appeared on their bodies. It is still unclear whether these wounds, or stigmata, are self-inflicted, or if they really come from God.

When we say that a person bears the stigma of guilt or failure, we really mean that the person has been marked by a particular experience. In the purely physical sense, a stigma is a mark or brand that is cut or burned onto the skin. There are many cultures that use stigmatisation, or scarring, to decorate the body, to signify membership in a tribe or social group or to designate slaves or criminals.

In the art of the Renaissance, St Francis is often shown at the moment of stigmatisation.

In the Christian religion, stigmatisation has a specific meaning: it refers to bleeding wounds that regularly appear in the same places – the head and feet, sides and forehead and the shoulders and back. The origin of these signs is connected to an ecstatic experience of the Passion of Christ, and the wounds correspond to those suffered by Jesus Christ when he was beaten and nailed to the cross. In his letter to the Galatians, contained in the New Testament, the Apostle Paul wrote that he bore the stigmata of Christ on his body. He was referring to the wounds that he had suffered in his mission to spread the word of Christ.

The first stigmata

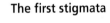

The first proven case of spontaneous stigmatisation was that of St Francis of Assisi (around 1181–1226), founder of the Franciscan order of monks. In mid-September, 1224, the saint went into solitude at Mount Laverna near Arezzo in Tuscany to fast and pray. In a vision, he saw a crucified angel. Deeply moved, he began to meditate on the Passion of Christ, and noticed how the marks of the crucifixion appeared on his skin. For the rest of his life, he tried to hide the wounds from his brothers, but many were able to observe them at the moment of his death, as he lay naked on the ground.

According to Brother Elias, the minister general of the young order, the stigmata took the form of nail punctures on both hands and feet. Thomas of Celano, the author of the first official biography of St Francis, spoke of nails running right through his body, formed by extensions of the flesh.

The Franciscans have long emphasised the uniqueness of St Francis's stigmata, and the Catholic Church has responded cautiously. Nevertheless, there have been other incidents of stigmatisation since St Francis. To date, 320 have been noted, most of them women.

In the Middle Ages, the most celebrated cases were Elisabeth of Spalbeck, who died in 1274; a Dominican monk named Gauthier of Strasbourg (1324–1390); and Catherine of Siena (1347-1380), who wrote down her visions and ecstasies in the so-called *Dialogo*, the *Book of Divine Providence*. In modern times, the most famous cases have been those of Therese Neumann (1898–1962) from Germany's Rhineland region, and an Italian Franciscan monk by the name of Father Pio (1887–1968).

St Catherine of Siena is one of the most famous cases of stigmatisation.

Hidden causes

Virtually all cases of stigmatisation share certain features. Wounds appear at regular intervals on specific days, mainly Fridays, and above all on Good Friday. Gripped by religious ecstasy, the stigmatised person goes through the stages of the Passion. Sometimes he or she mimics the scenes of suffering or describes them in detail. The wounds do not become infected, but remain open and do not respond to medical treatment.

Scientists and experts have advanced a number of explanations for stigmatisation. Some see it quite simple as a fraud, while others regard it as the effect of hysterical neuroses. Still others believe that a psycho-physiological mechanism is at work: a believer's obsession with the events of the Passion may allow images of the crucifixion to be transferred from the mind into bodily processes. In spite of its reservations, the Catholic Church admits that God might make use of an individual predisposition towards stigmatisation.

ECSTATIC LEVITATION

Is it possible that the feeling of nearness to God can literally lift a person off the ground? Many people have described such experiences, which generally occurred when they were deep in the ecstasy of prayer. Can certain individuals harness the power of levitation, or has God set aside physical principles?

The idea of humans flying through the air may sound like science fiction, but there are too many documented cases for us to dismiss it as impossible. The technical name for overcoming the force of gravity is levitation, and most accounts of this startling phenomenon are to be found in connection with the legends and biographies of saints. For example, a 13th-century life of St Francis of Assisi (around 1181–1226), tells how the saint's body would sometimes lose contact with the ground. Another biography, which appeared roughly a century after his death, reports that Francis would float among the trees during prayer.

Unfortunately, descriptions of St Francis's levitation are somewhat vague. For a more detailed account, we can turn to the story of the Spanish nun and mystic, St Teresa of Avila (1515–1582). St Teresa recorded her personal experiences of religious ecstasy, including her levitation. Intensely immersed in the nearness of God, she would sometimes float for up to half an hour at a distance of several centimetres or even as much as half a metre above the ground. She was seized with terror when this happened for the first time, and tried hard to resist. However, the force of levitation proved stronger than she was. St Teresa later described the experience as a feeling of 'blissful lightness'.

During the 17th century, the ecstatic experiences of Joseph of Copertino were verified by approximately 100 witnesses, who described his spectacular levitations. These flights began when Joseph was still a youth. He would rise vertically from the ground to a height of about 3 metres, cry out and lie stretched out flat in the air. He would then travel considerable distances, either alone or accompanied by others.

Descriptions of levitation are by no means confined to Christianity. The phenomenon occurs among mystics of several other religions, including Buddhism, Taoism and Islam. Such occurrences are often reported in India, where the practice of yoga is thought to contribute to levitation.

Above: *In one of his 28 frescoes on the life of Francis of Assisi, the Italian Renaissance painter Giotto shows the saint raised up by a cloud.*

Right: *Teresa of Avila's ecstatic encounter with the presence of God was portrayed in this famous work by the Italian Baroque sculptor Bernini.*

People who have experienced levitation have described it as a bodily manifestation of ecstasy. The determining factor seems to be a direct encounter with the presence of God. Levitation only seems to occur when the soul rises completely above the material world and rests in God. Levitation is not regarded as a necessary part of religious contemplation or ecstasy. For this reason, the Catholic Church does not regard it as a wonder or a criterion for individual holiness.

Powers of a medium?

The phenomenon of levitation does not only affect religious mystics. It is also said to occur in people who are not in a state of religious rapture, but are able to act as a medium and use their psycho-physiological powers, perhaps even command them at will.

One of the most famous cases concerns the spectacular feats of levitation performed by the Scotsman Daniel Dunglas Home in the mid-19th century. Home's feats were confirmed by a number of eyewitnesses on several occasions. A noted chemist and physicist, Sir William Crookes, looked into the events and published the results of his scientific studies in the *Quarterly Journal of Science*. He concluded that Home was able to harness immense physical powers, which Crookes saw as integral components of the human organism. Crookes provided a vivid description of Home's most spectacular feat of levitation: 'Once Home rose to a height of 20 metres, then floated out of the window on the third floor of a house, returning through another window'.

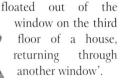

THE ENIGMA OF THE SHROUD OF TURIN

Is the ghostly image on the Shroud of Turin that of the dead Christ? Although the Catholic Church has never said this is the case, it does consider the shroud an object of veneration. Science has dated the shroud to the 13th century, but there are many things still to be explained about the celebrated cloth.

For centuries, devout Christians have believed that an ancient piece of linen, 4.34 m long and 1.09 m wide, is the burial cloth, or shroud, that was wrapped around the body of Jesus Christ after he was taken down from the cross. The shroud bears the faint outline of a crucified man, and the figure's facial features have been the inspiration behind the popular image of Christ as a bearded man. Since 1578, the celebrated shroud has been preserved in the cathedral of Turin, a city in northern Italy.

If the Shroud of Turin is indeed the burial cloth of Christ and bears the features of the saviour, it is by far the most precious relic of Christianity. It is certainly the most carefully guarded one. And yet, in spite of the measures taken by its guardians, the unexpected can happen. In April 1997, a fire broke out in the cathedral; fortunately, the shroud was undamaged, but, as a precaution, it has been stored elsewhere ever since.

Controversial dating

Naturally, the big question surrounding the Shroud of Turin is whether it is genuine or not. In order to answer this question, scientists have used a battery of modern techniques. The shroud has been subjected to chemical and microscopic analysis; X-ray, ultraviolet and infrared photography; and radiocarbon dating.

In 1983, the relic was passed on to the Vatican by its previous owner, the House of Savoy – the noble family who formerly ruled this part of Italy. Five years later, the Vatican gave permission for experts from the British Museum in London to examine the shroud. Independent testing was carried out by

The eerie image of the man imprinted on the Shroud of Turin has inspired religious artists since the Middle Ages.

laboratories in Oxford, Zürich and Tucson, Arizona. The experts concluded that the cloth dated from the 13th or 14th century, and could not have come into contact with the body of Christ.

However, other scientists disputed these findings. At conferences in 1989 and 1993, these scientists announced that they had examined the data from the laboratory analyses but come to different conclusions. A Russian scientist demonstrated that the fabric had been 'made younger' in 1532 when it was permeated with soot from a fire in Chambéry, France, where it was housed at

the time. Still other scientists considered the dating incorrect, since insufficient attention had been paid to the patina of the cloth, which consists of fungi and bacteria.

What do we know?

There are some certainties about the shroud. We know the image of the crucified person was not painted onto the cloth, and that the image is indelible. Drops of blood indicate that the corpse was wrapped in the shroud some two and a half hours after death at the latest. It has been determined that the blood comes from a male, for it was possible to isolate X and Y chromosomes, and the blood group is AB. The length of time in which the cloth was in contact with the corpse is known: the body was wrapped in it for not more than 36 hours. Any longer and the blood clots would have dissolved in the mixture of aloe and myrrh in which the cloth was soaked, and the cloth would have stuck together. What is unclear is how the corpse was freed from the cloth. The most important question has not been answered: how the image – which is negative rather than positive – came to be imprinted on the cloth. Nor do we know why the reverse shows only spots of blood. It is also remarkable that the image is hard to recognise in the original, while a negative clearly shows a face, limbs and body.

A French specialist in nuclear medicine believes that the image was produced by proton radiation released by a human body under the influence of an unknown source of energy. If we could discover the nature of this energy, we would have more information, not only about the origin of the Shroud of Turin, but its remarkable preservation.

THE MYSTERIOUS PASSION OF MARTHE ROBIN

The stories were astonishing: a French peasant girl who allegedly bore the stigmata of Christ, wept tears of blood and lived on a single communion wafer each day. Was she one of God's chosen ones? Sceptics argue that Marthe Robin was more likely the pawn of a manipulative clique.

The remarkable story of Marthe Robin began in 1902 on a farm near Châteauneuf-de-Galaure, a village located southwest of Grenoble in the French Alps. Marthe was the fifth child in the Robin family. When she was small, she contracted typhoid, which left her system chronically weakened. She left school at a very early age in order to help her parents run the farm. When she was 16, an inflammation of the brain left her comatose for two years. When she emerged from the coma, her body showed the first signs of paralysis. Following another period of coma in 1927 and a severe stomach illness, she began to eat and sleep less and less.

As long as Marthe was confined to her bed, the villagers and the parish priest took care of her, visiting her frequently and praying with her. Gradually, however, rumours began to circulate about mysterious occurrences; about how Marthe bore the stigmata of Christ, and how blood had flowed from her hands, feet, forehead and side on Good Friday. One rumour suggested that Marthe was possessed by the devil; apparently some visitors claimed to have witnessed the devil throwing Marthe out of bed. Finally, it was said that she no longer ate or drank, but lived off a single communion wafer each day, and yet did not lose weight. The stories soon multiplied: Marthe was stigmatised every Friday; Marthe could heal severe illnesses and had visions. It was not long before people began to flock to the Robin farm to witness the miracle with their own eyes. The parish priest informed the bishop and tried to organise the streams of visitors.

The organisation

In 1936, a priest named Finet was called to Marthe's bedside. He was to carry out an order, apparently given to Marthe by God, to found a school and a home in the name of brotherly love. He organised an initial appeal for donations and received enough funds to build a home that was to be run by pious lay-people.

By 1981, the organisation had collected enough money to build a dazzling basilica; an agricultural college for 1,500 students and an old-age home would also be affiliated to

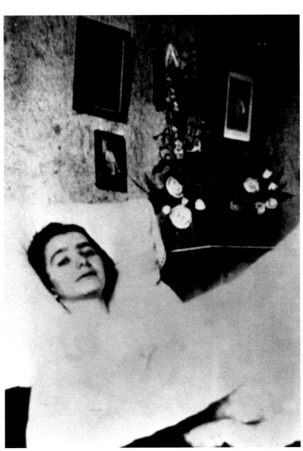

There are few photographs of Marthe Robin, who was extremely sensitive to light, and spent her days in a darkened room.

the foundation set up in Marthe's name. These institutions formed the nucleus of a Roman Catholic charity that has spread throughout the world.

In spite of this legacy of good works, the actions of Marthe Robin and her followers attracted criticism, even in clerical circles. Critics condemned the fact that the only people who could come near Marthe's bedside were those approved by Father Finet. The villagers of Châteauneuf-de-Galaure, who knew her best and had cared for her for many years, felt increasingly excluded. Many people were dismayed that visitors to Marthe had to pay an entrance fee, and endure days of religious exercises beforehand. These religious exercises met with almost unanimous rejection; participants claimed that they had to listen to daily eight-hour lecture sessions, which amounted to nothing more than indoctrination. After all this, even if a person managed to gain entry to Marthe's house, they were generally unable to confirm her stigmatisation, since they were kept at a distance that made it impossible to see any wounds. Nor could anyone find out whether Marthe really lived on a single communion wafer per day. She expressed her willingness to be treated by doctors, provided the bishop gave the order. But the order came too late. Marthe died in 1981 before she could be moved to a hospital.

The sceptical view

Medical science tells us that it is impossible for a person to survive without food and drink for several decades. Does this mean that the case of Marthe Robin amounts to an unexplained phenomenon or even a miracle? Preparations for her beatification – the first step on the road to sainthood – began nine years after her death. One after another, witnesses told of the religious passion that Marthe lived through – week after week – between Thursday evening and Monday morning. They all reported how she wept bloody tears, and how her soul left her body. But of course the only witnesses to these events were hand-picked by the foundation.

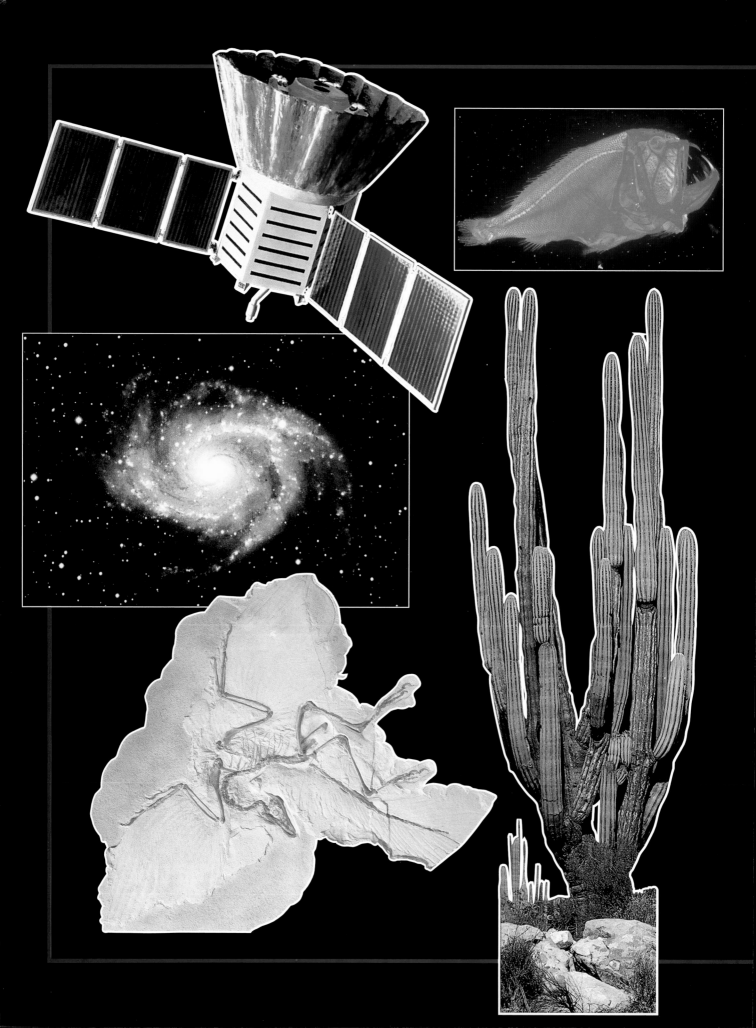

UNLOCKING NATURE'S SECRETS

Scientists in many disciplines are working tirelessly to advance the boundaries of knowledge and to find answers to the many questions that surround the natural world and the universe. From the smallest building blocks of matter to the endless expanses of the universe, researchers use the latest theories and technology to solve the riddles of plants and animals, of the earth and the cosmos. They study the structures of ant colonies, measure the slopes of volcanoes, drill into the permafrost layers of the polar regions or scan the night sky for evidence of black holes. But in spite of all the achievements of science, nature remains unpredictable and enigmatic. Humans will always be at the mercy of natural forces – however much we pride ourselves on taming our environment. And although we have amassed a vast body of knowledge that grows by the day, science is constantly confronted by new questions and new mysteries. Perhaps the greatest of these is the nature of the universe itself. What happened in the first moments when the universe was created? But first we will turn to the animal world, and look at the ways in which widely differing species have adapted to their habitats.

DO ANIMALS HAVE THE ABILITY TO REASON?

Humans like to think of themselves as the only creatures with intelligence. While the members of the animal kingdom may not have all the faculties that we possess, they are nevertheless capable of a startling range of actions and thought processes.

Is this chimpanzee's ability to combine symbols on a board proof of intelligence?

Kanzi loves orange juice, bananas and coffee with milk. Whatever he wants, he generally gets. He has learned more than 200 words and has attained the mental development of a two-and-a-half-year-old child. Kanzi also understands what he is told, even if he hears it on the telephone. It may be surprising to learn that Kanzi is a young bonobo, a pygmy chimpanzee, who lives in captivity at the language research centre of the University of Georgia, in the United States. Here, scientist Sue Savage-Rumbaugh heads a team of psychologists who are totally dedicated to Kanzi's welfare. These researchers live and work with the animal; if he becomes ill, they will even sleep beside him.

This remarkable primate communicates with his human companions by pointing to geometric symbols on a console, on which each symbol represents a word. Like all monkeys, Kanzi does not have the power of speech. But thanks to this system, he can form simple but meaningful sentences by pressing a sequence of two or three words on the console. But does this prove that Kanzi is

intelligent? It is difficult to answer this question. While the animal's ability to form sentences is certainly a considerable mental feat, Kanzi is unlikely to progress very much further in this direction. His vocabulary will stay more or less the same, and his capacity for thought will almost certainly never reach the level of a human's.

Clever energy-saver

Ironically, humans still struggle to find an adequate definition of intelligence. According to experts in this field, the capacity for thought includes such essential aspects as memory, attention, logic, spatial perception and the command of language. It is clear, though, that few animals have such abilities, but some animals do display startling evidence of something resembling intelligence. For example, when the Egyptian vulture (*Neophron percnopterus*) wants to open an ostrich egg – a favoured source of food – it picks up a stone in its beak and drops it onto the egg to crack the thick shell. Another example is the salmon (family Salmonidae),

various species of which inhabit the Pacific and Atlantic oceans: after several years in the open sea, the salmon uses its homing instinct to return unerringly to the same river in which it was born in order to breed. In the West African country of Ivory Coast, the abilities of chimpanzees (*Pan troglodytes*) are even more impressive: because the nuts that form their preferred diet have an extremely hard shell, these sociable primates use granite stones to crack them open. If they have to carry the stones a short distance, say less than 20 m, the apes will always choose the heavier stones. But over distances of more than 40 m they will choose the lighter stones, so as not to tire themselves out when carrying them.

For the Egyptian vulture and the salmon, there is certainly no need to speak of genius, for their behaviour stems from inherited automatism, a series of instinctive actions that are contained in the animal's genetic code. But the attempts of a chimpanzee to conserve its strength show that the animal is obviously making use of its judgement. If we think of the animal's actions in terms of a mathematical formula, where the weight of

Cracking the thick shell of an ostrich egg is child's play for this Egyptian vulture.

the stones, the place they are found and the distance they are carried are all variables, it suggests that intelligent thought processes may be at work.

The chimpanzee's impressive abilities are not all that surprising when we consider that – together with gorillas and orang-utans – chimpanzees are our closest living relatives on the evolutionary scale. From their earliest years, these animals learn at a significantly faster rate than human babies. They can

the movements of the trainer, who signals the word 'tandem' by holding up his crossed index fingers. He then throws up his arms in a gesture that is intended to mean 'creative'. Scarcely have the two dolphins registered the trainer's message than they dive to the bottom of the pool, where they proceed to swim in formation. Then they catapult out of the water in a fountain of spray, and spit a mighty jet of water, before disappearing together into the water.

Many people would say that this is just a well-staged piece of training. It is true that this trick is performed at the command of the trainer, but the details are left to the dolphins. It is they who have choreographed the routine. In other words, the animals have to communicate with each other and co-ordinate their movements so they can swim in tandem, swallow water and spit it out in unison. The most impressive thing is that these marine mammals do not always react in the same way to the trainer's command. Sometimes they decide to swim backwards or around the pool; it is just as if some form of animal freedom of choice is at work.

An astonishing memory

The near perfect co-ordination that the two dolphins demonstrate could be simply a matter of habit, or perhaps one animal is imitating the other perfectly. Behaviour patterns like these present scientists with a genuine riddle, for if we assume intelligence to be closely related to the capacity to grasp a given situation, then these dolphins must be extremely talented.

learn to eat with a spoon, use a screwdriver and even ride a bicycle. These precocious talents, which are acquired through training, might lead us to believe that the apes could, through education, become civilised beings like ourselves. However, when they reach sexual maturity their natural aggression starts to take over, and adult chimpanzees – particularly the males – become dangerous to humans.

Acrobatics in the water

At a research station for marine mammals in Hawaii, two dolphins (family Delphinidae) perform a series of lively acrobatic feats. Their antics are all the more remarkable because these highly intelligent creatures have developed their routine themselves – with a little help from their human trainer. With their heads out of the water, they watch

The synchronisation of these two dolphins resembles a water ballet. The dolphins themselves are responsible for this display of choreography.

Beating the rat race

When it comes to finding the fastest way through a maze, laboratory rats are masters of navigation. But this impressive ability does not necessarily indicate that these rodents possess the capacity for complex thought. The explanation is that rats have developed an extraordinary spatial intelligence, a talent which is essential if they are to find their way in the underground tunnels that are their natural habitat.

There is nothing simpler for a laboratory rat than finding its way through a maze. The rodent experiences the maze as a variation on its natural habitat.

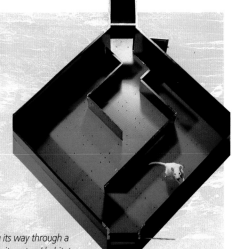

Above: *Ants live in colonies, and their activities are controlled by the strict rules required for communal living.*

Even in the wild, dolphins are noted for amazing feats. For example, fishermen came across a dolphin, whom they nicknamed Percy, far off the coast of Cornwall, in southwestern England. Like many dolphins, Percy enjoyed the company of humans and liked to follow in the wake of fishing boats or approach divers. He was particularly fond of one diver, and would spend hours swimming alongside him. Percy also liked to play with the fishermen's lines.

Although perhaps less spectacular, the behaviour of other animals is often much more subtle than it first appears. One example is the rooster and his

Above: *Hens possess the ability to decode a rooster's clucking and receive messages about the quality of food on offer.*

hens. An American scientist who has specialised in the study of the social behaviour of chickens has observed that a rooster in a chicken coop will not only announce to the hens with his clucking that there is something to eat, but by varying his calls he will offer comments on how interesting the food is. In order to test this hypothesis, the scientist fed his chickens a daily diet of worms, peas and peanuts. When the rooster saw the first two of these foods, he called to the hens with short, quick clucks, and they immediately came running. But if the chickens were only given peanuts, the rooster let out a slow cluck of disappointment, and only half of the hens reacted at all.

Collective intelligence

Insects have a fairly simple nervous system, but in groups they can achieve miracles. Many scientists suggest that insects can even grasp abstract and complex concepts, such as time. For example, researchers in the French city of Toulouse have taught ants to take food only at certain times and in certain places. Three times a day, the small colony comes out of its nest and picks up bread crumbs placed at three precise locations.

Equally impressive are the feats of honey-bees, who build elaborate networks of cells for breeding and food storage. The material used to build the cells is produced from their own bodies. The complex division of roles in a beehive even extends to so-called fanner bees, whose job is to make sure that the hive does not overheat.

Master of mimicry

While searching for the victims of a natural disaster (above), a dog looks to its fireman handler for guidance. It is with good reason that dogs are known as 'man's best friend', for they certainly like to do as we do. The behaviour of many household pets, above all cats and dogs, often seems intelligent, particularly when they are compared to our own behaviour. There are many stories of dogs that have crossed vast distances to find their way home after becoming lost on holiday, or of cats that do their business in a toilet, then flush it. But according to experts, such patterns of behaviour do not indicate that the animals can think. Many of their actions are the result of observation, where their ability to mimic humans is important.

THE MYSTERY OF WHALE STRANDINGS

Whales swim with enchanting grace, effortlessly covering enormous distances underwater. They are masters of navigation and can easily follow the same course year after year. But from time to time – like a ship with a broken rudder – whales mysteriously beach themselves. These strandings are almost invariably fatal. Experts are powerless to prevent these tragic events, but our understanding of whale navigation is increasing.

Marine mammals, especially whales, exert an enormous fascination for human beings. Not only do they include the largest animals on our planet, but some whales display human-like behaviour. Their outstanding sense of navigation enables dolphins (family Delphinidae) and many species of whale (order Cetacea) to cover large distances when migrating from their calving grounds – where they spend the summers, giving birth to their young – to the waters of the Arctic and Antarctic oceans, where a rich supply of fish and krill (tiny crustaceans that look like shrimps or prawns) is available in winter. Some species, like the blue whale (*Balaenoptera musculus*), can cover a distance of several thousand kilometres.

Perhaps the most heartbreaking sight in the natural world is a stranded whale. No-one knows what causes these giants to stray off course and beach themselves. Sometimes, it is a single animal; at other times, whole pods of whales come ashore. Once they are out of the water, the great weight of these animals literally crushes them to death.

Is this some kind of collective suicide? Most scientists think this is unlikely. Instead, research suggests that a technical defect in the animals' sense of orientation may come into play.

Using the ears to see

Certain animals – for example, dolphins, sperm whales and killer whales – use a sonar technique to locate obstacles, such as a rocky shoal, or to track down a school of fish. This sonic depth-finder works by emitting clicking sounds at short intervals within the ultrasonic range. These sound waves hit the contours of nearby objects and are reflected back to the whale. From information such as strength, direction and type of reflection, the whale's brain then calculates the distance of the object and compares it to sonar images stored in its memory. The sonar is effective within a radius of 800 m, enabling the sperm whale (*Physeter macrocephalus*) to hunt its favourite food, cephalopods – particularly squid – in the complete darkness of the deep sea. Researchers think that storms, pollution, noise from ships or even ear infections could impair the whale's sonar, effectively making the animal blind.

Some species – blue whales, for example – lack these sonic depth-finders, and must use other methods to navigate. According to the latest research, these animals may make use of the earth's magnetic field. This field has fluctuated over very long periods of time, and the changes are recorded in the layers of rock on the ocean floor. Magnetic signals emerge from the depths, depending on which layer is exposed. These signals guide the whales in their migrations. Unfortunately, some geomagnetic routes run towards the coast. Whales have been stranded along the Wash, for example, on the east coast of Great Britain, where the magnetic field curves towards the coast.

There is increasing evidence that whales have a kind of built-in compass. But we do not know how it works. The animal must be extremely sensitive to be able to detect fluctuations of the magnetic field, even in deep water. Research suggests the 'compass' may be located in the retina of the eye.

Conflicting agnetic signals could explain whale strandings, which often recur in the same place.

ANIMALS AT PLAY

Like humans, animals love to play. But animals face far more threats to their existence than we do. For wild creatures, play is a vital part of preparation for survival. Although animal play can seem brutal and dangerous, it is excellent preparation for life-and-death situations.

The animal kingdom is a tough place. We all know that life in the wild is a matter of kill or be killed, where only the strong survive. But there is also a lighter side to being an animal, where youngsters learn the rudiments of survival through play.

Play begins in the womb, long before a little mammal is ready to take on the world, when it will nudge and knock against its mother's belly. Well protected, the animal is preparing its body for new activities such as jumping, running or climbing. After birth, the animal is immediately plunged into an environment that is filled with

danger. Hungry predators with dangerous teeth or powerful beaks are waiting for the youngster, who will make tasty prey. The little creature is totally inexperienced but thirsty for adventure, teasing and full of boundless energy. As the careless youngster, engrossed in play, enjoys itself far away from the nest or burrow, out of reach of its mother, hungry hyenas, foxes, lions or birds of prey wait to pounce upon it and swallow it in a few gulps.

Although vital for the development of the young animal, play is also filled with danger. But, according to the experts, the risks taken by animals will pay off in the end. They believe that the experience of play provides a good opportunity for animals to equip themselves for life as an adult.

First, it can be said that playing definitely increases the chances of survival. Siberian ibexes, for example, who are true climbing artists, leap over deep gorges with ease, or chase one another down rocky slopes. To them, it is all play, but such activity is still close to their physical limits. For a young animal, however, the demands may appear to be extreme. A youngster that cannot keep up with the dangerous acrobatics is very quickly made to find its legs by its mother. If real danger appeared and the animal had to run for its life, it would stand a far better chance of surviving a deadly fall if it had already mastered all the secure footholds. For this reason, hard training disguised as play is absolutely imperative.

Learning to socialise

Secondly, playing is a great way to learn social behaviour. While the young animal is growing up, it has to find its place in the group, secure its social status or conquer a territory. A good example is the wolf (*Canis lupus*): wolf cubs from one litter will fight

For young wolves, mock battles are a good preparation for the coming conflicts for status within the pack.

over a feather or a piece of wood. In this way, they either learn to demand respect from one another or to submit to the strongest. Over the course of time, an entire behavioural catalogue develops, in which each animal learns its place in the pecking order. At the same time, this ensures good co-operation within the pack.

Animals that will lead a solitary life once they are fully grown – for example, a young fox – will prefer to play alone. Animals such

Fox cubs often play alone, an indication of the lifestyle they will lead as adults. As soon as they are fully grown, foxes become loners.

as this will fend for themselves later on and not hunt in a pack like wolves.

Animals at play do not want to get hurt. When two lion cubs fight, for example, it appears wild to an outsider. But the bites and blows are only pretence; playful gestures which appear to be brutal but are, in fact, perfectly controlled. The game is a ritual, in which all movements have a clearly defined significance, and can be enjoyed by the stronger as well as the weaker as they take turns being winner and loser. During

Lion cubs growl at one another, exchange paw blows and even bite. These actions may seem dangerous, but are practice for the real thing.

these practice fights, the animals adopt the so-called playful face, a relaxed expression that conveys friendly intent. Young wolves, for example, open their snouts when they fight, but their sharp teeth are covered by their lips and are not bared.

The joy of combat

This type of single combat, which stems purely from the joy of brawling, offers three advantages. Firstly, it allows for a reduction of violence and aggressiveness in a contest that is independent of the strength and the rank of both partners within the group. Secondly, it promotes physical endurance and skill in fighting, good training for later challenges from real rivals. And thirdly, when a creature of the same species plays the role of the willing victim, mock battles provide a wonderful opportunity to perfect individual hunting techniques. This includes patterns of behaviour such as concealment, stalking prey, pouncing, throwing down and the so-called death-bite.

Sexual experience is also part of growing up in the wild. Elephant seals get their initiation into sexuality through acts between brothers and sisters. Among monkeys, young males, having been aroused by the presence of females who are ready for mating, imitate copulation under the almost indifferent eyes of dominant males. These gestures are performed again and again in the same form and do not serve any reproductive function. They are only tolerated by the adult members up to a certain age, and after that they are immediately punished. Later, the young animal must assert its dominance over other males if it wants to mate.

Upon closer observation, it seems that the two sexes seem to prefer different pursuits. Females, for example, seem to play less than

In a gesture of simple exuberance, a young fur seal playfully pulls an amphibious lizard's tail.

males. Among macaques, we find that the the females like to occupy themselves in grooming and child care, while the males have only one thing in mind: playing catch. When we observe marmots, we see that in their fights with the females, the males are the ones that soon gain the upper hand. Consequently, young males often prefer to fight amongst themselves, if possible with a stronger partner.

A young Galápagos fur seal pulls an amphibious iguana by the tail; a raven slides down a little snowfield on his back over and over again; a baby monkey tickles his mother's nose: the natural world provides countless, often hilarious, examples of play. Play provides excellent training for life, but most importantly, play is fun.

Of players and spectators

Play has only been observed in mammals and birds. For other animal groups, such as reptiles, amphibians, fish or insects, play seems to be a foreign concept. Intensity and duration of play are clearly dependent on availability of food in the environment. If there is plenty of food around, the young ones can waste their energy in play. In times of scarcity, they automatically limit their fun, for they have to watch how they expend their energy.

If animals have enough to eat, like these baboons in Kenya, playful fights become a common way of working off excess energy.

ANIMAL COMMUNICATION

The mysteries of animal communication are still very far from being solved. And yet humans are gradually gaining a greater understanding of the many ways in which animals send messages to one another. From bird song to the dances of honeybees, the variety of animal communication is truly astounding. For specialists in animal behaviour, the vital question remains: do animals use language?

The nightingale, a master of imitation, can mimic the songs of other bird species.

On a rainy night, a frog concert fills the darkness. A forest clearing echoes with the beautiful song of a nightingale. The eerie howling of a coyote breaks the stillness of the dry and dusty desert .... The sounds of the natural world are all around us, evidence of the richness of the animal kingdom. These sounds, which may seem strange, humourous or even threatening, may be coded messages from animals. But is there such a thing as animal language? This is a tricky question to answer, even for experts in animal behaviour.

Scientists define language as a form of symbolic and creative communication. It is not just a succession of signals aiming for an immediate effect. Unlike humans, animals generally communicate only in three specific situations: to exchange information about sources of food, to strengthen the bonds between partners during the mating season or to call for help when danger threatens.

Dancing for joy

In some animals, communication takes place on such a sophisticated level that researchers have been forced to conclude that language is being used. For example, an amazing type of communication takes place among honeybees (*Apis mellifera*). When one of them discovers a source of food, it returns to the hive where it passes this information on to the other worker bees. This is done by means of certain dances, as the Austrian naturalist and zoologist Karl von Frisch discovered during the 1920s.

If the food is located less than 100 m from the hive, the bee will dance around in a circle to attract attention. The location of more distant food sources is conveyed through a waggling dance, in the form of a figure of eight. The speed of the dance indicates the distance of the food, and the number of rounds decreases as the distance becomes greater. For example, 40 rounds indicates 100 m, while 24 means more than 500 m). The orientation of the dance symbolises the direction of the food, while the dance's intensity and duration gives information on the richness of the food to be found. Finally, the dancer also reports to its fellow-workers about the quality of the food, for they only

The majestic humpback whale has a wide repertoire of sounds which it uses to communicate with its fellows.

need to sniff the messenger to recognise the scent of the blossoms. Once the message has been understood, the bees head for the food, and a new group of nectar-collectors will pass on the vital information. The honeybee's communication skill ensures that, within about an hour, some 10,000 insects can arrive on site.

Imitating humans

For humans, the most amazing animals are those that can imitate our speech. The parrot is a good example.

Because they are so good at imitations, these birds love to repeat almost any sound they hear. In fact, when someone repeats something that we have just said, we generally compare them to a parrot. But does the parrot's wonderful ability represent a genuine form of communication?

Through repetition, psychologist Irene Pepperberg teaches a grey parrot to name different objects.

To answer this question, American psychologist Irene Pepperberg taught an African grey parrot (*Psittacus erithacus*) from Gabon some very simple words: for example, 'cork' for his favourite toy, or 'carrot' for his favourite food. When she offered the parrot an object, she waited for the bird to say the correct word before she put it into his beak as a reward. In this way, the bird quickly learned a dozen words or so, and even grew capable of demanding an object which he couldn't see.

Pepperberg extended the programme when the parrot started speaking real sentences, such as 'wanna do tricks'. Eventually, the parrot learned to distinguish between over 300 objects by form, size and colour. In four out of five cases, the bird gave the correct answer to such questions as 'What is yellow?' or 'What colour is this box?'

Just like the parrot, members of the animal kingdom can make themselves heard in an amazing variety of ways. Every squeak, neigh and squawk probably contains some kind of message that can be understood by other members of a particular species. One of the most fascinating ranges of sound are the powerful noises – often referred to as songs – of the great whales, the travellers of the world's oceans. The songs of the humpback whales (*Megaptera novaeangliae*) and beluga whales (*Delphinapterus leucas*) are particularly impressive. These animals can sing for over half an hour without interruption, but what separates them from other species is the great variety of their sounds: a mixture of barking, squeaking, canary-like whistling, rasping, snorting, bawling, humming and trilling are continually combined in new ways. Instead of a monotonous refrain, there are melodious verses, whose meaning is still unknown. For centuries, seafarers believed that these mysterious sounds were the songs of mermaids or of the Sirens of the Greek myths – beautiful women who called to sailors and lured them onto deadly jagged rocks.

Because there are so many species of birds, interpreting their song presents a real challenge to scientists. In looking at the ways in which birds communicate, researchers have isolated the three levels on which birds identify themselves: the species-related level, the regional level and the individual level. The song of the nightingale, for example, has several sections, some of them alluring, others warning. Other parts of its song, however, are either individual compositions or imitations of other birds. The nightingale even makes the sounds of other animal species, for the bird is a master of mimicry.

The basics of language

To decide whether animal communication is really language, scientists must identify the basic features of language. One of the leaders in this area was the Swiss linguist Ferdinand de Saussure (1857–1913), who founded the modern study of linguistics.

According to Saussure, language is present if signals are transported on a level which he called 'double articulation'. This means that

Five types of communication

Every animal species communicates in its own way. However, all animal communication can be classified into five categories:
❏ Acoustic messages, such as singing, shouting, ultra- or infra-sound calls;
❏ Optical signals, such as patterns of fur, colour change or sign language;
❏ Emission of odours via chemical substances (many animals mark their paths in this way);
❏ Touch stimulus, as used by chicks to beg food from their parents;
❏ Electrical signals, such as those sent by some fish species to improve their orientation.

language is composed of a limited number of useless units – for example, vowels and consonants – which make up the alphabet. These can, however, be converted into an endless number of useful units, which make up our vocabulary. By using several different language signals, we can describe reality. For example, to describe a stretch of road, we might use the terms path, street, highway or lane. It is also possible to use one particular sign – for example, the blade of a knife or a blade of grass – to name different objects. However, the chief characteristic of animal communication systems is that every signal corresponds to only one message, and vice versa. Even very intelligent primates such as chimpanzees, gorillas or orang-utans have to extend their vocabulary when they want to communicate or understand something new.

Despite its high level of development, the orang-utan uses a very basic form of communication.

THE SOCIAL INSECTS: IS COLLECTIVE INTELLIGENCE AT WORK?

If you stand on a busy city street during rush hour, the flow of traffic and commuters appears to be chaotic and without purpose. A termite mound, ant hill or beehive might appear similarly chaotic, but there is something else at work here. They may be tiny, but insects are capable of astonishing feats of building and social organisation. By working together according to instinctive behaviour patterns, they are able to create some of nature's most amazing structures.

Their jaws have two pincers for grasping; on their heads, a pair of antennae serve as sensory organs for feeling and smelling; six legs and a skinny jointed waist complete the picture of one of nature's most efficient designs – the insect. There are countless species of insects, and new ones are named every year. The insect's body model is very adaptable, and its wide distribution is largely due to a social system which puts the colony rather than the individual in the foreground.

Colonial life

If we could enter a termite mound, it would be like passing through the doors of a huge fortress, a labyrinth or even a skyscraper, for some African species build towers up to 7 m high. Inside is a network of walkways and

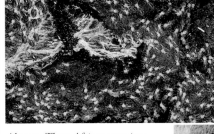

Above: *These African termites have no idea what their mound will look like when it is finished.*

chambers, the layout of which guarantees co-operation within the community. Termites even build an efficient ventilation system which allows the carbon dioxide exhaled by thousands of colony members to escape. However, you would look in vain if you tried to find the master builder who planned the structure. No individual directs any of the colony's actions – except the group itself.

Termites are blind from birth and lack individual intelligence. However, as a community they are brilliant builders. Together with ants, bees and wasps, they belong to the group of insects which forms colonies and whose

Deadly solitude

The social insects depend on one another for survival. For example, like the honeybee, the Australian honey ant (*Camponotus inflatus*) has a foregut in which it stores the food it has ingested (nectar or honeydew). However, the honey ant cannot digest this food any further, and it must be regurgitated on demand and fed to another member of the hive or to larvae. If there is no other ant to feed, the honey ant could literally die on a full stomach.

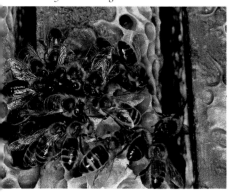

Below: *Honeybees can communicate the direction and distance of a food source. Humans are the only other beings that can do this.*

behaviour fascinates researchers. Scientists see in the behaviour of these insects many similarities to human societies – including hierarchical structures, with queens, drones or kings, workers and soldiers. For a long time, researchers thought that insect colonies functioned so well because the actions of individuals were controlled by instinct – built-in patterns of behaviour. In recent years, attention has focused on chemical substances called pheromones, which, when released into an animal's surroundings, influence the behaviour or development of other individuals of the same species.

Chemical messages

A termite mound starts to take shape when workers of the species *Bellicositermes* form little mud balls, mix them with saliva and then arrange them in small piles, apparently at random. Since the scent of saliva is strong, the termites make their mounds increasingly larger, and they eventually tower chimney-like towards the sky. If two columns are close together, the workers at the top of one chimney may become attracted by the pleasant scent of the neighbouring structure. Piles of earth are built up between them to make a rudimentary bridge, which is soon reinforced to form an arch.

The whole process takes place without an architect, manager or central programme, a phenomenon that scientists have dubbed the

Left: *This massive Australian termite mound, with its ventilation system, chambers, walkways and fungus cultures, is one of the most complicated structures in the animal kingdom.*

'ping-pong effect'. To put it another way, the work influences the worker, and vice versa. Although this explanation does not shed light on all the phases that are involved – especially the construction of the queen's chamber or the hard outer wall of the termite hill – it indicates the importance of chemical substances in the exchange of information between individuals. Without these chemical signals, there would be no community life. In a beehive, for example, the queen secretes a specific pheromone that renders the worker bees infertile by retarding the development of their ovaries. By licking the queen bee, the other bees absorb the chemical substance and spread it, guaranteeing that the queen will be the only one capable of reproducing.

Individual scents

Chemistry also explains how ants tell each other about food supplies. If one of them finds food, it secretes a pheromone from its abdomen, which then marks the way to the ant hill. As soon as another ant crosses this path, it will react in a similar manner. Soon, the little scent trail becomes a wide river.

Pheromones also enable insects to detect individuals of the same group. A termite, for example, uses its feelers, which are covered with smelling cells, to test the cuticle – the waxy outer layer covering the epidermis of insects – of all it meets. The exoskeleton of each type of termite, and of each individual

A chemical fingerprint

As the insect's waxy outer layer gives off a certain scent, scientists are able to define the fragrance of each species, even of individual colonies. Using organic solvents, the carbohydrate molecules of the cuticle are extracted and subjected to analysis by a chromatograph connected to a spectrometer. This method reveals the chemical make-up of the insect concerned.

colony, has a distinctive smell, which comes from specific carbohydrate molecules that form the cuticle.

Social insects

With the exception of humans, no other species has matched the achievements of the social insects – for example, the leaf-cutting ants of the species *Atta*. These industrious creatures cut and remove parts of leaves, and take them back to the colony, where they are used to raise crops of fungi. No other animal, not even the most intelligent ape, can tell another member of the species the direction where food is to be found and how far away it is. The honeybee holds this honour – thanks to their famous 'waggle' dances, first described in the 1920s.

Robot insects

Social insects have long been of great interest to computer scientists working in the field of artificial intelligence. In order to design large numbers of tiny robots, these researchers look carefully at the behaviour of termites or ants. Although these tiny creatures have limited capabilities as individuals, they can achieve miracles when they act co-operatively.

Rodney Brooks, a robot specialist at the Massachusetts Institute of Technology (MIT) has suggested that NASA send 30 insect-like robots to Mars in order to explore the planet's surface and collect rock samples. Aside from the cost savings, the advantage would be the relatively minor consequences if one

Robotics specialist Rodney Brooks has developed mechanical insects which can act as a team – just like termites or ants.

member were to malfunction. However, there is still no proof that robot insects can act in a co-ordinated manner.

'Monkey Medicine'

As our closest animal relatives, primates are fascinating for humans. We know that they possess a high order of intelligence and are capable of many complex tasks. However, primate researchers are starting to shed light on a little-known aspect of primate behaviour – their ability to treat their ailments, practise contraception and even to select the sex of their offspring.

The mountainous kingdom of Nepal, in southern Asia, contains some of the world's most breathtaking mountain scenery. More astonishing, though, are the antics of the macaques (members of the Eurasian monkey family), who live in the region. These primates have the strange habit of digging holes in the ground with their delicate fingers. When they reach a certain depth, the monkeys scoop up the earth at the bottom of the hole – and eat it.

Bernadette Mariott, an American scientist, has looked into this phenomenon. At first, she thought the monkeys were eating the insects or worms living in the soil. Then she noticed that the macaques were interested in the soil itself. After conducting a soil

Above: *The rhesus monkey is the best known of the macaque family. In Nepal, macaques prevent diarrhoea by eating mineral-rich soil.*

analysis, researchers were able to solve the riddle. It turns out that the soils of the macaque's habitat are rich in minerals, and have a particularly high concentration of kaolin, a substance which hinders diarrhoea. Somehow, the monkeys discovered the medicinal effects of the soil, and begun to treat their ailments with it.

Primate self-medication

The primate world is full of surprises. A good example are the chimpanzees (*Pan troglodytes*) that live deep in the mountains of Tanzania, in East Africa. Japanese researchers have documented the actions of a large female chimpanzee, which was obviously weak and in poor health, but which was able to find a natural medicine.

The animal did not have the strength even to pick up the ants that were within reach on the ground. Instead, she gathered her last reserves of strength and dragged herself to a little grove of trees. There, she grabbed a bunch of leaves of the tropical plant *Vernonia amygdalina* and chewed them carefully to get at the plant's bitter juice. Apparently, the

juice acts to ease cases of stomach and digestive upsets. After administering this natural 'medicine', the chimpanzee spat out the leaf fibres.

From a discreet distance, the Japanese researchers watched this amazing scene. The next day, they noticed that the chimpanzee was in good health and fed completely normally. Impressed by their discovery, they formulated a daring hypothesis, namely that primates such as the chimpanzees are able to heal themselves.

Chimpanzees know something about the healing powers of nature. Chimpanzees in Tanzania heal themselves with carefully selected plants.

Further observations of chimpanzees in other parts of Africa have lent support to the Japanese hypothesis. Generally, primates feed from fruits in the immediate vicinity, but they sometimes undertake a 20-minute walk in order to find a plant called *Aspilia*, which belongs to the aster family. This plant is certainly no delicacy, for the apes make a disgusted face and turn up their noses when they chew the leaves. At one point, researchers even surprised a male as it spat out bits of half-chewed plant.

What makes chimpanzees eat such foul-tasting food? Perhaps it is good for them. Together with biologists, primate researchers have analysed the red, oily juice contained in *Aspilia*. To their great surprise, they found that it contains a substance which destroys parasites and fungi – making it a kind of natural antibiotic.

Scientists from Japan and the United States have also noticed that chimpanzees eat more healing plants during the rainy season – the period when pneumonia and other infectious diseases are particularly threatening. This seems to imply that our primate cousins are aware of the health risks

Some research suggests that howler monkeys – in this case, the red howler monkey (Alouatta seniculus) – *can influence the sex of their babies.*

Below: *By eating the leaves of a certain tree, female howler monkeys of a Brazilian species called* muriki *can reduce their fertility. The leaves act like the human contraceptive pill.*

confronting them. This is a very daring hypothesis, but one which has not been dismissed by scientists.

Contraception

Alleged evidence of birth control has resulted in a more careful reaction from scientists. Here, attention has focused on the behaviour of the howler monkey (genus *Alouatta*), a group of primates which is indigenous to the Americas. For some time after birth, female howler monkeys in Brazil frequent a certain tree species, which has not yet been named . The monkeys eat a considerable quantity of the leaves, which contain certain chemical substances known as isoflamines, whose effect is similar to that of oestrogen and probably reduces the fertility of the females. Could this be a type of plant contraceptive?

Because 'monkey medicine' is a very new field of research, there are potentially many surprises in store. So the scientists organised conferences to share their findings, and extended their studies to other regions.

They soon found, for example, that some female howler monkeys in Costa Rica – a small nation in Central America – eat a herbaceous plant before and after mating, which they do not consume at any other time. Even though there is as yet no proof, researchers suggest that the females may use the plant to regulate their fertility, since they do not register any births in these periods.

Pick a gender

Of all the hypotheses so far put forward by primate researchers, the most far-fetched states that pregnant howler monkeys may be able to determine the sex of their young ones. More than 20 years of observation has demonstrated that, at a certain period, a large percentage of the females give birth to male offspring only. At other times, however, only females are produced. Again, scientists found that these females had eaten certain plants before and after mating. They suggest that the plants affect the acidity of vaginal mucus, perhaps inhibiting conception.

Managing the population

What is uncertain is the monkeys' reasons for determining the gender of their babies. The answer may be found in the complex structure of primate societies. In a troop of howler monkeys, only the males have a chance of eventually assuming a leadership role. Thus, a mother could secure a privileged position for herself within the group by producing male offspring. In the same way, when there is a shortage of females, the female who is responsible for producing offspring could strengthen her position in the hierarchy by producing female young (which will, in turn, become mothers) since this goes a long way towards ensuring the survival of the group.

It may not taste good, but Aspilia contains chemicals that fight parasites and fungi.

Learning from primates

Years of observation have allowed scientists to conclude that monkeys not only know about the healing effects of plants, but also have the ability to apply their knowledge. Some American biochemists are asking themselves why we humans don't follow the primates' example. Fascinated by the discovery that chimpanzees, for example, eat a tropical plant called *Aspilia* in order to rid themselves of parasites and fungi, scientists have carried out laboratory tests to isolate the plant's active substances. Initial test results suggest that these natural chemicals can apparently combat certain cancer cells, especially in the case of tumours affecting the lung and breast.

WHAT REALLY HAPPENED TO THE DINOSAURS?

While the dinosaurs may be dead, they are still very much alive in our imaginations. The success of films such as Jurassic Park *has reawakened interest in the great lizards. However, controversial new theories suggest that the dinosaurs may have been quite different from what we imagine.*

For nearly 200 years, palaeontologists have been trying to find the answers to the questions surrounding the extinction of the dinosaurs, the great lizards that once ruled our planet. Dinosaurs first appeared on earth about 230 million years ago, towards the end of the Triassic period. They reigned for about the next 165 million years. The only clues to help us reconstruct their world are tracks and fossilised bones, eggs and portions of skin. However, scientists are

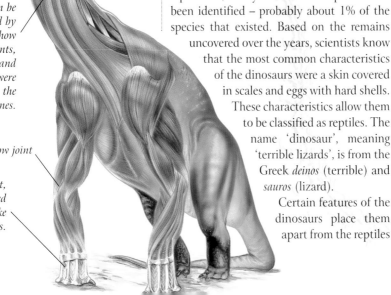

Nostrils

Chisel-like teeth

A flexible, giraffe-like neck allowed Brachiosaurus *to browse in the tree-tops.*

Like the cables of a crane, the muscles moved the neck.

The muscular system of the animal can be reconstructed by examining how ligaments, tendons and muscles were attached to the bones.

Elbow joint

Straight, column-shaped front foot, like an elephant's.

Top: *Dinosaur National Monument in the United States is one of the world's most important sites for fossilised dinosaur remains. Complete skeletons are embedded in the rock walls. At left is the fossil skeleton of* Archaeopteryx, *which is thought to be the ancestor of all birds.*

gradually putting together a picture of what these giant animals looked like and how they behaved. They are trying to understand how the dinosaurs were able to rule the earth for so long, and why they vanished so suddenly.

Scaly skins

Up to now, nearly 500 dinosaur species have been identified – probably about 1% of the species that existed. Based on the remains uncovered over the years, scientists know that the most common characteristics of the dinosaurs were a skin covered in scales and eggs with hard shells. These characteristics allow them to be classified as reptiles. The name 'dinosaur', meaning 'terrible lizards', is from the Greek *deinos* (terrible) and *sauros* (lizard).

Certain features of the dinosaurs place them apart from the reptiles

that we know today. Their legs, for example, were positioned vertically under the body, so that they walked like mammals and birds. This manner of locomotion is unknown in

Bird brains?

The dinosaurs may have been big, but they didn't have much upstairs. The largest sauropods had a tiny skull in relation to their body size, with a brain weighing a couple of grams at most. The most extreme case was *Stegosaurus*, which probably weighed around 1.5 tons, but had a brain the size of a chicken's egg. However, if the latest theories are correct – that the dinosaurs took care of their young, gave calls of recognition and developed hunting strategies – this would prove that their brains were much more complex than has been previously supposed.

modern reptiles, whose legs protrude from the sides of their bodies. Intriguingly, the skeletal structure of the dinosaurs is very similar to that of the birds. This has led some researchers to speculate that the dinosaurs may even have been warm-blooded animals.

In the late 1960s, palaeontologist Robert Bakker created controversy among dinosaur experts. He maintained that dinosaurs had the ability to keep their body temperatures at a constant level, irrespective of external fluctuations – unlike cold-blooded reptiles, whose body temperatures always adapt to their environments.

Bakker provided a number of arguments to back up his theory, suggesting that dinosaurs were in a position to survive the climatic changes which occurred on earth during their 165-million-year rule. According to Bakker, when the dinosaurs walked the earth, they displayed a number of features typical of warm-blooded species: they were very active animals with a large heart and lung volume; they grew fast; and they reproduced quickly. In addition, precise analyses of bone sections show similarities with mammal bones, but strong differences from reptiles.

Opponents of Bakker's theory, however, argued that the metabolisms of warm-blooded animals require food at regular intervals, and that this requirement is even

more important for the heavier animals. A lion, for example, has to eat ten times the amount of meat as a crocodile of the same size. If we consider that some sauropods (the very large plant-eating dinosaurs that stood on four legs) were larger than 15 elephants, they would have had to consume a vast amount of food each day. After all, a single elephant has to eat some 135–270 kg of food each day. However, there are a number of specialists who believe that the dinosaurs possessed a special metabolism which is no longer found among animals on earth.

The age of the giants

Another area of study focuses on how land animals grew to such gigantic proportions. One of the largest dinosaurs that has been found to date is *Brachiosaurus*. Although it was 23 m long and 12 m high, *Brachiosaurus* was by no means the largest of the great lizards. Behemoths such as *Supersaurus* and *Ultrasaurus* attained an overall length of 30 m and 35 m, respectively, and stood as tall as 15–17 m above the ground. Researchers have calculated that these creatures weighed up to 100 tons. But the hands-down winner in the heavyweight division was *Seismosaurus*, which may have been a cousin to *Diplodocus*. So far, only fragments have been found, but *Seismosaurus* was probably 40–50 m in length – equivalent to four or five buses placed end to end. Palaeontologists are still studying how muscles and tendons were attached to the bones, in order to determine how such giants could move at all.

At the other end of the size scale was *Compsognathus*, which was no bigger than a turkey. This small creature measured a mere 70 cm from the tip of its snout to the end of its tail, and stood only 30 cm in height. There is considerable evidence that some dinosaurs did not even reach the size of a dog. Incidentally, we know that the large sauropods only reached their great size after many millions of years of evolution. The advantage of this progressive gigantism may

Only about 70 cm in length, Compsognathus *is among the smallest dinosaurs yet discovered.*

have stemmed from the fact that a really large organism takes a long time to cool down. The reason for this is that even with a bigger body volume the animal still has a relatively small exterior, or heat-radiating surface. Thus, total heat loss is actually less than for smaller creatures. The body mass of the sauropods thus represented an excellent method of gigantothermia, a scientific term for this method of temperature regulation.

Unexplained extinction

In dinosaur research, the critical question remains why the dinosaurs disappeared from earth during the Mesozoic era, more than 65 million years ago. In an attempt to answer this question, Walter Alvarez, a geophysicist at the University of California at Berkeley, came up with the idea that the Mesozoic-era dinosaurs became extinct after the earth was struck by a meteorite. To back up his theory, Alvarez pointed to a discovery made near Gubbio in the region of Umbria, central Italy: a layer of clay containing carbon, marking the boundary of the Cretaceous and Tertiary geological periods. With the help of precise dating procedures, the age of this layer could be fixed at 65 million years. It stemmed from exactly the same time that the dinosaurs became extinct. Furthermore, the clay contained a lot of iridium, a rare precious metal normally present in tiny traces in the earth's crust, but present in high

A hind leg of Ultrasaurus *gives an indication of the general height of this dinosaur.*

concentrations in asteroids and cosmic dust. The samples collected by Alvarez showed 35 times the normal level of iridium.

Moreover, the clay contained peculiar quartz grains, which, when examined under a microscope, seemed to have been subjected

This artist's impression shows Tyrannosaurus rex, *one of the largest carnivorous dinosaurs, as a meteorite streaks fatefully across the sky.*

to unusual pressures. This could have been caused by a very high-velocity impact, which led Alvarez to conclude that a meteorite of a diameter of about 10 km had hit the earth at a speed of more than 100,000 km/h, forming a crater more than 150 km in diameter. The massive explosion threw up a thick cloud of dust, which soon covered the planet and plunged the earth into darkness. Without light, the vegetation died, spelling doom for the dinosaurs. After the dust had cleared, the survivors must have faced conditions that were harsh in the extreme. It is likely that the great energy of the impact led to huge storms and disastrous floods, as well as releasing waves of blazing heat. It is also likely that the oxygen and nitrogen in the air heated up to such an extent that nitric acid formed, creating an atmosphere hostile to

the existence of many organisms. Scientists know that nearly 50% of all life forms died out at the time the dinosaurs became extinct.

Eruption in India

Recent research seems to have corroborated Alvarez's hypothesis. Several sites have revealed an iridium anomaly from the late Cretaceous period. In 1990, an enormous impact crater was identified on the coast of Mexico's Yucatán Peninsula, which could have been created by a meteorite. And yet the meteorite hypothesis is still not accepted. Some scientists are looking at volcanic activity that took place on India's Deccan Plateau towards the end of the Cretaceous period. In less than 500,000 years, a mass of lava covering an area twice the size of France in a layer as thick as 4 km was deposited there in what must have been the most gigantic volcanic eruption of the past 200 million years. The resulting climate change would have destroyed much of life on earth.

Some believe the dinosaurs were already on their way out. They point to the fact that 70% of dinosaur species had become extinct by 65–73 million years before our time. There are also a number of palaeontologists who believe that the successors of the dinosaurs still roam the earth – as birds, crocodiles, turtles and other creatures.

Speed of growth

Considering their body size, the dinosaurs laid tiny eggs. The largest ones to have been discovered come

Reconstruction of the nest of a Maiasaurus, based on fossil eggs and embryos unearthed in Montana.

from sauropods weighing more than 10 tons. The eggs themselves have a volume of about 3 litres – about double the size of an ostrich egg. Scientists have carried out tests on fossil bones, which have revealed the existence of numerous channels for blood vessels – a guarantee of rapid growth. For example, it could have taken a mere 4 years for a 36-cm-long newborn *Maiasaurus* (which means 'good mother lizard') to grow to its adult length of 8 m.

Triceratops's bony neck plate may have served as a form of defence, a display or a means of keeping cool.

Nessie, the Yeti and Other Monsters of Our Time

From the abominable snowman and the Loch Ness Monster to a dwarf brontosaurus and the giant squid, there are innumerable reports of strange creatures living in remote corners of our planet. Are they imaginary, or could they be the descendants of prehistoric animals? A group of determined zoologists is trying to separate the facts from the fantasy.

In 1933, work was finally completed on a road running along the northern shore of Scotland's Loch Ness, a deep lake located to the southwest of the town of Inverness. The road gave travellers an unobstructed view of the lake's 35-km length. It was at this time that reports first began to circulate of a strange creature living in the depths. Soon eyewitnesses came forward with claims of having seen an animal appear on the surface of Loch Ness. These so-called sightings described an animal with a long neck and a small head, sometimes with one or more humps extending behind it on the surface.

Since the 1930s, the creature has entered popular folklore, and there have been many attempts to locate and photograph Nessie, as the Scots lovingly call their 'monster'. Some people have speculated that Nessie may be a long-necked seal, a giant amphibian or a descendant of *Plesiosaurus*, a kind of aquatic dinosaur. Nessie seems to surface regularly from the lake's peat-stained waters, and any alleged sightings invariably find a place in the newspapers. Moreover, journalists never miss the chance to report on the hunts that have been carried out over the years – not one of which has ever found a shred of evidence to support the idea that a monster lurks beneath the surface of Loch Ness.

Cryptic creatures

Nessie is just one of a menagerie of fantastic creatures, or monsters, that have been reported over the years. They vary widely in appearance and in the explanations advanced for their existence. Sometimes, these creatures are dismissed as optical illusions or figments of the imagination. However, representatives of the relatively new research discipline of cryptozoology (the study of hidden

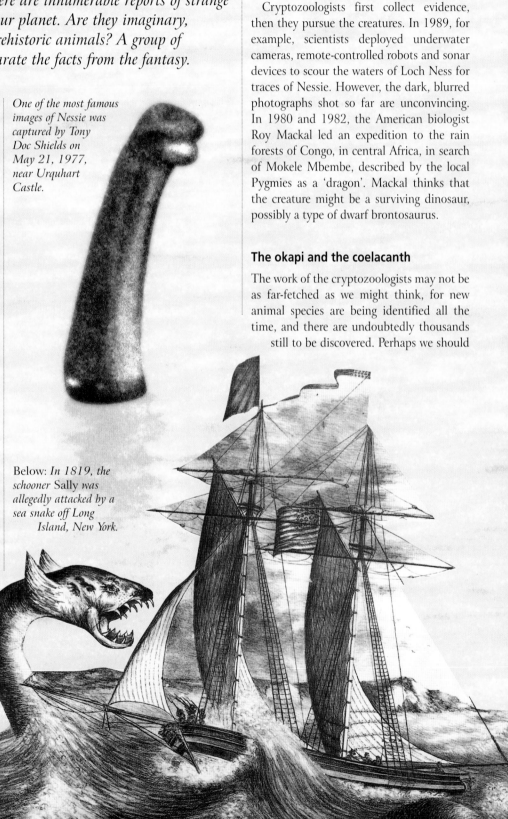

One of the most famous images of Nessie was captured by Tony Doc Shields on May 21, 1977, near Urquhart Castle.

Below: *In 1819, the schooner* Sally *was allegedly attacked by a sea snake off Long Island, New York.*

animals) regard them as unknown creatures awaiting zoological classification, possibly even survivors from a prehistoric age. These scientists tend to be stubborn individualists, but they have formed organisations such as the International Society of Cryptozoology (ISC), headquartered in Tucson, Arizona.

Cryptozoologists first collect evidence, then they pursue the creatures. In 1989, for example, scientists deployed underwater cameras, remote-controlled robots and sonar devices to scour the waters of Loch Ness for traces of Nessie. However, the dark, blurred photographs shot so far are unconvincing. In 1980 and 1982, the American biologist Roy Mackal led an expedition to the rain forests of Congo, in central Africa, in search of Mokele Mbembe, described by the local Pygmies as a 'dragon'. Mackal thinks that the creature might be a surviving dinosaur, possibly a type of dwarf brontosaurus.

The okapi and the coelacanth

The work of the cryptozoologists may not be as far-fetched as we might think, for new animal species are being identified all the time, and there are undoubtedly thousands still to be discovered. Perhaps we should not be so quick to dismiss reports of the Himalayan yeti or a monster in Loch Ness. Cryptozoologists consider the descriptions and illustrations provided by local people as important circumstantial evidence. The same is true of other eyewitness reports, even if these are often greatly exaggerated.

Such descriptions sometimes really do describe new species. This was so with the mountain gorillas (*Gorilla gorilla beringei*) of Central Africa, which were only discovered in the early 20th century. People living near the Virunga Mountains – situated between Uganda and the Democratic Republic of Congo – told of large monkey-like monsters who sometimes ran off with their women. After many years of scientific research, we know that the mountain gorillas are, in fact, gentle giants with no desire for contact with humans. The Komodo dragon (*Varanus komodoensis*), a type of monitor lizard living mainly on the Indonesian island of Komodo, was discovered by researchers in 1912, after fishermen and pearl divers told stories of mighty dragons or land crocodiles. In part these were well founded, for the Komodo dragon is a fierce and brutal killer. Quite different is the shy okapi (*Okapia johnstoni*), a relative of the giraffe which was discovered in 1901 in the dense rain forests of Congo. In 1938, fishermen off East London, in South Africa, netted a coelacanth (*Latimeria chalumnae*), a primitive bony fish thought to have been extinct since prehistoric times. Although the coelacanth is fairly common to the Comoro Islands, it is not popular as a food source. Because the fish did not represent a threat, no legends had been woven around it.

Monsters of the deep

The list of aquatic monsters is a long one, with Nessie only the best-known representative of this large family. From Ireland to China, from Alaska to Patagonia, many lakes are alleged to contain bizarre creatures. The oceans also have their share of strange beasts, but, in some cases at least, science is uncovering some of the facts

Almasti, the yeti of the Caucasus Mountains, was allegedly sighted in Dagestan, southern Russia, in 1941.

These plaster casts of Bigfoot's tracks were made in 1967 in northern California.

In the late 19th century, the crew of the French ship Alecton *tried to capture a giant squid: this was the first indication that this fabled animal might really exist.*

surrounding them. For example, it took a long time for scientists to confirm the existence of the giant squid (*Architeuthis*), the largest representative of the invertebrate family known today. Previously, the giant squid had belonged to the realm of fable.

Fascinated by seamen's tales of huge sea snakes and a creature with long arms, a Norwegian naturalist, Erik Pontoppidan, had included the giant squid in his 18th-century description of the natural history of Norway. In 1854, a huge, parrot-like beak was found on the coast of Jutland, in Denmark, where it came into the hands of Danish naturalist Japetus Steestrup. After analysing the remains, he described a new species of cephalopod: *Architeuthis*.

Towards the end of 1873, evidence turned up that proved the existence of the giant squid. The find was made by two fishermen who had set out from the Newfoundland coast in a rowing boat to investigate what they thought was a wreck. As they tried to pull alongside it with a grapnel, the 'wreck' suddenly moved. A large, hard jaw knocked into the side of the little boat and a long tentacle enfolded it. Only by quickly hacking off the tentacle did the fishermen save themselves. The piece was an incredible 6 m in length, and was covered in giant suction cups.

Occasionally, a giant squid is washed ashore. The largest beached cephalopod ever found had a body length of about 4 m and weighed about a ton. From the top of its head to the end of its 10 tentacles, the animal was more than 18 m long. Its eyes were over 20 cm in diameter – the largest organs of sight in the animal kingdom. But no-one has ever observed the behaviour of a living giant squid in its natural habitat.

Men of the mountains

While descriptions of sea monsters can no longer be assigned to the realms of fantasy, reports of so-called ape-men still present a puzzle. The most famous of these is the yeti, which is thought to inhabit the Himalaya Mountains of southern Asia. Various ape-men, known as hominoids, have been reported on the island of Sumatra (Orang-Pendek), in the Caucasus Mountains (Almasti) of Europe, in Australia (Yowie), North America (Bigfoot, also known as the Sasquatch), Africa and South America. Sceptics dismiss the idea that ape-men exist: after all, there would have to be enough of them to be able to reproduce.

Bigfoot, for example, has only left footprints. Plaster casts of these show that Bigfoot would take a shoe size of about 61. There are people who claim that Bigfoot, and others like him, are the surviving descendants of *Gigantopithecus*, a hominid who lived in South East Asia in prehistoric times and migrated to North America via the Bering Strait. Sceptics dismiss this idea as pure speculation.

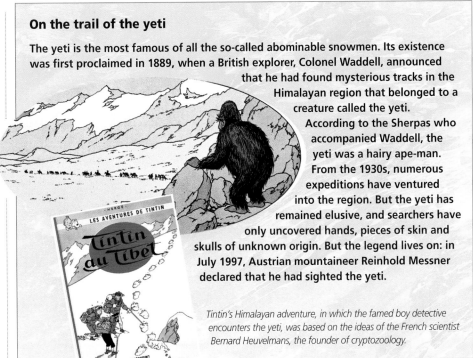

On the trail of the yeti

The yeti is the most famous of all the so-called abominable snowmen. Its existence was first proclaimed in 1889, when a British explorer, Colonel Waddell, announced that he had found mysterious tracks in the Himalayan region that belonged to a creature called the yeti.

According to the Sherpas who accompanied Waddell, the yeti was a hairy ape-man. From the 1930s, numerous expeditions have ventured into the region. But the yeti has remained elusive, and searchers have only uncovered hands, pieces of skin and skulls of unknown origin. But the legend lives on: in July 1997, Austrian mountaineer Reinhold Messner declared that he had sighted the yeti.

Tintin's Himalayan adventure, in which the famed boy detective encounters the yeti, was based on the ideas of the French scientist Bernard Heuvelmans, the founder of cryptozoology.

In the Caucasus Mountains of southern Europe, the local version of the yeti is known as Almasti. Since the late 1950s, Russian cryptozoologists have gathered the stories of local people, which mention sightings of hairy, ape-like creatures. In 1992, a French expedition attempted without success to track down one of these elusive creatures.

For more than a decade, British journalist Deborah Martyr has visited the Indonesian island of Sumatra in search of proof of the existence of Orang-Pendek. In the jungles of the Kerinci-Seblat National Park in the mountainous west of the island, she has interviewed local people, gathered reports of eyewitnesses and studied tracks. She believes that she knows the diet of the 'small man', and the sounds he makes. But neither she nor anyone else has caught more than a three-second glimpse of the creature.

According to cryptozoologists, myths and reality are often closely tied. A good example is the woolly mammoth, a large, hairy, extinct elephant that flourished during the Pleistocene epoch. In parts of Alaska and eastern Siberia, native people believe that the mammoths were chased out of the sea by a sea monster, and that they still live under the earth. Sometimes they come to the surface, and Inuit hunters can see their tusks peeping out from the ground. Then the hunters kill them with their harpoons. Reports of mammoths persist, so perhaps the efforts of the cryptozoologists will one day bear fruit.

Excavations of mammoths in the frozen swamps of Alaska and Siberia – this example was uncovered in 1977 – have fed legends of underground monsters.

THE LOST WORLD OF MOVILE CAVE

The inhabitants of Movile Cave are blind, virtually colourless and live in an almost unbreathable atmosphere. The accidental discovery of this subterranean 'island of life', cut off from the rest of the world for hundreds of thousands of years, affords biologists an unprecedented opportunity to study how animals adapt to hostile living conditions.

In 1986, Rumanian speleologist Christian Lascu was probing a cave system in the Dobruja region of eastern Rumania. Wearing a protective suit, he plunged into a pool of

A millipede with no pigmentation.

A blind water scorpion.

The spider Lascona christiani *was named after the discoverer of the cave.*

A colourless crustacean.

A transparent isopod, one of many species found nowhere else on earth.

Movile Cave is an isolated ecosystem. It includes sulphurous bacteria, which form a jelly-like film on the water, as well as fungi and several animal species. These creatures can survive in as little as 1% oxygen.

Sulphurous water rises from about 400 m.

The calcium carbonate rock above the cave is 25 m thick.

Many thousands of years ago, a unique ecosystem was trapped in Movile Cave.

sulphurous water and worked his way along a passage in the limestone rock. When he surfaced in a muddy cavity, he could hardly believe his eyes: in an atmosphere heavy with sulphur and containing almost no oxygen, he found an extraordinary animal world. Lascu saw spiders, isopods and other crustaceans, millipedes and worms, each of a kind not found anywhere else on earth. The cave explorer had discovered Movile Cave, an oasis of life cut off from the rest of the world for thousands of years.

As news of Lascu's discovery spread, biologists from all over the globe began to converge on the site. Tests determined that the subterranean cavity, situated beneath a

layer of about 25 m of limestone, was lined with a thick layer of clay, which had cut it off from the surface for at least 500,000 years. The cave dwellers had been isolated since primeval times, forming a closed system of life.

Older than humans

The main question was how the animals got there. According to the geological evidence, the cave was created when a karst region – easily eroded limestone layers – collapsed during an

earthquake about 5 million years ago. It is possible that the inhabitants of Movile were trapped in the cave by this sudden geological event.

At that time, the climate was very different, and Europe was covered with tropical forests. The human species had not yet developed, but there was already a rich and varied animal world. It is quite possible that the creatures of Movile Cave include some of these archaic organisms. Other organisms were able to enter the cave until around 500,000 years ago, at which time Movile was sealed off by a thick layer of clay. Today, about 60 species exist there, roughly half of which were previously unknown to science.

Perfect adaptation

Over millions of years, the community had to adapt to the difficult conditions in the cave. Most of the animals are white or very light in colour, for their skins have lost the ability to produce pigments. Deprived of the space to fly in, the insects lost their wings, while in the complete darkness beetles and spiders went blind.

One of the most astonishing things about this unique micro-world is the animals' diet. Because there are no plants to eat, so-called sulphur bacteria have become the basic food. The bacteria form a jelly-like film on the surface of the water, and serve as an organic breeding ground for fungi. The fungi are consumed by insects that would normally live on worms and plants. They, in turn, become the prey of carnivorous animals, and so the food chain is closed again.

So far, it is unclear how the animals successfully adapted to the sulphurous atmosphere, which contains almost no oxygen. Special metabolic adaptations must have evolved, but the processes involved require more study.

Elephants use infrasound (very low-frequency sound waves) to communicate with each other.

DO ANIMALS HAVE A SIXTH SENSE?

Many people say that animals can sense impending disasters. While it is uncertain whether animals have a third eye or a sixth sense, we need to look more carefully at the astonishing feats of which many of our animal friends are capable.

The stories are incredible, but true: the dog who travels hundreds of kilometres to return home; the cat that goes around the world to find its master; cows and horses that flee in panic before an approaching earthquake; or camels that panic shortly before a sandstorm. There are countless similar tales, all testifying to the extraordinarily sharp senses of perception among animals. The thing that is uncertain is whether they have certain abilities that human beings lack. Specialists in animal behaviour reject the idea that animals are capable of extrasensory percep-tion (ESP), for their senses of sight, smell, hearing, touch and taste are similar to our own. So how can we explain phenomena such as an uncannily accurate sense of direction or the premonition of impending disaster?

Among the millions of animals that populate our planet, there is a wide range of sensory perception. The night is almost impenetrable for humans, but the owl possesses specially equipped organs of sight which enable it to see equally well in darkness as in broad daylight. A rattlesnake can hunt for food during the night without any problems, as this reptile has heat-seeking sensory organs which register the heat given off by its prey.

Picking up sound waves

The human ear can pick up sound waves in a frequency range between 20 and 20,000 Hz (hertz). Elephants, however, can also hear low-frequency sounds below 20 Hz – so-called infrasound – enabling them to hear over distances of several hundred kilometres and thus communicate over long distances. The ears of dogs and cats are receptive to ultrasound – vibrations above 20 kilohertz – enabling them to detect enemies early and track down prey successfully.

Most animals, especially those mammals that are active during the night, have whiskers and sensory hairs which react with great sensitivity to touch and vibrations. A bird's feathers function like whiskers to convey information about air currents to the

A cat's whiskers register even the smallest vibration.

brain, which then directs the animal's flight movements accordingly. Some creatures can detect changes in air pressure – for example, the freshwater catfish – which explains their agitation before a thunderstorm.

An internal compass

Scientific studies have shown that carrier pigeons and other migratory birds are capable of registering fluctuations in the earth's magnetic field, which they use to judge their position. Even honeybees use a magnetic sensor when they build their hives, for new honeycombs are orientated the same way as existing ones. Other studies show that, during their seasonal walks, penguins orientate themselves by the position of the stars in the night sky. What is certain is that each species has its own range of perception and uses the information supplied by its senses according to its individual needs and environment.

The rattlesnake makes use of so-called thermo-receptors to detect the body warmth of its prey.

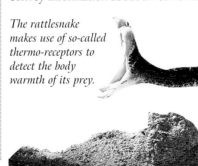

THE MIRACLE OF BIRD MIGRATION

The migration of birds takes place every year like clockwork. Nothing stops the great flocks of feathered creatures in their journeys to and from their breeding grounds. But scientists are baffled by the processes used by the birds to find their routes and to stay on track.

During their spring migrations, millions of birds cross the skies. They follow a strict ritual, leaving their winter quarters and moving to their summer locations, where they mate and reproduce. The journey can take many days to complete. The European fish eagle, for example, needs an average of 30–80 days for its migration from West Africa; the blackpoll warbler travels from North to South America in just 80–90 hours; the knot or Icelandic sandpiper, which belongs to the family of stilts, flies thousands of kilometres across the Atlantic from Europe to Greenland; and the cuckoo migrates in winter from Europe to tropical Africa.

Migratory birds almost never deviate from their course. They always depart from the

Carrier pigeons may use their specially developed sense of smell to orientate themselves.

same places each year. To scientists, the astonishing navigational ability of migratory birds is one of nature's greatest mysteries. We still don't know exactly how animals can travel round the world without getting lost. Nor do we know what navigational aids they use to keep their bearings in the boundless space of the skies. What is clear is that migrating birds face the same problems that seafarers, pilots and explorers must solve: knowing simultaneously where they are, which direction to go and how to get there. In other words, the birds must be able to

same place in order to arrive in exactly the same location as in the previous year. With admirable precision, they follow the same route again and again, resting mostly at the

Long-distance flier

The Arctic tern (*Sterna paradisaea*) is a small ocean bird that weighs barely 100 g. Yet it is a record long-distance flier. After ornithologists placed a ring on an Arctic tern caught in Brittany, western France, the bird later turned up in southeastern Australia, having covered a distance of over 20,000 km. The Arctic tern flies twice yearly on its migrations, travelling literally from one end of the world to the other.

determine their position and choose the correct direction of travel at the same time.

Because migratory birds have neither compasses nor air-traffic controllers to tell them where to go, how do they orientate themselves? Some keep to their northward course by aligning their flight with the position of the sun. In tests carried out on pigeons, scientists have demonstrated the critical importance of the sun.

An internal clock

Carrier pigeons have a kind of inner clock which enables them to find their way back home over many hundreds of kilometres. The decisive factor is the position of the sun. Laboratory tests have shown that it is possible to alter a bird's inner clock by artificially modifying the rhythm of day and night. A number of pigeons were released at noon after their inner clock had been set forward by six hours. The birds perceived the

sun to be already at its 6 p.m. position, which is much further in the west. As a result, the birds orientated their flight too much to the east. In another experiment, researchers exposed them to sunlight that had been re-directed using a mirror. The pigeons tried to follow the new direction of the light and therefore flew in the wrong direction.

Of course, the sun only plays a role for those birds that are active in the day. Those that migrate at night must use a different point of reference. The stars are a possibility, but the great migrations are not disturbed by the presence of clouds by day or night.

Many researchers favour the theory that the earth's magnetic field plays a role in bird navigation. The North Pole and the South Pole act like the two poles of a huge magnet, creating a field which acts on electrically charged particles from the sun, causing them to deviate. Carrier pigeons in particular are known to use the lines of the earth's magnetic field to orientate themselves. If a magnet is attached to a pigeon's head, the bird becomes completely disorientated if the sky turns cloudy, and is incapable of finding its way back home to its cote. However, scientists have to admit that the workings of the internal compass supposedly used by the birds remains a mystery.

A matter of smell?

Scientists must also tackle the problem of how the birds actually locate their routes. There are probably a variety of ways: some species doubtless possess a good visual memory, while the high resolution capacity of their eyes permits them to see objects from a large distance very clearly. But the visual capacity of other species is inadequate.

According to one Italian scientist, pigeons can partially orientate themselves by their sense of smell. They mentally map the smells around their cote, and estimate their exact position with the help of the wind – which brings known scents closer. Shearwaters, such as the great shearwater (*Puffinus gravis*), which visits the eastern North Atlantic in summer and autumn, also use their sense of smell to find their way back to their nesting

Animal travellers

Birds are not the only members of the animal kingdom to undertake long journeys. Many other animals migrate in order to locate food or to find a suitable environment for breeding.

In North America, the tiny monarch butterfly covers near-record distances – more than 4,000 km – during its migration; various species of sea turtle cover several thousand kilometres on the way back to their spawning grounds, where they will lay their eggs. In Tanzania's famous Serengeti National Park, the black wildebeest undertakes an epic journey of about 3,000 km in summer in order to reach the green summer pastures of the north; thereafter it returns to the south.

To reach the spot where it will lay its eggs, a sea turtle (above) often covers enormous distances.

Migrating wildebeest (right).

Monarch butterflies (left) fly great distances on their migrations.

older birds and 'beginners' – when the flock, flying in a southwesterly direction, moved to its annual winter location near the coast of the English Channel. The researchers loaded the captured birds on an aircraft, and flew them to Poland, 600 km further east, where they were released. The youngest crows, which were less than a year old and had no navigational experience, immediately took up their southwesterly course, according to their inherent sense of orientation. The experienced, older birds, however, were able to correct their course and flew purposefully towards the northern coast of France.

But what is the reason for bird migration? Contrary to popular belief, the birds do not only fly south in order to warm up in the sun. Most of them are actually quite resistant to

Mysterious migration

Despite years of study, we know little about long-distance migrations of birds. However, learning processes may play an important role. Experiments have shown conclusive behavioural differences between the young, inexperienced birds and the older ones. On an island in the North Sea, researchers captured a number of hooded crows – both

places on the other side of the ocean in the south. This is a promising area of research, but will require closer observation of various bird species.

cold. However, migration fulfils two vital functions: on the one hand, it safeguards the food supply; on the other, it guarantees the maintenance of the species, as it provides ideal conditions for reproduction. Birds that migrate over long distances and whose departure dates, flight duration and arrival dates tend to be very punctual, are called calendar birds.

ANIMAL ODDITIES

If you think that science has uncovered all the secrets of the animal kingdom, then think again. The natural world is full of creatures whose appearance, habits or way of life raise all kinds of questions for researchers. Whether it is a blind cave salamander, the elusive freshwater eel or South America's smelly bird, the hoatzin, nature has plenty of curiosities in store.

Above: *The pink cave olm has perfectly adapted to its life as a cave dweller. The creature is blind and almost transparent.*

Left: *To sustain itself, the hummingbird needs a lot of energy, which it gets from the nectar of flowers.*

As the rulers of the planet, humans like to think that it is the large creatures who will emerge victorious from the struggle for survival. However, nature teaches us the opposite: it is often the smallest species which are the toughest and most adaptable.

A perfect example is the water bear (species *Echiniscus* and *Macrobiotus*). These invertebrates, which measure less than 1 mm in length, are shaped like cylinders, with a transparent outer skin, known as the cuticle, covering their bodies. Water bears live primarily in fresh water, but can also be found in the coastal regions of the oceans. They are often found in damp mosses or patches of lichen on rocks, walls and roofs. In spite of – or perhaps because of – their small body size, these animals can adapt to the most extreme living conditions. If water is scarce, for example, they can expel a large part of their bodily fluids and shrink to egg-shaped cylinders. Water bears can live for a long time in this state of suspended animation, and can withstand very difficult conditions. In experiments, water bears have survived unharmed after immersion in ether, in 100% alcohol or in hydrogen sulphide; they seem perfectly happy in a vacuum or in an oven pre-heated to 150°C; and recover miraculously after a cold bath in liquid helium at a temperature of -272°C. It takes just a little water to bring them back to life. In a short time, the water bears are flourishing as if nothing had happened.

Small but active

Another record-breaking animal group is the hummingbirds, which are found mainly in the Americas. One species of hummingbird, the bee hummingbird (*Calypte helenae*), ranks as the world's smallest and lightest bird. With a length of only 6 cm and weighing less than 2 g, the bee hummingbird is barely visible when it is in flight.

Hummingbirds are the only birds that can fly backwards. They feed mainly on the nectar of flowers, a liquid that is rich in energy. Nectar is an ideal food source, for hummingbirds need an incredible amount of energy to sustain their body metabolism. A hummingbird's wings flap at a rate of about 80 times per second and its tiny heart beats more than 1,000 times per minute. This is why they must consume relatively large quantities of food: in the course of a day, a hummingbird consumes about half its body weight in nectar.

Forever young

We have to go deep underground to catch sight of the pink cave olm (*Proteus anguinus*), a species of salamander. The pink cave olm can only be found in the subterranean waters of the Dinaric Karst, a mountainous area composed of layers of fractured and eroded limestone in southern Slovenia (formerly part of Yugoslavia). The best known site where it can be found is the Adelsberg Cave near the town of Postojna. The caves are a hostile environment for any living creature, but the tiny cave olm has adapted perfectly to this sunless world: because it lacks the pigments that other animals have, its skin is a translucent, pale pink colour, through which the blood vessels can be clearly seen. Because of the lack of sunlight, the creature has no need for vision: its eyes, which are present in the embryos, disappear in later life, and become hidden

Inseparable

Apart from humans, few animals stay together for life. One that does is the tiny fluke (*Diplozoon paradoxum*), which grows only about 6–10 mm long. The fluke is a trematode, and lives as a parasite on the gills of carp, causing anaemia in its host.

When they mate, flukes literally stick together. Mating occurs very early between two individuals which are still in the larval state. Young worms that do not find sexual partners never mature sexually. With a sucker on the belly and a small elevation on the back, the animals attach themselves cross-wise and copulate. Thereafter they stay together and even grow together.

under the skin. In spite of the difficulty in finding food underground, the cave olm can reach the ripe old age of 30 years.

When scientists first observed the cave olm, they thought it was a larva which was about to change into an adult. However, further studies revealed that this was indeed the adult animal, which had retained its larval features – a phenomenon known to science as neoteny. Although it looks like a larva, the cave olm still has its outer gills, and it is capable of producing young.

Carrying the brood

There are many ways of reproducing and caring for the young, but one of the strangest belongs to the tongueless Surinam toad (*Pipa pipa*). These large amphibians are found in the northeastern part of South America – the animal is named for the former Dutch colony of Surinam – where they live in the basins of large rivers such as the Amazon or Orinoco. The Surinam toad has a very flat body and large webbed feet. It lives almost exclusively in water, where it sits motionless for long periods waiting for its prey to come within striking range.

The Surinam toad was first described at the beginning of the 18th century. Since that time, new reports of its peculiar mating habits have appeared time and again. It was not until 1960, though, that a research team succeeded in observing captive animals as they mated and laid their eggs.

During the mating ritual, the male toad's front legs clasp the female just in front of her hind legs; the pair then make a longitudinal

half-turn so that their bellies are turned towards the surface of the water. Under the pressure of her partner's gentle massage, the female lays about three to ten eggs, which fall onto the stomach of the male. After another half-turn back into the initial position, the eggs then reach the back of the female. At this point, the male holds the female firmly

Above: *The female Surinam toad* (Pipa pipa) *carries its eggs on its back while they develop.*

Below: *The European freshwater eel still poses a riddle for scientists. No-one has ever observed the eel mating or reproducing.*

and fertilises her. In the hours and days that follow, the skin on the mother's back gradually thickens, forming a kind of pocket or cell around each individual egg. After a while, the larvae or tadpoles hatch out, but they remain in their cells until they have grown to maturity, a process that takes about three months.

Secret wedding

Although it took long years of observation and study, researchers finally succeeded in decoding the mating behaviour of the Surinam toad. The situation is different for the European freshwater eel (*Anguilla anguilla*), whose reproduction is a mystery. To this day, no-one has ever observed a sexually active one, and nothing is known about the development of the fertilised egg to the larval stage. However, scientists have discovered a number of facts about the eel's life cycle.

When it is time for mating, the eel leaves European inland waters in autumn and

The coelacanth: discovery of a living fossil

On December 22, 1938, a fisherman off the coast of South Africa, near the port of East London, found a peculiar fish. The creature measured nearly 2 m in length, and was steel-blue, with white specks. By accident, naturalist Marjorie Courtenay-Latimer was present when the boat returned to harbour. She inspected the fish and realised that this was a very unusual animal. Tests showed that it was a creature thought to have become extinct 65 million years ago. This 'living fossil' was named *Latimeria chalumnae* after its discoverer, but we know it as the coelacanth. Subsequent research has shown that the coelacanth is commonly found around the Comoro Islands, and that it is quite familiar to the natives of the islands, who call it *kombessa*. Even today, the coelacanth is sold in local markets, although it is not considered a delicacy.

The coelacanth has a fleshy breast and its belly fins resemble limbs. For these reasons, scientists think that it may be a close relative of the amphibians that first colonised the land.

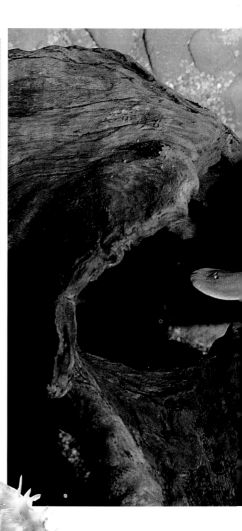

moves towards the salty open ocean, where it disappears into the depths. Scientists have no idea where the animal goes, although they assume that when it is time to mate, in the following spring, the eel will reappear in the eastern part of the Sargasso Sea, south of the island of Bermuda in the western Atlantic Ocean. This means that the animal covers a distance of about 7,000 km on its journey from the other side of the Atlantic. When it arrives in tropical waters, the eel finds the right conditions for reproduction – relatively warm water and a suitable salt content – in water about 5,000 m in depth. It seems that sexual maturation as well as the hatching of eggs requires a minimum temperature of 17°C and a pressure 40 times greater than that found in shallow coastal waters.

A critical role is played by the Gulf Stream, the warm-water current that flows along the eastern coast of North America from the Caribbean, and warms the shores of north-western Europe. The Gulf Stream carries the eel larvae, which are shaped like willow leaves, towards the home of their parents, a journey that takes as much as three years. In spring, when they reach the European coast, the young larvae change into so-called grass eels. The tide carries them into river mouths and they keep on travelling upstream. As they search for a suitable environment – for example, a lake or pond – the eels become darker in colour. They can get over large obstacles and even travel overland by wriggling through wet grass.

When the eel is between 7 and 20 years old, there will come a day, usually during summer, when it will stop eating. Its sexual organs start to develop, signalling that it is time for the great journey. The eel then returns to its spawning grounds in the Sargasso Sea, where it will die after mating has been concluded. To the best of our knowledge, there has not been a single case of a mature eel returning to Europe.

Reversing roles

The sea horse is one of the loveliest, but also one of the oddest, creatures in the ocean. Sea horses of the genus *Hippocampus* are, in fact, modified fish: they hold their bodies in a vertical position as they swim, with their

Sea horses look nothing like other fish. Unusually, the care of the young is the responsibility of the male.

Above: *A duck-billed platypus uses its front paws to propel itself forward, while the hind legs are used for steering.*

head bowed towards the front at right angles. Their skin is made up of bony plates, which form a protective armour. The end of the sea horse's body is drawn into a flexible tail without fins, which they use to cling onto plants. The creature's protruding telescope-like eyes look a bit like a chameleon's eyes. But the quality that separates sea horses from the majority of fish is the fact that the males look after the offspring, and they do so in a very special way.

A male sea horse has a large pouch on his stomach. During mating, the female inserts her laying tube into the pouch and lays her eggs. The male fertilises the eggs, one after another. The wall of the

which is attached to a poisonous gland. If the animal is handled by humans, it can deliver a painful sting, and the poison is powerful enough to kill a dog. As the female platypus has no teats, she suckles her young with the help of milk glands located under the skin. Milk trickles from these glands and runs into a hollow in the middle of her belly.

When the animal dives in search of food, folds of skin cover its eyes and ears. Tiny pores situated around its bill enable the platypus to detect electrical fields created by muscle movements. Thus, the animal can accurately detect its prey, such as insect larvae and small invertebrates, which may be hidden in the mud.

Beyond all categories

Another mammal that is difficult to classify is the aardvark (*Orycteropus afer*), which lives in the savannahs of southern Africa and the rain forests of Cameroon and Congo in Central Africa. Its name is derived from the Afrikaans words *aarde* (earth) and *vark* (pig), and comes from its pig-like snout and the fact that these nocturnal animals dig holes in which they rest during the day.

The aardvark has a large body, which is covered with a coat of bristly fur. A short neck supports its long, hairless head. Its great ears look like those of a rabbit or donkey, while the thick tail is long and muscular like that of a kangaroo. The aardvark has the ability to close its nostrils completely. This means that no ants or termites – the animal's favourite foods – can climb into its nose while it is eating.

abdominal pouch begins to thicken and increasingly fills with blood vessels, forming a type of nourishing placenta. After the eggs hatch, the larvae remain in their father's pouch until they have reached a length of about 5 mm. At this point, the young sea horses are set free in groups.

A mammal with a bill

In the waters of eastern Australia and Tasmania lives what must be the world's oddest mammal: the duck-billed platypus (*Ornithorhynchus anatinus*). The platypus has a wide shovel-like bill and webbed feet like a duck's; its rump looks like that of a mole; and its flat tail, which serves as fat storage, resembles that of a beaver. However, the animal's webbed feet have digging claws similar to a bird's. Strangest of all, this southern-hemisphere mammal also lays eggs!

A male platypus seldom reaches a length of over 50 cm and weighs less than 2 kg. To defend itself, the platypus has something very rare for mammals – a sting in its heel,

The primarily nocturnal aardvark uses its strong claws to open up termite mounds and ant hills. The aardvark's long tongue is also useful in reaching its prey. The animal's digging snout is protected by strong bristles.

Although it is an awkward flier, the hoatzin flutters from tree to tree looking for sources of food. The bird feeds mainly on leaves.

The aardvark's column-like teeth also put it in a class by itself. They continue to grow throughout the animal's life, and slowly wear down on the surface. Each tooth is composed of many hexagonal, parallel prisms, with a tube-like canal in the middle. This is why the order to which the aardvark belongs is called *Tubulidentata*, meaning 'tube teeth'.

Smelly but endearing

Scientists are still unsure how to classify the hoatzin (*Opisthocomus hoazin*), a bird which lives in the rain forests of northern South America. For a long time, it was regarded as a

prehistoric relic, and some ornithologists still regard it as a living fossil at the interface between reptiles and birds. The reason for this stems from the claws which the hoatzin chicks have on their wings. These are similar to those of *Archaeopteryx*, a winged and feathered dinosaur that is considered to be the oldest known fossil bird.

Apart from its blue face, round red eyes and spiky crest, the hoatzin has a number of other intriguing features. It is known as a gallinaceous bird because it belongs to the order *Galliformes*, which includes domestic fowl and pheasants. Most gallinaceous birds digest their food in a muscular stomach. The hoatzin, however, differs from its fellows in two ways. Firstly, its diet consists almost exclusively of leaves. Secondly, the leaves are ground to a mash in a huge muscular pouch in its oesophagus. The gases which it emits have earned it the nickname of 'stink-bird'.

The hoatzin live in flocks and keep in constant contact through their crowing calls. At breeding time, each pair builds a nest on branches close to the water, so the young can drop into the river in case of danger. Using their feet, their claw-like wings and their beaks, the young can then climb back up the tree and into their nest like reptiles.

An underground state

Communal life is a good way to protect the species. A good example of this is the naked mole rat (*Heterocephalus glaber*), which lives in underground colonies beneath the savannahs of East Africa. Naked mole rats grow to 10 cm in length, and their hairless bodies, which lack pigment, look like sausages. Their outsized front teeth mark them as rodents, while their small eyes show that they shun the light.

Naked mole rats live underground. They are hairless, except for a couple of tactile hairs at the tip of the snout.

A naked mole rat community functions much like an insect colony: presiding over a clan of 70 to 80 individuals, a relatively large and aggressive queen reserves the sole right of reproduction, and exercises strict control over her subjects. Younger animals have to look after and rear the young, gather material for nests, provide sufficient food such as roots and tubers, and maintain the colony's tunnel system. The older animals have to dig tunnels and must defend the colony against intruders, especially snakes, the main enemy of the naked mole rat. Living underground and in darkness, the naked mole rat has to be able to communicate with other members of the colony. For this reason, the animals make use of chemical, acoustic and tactile signals. Their repertoire of sounds is regarded as the most sophisticated of all the rodents.

An enterprising fish

If you take a fish out of water, it will soon die. One exception to this rule, however, is the resourceful mudskipper (genus *Periophthalmus*), which is found mainly in the tropics,

With its goggle eyes, thick head and fat tail, the mudskipper resembles a large tadpole.

where it dwells in coastal mangrove swamps. Mudskippers often come onto land at low tide in search of prey. They crawl or hop over the mud as they search for shellfish or insects.

While on land, mudskippers support themselves with strong, arm-shaped breast fins. They can also use their muscular tails like a spring. Even on land, mudskippers use their gills to breathe. Their breathing is made easier by the high humidity and good blood supply in their mouths.

SURVIVAL IN A FROZEN WORLD

After surviving 90 years buried in the frozen soil of Siberia, a tiny salamander has turned the spotlight on one of the miracles of the natural world. We are only beginning to learn how animals adapt to extremes, but this knowledge could be valuable in the future.

One autumn day in the early 20th century, a tiny Siberian salamander (*Ranodon sibiricus*) burrowed beneath the surface of the Siberian soil, in search of protection from the frosty climate and the coming winter. This was part of the animal's natural yearly cycle, for winter temperatures in Siberia can plunge as low as -70°C. Consequently, cold-blooded animals, such as salamanders, newts and frogs, must find protection if they are going to last through the long winter until the arrival of spring.

This particular winter must have been extremely harsh, as the animal was literally frozen solid, even though it had buried itself very deeply. The 12-cm-long amphibian was found by a gold prospector in a block of ice at a depth of nearly 9 m. When told of the find, Russian biologists hurried to the site. After freeing the animal from the ice, they were surprised to see signs of life. Eventually, the salamander stirred and set off in search of new adventures on the Arctic tundra.

Fixing a date

Daniil Berman and his colleagues from the Biological Institute in Magadan, eastern Siberia, used radiocarbon dating to find out how long the salamander had lain in its burrow. This procedure analyses the amount of carbon-14, a radioactive carbon isotope which is naturally present in the soil and corresponds to the carbon-14 content of the atmosphere. Based on the amount of decay recorded in the carbon-14, they concluded that the creature had slept for 90 years.

In the permafrost region of Siberia, winter temperatures can dip to a bone-chilling -70°C.

Few animals can survive such extreme conditions, for each organism contains a high proportion of fluids, which freeze at low temperatures. For example, the human body consists of up to 60% water. If it freezes, ice crystals form in the cells, causing irreparable internal damage to the cell membranes. Ice crystals outside the cells act like a pump to draw the body's vital water from its cells.

To wake up after 90 years in a deep-freeze requires incredible survival strategies. If we look closely at the Siberian salamander, we find that it has a relatively strongly developed liver, which makes up about a third of its body weight and stores plenty of glycogen (carbohydrates), also known as animal starch. When winter sets in, the liver converts these stored carbohydrates into glycerine, an alcohol compound. The presence of glycerine lowers the crystallisation temperature of water, preventing the formation of ice crystals in the animal's body. The glycerine acts as a natural anti-freeze, allowing the salamander to burrow into the permafrost (permanently frozen soil), where it can wait for spring. Another example is the North American wood frog (*Rana sylvatica*),

To keep warm, the North American wood frog produces a natural anti-freeze.

which also endures extreme cold in winter. This amphibian can tolerate temperatures as low as -8°C. Its natural anti-freeze system makes use of glucose, a form of sugar.

Scientists are interested in the ways organisms adapt to extreme living conditions. Even though cellular anti-freeze has been identified, its uses are limited. At present, it is only possible to preserve some tissue and cells – for example, blood vessels, sperm, embryos and red corpuscles – in liquid nitrogen (at -196°C). However, vital organs such as the liver or heart cannot survive such treatment. Such studies have important implications for the field of biotechnology; in agriculture, for example, the principle of cellular anti-freeze may be useful in the development of frost-resistant plants.

CHEMICAL WEAPONS IN THE PLANT WORLD

It is not just animals that make use of toxic substances in the struggle for survival. Many plants use chemicals to defend themselves against the unwelcome attentions of hungry herbivores. When we take a closer look, there seems to be no limit to their capacity for invention.

When we think of plant defences, we usually think of the thorns of a rose or the spines of a cactus. However, the use of chemical defences by plants is less well known, but evidence is emerging that plants can manufacture chemicals that discourage – sometimes permanently – the attentions of grazing animals or inquisitive humans.

In 1985, the University of Pretoria in South Africa asked zoologist Wouter van Hoven to conduct research into the deaths of more than 4,000 kudu (a southern African antelope with distinctive spiral horns). The affected herd was being kept for breeding purposes in a fenced area, but its members were dying fast. In contrast, kudu in the Kruger National Park, in northeastern South Africa, were not affected. When Van Hoven carried out autopsies on some of the dead

animals, the damage to the major organs, particularly the liver and stomach, pointed to poisoning as the cause of death.

A subsequent examination of the faeces of the dead animals solved the riddle: the kudu had eaten from the acacia trees growing in the fenced area. To the zoologist, it seemed that the acacias must be poisonous. In order to test his hypothesis, he cut into the trees. The sap which came out of the cuts was very high in tannin, which can have a poisonous effect when consumed.

Launching a counterattack

Many plants emit poisons in order to defend themselves against predators. This strategy is similar to that of the human immune system, which reacts by releasing antibodies as soon as disease-causing agents appear. For example, if tomatoes start to grow mouldy they can give off substances known as fungicides which will kill off the invaders. When mistletoe, which is semi-parasitic, settles on an oak tree, the plant uses its penetrating roots to extract vital water and mineral salts from its host. However, the oak tree will try to halt the growth of the mistletoe by producing tannins.

Research in South Africa has shown that the acacia tree can mount a chemical defence against herbivores. The trees also seem to have the ability to warn their neighbours of an attack.

An extremely effective defence mechanism can be observed in sorghum, a grain that is cultivated in many tropical and subtropical countries. In the epidermis – the external layer of its leaves – the sorghum plant stores a substance that forms the basis of prussic acid, which is extremely poisonous. This cyanogenic glycoside is a sugar compound of

Oak trees produce tannins to fight off invasions by semi-parasitic plants such as mistletoe.

hydrocyanic complexes. As soon as a herbivorous (plant-eating) animal injures the leaf, special enzymes cause hydrocyanic acid, or cyanide, to be released. This highly toxic substance inhibits the animal's breathing and usually results in death. White clover (*Trifolium repens*) also uses hydrocyanic acid to protect itself from herbivores.

Carried on the wind

But plants may have even more astonishing abilities. The trees identified by Wouter van Hoven were able to send warning signals to other trees. Van Hoven arrived at this conclusion when he noticed an increase in tannins not only in the injured trees but also in unharmed ones nearby. It appears that the first victims of the grazing kudu told their neighbours to produce poisonous substances more quickly. This strategy is successful, for animals usually leave the plants alone once the leaves begin to taste bitter.

But researchers are not clear about the nature of these signals. Botanists believe it is probably ethylene, a chemical substance that plays an important role in the ripening of fruits. It appears that the injured sections of the acacia trees produced ethylene and let the wind carry it to neighbouring trees.

PLANT ADAPTATIONS: DO TREES AND FLOWERS REMEMBER?

Plants of all shapes and sizes are symbols of growth and the unbroken force of life, standing proud in all weathers and conditions. Scientific studies have shown that plants may possess a kind of memory in which they can store and even learn from negative experiences such as injuries or extreme living conditions.

It is generally known that most plants are very sensitive to stress factors such as heat, drought, strong winds or frost. And just like animals and humans, plants also try to adapt in the best possible way to the prevailing living conditions.

We can observe plant survival strategies all around us. Many tree species, for example, give us a very clear picture of how plants cope with their environment. In a forest, beech trees do not develop branches on the lower third of the trunk, and the branches that do develop grow more or less straight upwards. But when a beech tree grows in a park, the most impressive thing about it is its prominent crown and branches, which often almost touch the ground. In very windswept areas, such as near the coast, the branches will grow in the direction of the wind in order to offer the least resistance to natural forces. At the same time, the tree develops a strong root network, anchoring the trunk and branches firmly to the ground.

Defensive strategies

But trees are not alone in their ability to adapt their metabolism to difficult conditions. Tomatoes and carrots can secrete poisonous substances as soon as they become infected with fungi or are injured by grazing animals. Another effective defence strategy is the covering of thorns which plants such as roses or cacti use to defend themselves. What is not yet known is whether plants store memories of bad experiences, and react in anticipation of similar events.

French biologists have tested the 'learning capabilities' of the bryony (*Bryonia dioica*), which belongs to a family of herbaceous climbing plants found in Europe and North Africa. When it is cut back, the bryony will slow down its growth. This effect is caused by the production of ethylene, a gaseous substance. The French team also found that the stem becomes hard and woody as the complex polymer lignin is stored in cell walls. Scientists use the term thigmomorphosis to describe these and other changes in plant characteristics triggered by touch.

The next task for the scientists was to find out whether the reactions of the bryony were genetically programmed. They made clones of certain stem sections, creating genetic copies of the plant. The results showed that the clones possessed the same structural characteristics as the mother plants. This implied that characteristic changes had been passed on to the genetic material, at least for the period of the experiment.

Experiments were also done on the devil's beggarstick, which belongs to the composite flower family. The results confirmed the hypothesis that plants do indeed have a form of memory. Under ideal conditions, devil's beggarstick shoots recovered after the young leaves were damaged with a needle. But if the plants, which thrive in humid conditions, were subsequently moved to a drier position, they wilted much faster than other plants of the same species whose growth period had been left undisturbed.

Above: *The bryony reacts to tactile stimuli by changing its growth and structure.*

Even in an environment of strong winds and drought, trees know how to adapt perfectly.

HOW PLANTS DEFY THE FORCE OF GRAVITY

Ever since Isaac Newton formulated the law of gravity in 1666, we have known that gravity attracts all matter towards the centre of the earth. How, then, do plants and trees effortlessly move water up to their highest parts?

In order for plants to survive, the stem and the leaves – those parts of the plant above the earth's surface – require water and mineral salts in solution. Both are taken from the soil by the roots and are transported in bundled vessels along the axis of the shoot right up into the leaves. During the day, water can rise up through the conducting vessels of trees at speeds of several metres per hour (about 1 m/h in a birch tree, and 43 m/h in oak trees). The water can reach heights of up to 100 m, as is the case with sequoia or eucalyptus trees. The final destination of the

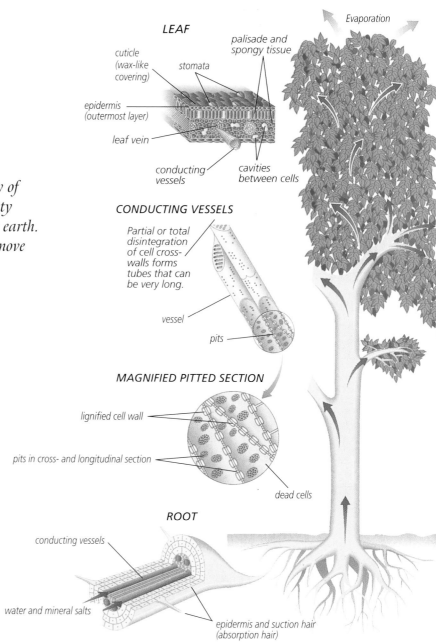

LEAF
cuticle (wax-like covering)
epidermis (outermost layer)
stomata
palisade and spongy tissue
Evaporation
leaf vein
conducting vessels
cavities between cells

CONDUCTING VESSELS
Partial or total disintegration of cell cross-walls forms tubes that can be very long.
vessel
pits

MAGNIFIED PITTED SECTION
lignified cell wall
pits in cross- and longitudinal section
dead cells

ROOT
conducting vessels
water and mineral salts
epidermis and suction hair (absorption hair)

Giant plants, such as the sequoia trees of California, can transport water to great heights without expending energy.

water is the leaves of the plant or tree. The leaves open to the atmosphere by means of so-called stomata – tiny pores on the surface of the leaf that control the movement of gases in and out of the plant.

The need for water

This enormous upward movement of water in plants goes against the force of gravity. The process responsible is a simple one, and is called transpiration or evaporation. Leaves continuously give off water vapour through the stomata, and this amount increases when the air outside is drier and the transpiring leaf surface is larger. Every

Plants absorb mineral salts from the soil with their roots. Through the conducting vessels, or ducts, the diameter of which shrink to as little as 0.1–0.5 mm in diameter, the sap moves up through the stem or trunk and twigs until it reaches the leaves. The water evaporates through the stomata.

day, a birch tree loses 60–70 litres of water through evaporation, and on hot summer days this can reach 300–400 litres. As a result, the leaves start to suffer a water deficit which, in turn, causes a suction effect further down in the conducting vessels of the plant. Tensile stress starts to build up in the conducting vessels, since water particles are held together by the molecular force of attraction, as well as by sticking to the extremely narrow walls of capillary vessels.

This leads to the formation of a siphon, formed with sufficient tensile strength to suck water to heights of 100–120 m without breaking off and without the tree having to exert any energy.

Within the plant, the water is transported via the dead cells of the conducting vessels – the so-called woody tissue or xylem – and by way of the small cavities in the cell walls. The flow of water can be easily disrupted on the long journey to the leaves. Disruptions are often caused by air bubbles, particularly at temperatures below zero, when gases which can usually escape become trapped in the frozen sap. When this happens, gases may block the transport of water and nutrients. Parasites such as fungi and bacteria can also obstruct the channels by narrowing or even destroying the conducting vessels.

A force from below

If a conducting vessel becomes blocked, the plant is usually in a position to deal with the blockage. Often, it will build a bridge across the affected area to allow the liquid in the conducting vessel to flow freely. In the case of the red oak (*Quercus rubra*), a species which is native to eastern North America, the large water ducts die off at the end of each annual growth period and are only rebuilt the following spring, when new growth begins.

The red oak, popular for its lovely autumn foliage, rebuilds its conducting vessels in spring.

In spring, there is a different transport mechanism which plays an important role. As the leaves have not yet unfolded, there is no evaporation suction. However, the roots actively create a pressure which can push water to a height of about 25 m. The process takes place when ions or sugar molecules are pumped into the water ducts from live root cells. The different concentrations create a passive flow of water particles.

AMAZING PLANTS

There are some 100,000 known species of plants on earth, and the list grows longer all the time as new species are named and classified. Plants have developed unique survival strategies that enable them to flourish in all the earth's climatic zones. They can cope with extremes of drought or cold, have developed sophisticated methods of reproduction and break all the records for long life and the attainment of size.

Anyone who has watched a cowboy movie will be familiar with the saguaro cactus (*Carnegiea gigantea*). Like a many-branched candelabra, the saguaro graces the deserts of Arizona, northern Mexico and southeastern California. Its ribbed columns can reach up to 15 m in height, and are the most striking features in these extremely dry landscapes, which would otherwise be stark and monotonous.

This saguaro cactus is a very good example of the phenomenon called stem succulence. In order to adapt to low rainfall in the environment where it is found, the plant's lateral buds have adapted into areoles – sunken areas on which spines grow. The spines are sharp thorns that are actually a form of leaf. In the bud axis, the cactus also has a specialised tissue that can quickly store large amounts of water.

Coping with drought

During periods of drought, the stem of the saguaro cactus becomes wrinkly. But as soon as the rains come to the desert, the plant's storage cells absorb a great amount of moisture, the tissues expand and the wrinkles disappear. The saguaro cactus can also use its extensive root system to replenish its water reserves rapidly. In order to reduce evaporation of valuable moisture, the surface of the plant is covered in a waxy layer known as the cuticle, which contains only a small number of the openings known as stomata, which on most plants permit the exchange of moisture and gases with the atmosphere.

Above: *With a sophisticated system of water conduction, the welwitschia can survive in the arid Namib Desert.*

The Namib Desert runs along the Atlantic coast of Namibia, in southwestern Africa. Rainfall is almost unknown in the Namib; with annual precipitation of under 50 mm and ground temperatures that can hit a blistering 70°C, it is one of the driest regions on earth.

The Namib is the only place on earth where the amazing *Welwitschia mirabilis* flourishes. This plant belongs to the family of gymnosperms, which

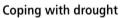

The saguaro cactus has a remarkable capacity for survival in arid climes.

also includes the world's coniferous trees. Scientists estimate that a welwitschia can live to be 1,000–2,000 years old. It consists of a bulb-like stem up to 1.5 m long, but which barely protrudes above ground level, and two giant, band-like leaves.

The only source of water in the Namib is nocturnal dew and the fog that drifts in from the Atlantic Ocean. Scientists used to think that the welwitschia absorbed this moisture through its leaves. However, we now know that the water condenses on the leaves at

The Arctic willow has adapted well to its environment, the icy regions of the far north.

dawn, but then runs along their waxy coating to the tips where it drips onto the ground and is absorbed by the plant's roots.

Survival artists in miniature

The Arctic regions are another kind of desert, one where plants must withstand extremes of cold and long periods of total darkness. The Arctic willow (*Salix arctica*) is found on Iceland, the Faeroe Islands, Greenland and Siberia. In some areas where the Arctic willow flourishes, the mercury can plummet to -60°C. This shrub reaches a maximum height of between 5 and 20 cm, but its branches can grow longer than 1 m. The plant's low profile is partly due to the strong winds that prevail in the Arctic regions and by the ice crystals that develop close to the ground. The Arctic willow grows very slowly, reducing its need for water and nutrients, which are very scarce in the Arctic regions. It flourishes in cracks in rocks and scree (piles of rock debris at the bottom of mountain slopes), where the ground is covered by a warmer layer of snow in winter and where it

is sheltered from the strong winds in summer.

Arctic willows bloom in late spring, when the layers of ice begin to melt. Their catkins are very hairy, and create a warm micro-climate around the tiny blossoms. The seeds ripen in late summer, then fall to the ground. They lie on the ground through the winter, and do not germinate until temperatures rise in the following spring. This phenomenon is known as dormancy, and is similar to the winter hibernation of many animals who live in cold climates.

Planned marriages

For many plants, sexual reproduction is essential to the survival of the species. The key phase in this process is pollination, in which the minute grains of pollen are transferred to the female organs of flowers – their stigmas. Sometimes the wind is the major means of transportation, as is the case with grasses and coniferous trees.

Generally, however, the vital task of pollination is carried out by animals. In most orchids, pollen is carried by flying insects. The woodcock orchid (*Ophrys scolopax*) has developed a particularly clever seduction technique for attracting wild bees. Its flowers imitate the scent, colour and form of female bees so perfectly that male bees simply cannot stay away once their attention has been caught. They alight on the lip of the flower and attempt to mate with the female they think is sitting there. This brings them into contact with the stamen, on which thousands of grains of pollen are found. The pollen is rubbed off onto the heads of the bees and held there. After their mating attempts have failed, the bees set off for the next flower. Their unwanted baggage rubs off on the stigma of the new flower. Pollination is complete, and the woodcock orchid is rewarded for its deception.

The corpse lily or Rafflesia, *native to the rain forests of Indonesia, has the largest flower in the world.*

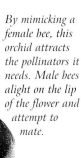

By mimicking a female bee, this orchid attracts the pollinators it needs. Male bees alight on the lip of the flower and attempt to mate.

Some plants need a single insect to carry out pollination. The vanilla plant (*Vanilla plonifolia*), for example, is indigenous to Mexico, where it is pollinated by a certain species of bee. When it is planted outside its natural habitat, the vanilla plant has to be pollinated by hand.

A smelly giant

The corpse lily (*Rafflesia arnoldii*) is found in the rain forests of Borneo and Sumatra, in Indonesia. This leafless plant has adapted to its habitat, in the process becoming a parasite. Because of this lifestyle, the corpse lily no longer has the typical organs of flowering plants, such as stems and roots. Instead, it consists only of cell fibres through which it draws water and nutrients from the roots of woody vines.

The *Rafflesia* flower is an impressive sight, reaching diameters of up to 1 m, with thick reddish petals covered in white spots. In the middle it has a round disc with a thick protruding edge, which forms the female organ. But instead of filling the air with sweet perfume, like most orchids, the corpse lily emits a smell of rotting flesh. This attracts its pollinators, carrion flies.

A living fossil

The maidenhair is named for its magnificent golden autumn hues. Called the ginkgo tree (*Ginkgo biloba*) by scientists, it is recognisable by its typical fan-like leaves, and is related to the conifers. Its dwarf branches carry large, long-stemmed seeds surrounded by fleshy integument, or 'rind'. The ginkgo tree is a native of China, but it was imported to Europe in the 18th century. The ginkgo is the last member of a family of plants that flourished 150–299 million years ago.

The healing powers of this ancient plant are well known today. The concentrated extract of its leaves is known to cause the dilation of the blood vessels, and it is beneficial for ailments of the circulatory system.

The ginkgo tree has lived on earth for about 200 million years.

Deadly traps

Wherever nutrients are scarce – particularly nitrogen and phosphates – plants have found unusual ways of taking in food. In temperate climates, such plants are generally found in moors and swampy locations. In the tropics, these unusual feeders tend to be epiphytic – that is, they live on other plants. Some epiphytes are carnivorous, catching small insects to provide themselves with extra sources of nitrogen. These fascinating plants have developed a variety of ways of trapping their prey.

One of the best known and impressive of these is the pitcher plant (genera *Sarracenia*, *Nepenthes* and *Darlingtonia*). The leaves have become modified to form pitchers with lids. These have a thick lip at the top containing nectar glands which secrete a syrup that attracts insects. The adjacent leaf is slippery, ensuring that the prey slips into the fluid inside the pitcher, where it drowns. Enzymes released by glands on the pitcher floor enable the nutrients to be absorbed by the plant.

The island of Borneo is home to the giant pitchers of *Nepenthes rajah*, which are about 35 cm long and 15 cm across. The plants prey mainly on insects, but also amphibians, birds and mammals.

The cecropia shelters rain forest ants in its branches and stems.

Pitcher plants are among the largest representatives of carnivorous plants.

Strength in unity

The cecropia (*Cecropia obtusa*), which is native to South America, is related to the mulberry family. It has evidently come to an agreement with the ants of the rain forest, giving them shelter and care. In return, the ants protect the plant from herbivores.

In order to attract the ants, the tree forms growths at the base of the leaf stems. These are known as Mullerian bodies, and they are rich in proteins and fats. The Mullerian bodies are regarded by the ants as a delicacy. The cecropia's stem and branches are hollow, like bamboo, with internal partitions. After the queen ant has eaten her way into the stem at a deformed spot where the wall is thin, the ants move inside.

A giant tree

The largest plant on earth is the mighty coast redwood (*Sequoia sempervirens*) of California. These towering trees once covered vast regions of the northwestern United States, but today redwood forests have shrunk to only about 10% of their original extent. Around half of North American redwood forests are located in national parks, where they are protected by federal law.

No other plant on earth can rival the redwood. The world's highest tree, simply known as Tall Tree, grows in Redwood National Park in California; at 112 m, it is the height of a 36-storey skyscraper. A related species, *Sequoiadendron giganteum*, is protected in Sequoia National Park, also in California. The thickest redwood is 25 m in circumference and weighs some 2,500 tons – equivalent to 500 elephants. The tree's characteristic reddish-brown bark can be half a metre in thickness, protecting the tree from virtually any foe – except humans.

The largest seed on earth

For the coco-de-mer (*Lodoicea maldivica*), also known as the sea coconut palm, fame has not been a good thing. Its giant seed – the largest seed in the world – has long been exploited for local tourism. Because of its unusual shape

The seeds of the coco-de-mer are relatively fatty and sometimes very hard.

and size – up to 20 kg in weight and 30 cm in diameter – the seed was useful as a container. Today, the sea coconut palm faces extinction.

PROBING THE MYSTERIES OF THE OCEAN DEPTHS

Incredibly, we now know more about the surface of the moon than we do about the many strange creatures that dwell near the ocean floor. Although the sunless depths of the oceans still conceal many secrets, scientists have begun to unravel the mysteries of this almost unfathomable world.

In the depths of the world's oceans lies a realm of icy cold, darkness and almost unimaginable pressure. Until the mid-19th century, scientists assumed that living things could not possibly survive in the deepest parts of the oceans. In 1841, the English biologist Edward Forbes even expressed the opinion that at depths below 550 m there lay the great oceanic vacuum, an unfathomable liquid hell, as empty as outer space.

Twenty years later, exploration proved that the opposite was true. To the astonishment of scientists, a variety of creatures were recovered from as deep as 1,800 m; these included worms that clung to undersea telegraph cables. In the years that followed, scientists all over the world cast their nets into the sea and trawled its depths. Their efforts were rewarded by the discovery of an assortment of monstrous fish, invertebrates camouflaged as plants and strange creatures seemingly from prehistoric times.

Based on these finds, oceanographers tried to draw up a classification of the remarkable denizens of the ocean depths. This presented a daunting task, since the regions of the oceans that lie below 2,000 m cover 60% of the surface of the earth – more than the area of all the continents put together. Gradually, the data gathered by scientific expeditions has expanded the general picture of deep-sea fauna, in spite of the huge blank spaces that still remain to be explored.

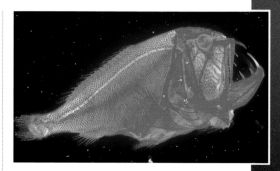

Although the fangtooth looks terrifying, this deep-sea dweller is no larger than a sardine.

A hostile world

In order to understand how animals can survive in such a hostile environment, scientists have had to enter the depths of the undersea world themselves.

If you were to descend towards the ocean floor, you would experience a rapid fall in temperature as you sank further from the surface, but below 2,000 m temperatures

stabilise at about 2°C. The water pressure increases by one bar (1 kg/cm^2) for every 10 m of depth – that is, by the average atmospheric pressure at sea level. At a depth of 5,000 m, the water pressure is 500 kg/cm^2; at 10,000 m – almost the bottom of the deepest trenches – the pressure is 1 ton/cm^2. This is equivalent to the weight of a car pressing down on your thumbnail.

In 1960, the Swiss deep-sea explorer Jacques Piccard and US Navy lieutenant Donald Walsh descended to a depth of 10,912 m in the Marianas Trench – the lowest point on the surface of the planet – on board *Trieste*, a specially built submersible craft known as a bathyscaphe. Piccard and Walsh's descent set a record that has never been surpassed. During the trip, they caught a tantalising glimpse of a flatfish quickly flitting out of the range of their searchlights.

Under pressure

In recent years, scientists have concentrated above all on the mesopelagial, or middle depths, of the ocean. This level is between 100 and 3,000 m below the surface. With the help of submarines and unmanned robot submersibles, they have managed to reveal some of the secrets of the lives of the deep-sea organisms that dwell here.

The first question that scientists have tried to answer is how animals manage to survive such extremes of pressure. To avoid being crushed, the denizens of the deep seas have adapted to the extreme conditions. Their body cavities do not contain gases, which can be compressed; instead their vital organs are filled with water or composed of water-rich tissue that cannot be deformed by pressure. In fact, scientists estimate that half the oceans' mesopelagial animals are gelatinous creatures, many of them jellyfish.

The giant squid

For decades, scientists have tried to solve the mystery of the giant squid, also known by its Latin name *Architeuthis*. For years, the creature was the object of rumour; the first giant squids were only netted in early 1997. These mighty creatures probably live many thousands of metres below the surface. So far, the longest remains that have been washed up on beaches were 20 m. Judging by the size of the scars left by their suction cups on sperm whales – their preferred prey – some individuals must reach lengths of 75 m.

Left: *The submersible* Nautilus *is one of the new generation of undersea craft used by scientists for exploring the ocean depths.*

Left: *The predatory viperfish has extra-long, needle-like teeth that resemble the fangs of a snake. With its cavernous mouth, the gulper (below) can swallow large creatures whole.*

Treasure in the depths

Some species have lived almost unchanged for long periods of time in the depths of the oceans. One of these is *Neopilina galatheae*, a snail about 4 cm long that was considered to have become extinct 250 million years ago. In 1952, it was discovered at a depth of about 4,000 m off the west coast of Central America and brought to the surface.

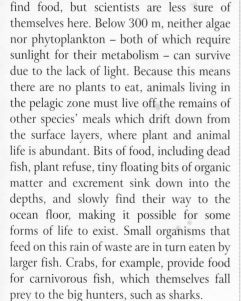

Another question is how these creatures find food, but scientists are less sure of themselves here. Below 300 m, neither algae nor phytoplankton – both of which require sunlight for their metabolism – can survive due to the lack of light. Because this means there are no plants to eat, animals living in the pelagic zone must live off the remains of other species' meals which drift down from the surface layers, where plant and animal life is abundant. Bits of food, including dead fish, plant refuse, tiny floating bits of organic matter and excrement sink down into the depths, and slowly find their way to the ocean floor, making it possible for some forms of life to exist. Small organisms that feed on this rain of waste are in turn eaten by larger fish. Crabs, for example, provide food for carnivorous fish, which themselves fall prey to the big hunters, such as sharks.

The struggle for survival

Because food is scarce, animals that dwell in the depths are primarily predators. Strange forms have evolved in order to ensure that scarce prey does not escape. The *Brotulidae*, for example, look like giant tadpoles with their thick, bullet-shaped heads and thin, tapering bodies. Other species have spines that are sometimes larger than their own bodies, which they presumably use as tactile organs. Many of the denizens of the deep have phosphorescent (light-emitting) organs which they light up to attract their prey or frighten predators.

Big mouths

But one of the most striking things about most of the deep-sea predators is their formidable mouths, typically with an array of long, needle-like teeth. The viperfish, a member of the Chauliodontidae family, or the fangtooth (*Anoplogaster cornuta*), are both excellent examples.

The group of species known as gulpers are aptly named. These fish are members of the Saccopharyngoidae family, and include the 1.8-m-long *Saccopharynx ampullaceus*. This creature has a wide mouth and a highly elastic throat and stomach. These outsized features allow it to swallow prey nearly twice its own size. The

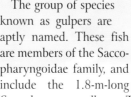

The dogfish can detect prey even if it is hidden below the sand. To do this, the fish uses electric sensory organs located around its mouth.

gulper's belly then swells enormously until the meal has been digested.

If we descend below 3,000 m, we enter a world where life is very scarce. At 4,000 m, the real deep-sea desert begins. Below here, there is only 1 g of living matter per 1 m^2 of water.

Surprisingly, species dwelling at such great depths are often larger than those in the pelagic zone. Many species of fish, like the grenadier fish (a member of the Macrouridae family) can grow to over 1 m in length. Their skin is often thickly covered with an armour of large spiny scales, which gives them their name. There is some evidence of larger species, but these are very much the exception – for example, the giant squid, which is thought to grow to a length of more than 20 m. There is also an unnamed species of shark, measuring some 5–7 m in length, which has been surprised by cameras at a depth of 4,500 m.

For creatures dwelling below 4,000 m, the carcasses of dead animals are an important source of food. Many fish, as well as carnivorous invertebrates, lie in wait on the muddy bottom for carcasses descending from the surface. Whether these are fish, seals or whales, the dead all reach the ocean floor in the end.

The scavengers of the depths are attracted by the smell of decay, as well as by the variations in pressure caused by the movements of a descending carcass. Among the most resourceful of these scavengers are the sand fleas (amphipods), cousins of the species that live on the coast or in fresh water. The deep-sea variety can reach a length of 14 cm. As soon as a carcass has been gnawed clean to the last bone, the animals take a rest in order to digest. Because they never know when they will get their next meal, their metabolism functions at high speed. They rapidly build up fat deposits, which serve as a source of energy until the next feast.

Plants or animals?

But not all deep-sea creatures obtain their food like this. There is a range of detritus-eating organisms attached to the ocean floor, for example, which take advantage of the rain of waste from above. These organisms have many arms, which they extend in the current to snag passing particles of food.

These creatures may appear to be lazy and sluggish, but they actually have very healthy appetites. Sponges, for example, were long considered to be plants, but we now know that they are simple animals which feed by filtering detritus-rich water through their tube-like bodies. The flow is created

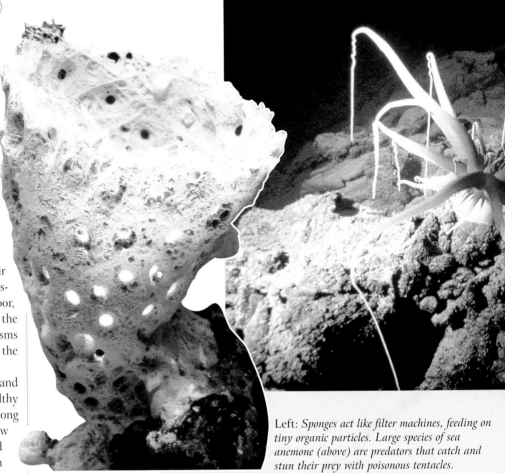

Left: *Sponges act like filter machines, feeding on tiny organic particles. Large species of sea anemone (above) are predators that catch and stun their prey with poisonous tentacles.*

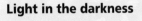

Light in the darkness

Many species of deep-sea fish are capable of producing light with the help of bacteria. The resultant

Deep-sea fish like the anglerfish (Melanocetus) *emit light to attract their prey.*

chemical reactions take place in special luminous organs. The reasons for this extravagant display of light are still not fully understood and seem to depend on the particular species. Some fish use light to attract sexual partners, just as glow-worms or fireflies do on land. Others have veritable chains of light that they use to frighten enemies. The fearsome anglerfish attracts its prey with a luminous thread that hangs in front of its mouth like bait.

by numerous cells equipped with flagella – long whiplike growths that also help the sponge to move.

Sea lilies, on the other hand, extend a wreath of arms, which are covered in tiny feet. The arms catch particles of food. These are then covered in slime and transported by an arrangement of fine hairs through food canals to the creature's central mouth.

Sea anemones have a completely different mode of feeding. They have an impressive crown of tentacles, which can grow up to 1 m in length, and are covered in tiny capsules, known as nematocysts. These break open when touched, and can paralyse the prey.

Tireless rubbish processors

Another way of feeding belongs to so-called detritivores (waste-eaters), which roam the ocean floor consuming the refuse that lies there. Some of these creatures even eat mud: the nutrients in the mud are extracted as the mud passes through the digestive tract.

The sea cucumbers are the aristocrats of the detritivores. Sea cucumbers are echinoderms, of the class Holothurioidea, and have adapted perfectly to life in the deep sea. In

fact, sea cucumbers comprise up to 80% of the species found on the ocean floor. Their fleshy, roller-shaped body resembles that of a cucumber or sausage. These animals cover large areas in search of food, and will consume even the smallest particles. In contrast to their cousins closer to the surface, they often make use of peculiar appendages, which serve as fins, to propel themselves.

Oases in the desert

The deepest parts of the world's oceans are truly a watery desert. Just as in the deserts on land, only a few organisms have adapted to this environment. However, there are a few places that boast an incredible wealth of species: here, huge bush-like collections of long, agile reddish worms wave to and fro in the current. We call these places oases, because they are the underwater equivalent of the life-giving water sources in a hot, sandy

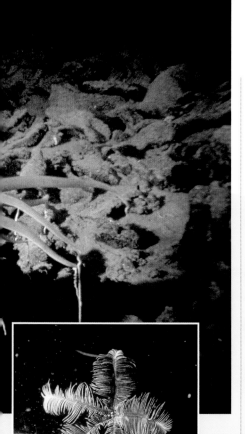

Above: *The sea lily catches digestible floating matter in its many arms, which pass it on to the creature's mouth through the movement of hair-like appendages.*

Below: Hot volcanic vents on the ocean floor support a unique community of living creatures. Among these are crabs, fish and tubeworms (right).

desert. Among the roughly 320 species that have been recorded in the deep-sea oases, 95% are not found anywhere else on earth.

Remarkably, these biological islands are found in the most hostile regions of the deep sea, near volcanic vents along the mid-ocean ridges. Here, sea water seeps through the oceanic crust, coming into contact with molten magma from the earth's core. The water becomes boiling hot and saturated with hydrogen sulphide gas before it is ejected through chimneys known as 'black smokers'. An impressive wealth of animal life thrives in this environment.

Hydrogen sulphide, recognisable by its 'rotten egg' smell, is normally poisonous to living beings. But the boiling hot water emitted by the volcanic springs contains specialised, sulphur-dioxidising bacteria of the species *Sulfolobus*, which thrive in this environment. The bacteria play a vital part in the unique ecosystem of the undersea oases by converting poisonous hydrogen sulphide

Riftia possesses no mouth, stomach, intestine or anus. Instead, bacteria live in specialised internal nutrient tissue, providing the worm's primitive circulatory systems with oxygen and hydrogen sulphide.

These deep-sea oases were only discovered in 1977, and still present scientists with many riddles. For example, why have so many species settled near hot springs, which appear suddenly with movements in the earth's crust, and only last for a limited time? The 'black smokers' are located far apart, and it is hard to believe that such creatures would be able to cover such large distances.

This squid lives at great depths and can inflate when danger threatens.

There are still many questions to be answered about the creatures of the depths. How do they manage to reproduce? How do healthy organisms flourish in an environment of cold and extreme pressure? Because it is so difficult to observe the lives of deep-sea creatures with any degree of precision,

gas into organic matter. In other words, they carry out the same function as green plants on the surface, which use sunlight to produce carbohydrates through the process of photosynthesis.

The sulphur-eating bacteria are the initial or primary producers and represent the beginning of the food chain. They find their way into the bodies of many of the oasis-dwellers, where they provide their hosts with energy-rich compounds. For example, a long tubeworm of the genus

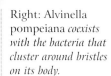

Right: Alvinella pompeiana *coexists with the bacteria that cluster around bristles on its body.*

it will be a long time before we have answers. It is impossible for divers to venture down into the deepest parts of the oceans, for the pressure would kill them. But scientists now use remote-controlled probes which can provide images around the clock. There are also plans to use fast-swimming robots to follow the faster creatures to collect data on their migratory and feeding habits.

TAKING STOCK OF LIFE ON EARTH

No-one knows the exact number of plant and animal species that live on our planet. Counting and classifying them is a lengthy and difficult task, but an urgent one at a time when many species' populations are in drastic decline, and others are threatened with extinction.

For more than two centuries, scholars have been attempting to collect and name all forms of life, as well as to describe their individual characteristics and establish their relationships with species that have already been identified.

The scientific name for this discipline is taxonomy, and its practitioners continue to discover new forms of life. But the process of taking stock of life on earth is a long way from completion. Roughly 1.5 million species of plant and animal are known, but it is estimated that there are another 10–100 million species still to be discovered and named. However, time is running out, since the worldwide destruction of the environment threatens large numbers of flora and fauna with extinction. Since each species is a potential supplier of genetic material and chemical substances which could be used by humans, their loss presents a serious danger.

Saving paradise

The tropical rain forest is the home of almost half of all plant species, a third of the birds and a significant portion of our planet's insects and micro-organisms. However, the rain forest is rapidly being cleared, a problem which worries ecologists and millions of people around the world. Each year, an area of about 200,000 km^2 is cleared – equivalent to more than a third of the area of Thailand. Every day, 600 giant rain forest trees are cut down. If this trend continues, it is estimated that 60,000 plant species and a similar number of animal species will become extinct within the next 30 years.

Other ecosystems are also in danger – for example, coastal mangrove forests and coral reefs. These fragile ecosystems support a huge number of marine animals and plants, many of which are found nowhere else on earth. Industrial pollution and raw sewage are fast destroying the mangroves. Of the 50,000 ha of mangrove forests that once covered the coastline of the Philippines, only 40,000 ha remain intact today. Similarly, 90% of the coral reefs in this region have fallen victim to pollution.

Unknown treasures

We will have to act quickly and decisively if we are to identify, preserve and make use of the species that are still unknown to science. Some of these could be sources of food and medicine. If, for example, the Madagascar rosy periwinkle (*Catharanthus roseus*) had become extinct before its discovery by botanists, we would never have been able to make use of vinblastin and vincristin, two substances extracted from the plant which are used in the treatment of cancer.

Similarly, there are certain species of sponge and coral, found at depths of 500 m, that may have cancer-inhibiting properties. We will have to work fast to save these organisms. Edible wild plants are also of significance, since they increase resistance to disease or improve flavour when crossbred with known food crops.

The rain forest is a vast source of genetic diversity (1).

Mangrove forests (2) and coral reefs (4) are among the earth's most diverse ecosystems.

The Madagascar rosy periwinkle (3) yields an anti-leukaemia drug.

CONTINENTS IN MOTION

The earth seems so firm that it is hard to believe that the continents are actually sliding over its surface. It took decades to convince sceptics that the earth's land masses are not fixed, but are constantly on the move. Mighty forces, whose origins lie deep in the interior of our planet, are ceaselessly at work pushing the continents about like the pieces of a puzzle.

We are all familiar with maps or pictures of the earth that show the continents and oceans. But why is Africa where it is on the map of the world, and not somewhere else? Why are the continents concentrated in the northern hemisphere? What forces created the huge rift – now occupied by the Pacific Ocean – between the Americas, Asia and Australia? Scientists once assumed that it originated in ages past when the moon split away from the earth and became our satellite. Just as we now know that the moon was never joined to the earth, we now have a better understanding of how the continents arrived at their positions.

Until the early 20th century, geologists ridiculed the idea that the continents might be mobile. The traditional picture of the earth saw the continents as fixed masses of land whose position on the globe had not changed over the aeons – except perhaps for a certain amount of rising and sinking. And yet there were certain facts that could not be explained by the theory of fixed continental masses. Some fossils, for example, indicated that related plant and animal species must have inhabited regions of the earth that are today separated by thousands of kilometres of ocean. We know that a dinosaur called *Mesosaurus* dwelt in the rivers and lakes of South America and South Africa around 280 million years ago. Since this small reptile had to travel on dry land and could not have crossed the ocean, scientists assumed that there must have been a land bridge between South America and Africa. According to this hypothesis, *Mesosaurus* must have crossed this bridge, which, at a later stage, must have sunk into the South Atlantic.

200 million years ago

140 million years ago

Today

In 50 million years?

The land bridge theory was first proposed by a German geophysicist on the basis of fossil evidence, but it was not supported by geological finds. In 1912, the German meteorologist Alfred Wegener (1880–1930) caused a sensation in the geological world when he claimed that the continents had once been joined in a single land mass – the original super-continent of Pangaea. In his view, the continents had not remained in one place since their formation, but were drifting over the surface of the planet at a speed of a few millimetres per year. Two years before,

'while observing the map of the world and noting the congruence between the Atlantic coasts of Africa and South America .... the

Alfred Wegener battled for recognition of his theory of continental drift.

initial idea of continental drift' had occurred to Wegener. However, he had rejected it right away, since he 'considered it improbable'. But in the autumn of 1911 he heard about 'previously unknown palaeontological finds indicating an early land bridge between Brazil and Africa'. Soon, he became obsessed by the idea, which came to be known as 'continental drift'.

Plate tectonics

Before Wegener came up with his theory, a number of other scientists had noticed that the coastlines of West Africa and eastern South America fit neatly together like two pieces of a jigsaw puzzle. There are similar correspondences in other regions of the earth – if not in the coastlines, then in the offshore continental shelves, which form the actual boundaries of the continents. But no-one could offer a convincing explanation of what forces had displaced these enormous puzzle pieces. Unfortunately, Wegener could not convince his sceptical colleagues of the validity of this point, and his pioneering theory was soon forgotten.

Wegener died in 1930 while on an expedition to Greenland. It would be more than two decades before American geologists returned to his idea of continental drift and developed it into the now widely-accepted

When the earth trembles

Most earthquakes are tectonic quakes, caused by the release of tensions that build up along faultlines, where the plates of the earth's crust rub against one another. Seismic stations register frequent and powerful earthquakes at so-called convergent edges of the plates – for example, under the Japanese islands on the northwestern edge of the Pacific Plate. It is here that the Pacific Plate pushes under the Eurasian Plate, and is swallowed into the earth's interior. This process is not a smooth one, and explains the frequent earthquakes and volcanic eruptions that shake the region.

In January 1995 the city of Kobe, Japan, was hit by a severe earthquake. Around 5,500 people were killed and thousands more were injured.

theory of plate tectonics, a concept which has revolutionised our understanding of the structure of the planet.

Gradually, researchers uncovered new and surprising similarities in plant and animal fossils that had been discovered in widely separated regions of the earth. But the real breakthrough came when new technologies opened up a field of research that had been unavailable for Alfred Wegener – the study of the ocean floor (also known as the oceanic crust). After World War II, scientists were able to use special ships and electronic equipment to systematically explore and map the ocean floor. Their efforts revealed many thousands of underwater peaks and thousands of kilometres of mountain ranges. Where these break the surface of the sea, they are often crowned with volcanic peaks – for example, in Hawaii or Iceland.

Researchers also discovered that, below the ocean, the earth's crust – with the exception of the continental shelves – is made of rock that is completely different to the continental crust. While the underlying rocks of the continental land masses consist of a wide variety of different and sometimes very old rocks, the geological structure of the oceanic crust is uniform, consisting mainly of volcanic rock of the basalt family, with transitions to plutonic rock (derived from volcanic magma). Furthermore, while rock strata (layers) up to 1,000 million years old are found on the continents, none of the rocks on the oceanic crust are older than 200 million years. As a rule, the youngest rocks lie in the separating zones that lie on either side of the mid-oceanic ridges. As the distance from these great undersea ranges increases, the age of the rocks on both sides also increases.

A conveyor belt under the sea

Based on several decades of observation and analysis, it appears that the oceanic crust is constantly being replenished. New material wells up in the region of the mid-oceanic

Below: *Along California's San Andreas Fault, the Pacific Plate and the North American Plate are shifting horizontally.*

Main forms of volcanic activity

1) and 4) When one plate is forced under another, it can melt in the hot interior of the earth's mantle. The resultant material is relatively viscous (thick), and can lead to explosive eruptions.

2) Above hot spots, where there is increased warmth conducted from the interior, volcanoes may occur in chains – due to plate movements.

LITHOSPHERE { Crust / Upper mantle

Subduction zone

Pacific Ridge

Mid-Atlantic Ridge

MANTLE

Hot spot

Convection currents in the earth's mantle

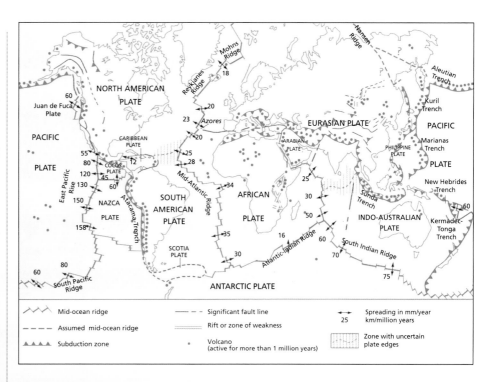

ridges – the gigantic volcanic ovens of the deep sea – and is pushed away from its source by pressure from below. The problem with this interpretation was that if the mid-oceanic ridges had continued to produce new oceanic crust over the aeons without the older crust disappearing again into the earth, then the surface of the earth would have long ago been covered in a solid layer of rock.

The challenge for geologists has been to explain where the old crust has gone. The answer lies in the so-called subduction zones, regions of the earth where the oceanic crust is literally swallowed under the continental crust at a rate of about 8–10 cm per year. The old crustal material is then re-absorbed into the earth's fiery mantle. Subduction zones appear on the ocean floor as longitudinal depressions or deep-sea trenches. In form, they are the opposite of the mid-oceanic ridges. Huge masses of rock are constantly being transported from the ridges to the trenches, as if by a conveyor belt. Scientists estimate the amount to be in the region of 40 thousand million tons per year, with another few thousand million tons of sea water carried along with the oceanic crust.

Since the 1960s, the theory of continental drift, or plate tectonics, has been greatly refined. The difference between Wegener's ideas and the theory of plate tectonics is that

3) and 5) On divergent plate edges, a runny basaltic magma rises and forms the mid-oceanic ridges on the ocean floor.

→ *Movement of plates*

→ *Rising magma*

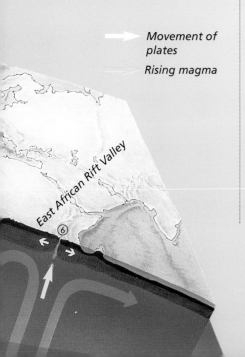

6) Continental rifts like the East African Rift Valley mark where the continental crust splits and where continental drift begins.

today we don't speak of six or seven drifting continents but of about a dozen mobile plates, which carry the land masses of the earth as if by piggyback. These gigantic plates consist of continental or oceanic crust and the upper mantle of the earth. Together they form the fixed crust of the earth, or the lithosphere. The lithosphere is 70–100 km thick, and is thicker under the continents than under the oceans.

Alfred Wegener was unable to pinpoint the forces which drive the continents apart. Today, we now know that the key role is played by convection currents – circulatory movements in the earth's mantle caused by temperature variations. To understand the principle of convection, think of water in a pot: hot water is less dense than cold water and rises to the surface when it is heated; on the surface, it cools, increasing in density, and sinks to the bottom of the pot. In the earth's mantle, it is solid matter, not molten rock, which moves. The asthenosphere, the zone of the earth's mantle directly beneath the lithosphere, is less rigid than the fixed crust, and contains a small amount of molten matter. The asthenosphere acts as the surface across which the plates slide. At times, the plates move at more than 10 cm a year.

In the interior of the plates there is almost no sign of their rapid drift. Deformations of the crust are found here too, but amounting to only a few millimetres per year. The most violent geological processes – for example, volcanoes, earthquakes and the formation of mountain ranges – take place on the edges of the plates. Depending on the direction of plate movement, three kinds of plate edge can be identified: divergent, in which plates move apart; conservative, in which plates slide past one another; and convergent, in which plates collide, with one plate being pulled downward by convection currents.

Divergent and convergent plate edges feature lively volcanic activity and powerful earthquakes. These tectonic phenomena are most dramatic on the convergent edges. Extensive sections of the edges between the (oceanic) Pacific Plate and the neighbouring continental plates, for example, are typical of a subduction zone. This region is known as the 'ring of fire', due to the many eruptions and earthquakes that occur here.

The collision of continental plates is marked by strong uplifts and deformations of the crust. These plates consist of relatively light rock that is more easily forced upwards. The world's highest mountain ranges lie in the 'crumple zones' of the continental plates. The best example is the mighty Himalayas of southern Asia, which were created when the Indo-Australian Plate ground its way into the larger Eurasian Plate.

JOURNEY TO THE CENTRE OF THE EARTH

Only in science-fiction stories are adventurers able to probe the secrets of the earth's interior. In the real world, we rely on technology to probe the secrets of our planet's molten core. Seismology – the branch of geology that is concerned with how and why earthquakes take place – has taught us much about the inner structure of the earth, but many details remain a mystery.

A scene from Jules Verne's Journey to the Centre of the Earth.

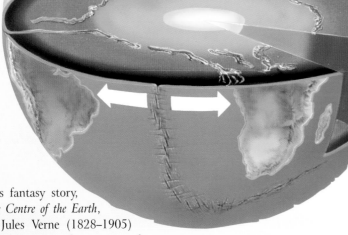

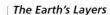

The Earth's Layers

1 – Inner core (*solid*)
 > 5,000°C
 iron, nickel and some other elements.

2 – Outer core (*molten*)
 > 3,500°C
 iron, nickel, silicon.

3 – Inner mantle (*solid*)
 2,100–2,900°C
 iron-magnesium-silicon and other silicate minerals with high-density ion packing.

4 – Outer mantle (*mainly solid; partly molten*)
 > 1,200°C
 peridotite (iron-magnesium-silicates).

5 – Crust: *continental crust, primarily granite; oceanic crust, basalt.*

In his famous fantasy story, *Journey to the Centre of the Earth*, French author Jules Verne (1828–1905) described the adventures of a group of explorers venturing into the earth's core. Verne's tale has become a classic of science fiction, but we know today that no human could survive the conditions that prevail deep beneath the earth's crust.

It should be no surprise that hell was thought to lie in the earth's interior. Drilling has revealed that temperature increases by about 3°C per 100 m of depth. At a depth of 10 km, temperatures of 300°C prevail. The world's deepest mines, by contrast, are only about 2 km in depth, and it is impossible for humans to work below this depth. Apart from the enormous cost, deep drilling has failed because of the technical problems caused by extreme heat. This means that scientists use other methods to explore the earth's interior: they examine rock fragments brought to the surface by volcanic eruptions; they carry out experiments which simulate conditions in the interior – for example, at extremely high temperatures and still higher pressures; and they analyse seismic waves to determine changes in their velocity and the manner of their propagation. This makes the seismograph – an instrument for detecting earth tremors – a valuable tool. It provides X-ray vision into the depths of the earth.

Deep underground, more than 5,000 km below the surface of the earth, our planet must consist of solid matter, most probably a mixture of iron and nickel. It also contains lighter elements such as sulphur, oxygen or silicon, since we know that the density of the inner core is lower than that of a pure iron–nickel alloy.

The movement of seismic waves in the inner core depends on their orientation – a typical property of crystalline matter – so that many scientists assume that the basic chemical components of the core are crystals. These prevail at temperatures of up to 7,000°C – so hot that most substances on the surface would instantly melt or vaporise. The outer core does not transmit certain seismic waves, which indicates that it may be in a molten state. But it may consist of materials unknown to us.

A lost continent?

Earthquake activity gives scientists useful opportunities to listen to the earth's interior with their instruments. But earthquakes are hard to predict, so man-made explosions are the next-best thing. In 1947, British forces blew up German-built fortifications on the island of Helgoland in the North Sea. The 'big bang' – the largest non-nuclear explosion in history – was not entirely successful from a military point of view, but it was valuable for geophysicists. It provided them with important new insights into the structure of the earth's crust underlying central Europe.

Man-made explosions provide a flood of data which can present new problems. In 1993, China conducted an underground nuclear test that provided scientists with a remarkably exact three-dimensional picture of the interior of our planet. At the same time, the data added another question to the list of the earth's riddles. Some scientists thought the data showed fragments of a continent that had been sucked from the surface to depths of more than 2,000 km. Whatever the truth may be, a journey to the earth's core would be just as exciting today as it would have been in Jules Verne's day.

OUR PLANET'S LIFE-GIVING ATMOSPHERE

Humans depend for survival on a mixture of gases which we call air and water. Without these two ingredients, life as we know it would not exist. The earth's covering of air and water means that our planet is probably the only one in the solar system where life has developed. But the earth's atmosphere was created out of a witches' brew of deadly gases, at a time when the earth was shaken by natural forces of unimaginable ferocity.

Seen from space, our planet presents a lovely sight. Wisps of cloud drift over the continents and the great blue oceans which cover almost three-quarters of the earth's surface. Because there is so much water, the earth is often referred to as the 'blue planet'. But it was not always this way. In the beginning, the earth was covered with black lava and grey ash. Its surface resembled that of the moon, and the thin crust was covered in countless craters caused by the impact of meteors or by the eruptions of thousands of volcanoes.

As well as lava and ash, every volcanic eruption spews out large amounts of volcanic gases from the earth's interior. These gases are composed primarily of water vapour, which typically makes up between three- and nine-tenths of volcanic gas. Scientists are not certain how much water vapour originates from ground water that comes into contact

Without its mantle of air and water, created mainly from volcanic gases, the earth could not have produced life.

with molten rock, and how much comes directly from the magma in the earth's mantle. Depending on the variety of molten matter, water vapour could make up between 0.1% and more than 7% of it. This may seem quite a small amount, but over the millions and billions of years of the geological time scale, even a small percentage can yield huge quantities. Today, the total quantity of molten matter produced by all the active volcanoes on earth in a year amounts to about 6–8 km^3. If the average water content of this matter is 1%, then the annual supply

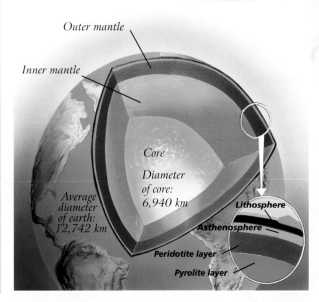

Outer mantle

Inner mantle

Core

Diameter of core: 6,940 km

Average diameter of earth: 12,742 km

Lithosphere

Asthenosphere

Peridotite layer

Pyrolite layer

The earth consists of several layers. The core is metallic, surrounded by several layers of mainly silicates and oxides. The earth's water masses and most atmospheric gases originate from these layers.

of juvenile water – as it is referred to – would be enough to fill a moderate-sized lake. However, if we start our calculations at the dawn of the ice ages, then the amount of juvenile water produced would have been enough to fill all the lakes on earth.

When the planet was developing, volcanic activity was more intense than it is today. This meant that much more water vapour was produced. At first, however, the surface of the planet would have been too hot to retain the water. Only after the temperature had cooled below boiling point could the water vapour from the volcanoes start to condense. When this took place, torrential rains flooded the planet and the oceans were born.

Oxygen versus carbon dioxide

After water vapour, the most important volcanic gas is carbon dioxide (CO_2), which is produced in even greater quantities than water vapour. When we breathe, we exhale carbon dioxide, and the gas is an essential component of the process of photosynthesis. When the earth was young, the atmosphere contained much more carbon dioxide than today because of constant volcanic activity. Oxygen (O_2), which today makes up 21% of the earth's atmosphere, was scarcely present in this primal atmosphere. The amount of carbon dioxide in the atmosphere has fallen steadily since those early days, while the

Why is the sky blue?

It's an obvious question, but not one that is easy to answer. The sky gets its colour from the blue, short-wave portion of sunlight, which is much more strongly dispersed by air molecules than the long-wave, red portion. The short-wave rays are diverted from their original course by the tiny particles of air. The larger particles of water in the air disperse light evenly, regardless of its wavelength. For this reason, clouds appear white or grey.

oxygen content has climbed to its present values. However, scientists around the world are concerned about the recent sharp rise in carbon dioxide levels which has resulted from industrialisation, population growth and the clearing of tropical forests.

In examining the formation of the earth's atmosphere, scientific attention has focused on the original proportion of carbon dioxide, and the ways in which oxygen gradually replaced it. So far, two distinct hypotheses have emerged. The first of these is based on biology. After the 'invention' of photosynthesis – the process by which plants use sunlight to convert carbon dioxide and water into organic compounds – primitive plants removed the carbon dioxide from the air and water, producing oxygen as a 'waste product'.

The second hypothesis suggests that torrential rains washed the carbon dioxide out of the atmosphere into the oceans, where it was trapped in calcium-rich sedimentary rock. As a result, the original carbon dioxide content – which, at the time when the earth's fixed crust was formed, could have been as high as 95% – gradually fell to today's value of less than 1%, while the oxygen content climbed to today's 21%. The first indication of a higher oxygen content in the earth's atmosphere comes from the red colour of sedimentary rock, which comes from finely distributed iron oxide, better known as rust.

The birth of life

It must have taken several hundred million years before the earth's mantle of air began to resemble what it is today. During that time, conditions would have been extremely hostile to life. Volcanic eruptions rocked the planet, while violent thunderstorms drifted overhead and deadly ultraviolet rays from the sun penetrated the gases and blanketed the earth's surface. Acid rain fell from an atmosphere poisoned by hydrogen sulphide, ammonia and methane and collected in oceans of near-boiling water. And yet, a miracle took place – the emergence of life.

In the 1950s, the American chemists Stanley L. Miller and Harold Urey carried out a series of pioneering experiments that showed decisively how the earliest forms of life were created. Miller and Urey succeeded in reproducing the primal atmosphere under laboratory conditions. They then subjected the gaseous mixture to electrical discharges that simulated the lightning that struck the earth 4–5 thousand million years ago. After a few days, the 'primal soup' in the test tubes was found to contain the amino acid glycine, one of the building blocks of protein.

The first steps towards the emergence of life probably took place in the mud on the ocean floor. This was the only place where primitive forms of life were protected from the sun's ultraviolet rays. Certain minerals may also have played an important role in uniting simple organic molecules. These had the ability to bind chemical substances, thus preventing the building blocks of life from being destroyed by energy-rich waves.

Venus and Mars: our closest neighbours

Mars, the desert planet.

In the last 20 years, a number of satellites and probes have provided scientists with a wealth of new knowledge on the planets of our solar system. Much of this data relates to the atmospheres of these planets. We now know that Mars and Venus, the two closest planets to the earth, both possess atmospheres fundamentally different to our own. On both planets, the carbon dioxide content in the lower and middle atmosphere

Venus, glowing hot.

fluctuates around 95%, while the oxygen content is less than 1%. This probably resembles the primal atmosphere of our planet some 4–5 thousand million years ago. But unlike the earth, Mars and Venus have remained hostile to life.

The Sahara covers the northern portion of the African continent, a vast area of sand dunes, rock and desolate gravel plain. For some time, the world's largest desert has been growing. In North Africa, the average rate of advance is 5 km per year. On the southern edge, drifting sand has encroached into the wetter Sahel region, which runs across Africa from the Atlantic to the Red Sea. Since 1900, the Sahara has grown by a total of about 1 million km².

The expansion of the Sahara is not unique. In many of the earth's arid regions, once-fertile land is gradually being turned into

During the terrible drought of the early 1980s, thousands of cattle died of hunger and thirst in Africa's Sahel region.

desert. Scientists do not agree on the exact causes of this progressive desertification, but what is certain is that it affects many thousands of people each year. Some experts argue that desertification is caused by the over-exploitation of natural resources by humans – for example, by clearing natural vegetation for use as fuel or by allowing livestock to consume scarce vegetation.

A cyclical process

As population growth continues in many poorer countries, such practices are likely to go on, and even to accelerate. However, there are other researchers who argue that the expansion of the Sahara and other deserts is a natural process, and is caused by climatic variations of the kind that have occurred frequently in the history of the earth.

Professor Marcel Boodt, director of the World Centre for the Study of Deserts, argues that we must look far back into the history of the earth's deserts if we are to

DESERTS ON THE MOVE: THE PROBLEM OF DESERTIFICATION

Why is the Sahara Desert ruthlessly advancing on the fertile landscape at its boundaries? Why is a third of the earth's land surface threatened by desertification? Is it due to the ecological sins of humanity, or is the alarming desertification of our planet a natural, unstoppable process?

Sahara

Sahel

Savannah zone

Tropical forests

understand their current phase of expansion. Twenty thousand years ago, during the coldest period of the ice ages, the Sahara extended in some places up to 500 km further south than its present boundary. At that time, these zones would have been too hot and dry for human occupation. Then, around 9,500 years ago – towards the end of the last ice age – the climate in this southern zone became wetter. This meant that the limit of the tropical summer-rainfall region pushed northwards, and, with it, the belt of savannah vegetation. Hollows became lakes, and their shores supported crocodiles, hippos and rhinoceros. About 4,500 years ago, the

warm period following the ice age came to an end and the earth cooled significantly. The land dried out and the deserts took over.

The alternation of wet and dry climatic periods may be tied to long-term variations in temperature. When temperatures are cooler, there is less evaporation and therefore also less rainfall. During the ice ages, for example, rainfall would have been only about half what it is today.

While the main reason for the advance and retreat of the world's deserts may lie

Green grass in the Sahel does not mean the region is out of danger.

with long-term climatic cycles, humans have certainly interfered with nature's balance. The Sahel is particularly vulnerable, and endured four droughts in the 20th century. The last major drought (1968–1985) led to widespread misery and starvation. After the drought, there was a partial recovery and greening along the southern edge of the Sahara, but no-one can predict if another drought is on its way or not. And it will take many decades before scientists can unravel the complex causes of desertification.

THE GREENHOUSE EFFECT

The ice caps melt and the seas rise, flooding cities, towns and farms, while blistering heat waves and devastating floods ravage the land. This may sound like science fiction, but such events are a possibility if the current global warming trend continues. The cause of this is a process of radiation and irradiation, warming and heat loss known as the greenhouse effect. Without it, there would probably be no life on earth, but our actions are placing great strains on this vital natural process.

Bleak prospects

Little progress has been made in reducing the build-up of greenhouse gases in the earth's atmosphere. If progress is not made soon, the average air temperature will continue to rise, with potentially dire effects. So far, the results of international climate conferences and conventions have been disappointing.

The greenhouse effect has received a great deal of attention in recent years. While it is often mentioned in newspapers, magazines and TV reports – sometimes as 'global warming' – most people are not sure exactly what it is, or whether it is a good or bad thing. One thing is certain, though: without the greenhouse effect, our planet would be a very different place. A few primitive creatures might possibly exist in certain sheltered areas, but there would be no human beings, and we would certainly not be in a position to discuss this phenomenon. But human activities have made it into a potentially serious problem.

The greenhouse effect is a term for the warming influence of the atmosphere. The atmosphere allows short-wave radiation from the sun to penetrate almost unimpeded to the surface of the earth. However, long-wave radiation reflected by the earth's surface is

Solar radiation (visible light, ultraviolet and infrared radiation)

Radiation into space

Solar energy absorbed by the atmosphere

Solar radiation reflected into space

Greenhouse gases

Radiation absorbed by the earth's surface

Stratosphere

Troposphere

Heat reflected by the atmosphere

Heat radiated by the earth

CO₂ and other greenhouse gases produced by human activity

Short-wave solar radiation (yellow) warms the earth, which emits long-wave heat radiation (red). Only a small part of this energy dissipates into space: most of it is absorbed in the atmosphere. This then becomes warmer, and returns a portion of the energy to the surface through irradiation.

The ozone hole

Another factor that contributes to the greenhouse effect is the destruction of the earth's ozone shield. The reason for this is an accumulation of ozone-destroying chlorofluorocarbons (CFCs) in the atmosphere. For several decades, these chlorine compounds were used as propellants

in aerosol spray cans, as cooling elements and in the production of plastics. The Montreal Protocol of 1987 set targets for phasing out the production and use of CFCs.

absorbed and converted to heat energy in the upper atmosphere, and then immediately returned to the lower layers of air. Think of a greenhouse on a sunny day: the glass roof allows the sunlight to reach the young plants, but it also keeps the heat inside, making a greenhouse a warm place even when it is cold outside. Without the greenhouse effect, the surface of our planet would be icy cold: the average temperature would probably be about -18°C. But, in fact, the average air temperature on earth is 15°C – a gain of more than 30°C! The earth's mantle of air acts as a permanent heat trap. The key role in this process is played by a number of gases, primarily nitrogen and oxygen, with traces of several other gases: water vapour takes up a significant but varying proportion, while

carbon dioxide, methane, nitrous oxide, ozone and the other so-called greenhouse gases only make up about 0.01% of dry air (air without water vapour).

Too much of a good thing

The greenhouse gases are known as trace gases because they normally only occur as traces – very small quantities – in the earth's atmosphere. The trace gases act like spices in a meal: if they are used sparingly, spices give the food the right flavour, but too much and the whole meal will be ruined. Of course, the amounts of greenhouse gases fluctuate due to natural causes, such as volcanic activity, but they have recently increased to an alarming extent.

An oil fire is an example of a global problem: burning fossil fuels, such as oil, gas and coal, increases the supply of carbon dioxide.

The origins of the problem lie with rapid industrialisation, the clearance of tropical forests and the burning of more and more petroleum, natural gas, coal and other fossil fuels. For example, since industrialisation took off in the late 19th century, world-wide emission of carbon dioxide (CO_2) – the main greenhouse gas – has increased by about 60 times since 1860, when roughly 340 million tons were emitted. Carbon dioxide, which is poisonous to humans, has also become much more concentrated due to the widespread clearing of the world's forests. This is because growing plants and trees bind CO_2 from the atmosphere, acting as toxic-waste depots in the CO_2 cycle. If there is less vegetation, particularly in the critical rain forest belt, then less carbon dioxide will be recycled, increasing concentrations in the atmosphere. With the other greenhouse gases, such as methane or ozone, the situation is even more dramatic; these gases represent about 15% of the human destruction of the earth's balance of energy.

Can nature help itself?

In greenhouses, the carbon dioxide content generally falls significantly below that in the outside environment, since rapidly growing plants require large amounts of CO_2. This is why gardeners must provide an artificial supply of the gas. High concentrations lead to rapid plant growth and therefore to a greater consumption of carbon dioxide. This seems to suggest a way for us to

Above: *Exhaust gases from automobiles are a major cause of global warming.*

dispose of our surplus greenhouse gas. From a practical point of view, however, this is impossible. The forests that could be used to consume the gas are shrinking at an alarming rate. This applies particularly to the tropical forests, which are the main consumers of carbon dioxide (and suppliers of oxygen) on our planet. When rain forests are converted to pasture or agricultural land, their CO_2 consumption falls to about a quarter of its former level.

The build-up of greenhouse gases goes on, but some scientists and politicians still see no reason to attack the problem at its roots and cut our emissions of carbon dioxide. Some experts believe the oceans may help us out of our self-inflicted misery, for the world's oceans store vast amounts of carbon dioxide. The storage capacity of the oceans is 60 times that of all the plants, and the colder the water, the more carbon dioxide it can absorb. The problem here is that the warming of the atmosphere will also warm the oceans, reducing their capacity to store carbon dioxide.

The role of water vapour, or the water in the atmosphere, has not yet been satisfactorily

explained. The thing we know for certain is that warm air can absorb more water vapour than cold air. The general warming caused by an increase in carbon dioxide content also results in an increased water-vapour content in the air. Because water vapour is a greenhouse gas, this means that the barriers to heat irradiation would become stronger and the warming of the lower atmosphere even more dramatic. Many scientists fear that this process could accelerate global warming, which has been estimated at 2–3°C. Rising temperatures are always calculated on the basis of average world values. A rise of 2–3°C would have the

Forest fires consume millions of hectares of trees each year. A bigger problem is forest clearance, which destroys carbon-dioxide storage capacity.

most serious consequences in the polar regions, where it would cause glaciers to melt. This would cause even more solar energy to be retained in the earth's heat-trap, since ice and snow reflect more solar rays than grass or bare rock.

Heavy industry is a major producer of greenhouse gases, such as methane, water vapour and carbon dioxide, but farmers also contribute to the problem.

THE GROWING OZONE HOLE

High above the earth, an invisible shield protects living beings from the sun's harmful ultraviolet radiation. This is the ozone layer, a fragile membrane that is under threat from a deadly brew of man-made chemicals. Unless we do something, a global catastrophe looms.

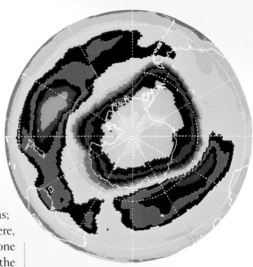

In this thermal image of the southern hemisphere taken by NASA, the pale violet and grey sections show the ozone hole over Antarctica. Research shows that the ozone layer above Antarctica almost disappears at certain times of the year. In 1994, the ozone hole covered 24 million km² and was three times the size of Australia.

Ozone is a peculiar gas: close to the ground it is a harmful substance, but at a height of 20–50 km above the earth's surface it forms a protective layer. For almost two decades, we have known that this invisible shield is crumbling. At first, a large hole formed above Antarctica. Researchers noted that the ozone content in this region had fallen to more than 70% below normal. This set alarm bells ringing, for the ozone layer acts as a protective radiation filter, without which living beings on earth would be over-exposed to the sun's energy-rich ultraviolet radiation. At present, the ozone supply seems to be diminishing by 3–4% each decade near the equator, and by more than double that amount at higher latitudes.

What's going on up there?

There are a lot of questions surrounding the ozone issue. Most people are unsure what the ozone layer is, how it is formed and where it is located. Ozone, which comes from the Greek word *ozein*, meaning 'to smell', is the name for the form of oxygen with three atoms (O_3; oxygen is O_2) compounded in a single molecule. The gas has a characteristic odour; it is poisonous and aggressive, and causes damage to plants and buildings even in small amounts. Air that becomes contaminated by ozone can cause eye irritation and lung complaints. For this reason, some countries monitor ozone levels during the summer months; if it rises above a safe level, environmental authorities issue an ozone warning. Usually, however, the ozone content in the lower layers of the atmosphere remains relatively low. A rise in ozone concentration occurs under certain weather conditions, such as in summer when automobile exhaust gases (which consist of a mixture of nitrogen and hydrocarbons) reacts with sunlight to produce more ozone than normal.

At the earth's surface, excess ozone is related to air pollution created by humans; in the upper layers of the atmosphere, however, pollutants drastically reduce ozone content. The ozone layer surrounding the earth is not a permanent, fixed layer. It fluctuates according to seasonal changes and longitude. It is more like a high-altitude laboratory in which ozone is constantly produced and destroyed. Like the phoenix, a mythical bird that rose from the ashes, the ozone dies and is constantly reborn.

During the day, when most of the sun's radiation passes unhindered through the upper atmosphere, energy-rich ultraviolet radiation collides with oxygen molecules (O_2), breaking many of them down into two single atoms. Some of these combine again immediately with other O_2 molecules that have remained intact during the ultraviolet bombardment. This two-step process leads to the creation of ozone molecules (O_3). Along with the production of ozone, there is also a natural process of decomposition of the gas. If this did not happen, there would

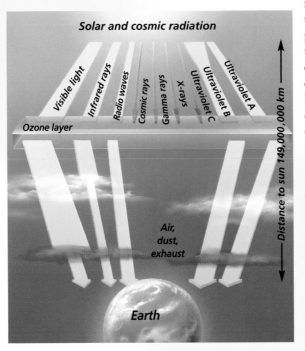

Solar and cosmic radiation

Visible light
Infrared rays
Radio waves
Cosmic rays
Gamma rays
X-rays
Ultraviolet C
Ultraviolet B
Ultraviolet A

Ozone layer

Air, dust, exhaust

Distance to sun 149,000,000 km

Earth

soon be far too much ozone. Decomposition occurs when other, soft ultraviolet radiation splits ozone molecules, releasing an oxygen atom which combines in a second step with another ozone molecule, forming two oxygen molecules. This process requires certain substances that act as catalysts, such as sulphur particles from volcanic eruptions.

A natural cycle

The production and decomposition of ozone is a natural cycle that has taken place over millions of years. In recent decades, though, the process has been disrupted, producing such lasting phenomena as the holes that have opened up in the ozone layer, first above Antarctica then over the northern polar regions. In the late 1970s, British scientists reported a dramatic reduction in ozone content over Antarctica towards the end of the polar winter. At first, they assumed that there was a problem with their equipment. However, their data proved to be correct, and triggered a desperate search for the causes.

Scientists have developed a number of theories to explain the depletion of the ozone layer. Some believed that ozone

Left: The atmosphere in general and the ozone layer in particular act like filters to protect life on earth from the sun's harmful ultraviolet radiation.

depletion stemmed from natural causes, such as meteor showers, solar flares or volcanic eruptions, while others felt that the balance between ozone production and decomposition had been upset by human activity. One theory suggests that ozone depletion is caused by aeroplane emissions. Modern jets fly at heights that are dangerously close to the ozone layer. However, it is also quite possible that aeroplane emissions may act as a kind of 'antidote', actually slowing down ozone depletion.

The main source of substances harmful to the ozone layer probably lies in the lower levels of the atmosphere. Because of human activities, this seems to be where harmful substances originate. Scientific attention has zeroed in on a particular group of chemicals that are believed to have a hugely destructive effect: the halogenated hydrocarbides (those containing chlorine, fluorine or bromine), among them chlorofluorocarbons – known as CFCs for short. For decades, these stable compounds were widely used in industry, in refrigeration systems, as aerosol propellants and in the production of insulating foam, aluminium and semiconductors.

As far as we know, these gases are harmless when released at ground level, but their effect changes radically when they rise into the upper layers of the atmosphere. As soon as CFCs arrive in the ozone layer, they are broken down by ultraviolet radiation; they then release chlorine, bromine and fluorine. These three chemicals cause chain reactions

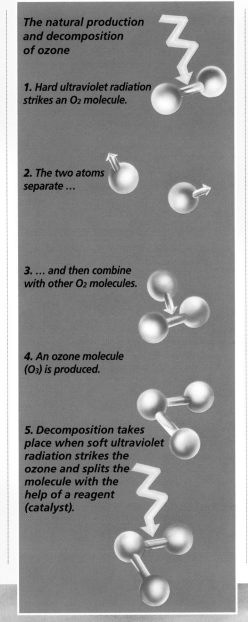

The natural production and decomposition of ozone

1. Hard ultraviolet radiation strikes an O2 molecule.

2. The two atoms separate …

3. … and then combine with other O2 molecules.

4. An ozone molecule (O3) is produced.

5. Decomposition takes place when soft ultraviolet radiation strikes the ozone and splits the molecule with the help of a reagent (catalyst).

Flying high

We still do not fully understand the role played by aircraft emissions on the depletion of the ozone layer. Just like car exhausts on the surface, aircraft engines emit a cocktail of gases – among them water vapour and carbon dioxide – which may play a role in the destruction of the ozone layer. According to one recent theory, nitrogen oxides from jet engines play a role in the decomposition of ozone, but at the same time they produce new ozone in the upper atmosphere through a complex chain reaction triggered by ultraviolet radiation.

that destroy ozone molecules. Above all, it is chlorine that has the most disastrous effects. One chlorine atom can destroy up to 10,000 ozone molecules before it is bound onto another substance.

Is time running out?

Although we have identified the culprits, the world community has been slow to deal with the problem. This may seem surprising, for ozone depletion poses catastrophic effects for human health and economic activity. Calculations indicate that a 5% reduction in ozone concentration (such as has been observed within a decade at high latitudes) can cause a 10% increase in the rate of skin cancer. Other probable health problems include increased risks of sunburn, eye disease and a weakening of the human immune system. If ozone depletion goes on, farmers will have to deal with falling harvests – as much as 20% in certain crops that are sensitive to ultraviolet radiation, such as soya beans. Even if all steps were immediately taken to prevent further depletion of the ozone layer, scientists fear that the worst is yet to come. This is because the harmful substances take years to rise up into the stratosphere.

The ozone hole above Antarctica attains its greatest size during the southern hemisphere's early summer.

Scientists release balloon probes to provide data on ozone content in the stratosphere.

In 1985, the first international agreement was signed: this was the Vienna Convention for the Protection of the Ozone Layer. Two years later came the Montreal Protocol on Substances that Deplete the Ozone Layer. These agreements placed restrictions on the production and use of CFCs, and committed the world community to an eventual ban. The production and use of these substances is now prohibited in industrial nations, while grace periods have been mandated for the development and implementation of replacement substances. For developing countries, the grace periods will extend into the middle of the 21st century. The signatories agreed that the production of some other substances will be frozen at 1995–1998 values. However, many countries still manufacture huge amounts of

CFCs, while others have not adhered to the terms of the protocol. In the states of the former Soviet Union, for example, CFCs are apparently produced in large quantities, and then smuggled into other countries. Despite international efforts to halt the damage, the upper atmosphere today contains about 50% more ozone-damaging chlorine than it did when ozone depletion was first noticed.

The situation seems more desperate than ever. In the past 25 years, the ozone layer has lost about a tenth of its original ozone content, and the trend is continuing. A noticeable reversal will probably only take place well into the 21st century. In the mid-1990s, scientists noted for the first time a reduction in ozone-damaging substances in the air at ground level. Because the gases need an average of three to four years to reach the stratosphere, this reduction will take several years to make a difference. Until

The high-altitude ER-2 reconnaissance aircraft can gather data from heights of 20 km.

then, the depletion of the ozone layer is likely to continue unchecked.

Ozone depletion is taking place all over the world. The major exceptions are the tropical and subtropical areas on either side of the equator. Almost all atmospheric ozone

A convenient scapegoat

Since its discovery, the ozone hole has been blamed for a range of illnesses. Some people have claimed that greater ultraviolet radiation caused by the ozone hole has blinded sheep in southern Argentina and endangered frog populations. However, numbers of amphibians have been declining in regions where the ozone layer is still intact. All over the world, many frog species are classified as endangered. The real culprits could be agricultural chemicals and drought.

is produced in these areas. The ozone is transported to the higher latitudes, which are naturally poorer in ozone.

Polar crisis

Sometimes the ozone layer becomes thinner, sometimes a real hole is detected. Since the 1970s, ozone depletion over Antarctica has been dramatic. In the late 1990s, the ozone layer over the South Pole grew dangerously thin, and was almost destroyed at heights of 15–20 km during the brief Antarctic spring and early summer (from September to mid-November). But it then

A French slogan urges efforts to save the ozone layer.

regularly closed again. The rapid depletion of the ozone layer over the South Pole may be connected to very low temperatures in the southern continent: the ozone-damaging substances are stored in ice particles in clouds in the stratosphere, so low temperatures tend to intensify the ozone-depletion process. The stratosphere above the North Pole is on average 10°C warmer than the corresponding layer above the South Pole. For this reason, the depletion of the northern ozone layer is taking place more slowly. Nevertheless, in the mid-1990s, ozone values up to 45% lower than normal were measured over the Arctic. The northern hemisphere ozone hole has been made worse by a succession of unusually cold winters and by several violent volcanic eruptions.

VOLCANOES: MOUNTAINS OF FIRE

Volcanoes reveal the terrifying and elemental power of nature. Few natural phenomena are as fascinating – or as unpredictable – as a volcanic eruption. Increasingly, volcanologists are making use of sophisticated technology to investigate the moods of these fiery mountains. In time, we may be able to predict when eruptions will take place.

Volcanologists were astonished when the first clouds of ash began to rise from the crater of Mount Pinatubo in the Philippines on April 2, 1991. Many of the volcanoes on Luzon – the largest island in the Philippines archipelago – are monitored by scientists, but no-one thought that Pinatubo, which had been dormant for centuries, would come to life again. When they reached the mountain, which lies to the northwest of Manila, scientists found that the magma level in the volcano was rising daily. On June 7, a catastrophe seemed to be approaching, and the experts convinced the local authorities to evacuate people living nearby. The evacuation was just in time, for one of the strongest volcanic eruptions of the 20th century began on June 12. In three days, the volcano released an amount of energy 100 times greater than that of the atomic bomb which levelled Hiroshima in 1945. Pinatubo's fury left at least 400 people dead and destroyed the homes of many thousands.

Every eruption is different

The eruption of Pinatubo should not have been a surprise. One of the characteristics of volcanoes in this part of the world is that they lie dormant for decades, even centuries, and then explode

Above: *With their fluid streams of magma, pure lava eruptions, like this one in the Pu'u O'o crater, Hawaii, are usually harmless.*

Below: *A section through a classical layered or stratified volcano. The name comes from the characteristic layers of lava and ash.*

Lava discharged in various sizes, from small pieces of ash to volcanic bombs

Lava streams of relatively sluggish magma

Cloud of ash and gases

Volcanic gases and water vapour cause a powerful explosion

Alternating layers of lava and ash

Side crater

Magma rising in a vent

Magma chamber

with almost no warning. The prelude to an eruption is hidden from view: magma, a molten mixture of rock, more or less rich in gases, slowly rises through vents from the depths of the earth, collecting at first in subterranean cavities known as magma chambers. The magma may remain here for only a few weeks, or for several thousand years, depending on how long it takes for the chamber to fill. When a volcano is ready to erupt, it often swells up like a balloon; cracks appear on its flanks, allowing water to seep through to the molten magma, where it immediately vaporises. When this takes place, an eruption inevitably follows.

The flows of magma that rise in the top vents of the volcano display a variety of physical and chemical qualities – for example, gas content, viscosity (thickness) and temperature, among other things. This affects the way the eruption happens. Volcanoes whose activity is primarily explosive are known as plinian, after the Roman author and naturalist Pliny the Elder (AD 23–79), who died in the eruption of Mount Vesuvius in AD 79, during which the nearby towns of Pompeii and Herculaneum were buried in ash. Plinian eruptions expel huge amounts of debris in the form of clouds of ash and molten avalanches. There are also fiery mountains that spit out floods of lava, and volcanoes that emit ash or lava according to their moods, sometimes building up beautiful, symmetrical cones.

Appearances are deceiving

Volcanoes differ not only in the nature, but also in the frequency, of their eruptions. A few of them are always on the boil – a good example is Stromboli, located on an island off the southwestern coast of Italy. Widely known as the 'lighthouse of the Mediterranean', Stromboli has set off spectacular but harmless fireworks roughly every quarter hour since humans began to record such events. Other volcanoes gather their forces over centuries, only to strike with merciless power. Many volcanoes appear to be highly active, but appearances can be deceiving: Pichincha, in Ecuador, constantly emits thick clouds of vapour from its pinnacle, but has not erupted since 1881.

Alarm signals

Volcanology is the study of volcanoes, and volcanologists – the scientists who specialise in this field – are not easy to deceive. They have developed a set of procedures to provide early warnings of coming eruptions. Among the alarm signals are earth tremors, ranging from a barely perceptible shaking to powerful volcanic quakes. In highly active volcanoes, these quakes generally appear a week to a month before an eruption. If a volcano rests for several decades or centuries, its warnings begin many months, or as much as a year, before an eruption.

Quakes are caused when the rising magma violently forces its way to the surface of the earth, distorting the external structure of the volcano by anything from a few centimetres to dozens of metres. Volcanologists now use

In order to understand better how a volcano works, volcanologists often need to get very close to its mouth (1).

Lasers are used to measure ground movements, providing early warning of eruptions (2).

Taking gas samples, here on Mt Etna in Italy, is routine work for a volcanologist (3).

It is uncertain whether the Puy chain in France's Auvergne region is really extinct (4).

①

②

③

laser technology to detect and measure the tiniest movements of the ground. Other instruments include: inclinometers, highly sensitive instruments for measuring slope, which register changes in the incline of the earth's surface; magnetometers, which measure fluctuations in the earth's magnetic field, which are related to movements of magma; extensometers, which follow the growth of cracks in the earth which develop as the volcano swells and expands; and sensors, which register the temperature of geysers, or hot springs.

At present, approximately 1,000 volcanoes around the world are being monitored by volcanologists. In order to improve the early warning system, it would be necessary to observe constantly the earth's most active volcanoes – there are 50 of these – and to keep an eye on those mountains of fire that have announced their presence at least once over the past 10,000 years, and which might suddenly come to life again. Technology now makes it possible to carry out round-the-clock observation, thanks to satellites that can quickly detect erupting clouds. Mobile observation equipment can also collect data automatically, and then transmit it by radio to central stations. Of course, all this instrumentation is expensive, but when we consider the fact that volcanic eruptions have claimed the lives of more than 100,000 people during the 20th century, as well as destroying incalculable amounts of property, improving our warning systems represents an investment in humanity's future.

Monitoring systems

Even experienced volcanologists should not come too close to active volcanoes, and many have paid with their lives for acts of daring. For this reason, French physicist and volcanologist Michel Halbwachs keeps his distance and relies on satellite data to monitor volcanic activity. In 1990, equipment in his laboratory in Chambéry detected a suspicious bubbling of gases. A microphone beneath the surface of Lake Kelud in Indonesia was transmitting a warning signal of an impending eruption. Residents of the area were evacuated immediately – and just in time.

④

OUR ODD-SHAPED PLANET

It took many thousands of years for people to accept the fact that the earth is round, and not as flat as a pancake or a discus. The fact is, though, that the shape of our planet is more like a wrinkled pear or an under-inflated football – full of bumps and dents. Data from satellites orbiting the planet has given scientists a much more exact picture of the earth's surface. While we can now measure the planet's dimensions with a much greater degree of precision, we are still not clear about the processes that have produced its irregularities.

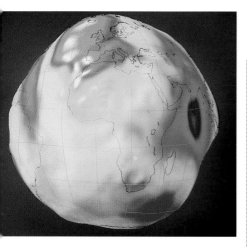

The earth is not flat, but it is not perfectly round either. Its shape has been created by gravity and centrifugal force. This computer-generated image shows the actual shape of the earth, complete with depressions (yellow, green and blue) and raised areas (red). To arrive at this shape, scientists used a theoretical form, known as a geoid, which is based on average sea levels.

For thousands of years, people thought that the earth was flat. Developments in science and the exploration of the planet changed this view, and the earth came to be seen as a perfect sphere – as we imagine it to be today. In recent years, though, we have discovered that our planet is shaped more like an egg: elliptical in cross-section and noticeably flattened at the poles. The polar radius – the distance from the centre of the earth to the surface at the poles – is about 15 km less than the earth's average radius. On either side of the equator, the earth bulges outward, with the equatorial radius at least 7 km longer than the average radius elsewhere on earth.

Like a drop of water

The earth's rotation creates centrifugal force, which means that a point on the equator is subject to greater acceleration than a point at the poles. Over millions of years the rotation of the earth has altered its shape – as a drop of water changes shape when it is shaken. In 1924, the International Union for Geodetics and Geophysics set out to describe the shape of the earth as exactly as possible by fixing the values of an international ellipsoid – a symmetrical geometric shape.

For several years, we have known that the true shape of the earth is very different from the ellipsoid. The breakthrough came from data gathered by satellites, which gave us a much more precise image of the main features of the earth's surface.

Because the raised parts of the earth's surface interfere with the exact calculation of the planet's shape, scientists have developed a theoretical earth that is covered by water. Their calculations are based on the earth's mean (average) sea level. Thus, they assume that the earth – like the sea – has a relatively smooth and uniform surface. The shape that results is known as a geoid. Strangely, this abstract shape is uneven, with bumps up to 100 m high or deep. Southern India is deformed by a 100-m-deep indentation; Indonesia stands on a 75-m-high bump; out in the Pacific Ocean there is another bump that rises 100 m above the surface of the geoid.

Scientists are focusing their studies on the make-up of the earth's core, and especially on gravitational variations that are related to the structure of the earth. We know that the distribution of mass over the crust of the earth is uneven, which implies that gravity must vary as well. In some places – under the oceans, for example – the crust of the earth is only a few kilometres thick. By contrast, under mountain ranges the crust is much thicker. In some areas, the crust consists of heavy rock, while in others the rock is much lighter. On land the force of gravity is above average. This may be why indentations seem to exist on land, while raised portions are found in oceanic areas.

The French astronomer and mathematician Alexis-Claude Clairaut (1713–1765) was sent to Lapland in 1736 to determine whether the earth was flatter in the polar regions.

A SHIFTING MAGNETIC FIELD

Contained in the rocks of the earth's crust is the evidence of startling shifts in the planet's magnetic field, which has completely reversed itself many times. By unlocking the secrets of these polar reversals, scientists are learning much about the events that have shaped our planet.

Migrating birds lose their way, radio communications break down and the night sky lights up red and green. This may sound like science fiction, but it is what might happen if the earth's magnetic field suddenly shifted. The last time this occurred was about 780,000 years ago. At that time, the earth's magnetic field altered by 180°, resulting in a reversal of its polarity. But this was not an unusual or a unique event. For several decades, scientists have known that the earth's magnetic field has shifted several times in the past. When seen on a geological time scale – the span of time since the rocks were created – these shifts have taken place at remarkably short intervals. However, the causes and timing of these magnetic shifts are still not clear to geophysicists.

A central dynamo

If you think back to school days, you may recall a simple scientific experiment. First, place a sheet of paper over a magnet; then spread iron filings over the paper. The iron filings will immediately orientate themselves toward the ends of the magnet, around which they form broken lines. These lines correspond to the lines of the magnet's field.

The earth also acts as a giant magnet. Its forces are distributed roughly as if a strong magnet were situated in the centre of the earth. The axes, or magnetic poles, are not aligned with the earth's rotational axis, but are located at an incline of about 11°. Thus, the north and south magnetic poles are located a considerable distance away from the geographic North Pole and South Pole.

To get an idea of the strength of the earth's magnetic field, imagine if every cubic metre of the earth's volume were to contain 200 m³ of magnetised steel rods. This would be about equal to the earth's magnetic field. But the magnetic field is not produced by fixed magnets. Instead, it is the result of electric currents produced by slow-moving molten matter, flowing on the edges of the earth's core. The process is like a dynamo. This is why scientists refer to the dynamo theory.

The memory of the rocks

Because the changes occurred so long ago, it is easy to think that we can know little about the shifts in the earth's magnetic field. The key to unlocking this mystery is contained in the rocks that make up the earth's crust. Certain rocks contain magnetic minerals –

Epochs and events

To understand changes in the earth's magnetic field, you have to take the long view. Before our present, 'normal' polarity was established, the last complete polar reversal took place 780,000 years ago. Before that, there was a period of almost 1.7 million years in which the magnetic poles were the opposite of what they are today. The periods of uniform polarity are known as epochs, and are named after scientists who study palaeo-magnetism. Within these epochs, the polarity has been known to reverse for several millennia. These events, like the one that took place between 910,000 and 980,000 years ago, are named after the places where they were discovered.

Folds of hardened lava are a reminder that the island of Hawaii was formed by volcanic action.

such as iron. When these rocks were formed, the prevailing direction of the magnetic field was frozen inside them. These types of rock remain magnetised through the ages. In igneous rocks – formed by volcanic action – magnetic particles orientate themselves in the molten magma like compass needles according to the earth's magnetic field. In sedimentary rocks – formed through the build-up of particles carried by water – the particles are deposited according to the magnetic field. As the volcanic magma or the waterborne sediments harden, the particles retain their magnetic orientation. Scientists use instruments known as magnetometers to measure this residual magnetism, which provides a 'map' of the fluctuations in the magnetic field.

Through examination of the magnetic orientation of parts of the earth's crust, geophysicists have determined that the earth's present magnetic epoch began 780,000 years ago. This epoch is named after the French physicist Bernard Brunhes, who in 1906 discovered a series of lava flows with reverse polarity. Brunhes's find caused a sensation, but it had no practical significance until the

1960s. Since that time, many other polarity reversals have been discovered. By recording the ages of these events, scientists have been able to develop a polarity time scale. This can be used to calculate the age of many rock series, and makes it possible to date with greater certainty rocks with little or no mineral content. The reverse polarity of the earth's magnetic field is the only way of dating many rock series.

The application of this procedure has achieved impressive results in the study of the basalt layers on both sides of the mid-ocean ridges. Here, rock series with normal and reverse polarity reveal a conspicuous, zebra-striped symmetry. The pattern shows that the ocean floor has been spreading, confirming the theory of continental drift.

The polarity scale shows us that the orientation of the earth's magnetic field usually remains steady for between several millennia and a million years. When polar reversal takes place, it happens suddenly. There have also been periods of quite short polar reversal, in which the magnetic field is out of balance for a few millennia without a complete polar reversal taking place. In these cases, the polar reversal from the northern to the southern hemisphere, or vice versa, only

The burning sky

One of the earth's most eerie natural displays is the pulsating bands of red, green and yellow light that appear in the skies of the polar regions. These are known as the aurora borealis (northern lights) and the aurora australis (southern lights). These atmospheric fireworks are set off when protons and free electrons released by the sun, and travelling at speeds of around 1,600 km/s, collide with atoms or molecules in the earth's atmosphere at altitudes of 80–1,000 km. The collisions cause the particles to light up. The aurora occur most frequently in two ring-shaped zones located 23° from the magnetic

The external magnetic field of the earth creates the spectacular phenomenon of the aurora borealis.

poles. In these areas, particles approaching the earth are drawn to the poles by the earth's magnetic field.

lasted for a few thousand years – which, in geological terms, is equivalent to the blink of an eye. A French-American team of scientists has even suggested a record time for reversal: analysis of 16-million-year-old samples of basalt has revealed that, at that time, the location of the magnetic poles wandered by several degrees each day! After a few weeks or months, the reversal was complete.

When they wander, the magnetic poles prefer certain routes, such as the north–south route through the Americas. The magnetic field seems to weaken before and during the migration, and can at times become chaotic, as if there were several magnetic poles at the same time. At present, the magnetic field is weakening noticeably. This could be a sign that a new polar reversal is approaching.

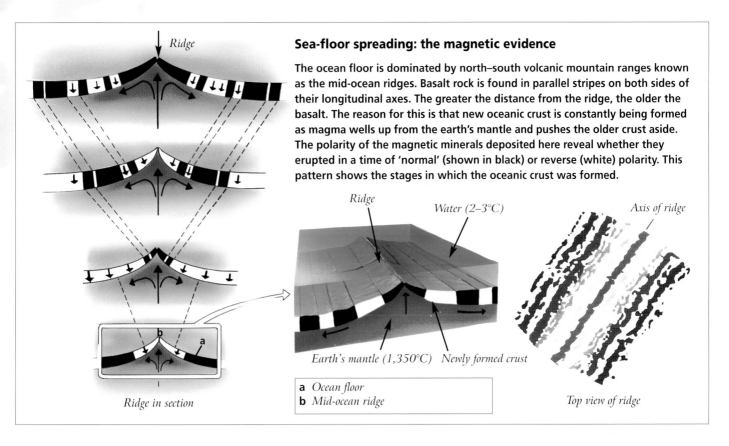

Sea-floor spreading: the magnetic evidence

The ocean floor is dominated by north–south volcanic mountain ranges known as the mid-ocean ridges. Basalt rock is found in parallel stripes on both sides of their longitudinal axes. The greater the distance from the ridge, the older the basalt. The reason for this is that new oceanic crust is constantly being formed as magma wells up from the earth's mantle and pushes the older crust aside. The polarity of the magnetic minerals deposited here reveal whether they erupted in a time of 'normal' (shown in black) or reverse (white) polarity. This pattern shows the stages in which the oceanic crust was formed.

Ridge

Ridge in section

Ridge

Water (2–3°C)

Axis of ridge

Earth's mantle (1,350°C)   Newly formed crust

a *Ocean floor*
b *Mid-ocean ridge*

Top view of ridge

IS THE EARTH SLOWING DOWN?

Around 370 million years ago, a year was 400 days long. Today, a year is only 365 days. The days are getting longer, because the earth is turning ever more slowly on its axis. One day, perhaps, it will even stop turning. However, we probably won't be around to find out.

The astronomer and mathematician Edmond Halley (1656–1742) was one of the most distinguished scientists of his time. Halley gave his name to the most impressive comet in the solar system, the orbit of which had first been observed in 1583, and his research embraced such fields as navigation, magnetism and diving.

Remarkably, Halley was the first scientist to conclude that the speed of the earth's rotation is slowing down. The rate at which this takes place is tiny, and cannot be detected within a lifetime. Nevertheless, it means that the days are actually getting longer. In 100 years, a day will be around 2 milliseconds longer. This may not seem like very much, but it adds up.

The slowing down in the rate of rotation only becomes meaningful when we measure it in geological terms – the span of time in which the rocks of our planet were created and gradually worn down. Today, the earth takes 24 hours to revolve around its axis. Four hundred million years ago, however, it only needed 22 hours. Since the path of the earth's orbit around the sun has remained constant, it is clear that at that time a year was 400 days long.

At the same time, we know that the moon is orbiting the earth more slowly, and is moving a few centimetres farther away every year. The moon's rate of rotation has slowed to the point where one side of it always faces the earth.

This set of interrelated phenomena is the result of complex interactions within the earth–moon system, including the tides and so-called tidal friction. The tides are caused by two things: centrifugal force, which is the tendency of rotating objects to move away from the centre of rotation; and by the force of gravity, particularly the gravitational pull of the moon (and to a lesser extent the sun). Variations in these forces exist at different positions on the earth, and are influenced by its changing relation to the moon, creating a cycle of change most noticeable in the tides. The sea ebbs and flows in rhythm, its level rising and falling twice daily anything from a few centimetres to more than 10 m, depending on the formation of the ocean bed, the size of the ocean and the shape of the coast. But the effect of the tides can also be seen in the movements of the atmosphere and in deformations in the earth's crust.

Applying the brakes?

The constant shifting in the planet's water masses as they move through channels and around islands produces friction, which absorbs energy. The same principle applies to the warping of the earth's crust. The forces of friction, or tidal friction, are applying the brakes to the earth's rotation. The moon's growing distance from the earth, which weakens the earth's hold on it, makes the moon slower, with the result that it lags behind the earth. The tides also seek to overtake the moon, rather than follow it. The moon pulls the masses of water back, applying the brakes. The effect is that the earth gradually loses the momentum it had when it came into being.

At some time in the future, then, our planet will lose its satellite. By that time, the earth will have slowed to the point where one side always faces the sun, dividing the planet into two hemispheres with extremes of climate. But it will take 4–5 thousand million years for this to happen.

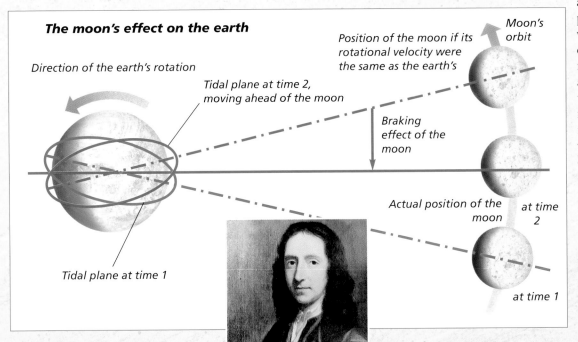

The moon's effect on the earth

Direction of the earth's rotation

Position of the moon if its rotational velocity were the same as the earth's

Moon's orbit

Tidal plane at time 2, moving ahead of the moon

Braking effect of the moon

Actual position of the moon

at time 2

Tidal plane at time 1

at time 1

Above: *Over time, the rotational velocity of the earth is gradually being reduced. The main cause is the moon, which creates the ebb and flow of the tides, and causes other disturbances. As a result, the tidal plane at time 1 is pulled backwards at time 2, which has a braking effect on the planet.*

Left: *Edmond Halley observed that the days are getting longer – in effect, that the earth's rotation is slowing.*

INVESTIGATING THE ORIGINS OF LIFE ON EARTH

The question of how life came to exist on earth presents scientists with one of the great mysteries. Long after it was formed, our planet was a desolate and lifeless place. Yet, in these unpromising conditions, a miracle took place and the first micro-organisms came into being. Many people have tried to explain this process, but there is much that is still unclear.

Chemist Stanley L. Miller reconstructed the atmospheric conditions under which organic molecules could have emerged.

Humans have long tried to explain the existence of life. Most explanations focused on how humans came to be on earth. But the very beginnings of life go back much, much further, and it is only in the last two centuries that scientists have begun to unlock this mystery.

As late as the 19th century, scholars explained the origin of life in terms of spontaneous generation: life emerged from inanimate matter without external influences, in a process which is constantly taking place. For example, in ancient times and in the Middle Ages it was believed that worms emerged not from eggs but directly from rotting meat; that toads and eels came from mud; and mice from wheat flour and soiled clothing. Many scientists were convinced that a mysterious life force converted inert matter into eggs or spores, out of which living beings then emerged.

Renowned French chemist Louis Pasteur (1822–1895), considered the founder of modern bacteriology, was the first to shoot down the idea of spontaneous generation. In an experiment

that created a big stir at the time, Pasteur mixed water with organic matter that would decompose in air, and placed the mixture in a glass container, which he then sealed and heated. Then he waited. The mixture remained clear. After the vessel was opened, air came into contact with the fluid, and decomposition began. Soon, the mixture had grown murky. Pasteur had assumed – correctly – that decomposition would only take place when airborne bacteria were allowed into the vessel.

Of course, Pasteur's experiment only proved how life that existed on earth could spread by itself. When it

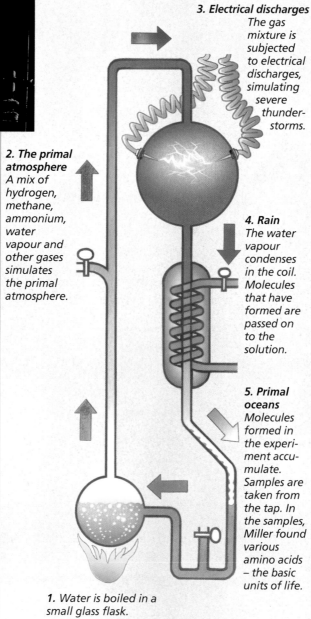

3. Electrical discharges
The gas mixture is subjected to electrical discharges, simulating severe thunder-storms.

2. The primal atmosphere
A mix of hydrogen, methane, ammonium, water vapour and other gases simulates the primal atmosphere.

4. Rain
The water vapour condenses in the coil. Molecules that have formed are passed on to the solution.

5. Primal oceans
Molecules formed in the experiment accumulate. Samples are taken from the tap. In the samples, Miller found various amino acids – the basic units of life.

1. Water is boiled in a small glass flask.

Above: *A mixture of inorganic gases and energy produce the building blocks of life.*

Miller's 'primordial soup'

In 1953, an experiment in a Chicago laboratory changed our understanding of the origin of life on earth. The experiment, which re-created the conditions in the primal atmosphere, was devised by Stanley L. Miller, at that time still a student at the University of Chicago. Miller filled a flask with water, which he boiled. The resulting vapour passed through a mixture of gases. For a week, he subjected this mixture to electrical discharges, simulating the electrical storms that raged over the surface of the planet. When Miller analysed the 'primordial soup', he found that significant amounts of the amino acid glycine, a building block of proteins and an organic molecule, had been formed.

came to the question of the very beginnings of life on earth, it was clear that many scientists believed that life could emerge from lifeless matter. The Russian scientist Aleksandr Ivanovitch Oparin (1894–1980) came up with an idea known as abiotic synthesis (from the Greek word *abios*, or 'lifeless'). Among the many and imaginative hypotheses on the origin of life, this is the only one that deserves to be called a theory according to scientific standards, since it is the only one to be experimentally confirmed, and it is widely accepted in the scientific community. For anybody without scientific training, however, Oparin's ideas are difficult to understand. In part, this is because of the complex chemical processes involved in the formation of the first organic molecules, but also because scientists are of the opinion that life on earth emerged under conditions in which no living being today would be able to survive for long.

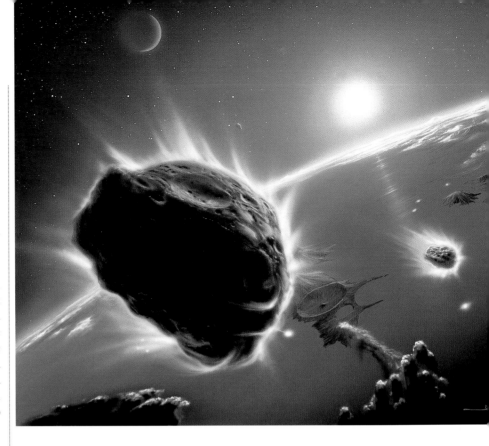

The primordial soup

What did the earth look like 4,000 million years ago, when life first began to emerge? There were constant volcanic eruptions; there was no protective ozone layer, and deadly ultraviolet rays from the sun met almost no resistance as they fell on the earth's surface; the atmosphere was poisoned by ammonia and methane, and acid rain fell to the ground, where it collected, forming an almost boiling hot ocean in which a solution of about 10% organic matter could be found. Although this sounds like a description of hell, it has come to be known to scientists as the 'primordial soup'.

Following in the footsteps of pioneering American chemist Stanley L. Miller, many scientists have reproduced the conditions of the primal atmosphere. By applying various sources of energy – for example, ultraviolet light or electricity – to its components, they have been able to produce various organic substances, such as amino acids, adenine, guanine, thymine, glucose or urea. Such experiments have proven that it was possible for organic compounds to emerge from inorganic ones in the primal atmosphere or the primal ocean, much as in a giant test tube. But it is still a long way from these basic compounds to cells and living beings.

The extraterrestrial factor

Half a century before Miller's experiments, Swedish chemist Svante Arrhenius (1859–1927) proposed a different model to explain the origins of life on earth: panspermatism. Arrhenius suggested that life on earth was created when living spores were transferred from one celestial body to another. Although Arrhenius's theories are not accepted today, it is possible that organic matter could have come from space – for example, via the meteorites that bombard the earth. Many meteorites, such as the Murchison meteorite which fell in Australia in 1969, contain more than 400 organic compounds. Each year, around 100 tons of meteorites strike the earth's surface, as well as around 20,000 tons of so-called micro-meteorites. In the primal phase of our planet's history, this cosmic bombardment would have been about 1,000–10,000 times greater.

Another possible source of organic matter is comets – celestial bodies that travel around the sun. Every time these cosmic wanderers

Vacuuming up the dust of the universe

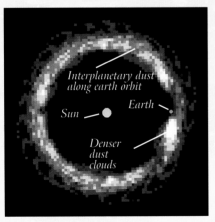

One theory of the origin of life suggests that the lifeless earth acted as a kind of vacuum cleaner, sucking up particles of cosmic dust. While the many meteorites that fall to earth contain certain organic compounds, the earth's orbital path passes through so-called chondrites, interplanetary clouds of dust which contain numerous organic compounds. Using data from the infrared observation satellite IRAS, scientists have developed a computer simulation (shown at left) that reconstructs this ring of dust.

For the most part, the cosmic matter consists of dust particles 0.001–0.1 mm in diameter, which probably originated in the distant reaches of the solar system. The earth's gravitational force gathers tons of this matter every year.

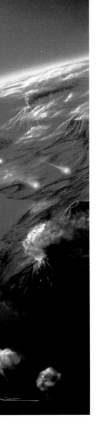

Left: *Meteorites may have transported complex organic compounds to earth, but the possibility that the building blocks of life came from space is still debated.*

pass close to the sun, they lose gases and particles of dust which can reach the earth. Comets are thought to consist of a solid frozen nucleus, and these hurtling 'cosmic snowballs' contain substantial proportions of organic compounds. Up to a third of Halley's comet, for example, may consist of hydrocarbons. In the opinion of Armand Delsemme, an astrophysicist at the University of Toledo in Ohio, the very existence of water and carbon can only be explained by constant replenishment from comets. However, his theory remains extremely controversial.

Life in the depths

Others believe that the depths of the ocean might have provided the best conditions for the emergence of the first micro-organisms. This is because the water would have protected them from ultraviolet rays and meteorites. We know that undersea volcanic vents, where sea water meets magma, furnish particularly favourable conditions for the creation of organic compounds. Around some volcanic vents, researchers have found basic substances such as nitrogen and carbon – at pressures 200–300 times that of the

What is life?

Strangely enough, life is not a simple thing to define. One of the general features of life is the chemical composition of all living beings: macro-molecules of carbon compounds, as well as molecules such as proteins, nucleic acids, carbohydrates or lipids, which consist of numerous atoms (at least 1,000) in various combinations. As a rule, these organic molecules can be divided into functional molecules that carry out vital functions, and information molecules (DNA) that carry genetic information – our genetic code. Probably, the decisive step towards the development of life came with the successful interaction of both kinds of molecules. The co-operation of the building blocks of life in ever larger and more complex units, such as the cellular organisation of living beings, represents perhaps the most important characteristic of life.

Mammals such as these donkeys represent an advanced stage in the development of life.

atmosphere, and at temperatures around 300°C. Certain minerals in the mud at the bottom of the ocean may also have played a role in combining simple molecules to form more complex ones. These minerals have the capacity to bind chemical substances, shielding the first building blocks of life from the destructive energy of the ocean waves.

Even if we accept the idea that the oceans were the cradle of the first life forms, there are still many questions. How did organic molecules that formed at the bottom of the ocean reach concentrations

Above: *Analyses of stromatolites – layered calcium crusts – proves that life has existed on earth for at least 3,600 million years.*

Left: *Undersea volcanic vents may have provided the right conditions for the emergence of life in the ocean depths.*

sufficient for the emergence of complex organisms? What caused the development from the lifeless organic molecules to the cell, the elementary unit of all living beings?

Today, scientists assume that amino acids, possibly affected by heat, joined in chains within the primordial soup. These chains in turn formed globules that were surrounded by thin membranes. These may well have had a resemblance to what we know as cell membranes. It is likely that at some point these membranes were able to allow the specialised intake and expulsion of substances – in other words, metabolism. Finally, there arose a means by which early life forms could reproduce, passing their biochemical properties on to their offspring.

The first living beings still depended on the nutrients provided by their environment. Then, 3–4 thousand million years ago, the first autotrophic organisms appeared. These were living beings capable of producing energy-rich substances from inorganic matter through photosynthesis. Because oxygen is a by-product of photosynthesis, this development transformed the atmosphere of the earth and opened the way for the evolution of life as we know it.

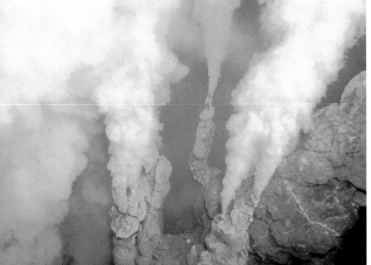

THE BIG BANG AND THE BIRTH OF THE UNIVERSE

According to astronomers and cosmologists, time and space began with a mighty cosmic explosion known as 'the big bang'. Although this name might not sound serious enough for the origins of the world, the theory is solid, and most scientists support it. But we will never know exactly what happened at the dawn of the universe, and the opponents of the big bang theory have some intriguing arguments.

An artist's interpretation of the big bang.

The universe started with a bang – the big bang, that is. This is the name that has been given to the explosion that created space and the stars. In spite of reservations, the big bang theory remains the most convincing and well-founded theory of the origin of the cosmos.

If we put it in specific terms, the history of the universe began 13 thousand million years ago. If we want to be really precise, we can say that the universe came into existence some 0.00000000000000000000000000000000000000000001 seconds (10^{-43} s) after the big bang. It is impossible to say what happened in the inconceivably short span of time before the big bang, since the known laws of physics did not yet apply. In order to form a picture of what happened, scientists rely on the insights of particle physics and astronomy.

The first three seconds

When it was 10^{-43} seconds 'old', the universe was infinitely dense and hot. Its temperature was almost 10^{32}°C – a one followed by 32 zeros. Matter and energy were inseparable and so densely bonded that they formed a mass less than 10^{-50} cm in radius.

But the newborn universe began to expand at a tremendous rate, and the more it expanded, the more it began to cool down. Gradually, matter and its opposite, anti-matter, emerged from the bundle of energy. After 10^{-10} seconds, the temperature had fallen to a thousand billion degrees Celsius (1,000,000,000,000,000°C) – impossible to conceive of, except in theory.

At this point, the cosmos contained all the basic particles – quarks, electrons, neutrinos – as well as particles of anti-matter. At

The origin of the universe

———— *13,000 mill. years*
First life on earth.
———— *9,000 mill. years*
Birth of the sun and planets.
———— *8,000 mill. years*
Birth of most galaxies, including the Milky Way.

———— *3,000 million years*
Evidence of quasars and some radio galaxies.

———— *1,000 million years*
Birth of the proto-galaxies; most of these remain outside the range of our instruments.
———— *800,000 years*
The universe becomes transparent. Matter releases radiation, later to be discovered in the form of microwave radiation in cosmic background radiation.

———— *200 seconds*
Helium and other light elements are created through nuclear fusion.

———— *1 second*
The universe is an undifferentiated mass of matter and energy. Its temperature is 10^{10}°C.

———— *10^{-35} seconds*
The universe has grown and its temperature is 10^{27}°C.

———— *10^{-43} seconds*
The radius of the universe is less than 10^{-50} cm.

———— *BIG BANG*

Radius of the universe ———→

10^6 seconds, the temperature had fallen to ten billion degrees. Particles of matter and anti-matter increasingly collided with one another. The more the temperature fell, the more matter and anti-matter was formed, which then collided and disappeared. But since there were more quarks and electrons than corresponding anti-matter particles, it was matter that finally prevailed. After about three seconds, the last positron (anti-electron) was destroyed and matter as we know it today existed. This consisted of electrons, protons and neutrons – the building blocks of the atom.

Above: *For a long time, the Mount Wilson Observatory in California housed the largest telescope on earth. Here, Edwin Hubble (left) collected the astronomical data which, on the basis of the red shift, showed that the galaxies were receding and the universe was expanding.*

The first light rays

After the fury of the first three seconds, the universe continued to expand and cool. Only 800,000 years after the big bang, the temperature had reached 3,000°C, and protons and electrons began to combine to form hydrogen atoms. At this point, energy became separated from matter, and the first photons – light quanta – were released. Over the next thousand million years, the stars took shape. In their cores, the furnace of nuclear fusion was ignited. This is the energy that fuels our sun.

As the temperature continued to sink, the first galaxies appeared, as did quasars – extremely bright objects on the edges of the universe. Galaxy after galaxy, the universe gradually took on its present form, until finally, 4.5 thousand million years ago, our solar system made its appearance.

Fleeing stars

This model of the origin of the universe was developed over several decades, and it is based on three basic observations: the receding galaxies observed by the American astronomer Edwin Hubble (1889–1953); the existence of cosmic background radiation; and the quantity of the element helium (He) that is present in space.

In 1929, after spending many nights taking photographs at the Mount Wilson Observatory in California, using what was then the world's largest telescope, Hubble made a fascinating discovery. On the basis of the so-called red shift, he discovered that the galaxies appear to be moving away from our

own, and that they are receding at a faster speed the farther away they are. Because the earth does not lie at the centre of the universe, this can only mean one thing: the spiral arms of the various galaxies are all expanding, like raisins in a rising cake dough.

The logical conclusion of Hubble's observation is that at some point in the past the universe consisted of a small but unimaginably dense mass of matter. Of course, it is too simple to say that the universe began from a single point: the processes that took place at the moment of the big bang will never be known with complete certainty.

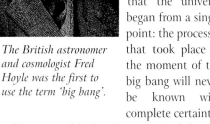

The British astronomer and cosmologist Fred Hoyle was the first to use the term 'big bang'.

The term 'big bang' was coined by the British astronomer Fred Hoyle (born 1915) who was actually an opponent of the theory. He developed an alternative, the 'steady state' theory, according to which the universe remains stable, since the decreasing density caused by expansion is balanced by the constant creation of new matter.

In 1946, our picture of the universe took another giant step forward. In that year,

the Russian–American astrophysicist George Gamow suggested that, if the theory of the big bang is correct, the receding energy would have to leave traces, in the form of cosmic noise or background radiation. After its journey of 13 thousand million years, this energy would have cooled almost to absolute zero, or -273°C. Indeed, the existence of this radiation was confirmed in 1965 by two American radio-astronomers, Arno Penzias and Robert Wilson. By chance, they detected a background radiation present in all parts of the heavens. Its temperature is -270°C, 3°C

The red shift

The red shift is a tool for measuring distance in the universe. To understand it, think of the sound of a police siren: the sound is higher as it approaches and lower as it recedes. This phenomenon is known as the Doppler effect, and it occurs not only with sound but also with light. As a result, the speed of a receding star is expressed as a shift towards the long-wave range of the spectrum in the light it emits – in other words, a shift towards red. In 1929, this occurrence allowed Edwin Hubble to show that the galaxies are moving apart, and that the farther away they are, the faster they are receding.

above absolute zero. In 1978, Penzias and Wilson shared the Nobel Prize for Physics for their discovery.

Years later, this uniformity of temperature became puzzling for the supporters of the big bang theory. Because background radiation was the first witness to the primal state of the cosmos, and it is the same everywhere in the universe today, it seemed to indicate that

In 1992, the satellite COBE *provided data that revealed irregularities in cosmic background radiation.*

The temperature of background radiation

It's cold out there in space. Scientists have calculated that the temperature of cosmic background radiation, or noise, is just 3°C above absolute zero. But how can noise have temperature? Basic physics tells us that if a body is warmed, its particles will move. The same principle applies to negatively charged electrons, which then emit electromagnetic waves of radio noise. Since the strength of this noise depends on temperature, it can, by analogy, be assigned a temperature value.

Arno Penzias and Robert Wilson received the Nobel Prize for Physics in 1978 for the discovery of cosmic background radiation.

matter was distributed uniformly in space. But our observations of the heavens tell us that matter is concentrated into galaxies containing billions of stars and planets. This raised the question of the origins of the universe's spiral galaxies. In other words, what caused the primal mass of matter to form concentrations?

An answer came from George Smoot and his team at the University of California at Berkeley. Smoot's team conducted intensive research into background radiation using data from the satellite *COBE*. In 1992, they discovered extremely small variations in temperature, which they interpreted as proof that the original state of space was not uniform, but must have contained clusters of matter that were the germs of future galaxies.

The light elements

The third pillar of the big bang theory rests on the quantity of helium present in the universe. The majority of chemical elements surrounding us are born in the interior of stars. Here, the atomic nuclei of two light elements are fused to form a heavy element, a process which becomes self-sustaining. However, helium accounts for 23% of all the matter in the universe. It is not possible that this all originated in the stars. We can only explain the existence of this amount of helium if we assume that it existed before the formation of the stars.

The age of the stars

Some believe the three pillars of the big bang theory to be unshakeable, but there are still many things we do not understand about the origins of the universe. One of the great weaknesses of the big bang theory is the fact that it is not possible to study the first moments of the cosmos – the very beginning of time and space. To re-create the conditions that existed at that time, we would need particle accelerators the size of the solar system itself. And even if we had such equipment, direct observations would not be possible, since the universe only became visible after it reached the age of 800,000 years. Before that time, it did not emit any light rays.

Many scientists regard the existence of quasars as another obstacle to the general

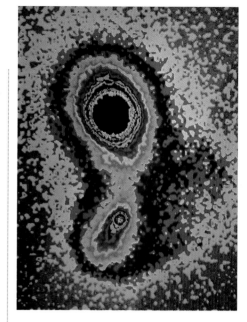

A false-colour radio map of Quasar QSO 0351 + 026. Distant objects like this one are the cores of active galaxies.

acceptance of the big bang theory. Quasars are the cores of active galaxies, and some scientists believe that their properties are in conflict with the theory.

Observations made by the Hubble Space Telescope have raised yet another problem. These observations have suggested that the universe is still relatively young. However, all astrophysical theories are based on the assumption that the universe must be at least 13 thousand million years old. This seeming contradiction has not yet been explained, but may be due to the misinterpretation of data. Scientists have recently solved another contradiction, in which some stars in our Milky Way appeared to be older than the universe. Using measurements transmitted from the satellite *Hipparchus*, scientists have found out that the stars in question were about 3 thousand million years younger than had been assumed. This meant that they did not contradict the big bang theory.

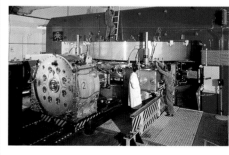

Only by using a particle accelerator – shown here at CERN, the European Centre for Nuclear Research – can we begin to understand the early phases of the universe.

WHAT DO WE REALLY KNOW ABOUT THE MOON?

To this day, astronomers are fascinated by the wonderful relationship between the earth and the moon. No other planet in the solar system possesses such a large satellite. But scientists still do not fully understand the interaction between these two celestial bodies. An even bigger mystery is how the moon came into existence. Is it the earth's sibling, its prisoner or perhaps its offspring?

When we look up into the night sky and see the familiar shape of the moon, it appears as natural and as permanent as the earth itself. But, like the earth, the moon was not always this way. It is natural to wonder where this celestial body came from, and there have been many theories advanced to explain the birth of the moon and its relationship to our planet. However, we still don't know exactly how the moon came to occupy the position that it does today.

In modern times, the first person to develop a theory about the moon was the scientist George Darwin (1845–1912), the son of the famous naturalist Charles Darwin (1809–1882). George Darwin held the view that the earth and moon had once been much closer together than today. In fact, he believed that they had been joined as a single planet rotating at incredibly high speed around its own axis – with one rotation taking about one or two hours. At that time, the earth was still very hot and molten, and the high speed of rotation caused it to bulge at the equator. Gradually, centrifugal force caused a 'drop' of terrestrial matter to detach itself and fly out into space. This piece of the earth became the moon, which continues to circle its mother planet as a faithful satellite. To provide evidence for his theory, Darwin pointed to the Pacific Ocean, which is shaped like a huge bowl. In his opinion, the Pacific represented the scar left behind when the moon broke away.

For decades, astronomers thought that Darwin's theory was more or less correct. Gradually, however, they came to realise that the separation of earth and moon could not have taken place in the way described by Darwin. The earth would have needed to be much more fluid than it in fact was, and the

motions of the earth–moon system would have to be different from those we observe.

The origins of the moon received more attention after World War II, when a new theory was developed. This assumed that when the solar system was formed, the moon was a small independent planet like the others. However, on one of its orbits it came a bit too close to the earth, was captured by the earth's gravitational pull and forced to follow the earth's orbit. This theory became very popular in professional circles for some time, even though it did have a central flaw: the 'capture' theory could not explain what had caused the moon to change its course.

In the 1960s, a third hypothesis was put forward. This was the so-called accretion theory (from the Latin *accretio*, meaning 'growth'). This model was based on the assumption that when the solar system was young numerous 'planetary embryos', or asteroids, disintegrated near the earth. The gravitational force of our planet then caused this asteroid debris to form a ring around the earth. Since these particles – some of them no larger than a speck of dust – attracted one another, they began to cluster together, finally forming the moon as we know it.

Telltale stones

In the eyes of many scientists, none of these theories was entirely satisfactory. In the 1960s, the advent of manned space flight and the beginnings of lunar exploration seemed to promise some answers to the questions surrounding the moon. After the first man landed on the moon in 1969, scientists hoped that samples of lunar rock would produce some reliable data. However, the lunar landings did not solve the moon's

DETACHMENT *According to George Darwin's model, a 'drop' detached itself from the rapidly rotating, fluid earth, forming the moon.*

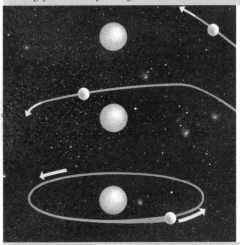

CAPTURE *When the orbit of the moon brought it too close to the earth, gravity captured it, causing the moon to circle the earth.*

ACCRETION *Small particles orbiting the earth came together through mutual gravitational attraction, eventually forming a celestial body – the moon.*

mysteries. On the contrary, for analysis of the 387 kg of rock samples brought back from the moon between 1969 and 1972 contradicted all known theories.

If the moon had once been part of the earth, as George Darwin suggested, then the chemical composition of its surface would have to be similar to that of the earth's crust. The lunar samples were indeed similar to the earth's crust, particularly in terms of silicon content, but scientists also detected some important differences. On the moon there are no alkali metals, such as sodium or potassium, which tend to form gases. But heat-resistant oxides – such as aluminium and calcium oxide – are present in abundant quantities. Both of these could indicate that the lunar mass was once subject to extreme

Rock samples gathered by astronauts on the moon reveal a different composition to the earth's crust.

A simulation of the birth of the moon

1 minute after collision

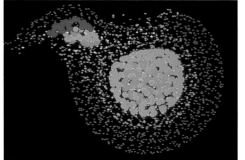

The earth is struck by an asteroid.

10 minutes after collision

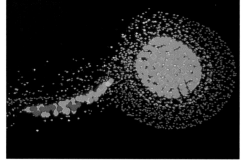

The asteroid's iron core (left) is temporarily thrown into space.

1 hour after collision

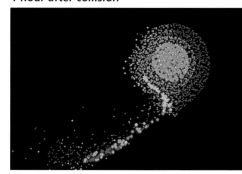

The iron core falls back to earth.

heat. But the moon does not have the slightest trace of water, which makes the detachment theory untenable.

Iron evidence

Finally, further rock analysis revealed that the moon contains only 10% iron, compared to the 30% iron content of the earth, whose core consists of concentrated iron. But if the moon was formed in the same region of the solar system as the earth – as the capture theory claims – then the different iron levels cannot be easily explained. The same applies to the accretion theory: if there had been a ring of dust circling the earth, it would have had to contain as much iron as the earth. So the question of the moon's origin remains a mystery. But we do know one thing: the earth and its satellite are the same age.

During the late 1970s, two American astronauts, working separately, presented a new version of the moon's history. In their opinion, the moon was formed when another celestial body collided with our earth at some time in its youth. At first glance, this hypothesis seemed rather far-fetched, since such collisions are statistically improbable.

Just a little bit

The earth and the moon are getting farther away from each other. The reason for this lies in the laws of physics: when two rotating bodies form a system – like the earth and the moon – the angular momentum of the system must stay constant. Angular momentum is derived from the product of mass, angular velocity and distance from the rotational axis. Because the tides slow down the rotation of the earth, angular velocity decreases, so the moon must either increase its mass – which is impossible – or its distance from the rotational axis. It has to move farther away from the earth, which it does – by 2–4 cm per year. This means that the two bodies were once much closer.

The earth and the moon move a few centimetres apart every year.

However, computer simulations carried out in the early 1980s seemed to confirm the astronauts' theory.

The theory states that some 4.5 thousand million years ago, an asteroid crossed the earth's orbit. Scientists estimate that this smaller celestial body, travelling at a speed of about 10 km/s, struck the earth frontally rather than sideways. This collision would have destroyed the asteroid, whose core was iron with a granite mantle, presumably pulverising it. However, the collision would have catapulted the very heavy core into space, whereupon it would have fallen back to earth again. This second collision would have been even stronger than the first. The iron mass would then have sunk into the still-molten surface of the earth. At the same

The interaction of moon and sun

The daily rise and fall of the tides is controlled by the moon, and, to a lesser extent, by the sun. The gravitational pull of both celestial bodies causes the masses of water in the earth's oceans to ebb and flow. The earth's rotation, as well as the differing coastal formations and depths of the oceans, cause extreme variations in tidal range. The difference between high and low tide levels in the Mediterranean is a few centimetres; in the Bay of Fundy in eastern Canada, it is an astonishing 20 m – the greatest in the world.

These images of a fishing harbour in the Bay of Fundy show the difference between high and low tide levels.

2–3 hours after collision

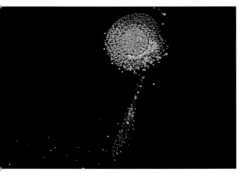

The iron core slowly sinks into the depths of the molten planet.

4 hours after collision

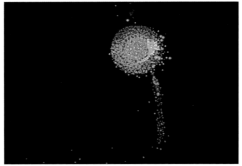

The remains of the core gradually fuse with the earth's core.

24 hours after collision

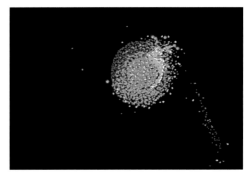

Over time, the moon is formed from particles released by the collision.

---

time, a gigantic cloud of vapourised matter, a mixture from the cores of both planets, rose up into space. The heat caused all alkali metals to disappear. The dust particles formed a ring orbiting the earth. Gradually, these particles could have given rise to a new celestial body – the moon – held in place by the pull of the earth's gravitational force.

The moon's balancing effect

The origin of the moon still presents a mystery, but one thing is certain: living in close association with its own satellite has important – and beneficial – consequences for the earth. For one thing, the moon influences the force of the tides, and scientists have demonstrated that tidal friction is actually slowing down the speed of the earth's rotation.

Tests carried out by astronauts have shown that the moon plays an important role in the earth's climate. Our planet has regularly alternating seasons, a phenomenon caused by the fact that its plane of rotation is not in line with its orbital plane around the sun, but is inclined at an angle of about 23° 27'. The presence of the moon exerts a stabilising influence on the inclination of the earth, with the result that it varies within a range of only about 1° 3'.

Without the balancing effect of our orbiting satellite, the inclination of the earth would be different, and would be subject to strong variations. This would have serious consequences – for example, extremes of climate – and our nights and days would last six months each. If this were the case, it is very doubtful whether the earth would be able to sustain life.

Alone in the solar system

Because life managed to emerge on earth, many scientists believed that this might also have occurred on other planets in the solar system. However, the chances of this happening seem fairly slim. We know that the moon functions as a kind of climatic regulator for the earth, because planets whose inclination is not controlled by a satellite can suffer sudden changes in climate. Calculations show variations in inclination of up to 90° on Mercury and up to 60° on Mars. Even if living organisms developed on these planets, they would hardly be capable of surviving these variations.

THE SEARCH FOR LIFE ON MARS

Of the nine planets in our solar system, Mars, the Red Planet, is considered to be the most similar to our own. But appearances are deceiving: exploration of the planet has determined that it is a barren place unsuited to life. Nevertheless, Mars provides scientists with a rich field of exploration, and it holds many secrets.

WILLS'S CIGARETTES.

IMAGINARY LANDSCAPE ON MARS.

Above: *Schiaparelli's Martian canals appeared on many products.*

Perhaps because it is relatively close to the earth – as little as 59 million kilometres at the closest point of its orbit – Mars has always fascinated humans. It is commonly known as the Red Planet, because of the colour of its arid, desert-like surface. It is considerably smaller than the earth, but larger than the moon. Until modern times, it was thought that it might be able to support life, and over the years many astronomers trained their telescopes hopefully in the direction of the Red Planet.

The Martian canals

One of the most famous observers of Mars was Italian astronomer Giovanni Schiaparelli (1835–1910). In the 1880s, after studying the planet through a telescope, Schiaparelli announced a truly sensational discovery: he claimed to have identified a pattern of geometric lines on its surface. The Italian thought he had found irrigation canals, and declared that there must be intelligent life on Mars. Although Schiaparelli's 'discovery'

Water has left unmistakable marks on the landscape of Mars.

was probably an optical illusion, the idea of Martian canals captured the imagination of the public. Writers such as H.G. Wells (1866–1946) took up this idea, and there soon emerged the myth of the little green men who had built the canals. Right up to the middle of the 20th century, there were many in the scientific community who considered there was some truth in Schiaparelli's thesis. Even if they did not accept the existence of the canals, there were many astronomers who believed that some form of life must exist on Mars.

It was not until the early 1960s, when the United States and the Soviet Union entered space, that we learned more about our planetary neighbour. The first probes to reach Mars sent back startling information. Contrary to what many had expected, there was no sign of life. The surface of the planet

Mars has numerous long, deep canyons that were carved out by wind and water.

turned out to be a barren, shimmering red desert, out of which some mountains tower as much as 27 km in height. The probes indicated that there was no water. Surface temperatures, which vary between -125 and 0°C, depending on the time of year, are hostile to life, and the planet's atmosphere, which consists almost entirely of carbon dioxide, is unbreathable. The fabled canals turned out to be mighty canyons – in the case of the Mariner Valley, more than 4,000 km in length. According to geologists, these chasms were once rivers, for only water can alter the landscape in this way.

The discovery that water once flowed on Mars was an important one, because water is fundamental for the development of life. The planet's water-eroded landforms implied that life might have existed at some point in the past. This led to an intensive search for any traces it might have left.

In 1971, The US launched the space probe *Mariner 9* – the first spacecraft to orbit the planet – which documented the presence of polar ice caps, made of water and carbon dioxide. This was of great interest to scientists, who considered the possibility that the ice might melt during the summer months. This might be sufficient to support a few particularly resistant micro-organisms.

In 1975, the US launched *Viking 1* and *2* to search for traces of life under the layers of dust on the Red Planet. When these probes landed, they collected soil samples. These were placed in a sterile container so that possible chemical changes in the atmosphere inside could be observed.

However, scientists were disappointed when the first results from Mars reached the laboratories on earth. The data gathered by the *Viking* probes was contradictory in almost every respect: while there were many indications of life, others pointed to the exact opposite. The search for life on Mars had suffered a bitter blow.

Evidence from the ice

In the mid-1980s, the discovery of a meteorite in the Antarctic added a new angle to the question of life on Mars. According to British geologists, the meteorite appeared to be almost 4 thousand million years old, and had come originally from Mars. In 1996, after subjecting the meteorite to detailed analyses, scientists from NASA (the US space authority) and Stanford University in

California came to the conclusion that the rock contained traces of simple forms of life – in the shape of single-celled, bacteria-like organisms. By extension, this meant that life had emerged on Mars more than 3 thousand million years ago.

But this did not turn out to be the hoped-for breakthrough. In 1997, other scientists announced that ALH84001 – as the rock was called – in fact provided no indications of life on Mars. The structures which had been thought to be fossils did resemble worms, but they were created through geological rather than biological processes. The controversial structures were probably broken parts of certain crystals. This left the question of life on Mars unanswered.

A rover on Mars

In spite of this disagreement, the exploration of Mars went on. In December 1996, NASA launched the 890-kg probe *Pathfinder*, which touched down on the Red Planet on July 4, 1997. *Pathfinder* carried a six-wheeled mini-rover, known as *Sojourner*, which glided down a ramp onto the frozen surface of Mars at Ares Vallis, where it soon began exploring its immediate environment. Back on earth, millions of people followed *Sojourner's* progress via images posted on the Internet.

The mobile robot's radius of activity was

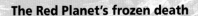

The Red Planet's frozen death

When it was born, Mars probably went through processes similar to those of our planet. But something went wrong. For a while, the vast quantities of carbon dioxide emitted by volcanoes was able to store the sun's heat and warm the surface of the planet. At this stage, water existed in the liquid state, and there may even have been some forms of life. But then the volcanoes died, and the concentration of carbon dioxide diminished. The water turned to ice, and Mars froze to death.

Like many planets, Mars was named after a Roman god.

about 100 m², and its life span, which had been set to last at least seven days, turned out to be several months. It had been designed so that it could ride over stones and other small obstacles, and carried a German-designed spectrometer which enabled it to study the make-up of the planet's surface.

The results sent back by *Sojourner* were of enormous significance for the scientists, but provided no trace of fossilised life forms. The new data has given rise to new questions – for example, why do some of the rocks contain much more silicon than ALH84001, and why does volcanic rock from Mars contain so much more sulphur than similar rocks found on our planet?

The work of *Sojourner* is only the beginning. The first manned flights to Mars are planned for some time after 2002. Perhaps the next wave of explorers will give us a more precise picture of the Red Planet.

Right: *A French cartoon from the early 20th century gives an amusing view of life on The Red Planet.*

The Viking *probes were tested in the desert to simulate conditions on Mars.*

IS THERE A TENTH PLANET IN OUR SOLAR SYSTEM?

In the infinite depths of space, all matter is in motion. As if moved by gears, the nine planets of our solar system orbit the sun, moving in their predictable elliptical paths. But something seems to be affecting the orbital path of Uranus, the seventh planet from the sun. Some astronomers are convinced that there could be another celestial body nearby. Is it possible that our solar system could have a tenth planet?

There are nine planets in our solar system. Of these, there are the four earth-like planets whose surfaces are solid (Mercury, Venus, Earth and Mars); the four giant planets with fluid or gaseous surfaces (Jupiter, Saturn, Uranus and Neptune); and Pluto, the most distant planet from the sun. Out of the nine, there is no doubt that Uranus, the seventh planet from the sun, behaves in the strangest way. Uranus takes 84 years to orbit the sun; because of the 98° tilt of its axis, 24 years of day alternate with 24 years of night, and the poles receive more heat than its equator. Uranus's orbital path is so irregular that it has been a rich source of information for astronomers for many years. Its striking deviations led to the discovery of Neptune in 1846 and Pluto in 1930.

But the unusual orbital path of Uranus cannot simply be attributed to the influence of Neptune and Pluto, and about 2% of the planet's deviations cannot be explained. It seems as if Uranus is being attracted by an unknown celestial body of about the same

The Vulcanus enigma

The possibility of a tenth planet is a tantalising one. But what if the tenth planet is not on the edge of our solar system, but right next to the sun? In the course of the past century, several astronomers have noticed the movements of a small point, similar to a planet, situated between Mercury and the sun. This hypothetical body has been named Vulcanus, but has never been definitely observed. The object may be a ring of dust or simply a passing asteroid.

Since research has produced no evidence, scientists are working on other hypotheses. Photographs made in the stellar observatory on the island of Hawaii between 1992 and 1994 indicate the existence of at least six primitive celestial bodies at a distance of several thousand million kilometres. If their existence is confirmed, these stars may prove that another planet could never have formed

It follows a broad orbital path, and then it disappears. Some scientists believe that a tenth planet reappears at regular intervals, accounting for the disturbances in the orbit of Uranus.

mass as the planet itself – which is 14 times greater than the mass of the earth. In other words, there might be a tenth planet in addition to the nine known planets.

Too far to see

If a mysterious celestial body exists, how do we explain the fact that the most powerful telescopes – for example, the Hubble Space Telescope – have not detected it? The answer is simple: if there is a tenth planet, we would have to look for it at the furthest reaches of our solar system, at least 4 thousand million kilometres beyond Pluto. This immense distance makes observation difficult. The only thing that is certain is that it is not a giant planet. If it were comparable to Uranus or Saturn, astronomers would have found it.

Astronomer Clyde Tombaugh, who discovered the planet Pluto in 1930, is convinced of the existence of the mysterious tenth planet.

beyond Neptune and Pluto because there is too little matter at that distance, and its concentration is too low. But for some astronomers, such as Clyde Tombaugh – who discovered Pluto in 1930 – there is reason enough to believe in the existence of the mysterious tenth planet.

THE SEARCH FOR INTELLIGENT LIFE IN THE UNIVERSE

Many people find it troubling to accept the idea that we are the only intelligent beings in the universe. For this reason, there is great interest in the possibility of contact with extraterrestrials. Movies and television often present stories of contact with aliens. But the serious side of this endeavour is the SETI programme, established to try to make contact with these alien civilisations. Scientists have been listening for radio signals for years, but have yet to pick up signs of life.

Ever since human beings began to peer into the depths of outer space, we have wondered whether there are other beings out there. While films and television are full of stories of UFOs and alleged cover-ups of contact with aliens, there is also a serious, scientific side to the issue. For decades, a number of astronomers and other scientists have been actively engaged in the search for extraterrestrial intelligence (SETI). The history of this endeavour began in 1960, when the physicists Giuseppe Cocconi and Philip Morrison suggested in the renowned British science journal *Nature* that we should listen to certain radio frequencies to intercept messages that might be arriving from extraterrestrial civilisations.

They did not say whether they thought this would lead anywhere. However, they were convinced that extraterrestrials must exist, and saw it as only a matter of time before we came into contact with them. Pursuing this idea to its logical conclusion, any extraterrestrial civilisation must have followed more or less similar scientific and technological paths to those of humans. The implication was that they, too, must be concerned about the existence of other intelligent beings – this would mean us – and that they would also try to establish contact. Following this logic, it makes sense to listen for their signals.

In popular accounts, extraterrestrials are often described as having large, bulbous heads.

Around the same time as Cocconi's and Morrison's article appeared in *Nature*, a young radio-astronomer named Frank Drake pointed the radio telescope in Green Bank, West Virginia, at two interesting stars – Tau Ceti and Epsilon Eridani – located about 12 light-years from earth. Both of these had been identified by Cocconi and Morrison as possible candidates. After some 150 hours of listening, Drake picked up signals apparently emanating from another intelligence. The signals took the form of strong static noise that filled the control room. Unfortunately, it turned out that the signals were routine transmissions from a US military aircraft.

A few years later, scientists in the Soviet Union tried their luck. In excited terms, the Soviet news agency TASS announced that a very promising radio signal with powerful field strength had been received during the night of April 12–13, 1965. But the Soviets too were soon to be disappointed. The so-called celestial radio emissions were later identified as emanating from quasars, extremely bright objects located at the centres of distant galaxies.

Communication difficulties

Communication is just one of the problems we would have in dealing with extraterrestrials. They would be subject to the same physical laws as we are, but their civilisation could be very different from our own. After all, human cultures have developed in different ways in different parts of the world. Many proponents of the SETI programme believe that there are extraterrestrial civilisations that are technologically far ahead of our own. In his novel *Contact*, Carl Sagan showed benevolent extraterrestrials who communicate with us out of sympathy. Like anthropologists studying a primitive tribe, they have to lower themselves to our level to communicate with us.

The radio telescope at Goldstone, California, which was used for NASA's Mega-SETI programme.

In spite of these initial failures, SETI was not abandoned. Between 1960 and 1990, scientists carried out about 60 listening programmes, all of which produced nothing. Admittedly, these were conducted over short periods of time, and they only concentrated on a few stars. The SETI specialists of the US space agency NASA (National Aeronautics and Space Administration) simply did not have the technical and financial means to carry out a large-scale search mission. Finally, in October 1992, the 500th anniversary of Columbus's landing in the Caribbean, new sources of finance were secured, and an ambitious follow-up project – to be called Mega-SETI – was planned.

Two powerful radio telescopes were to be used: one at Arecibo, on the island of Puerto Rico – the largest fixed dish in the world – and the other at Goldstone, California. A few months later, NASA was able to announce that a total of 164 signals had been received.

But money problems led to major cutbacks in Mega-SETI; government funding ended, and the organisers of the SETI programme had to look around for private money. This led to a comeback of Mega-SETI under the name META. The renowned US astronomer

Two versions of a confrontation with extraterrestrials: the landing scene from the film Close Encounters of the Third Kind *(above); and the cover of a 1950s science fiction magazine (left).*

Carl Sagan (1934–1996), widely known for popularising space and the stars, also claimed to have picked up signals, and in 1994 announced his support for the project.

The counter-argument

Both Mega-SETI and META produced little success, and the project did not enjoy wide support from the scientific community. The mathematician Frank Tipler, for example, attacked Sagan's convictions. He simply did not believe that extraterrestrial civilisations could exist. Tipler argued that there could not be intelligent extraterrestrials, since they would already have colonised us. Sagan countered that the goal of extraterrestrials need not be conquest. Perhaps we are simply too primitive to notice the messages from a non-earthly intelligence. In 1996, Sagan's novel about the search for extra-terrestrial life, *Contact*, was turned into a popular film, which tried to show that the intentions of extraterrestrials might be to help us.

The supporters of SETI assume that the existence of life is not unusual. In their opinion, humanity evolved through a series of by no means extraordinary events, and

that these could just as well have already taken place in the same or similar ways in other regions of the cosmos. According to this hypothesis, we are a fairly ordinary form of life that arose on an ordinary planet circling an ordinary star. The supporters of SETI validate this claim by pointing out that the universe contains some 100 thousand million galaxies, many of which possess 100 thousand million stars. Surely, they argue, uncounted thousands of these stars are circled, like our sun, by planets that are similar to our earth. This would mean that life-supporting conditions could exist on countless celestial bodies.

Perhaps we are unique

However, many biologists are sceptical about this argument. First, they do not believe that life is such a common thing. If we study the origins of life on our planet more carefully, we find that it is the result of complex and accidental events, and was by no means inevitable. Furthermore, it is questionable whether the laws of evolution automatically produce life forms that are similar to our own, and whether the humanoid form of life – what we call humanity – is indeed an ideal type. For example, the dinosaurs could very well have remained the rulers of earth had they not been destroyed by a meteorite or some other natural disaster.

Say hello to an alien

What would you say to an extraterrestrial if you met one? Humans not only listen for extraterrestrial signals, but also send special messages that might inform other intelligent life about the people and culture of our planet. From the 1960s to the 1980s, radio astronomers beamed a number of signals into space. These consisted of straightforward information coded in a series of 1s and 0s – the basic binary language used in all areas of computing. Once these signals have been correctly decoded, they will provide information about us and hopefully represent the first step in a dialogue. Admittedly, when they were asked to decode these messages, many distinguished scientists were unable to do so. Let us hope that any passing extraterrestrials have greater success.

A message sent from Arecibo, which consists of a series of 0s and 1s, contains important information about us and our environment. In this portion of the message we can recognise, among other things, the

Arecibo radio telescope; the solar system with the earth, which stands out from the other planets; a schematic figure of a human; and the structure of DNA – which contains our genetic code.

The French astronomer Jacques Laskar has observed that the earth is, in fact, not just an ordinary celestial body, since it forms a double system with the moon. Because of the size of the moon – its mass is about one-fifth that of the earth – our faithful satellite exerts a major influence on our planet. The moon stabilises the inclination of the earth's axis, ensuring that our planet does not wobble unpredictably in space. Without the moon to regulate the motion of the earth, it is quite possible that life would never have appeared on the earth.

SETI has also been criticised by experts who are familiar with the instruments used in radio astronomy. In their opinion, SETI uses instruments that are too old and not powerful enough. Radio waves may not be the best means of contacting other worlds. On the contrary, the pace of technological innovation shows that radio technology has not advanced as fast as other communication technologies.

Complicated conversation

Even if we contacted extraterrestrials, how would we communicate? Optimists believe that there will always be a way for intelligent beings to communicate with one another. However, pessimists point out that, even today, historians can decipher only a few words of ancient Etruscan, and that they still cannot decode the writing system used on Easter Island.

The study of an intergalactic language would certainly not be an easy undertaking. Even if we were to develop a basic cosmic vocabulary, we don't know if our interlocutors would understand our questions, or if our life experiences would simply be too far removed from one another.

One thing is certain: a conversation of this kind would take place across great spans of time. It would take 100 years for a message sent from a star 100 light-years away to reach us. Our answer would take another 100 years to reach that star. We will probably need a lot of patience to talk to extraterrestrials.

Two paths in the search for extraterrestrials

There are two very different groups of people engaged in the search for aliens or extraterrestrials. Astrophysicists and radio astronomers, who hope to intercept signals from intelligent beings in space using powerful radio telescopes, believe that somewhere in the far distant regions of space there might be other highly developed beings. The other group consists of the surprisingly large number of people – for the most part from the United States – who have allegedly already come into contact with aliens, together with those who believe in their reports. They support the theory that these extragalactic creatures are already among us. But, because of humanity's limited understanding, we are unable to prove their existence. They believe that ETs (extraterrestrials) are as baffling to us as primate researchers are in the eyes of the monkeys that they study: in other words, we might be able to see them, but we really cannot understand what they are doing.

A scene from Close Encounters of the Third Kind.

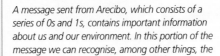

THE INFINITE BLACKNESS OF THE NIGHT SKY

Although it creeps over the sky every 24 hours, the night is still a special time for most people. Its darkness can produce contradictory feelings; it can bring peace and relief from the daily stresses, but it can also cause anxiety and fear. The darkness swallows colours, blurs shapes and makes familiar things appear strange. But why is the night so black? The answer to this simple question lies in cosmic distance.

Above: *Astronomers in the 16th century observe the moon using the instruments of their time.*

Although it dominates our solar system, the sun is just one star among billions in the universe. Of course, it is special for us: when it sets in the evening, the light goes out. This is a very familiar process for us, but why shouldn't the other stars take the sun's place after sunset, providing us with light until sunrise? Of course, this is impossible. The stars in the sky only light up like tiny pinpoints, and cannot banish the darkness. Sometimes the brightness of city lights even prevents us from seeing the stars.

Since the dawn of human society, we have been fascinated by the way the brightness of the day alternates with the darkness of the night. Over the centuries, many thinkers and scientists have tried to make sense of this natural process. In the 4th century BC, the Greek philosopher Aristotle (384–322 BC) described the universe as a huge, clearly bounded space which was coloured black and dotted with stars – including our own sun. During the day, the sun overpowered the other stars, so their little lights could only be seen at night. A century later, members of the Stoic school of Greek philosophy developed the idea of the cosmos as an endless ocean of nothingness, in which the stars were scattered too thinly to illuminate our nights.

From Galileo to Newton

This concept of a virtually empty sky lasted until well into the 17th century. In 1610, however, the Italian scientist Galileo Galilei (1564–1642) trained the telescope he had invented at the heavens. Galileo discovered that, contrary to what science maintained at that time, there is a huge number of stars. His observations included the mountains on the surface of the moon, the Milky Way and the moons of Jupiter.

Several decades later, in 1687, the English physicist, mathematician and astronomer Isaac Newton (1643–1727) offered his own explanation for Galileo's discovery. Newton claimed that the stars only stay in the sky because there is an infinite number of them. According to Newtonian physics, every mass attracts another mass with a force proportional to its size and the distance between

Sir Isaac Newton proposed the theory that the laws of gravity require the existence of an infinite number of stars.

them. This suggested that there must be stars everywhere, so they can attract one another. If this were not so, Newton reasoned, the gravitational force of the stars at the centre would pull those at the edges inward, and the entire world would collapse.

Of course, Newton's theory did not solve the mystery of why the night is black. In 1823, the German doctor and astronomer Wilhelm Olbers (1758–1840) reawakened interest in this question. His thesis rested on the idea that if there really were an infinite number of suns, then we should see a star no matter where in the sky we look. But a glance at the night sky immediately shows that there is no such mass of suns. Olbers tried to find an answer to this contradiction by attacking a hypothesis that had only recently been put forward by the Swiss astronomer Jean-Pierre Loys. The latter attributed the blackness of night to a fine fluid that is distributed in space and absorbs the light of stars like blotting paper. The scientific world was impressed by this explanation, since it fitted with the popular belief that the cosmos was filled with a fluid known as ether.

In the mid-19th century, the concept of cosmic ether was shot down by the discovery of the principle of conservation of energy.

This came about in 1848, when the English astronomer Sir John Herschel (1792–1871), who was expanding on the work of his father, Friedrich Wilhelm, pointed out that a fluid which absorbed the light of the stars would have to become very hot itself and emit even more light. It would be invisible light, since it would be in the infrared range of the spectrum, but the heat emissions would be not only noticeable, but unbearable. After this, the idea of ether filling the expanses of space was soon abandoned.

The intuition of a poet

The next phase in this story belongs not to a scientist or astronomer, but to a man of letters. Edgar Allan Poe (1809–1849) described his vision of the night sky in the essay *Eureka*: 'Were the succession of stars endless, then the background of the sky would present a uniform luminosity, like that displayed by the Galaxy – *since there could be absolutely no point in all that background, at which would not exist a star*. The only mode, therefore, in which, under such a state of affairs, we could comprehend the *voids* which our telescopes find in innumerable directions

Edwin Hubble discovered that the universe is expanding, which is the reason why billions of stars cannot be seen.

would be by supposing the distance of the invisible background so immense that no ray from it has yet been able to reach us at all.' Poe's flash of intuition was brilliant, but it would be many decades before the scientific world would accept it as fact.

In the 1920s, the American astronomer Edwin Hubble (1889–1953) took up this question. He explained that the army of stars reaches far beyond the regions accessible to the naked eye or even the most powerful telescopes. The reason for this is – as Edgar Allan Poe had correctly proposed – that the

Wilhelm Olbers believed that interstellar fluid, or ether, swallowed the light of the stars

light of distant stars has not yet arrived. Although it races towards us at a speed of 300,000 km per second, the light takes millions of years to cross the immense distances that separate the galaxies. For example, light emitted by the stars in Andromeda, the closest galaxy to our own, takes about 2 million years to cover the 19 trillion kilometres that separate Andromeda from us.

Shift to red

With his pioneering observations, Edwin Hubble not only confirmed Edgar Allan Poe's ideas, he also found himself confronted with another exciting phenomenon: the expanding universe. All galaxies, including our own Milky Way, are constantly moving away from each other. This recession of the stars, as it is known, was detected by the so-called red shift: light from the receding stars is shifted into the red range of the spectrum, and the shift is greater the higher the velocity

of the star. The most distant stars race with increasing speed, and thus they become increasingly red. Eventually, they enter the infrared range of the spectrum and cannot be detected by the human eye.

In 1927, the Belgian astrophysicist Georges Lemaître (1894-1966) came up with the idea of imagining the flight of the stars in terms of where they had come from. This idea led him to conclude that they must once have been much closer together. This led the way to the theory of the big bang, which is accepted by most people today. The big bang theory states that the universe formed 13 thousand million years ago in a vast cosmic explosion. At first, it was made of an infinitely small mass of inconceivably hot particles, which has been expanding and cooling ever since. In the course of time, new galaxies and stars are constantly being born, while others die out.

Edgar Allan Poe was the first to see that the reason for night's darkness lies in the dimensions of space.

As we can see, Aristotle was not entirely wrong. The universe does indeed have boundaries, since it had a beginning, and its population of stars is not infinite. Only the closest stars can penetrate the barriers of our night. The farther we look into space with our telescopes – for example, the Hubble Space Telescope – the longer the light we see has been travelling. If we could reach far enough back into time, in theory we would see the beginnings of the world.

THE RIDDLE OF BLACK HOLES

The most mysterious objects in the universe must certainly be the invisible and inconceivably dense objects known as black holes. Nothing can escape the grip of a black hole. But how can we be certain of their existence if we cannot see them?

To imagine a black hole, think of an abyss – small in size and yet unimaginably dense – that swallows everything that comes within its reach. The formal definition of a black hole is a star that has collapsed under its own weight several times, becoming more compact each time. Because of its extremely high density, this bottomless pit attracts even the smallest speck of dust that comes near. Nothing, absolutely nothing, can escape the pull of a black hole – not even light. In fact, this is why it is known as a black hole.

Ever since the name 'black hole' was coined, by the American astrophysicist John Weeler, astronomers have been trying to uncover the mysteries of this cosmic riddle. Even Albert Einstein (1879–1955), whose theory of relativity predicted the existence of black holes, was not quite sure if such an absurdity could really exist.

Physical forces of attraction

Ever since the revolution in physics initiated by Sir Isaac Newton (1643–1727), we know that there is a shared force of attraction between two bodies, and that this becomes stronger with the decrease in distance between them and with the increase in their mass. However, it is a huge leap from this basic principle to the idea that there might be stars so compact that nothing can resist the pull of their gravity.

Fortunately, we can turn to theoretical calculations to assist our imagination. These tell us, for example, that if our sun were to become a black hole, its mass would have to compact to 10^{30} kg – a one followed by 30 zeros – which would turn it into a ball 2 km in diameter. To put this into perspective, remember that the sun has a diameter of 1,392,000 km (measured at the equator).

And if the earth were to mutate into a black hole, it would have to find room for its present mass of 10^{25} kg in a ball just 2 cm in diameter – from its present diameter of 12,756 km (measured at the equator). But it is almost impossible for us to conceive of such immensely dense matter, and of the forces that are capable of compacting matter in this way.

Celestial furnaces

It is likely that we will begin to understand black holes once astronomers have learned more about the general processes at work in the universe, and particularly about the processes that produce and sustain stars. Like living beings, stars go through several stages. We know that stars are huge balls of gas, consisting primarily of hydrogen, and derive their energy from the conversion of hydrogen into helium. This takes place

An artist's impression of a black hole.

through nuclear fusion, which occurs only at extremely high temperatures and under immense pressures. Once the fusion process becomes self-sustaining, the energy that is produced balances the weight of the star's external surface. As a result, the star maintains a state of equilibrium: as long as it has enough fuel to keep its nuclear furnace burning, it will not collapse.

The next stage, however, begins when the fuel begins to dwindle. When this happens, the weight of the outside mantle begins to press in on the star, and it implodes (collapses in on itself) in stages. Each time this happens, it causes the temperature and

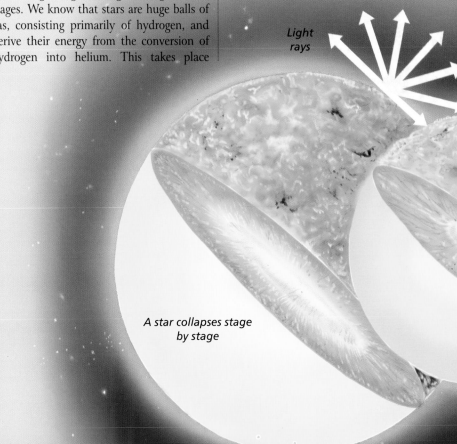

Light rays

A star collapses stage by stage

pressure inside the star to rise to the point where its reserves of helium are used up. After several collapses, the fiery celestial body becomes an old, compact star. If its radius then falls below a certain size – the so-called Schwarzschild radius – the pull of its gravitational force increases to the extent that it captures all matter and radiation. At this point, the star has become a black hole.

Indirect traces

In theoretical terms, this is what happens to stars which have at least three times the mass of our sun – as many in fact have, or will have in the future. But reality is more complex. One problem is the difficulty of discovering black holes. We cannot observe them, since they are invisible. So astrophysicists are forced to look for indirect indications of their existence. Their search is made easier by the phenomenon of so-called binary stars – pairs of stars which rotate around one another. If one of these becomes a black hole, the other begins a slow struggle to the death. Its matter is attracted by its partner until it is completely absorbed. Before it is absorbed,

however, the flow of dust forms a so-called accretion disc around the black hole. Within the disc, extremely hot matter is strongly accelerated, releasing radio waves. The disc rotates with a velocity directly proportional to the mass of the black hole, which can then be calculated.

This technique has already been used to determine the location of black holes – for example, in the galaxy M106, located 21 light-years from earth. Some astronomers even believe that there is a black hole in the centre of every galaxy.

Perhaps black holes will provide the key to another cosmic mystery, that of the hidden mass of the universe. Since galaxies rotate like giant centrifuges, the objects at their outside edges are only held in place by the total mass of the objects at the centre. Think of a carousel or merry-go-round at a fair: the faster it turns, the tighter you have to hold on. Similarly, the force that holds the stars at the edge of the galaxy has to increase as their velocity increases. This means that a greater mass is needed to exert this force.

According to astrophysicists' calculations, the mass of all matter in space is not sufficient to hold the distant stars. This has given rise to the idea that there is some invisible mass of matter that is capable of exerting sufficient force on all existing stars. It is possible that this force could be exerted by one or two gigantic black holes at the centre of the universe.

Right: *A black hole can be detected by the emissions occurring in its rotating accretion disc. These originate when particles collide.*

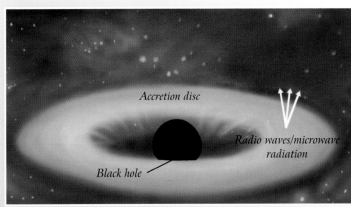

Accretion disc

Radio waves/microwave radiation

Black hole

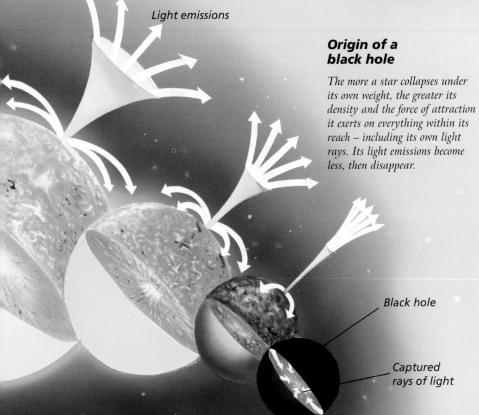

Light emissions

Origin of a black hole

The more a star collapses under its own weight, the greater its density and the force of attraction it exerts on everything within its reach – including its own light rays. Its light emissions become less, then disappear.

Black hole

Captured rays of light

What keeps the world together?

Until the 20th century, the workings of the universe could be explained according to the laws of gravity: two bodies of matter attract each other with a greater force the closer they are and the heavier they are. This law applies to our world, but only approximates conditions in the universe. Einstein's theory of relativity can be applied, however, when dealing with such infinitely large dimensions. This states that space and time are related values, and that time does not pass everywhere in the same way. Near a large star, time passes more slowly, and the space-time relationship becomes deformed. Time stops inside a black hole, making it a unique point in the structure of the relationship between space and time.

THE QUEST FOR DARK MATTER

Of all the secrets of the natural world, possibly the ultimate is the search for dark matter, a mysterious and invisible form of matter that many scientists believe actually holds the fabric of the universe together. At present, dark matter only exists in theory, and we may never know exactly what it is, for even our most powerful telescopes and measuring instruments can only capture a fraction of the full extent of the universe.

Even with the aid of the strongest telescopes, such as the Hubble Space Telescope, only about a tenth of the universe is visible. Astronomers cannot observe the rest simply because it does not emit visible light rays. Scientists have come to this conclusion on the basis of very careful calculations. After they estimated the mass of all visible objects and compared this figure to the minimum density the universe would have to have in order to remain in cohesion, they concluded that 90% of matter could not be detected. The name given to this mass is 'dark matter'.

The question of what constitutes dark matter is not a new one. The concept of dark matter was first considered in 1933, when astronomer Fritz Zwicky (1898–1974) of the California Institute of Technology (Caltech) found that he was unable to explain why the galaxy cluster in the constellation Coma Berenice, 300 million light years away, did not fall apart. According to his measurements, these galaxies contradicted all the laws of gravity and the most elementary principles of celestial mechanics, and they should have broken up an eternity ago, each galaxy going its own way. The only way that Zwicky could explain this anomaly was to suggest the existence of a mass of some substance that did not emit light, and whose force of gravity kept these galaxies together.

In recent years, astronomical observations have confirmed Zwicky's suspicion. The giant arms of the universe's spiral galaxies contain countless stars which should have flown off in all directions through the force of their own rotation. Since this has not happened, there must be something working against their centrifugal force. In this respect, scientists work from the basic assumption that the velocity of rotation of these stars increases with their increased distance from the core of the galaxy. However, the stars which are very far from the galactic core move with an astonishing speed, as if the force of an invisible material held them captive in a giant merry-go-round.

Dark stars

It is fascinating to wonder what this dark matter might be. One possibility is the existence of so-called brown dwarfs – dark stars that are compact enough to exert a force of attraction on other stars, even from a distance. Unlike the sun, which burns its hydrogen fuel in a thermonuclear reaction, converting it to light and heat while releasing helium, brown dwarfs are 'failed' stars, which have never attained a temperature high enough to trigger ignition. They are relatively small, dark and cold, and thus completely invisible. Nevertheless, some astronomers have succeeded in detecting these masked celestial bodies, since their mass – which lies somewhere between that of our sun and Jupiter – can bend the light rays of other stars. What is uncertain is if there are enough brown dwarf stars to make up the dark matter of the universe.

Another celestial body that might provide valuable clues to the nature of dark matter is a black hole. These are incredibly compact

In the 1930s astronomer Fritz Zwicky was one of the first scientists to propose the existence of dark matter.

former stars whose density is so great that they swallow everything that comes near, including their own light rays. Here, too, scientists must use indirect means in order to detect them, because black holes are invisible and absorb all nearby matter. One way to locate them is by picking up the radio signals released by matter that is about to be sucked in – like picking up a kind of cosmic distress call. But, as far as we know, there are not enough black holes in the universe to exert the combined forces of dark matter.

Speeding vagabonds

If we rule out brown dwarfs and black holes, then dark matter must consist not only of huge, dense objects, but also of gases such as molecular hydrogen or even particles of infinitely small dimensions. These include, for example, neutrinos – elementary particles released by the sun which race through the universe at the speed of light (300,000 km per second). Almost nothing can stop these wanderers: each second, 65 thousand million neutrinos strike every square centimetre of the earth's surface. Only one in a billion neutrinos passes through the earth. In spite of the sensitive instruments that are now available to scientists, neutrinos are very difficult to intercept and measure.

But it might still be worth the trouble. Current theory states that these particles have no mass. But if science succeeds one day in discovering that neutrinos do have mass – no matter how small this might be, even 10,000 times smaller than that of an electron – then their huge number could account for about 30% of dark matter.

Big bang or big crunch?

The question of dark matter holds great importance for the future of the universe. The theory of the 'big bang' – the original explosion that gave rise to the universe 13 thousand million years ago – claims that galaxies are moving away from each other in the same way raisins move apart in a cake dough when it rises. If the universe contains a large amount of matter, then the pull of gravity will slow down its expansion until it stops, and even reverses. This could be the beginning of the 'big crunch' – the reverse of the big bang – in which the universe collapses like a balloon when the air inside is released. But if existing matter is not sufficient to restrain the flight of the galaxies, then the universe is open and it will continue to expand for ever.

Astronomers have proposed a third version of this theory, in which the expansion of the universe is slowed by the gravitational forces of matter, but never completely stops. However, if we are to believe this scenario, the theoretical mass of the universe would still have to be about 100 times larger than the visible cosmos. Whatever model we choose to follow, it seems that dark matter will continue to play an important part.

Above: The cohesion of spiral galaxies, which rotate like spinning tops without collapsing, might be due to the existence of dark matter.

Hunting a brown dwarf

How do you track down something that can't be seen? Astronomers have had to be creative in their search for brown dwarf stars. In 1990, a French team from the EROS programme (Expérience de recherche d'objets sombre, or dark objects research experiment) observed the Large Magellanic Cloud, a star cluster located 170,000 light-years from earth. In 1992, they were joined by the American–Australian programme known as MACHO (Massive Compact Halo Objects). Each night for months, the astronomers photographed millions of stars. These images were analysed by computer for variations in brightness. As soon as an invisible celestial body, such as a brown dwarf, passes in front of a star, it does not block its light, but amplifies it. On the basis of this gravitational focusing effect, three kinds of light variations were detected – and perhaps the same number of brown dwarfs.

The Large Magellanic Cloud provides clues to the existence of brown dwarfs.

INDEX

Entries in *italics* indicate an illustration, photograph or map.

Abbreviations
bk. = background, l. = left,
c. = centre, t. = top, r. = right, b. = below

Front cover:
l. Archives Nationales, Paris/J.P. Germain/S.R.D.
c. Tabourdeau-Bossut/S.R.D.
r. Strange/ZEFA

Back cover:
bk.: D. Malin/A.A.O./Ciel et Espace

Interior:
10 t.l. G. Dagli Orti; t.r. R. Tournus; c.l. P. Vauthey/Sygma; c.r. J. M. Francillon/Explorer; b.l. Dumontier/Artephot; 12 *Le Monde* (17.11. 95); 13 t. L. Bessol/M.N.H.N.; c.l. M. Taraskoff; c.r. AP. Photo Color; 14 t. *Libération* (21.11.95); b. S.P.L./Cosmos (2); 15 t. The Bridgeman Art Library; c. E.T. Archive; b. Mary Evans Picture Library; 16 t. R. Pratta/Iconos/ Explorer; b.l. Musée de l'Homme; b.r. R.M.N.; 17 P. Vauthey/Sygma; 18 t. J. Clottes/Ministère de la Culture/Gamma; b. Broadcoast-Pellissier/ Gamma; 19 t. Harlingue/Viollet; c. Viollet; b. J. L. Charmet; 20 t. British Museum; b. G. Dagli Orti; 20/21 E. Lessing/Magnum; 21 t. R.M.N.; c. Bibliothèque Nationale de France; 22 G. Dagli Orti; 22/23 bk.: Novosti; 24 l. P. Hanny/ Gamma; c., r.: Sigma; 25 t. G. Dagli Orti; b. c. Hayaux du Tilly/Rapho; 26 J. L. Charmet; 26/27 Y. Travert/Diaf; 27 t. R. Burri/Magnum; b. Arch. Larousse/Giraudon; 28 Werner Forman Archive; 28/29 t. E. Lessing/Magnum; bk.: R. Percheron/Artephot; 29 l. G. Dagli Orti; r. E. Lessing/Magnum; 30 l. R.M.N.; r. Bibliothèque Nationale de France; 30/31 E. Lessing/ Magnum; 31 t. Scala; b. E. Lessing/Magnum; 32/33 D. Thierry/Diaf (4); 34 t., c.: G. Dagli Orti; b. Nimatallah/Artephot; 35 t. c. Oster/ Musée de l'Homme; c. The Bridgeman Art Library; 36 Ch. Gleizal/Mitchell Library, Sydney; 37 t. G. Dagli Orti; b. A. Held/ Artephot; 38 t. Bibliothèque Nationale de France; b. Fabbri/Artephot; 39 t. G. Dagli Orti; b. Lauros/Giraudon; 40 b. G. Dagli Orti; 41 t. Scala (2); b. G. Dagli Orti; 42 t. Dorka; b. G. Dagli Orti; 42/43 bk.: G. Gerster/Rapho; 43 l. G. Mandel/Artephot; r. Kazemi/Safir/Rapho; 44 t. G. Camps; b. P. Le Floc'h/Explorer; 45 J. C. Francillon/Explorer; 46 l. Nimatallah/Artephot; r. G. Dagli Orti; 46/47 Nimatallah/Artephot; 47 G. Dagli Orti; 48 t. G. Dagli Orti; b. Oronoz/ Artephot; 49 t., b.: G. Dagli Orti; c. R.M.N.; 50 t. Nimatallah/Artephot; b. E. Lessing/ Magnum; 51 Lauros/Giraudon; 52 R.M.N. (2); 53 t. G. Dagli Orti; b. Coll. Viollet; 54 t. Babey/Artephot; b. R.M.N. (2); 55–57 G. Dagli Orti (4); 58 Bibliothèque Nationale de France; 59 t. R.M.N.; b. Roger-Viollet; 60 t. AKG Photo, Paris; b. Oronoz/Artephot; 61 t. Oronoz/ Artephot; b. G. Dagli Orti; 62 R. Tournus; 62/63 bk.: R. Tournus; 63 t. Lauros/Giraudon; b. Cidim/S.R.D.; 64/65 c. Silverstone/Magnum; 65 F. Jourdan/Explorer; 66 l. A. Thomas/ Explorer; r. J. P. Courau/Explorer; 67 C. F. Baudry and P. Becquelin; 68 R. Nourry/ANA; 69 Bibliothèque Nationale de France; 70 Lauros/Giraudon; 70/71 Giraudon; 71 G. Dagli Orti; 72 t. Dorka; b. J. L. Charmet; 73 t. Dorka; b. J. L. Charmet; 74 t. Bibliothèque Nationale de France; b.l. S. Chirol; b.r. Lauros/Giraudon; 75 l. S. Chirol; r. Bibliothèque Nationale de France; 76 t. E.R.L./Sipa Icono; b. Bibliothèque Nationale de France; 77 t. Dumontier/ Artephot; c., b.: S. Chirol; 78 Dorka (2); 79 l. J. L. Charmet; r. Dorka; 80 Dorka (3); 81 t. Kommunalarchiv Herford, Stadt Herford; b. Bibliothèque Nationale de France; bk.: Archiv Gerstenberg; 82 Scala; 83 t. G. Dagli Orti; b. Central Library, Zürich; 84 l. Scala; r. Österreichische Nationalbibliothek; 85 t. Dorka; b. R. Mazin; 86 J. Guillard/Scope; 87 t. J. P. Germain/S.R.D.; c., b.: Bibliothèque Nationale de France; 88 l. Bridgeman/Giraudon; t.r., b.: Bibliothèque Nationale de France; 89 Oronoz/ Artephot; 90 X. Peron; 90/91 bk.: F. Varin/ Explorer; 91 X. Peron; 92 t. National Museum Copenhagen; b. Ville d'Aurillac; 93 Bibliothèque Nationale de France; 94 Lauros/ Giraudon; 95 r. Centre Jeanne-d'Arc; bk.: Giraudon; 96 t. Centre Jeanne-d'Arc; b.l. Bibliothèque Nationale de France; b.r. Arch. S.R.D.; 97 Giraudon; 98 t. R.M.N.; b. Bridgeman/Giraudon; 99 t. Coll. Viollet; c., b.: Arch. S.R.D.; 100 t. Giraudon; b.l. Oronoz/ Artephot; b.r. G. Dagli Orti; 101 l. G. Dagli Orti; r. Oronoz/Artephot; 102 t. Tabourdeau-Bossut/Arch. S.R.D.; b. Bibliothèque Nationale de France; 103 t.l., b.: Bibliothèque Nationale de France; t.r. NPG/Giraudon; 104 l. Oronoz/ Artephot; r. G. Dagli Orti; 105 t. Schneiders/ Artephot; b.l. Mary Evans Picture Library/ Explorer; b.r. Hulton Deutsch; 106 E.T. Archive; 107 t. Dorka; b. Coll. Viollet; 108 t.l. Lauros/Giraudon; t.r. Coll. Viollet; b. H. Josse; 109 l. S.R.D./J. P. Germain/Bibliothèque Nationale de France; r. Harlingue/Viollet; 110 P. Wysocki/Explorer; 110/111 t. J. L. Charmet; b. G. Dagli Orti; 111 Giraudon; 112 t. G. Dagli Orti; b. J. L. Charmet; 113–114 J. L. Charmet (5); 115 t. J. P. Germain/Photo S.R.D./B.H.V.P.; b. G. Dagli Orti; 116 t. G. Dagli Orti; b. Bibliothèque Nationale de France; 117 t. Coll. Viollet; b. Bibliothèque Nationale de France; 118 J. Guillard/Scope; 118/119 J. L. Charmet; 119 l. L. de Selva/Tapabor; r. G. Dagli Orti; 120 t. G. Dagli Orti; b. A.D.P.C./Artephot; 121 t. Lauros/Giraudon; b. G. Dagli Orti (2); 122 t.l. Vogel/Gamma; t.r. Duclos/Gamma; c. Liaison/Gamma; b.l. Gamma; b.r. Hashimoto/ Sygma; 124 l. c. Laurent/Gamma; r. Vogel/ Gamma; 124/125 t. D. Bruce/Cosmos; b. E. Baitel/Gamma; 126 t. Voulgaropoulos/Gamma; c. Photo News; b. Photo News/Gamma (2); 127 Keystone; 128 t. Keystone; c. Reglain/Gamma; b. Lochon/Gamma; 128/129 Roger-Viollet; 129 Coll. Viollet; 130 t. Museum Boijmans Van Beuningen, Rotterdam; b. Keystone; 130/131 Coll. Viollet; 131 t. Dorka; b. Labat-Viard/ Jerrican; 132 l. Rapho; r. C.N.R.I.; 133 t. Achtner/Sygma; b. Sygma; 134 Ciric; 134/135 REA; 135 l. Ciric; r. Gamma; 136 S.P.L./ Cosmos; 136/137 t. Keren/REA, bk.: I. Berry/ Magnum; 138 S.P.L./Cosmos; 138/139 Liaison/ Gamma; 139 Franquin/Editions Dupuis; 140 t. Limier/Jerrican; c. Picture Group/REA; b. Saba/ REA; 140/141 Leimdorfer/REA; 141 IDE; 142 l. S.E.P.L./Jerrican; 143 t. Gamma; c., b.: A.F.P.; 144 Gamma; 145 Giansanti/Sygma; 146 l. Giansanti/Sygma; c., r.: Gamma; 147 L. Christophe; 148 t., c.: Keystone; b. Associated Press/Tallandier; 148/149 L. Christophe; 149 Keystone (2); 150 t., b.: C. Angel/Gamma; c. Gamma; 151 t. Sygma; b. P. Chauvel/Sygma; 152 t. Max PPP/Reuter; b. A.F.P.; 153 t. Gamma; b. c. Abraityte/Sygma; 154 t. Morimoto/Gamma; c. Kurita/Gamma; b. Wada/ Gamma; 155 t. L. Christophe; b. c. Setboun/ Sygma; 156/157–158: Ph. Madelin (3); 159 A. Duclos/Gamma; 160 t. R. Boss/Sygma; c. Gamma; b. L. Vautrin/Gamma; 161 Hashimoto/ Sygma; 162 J. P. Guilloteau/Groupe Express; 163 t. Cosmos; b. *Waco Tribune Herald*/Sygma; 164 A.F.P.; 165 t. Max PPP/Reuter; c. Gamma; b. Epix/Sygma; 166 P. Marlow/Magnum; 166/ 167 l. Berry/Magnum; 167 c. A.F.P.; bk.: P. Marlow/Magnum; 168 Gamma; 169 t. Cosmos; c. Baldev/Sygma; b. Gamma; 170 t. Edimedia; b. H. Bamberger/Gamma; 170/171 Giraudon; 171 t. Starlight/Cosmos; b. P. Menzel/Cosmos; 172 t.l. G. Dagli Orti; t.r. Pagnotta/Cosmos; c. J. C. Chermann/Inserm; b.l. J. Burns/C.N.R.I.; b.r. Lavaud/Artephot; 174 Mary Evans/ Explorer; 174/175 t. Manceau/Rapho; 175 c. F. Bouillot/Marco Polo; b. Labat/Jerrican; 176 t. Ph. Roy/Explorer; b.l. D.R.; b.r. Gaillard/ Jerrican; 177 D. Aubert/Sygma; 178 Ch. Vioujard/Gamma; 178/179 t. J. C. Chermann/ Inserm; b. D. Brack/Black Star; 179 D. Vo Trung/Eurelios; 180 t. Béranger/B.S.I.P.; b. Laurent/B.S.I.P.; 181 t. G. Dagli Orti; c. P. Aventurier/Gamma; b. J. P. Germain/S.R.D.; 182 J-L Verdier; 182/183 B.S.I.P.; 183 b.l. Abeles/B.S.I.P.; b.r. Ryman-Cabannes/TOP; 184 l. Bibliothèque Nationale de France; r. Coll. Viollet; 185 t. N. Le Roy/Jacana; c. R. König/ Jacana; b. C. Carré/Jacana; 186 t. Taulin/ B.S.I.P.; b. Goivaux/Rapho; 187 Spot/S.D.P.; 188 t.l. Coll. ES/Explorer; b. J. L. Charmet; 189 t. ZEFA; b. R. Michaud/Rapho; 190 Coll. Viollet; 191 l. A. Pol/C.N.R.I.; r. Publiphoto/ C.N.R.I.; 192 t. J. Burns/C.N.R.I.; b. F. Gohier/ Explorer; 193 t. APA/B.S.I.P.; b. T. Holt/ Explorer; 194 t. Boyer/Viollet; b. Coll. Viollet; 195 t. Harlingue/Viollet; b. Taulin/B.S.I.P.; 196 J. L. Charmet; 197 J-L Verdier; 198 t. J. Y. Ruszniewski/Vandystadt; c. Bibliothèque Nationale de France; b. Giraudon; 199 t. G. Dagli Orti; b. Coll. Viollet; 200 F. Bouillot/ Marco Polo; 200/201 Ph. Plailly/Eurelios; 201 l. F. Bouillot/Marco Polo; r. R. Gaillarde/Gamma; 202 t. U. Andersen/Gamma; b. R. Gaillarde/ Gamma; 203 L. Christophe; 204 Sam Ogden; 205 t. Sam Ogden; b.l. Pagnotta/Cosmos; b.r. P. Menzel/Cosmos; 206 t. Dr. J. F. Demonet/455 Unit, Inserm/MRC Cyclotron Unit, London; b. Bibliothèque Nationale de France; 207 t. c. Huet/Hoa Qui; b. C. Abad/S.D.P.; 208 t. *Science et Vie Junior*/J.L. Verdier; b. Trigalou/PIX; 209 t. Harlingue/Viollet; b. Mary Evans/Explorer; 210 t. Phototake/C.N.R.I.; b. Arch. S.R.D.; 210/211 c. J. Challamel/Inserm; 211 t. J. L. Charmet; b. H. Gritscher/Rapho; 212 G. Dagli Orti; 212/213 Mary Evans Picture Library; 213 Bibliothèque Nationale de France; 214 t. P. Nief/Jacana; c. P. Montbazet/Explorer; b. Musée de l'Homme; 215 Fr. Bonvoust; 216 t.l. J. L. Dugast/Hoa Qui; t.r. G. Boutin/Hoa Qui; c. A. Dex/Publiphoto/C.N.R.I.; 217 A. de Surgy; 218 V. Hadengue/Hoa Qui; 218/219, 219: A. de Surgy; 220–222 E. Flandin (6); 223 t. D. Destable/Musée de l'Homme; b. Coll. Viollet; 224 t.l. F. Ancellet/Rapho; t.c., b.: C. Lenars; t. r. c. Delaplanche/Musée de l'Homme; 225 t.l. Dr. F Luisblanc; t.r. Musée de l'Homme; c.l. Lelièvre/Anako; b. J.L. Charmet; 226 t. J.L. Charmet; b. L. Christophe; 227 t. Coll. Viollet; b. G. Dagli Orti; 228 t. G. Dagli Orti; b. Alinari/ Viollet; 229 t. Scala; b. G. Sioen/Rapho; 230 t. Lavaud/Artephot; 230 b. Bridgeman Art Library 231–232 t.: R. & S. Michaud/Rapho (3); 232 b. G. Sioen/Rapho; 233 t. S. Grandadam/Hoa Qui; b. Simeone/Diaf; 234 t. c. Verin/Diaf; b. c. Lounes/Gamma; 235 G. Dagli Orti; 236 t., c.: Bibliothèque Nationale de France; b. P. Dupin/ Ciric; 237 C. Niedenthal/Rapho; 238 t. Sintesi/ Sipa Press; b. Alpha Diffusion/Sipa Press; 239 t. l. F. Origlia/Sygma; t.r. Deville-Gaillarde/ Gamma; b. A. Doclos/Gamma; 240 G. Bouquillon/Gamma; 241 G. Giansanti/Sygma; 242 J. L. Charmet; 242/243 *L'Illustration*/Sygma; 243 G. Giansanti/Sygma; 244 l. G. Dagli Orti; r. Oronoz/Artephot; 245 t. Giraudon; b. G. Dagli Orti; 246 G. Dagli Orti; 247 Keystone; 248 t.l. NASA/Cosmos; t.r. N. Wu/Gamma; c. A.A.O/ Ciel et Espace; b.l. Bruce Coleman; b.r. c. Vautier/ANA; 250 l. E. Ferorelli/Cosmos; r. Denis-Huot/Bios; 251 t. G. Lacz/Sunset; b. Ph. Plailly/Eurelios; 252 t. N.H.P.A./Sunset; c. J. M. Labat/PHO.N.E.; b. Hermeline/Cogis; 253 t. R. Harding; b. F. Gohier/PHO.N.E.; 254 l A.M. Loubsens/Colibri; r. Varin-Visage/Jacana; 255 t. Tui de Roy/The Roving Tortoise; c. G. Lacz/ Sunset; b. Labat/Ferrero/Jacana; 256 t. A. Jouffray/Colibri; b. Watt/Bios; 257 t. B. Sanders/ Nyt Pictures; b. Mc. Hugh/Jacana; 258 l. J. P. Hervy/Jacana; r. Audet/Sunset; 259 t. S. Cordier/ Jacana; b. Menzel/Cosmos; 260 t. Remy/Cogis; b. PHO.N.E.; 260/261 Seitre/Bios; 261 t. Mc. Hugh/Jacana; b. Fournet/Jacana; 262 t. L. Psihoyos/Cosmos; c. Bruce Coleman; b. J.L. Verdier/*Science et Vie Junior* No. 62; 263/263 bk.: L. Psihoyos/Cosmos; 263 t. D. Serrette/ M.N.H.N.; b. L. Psihoyos/Cosmos; 264 t. J.M. Nicollet/*Science et Vie Junior;* b.l. Seitre/Bios; b. r. L. Psihoyos/Cosmos; 265 t. Fortean Picture Library; b. J.L. Charmet; 266 Fortean Picture Library; 267 t. HERGE/Moulinsart, 1996; b. A.P.N.; 268 l. R. Macioszczyk; t.r., b.r.: J. C. Revy/Fovea; others P. Landmann/Gamma (3); 269 t.l. Fovea; t.r. Lanceau/Cogis; b. N.H.P.A./ Sunset; 270 Ziegler/Bios; 270/271 J. Warden/ Sunset; 271 t. A.N.T./Sunset; c.l. Animals Animals/Sunset; c.r. L. Renaud/Bios; 272 Seitre/Bios; 272/273 B. Pambour/Bios; 273 t. D. Heuclin/Bios; b. G. Lacz/Sunset; 274 t. J. Schauer; b. D. Heuclin/Bios; 274/275 H. Klein/ Bios; 275 S.T.F./Sunset; 276 t. N.H.P.A./Sunset; b. Animals Animals/Sunset (2); 277 l. L. Weisman/ANA; r. Animals Animals/Sunset; 278 t. P. Petit/Jacana; b. Dr. P. van Wyk/A.B.P.L.; 279 t. N. Le Roy/Jacana; b. D. Heuclin/Bios; 280 l. F. Gilson/Bios; r. *Sciences et Avenir*; 281 l. D. Lecourt/Jacana; t.r. H. Klein/ Bios; b.r. M. Vautier/ANA; 282 t. P. Pernot/ Bios; c. Seitre/Bios; b. N. & P. Mioulane/MAP; 283 l. Y. Monel/MAP; t.r. Seitre/Bios; t. c. A. Descat/MAP; b. G. Martin/Bios; 284 N. Wu/ Gamma; 284/285 Ph. Nargeolet/Ifremer; 285 t. P. Zahl/Jacana; c., b.: N. Wu/Gamma; 286–287: Ifremer (8); 288 l. Hoogervost/Bios; t.r. R. Morrison/Jacana; c.r. M. Gunther/Bios; b.r. P. Laboute/Jacana; 289 l. J-L. Verdier; r. Prussian State Archives; 290 l. Hosaka Naoto/Gamma; r. D. Parker/Cosmos; 290/291 Yves Larvor/*Science et Vie Junior* No. 15; 292 t. Photo Hachette/ Arch. S.R.D.; b. J-L. Verdier; 293 t. S.P.L./ Cosmos; b. J-L Verdier; bk.: Ph. Bourseiller/Hoa Qui; 294 t. D. Frazier/Cosmos; b.l. NASA/Ciel et Espace; b.r. Arch. S.R.D.; 295 l. Rannou/ Gamma; r. J.C. Martineau/Editing; bk.: Régis Macioszczyk; 296 t. Régis Macioszczyk; b. Jerrican; 297 t. Van der Stockt/Gamma; c.l. Gamma; c.r. P. Lorne/Explorer; b. Schuster/ Explorer; 298 t. NASA/Cosmos; b. Michel Loppé; 299 t. J-L. Verdier; b. J. Warden/Cosmos; 300 t. P. Bourseiller/Sygma; b.l. NASA/Ciel et Espace; b.r. F. Chazot/Explorer; 301 t. Krafft/Hoa Qui; b. Yves Larvor/*Science et Vie Junior* No. 15; 302 from top.: Krafft/Hoa Qui, R. Ressmeyer/Cosmos, F. X. Marit/Cosmos, J. Damase/Explorer; 303t. G.R.G.S./C.N.E.S.; b. Harlingue/Viollet; 304 Krafft/Hoa Qui; 305 t. J. Warden/Cosmos; b. J-L. Verdier; 306t. R. Macioszczyk; b. S.P.L./ Cosmos; 307l. R. Ressmeyer/Cosmos; r. R. Macioszczyk; 308t. A.P.B./Ciel et Espace; b. S.P.L./Cosmos; 309t. Ch. Errath/Jacana; c. J. Reader/Cosmos; b. Ifremer; 310t. c. Freeman/ ANA; b. Régis Macioszczyk; 311t.l. A. Barrington/Cosmos; t.r. R. Ress-meyer/Cosmos; b. S.P.L./Cosmos; 312t.l. NASA/Cosmos; t.r. S.P.L./Cosmos; b.l. D.I.T.E.; b.r. CERN; 313 R. Macioszczyk; 314t. S.P.L./Cosmos; b. NASA/ Cosmos; 314/315 AGW Cameron und W. Benz/*Science et Vie Junior* No. 4; 315 R. Estall; 316t. Mary Evans Picture Library/Explorer; c. S.P.L./Cosmos; b. NASA/Ciel et Espace; 317 t. G. Dagli Orti; c. Coll. Soazig/D.R./Explorer; b. NASA/Arch. S.R.D.; 318t. D. Galland/*Science et Vie Junior* No. 25; b. S. Brunier/Ciel et Espace; 319t. S.P.L./Cosmos; b. S. Brunier/Ciel et Espace; 320t. L. Christophe; b. Mary Evans Picture Library; 320/321 bk.: S. Brunier/Ciel et Espace; 321t. NAIC/Ciel et Espace; b. L. Christophe; 322t. Coll. Viollet; b. J. L. Charmet/Explorer; 322/323 Schad/Explorer; 323t.l. Arch. S.R.D.; t.r. Prussian State Archives; b.l. Bettmann; 324 Manchu/Ciel et Espace; 324/325, 325: J-L. Verdier/*Science et Vie Junior* No. 72; 326 Coltech/ Ciel et Espace; 326/327 S. Brunier/Ciel et Espace; 327l. A.A.O./Ciel et Espace; r. Ciel et Espace

Illustrations:
182,197 J-L Verdier in *Science et Vie Junior* No. 67; 268 R. Macioszczyk in G. Galland/*Science et Vie Junior* No. 42; 289, 292, 293 J-L. Verdier in *Pour la Science* No. 206; 295, 296 R. Macioszczyk in *Eureka* (28.3.95); 298 M. L. Laraque; 299, 305 J-L. Verdier; 306, 307 R. Macioszczyk in Ph. Fassier/*Science et Vie Junior* No. 2; 310 R. Macioszczyk in *Pour la Science* No. 158; 313 R. Macioszczyk in E. Noviant/*Science et Vie Junior* No. 4; 324–325 J-L Verdier